Deviant Behavior

A Text-Reader in the Sociology of Deviance

6th Edition

Delos H. Kelly
California State University, Los Angeles
Edward J. Clarke
Vanguard University

WORTH PUBLISHERS

Deviant Behavior, sixth edition
Copyright © 2003 by Worth Publishers; © 1996 by St. Martin's Press, Inc.

Manufactured in the United States of America

ISBN: 1-57259-749-6
First Printing: 2002

Executive Editor: Alan McClare
Sponsoring Editor: Laura J. Edwards
Marketing Manager: Jeffrey Rucker
Production Editor: Margaret Comaskey
Art Director: Barbara Reingold
Text and Cover Design: Lee Ann Mahler
Production Manager: Barbara Anne Seixas
Composition: Northeastern Graphic Services, Inc.
Printing and Binding: R. R. Donnelley & Sons Company

Acknowledgments start on page 669 and constitute an extension of the copyright page.

Library of Congress Cataloging-in-Publication Data

Deviant behavior : a text-reader in the sociology of deviance / [compiled by] Delos H.
Kelly, Edward Clarke.— 6th ed.
    p. cm.
  Includes index.
  ISBN 1-57259-749-6 (pbk.)
    1. Deviant behavior. I. Kelly, Delos H. II. Clarke, Edward J.

HM811 .D54 2002
302.5'42—dc21

2002066173

Worth Publishers
41 Madison Avenue
New York, NY 10010
http://www.worthpublishers.com

For Alison Michele and for Crickett

Contents

PART II

Understanding Deviance: Theories and Perspectives 77

PART

Becoming Deviant   237

PART**IV**

The Production of Institutional Careers and Identities   295

Organizational Structures, Ideologies, Social-Control Agents, and
Recruitment: The Institutional Backdrop   **295**

PART—**V**—

Building Deviant Careers and Identities 483

PART **VI**

Changing Deviance   631

Transforming Deviance: Conceptions, Actors, and Organizations   **632**

Preface

Some anthologies dealing with the subject of deviance emphasize the ways in which society responds to deviant behavior. Others, by examining why certain individuals violate the social norm, focus on the motivational element. A few trace the evolution of deviant categories. *Deviant Behavior* has been designed to integrate and balance these concerns in a single volume—to explore, through carefully selected readings, the ramifications of deviance for the individual (the *actor*) and for society.

Part I considers the ways society defines deviance and the deviant. Of particular interest is the role that specific individuals—especially those who hold political power or who serve as enforcers of the law—play in the labeling of actors and acts as deviant. It will become clear to the reader that no individual and no behavior is inherently deviant; it is society's perception of an actor or an act as deviant that affixes the label. Deviance, in other words, is in the eye of the beholder.

Why does socially prohibited behavior occur—and persist—despite society's efforts to eliminate or discourage it? How can we make sense of deviance? Sociologists approach these questions from a number of different theoretical perspectives. Part II presents readings by major theorists representing the most important of these perspectives. The introduction to the section furnishes students with the theoretical framework upon which to build an understanding and an appreciation of these key thinkers. This section contains several empirical pieces that underscore the important relationship that must exist between theory and deviance research. The writings also illustrate how researchers go about their work.

Part III analyzes how a deviant career may be initiated in a private domain; it depicts, for example, how actors may employ a range of strategies to conceal potentially discrediting information about themselves—attempts that may not only fail but can result in some type of institutional control and processing. And if actors actually fail in their attempts at accommodation, they may find themselves institutionalized, and thereafter their careers become shaped, to a great extent, by the interactional experiences they encounter within the institution.

Part IV explores the workings of several such people-processing and people-changing facilities—ranging from the schools to the police—to examine how such agencies handle clients and how clients, in turn, may adapt their behavior and their view of self and personal identities to their surroundings.

For certain types of deviance, institutional controls are far less significant than the traditions and norms of deviant subcultures and enterprises. Part V examines the ways in which such structures shape the career of the bookie, the drug dealer, and others.

Part VI analyzes the processes by which deviant categories, actors, and organizations can be altered or transformed. The first selection offers contemporary accounts of how selected deviant conceptions and categories have undergone significant changes. Clearly, if the underlying content of the prevailing images changes, so, too, must the picture of deviance change. Thus activities that may have been seen as deviant at one time may now be perceived as acceptable or even normal by various audiences. The last two readings describe various personal and institutional barriers that confront those who desire to move from a deviant to a nondeviant status—in particular, society's reluctance to accept as "normal" anyone who has borne the stigma of deviance. The remaining piece outlines specific ways in which deviant organizations, decision makers, and structures could be controlled, sanctioned, or even rehabilitated. It focuses on the police.

Overall, then, this book explores the establishment and maintenance of deviant categories; the motivations behind deviant behavior; the identification as deviant of individuals and of particular segments of society, by formal and informal means; the effects of institutionalization upon the deviant; and the efforts of deviants to eradicate the label society has placed upon them. Attention is also given to the ways in which deviant categories and structures can be altered.

We would like to thank many people for their help in preparing the sixth edition of this book, particularly our initial sponsoring editor, Laura Edwards, and production editor, Margaret Comaskey. Decisions about adding and deleting material from edition to edition are always made with apprehension. It is difficult to presume to make the right choices for both the people you hope will give your book a fresh examination and the people who have been loyal and contented users of previous editions. Suggestions from the following individuals helped make our deliberations considerably easier: Martin Weinberg, Indiana University; Ruth Sedlitz, University of New Orleans; Keith Durkin, Ohio Northern University; Al McLeod, California State University, Fresno; and Julia Hall, Drexel University.

Delos H. Kelly

Edward J. Clarke

Deviant Behavior

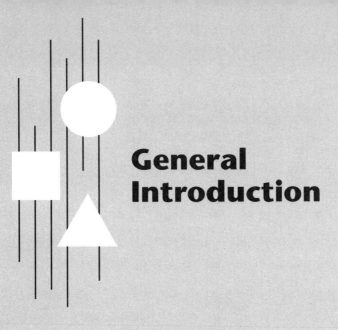

General Introduction

We all carry in our minds images of deviance and the deviant. To some, deviants are murderers and rapists. Other would include in the list prostitutes, child molesters, wife beaters, and homosexuals. With regard to the motivations behind deviant behavior, some of us would place the blame on the family, while others would emphasize genetic or social factors, especially poverty.

Creating Deviance

Regardless of what kinds of behavior we consider deviant or what factors we believe cause deviance, we must recognize that deviance *and* the deviant emerge out of a continuous process of interaction among people. For deviance to become a public fact, however, several conditions need to be satisfied: (1) some deviant category (e.g., mores and laws) must exist; (2) a person must be viewed as violating the category; and (3) someone must attempt to enforce this violation of the category. If the individuals demanding enforcement are successful in their efforts to label the violator, the social deviant has been created.

The Creation of Deviant Categories

As far as deviant categories are concerned, relatively little attention has been focused on their evolution. Formal and informal codes of conduct are generally accepted as "givens," and investigators concentrate on the examination of *why* the categories are violated and *how* they are enforced. An approach of this kind is inadequate, however, particularly in view of the fact that new categories are continually evolving and old ones are being modified. Obviously,

1

as the definitions or categories of deviance change, the picture of deviance must also be altered. The changing content of the laws governing cocaine provides an example. If there are no penalties for possessing and using cocaine, one cannot be formally charged and processed for doing so.

In studying deviance, then, a central question needs to be raised: How (and why) do *acts* become defined as deviant?[1] Providing answers to this question requires an examination of how deviance is defined, how the definitions are maintained, and how violators of the definitions are processed and treated. This entails a historical and ongoing analysis of those legislative and political processes that affect the evolution, modification, and enforcement of deviant categories. Central focus must be placed on those who possess the power and resources not only to define deviance but also to apply a label of deviance to a violator and to make the label stick. These processes are highlighted in Part I and will be evident in the discussion of the "radical-conflict theory" in Part II.

Reactions to Violators of Deviant Categories

In terms of the *actor*, an equally important question can be asked: How (and why) do violators of various types of deviant categories (mores, laws, and regulations) become labeled as deviant? Answering this question requires an examination of the interaction occurring between an *actor* and an *audience*. A simple paradigm (Figure 1) can illustrate how the deviant is reacted to and thus socially created. This paradigm can be applied to most of the selections in this volume.

The Interactional Paradigm   A young man (the social *actor*) is seen selling or snorting cocaine (the *act*, a violation of a deviant category) by a police officer (a social *audience*, an enforcer of the deviant category) and is arrested. The youth's deviation thus becomes a matter of public record, and a deviant career is initiated—a career that may be solidified and perpetuated by legal and institutional processing. Another officer, however, might ignore the offense. In the first case, then, the violator is initially labeled as a "deviant," whereas in the second he is not. Figure 1 indicates that audience response not only is critical, but depends on several factors. The example also helps to underscore the fact that there is nothing inherently deviant about any act or actor—their meanings are derived from the interpretations *others* place on them. Hence the notion is put forth that "deviance lies in the eyes of the beholder." This example can be extended by considering the fourth element of the paradigm: *third parties*, or witnesses. Specifically, a young man may be observed selling or snorting cocaine by a peer, and the peer may choose to ignore the offense. Another peer, however, may not only consider the act illegal or deviant but may decide to do something about it. The peer lacks the power to arrest; he can, however, bring in third parties in an effort to create a shared attitude toward the cocaine user—namely, that he is a

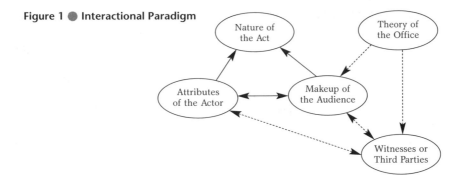

Figure 1 ● Interactional Paradigm

"criminal" or "deviant." The peer may turn to other peers, and they may decide to call the police and have the user arrested. If this happens, the person's "deviance" becomes a public fact.

Thus, the label "deviant" is a status conferred on a person by an observer or observers. Although an understanding of this process requires an examination of the way the four basic elements of the paradigm interact with one another, such an examination is not sufficient. An awareness of the *theory of the office* that a particular agent or audience operates out of is also necessary, especially if the occupant of the office is an agent of social control. The preceding example, as well as the "organizational paradigm" highlighted in Figure 2, can be used to illustrate this requirement. This paradigm represents a refinement of the "interactional paradigm" described in Figure 1. Here we are focusing on the audience, particularly in terms of how an institution expects certain outcomes on the part of its agents. This paradigm will be generally applied throughout this volume.

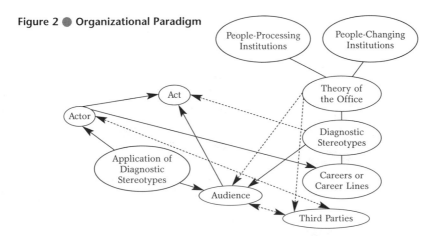

Figure 2 ● Organizational Paradigm

The Organizational Paradigm   Although it might be assumed that the police officer in our examples operates on the basis of his or her own initiative, this is frequently far from the truth. The officer, like any institutional or bureaucratic agent concerned with the processing (through the courts) or rehabilitating (in correctional facilities) of clients, is guided and generally constrained by a theory of the office, or "working ideology." The officer, through informal (contacts with other officers) and formal (police academies) socialization experiences, learns how to identify and classify deviants or suspected deviants. These institutional, or "diagnostic," stereotypes (Scheff, 1966) constitute a basic ingredient of a department's official perspective. The officer, for example, learns how to recognize the "typical" case of child molestation, runaway, or rape. These "normal crimes" (Sudnow, 1965), or "social type designations," not only help the officer make sense out of events, they also provide criteria upon which a suspect can be initially identified, classified, and then selected out to play the role of the deviant.

An institution's stereotypes are basic to the *rate production process*—the creation of a body of institutional statistics. If, for example, a police chief feels that homosexual behavior is morally wrong or criminal, not only will this one individual's conception become embedded within the theory of the office, but the officers will be required to zero in on such activity. This response will produce a set of crime statistics exhibiting an unusually high arrest rate for homosexual exchanges. Similarly, if a police chief formally or informally communicates to department personnel that African-Americans, Hispanics, Native Americans, and other minorities constitute the "real" deviants, delinquents, and criminals, such people will be disproportionately selected out to play the role of the deviant—that is, they will become more vulnerable to institutional processing. This, too, will produce a set of statistics reflecting a heavy concentration of these individuals. The statistics can, in turn, serve as justification for heavy and continued surveillance in areas containing such groups. Examples of this phenomenon abound.

If we are to approach an understanding of what causes deviance, and particularly of the ways in which institutional careers arise and are perpetuated, then we need initially to analyze and dissect the existing structure of the institutions of social control. To obtain an understanding of how institutions operate requires, as suggested by Figure 2, sensitization to several basic organizational elements and processes: (1) the institution's theory of the office, (2) the content of the institutional stereotypes embedded within the theory of the office and used to identify clients for typing and processing, (3) the existing careers or career lines (and associated role expectations) into which the identified clients are placed, (4) the socialization of institutional agents and their application of diagnostic stereotypes to clients, and (5) the effects of institutional typing and processing, from the perspectives of both the client and the institution.

Understanding Deviance

In the discussion of the creation of deviance it was argued that some deviant category must exist, a person must be viewed as violating the category, and someone must make a demand for enforcement. Thus far, too, the focus has been upon the evolution and change of deviant categories, as well as on the interactional aspects—how and why violators of categories may be reacted to. Missing from this analysis, however, is a concern for the motivational aspects—the reasons why people may violate deviant categories. This concern has been generally ignored by the labeling or interactionist proponents. Their main interest revolves around examining audience reactions and the impact of those reactions on people. Implicit in such a stand is the idea that the reasons for behavior are relatively unimportant. If, however, we are to approach a more complete understanding of deviance from a dynamic perspective, attention must also be given to motivation. Such a view provides us with an opportunity continually to analyze how behavior and labels interact with each other.

Violations of Deviant Categories

Traditionally, writers have concentrated on trying to explain why people may violate various types of deviant categories. Some have spent their time trying to explain group or structural rates of deviance, and others have concentrated on those processes by which individuals learn culture and traditions. These efforts have produced many schools of thought, each with its own set of assumptions. The "anomie" theorists, for example, argue that blocked opportunity can produce a tendency or strain toward deviation. The "conflict" theorists, by contrast, contend that the powerless may consciously violate the laws formulated by the powerful. Understanding deviance, then, requires that we investigate those reasons why people may violate deviant categories and by their violations bring upon themselves a particular labeling. The selections in Part II offer some representative attempts to explore this question.

Becoming Deviant

With regard to the process of becoming deviant, an initial distinction can be made between *private* and *public* settings. A husband may violate a particular set of expectations by acting strangely. The wife may try to make sense out of such behavior by rationalizing it away or neutralizing it. She may argue to herself and others that her husband has experienced some personal setbacks and that the peculiar behavior will pass. At this stage the wife is trying to develop a counterdefinition of the situation, and she is also refusing to impute a deviant label to her spouse. The husband's behavior may grow increasingly violent, though, to the point where the wife finds it necessary to bring in agents of social control. She may call the police (third parties) or ultimately have her husband committed to a mental institution. If this should happen, not only have the wife's tolerance limits been exceeded but her attempts at various strategies of *accommodation* (e.g., neutralization or rationalization) have failed. The husband may then be typed as, for example, a schizophrenic and processed in accordance with the establishment's expectations of what the schizophrenic career should entail. The patient is expected, thereafter, to live up to his institutional role—to accept the label and act accordingly. The case of McMurphy in *One Flew Over the Cuckoo's Nest* (Kesey, 1962) describes what may happen when a patient protests against his assigned label. Because McMurphy rejects the "sick role," he becomes embroiled in a running battle with Big Nurse, the institution's agent. In our example, a similar situation may evolve with respect to the husband's response: he may repudiate the institutional tag, he may try to ignore it, or he may accept it. His response, like the responses of observers, is frequently difficult to predict.

In private settings, attempts may be made to regulate and control behavior, and these efforts may be successful. However, once third parties or social-control agents (e.g., the police or psychiatrists) are called in, the individual is frequently on his or her way to becoming an institutional deviant—that is, the organizational paradigm becomes operative, not only from the institution's viewpoint but from the actor's perspective. In particular, if a mental institution is involved, the client becomes viewed as a "mental patient"; this label becomes the patient's *master status* (Becker, 1963), and people will then often react to the person on the basis of the label rather than regarding him or her as sane or "normal." The changing of one's status, or the *status degradation ceremony* (Garfinkel, 1956), also affects the views others have of the "deviant" (one's public identity), as well as how the actor views himself or herself (one's personal identity). The change frequently affects the person's self-esteem (how one views self, positively or negatively, relative to others on selected criteria).

Institutional and Noninstitutional Careers

An important distinction should be made between *institutional* and *noninstitutional* careers. A noninstitutional career is one that a person pursues primarily as a matter of choice. The individual takes an active role in structuring and presenting a specific image of self to others. The bookie, gambler, con artist, nudist, skid row alcoholic, and homosexual provide examples. Such individuals generally progress through some semblance of a career: once they gain entry or exposure, they begin to learn the existing culture and traditions. The bookie, for instance, may start out as a runner, "learn the ropes," and then move into other phases of the bookmaking operation. Similarly, the skid row alcoholic who wants to become an accepted member of the "bottle-gang culture" will become familiar with the norms prevalent among the skid row inhabitants, particularly norms that relate to the procurement and consumption of alcohol. Violations of the normative code frequently cause a person to be excluded from the group (Rubington, 1973). As with the sanctioning of "deviants" by "nondeviants," the "labeled deviants" have ways of punishing those who deviate from their own code.

Institutional careers, by contrast, involve those in which the individual plays a relatively passive role. Here, the career is initiated and perpetuated by some socializing or social-control institution; this process was briefly noted in the discussion of how one becomes deviant. The careers of the "school misfit," mental patient, delinquent, and criminal are of this type. The major difference between institutional careers and noninstitutional careers concerns the role of the actor, particularly in the matter of choice and in the means of gaining entry. Once the institutional career begins, though, the mental patient, like the skid row alcoholic, is expected to learn and act in accordance with the existing subculture and its traditions.

Institutional and noninstitutional careers are not mutually exclusive. Frequently, a degree of overlap exists between the two. The skid row alcoholic, for example, may be arrested and sent to an alcoholic ward, where his or her behavior becomes subject to institutional or bureaucratic control. Similarly, the prostitute may be arrested and taken to jail. In both instances the activities become a matter of institutional knowledge and record. A secret homosexual, by contrast, may never directly experience the effects of institutional processing.

The Effects of Institutional and Noninstitutional Careers

The distinction between institutional and noninstitutional careers provides a backdrop against which a person's reactions can be assessed. How, for example, is a person likely to respond to institutional typing and processing as a deviant? Will he or she reject or accept the institutional label? Answering these questions requires a consideration of how the "status degradation ceremony" affects an actor's personal and public identity. If the deviant rejects the label, a discrepancy (or *identity crisis*) occurs between one's personal and public identities—that is, between one's view of self as normal and the institution's view of one as a deviant. Obviously, unless some personal gain can be realized, such as the enhancement of one's prestige or status in the eyes of others, most persons will reject a deviant label imputed to them. Maintaining an image of self that is at odds with the institution's image is not without its costs, though, and eventually the individual may come to accept the label and bring his or her behavior into line with institutional expectations. Lemert (1951) argues that *acceptance of the label* is a critical step on the way to secondary or *career* deviance. Not only do some individuals change their view of self—for instance, from that of "normal" to that of "schizophrenic"—but they often change their mode of dress, mannerisms, and circle of acquaintances. Acceptance of the label, it should be noted, is an important precondition to being certified as "sane" or "rehabilitated" by institutions.

Involvement in noninstitutional careers or activities affects both the participants and other members of society. The covert gay or lesbian teacher, for example, engages in sexual activity that some would consider deviant, and a discrepancy may evolve between her personal and public identities. Privately she may view herself as gay and a normal female, but publicly she is viewed and responded to as a heterosexual teacher. As with the institutional deviant, however, an identity crisis may arise. She may decide to "come out" and admit her sexual preference to others. Such a strategy is not without its costs. She may be ostracized by her family, friends, and acquaintances; and, more than likely, she will be either discriminated against on her job or perhaps fired. In view of these possibilities, she may decide to keep her sexual preference hidden and become involved in a gay subculture. Such involvement can provide her with a degree of social support, as well as appropriate rationalizations to legitimize her way of life. Still, she (and other noninstitutional deviants) is aware not only that she is engaging in potentially discrediting behavior but also that she must operate in a society in which many hostile elements remain.

Changing Deviance

Identity problems do not cease when one leaves an institution or decides to "go straight." Public or known ex-deviants, whether of the institutional or noninstitutional variety, continue to be viewed as deviants. What Simmons (1969) calls a "lingering of traces" quite frequently occurs, especially among those who carry an institutionally bestowed label. Institutions, it has been pointed out, are most efficient in assigning deviant labels; they are notoriously inefficient when it comes to removing labels and their associated stigma (Goffman, 1963). Former deviants must continue to bear the brunt of the label—with the result that their behavioral patterns are much less likely to change.

The probability of rehabilitating someone who does not view his or her activity or career as deviant is poor. Many noninstitutional deviants—such as prostitutes, gamblers, and homosexuals—feel little need to "repent"; they believe that the pressure they face and the difficulties they experience result from the intolerance of society. In fact, many of these individuals feel strongly that it is society that should be rehabilitated. On the other hand, some noninstitutional deviants—as well as some institutional deviants, such as mental patients, criminals, and delinquents—may try to transform their "deviant" identity. If they do, they can expect to encounter certain barriers. Job applications, for example, frequently require prospective employees to list any arrests, convictions, or periods of institutionalization—circumstances that can bar entry into many occupations. Such roadblocks can produce feelings of frustration and inferiority. What many ex-deviants soon realize is that even if they change, they will still be effectively discriminated against because of past activities or involvement with stigmatizing institutions. They also learn very quickly that the social and political establishment is virtually unchanging—that the burden of change falls upon *them*.

Summary and Organization of This Volume

This book explores the subject of deviance in a number of ways—by focusing in turn on society, on the individual, and on institutions of control and rehabilitation. Part I describes how deviant categories evolve and how people who violate these categories become defined as social deviants. Part II analyzes why people may elect to violate deviant categories—violations that can initiate the defining or labeling process. Part III deals with the deviant career, particularly as it arises in private, noninstitutional settings. Part IV describes how careers may become initiated and perpetuated by institutions, while Part V examines the rise and furtherance of noninstitutional careers. Finally, Part VI discusses how conceptions, careers, and organizational structures may be altered. Throughout, a major focus is on the impact that involvement in institutional as well as noninstitutional activities and careers has upon actors, audiences, and third parties.

Note

1. For an excellent discussion of questions such as these, see particularly Ronald L. Akers, "Problems in the Sociology of Deviance: Social Definitions and Behavior." *Social Forces*, 46 (June 1968), 455–465.

References

Becker, Howard S. *Outsiders: Studies in the Sociology of Deviance*. New York: Free Press, 1963.
Garfinkel, Harold. "Conditions of Successful Degradation Ceremonies." *American Journal of Sociology*, 61 (March 1956), 420–424.
Goffman, Erving. "The Moral Career of the Mental Patient," *Psychiatry* 22 (1959), 123–142.
——— *Stigma: Notes on the Management of Spoiled Identity*. Englewood Cliffs, N.J.: Prentice Hall, 1963.
Kesey, Ken. *One Flew Over the Cuckoo's Nest*. New York: Viking, 1962.
Lemert, Edwin. *Social Pathology*. New York: McGraw-Hill, 1951.
Rubington, Earl. "Variations in Bottle-Gang Controls." In Earl Rubington and Martin S. Weinberg, eds., *Deviance: The Interactionist Perspective*. New York: Macmillan, 1973.
Scheff, Thomas J. "Typification in the Diagnostic Practices of Rehabilitation Agencies." In Marvin B. Sussman, ed., *Sociology and Rehabilitation*. Washington, D.C.: American Sociological Association, 1966.
Simmons, J. L. *Deviants*. Berkeley: Glendessary, 1969.
Sudnow, David. "Normal Crimes: Sociological Features of the Penal Code," *Social Problems*, 12 (Winter 1965), 255–270.

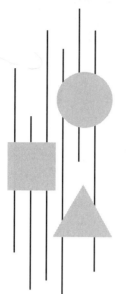

Creating Deviance

As noted in the general introduction, approaching an understanding of deviance requires an examination of several interrelated factors. An initial concern involves the way in which the subject matter is to be approached, viewed, and subsequently defined. Does the theorist or researcher, for example, conceptualize and define deviance and the deviant in individual terms, or does he or she invoke some type of structural view? Similarly, is there something inherently deviant about certain acts or actors, or do their meanings derive from the interpretations and reactions of others? If the latter, then not only should the student of deviance be aware that a specific image is being advanced (i.e., the notion that deviance and the deviants are social constructs), but he or she must also recognize the need to examine the evolution of deviant categories and the ways in which violators of the categories may be perceived and responded to. As noted earlier, for deviance to become a social fact, a person must be viewed as violating some deviant category and thereafter be labeled as deviant by a social observer.

The first three selections introduce major conceptual and definitional issues within the field of deviance and social control and offer some important analytic tools. The following three selections illustrate how the concepts are utilized. These articles demonstrate the process and the basis for selecting out particular individuals and acts as deviant and how, for example, the medical institution has been co-opted as an important agent of social control. In addition, more systematic attention is given to the basic process involved in the construction of the social deviant: (1) the creation of deviant categories and (2) the reactions to violators of deviant categories.

Conceptions, Entrepreneurs, and Power

The idea that deviant categories can be viewed as social constructs represents a particular image of deviance. Such a view also suggests the possibility of competing conceptions. Jack P. Gibbs, in "Conceptions of Deviant Behavior: The Old and the New," acknowledges these points but stresses that the traditional conceptions continue to dominate. How one comes to "think about" a specific phenomenon influences the definitions that are developed, as well as the theory or explanation that may result. For example, in the area of deviance, do we locate pathological or deviant-producing stimuli within the actor or do we look elsewhere, perhaps to society in general? Gibbs maintains that the former viewpoint is favored in the fields of crime and deviance. Historically, the dominant conception has been one of individual pathology. Gibbs then proceeds to compare what he terms the "older conceptions" (e.g., the idea that deviants or criminals possess some *internal* trait that distinguishes them from nondeviants) with the "new conception" (i.e., the view that the essential characteristic of a deviant or deviant act is *external* to the actor and the act). This new perspective emphasizes the *character of the reaction* that a specific act or actor may elicit. If the responses are of a certain kind, deviance comes into being. Gibbs then offers several criticisms of the new conception. Is, for example, this perspective intended to be a substantive theory of deviant behavior, or is it primarily a definitional/conceptual treatment of it? Even if the perspective is viewed as an explanatory framework, Gibbs maintains that several questions have not been answered adequately. "Why," for example, "is the act in question considered deviant and/or criminal in some societies but not in others?"

In "Positive Deviance: A Classificatory Model," Druann Maria Heckert goes well beyond seeing deviance as simply a negative social fact. Norms can be exceeded as well as they can be violated. The tendency is to see deviance as norm violation and, therefore, as negative. This inclination is reflected in the meager accumulation of literature focusing on positive deviance over the past 60 years. Important to note is that, although positive deviance is behavior that people judge to be superior, negative evaluations continue to play an important role. For example, social movements and transforming leaders are often originally labeled as negative entities, and even when the deviance is seen for the most part as positive, derogatory assumptions often follow. Heckert offers a classification scheme that differentiates between various types of positive deviance.

The Gibbs and Heckert articles sensitize one to the fact that the underlying images and conceptions of deviance have changed, and they highlight the manner in which social observers—either individually or collectively—ascribe meaning to the actions of others. Thus, deviance is very much a product of initiative on the part of observers. Logically, then, the reactors and decision makers must become the object of direct study. What, for example, can we say about the content of their conceptions and belief systems? The selection by Howard S. Becker, "Moral Entrepreneurs: The Creation and Enforcement of Deviant Categories," adds some refinements to these issues. Becker also provides an excellent general overview of how deviant categories, particularly rules, evolve. Central to his analysis is the role of *moral entrepreneurs*, whom he categorizes into *rule creators* and *rule enforcers*. Rule creators are individuals who see some "evil" in society and feel that the evil can be corrected only by legislating against it. Frequently their efforts result in the passage of a new law—that is, the creation of a new deviant category. Becker offers several interesting examples that describe this legislative-political phenomenon. He argues that a successful crusade will not only result in "the creation of a new set of rules" but will often give rise to "a new set of enforcement agencies and officials." It becomes the function of these officials to enforce the new rules. Becker concludes his analysis by offering several comments relating to rule enforcers. He contends, for example, that enforcers are concerned primarily with enforcing the law and not its contents; they are also interested in justifying their own position in the organization, as well as in gaining respect from their clients. Many of these same phenomena can be observed in several other selections, especially those that deal with institutional incarceration and deviance.

Conceptions of Deviant Behavior: The Old and the New

Jack P. Gibbs

The ultimate end of substantive theory in any science is the formulation of empirical relations among classes of phenomena, e.g., X varies directly with Y, X is present if and only if Y is present. However, unless such propositions are arrived at by crude induction of sheer intuition, there is a crucial step before the formulation of a relational statement. This step can be described as the way the investigator comes to perceive or "think about" the phenomena under consideration. Another way to put it is the development of a "conception."

There is no clear-cut distinction between, on the one hand, a conception of a class of phenomena and, on the other, formal definitions and substantive theory. Since a conception emphasizes the predominant feature of a phenomenon, it is not entirely divorced from a definition of it; but the former is not identical with the latter. Thus, for example, the notion of exploitation looms large in the Marxian conception of relations among social classes; but exploitation is or may be only one feature of class relations, and it does not serve as a formal definition of them. Further, in certain fields, particularly the social sciences, a conception often not only precedes but also gives rise to operational definitions. As the case in point, if an operational definition of social class relies on the use of "reputational technique," the investigator's conception of social class is in all probability non-Marxian.

What has been said of the distinction between definitions and conceptions holds also for the relation between the latter and substantive theory. A conception may generate a particular theory, but it is not identical with it. For one thing, a conception contains definitional elements and is therefore partially tautological, which means that in itself a conception is never a clear-cut empirical proposition. Apart from its tautological character, a conception is too general to constitute a testable idea. Nonetheless, a conception may generate substantive theory, and it is certainly true that theories reflect conceptions. Durkheim's work is a classic illustration. His theory on suicide clearly reflects his view of society and social life generally.

14

In a field without consensus as to operational definitions and little in the way of systematic substantive theory, conceptions necessarily occupy a central position. This condition prevails in most of the social sciences. There, what purport to be definitions of classes of phenomena are typically general and inconsistent to the point of lacking empirical applicability (certainly in the operational sense of the world). Moreover, what passes for a substantive theory in the social sciences is more often than not actually a loosely formulated conception. These observations are not intended to deride the social sciences for lack of progress. All fields probably go through a "conceptions" stage; it is only more apparent in some than in others.

Of the social sciences, there is perhaps no better clear-cut illustration of the importance of conceptions than in the field identified as criminology and the study of deviant behavior. As we shall see, the history of the field can be described best in terms of changing conceptions of crime, criminals, deviants, and deviation. But the purpose of this paper is not an historical account of major trends in the field. If it is true that conceptions give rise to formal definitions and substantive theory, then a critical appraisal of conceptions is important in its own right. This is all the more true in the case of criminology and the study of deviant behavior, where conceptions are frequently confused with substantive theories, and the latter so clearly reflect the former.

Older Conceptions

In recent years there has been a significant change in the prevailing conception of deviant behavior and deviants. Prior to what is designated here as the "new perspective," it commonly was assumed that there is something inherent in deviants which distinguishes them from non-deviants.[1] Thus, from Lombroso to Sheldon, criminals were viewed as biologically distinctive in one way or another.[2] The inadequacies of this conception are now obvious. After decades of research, no biological characteristic which distinguishes criminals has been discovered, and this generalization applies even to particular types of criminals (e.g., murderers, bigamists, etc.). Consequently, few theorists now even toy with the notion that all criminals are atavistic, mentally defective, constitutionally inferior. But the rejection of the biological conception of crime stems from more than research findings. Even casual observation and mild logic cast doubt on the idea. Since legislators are not geneticists, it is difficult to see how they can pass laws in such a way as to create "born criminals." Equally important, since most if not all "normal" persons have violated a law at one time or another,[3] the assertion that criminals are so by heredity now appears most questionable.

Although the biological conception generally has been rejected, what is here designated as the analytic conception of criminal acts largely has escaped criticism. Rather than view criminal acts as nothing more or less than behavior contrary to legal norms, the acts are construed as somehow injurious to society. The shift from the biological to the analytical conception is thus from the actors to the characteristics of their acts, with the idea being that some acts are inherently "criminal" or at least that criminal acts share intrinsic characteristics in common.

The analytical conception is certainly more defensible than the biological view, but it is by no means free of criticism. Above all, the "injurious" quality of some deviant acts is by no means conspicuous, as witness Durkheim's observation:

> . . . there are many acts which have been and still are regarded as criminal without in themselves being harmful to society. What social danger is there in touching a tabooed object, an impure animal or man, in letting the sacred fire die down, in eating certain meats, in failure to make the traditional sacrifice over the grave of parents, in not exactly pronouncing the ritual formula, in not celebrating holidays, etc.?[4]

Only a radical functionalism would interpret the acts noted by Durkheim as literally injuring society in any reasonable sense of the word. The crucial point is that, far from actually injuring society or sharing some intrinsic feature in common, acts may be criminal or deviant because and only because they are proscribed legally and/or socially. The proscription may be irrational in that members of the society cannot explain it, but it is real nonetheless. Similarly, a law may be "arbitrary" in that it is imposed by a powerful minority and, as a consequence, lacks popular support and is actively opposed. But if the law is consistently enforced (i.e., sanctions are imposed regularly on violators), it is difficult to see how it is not "real."

The fact that laws may appear to be irrational and arbitrary has prompted attempts to define crime independently of legal criteria, i.e., analytically. The first step in this direction was Garofalo's concept of natural crime—acts which violate prevailing sentiments of pity and probity.[5] Garofalo's endeavor accomplished very little. Just as there is probably no act which is contrary to law universally, it is equally true that no act violates sentiments of pity and probity in all societies. In other words, cultural relativity defeats any attempt to compile a list of acts which are crimes universally. Also, it is hard to see why the violation of a rigorously enforced traffic regulation is not a crime even though unrelated to sentiments of pity and probity. If it is not a crime, what is it?

The search for an analytic identification of crime continued in Sellin's proposal to abandon legal criteria altogether in preference for "conduct norms."[6] The rationale for the proposal is simple. Because laws vary and may be "arbitrary" in any one society, a purely legal definition of crime is not suited for scientific study. But Sellin's observations on the arbitrariness of laws apply in much the same way to conduct norms. Just as the content of criminal law varies from one society to the next and from time to time, so does the content of extra-legal norms. Further, the latter may be just as arbitrary as criminal laws. Even in a highly urbanized society such as the United States, there is evidently no rationale or utilitarian reason for all of the norms pertaining to mode of dress. True, there may be much greater conformity to conduct norms than to some laws, but the degree of con-formity is hardly an adequate criterion of the "reality" of norms, legal or extra-legal. If any credence whatever can be placed in the Kinsey report, sexual taboos may be violated frequently and yet remain as taboos. As a case in point, even if adultery is now common in the United States, it is significant that the participants typically attempt to conceal their acts. In brief, just as laws may be violated frequently and are "unreal" in that sense, the same applies to some conduct norms; but in neither case do they cease to be norms. They would cease to be norms if and only if one defines de-viation in terms of statistical regularities in behavior, but not even Sellin would subscribe to the notion that normative phenomena can or should be defined in statistical terms.

In summary, however capricious and irrational legal and extra-legal norms may appear to be, the inescapable conclusion is that some acts are criminal or deviant for the very simple reason that they are proscribed.

The New Conception

Whereas both the pathological and the analytical conceptions of deviation assume that some intrinsic feature characterizes deviants and/or deviant acts, an emerging perspective in sociology flatly rejects any such assump-tion. Indeed, as witness the following statements by Kitsuse, Becker, and Erikson, exactly the opposite position is taken.

Kitsuse: Forms of behavior *per se* do not differentiate deviants from non-deviants; it is the responses of the conventional and conforming mem-bers of the society who identify and interpret behavior as defiant which sociologically transform persons into deviants.[7]

Erikson: From a sociological standpoint, deviance can be defined as conduct which is generally thought to require the attention of social control agencies—that is, conduct about which "something should be done." Deviance is not a property *inherent in* certain forms of behavior; it is a property *conferred upon* these forms by the audiences which directly or indirectly witness them. Sociologically, then, the critical variable in the study of deviance is the social *audience* rather than individual *person,* since it is the audience which eventually decides whether or not any given action or actions will become a visible case of deviation.[8]

Becker: From this point of view, deviance is *not* a quality of the act a person commits, but rather a consequence of the application by others of rules and sanctions to an "offender." The deviant is one to whom that label has successfully been applied; deviant behavior is behavior that people so label.[9]

The common assertion in the above statements is that acts can be identified as deviant or criminal only by reference to the character of reaction to them by the public or by the official agents of a politically organized society. Put simply, if the reaction is of a certain kind, then and only then is the act deviant. The crucial point is that the essential feature of a defiant or deviant act is *external* to the actor and the act. Further, even if the act or actors share some feature in common other than social reactions to them, the feature neither defines nor completely explains deviation. To take the extreme case, even if Lombroso had been correct in his assertion that criminals are biologically distinctive, the biological factor neither identifies the criminal nor explains criminality. Purely biological variables may explain why some persons commit certain acts, but they do not explain why the acts are crimes. Consequently, since criminal law is spatially and temporally relative, it is impossible to distinguish criminals from noncriminals (assuming that the latter do exist, which is questionable) in terms of biological characteristics. To illustrate, if act X is a crime in society A but not a crime in society B, it follows that, even assuming Lombroso to have been correct, the anatomical features which distinguish the criminal in society A may characterize the noncriminal in society B. In both societies some persons may be genetically predisposed to commit act X, but the act is a crime in one society and not in the other. Accordingly, the generalization that all persons with certain anatomical features are criminals would be, in this instance, false. True, one may assert that the "born criminal" is predisposed to violate the laws of his own society, but this assumes either that "the genes" know what the law is or that the members of the legislature are geneticists (i.e., they deliberately enact laws in such a way that the "born criminal" will violate them). Either assumption taxes credulity.

The new perspective of deviant behavior contradicts not only the biological but also the analytical conception. Whereas the latter seeks to find something intrinsic in deviant or, more specifically, criminal acts, the new conception denies any such characterization. True, the acts share a common denominator—they are identified by the character of reaction to them—but this does not mean that the acts are "injurious" to society or that they are in any way inherently abnormal. The new conception eschews the notion that some acts are deviant or criminal in all societies. For that matter, the reaction which identifies a deviant act may not be the same from one society or social group to the next. In general, then, the new conception of deviant behavior is relativistic in the extreme.

• • •

Notes

1. Throughout this paper crime is treated as a sub-class of deviant behavior. Particular issues may be discussed with reference to crime, but on the whole the observations apply to deviant behavior generally.

2. Although not essential to the argument, it is perhaps significant that the alleged biological differentiae of criminals have been consistently viewed as "pathological" in one sense or another.

3. See Edwin H. Sutherland and Donald R. Cressey, *Principles of Criminology,* 6th ed., Chicago: J.B. Lippincott, 1960, p. 39.

4. Emile Durkheim, *The Division of Labor in Society,* trans. George Simpson, Glencoe, Illinois: The Free Press, 1949, p. 72.

5. Raffaele Garofalo, *Criminology,* Boston: Little, Brown & Co., 1914, Chapter I.

6. Thorsten Sellin, *Culture Conflict and Crime,* New York: Social Science Research Council, Bulletin 14, 1938.

7. John I. Kitsuse, "Societal Reaction to Deviant Behavior: Problems of Theory and Method," *Social Problems,* 9 (Winter, 1962), p. 253.

8. Kai T. Erikson, "Notes on the Sociology of Deviance," *Social Problems,* 9 (Spring, 1962), p. 308.

9. Howard S. Becker, *Outsiders,* New York: The Free Press of Glencoe, 1963, p. 9.

Positive Deviance: A Classificatory Model

Druann Maria Heckert

Introduction

Positive deviance has been variously defined in the literature. Additionally, divergent examples, ranging from extreme intelligence to accomplished athletes have been advanced as pertinent examples of positive deviance. While the actors and/or actions that have been mentioned in the literature do have in common that there has been a deviation in a positive direction, the diversity of the examples is great. Consequently, a classificatory model, developed from examples that have been cited in the literature on positive deviance is presented. The types (i.e., ideal types) include the following: altruism, charisma, innovation, supra-conforming behavior, and innate characteristics. The category of ex-deviants is also advanced.

Positive Deviance

Not specifically utilizing the term, Sorokin (1950) had by 1950 recognized the validity of the concept. Convinced that Western culture had entered a "declining sensate phase," Sorokin felt that a negative orientation permeated these societies. This stance also dominated the social sciences. According to Sorokin:

> For decades Western social science has been cultivating . . . an ever-increasing study of crime and criminals; of insanity and the insane; of sex perversion and perverts; of hypocrisy and hypocrites. . . . In contrast to this, Western social science has paid scant attention to positive types of human beings, their positive achievements, their heroic actions, and their positive relationships. The criminal has been "researched" incomparably more thoroughly than the saint or the altruist; the idiot has been studied much more carefully than the genius; perverts and failures have been investigated much more intensely than integrated persons or heroes. (1950)

Sorokin (1950) suggested that a more thorough understanding of positive types of individuals was essential, especially in terms of the ability of humans to understand the negative.

Various conceptualizations of positive deviance have emerged during the last several decades. One important point is that, unlike the scholarly theorizing regarding deviance (negative deviance), in general, certain analysts (Best, Luckenbill 1982; Goode 1991; Sagarin 1985) contend that positive deviance does not exist. For example, in an acerbic denunciation, Sagarin (1985) contended that positive deviance is an oxymoron and should occupy no place in the study of deviance and Goode (1991) also proclaimed that the concept was not viable. Nevertheless, this opinion is not universally accepted.

Currently, existing literature in positive deviance is scant in comparison to the voluminous literature in negative deviance. However, social scientists have advanced the point of view that the concept of positive deviance is important, and furthermore, pertinent to the study of deviance, in general. According to Ben-Yehuda (1990), " . . . it will open new and exciting theoretical and empirical windows for research." Considering the multitude and the divergency of definitions and definitional approaches to the concept of deviance, it should not be surprising that there has also been a variety of definitions/definitional approaches offered for positive deviance. As such, these can be separated into the following categories: discussions of positive deviance that do not specifically use the terminology, definitions postulating a norm-violation perspective, definitions that utilize a labeling or societal reaction approach, and definitions that advocate a single or unique form of behavior only.

Certain theorists (Katz 1972; Lemert 1951; Liazos 1975; Sorokin 1950; Wilkins 1965) have recognized the validity of analyzing positive forms of behaviors within the general context of the study of deviance. Nevertheless, they did not employ the term positive deviance. For example, Wilkins (1965) wrote that some types of deviance are functional to society. Geniuses, reformers, and religious leaders are all examples of deviants, in addition to those examples more often thought about, such as criminals. Wilkins (1965) suggested that deviance could be examined by utilizing the analogy of a continuous distribution which ranged from bad to good. Normal behaviors constitute the major portion of the continuum; at the negative end are acts such as serious crimes and at the good end are behaviors such as those performed by saints. For example, regarding intelligence, most people fall into the middle part of the continuum, while there are a small number of those of very low intelligence (negative deviants) as well as a very small number of geniuses (positive deviants).

Perhaps, not always explicitly stating a preference of a specific paradigm, some theorists (Sorokin 1950; Wilkins 1965; Winslow 1970) have offered a view of positive deviance as that which violates norms, in that norms are exceeded. Similar to Wilkins (1965), Winslow (1970) noted that deviance can be constructed as a concept which is "relative to statistical norms." When deviance is conceptualized as approximating a normal curve, normative acts are in the middle of this curve. At one extreme end of the curve, beyond tolerance limits, are disapproved behaviors, such as mental illness and suicide. Positive deviance refers to approved deviation, beyond the tolerance limits, such as wealth, health, wisdom, virtue, and patriotism.

On the other hand, while not always stating their adoption of the paradigm, various theorists (Freedman, Doob 1968; Hawkins, Tiedeman 1975; Norland, Hepburn, Monette 1976; Scarpitti, McFarlane 1975; Steffensmeier, Terry 1975) have explained positive deviance from a labeling or societal reaction paradigmatic stance and in synthesis with a non-Marxist Conflict approach, so does Ben-Yehuda (1990). As an example, Freedman and Doob (1968) analyzed positive deviance from a psychological frame of reference, while for all intents and purposes proffering a labeling approach. From their point of view, deviance is an ephemeral characteristic which varies by situation. Differences are important. Various characteristics can be labeled deviant if others involved in a situation in which the individual is enmeshed do not share the same trait. As Freedman and Doob wrote:

> Gulliver was as deviant among the Brobdingnags when he was unimaginably small and weak then when he lived in Lilliput where he was fantastically big and powerful. The genius is as deviant as the idiot. . . . It is perhaps remarkable that the term "exceptional" children is used to refer not only to the unusually intelligent, but also the mentally retarded, the physically handicapped, the emotionally disturbed and so on. (1968)

The reaction of others is significant since certain acts will require a major difference from the norm to be judged deviant while with other acts, only a small variation from the norm will result in a designation of deviance. Simply put, as Steffensmeier and Terry (1975) noted, "Deviance consists of differentially valued phenomenon." Optimally desirable phenomena include great beauty or heroism as examples of positively valued behaviors.

As a final approach, some theorists (Ewald 1981; Buffalo, Rodgers 1971) have suggested that positive deviance refers to only a very specific type of action. Ewald advanced the idea of positive deviance as excessive conformity when he wrote:

> Positive deviance is where the relationship to societal norms is not one of blatant violation but rather extension, intensification, or enhancement of social rules. In this case, the zealous pursuit or overcommitment to normative prescriptions is what earns the individual or group the label of deviant. The individual or group is essentially true to normative standards but simply goes "too far" in that plausible or actual results are judged inappropriate by the general culture. (1981)

In a nutshell, positive deviance has been conceptualized as follows: from a norm-violation stance, from a labeling perspective, and from the reference of describing only one type of act. Some integration can be achieved with the norm-violation and reactionist approaches. Therefore, positive deviance is defined as behavior that people label (publicly evaluate) in a superior sense. That labeling will typically occur because the behavior departs from that which is considered normative in the particular case.

Examples of Positive Deviance

A myriad of behaviors and/or actions have been advanced as examples of positive deviance. Specifically, the following have been referred to as examples of positive deviance: Nobel Prize winners (Szasz 1970), the gifted (Huryn 1986), motion picture stars (Lemert 1951), superstar athletes (Scarpitti, McFarlane 1975), pro quarterbacks (Steffensmeier, Terry 1975), geniuses (Hawkins, Tiedeman 1975), exceptionally beautiful women (Lemert 1951), reformers (Wilkins 1965), altruists (Sorokin 1950), Congressional Medal of Honor winners (Steffensmeier, Terry 1975), religious leaders (Wilkins 1965), straight-A students (Hawkins, Tiedeman 1975), zealous weight lifters and runners (Ewald 1981), innovative/creative people, such as Freud or Darwin (Palmer 1990), and social idealists (Scarpitti, McFarlane 1975).

These behaviors and/or actions are similar to the extent that they are all examples of positive deviance. Consequently, people will label (publicly evaluate) the behaviors and/or actors in a superior manner. In essence, there is a departure from that which is deemed to be normative in a society. As a result of the behavior being non-normative, several potential consequences ensure the similarity of the divergent types of positive deviance. For example, positive deviants due to the fact that in essence they are as different from "normal" as negative deviants and perhaps threatening to the dominant social order, can, at times, be originally labeled negative deviants (e.g., the French Impressionists, Galileo, civil rights leaders) by the powers that be. Also, even many types of positive deviance, that are for the most part viewed positively, often concomitantly, are subject in some respects to negative treatment. For example, inordinately intelligent individuals are considered positive deviants, according to Scarpitti and McFarlane (1975). Nevertheless, derogatory traits are often imputed to them. This process is intuitively obvious to the gifted child who is simultaneously termed gifted, yet perniciously assumed to be "geeky" or socially unacceptable to peers. In essence, various types of positive deviance share many attributes in common. Perhaps, positive deviants even have similarities to negative deviants that they do not share with non-deviants.

Nevertheless, a problem emerges due to the diversity of behaviors and/or actors that have been posited to be examples of positive deviants. In reality, a Congressional Medal of Honor winner, a charismatic religious leader, and a beauty queen winner are actually quite disparate. Comparatively, the mentally ill, criminals, and the physically handicapped are also different. Consequently, to delve further into the nature of positive deviance, a typology of positive deviance would assist in the elucidation of positive deviance.

Positive Deviance: A Classificatory Model

The following types of positive deviance are advanced: altruism, charisma, innovation, supra-conformity, and innate characteristics. This classificatory scheme was developed by examining and categorizing the examples provided in the existing literature on positive deviance. The typology may not yet be exhausted at this point; indeed, another potential type of positive deviant, the ex-deviant, is suggested. Additionally, other types of positive deviance could also be postulated at some further point. This model is composed of ideal types.

Altruism

The first form of positive deviance postulated is altruism. Sorokin (1950) specifically discussed altruists in general (including saints and good neighbors as examples), Scarpitti and McFarlane (1975) mentioned self-sacrificing heroes, and in a variation on that particular theme, Steffensmeier and Terry (1975) referred to Congressional Medal of Honor winners. Interestingly, while altruism has been primarily researched by psychologists in the modern era, Auguste Comte (1966) was the first social scientist to use and analyze the concept. Altruism involves an act undertaken voluntarily to assist another person or other people without any expectation of reward (Leeds 1963; Cialdini, Kerrick, Bauman 1982; Grusec 1981; Macaulay, Berkowitz 1970). As Sorokin so eloquently noted,

> Genuine altruism is pure also in its motivation: altruistic actions are performed for their own sake, quite apart from any consideration of pleasures of utility. (1948)

Rosenhan (1970) has dichotomized altruism into normal altruism which includes acts such as donating small amounts of money and does not require much effort and autonomous altruism, which refers to actors, such as abolitionists who did exert themselves and sacrifice themselves to a much greater degree. Autonomous altruism is more descriptive of positive deviance.

Charisma

Charisma is the second type of positive deviance. Sorokin (1950) discussed the historical examples of Gandhi and Jesus as examples, and Wilkins (1965) cited religious leaders in general as positive deviants. According to the seminal work of Weber (1947), the charismatic claim to legitimate authority (as opposed to rational-legal or traditional authority) is rooted in the devotion of followers to the believed (not necessarily tangible) extraordinary qualities of their leader and the authority is based on the willingness of the followers to obey their leader. More comprehensively, Weber wrote:

> The term "charisma" will be applied to a certain quality of an individual personality by virtue of which he is set apart from ordinary men and treated as endowed with supernatural, superhuman, or at least specifically exceptional powers of qualities. These are such as are not accessible to the ordinary person, but are regarded as of divine origin or as exemplary, and on the basis of them the individual concerned is treated as a leader. . . . How the quality in question would be ultimately judged from any ethical, esthetic, or their such point of view is naturally entirely indifferent for purposes of definition. What is alone important is how the individual is actually regarded by those subject to charismatic authority by his "followers" or "disciples." (1947)

One important point that Weber (1947) made was that this quality can be attributed by followers to people perceived as having gifts in different areas, including, for example, intellectuals, shamans (magicians), war leaders, heroes, and prophets. Essentially, the charismatic relationship is composed of two important elements: a situation in which there is a following that wants to be led and a leader who has the capability to catalyze their needs and/or desires.

Innovation

Innovation is another form of positive deviance. As examples, Szasz (1970) discussed Nobel Prize winners, Palmer (1990) analyzed innovative/creative figures including Freud and Darwin, and Wilkins (1965) suggested reformers. In essence, innovation (or invention) has been basically defined as the combining of already existing cultural elements in a novel manner, or the modifying of already existing cultural elements to produce a new one (Lenski, Lenski 1982; Linton 1936; Ogburn 1964; Rogers, Shoemaker 1971). Innovations cover a myriad of areas, as they range from the abstract to the pragmatic, and from art to technology. As Kallen (1964) notes, innovations are a fundamental factor of a society as innovations can occur in these crucial areas of culture: food, clothing, shelter, defense, disease prevention, production, recreation, religion, science, thought, literature, and art. Innovators, as positive deviants, profoundly impact the life of a culture. The willingness of a society to foster change, which is a condition present to a greater extent in modern societies, will relate to the acceptance of the innovator.

Supra-Conformity

A fourth kind of positive deviance is supra-conformity. Hawkins and Tiedeman (1975) pointed to straight-A students, Ewald (1981) analyzed zealous weight lifters and runners, and Scarpitti and McFarlane (1975) mentioned extreme moralists. Additionally, Buffalo and Rodgers (1971) and Ewald

(1981) have utilized the concept of positive deviance to suggest only supra-conforming behavior. Supra-conformity is behavior that is at the level of the idealized within a culture. That is, as Gibbs noted,

> Collective evaluations refer to what behavior *ought to be* in a society, whereas collective expectations denote what behavior actually *will be*. (1965)

In relation to the normative structure of a society, there is a tendency for the idealized version of the norms to be attained less often than the realized versions of the norm (Homans 1950; Johnson 1978; White 1961). In other words, norms operate at two levels—the ideal, which most people believe is better but few achieve, and the realistic version, which most people can achieve. The negative deviant fails to abide by either level; the "normal" person operates at the realistic level, but does not achieve the idealized level; and the positive deviant is able to attain or behave at the idealized level. Cohen expressed this idea in the following manner when he noted that only a small percentage of people can reach that which is idealized in a society:

> The ideal is one thing, the practice another. In other words, persons may be variously socialized into the ideological traditions of their society so that the two—ideology and its achievement—are not simply the same thing from different perspectives, but are quite independently variable entities. (1966)

Thus, a supra-conformist demonstrates desire and ability to pursue, perhaps, even in quixotic style if necessary that which is idealized for a particular norm.

Innate Characteristics

Finally, innate characteristics constitute a fifth kind of positive deviance. Certain actions/actors, that are positive deviance, are at least partially rooted in innate characteristics. Examples that have been referred to as positive deviance include beautiful women (Hawkins, Tiedeman 1975; Lemert 1951), superstar athletes (Scarpitti, McFarlane 1975), and movie stars (Lemert 1951). The use of the terminology, innate characteristics, is actually not the best choice to described this type of positive deviance. These traits (e.g., beauty, intelligence, talent) are innate to a certain, as to yet, unspecifiable extent, and to a certain, as to yet, unspecifiable extent, are modified by environmental conditions. In addition, these characteristics are culturally defined. For example, Rebelsky and Daniel (1976) clearly note that intelligence is culturally defined and according to Morse, Reis, Gruzen, and Wolff (1974), attractiveness is culturally defined, as individuals from the same cultural background do tend to coincide in their assessment of what is physically attractive. As such, innate characteristics can be considered a fifth type of positive deviance. As Scarpitti and McFarlane noted,

Deviant attributes often are the products of one's biological inheritance, which accounts for such conditions as rare beauty, extraordinary intelligence, or dwarfism. (1975)

Another Potential Type: The Ex-Deviant

The potential for new types of positive deviance, not previously cited in the literature, certainly exists. For example, the ex-deviant might possibly be deemed a positive deviant. The previously stigmatized person, labeled in a negative fashion, that manages to convert to a status of normative person is essentially a novel way to think of a positive deviant. According to Pfuhl and Henry, destigmatization

> . . . refers to the processes used to negate or expunge a deviant identity and replace it with one that is essentially non-deviant or normal. (1993)

Subsumed as types of destigmatization are purification " . . . whereby one's defective self is replaced by a moral or 'normal' self, either by sacred or secular norms" and transcendence whereby the deviant manages " . . . to display a 'better' self rather than to eliminate the former self." An example of destigmatization is an ex-convict; an example of transcendence is an accomplished person with a physical disability. Purification essentially involves a destigmatization by which the person exits a stigmatized role. While the previous stigmatization might still taint the individual, society tends to positively evaluate the purification. As such, an ex-deviant might potentially be considered in relation to the concept of positive deviance.

More specifically, Ebaugh has defined the ex-role as,

> The process of disengagement from a role that is central to one's self-identity and the reestablishment of an identity in a new role that takes into account one's ex-role. (1988)

As Ebaugh (1988) notes, certain ex-roles are in fact potentially stigmatizing as they are not generally culturally construed as positive role changes (e.g., ex-spouse, ex-nun). On the other hand, other role changes are societally constructed as positive in that the deviant has been rehabilitated to a more positive status (e.g., ex-alcoholic, ex-prostitute, ex-convict). Additionally, those role changes viewed as socially positive are deemed to be more within the control of individuals.

Crucially, the exiting process is a fairly difficult one, mediated by various factors. Ebaugh (1988) hypothesizes that the role exit is a fairly long-term process generally consisting of the following stages: first doubts, or doubting the previous role; seeking and evaluating alternatives to the role (including "conscious cuing, anticipatory socialization, role rehearsal, and shifting reference groups"); turning points; and establishing the ex-role. Even while the role exit from deviant to non-deviant is positively evaluated and labeled, the person still often experiences the remnants of the stigmatization that typically accompanies the previous role. Thus, there is a tenuousness to exiting a role. Perhaps, the fragile and difficult path from deviant to ex-deviant produces the positive evaluation of the category of ex-deviant.

One of the most dramatic role changes is that of ex-convict. Irwin and Austin have outlined the extraordinary difficulty in the transformation of an incarcerated individual to an ex-convict who does not relapse, as follows:

> During this period of supervision, many released inmates experience tremendous difficulties in adjusting to the outside world without being rearrested and returning to prison and jail. In general, most inmates are rearrested at least once after being released from prison. (1997)

Among the most critical factors in facilitating recidivism, or impending rehabilitation, according to Irwin and Allen (1997) are the following: the trauma of reentering the world after being incarcerated in a total institution; the difficulty of attaining employment for the all too often undereducated and underskilled ex-convict; the intensive supervision and law enforcement mandate of parole agents; drug testing; intensive supervision programs; and electronic monitoring. While Irwin and Allen (1997) conclude that the majority of incarcerated individuals do intend to lead a conforming life after their release from prison, these difficult obstacles result in most inmates ending up dependent, drifting between conventionality and criminality, and dereliction. Some do make it.

How do the formerly incarcerated achieve the positively evaluated status of returning to conformity? Irwin and Allen conclude:

> They usually do so only because of the random chance of securing a good job and a niche in some conventional social world by virtue of their own individual efforts to "straighten up" often with the help of their family, friends, or primary assistance organization. But even members of this group are likely to face periodic obstacles in being accepted fully as a citizen. (1997)

Shover (1983) has most extensively analyzed the successful passage, from the perspective of ex-convicts (in this case, ordinary property offenders). According to ex-convicts, two types of changes assisted the transition from the negative status of convict to ex-convict: temporal changes and interpersonal changes. The temporal changes, perhaps congruent to a certain extent with the processes of adult maturation, included the following: an identity shift, in the confrontation with a past of unsuccessful criminality; a perception that their time had not been well spent and that time was not infinite; a lessening of youthful material goals; and a sense of tiredness at the thought of dealing with a criminal justice system that while not omnipotent, is certainly potent. Additionally, interpersonal contingencies primarily revolved around involvement with a significant relationship and secure employment. Essentially, these were the factors identified by one group of ex-deviants as the most pertinent in their advancing beyond their formerly negative status.

Thus, the ex-deviant transcends the stigmatization that Goffman (1963) deemed so critical in shaping the individual. While the ex-deviant still may be tinged with a previous status, this particularly unique category is another potential type of positive deviance. Perhaps, other types will be outlined in the future.

Conclusion

One point should be noted. Various actions or actors probably transcend more than one category. As an example, Mother Theresa lived a life of altruism (rather than just having engaged in one dramatic altruistic incident), yet was also a supra-conformist, as she abided by the idealized norms of religious adherents, rather than just the expected behavioral norms. Additionally, while Martin Luther King was primarily a charismatic leader, he was innovative in that he combined cultural elements in a new way, by applying the techniques of nonviolent civil disobedience to the civil rights movement. At the same time, with his specifically exquisite oratorical skills, he also fits into the category of having been a possessor of innate characteristics. All in all, many actions and/or actors can be explained by more than one type. Nevertheless, the present typology seems the best way to begin the categorization of positive deviance, since as previously noted, each type can be considered an ideal type.

Hopefully, this typology will help to clarify the concept of positive deviance and facilitate the emergence of other questions and other issues especially those issues that have been suggested in relationship to deviance (negative deviance). For example, various theorists contrast major forms of deviance, with minor ones. Curra (1994) and Raybeck (1991) differentiate between soft deviance, or unique behaviors not consistent with social norms but not threatening to the social system, and hard deviance, or more serious and ominous forms of behavior. Along these same lines, Thio (1988) contrasts higher-consensus deviance with lower-consensus deviance, depending on the seriousness of the act and the degree of societal consensus in relationship to the perception of the act. In reference to examples of positive deviance that have been cited in the literature, most are probably soft deviance, in that the acts do not generally harm others and are not reacted to as serious. For example, altruists and straight-A students do not potentially harm others. In some cases, the predominant paradigms ensconced in the social order are potentially challenged by such examples of positive deviants as innovators in any realm of the social order, from science to art to politics to religion, or by reformers. This phenomenon might address the issue of why certain positive deviants are not generally easily accepted in their time and place. Deviance is relative; many positive deviants also experience this relativity in that the initial reception to their actions is negative. In this sense, these types of positive deviants can potentially, at least, be deemed hard deviance, in the sense that the social order is challenged.

Another interesting issue is the following and also relates to the relativity of deviance. Are certain actions and/or actors (or categories of positive deviance) more likely to be positively labeled, negatively labeled, or neutrally labeled at first? Perhaps, since innovation can be more psychologically threatening to a culture, innovation is more often negatively labeled in the beginning. On the other hand, altruism, because it involves self-sacrifice, and is not usually potentially threatening to society, is more often positively evaluated at first. In addition, physical attractiveness as a form of innate characteristic seems usually to result in an initial positive label and minimal negative treatment. According to Dion, Berscheid, and Walster (1972) "what is beautiful is good" since the attractive are the recipients of ubiquitous advantageous treatment, extending to various parts of their life.

Additionally, the notion of stigma, outlined by Goffman (1963) has been central to the examination of deviance. The ambivalence toward positive deviance does raise the possibility that stigma is applicable in this case, also. The central reason is that positive deviants are also different. For example, as previously suggested, the entire social construction of the "geek" with its accompanying stereotypes, would suggest that straight-A students and/or the gifted are not entirely positively received. The sword is dual-edged in that while there is positive treatment, the stigmatization is also profound and quite potentially has a negative impact on individuals so categorized. The clownish, or not completely human construction of the geek (or nerd or dweeb or dork) is perhaps similar to the village idiot or the in-group deviant, as presented by Goffman (1963), a "mascot" not fully rejected and partially admired for academic acumen, yet not fully accepted. Positive deviants are different; due to their difference, the possibility of stigmatization is great.

Another useful way to think about deviance, that might also be pertinent to positive deviance, is the manner in which deviance is functional to society. Cohen (1966) has maintained that deviance can contribute to society in the following manner: opposing red tape and dealing with anomalies, serving as a safety valve, clarifying the rules, uniting a group in opposition to the deviant, uniting a group in support of the deviant, accentuating conformity, and performing as a warning sign to society. Along these same lines, perhaps, positive deviance also provides some of the same opportunities to benefit the social order. For example, reformers clearly provide a warning signal to society that the social order is in dire need of change. As another example, positive deviants accent conformity. As Cohen (1966) describes, "The good deed, as Shakespeare noted, shines brightest in a naughty world." Thus, as deviants (negative deviants) are a reference for the contrast between bad and good, so can positive deviants, ranging from straight-A students to altruists serve as a reference. Altruists also contrast with conforming behavior, serving as a guide for human potentiality. As such, positive deviance, like deviance, also contributes to the social order of society.

The concept of positive deviance needs to be further expanded. Yet, it does appear that critical ideas related to deviance could also be applied to positive deviance. Additionally, this typology posits that there is more than one type of positive deviance. Each type needs to be examined further— within a framework and within the parameters of positive deviance and of deviance theory—as a unique and as an important entity.

References

Ben-Yehuda N 1990 Positive and negative deviance: more fuel for a controversy *Deviant Behavior* 11 221–243

Best J, DF Luckenbill 1982 *Organizing Deviance* Englewood Cliffs, NJ: Prentice-Hall

Buffalo MD, JW Rodgers 1971 Behavioral norms, moral norms, and attachment: problems of deviance and conformity *Social Problems* 19 101–113

Cialdini RJ, DT Kerrick, DJ Bauman 1982 Effects of mood on prosocial behavior in children and adults. Pp 339–359 N Eisenberg ed *The Development of Prosocial Behavior* NY: Academic Press

Cohen AK 1966 *Deviance and Control* Englewood Cliffs, NJ: Prentice-Hall

Comte A 1966 *System of Positive Polity. Vol. 1. General Views of Positivism and Introductory Principles* Tr. JH Bridges NY: Burt Franklin

Curra J 1994 *Understanding Social Deviance: From the Near Side to the Outer Limits* NY: Harper Collins

Dion K, E Berscheid, E Walster 1972 What is beautiful is good *J Personality Social Psychol* 24 285–290

Ebaugh HRF 1988 *Becoming an Ex: The Process of Role Exit* Chicago: U Chicago Press

Ewald 1981 *The Extension of the Becker Model of Socialization to Positive Deviance: The Cases of Weight Lifting and Running.* Unpublished Ph.D. Dissertation: Ohio State U

Freedman JL, AN Doob 1968 *Deviancy: The Psychology of Being Different* NY: Academic Press

Gibbs JP 1965 Norms: the problem of definition and classification *Amer J Sociology* 70 586–594

Goffman E 1963 *Stigma: Notes on the Management of Spoiled Identity* Englewood Cliffs, NJ: Prentice-Hall

Goode E 1991 Positive deviance: a viable concept *Deviant Behavior* 12 289–309

Grusec JE 1981 Socialization processes and the development of altruism. Pp. 65–90 P Rushton, RM Sorrentino eds *Altruism and Helping Behavior* Hillsdale, NJ: Lawrence Erlbaum

Hawkins R, G Tiedeman 1975 *The Creation of Deviance* Columbus, OH: Charles E Merrill Pub

Homans GC 1950 *The Human Group* NY: Harcourt, Brace, and Company

Huryn JS 1986 Giftedness as deviance: a test of interaction theories *Deviant Behavior* 7 175–186

Irwin J, J Austin 1997 *It's About Time: America's Imprisonment Binge* 2nd ed Belmont, CA: Wadsworth

Johnson EH 1978 *Crime, Correction, and Society* NY: Harcourt, Brace, and Company

Kallen HM 1964 Innovation. Pp. 427–430 A Etzioni, E Etzioni eds *Social Change* NY: Basic Books

Katz J 1972 Deviance, charisma, and rule-defined behavior *Social Problems* 20 186–202

Leeds R 1963 Altruism and the norm of giving *Merrill-Palmer Qrtly* 9 229–40

Lemert EM 1951 *Social Pathology* NY: McGraw-Hill

Lenski G, J Lenski 1982 *Human Societies* NY: McGraw-Hill

Liazos A 1975 The poverty of the sociology of deviance: nuts, sluts, and perverts. Pp. 9–29 DJ Steffensmeier, RM Terry eds *Examining Deviance Experimentally* NY: Alfred Publishing

Linton R 1936 *The Study of Man* NY: C Appleton-Century

Macauley JR, L Berkowitz 1970 Overview. Pp. 1–9 J Macauley, L Berkowitz eds *Altruism and Helping Behavior* NY: Academic Press

Morse ST, HT Reis, J Gruzen, E Wolff 1974 The eye of the beholder: determinants of physical attractiveness judgments in the United States and South Africa *J Personality* 42 528–41

Norland S, JR Hepburn, D Monette 1976 The effects of labeling and consistent differentiation in the construction of positive deviance *Sociology Soc Res* 61 83–95

Ogburn WF 1964 *On Culture and Social Change: Selected Papers* OD Duncan ed. Chicago: U Chicago Press

Palmer S 1990 *Deviant Behavior* NY: Plenum Press

Pfuhl E, S Henry 1993 *The Deviance Process* 3rd ed NY: Aldine de Gruyter

Raybeck D 1991 Deviance: anthropological perspectives. Pp. 51–72 M Freilich, D Raybeck, J Savishinsky eds *Deviance: Anthropological Perspectives* NY: Bergin and Garvey

Rebelsky FA, PA Daniel 1976 Cross-cultural studies of infant intelligence. Pp. 279–97 M Lewis ed *Origins of Intelligence* NY: Plenum Press

Rogers EM, FF Shoemaker 1971 *Communication of Innovations* NY: Free Press of Glencoe

Rosenhan D 1970 The naturalistic socialization of altruistic autonomy. Pp. 251–68 J Macauley, L Berkowitz eds *Altruism and Helping Behavior* NY: Academic Press

Sagarin E 1985 Positive deviance: an oxymoron *Deviant Behavior* 6 169–181

Scarpitti FR, PT McFarlane 1975 *Deviance: Action, Reaction, Interaction* Reading, MA: Addison-Wesley

Shover N 1983 The later stages of ordinary property offender careers *Social Problems* 31 208–218

Sorokin PA 1948 *The Reconstruction of Humanity* Boston: Beacon Press

—— 1950 *Altruistic Love* Boston: Beacon Press

Steffensmeier DJ, RM Terry 1975 *Examining Deviance Experimentally* Port Washington, NY: Alfred Publishing

Szasz TS 1970 *The Manufacture of Madness* NY: Harper and Row

Thio A 1988 *Deviant Behavior* 3rd ed NY: Harper Collins

Weber M 1947 *The Theory of Social and Economic Organization* Trs. AM Henderson, T Parsons NY: Free Press

White W 1961 *Beyond Conformity* Westport, CT: Greenwood Press

Wilkins LT 1965 *Social Deviance* Englewood Cliffs, NJ: Prentice-Hall

Winslow RW 1970 *Society in Transition: A Social Approach to Deviance* NY: Free Press

Moral Entrepreneurs: The Creation and Enforcement of Deviant Categories

Howard S. Becker

Rule Creators

The prototype of the rule creator, but not the only variety as we shall see, is the crusading reformer. He is interested in the content of rules. The existing rules do not satisfy him because there is some evil which profoundly disturbs him. He feels that nothing can be right in the world until rules are made to correct it. He operates with an absolute ethic; what he sees is truly and totally evil with no qualification. Any means is justified to do away with it. The crusader is fervent and righteous, often self-righteous.

It is appropriate to think of reformers as crusaders because they typically believe that their mission is a holy one. The prohibitionist serves as an excellent example, as does the person who wants to suppress vice and sexual delinquency or the person who wants to do away with gambling.

These examples suggest that the moral crusader is a meddling busybody, interested in forcing his own morals on others. But this is a one-sided view. Many moral crusades have strong humanitarian overtones. The crusader is not only interested in seeing to it that other people do what he thinks [is] right. He believes that if they do what is right it will be good for them. Or he may feel that his reform will prevent certain kinds of exploitation of one person by another. Prohibitionists felt that they were not simply forcing their morals on others, but attempting to provide the conditions for a better way of life for people prevented by drink from realizing a truly good life. Abolitionists were not simply trying to prevent slave owners from doing the wrong thing; they were trying to help slaves achieve a better life. Because of the importance of the humanitarian motive, moral crusaders (despite their relatively single-minded devotion to their particular cause) often lend their support to other humanitarian crusades. Joseph Gusfield has pointed out that:

> The American temperance movement during the 19th century was a part of a general effort toward the improvement of the worth of the

33

human being through improved morality as well as economic conditions. The mixture of the religious, the equalitarian, and the humanitarian was an outstanding facet of the moral reformism of many
movements. Temperance supporters formed a large segment of movements such as sabbatarianism, abolition, woman's rights, agrarianism,
and humanitarian attempts to improve the lot of the poor. . . .

In its auxiliary interests the WCTU revealed a great concern for the
improvement of the welfare of the lower classes. It was active in campaigns to secure penal reform, to shorten working hours and raise
wages for workers, and to abolish child labor and in a number of other
humanitarian and equalitarian activities. In the 1880's the WCTU
worked to bring about legislation for the protection of working girls
against the exploitation by men.[1]

As Gusfield says,[2] "Moral reformism of this type suggests the approach
of a dominant class toward those less favorably situated in the economic
and social structure." Moral crusaders typically want to help those beneath
them to achieve a better status. That those beneath them do not always like
the means proposed for their salvation is another matter. But this fact—that
moral crusades are typically dominated by those in the upper levels of the
social structure—means that they add to the power they derive from the legitimacy of their moral position, the power they derive from their superior
position in society.

Naturally, many moral crusades draw support from people whose motives are less pure than those of the crusader. Thus, some industrialists supported Prohibition because they felt it would provide them with a more
manageable labor force.[3] Similarly, it is sometimes rumored that Nevada
gambling interests support the opposition to attempts to legalize gambling
in California because it would cut so heavily into their business, which depends in substantial measure on the population of Southern California.[4]

The moral crusader, however, is more concerned with ends than with
means. When it comes to drawing up specific rules (typically in the form of
legislation to be proposed to a state legislature or the Federal Congress), he
frequently relies on the advice of experts. Lawyers, expert in the drawing of
acceptable legislation, often play this role. Government bureaus in whose
jurisdiction the problem falls may also have the necessary expertise, as did
the Federal Bureau of Narcotics in the case of the marihuana problem.

As psychiatric ideology, however, becomes increasingly acceptable, a
new expert has appeared—the psychiatrist. Sutherland, in his discussion of
the natural history of sexual psychopath laws, pointed to the psychiatrist's
influence.[5] He suggests the following as the conditions under which the
sexual psychopath law, which provides that a person "who is diagnosed as
a sexual psychopath may be confined for an indefinite period in a state hospital for the insane,"[6] will be passed.

First, these laws are customarily enacted after a state of fear has been
aroused in a community by a few serious sex crimes committed in

quick succession. This is illustrated in Indiana, where a law was passed following three or four sexual attacks in Indianapolis, with murder in two. Heads of families bought guns and watch dogs, and the supply of locks and chains in the hardware stores of the city was completely exhausted. . . .

A second element in the process of developing sexual psychopath laws is the agitated activity of the community in connection with the fear. The attention of the community is focused on sex crimes, and people in the most varied situations envisage dangers and see the need of and possibility for their control. . . .

The third phase in the development of those sexual psychopath laws has been the appointment of a committee. The committee gathers the many conflicting recommendations of persons and groups of persons, attempts to determine "facts," studies procedures in other states, and makes recommendations, which generally include bills for the legislature. Although the general fear usually subsides within a few days, a committee has the formal duty of following through until positive action is taken. Terror which does not result in a committee is much less likely to result in a law.[7]

In the case of sexual psychopath laws, there usually is no government agency charged with dealing in a specialized way with sexual deviations. Therefore, when the need for expert advice in drawing up legislation arises, people frequently turn to the professional group most closely associated with such problems:

In some states, at the committee stage of the development of a sexual psychopath law, psychiatrists have played an important part. The psychiatrists, more than any others, have been the interest group back of the laws. A committee of psychiatrists and neurologists in Chicago wrote the bill which became the sexual psychopath law of Illinois; the bill was sponsored by the Chicago Bar Association and by the state's attorney of Cook County and was enacted with little opposition in the next session of the State Legislature. In Minnesota all the members of the governor's committee except one were psychiatrists. In Wisconsin the Milwaukee Neuropsychiatric Society shared in pressing the Milwaukee Crime Commission for the enactment of a law. In Indiana the attorney-general's committee received from the American Psychiatric Association copies of all the sexual psychopath laws which had been enacted in other states.[8]

The influence of psychiatrists in other realms of the criminal law has increased in recent years.

In any case, what is important about this example is not that psychiatrists are becoming increasingly influential, but that the moral crusader, at some point in the development of his crusade, often requires the services of a professional who can draw up the appropriate rules in an appropriate form. The crusader himself is often not concerned with such details. Enough for him that the main point has been won; he leaves its implementation to others.

By leaving the drafting of the specific rule in the hands of others, the crusader opens the door for many unforeseen influences. For those who draft legislation for crusaders have their own interests, which may affect the legislation they prepare. It is likely that the sexual psychopath laws drawn by psychiatrists contain many features never intended by the citizens who spearheaded the drives to "do something about sex crimes," features which do however reflect the professional interests of organized psychiatry.

• • •

Rule Enforcers

The most obvious consequence of a successful crusade is the creation of a new set of rules. With the creation of a new set of rules we often find that a new set of enforcement agencies and officials is established. Sometimes, of course, existing agencies take over the administration of the new rule, but more frequently a new set of rule enforcers is created. The passage of the Harrison Act presaged the creation of the Federal Narcotics Bureau, just as the passage of the Eighteenth Amendment led to the creation of police agencies charged with enforcing the Prohibition Laws.

With the establishment of organizations of rule enforcers, the crusade becomes institutionalized. What started out as a drive to convince the world of the moral necessity of a new rule finally becomes an organization devoted to the enforcement of the rule. Just as radical political movements turn into organized political parties and lusty evangelical sects become staid religious denominations, the final outcome of the moral crusade is a police force. To understand, therefore, how the rules creating a new class of outsiders are applied to particular people we must understand the motives and interests of police, the rule enforcers.

Although some policemen undoubtedly have a kind of crusading interest in stamping out evil, it is probably much more typical for the policeman to have a certain detached and objective view of his job. He is not so much concerned with the content of any particular rule as he is with the fact that it is his job to enforce the rule. When the rules are changed, he punishes what was once acceptable behavior just as he ceases to punish behavior that has been made legitimate by a change in the rules. The enforcer, then, may not be interested in the content of the rule as such, but only in the fact that the existence of the rule provides him with a job, a profession, and a *raison d'être*.

Since the enforcement of certain rules provides justification for his way of life, the enforcer has two interests which condition his enforcement activity: first, he must justify the existence of his position and, second, he must win the respect of those he deals with.

These interests are not peculiar to rule enforcers. Members of all occupations feel the need to justify their work and win the respect of others. Musicians would like to do this but have difficulty finding ways of successfully impressing their worth on customers. Janitors fail to win their tenants' respect, but develop an ideology which stresses the quasi-professional responsibility they have to keep confidential the intimate knowledge of tenants they acquire in the course of their work.[9] Physicians, lawyers, and other professionals, more successful in winning the respect of clients, develop elaborate mechanisms for maintaining a properly respectful relationship.

In justifying the existence of his position, the rule enforcer faces a double problem. On the one hand, he must demonstrate to others that the problem still exists: the rules he is supposed to enforce have some point, because infractions occur. On the other hand, he must show that his attempts at enforcement are effective and worthwhile, that the evil he is supposed to deal with is in fact being dealt with adequately. Therefore, enforcement organizations, particularly when they are seeking funds, typically oscillate between two kinds of claims. First, they say that by reason of their efforts the problem they deal with is approaching solution. But, in the same breath, they say the problem is perhaps worse than ever (though through no fault of their own) and requires renewed and increased effort to keep it under control. Enforcement officials can be more vehement than anyone else in their insistence that the problem they are supposed to deal with is still with us, in fact is more with us than ever before. In making these claims, enforcement officials provide good reason for continuing the existence of the position they occupy.

We may also note that enforcement officials and agencies are inclined to take a pessimistic view of human nature. If they do not actually believe in original sin, they at least like to dwell on the difficulties in getting people to abide by rules, on the characteristics of human nature that lead people toward evil. They are skeptical of attempts to reform rule-breakers.

The skeptical and pessimistic outlook of the rule enforcer, of course, is reinforced by his daily experience. He sees, as he goes about his work, the evidence that the problem is still with us. He sees the people who continually repeat offenses, thus definitely branding themselves in his eyes as outsiders. Yet it is not too great a stretch of the imagination to suppose that one of the underlying reasons for the enforcer's pessimism about human nature and the possibilities of reform is that fact that if human nature were perfectible and people could be permanently reformed, his job would come to an end.

In the same way, a rule enforcer is likely to believe that it is necessary for the people he deals with to respect him. If they do not, it will be very difficult to do his job; his feeling of security in his work will be lost. Therefore, a good deal of enforcement activity is devoted not to the actual enforcement of rules, but to coercing respect from the people the enforcer deals with. This means that one may be labeled as deviant not because he has actually broken a rule, but because he has shown disrespect to the enforcer of the rule.

Westley's study of policemen in a small industrial city furnishes a good example of this phenomenon. In his interview, he asked policemen, "When do you think a policeman is justified in roughing a man up?" He found that "at least 37% of the men believed that it was legitimate to use violence to coerce respect."[10] He gives some illuminating quotations from his interviews:

> Well, there are cases. For example, when you stop a fellow for a routine questioning, say a wise guy, and he starts talking back to you and telling you you are no good and that sort of thing. You know you can take a man in on a disorderly conduct charge, but you can practically never make it stick. So what you do in a case like that is to egg the guy on until he makes a remark where you can justifiably slap him and, then, if he fights back, you can call it resisting arrest.

> Well, a prisoner deserves to be hit when he goes to the point where he tries to put you below him.

> You've gotta get rough when a man's language becomes very bad, when he is trying to make a fool of you in front of everybody else. I think most policemen try to treat people in a nice way, but usually you have to talk pretty rough. That's the only way to set a man down, to make him show a little respect.[11]

What Westley describes is the use of an illegal means of coercing respect from others. Clearly, when a rule enforcer has the option of enforcing a rule or not, the difference in what he does may be caused by the attitude of the offender toward him. If the offender is properly respectful, the enforcer may smooth the situation over. If the offender is disrespectful, then sanctions may be visited on him. Westley has shown that this differential tends to operate in the case of traffic offenses, where the policeman's discretion is perhaps at a maximum.[12] But it probably operates in other areas as well.

Ordinarily, the rule enforcer has a great deal of discretion in many areas, if only because his resources are not sufficient to cope with the volume of rule-breaking he is supposed to deal with. This means that he cannot tackle everything at once and to this extent must temporize with evil. He cannot do the whole job and knows it. He takes his time, on the assumption that the problems he deals with will be around for a long while. He establishes priorities, dealing with things in their turn, handling the most pressing problems immediately and leaving others for later. His attitude toward his work, in short, is professional. He lacks the naive moral fervor characteristic of the rule creator.

If the enforcer is not going to tackle every case he knows of at once, he must have a basis for deciding when to enforce the rule, which persons committing which acts to label as deviant. One criterion for selecting people is the "fix." Some people have sufficient political influence or know-how to be able to ward off attempts at enforcement, if not at the time of apprehension then at a later stage in the process. Very often, this function is professionalized; someone performs the job on a full-time basis, available to anyone who wants to hire him. A professional thief described fixers this way:

> There is in every large city a regular fixer for professional thieves. He has no agents and does not solicit and seldom takes any case except that of a professional thief, just as they seldom go to anyone except him. This centralized and monopolistic system of fixing for professional thieves is found in practically all of the large cities and many of the small ones.[13]

Since it is mainly professional thieves who know about the fixer and his operations, the consequence of this criterion for selecting people to apply the rules to is that amateurs tend to be caught, convicted, and labeled deviant much more frequently than professionals. As the professional thief notes:

> You can tell by the way the case is handled in court when the fix is in. When the copper is not very certain he has the right man, or the testimony of the copper and the complainant does not agree, or the prosecutor goes easy on the defendant, or the judge is arrogant in his decisions, you can always be sure that someone has got the work in. This does not happen in many cases of theft, for there is one case of a professional to twenty-five or thirty amateurs who know nothing about the fix. These amateurs get the hard end of the deal every time. The coppers bawl out about the thieves, no one holds up his testimony, the judge delivers an oration, and all of them get credit for stopping a crime wave. When the professional hears the case immediately preceding his own, he will think, "He should have got ninety years. It's the damn amateurs who cause all the heat in the stores." Or else he thinks, "Isn't it a damn shame for that copper to send that kid away for a pair of hose, and in a few minutes he will agree to a small fine for me for stealing a fur coat?" But if the coppers did not send the amateurs away to strengthen their records of convictions, they could not sandwich in the professionals whom they turn loose.[14]

Enforcers of rules, since they have no stake in the content of particular rules themselves, often develop their own private evaluation of the importance of various kinds of rules and infractions of them. This set of priorities may differ considerably from those held by the general public. For instance, drug users typically believe (and a few policemen have personally confirmed it to me) that police do not consider the use of marihuana to be as important a problem or as dangerous a practice as the use of opiate drugs. Police base this conclusion on the fact that, in their experience, opiate users commit other crimes (such as theft or prostitution) in order to get drugs, while marihuana users do not.

Enforcers then, responding to the pressures of their own work situation, enforce rules and create outsiders in a selective way. Whether a person who commits a deviant act is in fact labeled a deviant depends on many things extraneous to his actual behavior: whether the enforcement official feels that at this time he must make some show of doing his job in order to justify his position, whether the misbehaver shows proper deference to the enforcer, whether the "fix" has been put in, and where the kind of act he has committed stands on the enforcer's list of priorities.

The professional enforcer's lack of fervor and routine approach to dealing with evil may get him into trouble with the rule creator. The rule creator, as we have said, is concerned with the content of the rules that interest him. He sees them as the means by which evil can be stamped out. He does not understand the enforcer's long-range approach to the same problems and cannot see why all the evil that is apparent cannot be stamped out at once.

When the person interested in the content of a rule realizes or has called to his attention the fact that enforcers are dealing selectively with the evil that concerns him, his righteous wrath may be aroused. The professional is denounced for viewing the evil too lightly, for failing to do his duty. The moral entrepreneur, at whose instance the rule was made, arises again to say that the outcome of the last crusade has not been satisfactory or that the gains once made have been whittled away and lost.

Notes

1. Joseph R. Gusfield, "Social Structure and Moral Reform: A Study of the Woman's Christian Temperance Union," *American Journal of Sociology,* LXI (November, 1955), 223.

2. *Ibid.*

3. See Raymond G. McCarthy, editor, *Drinking and Intoxication* (New Haven and New York: Yale Center of Alcohol Studies and The Free Press of Glencoe, 1959), pp. 395–396.

4. This is suggested in Oscar Lewis, *Sagebrush Casinos: The Story of Legal Gambling in Nevada* (New York: Doubleday and Co., 1953), pp. 223–234.

5. Edwin H. Sutherland, "The Diffusion of Sexual Psychopath Laws," *American Journal of Sociology,* LVI (September, 1950), 142–148.

6. *Ibid.,* pp. 142.

7. *Ibid.,* pp. 143–145.

8. *Ibid.,* pp. 145–146.

9. See Ray Gold, "Janitors Versus Tenants: A Status-Income Dilemma," *American Journal of Sociology,* LVII (March, 1952), 486–493.

10. William A. Westley, "Violence and the Police," *American Journal of Sociology,* LIX (July, 1953), 39.

11. *Ibid.*

12. See William A. Westley, "The Police: A Sociological Study of Law, Custom, and Morality" (unpublished Ph.D. dissertation, University of Chicago, Department of Sociology, 1951).

13. Edwin H. Sutherland (editor), *The Professional Thief* (Chicago: University of Chicago Press, 1937), pp. 87–88.

14. *Ibid.,* pp. 91–92.

The Production of Deviant Categories and Actors

Quite clearly, in cases where the moral entrepreneurs and their crusades succeed, society is often confronted with a new deviant category and a corresponding enforcement or social-control apparatus. Becker's general discussion of the dynamics behind the passage of various laws (e.g., the Eighteenth Amendment and sexual psychopath laws) offers illustrations of this.

As a social construction, deviance can be shaped. Groups' ability to guide the construction of deviant categories is closely linked to power structures within society, especially political power. Justin L. Tuggle and Malcolm D. Holmes, in "Blowing Smoke: Status Politics and the Shasta County Smoking Ban," explore the relationship between social status and the creation of deviant categories. Central to their article is the idea that by defining particular acts or activities as deviant, certain groups may be disadvantaged differentially. In the case presented by Tuggle and Holmes, the campaign against smoking targeted the working class, since smoking was a defining characteristic of this group. What emerges from their exploration as being a central concern is the observation that those from higher socioeconomic positions are most likely to be those who prevail in contests concerned with defining deviant categories.

Steven Spitzer, in "The Production of Deviance in Capitalist Society," offers another account of how deviant categories and populations are created. A basic thesis of Spitzer is the argument that most traditional theories of deviance, given their preoccupation with the dramatic and predatory forms of social behavior, have neglected to focus on how deviance and deviant populations are constructed socially. He argues that instead of accepting prevailing definitions as givens, one must become aware of the processes by which deviance is "subjectively constructed" and the way in which deviants are "objectively handled," as well as the "structural bases of behavior and characteristics which come to official attention." Spitzer goes on to provide an insightful account of deviance production and control in capitalist societies. Most insightful, and particularly relevant to Part IV of this book, is his discussion of not only how "problem populations" are produced by the state but how these populations, once constructed, are transformed into deviants and become the objects of official social control. Spitzer cites several factors that influence the rate at which problem populations are transformed into deviants. For example, increasingly large and threatening problem populations are more likely to be controlled through some type of deviance processing.

Spitzer concludes by discussing two rather distinct groups that evolve as a result of social control efforts: the *social junk* and the *social dynamite*. Social junk is relatively costly (e.g., the aged, the mentally ill, the handicapped), yet not especially threatening to the established order. Social dynamite, however, is more threatening as it possesses the potential to call into question such factors as domination and the current mode of production. Spitzer notes further that the social dynamite, given its more youthful, alienated, and politically volatile nature, is more apt to be controlled through a rapid deployment of control resources; this often results in eventual processing through the legal system. The social junk, by contrast, is more likely to be handled by some agency of the welfare state.

Peter Conrad, in "The Discovery of Hyperkinesis: Notes on the Medicalization of Deviant Behavior," provides another historical account of how conceptions of behavior can change. His initial comments are given to the ways in which selected forms of behavior (e.g., alcoholism and drug addiction) become defined as a medical problem or illness and how, thereafter, the medical profession is mandated or licensed to provide the appropriate treatment. Conrad's focus is given to hyperkinesis, particularly its discovery. In his analysis, he describes the various *clinical* (e.g., the effects of amphetamine drugs on children's behavior) and *social* (e.g., the pharmaceutical revolution and associated government action) factors that gave rise to the creation of this new medical diagnostic category. He then moves to a discussion of how deviant behavior on the part of children became conceptualized as a medical problem, as well as why this happened. Conrad concludes with a discussion of some of the important implications that flow from the medicalization of deviant behavior. For example, the medical profession "has not only a monopoly on anything that can be conceptualized as illness," but also the power to define deviant behavior as a medical problem, so that certain procedures can be done that otherwise would not be allowed (e.g., cutting on the body). Moreover, society has a tendency to individualize social problems. Instead of looking to defects of social systems for causes and solutions, we look within the individuals or, instead of analyzing the social situation that affects a perceived difficult child, we prescribe a stimulant medication. Such a treatment strategy, Conrad asserts, deflects our attention away from the real possibility that the family or classroom situation may be the problem. This tendency to characterize problems in individual, clinical, or medical terms, instead of structural-organizational terms, is often the norm.

The selections by Spitzer and Conrad illustrate how, as a result of changing perceptions, behavior may not only become increasingly defined as deviant but may also become criminalized or medicalized. When this occurs, we can speak of the creation of deviant, criminal, or medical categories. And once the categories are in place, we can begin to analyze how others react to the violators of the categories. Many of the selections in Part IV and Part V offer specific illustrations of how actors may be responded to.

Blowing Smoke: Status Politics and the Shasta County Smoking Ban

Justin L. Tuggle
Malcolm D. Holmes

Over the past half century, perceptions of tobacco and its users have changed dramatically. In the 1940s and 1950s, cigarette smoking was socially accepted and commonly presumed to lack deleterious effects (see, e.g., Ram 1941). Survey data from the early 1950s showed that a minority believed cigarette smoking caused lung cancer (Viscusi 1992). By the late 1970s, however, estimates from survey data revealed that more than 90% of the population thought that this link existed (Roper Organization 1978). This and other harms associated with tobacco consumption have provided the impetus for an antismoking crusade that aims to normatively redefine smoking as deviant behavior (Markle and Troyer 1979).

There seems to be little question that tobacco is a damaging psychoactive substance characterized by highly adverse chronic health effects (Steinfeld 1991). In this regard, the social control movement probably makes considerable sense in terms of public policy. At the same time, much as ethnicity and religion played a significant role in the prohibition of alcohol (Gusfield 1963), social status may well play a part in this latest crusade.

Historically, attempts to control psychoactive substances have linked their use to categories of relatively powerless people. Marijuana use was associated with Mexican Americans (Bonnie and Whitebread 1970), cocaine with African Americans (Ashley 1975), opiates with Asians (Ben-Yehuda 1990), and alcohol with immigrant Catholics (Gusfield 1963). During the heyday of cigarette smoking, it was thought that

> Tobacco's the one blessing that nature has left for all humans to enjoy. It can be consumed by both the "haves" and "have nots" as a common leveler, one that brings all humans together from all walks of life regardless of class, race, or creed. (Ram, 1941, p. 125)

But in contrast to this earlier view, recent evidence has shown that occupational status (Ferrence 1989; Marcus et al. 1989; Covey et al. 1992), education (Ferrence 1989; Viscusi 1992) and family income (Viscusi 1992) are

43

related negatively to current smoking. Further, the relationships of occupation and education to cigarette smoking have become stronger in later age cohorts (Ferrence 1989). Thus we ask, *is the association of tobacco with lower-status persons a factor in the crusade against smoking in public facilities?* Here we examine that question in a case study of a smoking ban implemented in Shasta County, California.

Status Politics and the Creation of Deviance

Deviance is socially constructed. Complex pluralistic societies have multiple, competing symbolic-moral universes that clash and negotiate (Ben-Yehuda 1990). Deviance is relative, and social morality is continually restructured. Moral, power, and stigma contests are ongoing, with competing symbolic-moral universes striving to legitimize particular lifestyles while making others deviant (Schur 1980; Ben-Yehuda 1990).

The ability to define and construct reality is closely connected to the power structure of society (Gusfield 1963). Inevitably, then, the distribution of deviance is associated with the system of stratification. The higher one's social position, the greater one's moral value (Ben-Yehuda 1990). Differences in lifestyles and moral beliefs are corollaries of social stratification (Gusfield 1963; Zurcher and Kirkpatrick 1976; Luker 1984). Accordingly, even though grounded in the system of stratification, status conflicts need not be instrumental; they may also be symbolic. Social stigma may, for instance, attach to behavior thought indicative of a weak will (Goffman 1963). Such moral anomalies occasion status degradation ceremonies, public denunciations expressing indignation not at a behavior per se, but rather against the individual motivational type that produced it (Garfinkle 1956). The denouncers act as public figures, drawing upon communally shared experience and speaking in the name of ultimate values. In this respect, status degradation involves a reciprocal element: Status conflicts and the resultant condemnation of a behavior characteristic of a particular status category symbolically enhances the status of the abstinent through the degradation of the participatory (Garfinkle 1956; Gusfield 1963).

Deviance creation involves political competition in which moral entrepreneurs originate moral crusades aimed at generating reform (Becker 1963; Schur 1980; Ben-Yehuda 1990). The alleged deficiencies of a specific social group are revealed and reviled by those crusading to define their behavior as deviant. As might be expected, successful moral crusades are generally dominated by those in the upper social strata of society (Becker 1963). Research on the anti-abortion (Luker 1984) and antipornography (Zurcher and Kirkpatrick 1976) crusades has shown that activists in these movements are of lower socioeconomic status than their opponents, helping explain the limited success of efforts to redefine abortion and pornography as deviance.

Moral entrepreneurs' goals may be either assimilative or coercive reform (Gusfield 1963). In the former instance, sympathy to the deviants' plight engenders integrative efforts aimed at lifting the repentant to the superior moral plane allegedly held by those of higher social status. The latter strategy emerges when deviants are viewed as intractably denying the moral and status superiority of the reformers' symbolic-moral universe. Thus, whereas assimilative reform may employ educative strategies, coercive reform turns to law and force for affirmation.

Regardless of aim, the moral entrepreneur cannot succeed alone. Success in establishing a moral crusade is dependent on acquiring broader public support. To that end, the moral entrepreneur must mobilize power, create a perceived threat potential for the moral issue in question, generate public awareness of the issue, propose a clear and acceptable solution to the problem, and overcome resistance to the crusade (Becker 1963; Ben-Yehuda 1990).

The Status Politics of Cigarette Smoking

The political dynamics underlying the definition of deviant behaviors may be seen clearly in efforts to end smoking in public facilities. Cigarettes were an insignificant product of the tobacco industry until the end of the 19th century, after which they evolved into its staple (U.S. Department of Health and Human Services 1992). Around the turn of the century, 14 states banned cigarette smoking and all but one other regulated sales to and possession by minors (Nuehring and Markle 1974). Yet by its heyday in the 1940s and 1950s, cigarette smoking was almost universally accepted, even considered socially desirable (Nuehring and Markle 1974; Steinfeld 1991). Per capita cigarette consumption in the United States peaked at approximately 4,300 cigarettes per year in the early 1960s, after which it declined to about 2,800 per year by the early 1990s (U.S. Department of Health and Human Services 1992). The beginning of the marked decline in cigarette consumption corresponded to the publication of the report to the surgeon general on the health risks of smoking (U.S. Department of Health, Education and Welfare 1964). Two decades later, the hazards of passive smoking were being publicized (e.g., U.S. Department of Health and Human Services 1986).

Increasingly, the recognition of the apparent relationship of smoking to health risks has socially demarcated the lifestyles of the smoker and non-smoker, from widespread acceptance of the habit to polarized symbolic-moral universes. Attitudes about smoking are informed partly by medical issues, but perhaps even more critical are normative considerations (Nuehring and Markle 1974); more people have come to see smoking as socially reprehensible and deviant, and smokers as social misfits (Markle and Troyer 1979). Psychological assessments have attributed an array of negative evaluative characteristics to smokers (Markle and Troyer 1979). Their habit is increasingly thought unclean and intrusive.

Abstinence and bodily purity are the cornerstones of the nonsmoker's purported moral superiority (Feinhandler 1986). At the center of their symbolic-moral universe, then, is the idea that people have a right to breathe clean air in public spaces (Goodin 1989). Smokers, on the other hand, stake their claim to legitimacy in a precept of Anglo-Saxon political culture—the right to do whatever one wants unless it harms others (Berger 1986). Those sympathetic to smoking deny that environmental tobacco smoke poses a significant health hazard to the nonsmoker (Aviado 1986). Yet such arguments have held little sway in the face of counter-claims from authoritative governmental agencies and high status moral entrepreneurs.

The development of the antismoking movement has targeted a lifestyle particularly characteristic of the working classes (Berger 1986). Not only has there been an overall decline in cigarette smoking, but, as mentioned above, the negative relationships of occupation and education to cigarette smoking have become more pronounced in later age cohorts (Ferrence 1989). Moreover, moral entrepreneurs crusading against smoking are representatives of a relatively powerful "knowledge class," comprising people employed in areas such as education and the therapeutic and counseling agencies (Berger 1986).

Early remedial efforts focused on publicizing the perils of cigarette smokers, reflecting a strategy of assimilative reform (Neuhring and Markle 1974; Markle and Troyer 1979). Even many smokers expressed opposition to cigarettes and a generally repentant attitude. Early educative efforts were thus successful in decreasing cigarette consumption, despite resistance from the tobacco industry. Then, recognition of the adverse effects of smoking on nonusers helped precipitate a turn to coercive reform measures during the mid 1970s (Markle and Troyer 1979). Rather than a repentant friend in need of help, a new definition of the smoker as enemy emerged. Legal abolition of smoking in public facilities became one locus of social control efforts, and smoking bans in public spaces have been widely adopted in recent years (Markle and Troyer 1979; Goodin 1989).

The success of the antismoking crusade has been grounded in moral entrepreneurs' proficiency at mobilizing power, a mobilization made possible by highly visible governmental campaigns, the widely publicized health risks of smoking, and the proposal of workable and generally acceptable policies to ameliorate the problem. The success of this moral crusade has been further facilitated by the association of deviant characteristics with those in lower social strata, whose stigmatization reinforces existing relations of power and prestige. Despite the formidable resources and staunch opposition of the tobacco industry, the tide of public opinion and policy continues to move toward an antismoking stance.

Research Problem

The study presented below is an exploratory examination of the link between social status and support for a smoking ban in public facilities. Based on theorizing about status politics, as well as evidence about patterns of cigarette use, it was predicted that supporters of the smoking ban would be of higher status than those who opposed it. Further, it was anticipated that supporters of the ban would be more likely to make negative normative claims denouncing the allegedly deviant qualities of smoking, symbolically enhancing their own status while lowering that of their opponents.

The site of this research was Shasta County, California. The population of Shasta County is 147,036, of whom 66,462 reside in its only city, Redding (U.S. Bureau of the Census 1990). This county became the setting for the implementation of a hotly contested ban on smoking in public buildings.

In 1988, California voters passed Proposition 99, increasing cigarette taxes by 25 cents per pack. The purpose of the tax was to fund smoking prevention and treatment programs. Toward that end, Shasta County created the Shasta County Tobacco Education Program. The director of the program formed a coalition with officials of the Shasta County chapters of the American Cancer Society and American Lung Association to propose a smoking ban in all public buildings. The three groups formed an organization to promote that cause, Smoke-Free Air For Everyone (SAFE). Unlike other bans then in effect in California, the proposed ban included restaurants and bars, because its proponents considered these to be places in which people encountered significant amounts of secondhand smoke. They procured sufficient signatures on a petition to place the measure on the county's general ballot in November 1992.

The referendum passed with a 56% majority in an election that saw an 82% turnout. Subsequently, the Shasta County Hospitality and Business Alliance, an antiban coalition, obtained sufficient signatures to force a special election to annul the smoking ban. The special election was held in April 1993. Although the turnout was much lower (48%), again a sizable majority (58.4%) supported the ban. The ordinance went into effect on July 1, 1993.

Analytic Strategy

Three sources of data were analyzed in our effort to ascertain the moral and status conflicts underlying the Shasta County smoking ban. The first was interviews with five leading moral entrepreneurs and five prominent status quo defenders.[1] These individuals were selected through a snowball

[1]Although the term moral entrepreneur is well established in the literature on deviance, there seems to be little attention to or consistency in a corresponding term for the interest group(s) opposing them. Those that have been employed, such as "forces for the status quo" (Markle and Troyer 1979), tend to be awkward. "Status quo defenders" is used here for lack of a simpler or more common term.

sample, with the original respondents identified through interviews with business owners or political advertisements in the local mass media. The selected respondents repeatedly surfaced as the leading figures in their respective coalitions. Semistructured interviews were conducted to determine the reasons underlying their involvement. These data were critical to understanding how the proposed ban was framed by small groups of influential proponents and opponents; it was expected that their concerns would be reflected in the larger public debate about the ban.

A second source of data was letters to the editor of the local paper, the *Record Searchlight*. There were 105 letters published during the periods leading up to the two elections. The editor stated that all letters concerning the ban were published, with none being shortened or otherwise edited. The letters were content-analyzed, with each specific mention of individual rights, health, negative normative evaluations, and purported business effects of the ban being recorded, along with whether the writer was pro- or antiban. The content analysis provides a broader picture of the issues underlying the public debate about the proposed ban. It is particularly noteworthy that most proban writers were nonsmokers and most antiban writers were smokers.[2]

To identify socioeconomic status differences underlying their competing positions on the smoking ban, a measure of each letter writer's personal wealth was obtained. Public documents in the Shasta County Tax Assessor's office provided the number of properties owned by each letter writer and the value of each property. These values were summed to obtain the owner's cumulative property value. There were 57 proban property owners and 31 antiban owners included in the analysis.[3] Whereas the content analysis examined the ideological and symbolic framework of the debate, this comparison permitted an assessment of whether differences in economic status distinguished the pro- and antiban writers, reflecting the negative relationship between socioeconomic status variables and smoking.

Findings

Moral Entrepreneur/Status Quo Defender Interviews

The moral entrepreneurs and status quo defenders interviewed represented clearly different interests. The former group included three high-level administrators in the county's chapters of the American Cancer

---

[2]Most of the pro- and antiban letter writers indicated in their letters whether they smoked. Not surprisingly, among those who revealed their smoking behavior, virtually all ban supporters were nonsmokers, whereas ban opponents were smokers.

[3]Persons who wrote multiple letters were included in the property value analysis only once; there were 10 multiple letter writers, all of whom were proban. Renters were excluded from the analysis; there were 4 renters among the proban writers and 3 among those who were antiban.

Society and American Lung Association. A fourth was an administrator for the Shasta County Tobacco Education Project. The last member of this group was a pulmonary physician affiliated with a local hospital. The latter group included four bar and/or restaurant owners and an attorney who had been hired to represent their interests. Thus the status quo defenders were small business owners who might see their economic interests affected adversely by the ban. Importantly, they were representatives of a less prestigious social stratum than the moral entrepreneurs.

The primary concern of the moral entrepreneurs was health. As one stated,

> I supported the initiative to get the smoking ban on the ballot because of all the health implications that secondhand smoke can create. Smoking and secondhand smoke are the most preventable causes of death in this nation.

Another offered that

> On average, secondhand smoke kills 53,000 Americans each year. And think about those that it kills in other countries! It contains 43 cancer-causing chemical agents that have been verified by the Environmental Protection Agency. It is now listed as a Type A carcinogen, which is in the same category as asbestos.

Every one of the moral entrepreneurs expressed concern about health issues during the interviews. This was not the only point they raised, however. Three of the five made negative normative evaluations of smoking, thereby implicitly degrading the status of smokers. They commented that "smoking is no longer an acceptable action," that "smoke stinks," or that "it is just a dirty and annoying habit." Thus, whereas health was their primary concern, such comments revealed the moral entrepreneurs' negative view of smoking irrespective of any medical issues. Smokers were seen as engaging in unclean and objectionable behavior—stigmatized qualities defining their deviant social status.

The stance of the status quo defenders was also grounded in two arguments. All of them expressed concern about individual rights. As one put it,

> I opposed that smoking ban because I personally smoke and feel that it is an infringement of my rights to tell me where I can and cannot smoke. Smoking is a legal activity, and therefore it is unconstitutional to take that right away from me.

Another argued that

> Many people have died for us to have these rights in foreign wars and those also fought on American soil. Hundreds of thousands of people thought that these rights were worth dying for, and now some small group of people believe that they can just vote away these rights.

Such symbolism implies that smoking is virtually a patriotic calling, a venerable habit for which people have been willing to forfeit their lives in time of war. In the status quo defenders' view, smoking is a constitutionally protected right.

At the same time, each of the status quo defenders was concerned about more practical matters, namely business profits. As one stated, "my income was going to be greatly affected." Another argued,

> If these people owned some of the businesses that they are including in this ban, they would not like it either. By taking away the customers that smoke, they are taking away the mainstay of people from a lot of businesses.

The competing viewpoints of the moral entrepreneurs and status quo defenders revealed the moral issues—health versus individual rights—at the heart of political conflict over the smoking ban. Yet it appears that status issues also fueled the conflict. On the one hand, the moral entrepreneurs denigrated smoking, emphasizing the socially unacceptable qualities of the behavior and symbolically degrading smokers' status. On the other hand, status quo defenders were concerned that their livelihood would be affected by the ban. Interestingly, the occupational status of the two groups differed, with the moral entrepreneurs representing the new knowledge class, the status quo defenders a lower stratum of small business owners. Those in the latter group may not have been accorded the prestige and trust granted those in the former (Berger 1986). Moreover, the status quo defenders' concern about business was likely seen as self-aggrandizing.

Letters to the Editor

Soon after the moral entrepreneurs went public with their plan to end smoking in public buildings, the general populace became engaged in the debate. Of course the dialogue was carried on in many arenas, most of which left no observable record. A noteworthy exception is letters to the editor, where the competing viewpoints were again exhibited.

As to be expected, the proban writers ($n = 71$) emphasized the issue of health. Sixty nine percent of the proban writers raised this issue, whereas it was mentioned in approximately 18% of the antiban letters ($n = 34$). This substantial difference in the proportion of letters mentioning health from the two camps was statistically significant ($p < .0005$) in the test for differences in proportions (see Blalock 1979, pp. 232–234).[4] Analyzed differently,

---

[4]Significance tests are generally employed to make inferences from samples to populations. In this respect, they are unnecessary with these data because the population of letters is included. That fact notwithstanding, they may also be used to make inferences about causal processes that generate population data (see Blalock 1979, pp. 241–243). The latter use is consistent with our aims and, accordingly, they were reported here. One-tailed tests were reported because all findings were consistent with expectations.

health was mentioned 1.56 times on average (mean) in the proban letters, compared with only .26 times in the antiban letters ($t = 5.39$; $df = 103$; $p < .0005$). That is, proban writers were six times more likely than those who opposed it to mention this concern.

The issue of individual rights also appeared frequently in the letters to the editor, with debate focusing on the right to smoke versus the right not to be subjected to cigarette smoke. Because the issue of individual rights was a cornerstone of the status quo defenders' argument, it is not surprising that this concern was expressed more frequently by the antiban writers. Individual rights were mentioned in approximately 76% of antiban letters, compared with 48% of proban letters. The difference in the proportion of pro- and antiban letters raising this issue was statistically significant ($p < .005$). It was mentioned an average of 1.97 times in the antiban letters and 1.21 times in those supporting the ban ($t = 1.98$; $df = 103$; $p < .025$). Although a substantial difference in the pro- and antiban writers' views again surfaced, it was smaller than observed with respect to health because both sides had concerns about individual rights—that to smoke versus that to clean air.

In addition to concerns about health and individual rights, normative negative evaluations surfaced. For example, one proban writer called smokers "ignorant" and alleged that they used "nicotine-stained lies." On the other side, an antiban writer called ban supporters "clean air freaks." More than 22% of proban letters included such comments, compared with about 15% of those opposing the ban. Although consistent with expectations, this difference is not statistically different. On average, the proban letters contained .38 negative normative evaluations, compared with .15 of the antiban commentaries ($t = 1.94$; $df = 103$; $p < .05$). Thus they appeared two and one half times as often in the proban letters. Letter writers from both sides made negative normative evaluations questioning the character of their opponents, implicitly attacking their social credibility and status. But, like the moral entrepreneurs, proban writers made such claims more frequently.

The pro- and antiban writers were about equally likely to mention possible business effects of the ban (22.5% and 26.4%, respectively), with the issue mentioned an average of .44 times in the letters of both sides. Concerns about business consequences were not as paramount for antiban writers from the general public as for the status quo defenders, who had vested business interests. The antiban writers who mentioned the issue shared the status quo defenders' view that the ban would adversely affect the business of restaurants and bars. The proban writers who mentioned business effects were of the opinion that there would be no impact or that business would actually improve as a result of the ban.

For the public, then, it appears that the primary issues were ethical and moral—the right to health versus the right to smoke. Nonetheless, negative normative evaluations were also employed as a technique of status degradation, especially by those supporting the ban.

Letter Writers' Cumulative Property Value

To better understand the potential status conflicts underlying the opposing viewpoints on the ban, the letter writers' cumulative property values were compared. Here substantial differences in the backgrounds of the pro- and antiban writers appeared. The median cumulative property value for the proban writers was $101,516, compared with $68,766 for the antiban writers.

Table 1 presents a cross-classification of ban support by authors' property value. Here it may be seen clearly that, in general, as property value increased, support for the ban increased. Not only is the positive relationship significant ($p < .05$), Cramer's V (.375) shows that it is fairly strong. A slight nonlinearity appears in the $150,000 to $199,999 property value category, where antiban writers outnumbered proban writers. This irregularity probably occurred because of several bar and restaurant owners in this income range, who feared their business interests would be affected adversely and were among the antiban letter writers.

Comparison of the cumulative property values reveals a difference not discernible from the content of the letters—economic status appears to have been an important determinant of support for the smoking ban. This relationship clearly corresponds to the negative one between socioeconomic status and smoking.

Summary and Discussion

This research has examined the moral and status politics underlying the implementation of a smoking ban in Shasta County, California. Moral entrepreneurs crusading for the ban argued that secondhand smoke damages

---

Table 1 Frequencies and column percentages for the cross-classification of support for the smoking ban by letter writer's property value ($N = 88$)

	Letter writer's property value in dollars				
Support for ban	1 to 49,999 (%)	50,000 to 99,999 (%)	100,000 to 149,999 (%)	150,000 to 199,999 (%)	200,000 and up (%)
Proban	10 (43.5)	19 (73.1)	13 (86.7)	4 (40.0)	11 (78.6)
Antiban	13 (56.5)	7 (26.9)	2 (13.3)	6 (60.0)	3 (21.4)
Total	23	26	15	10	14

Note. $\chi^2 = 12.37$; $df = 3$; $p < .05$; Cramer's V = .375.

health, implicitly grounding their argument in the principle that people have a right to a smoke-free environment. Status quo defenders countered that smokers have a constitutional right to indulge wherever and whenever they see fit. Public discourse echoed these themes, as seen in the letters to the editor of the local newspaper. Thus debate about the smoking ban focused especially on health versus smokers' rights; yet evidence of social status differences between the competing symbolic-moral universes also surfaced. Competing symbolic-moral universes are defined not only by different ethical viewpoints on a behavior, but also by differences in social power—disparities inevitably linked to the system of stratification (Ben-Yehuda 1990). Those prevailing in moral and stigma contests typically represent the higher socioeconomic echelons of society.

The moral entrepreneurs who engineered the smoking ban campaign were representatives of the prestigious knowledge class, including among their members officials from the local chapters of respected organizations at the forefront of the national antismoking crusade. In contrast, the small business owners who were at the core of the opposing coalition, of status quo defenders, represented the traditional middle class. Clearly, there was an instrumental quality to the restaurant and bar owners' stance, because they saw the ban as potentially damaging to their business interests. But they were unable to shape the public debate, as demonstrated by the letters to the editor.

An even more distinct difference in social status appears when the cumulative property values of the two letter-writing camps is compared. There was a significant gap between the property values of the pro- and antiban writers, with a fairly strong positive relationship appearing when property value and support for the ban are cross-tabulated. Although the letter writers were probably not representative of the population of Shasta County, insofar as nearly all were property owners, this finding plainly parallels the negative relationships between indicators of socioeconomic status and smoking.

In many respects, the status conflicts involved in the passage of the Shasta County smoking ban were symbolic. The moral entrepreneurs focused attention on the normatively undesirable qualities of cigarette smoking, and their negative normative evaluations of smoking were reflected in public debate about the ban. Those who wrote in support of the ban more frequently offered negative normative evaluations than antiban writers; their comments degraded smoking and, implicitly, smokers. Since the advent of the antismoking crusade in the United States, smoking has come to be seen as socially reprehensible, smokers as social misfits characterized by negative psychological characteristics (Markle and Troyer 1979).

Ultimately, a lifestyle associated with the less educated, less affluent, lower occupational strata was stigmatized as a public health hazard and targeted for coercive reform. Its deviant status was codified in the ordinance banning smoking in public facilities, including restaurants and bars. The ban symbolized the deviant status of cigarette smokers, the prohibition visibly demonstrating the community's condemnation of their behavior. Further, the smoking ban symbolically amplified the purported virtues of the abstinent lifestyle. A political victory such as the passage of a law is a prestige-enhancing symbolic triumph that is perhaps even more rewarding than its end result (Gusfield 1963). The symbolic nature of the ban serendipitously surfaced in another way during one author's unstructured observations in 42 restaurants and 21 bars in the area: Whereas smoking was not observed in a single restaurant, it occurred without sanction in all but one of the bars. Although not deterring smoking in one of its traditional bastions, the ban called attention to its deviant quality and, instrumentally, effectively halted it in areas more commonly frequently by the abstemious.

Although more systematic research is needed, the findings of this exploratory case study offer a better understanding of the dynamics underlying opposition to smoking and further support to theorizing about the role of status politics in the creation of deviant types. Denunciation of smoking in Shasta County involved not only legitimate allegations about public health, but negative normative evaluations of those engaged in the behavior. In the latter regard, the ban constituted a status degradation ceremony, symbolically differentiating the pure and abstinent from the unclean and intrusive. Not coincidentally, the stigmatized were more likely found among society's lower socioeconomic strata, their denouncers among its higher echelons.

Certainly the class and ethnic antipathies underlying attacks on cocaine and opiate users earlier in the century were more manifest than those revealed in the crusade against cigarette smoking. But neither are there manifest status conflicts in the present crusades against abortion (Luker 1984) and pornography (Zurcher and Kirkpatrick 1976); yet the underlying differences of status between opponents in those movements are reflected in their markedly different symbolic-moral universes, as was the case in the present study.

This is not to suggest that smoking should be an approved behavior. The medical evidence seems compelling: Cigarette smoking is harmful to the individual smoker and to those exposed to secondhand smoke. However, the objective harms of the psychoactive substance in question are irrelevant to the validity of our analysis, just as they were to Gusfield's (1963) analysis of the temperance movement's crusade against alcohol use. Moreover, it is not our intention to imply that the proban supporters consciously intended to degrade those of lower social status. No doubt they were motivated primarily by a sincere belief that smoking constitutes a public health hazard. In the end, however, moral indignation and social control flowed down the social hierarchy. Thus we must ask: Would cigarette smoking be defined as deviant if there were a positive correlation between smoking and socioeconomic status?

References

Ashley, Richard. 1975. *Cocaine: Its History, Uses, and Effects.* New York: St. Martin's Press.

Aviado, Domingo M. 1986. "Health Issues Relating to 'Passive' Smoking." Pp. 137–165 in *Smoking and Society: Toward a More Balanced Assessment,* edited by Robert D. Tollison. Lexington, MA: Lexington Books.

Becker, Howard S. 1963. *Outsiders: Studies in the Sociology of Deviance.* New York: Free Press.

Ben-Yehuda, Nachman. 1990. *The Politics and Morality of Deviance: Moral Panics, Drug Abuse, Deviant Science, and Reversed Stigmatization.* Albany, NY: State University of New York Press.

Berger, Peter L. 1986. "A Sociological View of the Antismoking Phenomenon." Pp. 225–240 in *Smoking and Society: Toward a More Balanced Assessment,* edited by Robert D. Tollison. Lexington, MA: Lexington Books.

Blalock, Hubert M. Jr. 1979. *Social Statistics* 2d ed, Rev. New York: McGraw-Hill.

Bonnie, Richard J., and Charles H. Whitebread II. 1970. "The Forbidden Fruit and the Tree of Knowledge: An Inquiry into the Legal History of American Marihuana Prohibition." *Virginia Law Review* 56:971–1203.

Covey, Lirio S., Edith A. Zang, and Ernst L. Wynder. 1992. "Cigarette Smoking and Occupational Status: 1977 to 1990." *American Journal of Public Health* 82:1230–1234.

Feinhandler, Sherwin J. 1986. *The Social Role of Smoking* Pp. 167–187 in *Smoking and Society: Toward a More Balanced Assessment,* edited by Robert D. Tollison. Lexington, MA: Lexington Books.

Ferrence, Roberta G. 1989. *Deadly Fashion: The Rise and Fall of Cigarette Smoking in North America.* New York: Garland.

Garfinkle, Harold. 1956. "Conditions of Successful Degradation Ceremonies." *American Journal of Sociology* 61:402–424.

Goffman, Erving. 1963. *Stigma: Notes on the Management of Spoiled Identity.* Englewood Cliffs, NJ: Prentice-Hall.

Goodin, Robert E. 1989. *No Smoking: The Ethical Issues.* Chicago: University of Chicago Press.

Gusfield, Joseph R. 1963. *Symbolic Crusade: Status Politics and the American Temperance Movement.* Urbana, IL: University of Illinois Press.

Luker, Kristin. 1984. *Abortion and the Politics of Motherhood.* Berkeley, CA: University of California.

Marcus, Alfred C., Donald R. Shopland, Lori A. Crane, and William R. Lynn. 1989. "Prevalence of Cigarette Smoking in United States: Estimates From the 1985 Current Population Survey." *Journal of the National Cancer Institute* 81:409–414.

Markle, Gerald E., and Ronald J. Troyer. 1979. "Smoke Gets in Your Eyes: Cigarette Smoking as Deviant Behavior." *Social Problems* 26:611–625.

Neuhring, Elane, and Gerald E. Markle. 1974. "Nicotine and Norms: The Re-Emergence of a Deviant Behavior." *Social Problems* 21:513–526.

Ram, Sidney P. 1941. How to Get More Fun Out of Smoking. Chicago: Cuneo.

Roper Organization. 1978, May. *A Study of Public Attitudes Toward Cigarette Smoking and the Tobacco Industry in 1978, Volume 1.* New York: Roper.

Schur, Edwin M. 1980. *The Politics of Deviance: Stigma Contests and the Uses of Power.* New York: Random House.

Steinfeld, Jesse. 1991. "Combating Smoking in the United States: Progress Through Science and Social Action." *Journal of the National Cancer Institute* 83:1126–1127.

U.S. Bureau of the Census. 1990. *General Population Characteristics.* Washington, DC: U.S. Government Printing Office.

U.S. Department of Health, Education and Welfare. 1964. *Smoking and Health: Report of the Advisory Committee to the Surgeon General of the Public Health Service.* Washington, DC: U.S. Government Printing Office.

U.S. Department of Health and Human Services. 1986. *The Health Consequences of Involuntary Smoking. A Report of the Surgeon General.* Washington, DC: U.S. Government Printing Office.

U.S. Department of Health and Human Services. 1992. *Smoking and Health in the Americas. A 1992 Report of the Surgeon General, in Collaboration with the Pan American Health Organization.* Washington, DC: U.S. Government Printing Office.

Viscusi, W. Kip. 1992. *Smoking: Making the Risky Decision.* New York: Oxford University Press.

Zurcher, Louis A. Jr., and R. George Kirkpatrick. 1976. *Citizens for Decency: Antipornography Crusades as Status Defense.* Austin, TX: University of Texas Press.

5 The Production of Deviance in Capitalist Society

Steven Spitzer

• • •

The concept of deviance production offers a starting point for the analysis of both deviance and control. But for such a construct to serve as a critical tool it must be grounded in a historical and structural investigation of society. For Marx, the crucial unit of analysis is the mode of production that dominates a given historical period. If we are to have a Marxian theory of deviance, therefore, deviance production must be understood in relationship to specific forms of socio-economic organization. In our society, productive activity is organized capitalistically, and it is ultimately defined by "the process that transforms on the one hand, the social means of subsistence and of production into capital, on the other hand the immediate producers into wage labourers" (Marx, 1967:714).

There are two features of the capitalist mode of production important for purposes of this discussion. First, as a mode of production it forms the foundation or infrastructure of our society. This means that the starting point of our analysis must be an understanding of the economic organization of capitalist societies and the impact of that organization on all aspects of social life. But the capitalist mode of production is an important starting point in another sense. It contains contradictions which reflect the internal tendencies of capitalism. These contradictions are important because they explain the changing character of the capitalist system and the nature of its impact on social, political, and intellectual activity. The formulation of a Marxist perspective on deviance requires the interpretation of the process through which the contradictions of capitalism are expressed. In particular, the theory must illustrate the relationship between specific contradictions, the problems of capitalist development, and the production of a deviant class.

The superstructure of society emerges from and reflects the ongoing development of economic forces (the infrastructure). In class societies this superstructure preserves the hegemony of the ruling class through a system of class controls. These controls, which are institutionalized in the family, church, private associations, media, schools, and the state, provide a mechanism for coping with the contradictions and achieving the aims of capitalist development.

Among the most important functions served by the superstructure in capitalist societies is the regulation and management of problem populations. Because deviance processing is only one of the methods available for social control, these groups supply raw material for deviance production, but are by no means synonymous with deviant populations. Problem populations tend to share a number of social characteristics, but most important among these is the fact that their behavior, personal qualities, and/or position threaten the *social relations of production* in capitalist societies. In other words, populations become generally eligible for management as deviant when they disturb, hinder, or call into question any of the following:

1. capitalist modes of appropriating the product of human labor (e.g. when the poor "steal" from the rich)
2. the social conditions under which capitalist production takes place (e.g. those who refuse or are unable to perform wage labor)
3. patterns of distribution and consumption in capitalist society (e.g. those who use drugs for escape and transcendence rather than sociability and adjustment)
4. the process of socialization for productive and non-productive roles (e.g. youth who refuse to be schooled or those who deny the validity of "family life")[1]
5. the ideology which supports the functioning of capitalist society (e.g. proponents of alternative forms of social organization)

Although problem populations are defined in terms of the threat and costs that they present to the social relations of production in capitalist societies, these populations are far from isomorphic with a revolutionary class. It is certainly true that some members of the problem population may under specific circumstances possess revolutionary potential. But this potential can only be realized if the problematic group is located in a position of functional indispensability within the capitalist system. Historically, capitalist societies have been quite successful in transforming those who are problematic and indispensable (the protorevolutionary class) into groups who are either problematic and dispensable (candidates for deviance processing), or indispensable but not problematic (supporters of the capitalist order). On the other hand, simply because a group is manageable does not mean that it ceases to be a problem for the capitalist class. Even though dispensable problem populations cannot overturn the capitalist system, they can represent a significant impediment to its maintenance and growth. It is in this sense that they become eligible for management as deviants.

Problem populations are created in two ways—either directly through the expression of fundamental contradictions in the capitalist mode of production or indirectly through disturbances in the system of class rule. An example of the first process is found in Marx's analysis of the "relative surplus-population."

Writing on the "General Law of Capitalist Accumulation" Marx explains how increased social redundance is inherent in the development of the capitalist mode of production:

> With the extension of the scale of production, and the mass of the labourers set in motion, with the greater breadth and fullness of all sources of wealth, there is also an extension of the scale on which greater attraction of labourers by capital is accompanied by their greater repulsion. . . . The labouring population therefore produces, along with the accumulation of capital produced by it, the means by which itself is made relatively superfluous, . . . and it does this to an always increasing extent (Marx, 1967:631).

In its most limited sense the production of a relative surplus-population involves the creation of a class which is economically redundant. But insofar as the conditions of economic existence determine social existence, this process helps explain the emergence of groups who become both threatening and vulnerable at the same time. The marginal status of these populations reduces their stake in the maintenance of the system while their powerlessness and dispensability renders them increasingly susceptible to the mechanisms of official control.

The paradox surrounding the production of the relative surplus-population is that this population is both useful and menacing to the accumulation of capital. Marx describes how the relative surplus-population "forms a disposable industrial army, that belongs to capital quite as absolutely as if the latter had bred it at its own cost," and how this army "creates, for the changing needs of the self-expansion of capital, a mass of human material always ready for exploitation" (Marx, 1967:632).

On the other hand, it is apparent that an excessive increase in what Marx called the "lowest sediment" of the relative surplus-population might seriously impair the growth of capital. The social expenses and threat to social harmony created by a large and economically stagnant surplus-population could jeopardize the preconditions for accumulation by undermining the ideology of equality so essential to the legitimation of production relations in bourgeois democracies, diverting revenues away from capital investment toward control and support operations, and providing a basis for political organization of the dispossessed.[2] To the extent that the relative surplus-population confronts the capitalist class as a threat to the social relations of production, it reflects an important contradiction in modern capitalist societies: a surplus-population is a necessary product of and condition for the accumulation of wealth on a capitalist basis, but it also creates a form of social expense which must be neutralized or controlled if production relations and conditions for increased accumulation are to remain unimpaired.

Problem populations are also generated through contradictions which develop in the system of class rule. The institutions which make up the superstructure of capitalist society originate and are maintained to guarantee the interests of the capitalist class. Yet these institutions necessarily reproduce, rather than resolve, the contradictions of the capitalist order. In a dialectical fashion, arrangements which arise in order to buttress capitalism are transformed into their opposite—structures for the cultivation of internal threats. An instructive example of this process is found in the emergence and transformation of educational institutions in the United States.

The introduction of mass education in the United States can be traced to the developing needs of corporate capitalism (cf. Karier, 1973; Cohen and Lazerson, 1972; Bowles and Gintis, 1972; Spring, 1972). Compulsory education provided a means of training, testing and sorting, and assimilating wage-laborers, as well as withholding certain populations from the labor market. The system was also intended to preserve the values of bourgeois society and operate as an "inexpensive form of police" (Spring, 1973: 31). However, as Gintis (1973) and Bowles (1973) have suggested, the internal contradictions of schooling can lead to effects opposite of those intended. For the poor, early schooling can make explicit the oppressiveness and alienating character of capitalist institutions, while higher education can instill critical abilities which lead students to "bite the hand that feeds them." In both cases educational institutions create troublesome populations (i.e. dropouts and student radicals) and contribute to the very problems they were designed to solve.

After understanding how and why specific groups become generally bothersome in capitalist society, it is necessary to investigate the conditions under which these groups are transformed into proper objects for social control. In other words, we must ask what distinguishes the generally problematic from the specifically deviant. The rate at which problem populations are converted into deviants will reflect the relationship between these populations and the control system. This rate is likely to be influenced by the:

(1) *Extensiveness and Intensity of State Controls.* Deviance processing (as opposed to other control measures) is more likely to occur when problem management is monopolized by the state. As state controls are applied more generally, the proportion of official deviants will increase.

(2) *Size and Level of Threat Presented by the Problem Population.* The larger and more threatening the problem population, the greater the likelihood that this population will have to be controlled through deviance processing rather than other methods. As the threat created by these populations exceeds the capacities of informal restraints, their management requires a broadening of the reaction system and an increasing centralization and coordination of control activities.

(3) *Level of Organization of the Problem Population.* When and if problem populations are able to organize and develop limited amounts of political power, deviance processing becomes increasingly less effective as a tool for social control. The attribution of deviant status is most likely to occur when a group is relatively impotent and atomized.

(4) *Effectiveness of Control Structures Organized through Civil Society.* The greater the effectiveness of the organs of civil society (i.e. the family, church, media, schools, sports) in solving the problems of class control, the less the likelihood that deviance processing (a more explicitly political process) will be employed.

(5) *Availability and Effectiveness of Alternative Types of Official Processing.* In some cases the state will be able effectively to incorporate certain segments of the problem population into specially created "pro-social" roles. In the modern era, for example, conscription and public works projects (Piven and Cloward, 1971) helped neutralize the problems posed by troublesome populations without creating new or expanding old deviant categories.

(6) *Availability and Effectiveness of Parallel Control Structures.* In many instances the state can transfer its costs of deviance production by supporting or at least tolerating the activities of independent control networks which operate in its interests. For example, when the state is denied or is reluctant to assert a monopoly over the use of force, it is frequently willing to encourage vigilante organizations and private police in the suppression of problem populations. Similarly, the state is often benefited by the policies and practices of organized crime, insofar as these activities help pacify, contain, and enforce order among potentially disruptive groups (Schelling, 1967).

(7) *Utility of Problem Populations.* While problem populations are defined in terms of their threat and costs to capitalist relations of production, they are not threatening in every respect. They can be supportive economically (as part of a surplus labor pool or dual labor market), politically (as evidence of the need for state intervention), and ideologically (as scapegoats for rising discontent). In other words, under certain conditions capitalist societies derive benefits from maintaining a number of visible and uncontrolled "troublemakers" in their midst. Such populations are distinguished by the fact that while they remain generally bothersome, the costs that they inflict are most immediately absorbed by other members of the problem population. Policies evolve, not so much to eliminate or actively suppress these groups, but to deflect their threat away from targets which are sacred to the capitalist class. Victimization is permitted and even encouraged, as long as the victims are members of an expendable class.

Two or more or less discrete groupings are established through the operations of official control. These groups are a product of different operating assumptions and administrative orientations toward the deviant population. On the one hand, there is *social junk* which, from the point of view of the dominant class, is a costly yet relatively harmless burden to society. The discreditability of social junk resides in the failure, inability, or refusal of this group to participate in the roles supportive of capitalist society. Social junk is most likely to come to official attention when informal resources have been exhausted or when the magnitude of the problem becomes significant enough to create a basis for "public concern." Since the threat presented by social junk is passive, growing out of its inability to compete and its withdrawal from the prevailing social order, controls are usually designed to regulate and contain rather than eliminate and suppress the problem. Clear-cut examples of social junk in modern capitalist societies might include the officially administered aged, handicapped, mentally ill, and mentally retarded.

In contrast to social junk, there is a category that can be roughly described as *social dynamite.* The essential quality of deviance managed as social dynamite is its potential actively to call into question established relationships, especially relations of production and domination. Generally, therefore, social dynamite tends to be more youthful, alienated, and politically volatile than social junk. The control of social dynamite is usually premised on an assumption that the problem is acute in nature, requiring a rapid and focused expenditure of control resources. This is in contrast to the handling of social junk frequently based on a belief that the problem is chronic and best controlled through broad reactive rather than intensive and selective measures. Correspondingly, social dynamite is normally processed through the legal system with its capacity for active intervention, while social junk is frequently (but not always)[3] administered by the agencies and agents of the therapeutic and welfare state.

Many varieties of deviant populations are alternatively or simultaneously dealt with as either social junk and/or social dynamite. The welfare poor, homosexuals, alcoholics, and "problem children" are among the categories reflecting the equivocal nature of the control process and its dependence on the political, economic, and ideological priorities of deviance production. The changing nature of these priorities and their implications for the future may be best understood by examining some of the tendencies of modern capitalist systems.

•   •   •

Notes

1. To the extent that a group (e.g. homosexuals) blatantly and systematically challenges the validity of the bourgeois family it is likely to become part of the problem population. The family is essential to capitalist society as a unit for consumption, socialization, and the reproduction of the socially necessary labor force (cf. Frankford and Snitow, 1972; Secombe, 1973; Zaretsky, 1973).

2. O'Connor (1973) discusses this problem in terms of the crisis faced by the capitalist state in maintaining conditions for profitable accumulation and social harmony.

3. It has been estimated, for instance, that one-third of all arrests in America are for the offense of public drunkenness. Most of these apparently involve "sick" and destitute "skid row alcoholics" (Morris and Hawkins, 1969).

References

Baran, Paul, and Paul M. Sweezy. 1966. Monopoly Capital. New York: Monthly Review Press.

Becker, Howard S. 1967. "Whose side are we on?" Social Problems 14(Winter): 239–247.

Becker, Howard, S., and Irving Louis Horowitz. 1972. "Radical politics and sociological research: Observations on methodology and ideology." American Journal of Sociology 78(July): 48–66.

Blauner, Robert. 1969. "Internal colonialism and ghetto revolt." Social Problems 16(Spring): 393–408.

Bowles, Samuel. 1973. "Contradictions in United States higher education." Pp. 165–199 in James H. Weaver (ed.), Modern Political Economy: Radical versus Orthodox Approaches. Boston: Allyn and Bacon.

Bowles, Samuel, and Herbert Gintis. 1972. "I.Q. in the U.S. class structure." Social Policy 3(November/December): 65–96.

Bureau of Prisons. 1972. National Prisoner Statistics. Prisoners in State and Federal Institutions for Adult Felons. Washington, D.C.: Bureau of Prisons.

Cohen, David K., and Marvin Lazerson. 1972. "Education and the corporate order." Socialist Revolution (March/April): 48–72.

Foucault, Michel. 1965. Madness and Civilization. New York: Random House.

Frankford, Evelyn, and Ann Snitow. 1972. "The trap of domesticity: Notes on the family." Socialist Revolution (July/August): 83–94.

Gintis, Herbert. 1973. "Alienation and power." Pp. 431–465 in James H. Weaver (ed.), Modern Political Economy: Radical versus Orthodox Approaches. Boston: Allyn and Bacon.

Gorz, Andre. 1970. "Capitalist relations of production and the socially necessary labor force." Pp. 155–171 in Arthur Lothstein (ed.), All We Are Saying. . . . New York: G. P. Putnam.

Gross, Bertram M. 1970. "Friendly fascism: A model for America." Social Policy (November/December): 44–52.

Helmer, John, and Thomas Vietorisz. 1973. "Drug use, the labor market and class conflict." Paper presented at Annual Meeting of the American Sociological Association.

Karier, Clarence J. 1973. "Business values and the educational state." Pp. 6–29 in Clarence J. Karier, Paul Violas, and Joel Spring (eds.), Roots of Crisis: American Education in the Twentieth Century. Chicago: Rand McNally.

Liazos, Alexander. 1972. "The poverty of the sociology of deviance: Nuts, sluts and preverts." Social Problems 20(Summer): 103–120.

Mandel, Ernest. 1968. Marxist Economic Theory (Volume I). New York: Monthly Review Press.

Marcuse, Herbert. 1964. One-Dimensional Man. Boston: Beacon Press.

Marx, Karl. 1964. Class Struggles in France, 1848–1850. New York: International Publishers; 1967. Capital (Volume I). New York: International Publishers.

Matza, David. 1969. Becoming Deviant. Englewood Cliffs, N.J.: Prentice Hall.

McIntosh, Mary. 1973. "The growth of racketeering." Economy and Society (February): 35–69.

Morris, Norval, and Gordon Hawkins. 1969. The Honest Politician's Guide to Crime Control. Chicago: University of Chicago Press.

Musto, David F. 1973. The American Disease: Origins of Narcotic Control. New Haven: Yale University Press.

National Institute of Mental Health. 1970. Trends in Resident Patients—State and County Mental Hospitals 1950–1968. Biometry Branch, Office of Program Planning and Evaluation. Rockville, Maryland: National Institute of Mental Health.

O'Connor, James. 1973. The Fiscal Crisis of the State. New York: St. Martin's Press.

Piven, Frances, and Richard A. Cloward. 1971. Regulating the Poor: The Functions of Public Welfare. New York: Random House.

Rimlinger, Gaston V. 1961. "Social security, incentives, and controls in the U.S. and U.S.S.R." Comparative Studies in Society and History 4(November): 104–124; 1966. "Welfare policy and economic development: A comparative historical perspective." Journal of Economic History (December): 556–571.

Schelling, Thomas. 1967. "Economics and criminal enterprise." Public Interest (Spring): 61–78.

Secombe, Wally. 1973. "The housewife and her labour under capitalism." New Left Review (January-February): 3–24.

Spring, Joel. 1972. Education and the Rise of the Corporate State. Boston: Beacon Press; 1973. "Education as a form of social control." Pp. 30–39 in Clarence J. Karier, Paul Violas, and Joel Spring (eds.), Roots of Crisis: American Education in the Twentieth Century. Chicago: Rand McNally.

Turk, Austin T. 1969. Criminality and Legal Order. Chicago: Rand McNally.

Zaretsky, Eli. 1973. "Capitalism, the family and personal life: Parts 1 & 2." Socialist Revolution (January–April/May–June): 69–126, 19–70.

The Discovery of Hyperkinesis: Notes on the Medicalization of Deviant Behavior

Peter Conrad

Introduction

The increasing medicalization of deviant behavior and the medical institution's role as an agent of social control has gained considerable notice (Freidson, 1970; Pitts, 1968; Kittrie, 1971; Zola, 1972). By medicalization we mean defining behavior as a medical problem or illness and mandating or licensing the medical profession to provide some type of treatment for it. Examples include alcoholism, drug addiction and treating violence as a genetic or brain disorder. This redefinition is not a new function of the medical institution: psychiatry and public health have always been concerned with social behavior and have traditionally functioned as agents of social control (Foucault, 1965; Szasz, 1970; Rosen, 1972). . . .

This paper describes how certain forms of behavior in children have become defined as a medical problem and how medicine has become a major agent for their social control since the discovery of hyperkinesis. By discovery we mean both origin of the diagnosis and treatment for this disorder, and discovery of children who exhibit this behavior. The first section analyzes the discovery of hyperkinesis and why it suddenly became popular in the 1960's. The second section will discuss the medicalization of deviant behavior and its ramifications.

The Medical Diagnosis of Hyperkinesis

Hyperkinesis is a relatively recent phenomenon as a medical diagnostic category. Only in the past two decades has it been available as a recognized diagnostic category and only in the last decade has it received widespread notice and medical popularity. However, the roots of the diagnosis and treatment of this clinical entity are found earlier.

Hyperkinesis is also known as Minimal Brain Dysfunction, Hyperactive Syndrome, Hyperkinetic Disorder of Childhood, and by several other diagnostic categories. Although the symptoms and the presumed etiology vary, in general the behaviors are quite similar and greatly overlap.[1] Typical symptom patterns for diagnosing the disorder include: extreme excess of motor activity (hyperactivity); very short attention span (the child flits from activity to activity); restlessness; fidgetiness; often wildly oscillating mood swings (he's fine one day, a terror the next); clumsiness; aggressive-like behavior; impulsivity; in school he cannot sit still, cannot comply with rules, has low frustration level; frequently there may be sleeping problems and acquisition of speech may be delayed (Stewart et al., 1966, 1970; Wender, 1971). Most of the symptoms for the disorder are deviant behaviors.[2] It is six times as prevalent among boys as among girls. We use the term hyperkinesis to represent all the diagnostic categories of this disorder.

The Discovery of Hyperkinesis

It is useful to divide the analysis into what might be considered *clinical factors* directly related to the diagnosis and treatment of hyperkinesis and *social factors* that set the context for the emergence of the new diagnostic category.

Clinical Factors

Bradley (1937) observed that amphetamine drugs had a spectacular effect in altering the behavior of school children who exhibited behavior disorders or learning disabilities. Fifteen of the thirty children he treated actually became more subdued in their behavior. Bradley termed the effect of this medication paradoxical, since he expected that amphetamines would stimulate children as they stimulated adults. After the medication was discontinued the children's behavior returned to premedication level.

A scattering of reports in the medical literature on the utility of stimulant medications for "childhood behavior disorders" appeared in the next two decades. The next significant contribution was the work of Strauss and his associates (Strauss and Lehtinen, 1947) who found certain behavior (including hyperkinesis behaviors) in postencephalitic children suffering from what they called minimal brain injury (damage). This was the first time these behaviors were attributed to the new organic distinction of minimal brain damage.

This disorder still remained unnamed or else it was called a variety of names (usually just "childhood behavior disorder"). It did not appear as a specific diagnostic category until Laufer et al. (1957) described it as the "hyperkinetic impulse disorder" in 1957. Upon finding "the salient characteristics of the behavior pattern . . . are strikingly similar to those with clear cut organic causation" these researchers described a disorder with no clear-cut history or evidence for organicity (Laufer et al., 1957).

In 1966 a task force sponsored by the U.S. Public Health Service and the National Association for Crippled Children and Adults attempted to clarify the ambiguity and confusion in terminology and symptomology in diagnosing children's behavior and learning disorders. From over three dozen diagnoses, they agreed on the term "minimal brain dysfunction" as an overriding diagnosis that would include hyperkinesis and other disorders (Clements, 1966). Since this time M.B.D. has been the primary formal diagnosis or label.

In the middle 1950's a new drug, Ritalin, was synthesized, that has many qualities of amphetamines without some of their more undesirable side effects. In 1961 this drug was approved by the F.D.A. for use with children. Since this time there has been much research published on the use of Ritalin in the treatment of childhood behavior disorders. This medication became the "treatment of choice" for treating children with hyperkinesis.

Since the early sixties, more research appeared on the etiology, diagnosis and treatment of hyperkinesis (cf. DeLong, 1972; Grinspoon and Singer, 1973; Cole, 1975)—as much as three-quarters concerned with drug treatment of the disorder. There had been increasing publicity of the disorder in the mass media as well. The *Reader's Guide to Periodical Literature* had no articles on hyperkinesis before 1967, one each in 1968 and 1969, and a total of forty for 1970 through 1974 (a mean of eight per year).

Now hyperkinesis has become the most common child psychiatric problem (Gross and Wilson, 1974:142); special pediatric clinics have been established to treat hyperkinetic children, and substantial federal funds have been invested in etiological and treatment research. Outside the medical profession, teachers have developed a working clinical knowledge of hyperkinesis' symptoms and treatment (cf. Robin and Bosco, 1973); articles appear regularly in mass circulation magazines and newspapers so that parents often come to clinics with knowledge of this diagnosis. Hyperkinesis is no longer the relatively esoteric diagnostic category it may have been twenty years ago; it is now a well-known clinical disorder.

Social Factors

The social factors affecting the discovery of hyperkinesis can be divided into two areas: (1) The Pharmaceutical Revolution; (2) Government Action.

(1) The Pharmaceutical Revolution. Since the 1930's the pharmaceutical industry has been synthesizing and manufacturing a large number of psychoactive drugs, contributing to a virtual revolution in drug making and drug taking in America (Silverman and Lee, 1974).

Psychoactive drugs are agents that affect the central nervous system. Benzedrine, Ritalin, and Dexedrine are all synthesized psychoactive stimulants which were indicated for narcolepsy, appetite control (as "diet pills"), mild depression, fatigue, and more recently hyperkinetic children.

Until the early sixties there was little or no promotion and advertisement of any of these medications for use with childhood disorders.[3] Then two major pharmaceutical firms (Smith, Kline and French, manufacturer of Dexedrine, and CIBA, manufacturer of Ritalin) began to advertise in medical journals and through direct mailing and efforts of the "detail men." Most of this advertising of the pharmaceutical treatment of hyperkinesis was directed to the medical sphere; but some of the promotion was targeted for the educational sector also (Hentoff, 1972). This promotion was probably significant in disseminating information concerning the diagnosis and treatment of this newly discovered disorder.[4] Since 1955 the use of psychoactive medications (especially phenothiazines) for the treatment of persons who are mentally ill, along with the concurrent dramatic decline in inpatient populations, has made psychopharmacology an integral part of treatment for mental disorders. It has also undoubtedly increased the confidence in the medical profession for the pharmaceutical approach to mental and behavioral problems.

(2) Government Action. Since the publication of the U.S.P.H.S. report on M.B.D. there have been at least two significant governmental reports on treating school children with stimulant medications for behavior disorders. Both of these came as a response to the national publicity created by the *Washington Post* report (1970) that five to 10 percent of the 62,000 grammar school children in Omaha, Nebraska were being treated with "behavior modification drugs to improve deportment and increase learning potential" (quoted in Grinspon and Singer, 1973). Although the figures were later found to be a little exaggerated, it nevertheless spurred a Congressional investigation (U.S. Government Printing Office, 1970) and a conference sponsored by the Office of Child Development (1971) on the use of stimulant drugs in the treatment of behaviorally disturbed school children.

The Congressional Subcommittee on Privacy chaired by Congressman Cornelius E. Gallagher held hearings on the issue of prescribing drugs for hyperactive school children. In general, the committee showed great concern over the facility in which the medication was prescribed; more specifically that some children at least were receiving drugs from general practitioners whose primary diagnosis was based on teachers' and parents' reports that the child was doing poorly in school. There was also a concern with the absence of follow-up studies on the long-term effects of treatment.

The H.E.W. committee was a rather hastily convened group of professionals (a majority were M.D.'s) many of whom already had commitments to drug treatment for children's behavior problems. They recommended that only M.D.'s make the diagnosis and prescribe treatment, that the pharmaceutical companies promote the treatment of the disorder only through medical channels, that parents should not be coerced to accept any particular treatment and that long-term follow-up research should be done. This report served as blue ribbon approval for treating hyperkinesis with psychoactive medications.

Discussion

We will focus discussion on three issues: How children's deviant behavior became conceptualized as a medical problem; why this occurred when it did; and what are some of the implications of the medicalization of deviant behavior.

How does deviant behavior become conceptualized as a medical problem? We assume that before the discovery of hyperkinesis this type of deviance was seen as disruptive, disobedient, rebellious, anti-social or deviant behavior. Perhaps the label "emotionally disturbed" was sometimes used, when it was in vogue in the early sixties, and the child was usually managed in the context of the family or the school or in extreme cases, the child guidance clinic. How then did this constellation of deviant behaviors become a medical disorder?

The treatment was available long before the disorder treated was clearly conceptualized. It was twenty years after Bradley's discovery of the "paradoxical effect" of stimulants on certain deviant children that Laufer named the disorder and described its characteristic symptoms. Only in the late fifties were both the diagnostic label and the pharmaceutical treatment available. The pharmaceutical revolution in mental health and the increased interest in child psychiatry provided a favorable background for the dissemination of knowledge about this new disorder. The latter probably made the medical profession more likely to consider behavior problems in children as within their clinical jurisdiction.

There were agents outside the medical profession itself that were significant in "promoting" hyperkinesis as a disorder within the medical framework. These agents might be conceptualized in Becker's terms as "moral entrepreneurs," those who crusade for creation and enforcement of the rules (Becker, 1963).[5] In this case the moral entrepreneurs were the pharmaceutical companies and the Association for Children with Learning Disabilities.

The pharmaceutical companies spent considerable time and money promoting stimulant medications for this new disorder. From the middle 1960's on, medical journals and the free "throwaway" magazines contained elaborate advertising for Ritalin and Dexedrine. These ads explained the utility of treating hyperkinesis and urged physician to diagnose and treat hyperkinetic children. The ads run from one to six pages. For example, a two-page ad in 1971 stated:

> MBD . . . MEDICAL MYTH OR DIAGNOSABLE DISEASE ENTITY
> What medical practitioner has not, at one time or another, been called upon to examine an impulsive, excitable hyperkinetic child? A child with difficulty in concentrating. Easily frustrated. Unusually aggressive. A classroom rebel. In the absence of any organic pathology, the conduct of such children was, until a few short years ago, usually dismissed as . . . spunkiness, or evidence of youthful vitality. But it is now evident that in many of these children the hyperkinetic syndrome exists as a distinct medical entity. This syndrome is readily diagnosed through patient histories, neurologic signs, and psychometric testing—has been classified by an expert panel convened by the United States Department of Health, Education and Welfare as Minimal Brain Dysfunction, MBD.

The pharmaceutical firms also supplied sophisticated packets of "diagnostic and treatment" information on hyperkinesis to physicians, paid for professional conferences on the subject, and supported research in the identification and treatment of the disorder. Clearly these corporations had a vested interest in the labeling and treatment of hyperkinesis; CIBA had $13 million profit from Ritalin alone in 1971, which was 15 percent of the total gross profits (Charles, 1971; Hentoff, 1972).

The other moral entrepreneur, less powerful than the pharmaceutical companies, but nevertheless influential, is the Association for Children with Learning Disabilities. Although their focus is not specifically on hyperkinetic children, they do include it in their conception of Learning Disabilities along with aphasia, reading problems like dyslexia and perceptual motor problems. Founded in the early 1950's by parents and professionals, it has functioned much as the National Association for Mental Health does for mental illness: promoting conferences, sponsoring legislation, providing social support. One of the main functions has been to disseminate information concerning this relatively new area in education, Learning Disabilities. While the organization does have a more educational than medical perspective, most of the literature indicates that for hyperkinesis members have adopted the medical model and the medical approach to the problem. They have sensitized teachers and schools to the conception of hyperkinesis as a medical problem.

The medical model of hyperactive behavior has become very well accepted in our society. Physicians find treatment relatively simple and the results sometimes spectacular. Hyperkinesis minimizes parents' guilt by emphasizing "it's not their fault, it's an organic problem" and allows for nonpunitive management or control of deviance. Medication often makes a child less disruptive in the classroom and sometimes aids a child in learning. Children often like their "magic pills" which make their behavior more socially acceptable and they probably benefit from a reduced stigma also.

The Medicalization of Deviant Behavior

Pitts has commented that "medicalization is one of the most effective means of social control and that it is destined to become the main mode of *formal* social control" (1971:391). Kittrie (1971) has termed it "the coming of the therapeutic state."

Medicalization of mental illness dates at least from the seventeenth century (Foucault, 1965; Szasz, 1970). Even slaves who ran away were once considered to be suffering from the disease *drapedomania* (Chorover, 1973). In recent years alcoholism, violence, and drug addiction as well as hyperactive behavior in children have all become defined as medical problems, both in etiology or explanation of the behavior and the means of social control or treatment.

There are many reaons why this medicalization has occurred. Much scientific research, especially in pharmacology and genetics, has become technologically more sophisticated, and found more subtle correlates with human behavior. Sometimes these findings (as in the case of XYY chromosomes and violence) become etiological explanations for deviance. Pharmacological technology that makes new discoveries affecting behavior (e.g., antabuse, methadone and stimulants) are used as treatment for deviance. In part this application is encouraged by the prestige of the medical profession and its attachment to science. As Freidson notes, the medical profession has first claim to jurisdiction over anything that deals with the functioning of the body and especially anything that can be labeled illness (1970:251). Advances in genetics, pharmacology and "psychosurgery" also may advance medicine's jurisdiction over deviant behavior.

Second, the application of pharmacological technology is related to the humanitarian trend in the conception and control of deviant behavior. Alcoholism is no longer sin or even moral weakness, it is now a disease. Alcoholics are no longer arrested in many places for "public drunkenness," they are now somehow "treated," even if it is only to be dried out. Hyperactive children are now considered to have an illness rather than to be disruptive, disobedient, overactive problem children. They are not as likely to be that "bad boy" of the classroom; they are children with a medical disorder. Clearly there are some real humanitarian benefits to be gained by such a medical conceptualization of deviant behavior. There is less condemnation of the deviants (they have an illness, it is not their fault) and perhaps less social stigma. In some cases, even the medical treatment itself is more humanitarian social control than the criminal justice system.

There is, however, another side to the medicalization of deviant behavior. The four aspects of this side of the issue include (1) the problem of expert control; (2) medical social control; (3) the individualization of social problems; and (4) the "depoliticization" of deviant behavior.

1. *The problem of expert control.* The medical profession is a profession of experts; they have a monopoly on anything that can be conceptualized

as illness. Because of the way the medical profession is organized and the mandate it has from society, decisions related to medical diagnoses and treatment are virtually controlled by medical professionals.

Some conditions that enter the medical domain are not *ipso facto* medical problems, especially deviant behavior, whether alcoholism, hyperactivity or drug addiction. By defining a problem as medical it is removed from the public realm where there can be discussion by ordinary people and put on a plane where only medical people can discuss it. As Reynolds states,

> The increasing acceptance, especially among the more educated segments of our populace, of technical solutions—solutions administered by disinterested politically and morally neutral experts—results in the withdrawal of more and more areas of human experience from the realm of public discussion. For when drunkenness, juvenile delinquency, sub par performance and extreme political beliefs are seen as symptoms of an underlying illness or biological defect the merits and drawbacks of such behavior or beliefs need not be evaluated (1973:200–221).

The public may have their own conceptions of deviant behavior but that of the experts is usually dominant.

2. *Medical social control.*   Defining deviant behavior as a medical problem allows certain things to be done that could not otherwise be considered; for example, the body may be cut open or psychoactive medications may be given. This treatment can be a form of social control.

In regard to drug treatment Lennard points out: "Psychoactive drugs, especially those legally prescribed, tend to restrain individuals from behavior and experience that are not complementary to the requirements of the dominant value system" (1971:57). These forms of medical social control presume a prior definition of deviance as a medical problem. Psychosurgery on an individual prone to violent outbursts requires a diagnosis that there was something wrong with his brain or nervous system. Similarly, prescribing drugs to restless, overactive and disruptive school children requires a diagnosis of hyperkinesis. These forms of social control, what Chorover (1973) has called "psychotechnology," are very powerful and often very efficient means of controlling deviance. These relatively new and increasingly popular forms of social control could not be utilized without the medicalization of deviant behavior. As is suggested from the discovery of hyperkinesis, if a mechanism of medical social control seems useful, then the deviant behavior it modifies will develop a medical label or diagnosis. No overt malevolence on the part of the medical profession is implied: rather it is part of a complex process, of which the medical profession is only a part. The larger process might be called the individualization of social problems.

3. *The individualization of social problems.*   The medicalization of deviant behavior is part of a larger phenomenon that is prevalent in our society, the individualization of social problems. We tend to look for causes and solu-

tions to complex social problems in the individual rather than in the social system. This view resembles Ryan's (1970) notion of "blaming the victim"; seeing the causes of the problem in individuals rather than in the society where they live. We then seek to change the "victim" rather than the society. The medical perspective of diagnosing an illness in an individual lends itself to the individualization of social problems. Rather than seeing certain deviant behaviors as symptomatic of problems in the social system, the medical perspective focuses on the individual diagnosing and treating the illness, generally ignoring the social situation.

Hyperkinesis serves as a good example. Both the school and the parents are concerned with the child's behavior; the child is very difficult at home and disruptive in school. No punishments or rewards seem consistently to work in modifying the behavior; and both parents and school are at their wits' end. A medical evaluation is suggested. The diagnoses of hyperkinetic behavior leads to prescribing stimulant medications. The child's behavior seems to become more socially acceptable, reducing problems in school and at home.

But there is an alternate perspective. By focusing on the symptoms and defining them as hyperkinesis we ignore the possibility that behavior is not an illness but an adaption to a social situation. It diverts our attention from the family or school and from seriously entertaining the idea that the "problem" could be in the structure of the social system. And by giving medications we are essentially supporting the existing systems and do not allow this behavior to be a factor of change in the system.

4. *The depoliticization of deviant behavior.* Depoliticization of deviant behavior is a result of both the process of medicalization and individualization of social problems. To our western world, probably one of the clearest examples of such a depoliticization of deviant behavior occurred when political dissenters in the Soviet Union were declared mentally ill and confined in mental hospitals (cf. Conrad, 1972). This strategy served to neutralize the meaning of political protest and dissent, rendering it the ravings of mad persons.

The medicalization of deviant behavior depoliticizes deviance in the same manner. By defining the overactive, restless and disruptive child as hyperkinetic we ignore the meaning of behavior in the context of the social system. If we focused our analysis on the school system we might see the child's behavior as symptomatic of some "disorder" in the school or classroom situation, rather than symptomatic of an individual neurological disorder.

Conclusion

I have discussed the social ramifications of the medicalization of deviant behavior, using hyperkinesis as the example. A number of consequences of this medicalization have been outlined, including the depoliticization of deviant behavior, decision-making power of experts, and the role of medicine as an agent of social control. In the last analysis medical social control may be the central issue, as in this role medicine becomes a *de facto* agent of the *status quo*. The medical profession may not have entirely sought this role, but its members have been, in general, disturbingly unconcerned and unquestioning in their acceptance of it. With the increasing medical knowledge and technology it is likely that more deviant behavior will be medicalized and medicine's social control function will expand.

Notes

1. The U.S.P.H.S. report (Clements, 1966) included 38 terms that were used to describe or distinguish the conditions that it labeled Minimal Brain Dysfunction. Although the literature attempts to differentiate M.B.D., hyperkinesis, hyperactive syndrome, and several other diagnostic labels, it is our belief that in practice they are almost interchangeable.

2. For a fuller discussion of the construction of the diagnosis of hyperkinesis, see Conrad (1976), especially Chapter 6.

3. The American Medical Association's change in policy in accepting more pharmaceutical advertising in the late fifties may have been important. Probably the F.D.A. approval of the use of Ritalin for children in 1961 was more significant. Until 1970, Ritalin was advertised for treatment of "functional behavior problems in children." Since then, because of an F.D.A. order, it has only been promoted for treatment of M.B.D.

4. The drug industry spends fully 25 percent of its budget on promotion and advertising. See Coleman et al. (1966) for the role of the detail men and how physicians rely upon them for information.

5. Freidson also notes the medical professional role as moral entrepreneur in this process also:

> The profession does treat the illnesses laymen take to it, but it also seeks to discover illness of which the laymen may not even be aware. One of the greatest ambitions of the physician is to discover and describe a "new" disease or syndrome . . . (1970:252).

References

Becker, Howard S. 1963. *Outsiders: Studies in the Sociology of Deviance.* New York: Free Press.

Bradley, Charles. 1937. "The Behavior of Children Receiving Benzedrine." *American Journal of Psychiatry,* 94 (March): 577–585.

Charles, Alan. 1971. "The Case of Ritalin." *New Republic,* 23 (October): 17–19.

Chorover, Stephen L. 1973. "Big Brother and Psychotechnology." *Psychology Today* (October): 43–54.

Clements, Samuel D. 1966. "Task Force I: Minimal Brain Dysfunction in Children." National Institute of Neurological Diseases and Blindness, Monograph no. 3. Washington, D.C.: U.S. Department of Health, Education and Welfare.

Cole, Sherwood. 1975. "Hyperactive Children: The Use of Stimulant Drugs Evaluated." *American Journal of Orthopsychiatry,* 45 (January): 28–37.

Coleman, James, Elihu Katz, and Herbert Menzel. 1966. *Medical Innovation.* Indianapolis: Bobbs-Merrill.

Conrad, Peter. 1972. "Ideological Deviance: An Analysis of the Soviet Use of Mental Hospitals for Political Dissenters." Unpublished manuscript.

Conrad, Peter 1976. *Identifying Hyperactive Children: A Study in the Medicalization of Deviant Behavior.* Lexington, Mass.: D.C. Heath and Co.

DeLong, Arthur R. 1972. "What Have We Learned from Psychoactive Drugs Research with Hyperactives?" *American Journal of Diseases in Children,* 123 (February): 177–180.

Foucault, Michel. 1965. *Madness and Civilization.* New York: Pantheon.

Freidson, Eliot. 1970. *Profession of Medicine: A Study of the Sociology of Applied Knowledge*. New York: Dodd, Mead.

Grinspoon, Lester and Susan Singer. 1973. "Amphetamines in the Treatment of Hyperactive Children." *Harvard Educational Review,* 43 (November): 515–555.

Gross, Mortimer B. and William E. Wilson. 1974. *Minimal Brain Dysfunction.* New York: Brunner Mazel.

Hentoff, Nat. 1972. "Drug Pushing in the Schools: The Professionals." *The Village Voice,* 22 (May): 21–23.

Kittrie, Nicholas. 1971. *The Right to Be Different.* Baltimore: Johns Hopkins Press.

Laufer, M. W., Denhoff, E., and Solomons, G. 1957. "Hyperkinetic Impulse Disorder in Children's Behavior Problems." *Psychosomatic Medicine,* 19 (January): 38–49.

Lennard, Henry L. and Associates. 1971. *Mystification and Drug Misuse.* New York: Harper and Row.

Office of Child Development. 1971. "Report of the Conference on the Use of Stimulant Drugs in Treatment of Behaviorally Disturbed Children." Washington, D.C.: Office of Child Development, Department of Health, Education and Welfare, January 11–12.

Pitts, Jesse. 1968. "Social Control: The Concept." In David Sills (ed.), *International Encyclopedia of the Social Sciences.* Vol. 14. New York: Macmillan.

Reynolds, Janice M. 1973. "The Medical Institution." In Larry T. Reynolds and James M. Henslin, *American Society: A Critical Analysis.* New York: David McKay.

Robin, Stanley S. and James J. Bosco. 1973. "Ritalin for School Children: The Teacher's Perspective." *Journal of School Health,* 47 (December): 624–628.

Rosen, George. 1972. "The Evolution of Social Medicine." In Howard E. Freeman, Sol Levine, and Leo Reeder, *Handbook of Medical Sociology.* Englewood Cliffs, N.J.: Prentice-Hall.

Ryan, William. 1970. *Blaming the Victim.* New York: Vintage.

Silverman, Milton and Philip R. Lee. 1974. *Pills, Profits and Politics.* Berkeley: University of California Press.

Sroufe, L. Alan and Mark Stewart. 1973. "Treating Problem Children with Stimulant Drugs." *New England Journal of Medicine,* 289 (August 23): 407–421.

Stewart, Mark A. 1970. "Hyperactive Children." *Scientific American,* 222 (April): 794–798.

Stewart, Mark A., A. Ferris, N. P. Pitts, and A. G. Craig. 1966. "The Hyperactive Child Syndrome." *American Journal of Orthopsychiatry* 26 (October): 861–867.

Strauss, A. A. and L. E. Lehtinen. 1947. *Psychopathology and Education of the Brain-Injured Child.* Vol. 1. New York: Grune and Stratton.

Szasz, Thomas S. 1970. *The Manufacture of Madness.* New York: Harper and Row.

U.S. Government Printing Office. 1970. "Federal involvement in the Use of Behavior Modification Drugs on Grammar School Children of the Right to Privacy Inquiry: Hearing Before a Subcommittee of the Committee on Government Operations." Washington, D.C.: 91st Congress, 2nd session (September 29).

Wender, Paul. 1971. *Minimal Brain Dysfunction in Children.* New York: John Wiley and Sons.

Zola, Irving. 1972. "Medicine as an Institution of Social Control." *Sociological Review,* 20 (November): 487–504.

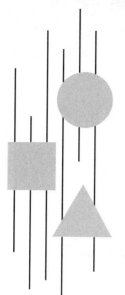

Understanding Deviance: Theories and Perspectives

Part I introduced a specific concern for the ways in which deviant categories arise, as well as the ways in which violators of existing categories may be reacted to. Missing from this introduction was a concern for *why* actors may exhibit behavior in violation of established norms, rules, regulations, and laws—violations that may cause them to be initially labeled as deviants. We believe that to approach a more complete understanding of deviance in terms of social processes, we must not only analyze the creation of deviant categories and the reactions to violators of categories; we must also examine the motivations for deviance. The selections in this part represent some of the major attempts to accomplish this goal.

Explanations of the motivations for deviance have taken various forms. Some observers would place the blame on a defective family structure or arrested personality adjustment; others would emphasize such conditions as poverty or racism; and there are proponents of the thesis that individuals are born deviant. It should be recognized, however, that no single factor can adequately explain why actors commit deviant acts. For example, findings in the area of delinquency research generally conclude that a combination of family, school, and peer variables is the most likely source of motivations for youth crime and deviance.

The actual attempts at understanding or explaining motivations for deviancy can, for our purposes, be roughly grouped into seven categories: (1) functionalist, (2) social conflict, (3) cultural transmission, (4) opportunity, (5) control, (6) interactionist, and (7) integrated approaches. Of the approaches reviewed here, certain divisions should be recognized. Functionalist, control, and opportunity frameworks are basically structural approaches. Structural perspectives seek to understand deviance in society by viewing deviance as a part of the larger social context and asking questions that probe the influence of deviance on social structures and the contribution of social structures to deviance. The cultural transmission and interactionist views are concerned primarily with how, through social-psychological-symbolic processes, actors learn existing cultures and traditions and incorporate them into their self-identity. Conflict theorists focus attention on the struggles and tensions between groups. Special consideration is given to how the powerful influence the creation of deviant categories that result in systematic disadvantage for opposing, less powerful groups. Although each of these approaches explicitly emphasizes certain underlying themes, concepts, or processes, there is frequently an implied or direct overlap among the various models. Such links are demonstrated in integrated approaches combining important elements from various perspectives.

The Functionalist Perspective

Social scientists who use a functionalist model contend that deviance is an integral part of any social system and that such behavior satisfies some societal need. In terms of sociological analysis, advocates of this model maintain that deviance serves the important function of demarcating and maintaining current boundaries of acceptable behavior. These particular conceptions are embedded in Emile Durkheim's work.

In his statement "The Normal and the Pathological," Durkheim argues that crime not only inheres in all societies but also serves a useful function for the collective conscience, particularly in maintaining the social system. And although forms and definitions of criminal and deviant behavior (i.e., the *collective types* or deviant categories) may vary from society to society, such behaviors do provide members with a basis for punishing violators of the prevailing normative codes. Punishment serves as an important reminder to others that certain behaviors are acceptable while others are not. Thus, achievement of an understanding of deviance and its categories requires an examination of the prevailing definitions of conformity.

In "On the Sociology of Deviance," Kai T. Erikson argues that behavior that may be acceptable within a family setting may not be perceived as such by the larger community. Furthermore, conduct that may be viewed unfavorably by the community may actually go unnoticed in other parts of the culture. In varying situations, then, different standards are used to assess whether or not an actor's behavior exceeds a social unit's "tolerance limits." If it does, the violator may be sanctioned negatively. In a sense, a community or social unit is concerned with the maintenance of its boundaries. Erikson argues that interactions occurring between a potential deviant and a community's official agents play an especially important role in "locating and publicizing the group's outer edges." Such confrontations are not without their individual and structural ramifications, however. Not only may a social actor be selected out, formally processed, and cast into a new status (e.g., that of a criminal), but if the violator is a member of a deviant group, the confrontation and resultant sanctioning may operate in such a way as to actually enhance an actor's esteem in the eyes of his or her peers, as well as to solidify and make more obvious the underlying structure, identity, and character of the group. Erikson goes on to offer some interesting observations. For example, he comments on the fact that even though selected institutions have been created to combat deviance, they, like many deviant groups, often operate in such a way as to encourage, promote, and perpetuate it.

7 The Normal and the Pathological

Emile Durkheim

Crime is present not only in the majority of societies of one particular species but in all societies of all types. There is no society that is not confronted with the problem of criminality. Its form changes; the acts thus characterized are not the same everywhere; but, everywhere and always, there have been men who have behaved in such a way as to draw upon themselves penal repression. If, in proportion as societies pass from the lower to the higher types, the rate of criminality, i.e., the relation between the yearly number of crimes and the population, tended to decline, it might be believed that crime, while still normal, is tending to lose this character of normality. But we have no reason to believe that such a regression is substantiated. Many facts would seem rather to indicate a movement in the opposite direction. From the beginning of the [nineteenth] century, statistics enable us to follow the course of criminality. It has everywhere increased. In France the increase is nearly 300 per cent. There is, then, no phenomenon that presents more indisputably all the symptoms of normality, since it appears closely connected with the conditions of all collective life. To make of crime a form of social morbidity would be to admit that morbidity is not something accidental, but, on the contrary, that in certain cases it grows out of the fundamental constitution of the living organism; it would result in wiping out all distinction between the physiological and the pathological. No doubt it is possible that crime itself will have abnormal forms, as, for example, when its rate is unusually high. This excess is, indeed, undoubtedly morbid in nature. What is normal, simply, is the existence of criminality, provided that it attains and does not exceed, for each social type, a certain level, which it is perhaps not impossible to fix in conformity with the preceding rules.[1]

Here we are, then, in the presence of a conclusion in appearance quite paradoxical. Let us make no mistake. To classify crime among the phenomena of normal sociology is not to say merely that it is an inevitable, although regrettable phenomenon, due to the incorrigible wickedness of men; it is to affirm that it is a factor in public health, an integral part of all healthy societies. This result is, at first glance, surprising enough to have puzzled even ourselves for a long time. Once this first surprise has been overcome, however, it is not difficult to find reasons explaining this normality and at the same time confirming it.

In the first place crime is normal because a society exempt from it is utterly impossible. Crime, we have shown elsewhere, consists of an act that offends certain very strong collective sentiments. In a society in which criminal acts are no longer committed, the sentiments they offend would have to be found without exception in all individual consciousnesses, and they must be found to exist with the same degree as sentiments contrary to them. Assuming that this condition could actually be realized, crime would not thereby disappear; it would only change its form, for the very cause which would thus dry up the sources of criminality would immediately open up new ones.

Indeed, for the collective sentiments which are protected by the penal law of a people at a specified moment of its history to take possession of the public conscience or for them to acquire a stronger hold where they have an insufficient grip, they must acquire an intensity greater than that which they had hitherto had. The community as a whole must experience them more vividly, for it can acquire from no other source the greater force necessary to control these individuals who formerly were the most refractory. For murderers to disappear, the horror of bloodshed must become greater in those social strata from which murderers are recruited; but, first it must become greater throughout the entire society. Moreover, the very absence of crime would directly contribute to produce this horror; because any sentiment seems much more respectable when it is always and uniformly respected.

One easily overlooks the consideration that these strong states of the common consciousness cannot be thus reinforced without reinforcing at the same time the more feeble states, whose violation previously gave birth to mere infraction of convention—since the weaker ones are only the prolongation, the attenuated form, of the stronger. Thus robbery and simple bad taste injure the same single altruistic sentiment, the respect for that which is another's. However, this same sentiment is less grievously offended by bad taste than by robbery; and since, in addition, the average consciousness has not sufficient intensity to react keenly to the bad taste, it is treated with greater tolerance. That is why the person guilty of bad taste is merely blamed, whereas the thief is punished. But, if this sentiment grows stronger, to the point of silencing in all consciousnesses the inclination which disposes man to steal, he will become more sensitive to the offenses which, until then, touched him but lightly. He will react against them, then, with more energy; they will be the object of greater opprobrium, which will transform certain of them from the simple moral faults that they were and give them the quality of crimes. For example, improper contracts, or contracts improperly executed, which only incur public blame or civil damages, will become offenses in law.

Imagine a society of saints, a perfect cloister of exemplary individuals. Crimes, properly so called, will there be unknown; but faults which appear venial to the layman will create there the same scandal that the ordinary offense does in ordinary consciousnesses. If, then, this society has the power to judge and punish, it will define these acts as criminal and will treat them as such. For the same reason, the perfect and upright man judges his smallest failings with a severity that the majority reserve for acts more truly in the nature of an offense. Formerly, acts of violence against persons were more frequent than they are today, because respect for individual dignity was less strong. As this has increased, these crimes have become more rare; and also, many acts violating this sentiment have been introduced into the penal law which were not included there in primitive times.[2]

In order to exhaust all the hypotheses logically possible, it will perhaps be asked why this unanimity does not extend to all collective sentiments without exception. Why should not even the most feeble sentiment gather enough energy to prevent all dissent? The moral consciousness of the society would be present in its entirety in all the individuals, with a vitality sufficient to prevent all acts offending it—the purely conventional faults as well as the crimes. But a uniformity so universal and absolute is utterly impossible; for the immediate physical milieu in which each one of us is placed, the hereditary antecedents, and the social influences vary from one individual to the next, and consequently diversify consciousnesses. It is impossible for all to be alike, if only because each one has his own organism and that these organisms occupy different areas in space. That is why, even among the lower peoples, where individual originality is very little developed, it nevertheless does exist.

Thus, since there cannot be a society in which the individuals do not differ more or less from the collective type, it is also inevitable that, among these divergences, there are some with a criminal character. What confers this character upon them is not the intrinsic quality of a given act but that definition which the collective conscience lends them. If the collective conscience is stronger, if it has enough authority practically to suppress these divergences, it will also be more sensitive, more exacting; and, reacting against the slightest deviations with the energy it otherwise displays only against more considerable infractions, it will attribute to them the same gravity as formerly to crimes. In other words, it will designate them as criminal.

Crime is, then, necessary; it is bound up with fundamental conditions of all social life, and by that very fact it is useful, because these conditions of which it is part are themselves indispensable to the normal evolution of morality and law.

Indeed, it is no longer possible today to dispute the fact that law and morality vary from one social type to the next, nor that they change within the same type if the conditions of life are modified. But, in order that these transformations may be possible, the collective sentiments at the basis of morality must not be hostile to change, and consequently must have but moderate energy. If they were too strong, they would no longer be plastic. Every pattern is an obstacle to new patterns, to the extent that the first pattern is inflexible. The better a structure is articulated, the more it offers a healthy resistance to all modification; and this is equally true of functional, as of anatomical, organization. If there were no crimes, this condition could not have been fulfilled; for such a hypothesis presupposes that collective sentiments have arrived at a degree of intensity unexampled in history. Nothing is good indefinitely and to an unlimited extent. The authority which the moral conscience enjoys must not be excessive; otherwise no one would dare criticize it, and it would too easily congeal into an immutable form. To make progress, individual originality must be able to express itself. In order that the originality of the idealist whose dreams transcend his century may find expression, it is necessary that the originality of the criminal, who is below the level of his time, shall also be possible. One does not occur without the other.

Nor is this all. Aside from this indirect utility, it happens that crime itself plays a useful role in this evolution. Crime implies not only that the way remains open to necessary changes but that in certain cases it directly prepares these changes. Where crime exists, collective sentiments are sufficiently flexible to take on a new form, and crime sometimes helps to determine the form they will take. How many times, indeed, it is only an anticipation of future morality—a step toward what will be! According to Athenian law, Socrates was a criminal, and his condemnation was no more than just. However, his crime, namely, the independence of his thought, rendered a service not only to humanity but to his country. It served to prepare a new morality and faith which the Athenians needed, since the traditions by which they had lived until then were no longer in harmony with the current conditions of life. Nor is the case of Socrates unique; it is reproduced periodically in history. It would never have been possible to establish the freedom of thought we now enjoy if the regulations prohibiting it had not been violated before being solemnly abrogated. At that time, however, the violation was a crime, since it was an offense against sentiments still very keen in the average conscience. And yet this crime was useful as a prelude to reforms which daily became more necessary. Liberal philosophy had as its precursors the heretics of all kinds who were justly punished by secular authorities during the entire course of the Middle Ages and until the eve of modern times.

From this point of view the fundamental facts of criminality present themselves to us in an entirely new light. Contrary to current ideas, the criminal no longer seems a totally unsociable being, a sort of parasitic element, a strange and unassimilable body, introduced into the midst of society.[3] On the contrary, he plays a definite role in social life. Crime, for its part, must no longer be conceived as an evil that cannot be too much suppressed. There is no occasion for self-congratulation when the crime rate drops noticeably below the average level, for we may be certain that this apparent progress is associated with some social disorder. Thus, the number of assault cases never falls so low as in times of want.[4] With the drop in the crime rate, and as a reaction to it, comes a revision, or the need of a revision in the theory of punishment. If, indeed, crime is a disease, its punishment is its remedy and cannot be otherwise conceived; thus, all the discussions it arouses bear on the point of determining what the punishment must be in order to fulfil this role of remedy. If crime is not pathological at all, the object of punishment cannot be to cure it, and its true function must be sought elsewhere.

Notes

1. From the fact that crime is a phenomenon of normal sociology, it does not follow that the criminal is an individual normally constituted from the biological and psychological points of view. The two questions are independent of each other. This independence will be better understood when we have shown, later on, the difference between psychological and sociological facts.

2. Calumny, insults, slander, fraud, etc.

3. We have ourselves committed the error of speaking thus of the criminal, because of a failure to apply our rule (*Division du travail social,* pp. 395–96).

4. Although crime is a fact of normal sociology, it does not follow that we must not abhor it. Pain itself has nothing desirable about it; the individual dislikes it as society does crime, and yet it is a function of normal physiology. Not only is it necessarily derived from the very constitution of every living organism, but it plays a useful role in life, for which reason it cannot be replaced. It would, then, be a singular distortion of our thought to present it as an apology for crime. We would not even think of protesting against such an interpretation, did we not know to what strange accusations and misunderstandings one exposes oneself when one undertakes to study moral facts objectively and to speak of them in a different language from that of the layman.

8 On the Sociology of Deviance

Kai T. Erikson

Human actors are sorted into various kinds of collectivity, ranging from relatively small units such as the nuclear family to relatively large ones such as a nation or culture. One of the most stubborn difficulties in the study of deviation is that the problem is defined differently at each one of these levels: behavior that is considered unseemly within the context of a single family may be entirely acceptable to the community in general, while behavior that attracts severe censure from the members of the community may go altogether unnoticed elsewhere in the culture. People in society, then, must learn to deal separately with deviance at each one of these levels and to distinguish among them in his own daily activity. A man may disinherit his son for conduct that violates old family traditions or ostracize a neighbor for conduct that violates some local custom, but he is not expected to employ either of these standards when he serves as a juror in a court of law. In each of the three situations he is required to use a different set of criteria to decide whether or not the behavior in question exceeds tolerable limits.

In the next few pages we shall be talking about deviant behavior in social units called "communities," but the use of this term does not mean that the argument applies only at that level of organization. In theory, at least, the argument being made here should fit all kinds of human collectivity—families as well as whole cultures, small groups as well as nations—and the term "community" is only being used in this context because it seems particularly convenient.[1]

The people of a community spend most of their lives in close contact with one another, sharing a common sphere of experience which makes them feel that they belong to a special "kind" and live in a special "place." In the formal language of sociology, this means that communities are boundary maintaining: each has a specific territory in the world as a whole, not only in the sense that it occupies a defined region of geographical space but also in the sense that it takes over a particular niche in what might be

85

called cultural space and develops its own "ethos" or "way" within that compass. Both of these dimensions of group space, the geographical and the cultural, set the community apart as a special place and provide an important point of reference for its members.

When one describes any system as boundary maintaining, one is saying that it controls the fluctuation of its consistent parts so that the whole retains a limited range of activity, a given pattern of constancy and stability, within the larger environment. A human community can be said to maintain boundaries, then, in the sense that its members tend to confine themselves to a particular radius of activity and to regard any conduct which drifts outside that radius as somehow inappropriate or immoral. Thus the group retains a kind of cultural integrity, a voluntary restriction on its own potential for expansion, beyond that which is strictly required for accommodation to the environment. Human behavior can vary over an enormous range, but each community draws a symbolic set of parentheses around a certain segment of that range and limits its own activities within that narrower zone. These parentheses, so to speak, are the community's boundaries.

Now people who live together in communities cannot relate to one another in any coherent way or even acquire a sense of their own stature as group members unless they learn something about the boundaries of the territory they occupy in social space, if only because they need to sense what lies beyond the margins of the group before they can appreciate the special quality of the experience which takes place within it. Yet how do people learn about the boundaries of their community? And how do they convey this information to the generations which replace them?

To begin with, the only material found in a society for marking boundaries is the behavior of its members—or rather, the networks of interaction which like these members together in regular social relations. And the interactions which do the most effective job of locating and publicizing the group's outer edges would seem to be those which take place between deviant persons on the one side and official agents of the community on the other. The deviant is a person whose activities have moved outside the margins of the group, and when the community calls him to account for that vagrancy it is making a statement about the nature and placement of its boundaries. It is declaring how much variability and diversity can be tolerated within the group before it begins to lose its distinctive shape, its unique identity. Now there may be other moments in the life of the group which perform a similar service: wars, for instance, can publicize a group's boundaries by drawing attention to the line separating the group from an adversary, and certain kinds of religious ritual, dance ceremony, and other traditional pageantry can dramatize the difference between "we" and "they" by portraying a symbolic encounter between the two. But on the whole, members of a community inform one another about the placement of their boundaries by participating in the confrontations which occur when persons who venture out to the edges of the group are met by policing agents whose special business it is to guard the cultural integrity of the community. Whether these confrontations take the form of criminal trials, excommunication hearings, courts-martial, or even psychiatric case conferences, they act as boundary-maintaining devices in the sense that they demonstrate to whatever audience is concerned where the line is drawn between behavior that belongs in the special universe of the group and behavior that does not. In general, this kind of information is not easily relayed by the straightforward use of language. Most readers of this paragraph, for instance, have a fairly clear idea of the line separating theft from more legitimate forms of commerce, but few of them have ever seen a published statute describing these differences. More likely than not, our information on the subject has been drawn from publicized instances in which the relevant laws were applied—and for that matter, the law itself is largely a collection of past cases and decisions, a synthesis of the various confrontations which have occurred in the life of the legal order.

It may be important to note in this connection that confrontations between deviant offenders and the agents of control have always attracted a good deal of public attention. In our own past, the trial and punishment of offenders were staged in the market place and afforded the crowd a chance to participate in a direct, active way. Today, of course, we no longer parade deviants in the town square or expose them to the carnival atmosphere of a Tyburn, but it is interesting that the "reform" which brought about this change in penal practice coincided almost exactly with the development of newspapers as a medium of mass information. Perhaps this is no more than an accident of history, but it is nonetheless true that newspapers (and now radio and television) offer much the same kind of entertainment as public hangings or a Sunday visit to the local gaol. A considerable portion of what we call "news" is devoted to reports about deviant behavior and its consequences, and it is no simple matter to explain why these items should be considered newsworthy or why they should command the extraordinary attention they do. Perhaps they appeal to a number of psychological perversities among the mass audience, as commentators have suggested, but at the same time they constitute one of our main sources of information about the normative outlines of society. In a figurative sense, at least, morality and immorality meet at the public scaffold, and it is during this meeting that the line between them is drawn.

Boundaries are never a fixed property of any community. They are always shifting as the people of the group find new ways to define the outer limits of their universe, new ways to position themselves on the larger cultural map. Sometimes changes occur within the structure of the group which require its members to make a new survey of their territory—a change of leadership, a shift of mood. Sometimes changes occur in the surrounding environment, altering the background against which the people of the group have measured their own uniqueness. And always, new generations are moving in to take their turn guarding old institutions and need to be informed about the contours of the world they are inheriting. Thus single encounters between the deviant and his community are only fragments of an ongoing social process. Like an article of common law, boundaries remain a meaningful point of reference only so long as they are repeatedly tested by persons on the fringes of the group and repeatedly defended by persons chosen to represent the group's inner morality. Each time the community moves to censure some act of deviation, then, and convenes a formal ceremony to deal with the responsible offender, it sharpens the authority of the violated norm and restates where the boundaries of the group are located.

For these reasons, deviant behavior is not a simple kind of leakage which occurs when the machinery of society is in poor working order, but may be, in controlled quantities, an important condition for preserving the stability of social life. Deviant forms of behavior, by marking the outer edges of group life, give the inner structure its special character and thus supply the framework within which the people of the group develop an orderly sense of their own cultural identity. Perhaps this is what Aldous Huxley had in mind when he wrote:

> Now tidiness is undeniably good—but a good of which it is easily possible to have too much and at too high a price. . . . The good life can only be lived in a society in which tidiness is preached and practised, but not too fanatically, and where efficiency is always haloed, as it were, by a tolerated margin of mess.[2]

This raises a delicate theoretical issue. If we grant that human groups often derive benefit from deviant behavior, can we then assume that they are organized in such a way as to promote this resource? Can we assume, in other words, that forces operate in the social structure to recruit offenders and to commit them to long periods of service in the deviant ranks? This is not a question which can be answered with our present store of empirical data, but one observation can be made which gives the question an interesting perspective—namely, that deviant forms of conduct often seem to derive nourishment from the very agencies devised to inhibit them. Indeed, the agencies built by society for preventing deviance are often so poorly equipped for the task that we might well ask why this is regarded as their "real" function in the first place.

It is by now a thoroughly familiar argument that many of the institutions designed to discourage deviant behavior actually operate in such a way as to perpetuate it. For one thing, prisons, hospitals, and other similar agencies provide aid and shelter to large numbers of deviant persons, sometimes giving them a certain advantage in the competition for social resources. But beyond this, such institutions gather marginal people into tightly segregated groups, give them an opportunity to teach one another the skills and attitudes of a deviant career, and even provoke them into using these skills by reinforcing their sense of alienation from the rest of society.[3] Nor is this observation a modern one:

> The misery suffered in gaols is not half their evil; they are filled with every sort of corruption that poverty and wickedness can generate; with all the shameless and profligate enormities that can be produced by the impudence of ignominy, the range of want, and the malignity of despair. In a prison the check of the public eye is removed; and the power of the law is spent. There are few fears, there are no blushes. The lewd inflame the more modest; the audacious harden the timid. Everyone fortifies himself as he can against his own remaining sensibility; endeavoring to practise on others the arts that are practised on himself; and to gain the applause of his worst associates by imitating their manners.[4]

These lines, written almost two centuries ago, are a harsh indictment of prisons, but many of the conditions they describe continue to be reported in even the most modern studies of prison life. Looking at the matter from a long-range historical perspective, it is fair to conclude that prisons have done a conspicuously poor job of reforming the convicts placed in their custody; but the very consistency of this failure may have a peculiar logic of its own. Perhaps we find it difficult to change the worst of our penal practices because we *expect* the prison to harden the inmate's commitment to deviant forms of behavior and draw him more deeply into the deviant ranks. On the whole, we are a people who do not really expect deviants to change very much as they are processed through the control agencies we provide for them, and we are often reluctant to devote much of the community's resources to the job of rehabilitation. In this sense, the prison which graduates long rows of accomplished criminals (or, for that matter, the state asylum which stores its most severe cases away in some back ward) may do serious violence to the aims of its founders; but it does very little violence to the expectations of the population it serves.

These expectations, moreover, are found in every corner of society and constitute an important part of the climate in which we deal with deviant forms of behavior.

To begin with, the community's decision to bring deviant sanctions against one of its members is not a simple act of censure. It is an intricate rite of transition, at once moving the individual out of his ordinary place in society and transferring him into a special deviant position.[5] The ceremonies which mark this change of status, generally, have a number of related phases. They supply a formal stage on which the deviant and his community can confront one another (as in the criminal trial); they make an announcement about the nature of his deviancy (a verdict or diagnosis, for example); and they place him in a particular role which is thought to neutralize the harmful effects of his misconduct (like the role of prisoner or patient). These commitment ceremonies tend to be occasions of wide public interest and ordinarily take place in a highly dramatic setting.[6] Perhaps the most obvious example of a commitment ceremony is the criminal trial, with its elaborate formality and exaggerated ritual, but more modest equivalents can be found wherever procedures are set up to judge whether or not someone is legitimately deviant.

Now an important feature of these ceremonies in our own culture is that they are almost irreversible. Most provisional roles conferred by society— those of the student or conscripted soldier, for example—include some kind of terminal ceremony to mark the individual's movement back out of the role once its temporary advantages have been exhausted. But the roles allotted the deviant seldom make allowance for this type of passage. He is ushered into the deviant position by a decisive and often dramatic ceremony, yet is retired from it with scarcely a word of public notice. And as a result, the deviant often returns home with no proper license to resume a normal life in the community. Nothing has happened to cancel out the stigmas imposed upon him by earlier commitment ceremonies; nothing has happened to revoke the verdict or diagnosis pronounced upon him at that time. It should not be surprising, then, that the people of the community are apt to greet the returning deviant with a considerable degree of apprehension and distrust, for in a very real sense they are not at all sure who he is.

A circularity is thus set into motion which has all the earmarks of a "self-fulfilling prophesy," to use Merton's fine phrase. On the one hand, it seems quite obvious that the community's apprehensions help reduce whatever chances the deviant might otherwise have had for a successful return home. Yet at the same time, everyday experience seems to show that these suspicions are wholly reasonable, for it is a well-known and highly publicized fact that many if not most ex-convicts return to crime after leaving prison and that large numbers of mental patients require further treatment after an initial hospitalization. The common feeling that deviant persons never really change, then, may derive from a faulty premise; but the feeling is expressed so frequently and with such conviction that it eventually creates the facts which later "prove" it to be correct. If the returning deviant encounters this circularity often enough, it is quite understandable that he, too, may begin to wonder whether he has fully graduated from the deviant role, and he may respond to the uncertainty by resuming some kind of deviant activity. In many respects, this may be the only way for the individual and his community to agree what kind of person he is.

Moreover this prophesy is found in the official policies of even the most responsible agencies of control. Police departments could not operate with any real effectiveness if they did not regard ex-convicts as a ready pool of suspects to be tapped in the event of trouble, and psychiatric clinics could not do a successful job in the community if they were not always alert to the possibility of former patients suffering relapses. Thus the prophesy gains currency at many levels within the social order, not only in the poorly informed attitudes of the community at large, but in the best informed theories of most control agencies as well.

In one form or another this problem has been recognized in the West for many hundreds of years, and this simple fact has a curious implication. For if our culture has supported a steady flow of deviation throughout long periods of historical change, the rules which apply to any kind of evolutionary thinking would suggest that strong forces must be at work to keep the flow intact—and this because it contributes in some important way to the survival of the culture as a whole. This does not furnish us with sufficient warrant to declare that deviance is "functional" (in any of the many senses of that term), but it should certainly make us wary of the assumption so often made in sociological circles that any well-structured society is somehow designed to prevent deviant behavior from occurring.[7]

It might be then argued that we need new metaphors to carry our thinking about deviance onto a different plane. On the whole, American sociologists have devoted most of their attention to those forces in society which seem to assert a centralizing influence on human behavior, gathering people together into tight clusters called "groups" and bringing them under the jurisdiction of governing principles called "norms" or "standards." The questions which sociologists have traditionally asked of their data, then, are addressed to the uniformities rather than the divergencies of social life: how is it that people learn to think in similar ways, to accept the same group moralities, to move by the same rhythms of behavior, to see life with the same eyes? How is it, in short, that cultures accomplish the incredible alchemy of making unity out of diversity, harmony out of conflict, order out of confusion? Somehow we often act as if the differences between people can be taken for granted, being too natural to require comment, but that the symmetry which human groups manage to achieve must be explained by referring to the molding influence of the social structure.

But variety, too, is a product of the social structure. It is certainly remarkable that members of a culture come to look so much alike; but it is also remarkable that out of all this sameness a people can develop a complex division of labor, move off into diverging career lines, scatter across the surface of the territory they share in common, and create so many differences of temper, ideology, fashion, and mood. Perhaps we can conclude, then, that two separate yet often competing currents are found in any society: those forces which promote a high degree of conformity among the people of the community so that they know what to expect from one another, and those forces which encourage a certain degree of diversity so that people can be deployed across the range of group space to survey its potential, measure its capacity, and, in the case of those we call deviants, patrol its boundaries. In such a scheme, the deviant would appear as a natural product of group differentiation. He is not a bit of debris spun out by faulty social machinery, but a relevant figure in the community's overall division of labor.

Notes

1. In fact, the first statement of the general notion presented here was concerned with the study of small groups. See Robert A. Dentler and Kai T. Erikson, "The Functions of Deviance in Groups," *Social Problems,* VII (Fall 1959), pp. 98–107.

2. Aldous Huxley, *Prisons: The "Carceri" Etchings by Piranesi* (London: The Trianon Press, 1949), p. 13.

3. For a good description of this process in the modern prison, see Gresham Sykes, *The Society of Captives* (Princeton, N.J.: Princeton University Press, 1958). For discussions of similar problems in two different kinds of mental hospital, see Erving Goffman, *Asylums* (New York: Bobbs-Merrill, 1962) and Kai T. Erikson, "Patient Role and Social Uncertainty: A Dilemma of the Mentally Ill," *Psychiatry,* XX (August 1957), pp. 263–274.

4. Written by "a celebrated" but not otherwise identified author (perhaps Henry Fielding) and quoted in John Howard, *The State of the Prisons,* London, 1777 (London: J. M. Dent and Sons, 1929), p. 10.

5. The classic description of this process as it applies to the medical patient is found in Talcott Parsons, *The Social System* (Glencoe, Ill.: The Free Press, 1951).

6. See Harold Garfinkel, "Successful Degradation Ceremonies," *American Journal of Sociology,* LXI (January 1956), pp. 420–424.

7. Albert K. Cohen, for example, speaking for a dominant strain in sociological thinking, takes the question quite for granted: "It would seem that the control of deviant behavior is, by definition, a culture goal." See "The Study of Social Disorganization and Deviant Behavior" in Merton et al., *Sociology Today* (New York: Basic Books, 1959), p. 465.

The Conflict Perspective

A basic premise underlying conflict perspectives is that the life experiences of groups are generally shaped by those who have power over them. From a conflict perspective, then, it is important to understand the different life experiences of groups within the population. In a diverse society such as ours, socializing experiences vary a great deal, and people are often confronted with conflicting definitions of a situation. In some cases, acting in accordance with one's own values may result in being defined as deviant by those others who are successful in attaching the label (those with power). In other cases, populations become eligible for control by those who are able to create deviant categories intended to "manage" certain groups. These ideas are illustrated and elaborated upon in the following three selections.

In "The Conflict of Conduct Norms," Thorsten Sellin argues that actors are members of numerous groups and are, therefore, exposed to many different sets of conduct norms and values. Among those who migrate from one society to another, the sense of cultural conflict may be particularly severe. Migrants frequently find themselves constrained and regulated by a new and unfamiliar set of values. Sellin cites, as an example, the case in which a father kills the seducer of his daughter. In Sicily, killing a seducer is acceptable; in the United States it is considered murder. A lack of consensus with respect to existing norms, then, may not only give rise to cultural conflicts of various types but may also result in the application of deviant labels to those who violate deviant categories.

Jeffrey H. Reiman, in "A Radical Perspective on Crime," offers a contemporary statement on the conflict model. He maintains that laws and the associated criminal justice system operate in such a manner as to support the established social and economic order. Concentrating on the individual wrongdoer, Reiman argues, is a particularly effective way of attaining this end. By blaming the individual, the criminal justice system simultaneously diverts our attention away from the possible evils of the social order and acquits society of any criminality or injustice. Further, Reiman argues that various types of social arrangements actually sustain and benefit from the perpetuation of the ideology of individual failure or blame. Reiman uses portions of Cloward and Ohlin's theory to buttress his case. For example, even though people are encouraged to succeed, many do fail, and especially those from the lower classes. As Reiman puts it: " . . . many are called but few are chosen." Involvement in criminal activities does offer an outlet for those experiencing failure and frustration. Thus, not only is society structured in such a way as to actually produce crime, but those who "reap the benefits of the competition for success" (i.e., those who enjoy a high standard of living) do not have to pay for the costs of this competition. The bill is paid by the poor. In fact, the affluent, Reiman argues, deny that they benefit from an economic system that produces a high degree of suffering and frustration for the poor.

This bias against the poor is manifested in other ways. Reiman speaks specifically of the bonuses associated with such a bias. For example, an image is conveyed that the real threat to a decent society comes from the poor. Another important bonus for the powerful is that the bias generates persistent hostility toward the poor. Reiman then notes some of the indignities that the poor suffer at the hands of the welfare system and its agents. Aid, instead of being viewed as an act of justice, is perceived as an act of charity. Many of these points, we might add, will be elaborated on in Part VI, particularly in our discussion of the need to rehabilitate institutions and social systems.

In their article, "Differential Punishing of African Americans and Whites Who Possess Drugs: A Just Policy or a Continuation of the Past?," Rudolph Alexander, Jr., and Jacquelyn Gyamerah address the issue of race and punishment. Their purpose is to set current charges of racial discrimination in broader historical context that reaches back to slavery and the reconstruction period. They argue that the origins of differential criminal treatment of African Americans can be traced to the need to control slaves. This required different sets of laws that applied to whites and slaves. Laws for slaves were more extensive with far greater limitations, and violations were sanctioned more severely. Alexander and Gyamerah draw our attention to the fact that all groups do not share equal voice in shaping social policy. The article serves as illustration for Reiman's "Radical Conflict Approach" in that (1) populations have been the target for management and (2) management strategies can be employed that differentially impact the target group (such as adding behaviors that are likely a part of the target population to the list of deviance). The "Conflict of Conduct Norms," as presented by Sellin is also illustrated here. Alexander and Gyamerah show how the dominant group is able to shape perceptions, laws, and sanctions related to deviance. Notice that when the dominant group is disadvantaged, laws may, in fact, change to relieve the disadvantage.

9 The Conflict of Conduct Norms

Thorsten Sellin

Culture Conflicts as Conflicts of Cultural Codes

. . . There are social groups on the surface of the earth which possess complexes of conduct norms which, due to differences in the mode of life and the social values evolved by these groups, appear to set them apart from other groups in many or most respects. We may expect conflicts of norms when the rural dweller moves to the city, but we assume that he has absorbed the basic norms of the culture which comprises both town and country. How much greater is not the conflict likely to be when Orient and Occident meet, or when the Corsican mountaineer is transplanted to the lower East Side of New York. Conflicts of cultures are inevitable when the norms of one cultural or subcultural area migrate to or come in contact with those of another.

Conflicts between the norms of divergent cultural codes may arise

1. when these codes clash on the border of contiguous culture areas;
2. when, as may be the case with legal norms, the law of one cultural group is extended to cover the territory of another; or
3. when members of one cultural group migrate to another.[1]

Speck, for instance, notes that "where the bands popularly known as Montagnais have come more and more into contact with Whites, their reputation has fallen lower among the traders who have known them through commercial relationships within that period. The accusation is made that they have become less honest in connection with their debts, less trustworthy with property, less truthful, and more inclined to alcoholism and sexual freedom as contacts with the frontier towns have become easier for them. Richard White reports in 1933 unusual instances of Naskapi breaking into traders' store houses."[2]

Similar illustrations abound in the works of the cultural anthropologists. We need only to recall the effect on the American Indian of the culture

95

conflicts induced by our policy of acculturation by guile and force. In this instance, it was not merely contact with the white man's culture, his religion, his business methods, and his liquor, which weakened the tribal mores. In addition, the Indian became subject to the white man's law and this brought conflicts as well, as has always been the case when legal norms have been imposed upon a group previously ignorant of them. Maunier[3] in discussing the diffusion of French law in Algeria, recently stated: "In introducing the *Code Penal* in our colonies, as we do, we transform into offenses the ancient usages of the inhabitants which their customs permitted or imposed. Thus, among the Khabyles of Algeria, the killing of adulterous wives is ritual murder committed by the father or brother of the wife and not by her husband, as elsewhere. The woman having been sold by her family to her husband's family, the honor of her relatives is soiled by her infidelity. Her father or brother has the right and the duty to kill her in order to cleanse by her blood the honor of her relatives. Murder in revenge is also a duty, from family to family, in case of murder of or even in case of insults to a relative: the vendetta, called the *rekba* in Khabylina, is imposed by the law of honor. But these are crimes in French law! Murder for revenge, being premeditated and planned, is assassination, punishable by death! . . . What happens, then, often when our authorities pursue the criminal, guilty of an offense against public safety as well as against morality: public enemy of the French order, but who has acted in accord with a respected custom? The witnesses of the assassination, who are his relatives, or neighbors, fail to lay charges against the assassin; when they are questioned, they pretend to know nothing; and the pursuit is therefore useless. A French magistrate has been able to speak of the conspiracy of silence among the Algerians; a conspiracy aiming to preserve traditions, always followed and obeyed, against their violation by our power. This is the tragic aspect of the conflict of laws. A recent decree forbids the husband among the Khabyles to profit arbitrarily by the power given him according to this law to repudiate his wife, demanding that her new husband pay an exorbitant price for her—this is the custom of the *lefdi.* Earlier, one who married a repudiated wife paid nothing to the former husband. It appears that the first who tried to avail himself of the new law was killed for violating the old custom. The abolition of the ancient law does not always occur without protest or opposition. That which is a crime was a duty; and the order which we cause to reign is sometimes established to the detriment of 'superstition'; it is the gods and the spirits, it is believed, that would punish any one who fails to revenge his honor."

When Soviet law was extended to Siberia, similar effects were observed. Anossow[4] and Wirschubski[5] both relate that women among the Siberian tribes, who, in obedience to the law, laid aside their veils, were killed by their relatives for violating one of the most sacred norms of their tribes.

We have noted that culture conflicts are the natural outgrowth of processes of social differentiation, which produce an infinity of social

groupings, each with its own definitions of life situations, its own interpretations of social relationships, its own ignorance or misunderstanding of
the social values of other groups. The transformation of a culture from a
homogeneous and well-integrated type to a heterogeneous and disinte-
grated type is therefore accompanied by an increase of conflict situations.
Conversely, the operation of integrating processes will reduce the number
of conflict situations. Such conflicts within a changing culture may be distinguished from those created when different cultural systems come in
contact with one another, regardless of the character or stage of development of these systems. In either case, the conduct of members of a group
involved in the conflict of codes will in some respects be judged abnormal
by the other group.

The Study of Culture Conflicts

In the study of culture conflicts, some scholars have been concerned with
the effect of such conflicts on the conduct of specific persons, an approach
which is naturally preferred by psychologists and psychiatrists and by sociologists who have used the life history technique. These scholars view
the conflict as internal. Wirth[6] states categorically that a culture "conflict
can be said to be a factor in delinquency only if the individual feels it or
acts as if it were present." Culture conflict is mental conflict, but the character of this conflict is viewed differently by the various disciplines which
use this term. Freudian psychiatrists[7] regard it as a struggle between deeply
rooted biological urges which demand expression and the culturally created rules which give rise to inhibitive mechanisms which thwart this expression and drive them below the conscious level of the mind, whence
they rise either by ruse in some socially acceptable disguise, as abnormal
conduct when the inhibiting mechanism breaks down, or as neuroses when
it works too well. The sociologist, on the other hand, thinks of mental conflict as being primarily the clash between antagonistic conduct norms incorporated in personality. "Mental conflict in the person," says Burgess in
discussing the case presented by Shaw in *The Jack-Roller*, "may always be
explained in terms of the conflict of divergent cultures."[8]

If this view is accepted, sociological research on culture conflict and its
relationships to abnormal conduct would have to be strictly limited to a
study of the personality of cultural hybrids. Significant studies could be
conducted only by the life-history case technique applied to persons in
whom the conflict is internalized, appropriate control groups being utilized,
of course. . . .

The absence of mental conflict, in the sociological sense, may, however,
be well studied in terms of culture conflict. An example may make this
clear. A few years ago a Sicilian father in New Jersey killed the sixteen-
year-old seducer of his daughter, expressing surprise at his arrest since he

had merely defended his family honor in a traditional way. In this case a mental conflict in the sociological sense did not exist. The conflict was external and occurred between cultural codes or norms. We may assume that where such conflicts occur violations of norms will arise merely because persons who have absorbed the norms of one cultural group or area migrate to another and that such conflict will continue so long as the acculturation process has not been completed. . . . Only then may the violations be regarded in terms of mental conflict.

If culture conflict may be regarded as sometimes personalized, or mental, and sometimes as occurring entirely in an impersonal way solely as a conflict of group codes, it is obvious that research should not be confined to the investigation of mental conflicts and that contrary to Wirth's categorical statement that it is impossible to demonstrate the existence of a culture conflict "objectively . . . by a comparison between two cultural codes"[9] this procedure has not only a definite function, but may be carried out by researchers employing techniques which are familiar to the sociologist.

The emphasis on the life history technique has grown out of the assumption that "the experiences of one person at the same time reveals the life activities of his group" and that "habit in the individual is an expression of custom in society."[10] This is undoubtedly one valid approach. Through it we may hope to discover generalizations of a scientific nature by studying persons who (1) have drawn their norms of conduct from a variety of groups with conflicting norms, or (2) who possess norms drawn from a group whose code is in conflict with that of the group which judges the conduct. In the former case alone can we speak of mental or internal culture conflict; in the latter, the conflict is external.

If the conduct norms of a group are, with reference to a given life situation, inconsistent, or if two groups possess inconsistent norms, we may assume that the members of these various groups will individually reflect such group attitudes. Paraphrasing Burgess, the experiences of a group will reveal the life activities of its members. While these norms can, no doubt, be best established by a study of a sufficient number of representative group members, they may for some groups at least be fixed with sufficient certainty to serve research purposes by a study of the social institutions, the administration of justice, the novel, the drama, the press, and other expressions of group attitudes. The identification of the groups in question having been made, it might be possible to determine to what extent such conflicts are reflected in the conduct of their members. Comparative studies based on the violation rates of the members of such groups, the trends of such rates, etc., would dominate this approach to the problem.

In conclusion, then, culture conflict may be studied either as mental conflict or as a conflict of cultural codes. The criminologist will naturally tend to concentrate on such conflicts between legal and nonlegal conduct norms. The concept of conflict fails to give him more than a general framework of reference for research. In practice, it has, however, become nearly synonymous with conflicts between the norms of cultural systems or areas. Most researches which have employed it have been done on immigrant or race groups in the United States, perhaps due to the ease with which such groups may be identified, the existence of more statistical data recognizing such groupings, and the conspicuous differences between some immigrant norms and our norms.

Notes

1. This is unfortunately not the whole story, for with the rapid growth of impersonal communication, the written (press, literature) and the spoken word (radio, talkie), knowledge concerning divergent conduct norms no longer grows solely out of direct personal contact with their carriers. And out of such conflicts grow some violations of custom and of law which would not have occurred without them.

2. Speck, Frank G. "Ethical Attributes of the Labrador Indians." *American Anthropologist.* N. S. 35:559–94. October–December 1933. P. 559.

3. Maunier, René. "La diffusion du droit français en Algérie." Harvard Tercentenary Publications, *Independence, Convergence, and Borrowing in Institutions, Thought, and Art.* Cambridge: Harvard University Press. 1937. Pp. 84–85.

4. Anossow, J.J. "Die volkstümlichen Verbrechen im Strafkodex der USSR." *Monatsschrift für Kriminalpsychologie und Strafrechtsreform.* 24:534–37. September 1933.

5. Wirschubski, Gregor. "Der Schutz der Sittlichkeit im Sowjetstrafrecht." *Zeitschrift für die gesamte Strafrechtswissenschaft.* 51:317–28. 1931.

6. Wirth, Louis. "Culture Conflict and Misconduct." *Social Forces.* 9:484–92. June 1931. P. 490. Cf. Allport, Floyd H. "Culture Conflict versus the Individual as Factors in Delinquency." *Ibid.* Pp. 493–97.

7. White, William A. *Crimes and Criminals.* New York: Farrar & Rinehart. 1933. Healy, William. *Mental Conflict and Misconduct.* Boston: Little, Brown & Co. 1917. Alexander, Franz and Healy, William. *Roots of Crime.* New York: Alfred A. Knopf. 1935.

8. Burgess, Ernest W. in Clifford R. Shaw's *The Jack-Roller.* Chicago: University of Chicago Press. 1930. Pp. 184–197, p. 186.

9. Wirth, Louis. *Op. cit.* P. 490. It should be noted that Wirth also states that culture should be studied "on the objective side" and that "the sociologist is not primarily interested in personality but in culture."

10. Burgess, Ernest W. *Op. cit.* P. 186.

10 A Radical Perspective on Crime

Jeffrey H. Reiman

The Implicit Ideology of Criminal Justice

Every criminal justice system conveys a subtle, yet powerful message in support of established institutions. It does this for two interconnected reasons.

First, because it concentrates on *individual* wrongdoers. This means that *it diverts our attention away from our institutions, away from consideration of whether our institutions themselves are wrong or unjust or indeed "criminal."*

Second, because the criminal law is put forth as the *minimum neutral ground rules* for any social living. We are taught that no society can exist without rules against theft and violence, and thus the criminal law is put forth as politically neutral, as the minimum requirements of *any* society, as the minimum obligations that any individual owes his fellows to make social life of any decent sort possible. Thus, it not only diverts our attention away from the possible injustice of our social institutions, but *the criminal law bestows upon those institutions the mantle of its own neutrality.* Since the criminal law protects the established institutions (e.g., the prevailing economic arrangements are protected by laws against theft, etc.), attacks on those established institutions become equivalent to violations of the minimum requirements for any social life at all. In effect, *the criminal law enshrines the established institutions as equivalent to the minimum requirements for any decent social existence—and it brands the individual who attacks those institutions as one who has declared war on* all *organized society and who must therefore be met with the weapons of war.*

This is the powerful magic of criminal justice. By virtue of its focus on *individual* criminals, it diverts us from the evils of the *social* order. By virtue of its presumed neutrality, it transforms the established social (and economic) order from being merely *one* form of society open to critical comparison with others into *the* conditions of *any* social order and thus immune from criticism. Let us look more closely at this process.

What is the effect of focusing on individual guilt? Not only does this divert our attention from the possible evils in our institutions, but it puts forth half the problem of justice as if it were the *whole* problem. To focus on individual guilt is to ask whether or not the individual citizen has fulfilled his obligations to his fellow citizens. *It is to look away from the issue of whether his fellow citizens have fulfilled their obligations to him.*

To look only at individual responsibility is to look away from social responsibility. To look only at individual criminality is to close one's eyes to social injustice and to close one's ears to the question of whether our social institutions have exploited or violated the individual. *Justice is a two-way street—but criminal justice is a one-way street.*

Individuals owe obligations to their fellow citizens because their fellow citizens owe obligations to them. Criminal justice focuses on the first and looks away from the second. *Thus, by focusing on individual responsibility for crime, the criminal justice system literally acquits the existing social order of any charge of injustice!*

This is an extremely important bit of ideological alchemy. It stems from the fact [that] the same act can be criminal or not, unjust or just, depending on the conditions in which it takes place. Killing someone is ordinarily a crime. But if it is in self-defense or to stop a deadly crime, it is not. Taking property by force is usually a crime. But if the taking is just retrieving what has been stolen, then no crime has been committed. Acts of violence are ordinarily crimes. But if the violence is provoked by the threat of violence or by oppressive conditions, then, like the Boston Tea Party, what might ordinarily be called criminal is celebrated as just. This means that when we call an act a crime *we are also making an implicit judgment about the conditions in response to which it takes place.* When we call an act a crime, we are saying that the conditions in which it occurs are not themselves criminal or deadly or oppressive or so unjust as to make an extreme response reasonable or justified, that is, to make such a response non-criminal.

This means that when the system holds an individual responsible for a crime, *it is implicitly conveying the message that the social conditions in which the crime occurred are not responsible for the crime,* that they are not so unjust as to make a violent response to them excusable. The criminal justice system conveys as much by what it does not do as by what it does. By holding the individual responsible, *it literally acquits the society of criminality or injustice.*

Judges are prone to hold that an individual's responsibility for a violent crime is diminished if it was provoked by something that might lead a "reasonable man" to respond violently and that criminal responsibility is eliminated if the act was in response to conditions so intolerable that any "reasonable man" would have been likely to respond in the same way. In this vein, the law acquits those who kill or injure in self-defense and treats lightly those who commit a crime when confronted with extreme provocation. The law treats leniently the man who kills his wife's lover and the woman who kills her brutal husband, even when neither has acted directly in self-defense. By this logic, when we hold an individual completely responsible for a crime, we are saying that the conditions in which it occurred are such that a "reasonable man" should find them tolerable. In other words, by focusing on individual responsibility for crimes, *the criminal justice system broadcasts the message that the social order itself is reasonable and not intolerably unjust.*

Thus the criminal justice system serves to focus moral condemnation on individuals and to deflect it away from the social order that may have either violated the individual's rights or dignity or literally pushed him or her to the brink of crime. This not only serves to carry the message that our social institutions are not in need of fundamental questioning, but it further suggests that the justice of our institutions is obvious, not to be doubted. Indeed, since it is deviations from these institutions that are crimes, the established institutions become the implicit standard of justice from which criminal deviations are measured.

This leads to the second way in which a criminal justice system always conveys an implicit ideology. It arises from the presumption that the criminal law is nothing but the politically neutral minimum requirements of any decent social life. What is the consequence of this?

Obviously, as already suggested, this presumption transforms the prevailing social order into justice incarnate and all violations of the prevailing order into injustice incarnate. This process is so obvious that it may be easily missed.

Consider, for example, the law against theft. It does indeed seem to be one of the minimum requirements of social living. As long as there is scarcity, any society—capitalist or socialist—will need rules preventing individuals from taking what does not belong to them. But the law against theft is more: it is a law against stealing what individuals *presently* own. *Such a law has the effect of making present property relations a part of the criminal law.*

Since stealing is a violation of the law, this means that present property relations become the implicit standard of justice against which criminal deviations are measured. Since criminal law is thought of as the minimum requirements of any social life, this means that present property relations become equivalent to the minimum requirements of *any* social life. And the criminal who would alter the present property relations becomes nothing less than someone who is declaring war on all organized society. The question of whether this "war" is provoked by the injustice or brutality of the society is swept aside. Indeed, this suggests yet another way in which the criminal justice system conveys an ideological message in support of the established society.

Not only does the criminal justice system acquit the social order of any charge of injustice, it specifically cloaks the society's own crime-producing tendencies. I have already observed that by blaming the individual for a crime, the society is acquitted of the charge of injustice. I would like to go further now and argue that by blaming the individual for a crime, the society is acquitted of the charge of complicity in that crime! This is a point worth developing, since many observers have maintained that modern competitive societies such as our own have structural features that tend to generate crime. Thus, holding the individual responsible for his or her crime serves the function of taking the rest of society off the hook for their role in sustaining and benefiting from social arrangements that produce crime. Let us take a brief detour to look more closely at this process.

Cloward and Ohlin argue in their book *Delinquency and Opportunity*[1] that much crime is the result of the discrepancy between social goals and the legitimate opportunities available for achieving them. Simply put, in our society everyone is encouraged to be a success, but the avenues to success are open only to some. The conventional wisdom of our free enterprise democracy is that anyone can be a success if he or she has the talent and the ambition. Thus, if one is not a success, it is because of their own short-comings: laziness or lack of ability or both. On the other hand, opportunities to achieve success are not equally open to all. Access to the best schools and the best jobs is effectively closed to all but a few of the poor and begins to open wider only as one goes up the economic ladder. The result is that many are called but few are chosen. And many who have taken the bait and accepted the belief in the importance of success and the belief that achieving success is a result of individual ability must cope with the feelings of frustration and failure that result when they find the avenues to success closed. Cloward and Ohlin argue that one method of coping with these stresses is to develop alternative avenues to success. Crime is such an alternative. Crime is a means by which people who believe in the American dream pursue it when they find the traditional routes barred. Indeed, it is plain to see that the goals pursued by most criminals are as American as apple pie. I suspect that one of the reasons that American moviegoers enjoy gangster films—movies in which gangsters such as Al Capone, Bonnie and Clyde, or Butch Cassidy and the Sundance Kid are the heroes, as distinct from police and detective films whose heroes are defenders of the law—is that even where they deplore the hero's methods, they identify with his or her notion of success, since it is theirs as well, and respect the courage and cunning displayed in achieving that success.

It is important to note that the discrepancy between success goals and legitimate opportunities in America is not an aberration. It is a structural feature of modern competitive industrialized society, a feature from which many benefits flow. Cloward and Ohlin write that

> . . . a crucial problem in the industrial world . . . is to locate and train the most talented persons in every generation, irrespective of the vicissitudes of birth, to occupy technical work roles. . . . Since we cannot know in advance who can best fulfill the requirements of the various occupational roles, the matter is presumably settled through the process of competition. But how can men throughout the social order be motivated to participate in this competition? . . .

> One of the ways in which the industrial society attempts to solve this problem is by defining success-goals as potentially accessible to all, regardless of race, creed, or socioeconomic position.[2]

But since these universal goals are urged to encourage a competition to weed out the best, there are necessarily fewer openings than seekers. And since those who achieve success are in a particularly good position to exploit their success to make access for their own children easier, the competition is rigged to work in favor of the middle and upper classes. As a result, "many lower-class persons . . . are the victims of a contradiction between the goals toward which they have been led to orient themselves and socially structured means of striving for these goals."[3]

> [The poor] experience desperation born of the certainty that their position in the economic structure is relatively fixed and immutable—a desperation made all the more poignant by their exposure to a cultural ideology in which failure to orient oneself upward is regarded as a moral defect and failure to become mobile as proof of it.[4]

The outcome is predictable. "Under these conditions, there is an acute pressure to depart from institutional norms and to adopt illegitimate alternatives."[5]

In brief, this means that the very way in which our society is structured to draw out the talents and energies that go into producing our high standard of living has a costly side effect: it produces crime. But by holding individuals responsible for this crime, those who enjoy that high standard of living can have their cake and eat it. They can reap the benefits of the competition for success and escape the responsibility of paying for the costs of that competition. By holding the poor crook legally and morally guilty, the rest of society not only passes the costs of competition on to the poor, but they effectively deny that they (the affluent) are the beneficiaries of an economic system that exacts such a high toll in frustration and suffering.

Willem Bonger, the Dutch Marxist criminologist, maintained that competitive capitalism produces egotistic motives and undermines compassion for the misfortunes of others and thus makes human beings literally *more capable of crime*—more capable of preying on their fellows without moral inhibition or remorse—than earlier cultures that emphasized cooperation rather than competition.[6] Here again, the criminal justice system relieves those who benefit from the American economic system of the costs of that system. By holding criminals morally and individually responsible for their crimes, we can forget that the motives that lead to crime—the drive for success at any cost, linked with the beliefs that success means outdoing others and that violence is an acceptable way of achieving one's goals—are the same motives that powered the drive across the American continent and that continue to fuel the engine of America's prosperity.

David Gordon, a contemporary political economist, maintains "that nearly all crimes in capitalist societies represent perfectly *rational* responses to the structure of institutions upon which capitalist societies are based."[7] That is, like Bonger, Gordon believes that capitalism tends to provoke crime in all economic strata. This is so because most crime is motivated by a desire for property or money and is an understandable way of coping with the pressures of inequality, competition, and insecurity, all of which are essential ingredients of capitalism. Capitalism depends, Gordon writes,

> . . . on basically competitive forms of social and economic interaction and upon substantial inequalities in the allocation of social resources. Without inequalities, it would be much more difficult to induce workers to work in alienating environments. Without competition and a competitive ideology, workers might not be inclined to struggle to improve their relative income and status in society by working harder. Finally, although rights of property are protected, capitalist societies do not guarantee economic security to most of their individual members. Individuals must fend for themselves, finding the best available opportunities to provide for themselves and their families. . . . Driven by the fear of economic insecurity and by a competitive desire to gain some of the goods unequally distributed throughout the society, many individuals will eventually become "criminals."[8]

To the extent that a society makes crime a reasonable alternative for a large number of its members from all classes, that society is itself not very reasonably or humanely organized and bears some degree of responsibility for the crime it encourages. Since the criminal law is put forth as the minimum requirements that can be expected of any "reasonable man," its enforcement amounts to a denial of the real nature of the social order to which Gordon and the others point. Here again, by blaming the individual criminal, the criminal justice system serves implicitly but dramatically to acquit the society of its criminality.

The Bonus of Bias

We turn now to consideration of the additional ideological bonus that is derived from the criminal justice system's bias against the poor. This bonus is a product of the association of crime and poverty in the popular mind. This association, the merging of the "criminal classes" and the "lower classes" into the "dangerous classes," was not invented in America. The word "villain" is derived from the Latin *villanus,* which means a farm servant. And the term "villein" was used in feudal England to refer to a serf who farmed the land of a great lord and who was literally owned by that lord.[9] In this respect, our present criminal justice system is heir to a long and hallowed tradition.

The value of this association was already seen when we explored the "average citizen's" concept of the Typical Criminal and the Typical Crime. It is quite obvious that throughout the great mass of middle America, far more fear and hostility are directed toward the predatory acts of the poor than the rich. Compare the fate of politicians in recent history who call for tax reform, income redistribution, prosecution of corporate crime, and any sort of regulation of business that would make it better serve American social goals with that of politicians who erect their platform on a call for "law and order," more police, less limits on police power, and stiffer prison sentences for criminals—and consider this in light of what we have already seen about the real dangers posed by corporate crime and business-as-usual.

In view of all that has been said already, it seems clear that Americans have been systematically deceived as to what are the greatest dangers to their lives, limbs and possessions. The very persistence with which the system functions to apprehend and punish poor crooks and ignore or slap on the wrist equally or more dangerous individuals is testimony to the sticking power of this deception. That Americans continue to tolerate the gentle treatment meted out to white-collar criminals, corporate price fixers, industrial polluters, and political-influence peddlers, while voting in droves to lock up more poor people faster and longer, indicates the degree to which they harbor illusions as to who most threatens them. It is perhaps also part of the explanation for the continued dismal failure of class-based politics in America. American workers rarely seem able to forget their differences and unite to defend their shared interests against the rich whose wealth they produce. Ethnic divisions serve this divisive function well, but undoubtedly the vivid portrayal of the poor—and, of course, the blacks—as hovering birds of prey waiting for the opportunity to snatch away the workers' meager gains serves also to deflect opposition away from the upper class. A politician who promises to keep their communities free of blacks and their prisons full of them can get their votes even if the major portion of his or her policies amount to continuation of favored treatment of the rich at their expense. Surely this is a minor miracle of mind control.

The most important "bonus" derived from the identification of crime and poverty is that it paints the picture that the threat to decent middle Americans comes from those below them on the economic ladder, not those above. For this to happen the system must not only identify crime and poverty, but *it must also fail to reduce crime so that it remains a real threat.* By doing this, it deflects the fear and discontent of middle Americans, and their possible opposition, away from the wealthy. The two politicians who most clearly gave voice to the discontent of middle Americans in the post-World War II period were George Wallace and Spiro Agnew. Is it any accident that their politics were extremely conservative and their anger reserved for the poor (the welfare chiselers) and the criminal (the targets of law and order)?

There are other bonuses as well. For instance, if the criminal justice system functions to send out a message that bestows legitimacy on present property relations, the dramatic impact is mightily enhanced if the violator of the present arrangements is propertyless. In other words, the crimes of the well-to-do "redistribute" property among the haves. In that sense, they do not pose a symbolic challenge to the larger system in which some have much and many have little or nothing. If the criminal threat can be portrayed as coming from the poor, then the punishment of the poor criminal becomes a morality play in which the sanctity of legitimacy of the system in which some have plenty and others have little or nothing is dramatically affirmed. It matters little who the poor criminals really rip off. What counts is that middle Americans come to fear that those poor criminals are out to steal what they own.

There is yet another and, I believe, still more important bonus for the powerful in America, produced by the identification of crime and poverty. It might be thought that the identification of crime and poverty would produce sympathy for the criminals. My suspicion is that it produces or at least reinforces the reverse: *hostility toward the poor.*

Indeed, there is little evidence that Americans are very sympathetic to criminals or poor people. I have already pointed to the fact that very few Americans believe poverty to be a cause of crime. Other surveys find that most Americans believe that police should be tougher than they are now in dealing with crime (83 percent of those questioned in a 1972 survey); that courts do not deal harshly enough with criminals (75 percent of those questioned in a 1969 survey); that a majority of Americans would like to see the death penalty for convicted murderers (57 percent of those questioned in November 1972); and that most would be more likely to vote for a candidate who advocated tougher sentences for law-breakers (83 percent of those questioned in a 1972 survey).[10] Indeed, the experience of Watergate seems to suggest that sympathy for criminals begins to flower only when we approach the higher reaches of the ladder of wealth and power. For some poor ghetto youth who robs a liquor store, five years in the slammer is our idea of tempering justice with mercy. When a handful of public officials try to walk off with the U.S. Constitution, a few months in a minimum security prison will suffice. If the public official is high enough, resignation from office and public disgrace tempered with a $60,000-a-year pension is punishment enough.

My view is that since the criminal justice system—in fact and fiction—deals with *individual legal* and *moral* guilt, the association of crime with poverty does not mitigate the image of individual moral responsibility for crime, the image that crime is the result of an individual's poor character. My suspicion is that it does the reverse: it generates the association of poverty and individual moral failing and thus *the belief that poverty itself is a sign of poor or weak character.* The clearest evidence that Americans hold this belief is to be found in the fact that attempts to aid the poor are regarded as acts of charity rather than as acts of justice. Our welfare system has all the demeaning attributes of an institution designed to give handouts to the undeserving and none of the dignity of an institution designed to make good on our responsibilities to our fellow human beings. If we acknowledged the degree to which our economic and social institutions themselves breed poverty, we would have to recognize our own responsibilities toward the poor. If we can convince ourselves that the poor are poor because of their own shortcomings, particularly moral shortcomings like incontinence or indolence, then we need acknowledge no such responsibility to the poor. Indeed, we can go further and pat ourselves on the back for our generosity and handing out the little that we do, and of course, we can make our recipients go through all the indignities that mark them as the undeserving objects of our benevolence. By and large, this has been the way in which Americans have dealt with their poor.[11] It is a way that enables us to avoid asking the question of why the richest nation in the world continues to produce massive poverty. It is my view that this conception of the poor is subtly conveyed by the way our criminal justice system functions.

Obviously, no ideological message could be more supportive of the present social and economic order than this. It suggests that poverty is a sign of individual failing, not a symptom of social or economic injustice. It tells us loud and clear that massive poverty in the midst of abundance is not a sign pointing toward the need for fundamental changes in our social and economic institutions. It suggests that the poor are poor because they deserve to be poor, or at least because they lack the strength of character to overcome poverty. When the poor are seen to be poor in character, then economic poverty coincides with moral poverty and the economic order coincides with the moral order—as if a divine hand guided its workings, capitalism leads to everyone getting what they morally deserve!

If this association takes root, then when the poor individual is found guilty of a crime, the criminal justice system acquits the society of its responsibility not only for the crime *but for poverty as well.*

With this, the ideological message of criminal justice is complete. The poor rather than the rich are seen as the enemies of the mass of decent middle Americans. Our social and economic institutions are held to be responsible for neither crime nor poverty and thus are in need of no fundamental questioning or reform. The poor are poor because they are poor of character. The economic order and the moral order are one. And to the extent that this message sinks in, the wealthy can rest easily—even if they cannot sleep the sleep of the just.

Thus, we can understand why the criminal justice system creates the image of crime as the work of the poor and fails to stem it so that the threat of crime remains real and credible. The result is ideological alchemy of the highest order. The poor are seen as the real threat to decent society. The ultimate sanctions of criminal justice dramatically sanctify the present social and economic order, and *the poverty of criminals makes poverty itself an individual moral crime!*

Such are the ideological fruits of a losing war against crime whose distorted image is reflected in the criminal justice carnival mirror and widely broadcast to reach the minds and imaginations of America.

Notes

1. Richard A. Cloward and Lloyd E. Ohlin, *Delinquency and Opportunity: A Theory of Delinquent Gangs* (New York: The Free Press, 1960), esp. pp. 77–107.

2. Ibid., p. 81.

3. Ibid., p. 105.

4. Ibid., p. 107.

5. Ibid., p. 105.

6. Willem Bonger, *Criminality and Economic Conditions,* abridged and with an introduction by Austin T. Turk (Bloomington, Indiana: Indiana University Press, 1969), pp. 7–12, 40–47. Willem Adriaan Bonger was born in Holland in 1876 and died by his own hand in 1940 rather than submit to the Nazis. His *Criminalité et conditions économiques* first appeared in 1905. It was translated into English and published in the United States in 1916. Ibid., pp. 3–4.

7. David M. Gordon, "Capitalism, Class and Crime in America," *Crime and Delinquency* (April 1972), p. 174.

8. Ibid., p. 174.

9. William and Mary Morris, *Dictionary of Word and Phrase Origins,* II (New York: Harper & Row, 1967), p. 282.

10. *Sourcebook,* pp. 203, 204, 223, 207; see also p. 177.

11. Historical documentation of this can be found in David J. Rothman, *The Discovery of the Asylum: Social Order and Disorder in the New Republic* (Boston: Little, Brown, 1971); and in Frances Fox Piven and Richard A. Cloward, *Regulating the Poor: The Functions of Public Welfare* (New York: Pantheon, 1971), which carries the analysis up to the present.

Differential Punishing of African Americans and Whites Who Possess Drugs: A Just Policy or a Continuation of the Past?

Rudolph Alexander, Jr.
Jacquelyn Gyamerah

Five African Americans in Minnesota were arrested and charged with possession of a cocaine base, known on the street as crack. The statute that they were charged under provided that possession of 3 or more grams of crack cocaine was a third-degree felony, punishable by up to 20 years of incarceration. In addition, the same statute provided that possession of 10 grams or more of a cocaine powder was a third-degree felony. Less than 10 grams of cocaine powder was a fifth-degree felony, punishable by up to 5 years. In Hennepin County in 1988, 97% of the persons arrested for cocaine base or crack were African Americans, and 80% of the persons arrested for cocaine powder were White. Because of these statistics and differential punishments, the five African Americans contested the constitutionality of the statute. After hearing the presentation of the issues, the Minnesota Supreme Court upheld the challenge and ruled the statute unconstitutional (*State v. Russell*, 1991).

The issue of whether African Americans are punished more severely than are White Americans by the criminal justice system and whether the system is racist has been debated in the literature (Blumstein, 1982; Johnson, 1992, Peterson & Hagan, 1984). On one hand, some criminal justice professionals have called the charge of a racist criminal justice system a myth (Langan, 1985; Wilbanks, 1987) or have stated that the evidence is mixed (Petersilia, 1983; Peterson & Hagan, 1984). However, other professionals have stated that the U.S. criminal justice system indeed is racist (Christianson, 1981/1991; Miller, 1991), and this racism traces itself back to slavery and the reconstruction period and continues today (Johnson & Secret, 1990). The purpose of this article is to recount this history, to discuss within this historical context the Minnesota case and the major federal cases involving charges of racial discrimination in the criminal justice system, and to propose a change in policy regarding possession of crack.

The Origins and Course of Differential Punishing of African Americans

The genesis of differential criminal treatment of African Americans is the slavery period in the United States. Controlling slaves required slave owners to subject slaves to sanctions for behaviors that were not offenses if committed by Whites. Punishable offenses for slaves included leaving the plantation without a pass, being out of their quarters after curfew, and being in a group of more than five slaves without a White man present. Slaves could not own firearms or animals, buy alcohol, give medicine to Whites, work in a drugstore, or work in a printing shop (Sellin, 1976). Moreover, slaves could not address a White person rudely or strike a White person even in self-defense, and these offenses were punishable crimes (Meier & Rudwick, 1976).

Slave-holding legislators did not view their traditional courts for free Whites as adequate for controlling slaves. Punishment for slaves had to be harsher than punishment for Whites because of a need to instill fear and obedience in slaves. As a result, state legislators created special courts to try slaves. These courts were called "Negro courts" and the judges were a combination of county justices and slave owners. For instance, Louisiana tried slaves for noncapital offenses before a court consisting of one justice and four slave holders. Mississippi tried slaves before a court consisting of two justices and five slave holders. Georgia tried slaves before three justices. Punishments decreed in these courts were swift and consisted primarily of whippings (Haunton, 1972/1992). In 1850, Georgia abolished its Negro courts and allowed its regular legal system to handle offenses by slaves, but in the other slave states the Negro courts existed to the end of slavery (Sellin, 1976).

Following slavery and the Civil War, both Presidents Lincoln and Johnson provided considerable latitude to Southern states to address the South's depressed economies, which were no longer going to be based on slave labor. Southern legislators responded with a series of laws, called the Black Codes, designed to reenslave African Americans and reestablish White supremacy (Levesque, 1989/1992; Wilson, 1980). As an example, the vagrancy law was vigorously enforced. Any African American without a permanent address or unemployed could be arrested and fined. If unable to pay the fine, he or she would be bound out to a plantation or leased (Adamson, 1983; Sisk, 1958/1992; Wilson, 1980). As W.E.B. Dubois wrote in 1901, many African Americans in the rural South were peons, "bound by law and custom to economic slavery, from which the only escape is death or the penitentiary" (Dubois, 1970, p. 124).

Wanting to increase the numbers of Africans in prisons in order to control them more effectively, Southern states enacted a series of laws targeting African Americans for differential punishments. As an example, several states increased the penalties for stealing livestock, making such acts grand larceny. Thus, stealing pigs or chickens could be punished by up to 10 years of incarceration (Adamson, 1983). To counter some of these unfair laws, Congress passed the first of a series of civil rights acts and the Fourteenth Amendment. Although the Fourteenth Amendment exists for all Americans, its origin was to address the legal problems of African Americans. As Jacob M. Howard, a member of the Senate Joint Committee on Reconstruction, reportedly wrote, the Fourteenth Amendment "prohibits the hanging of a black man for a crime for which the white man is not to be hanged" (Meltsner, 1973, p. 74).

However, the Fourteenth Amendment failed to provide this protection to African Americans because states continue to punish African Americans more seriously than Whites. The effect of targeting African Americans is seen in their increase in the penal systems. For example, in 1875, North Carolina had 569 African Americans in its penal institutions but only 78 Whites (Sellin, 1976). Similarly, Louisiana had 1,143 persons in its penal institutions in 1901 and 984 were African Americans (Sellin, 1976). In addition, Alabama created its "chain gang" in the 1920s, discarding its lease system. By the end of 1941, Alabama had 25 camps and all 1,717 prisoners in these camps were African Americans (Sellin, 1976). South Carolina's chain gangs in 1926 contained 1,017 African Americans and 298 Whites (Sellin, 1976). These disparate numbers suggest either that African Americans were committing more crimes or states were imposing punishments on African Americans that were not generally imposed on Whites. This latter explanation seems more correct.

For instance, all the persons executed by South Carolina and Virginia for *attempted rape* were African Americans (Bowers, 1984). In one case upholding a death sentence for an African American for attempted rape, the Virginia Supreme Court stressed that prompt convictions and severe penalties were needed in rape or attempted rape cases to decrease the likelihood of lynch law (*Hart v. Commonwealth,* 1921). The court's observation reveals the racial overtones in sexual assault cases, but it does not explain other instances where African Americans were punished more severely than Whites. For example, a few individuals have been executed for armed robbery in this country, and all but one were African Americans (Bowers, 1984).

A few laws were written during slavery that targeted African Americans and survived into the 20th century. For example, Georgia passed an anti-slave insurrection law involving printed materials in 1861, and the penalty was death. The law was broadened in 1871 to include speech and a lesser penalty was included ranging from 5 to 20 years. The law was used in the 1930s in Atlanta, Georgia to try an African American named Angelo Herndon who advocated social equality and self-determination for all African Americans. The prosecutor sought the death penalty for the defendant, but the jury recommended mercy and a sentence of 18 to 20 years at hard labor (Herndon, 1937).

Placed in an overall context of discriminatory responses by the criminal justice system, the issue of differential punishing of African Americans for possessing crack cocaine seems to be a continuation of historical policy. As one article revealed, White individuals use illicit drugs in substantial numbers, but their arrest numbers are substantially lower than for African Americans ("More Whites Use Drugs," 1992). Furthermore, when Whites are arrested and subsequently convicted, they, as the Minnesota case suggests, may face lesser punishment.

The following discussion explores the Minnesota case in more detail and the analytic framework used by courts to decide whether African Americans have been denied their Fourteenth Amendment right to equal protection of the law.

State v. Russell

In 1989 and 1990, the Minnesota legislature grappled with the issue of drug possession and prescribing appropriate penalties. Following legislative testimonies, it decided that possession of 3 or more grams of cocaine base [hereinafter referred to as crack cocaine] was a third-degree felony (Minnesota Statute § 152.023, 1989), and according to its criminal law, a third-degree felony is punishable by up to 20 years. The following year, the Minnesota legislature decreed that possession of 10 or more grams of cocaine powder was a third-degree felony and less than 10 grams of cocaine powder was a fifth-degree felony (Minnesota Statute § 152.025, 1990) and punishable by up to 5 years. Essentially, possession of 3 grams of crack could be punishable by up to 20 years, but an equal amount of cocaine powder was punishable only by up to 5 years.

Five African Americans, charged with possessing three or more grams of crack and facing up to 20 years in the state penitentiary, asked a trial judge to dismiss charges against them. Particularly, the Black defendants contended that there is no substantial difference between crack cocaine and cocaine powder, but the statutes punished them differently and more harshly for crack. Because 97% of the persons arrested for possession of crack in 1988 were African Americans and 80% of those arrested during that same year for cocaine powder were Whites, the statutes had a discriminatory impact and violated the equal protection clauses of both the U.S. and Minnesota Constitutions.

The trial judge, an African American woman, dismissed the charges and certified the following question to the Minnesota Supreme Court for a ruling: Does Minnesota Statute § 152.023, Subdivision 2(1)(1989), as it is applied, violate the equal protection clauses of the Fourteenth Amendment of the United States Constitution and the Minnesota Constitution, Article 1, Section 2? After considering its precedents, a majority of the justices held that the statute in question violated the Minnesota Constitution.

The majority justices arrived at its decision by noting differences in Minnesota's rational basis test and the federal test when challenges are made that a statute violates equal protection of the law. The federal rational basis test requires that (a) the statute serves a legitimate purpose and that (b) it was reasonable for legislators to believe that the statute would serve that purpose. However, Minnesota's rational basis test is substantially higher and requires that

> (1) the distinctions which separate those included within the classification from those excluded must not be manifestly arbitrary or fanciful but must be genuine and substantial, thereby providing a natural and reasonable basis to justify legislation adapted to peculiar conditions and needs; (2) the classification must be genuine and relevant to the purpose of the law; that is there must be an evident connection between the distinctive needs peculiar to the class and the prescribed remedy; and (3) the purpose of the statute must be one that the state can legitimately attempt to achieve. (*State v. Russell*, 1991, p. 888)

Hence, Minnesota's rational basis test is less deferential to the state than the federal test and requires a reasonable connection between the *actual* effects and the statutory aims.

Accordingly, the challenged statute was unconstitutional under Minnesota's rational basis test for three reasons. First, the statute failed to distinguish genuinely and substantially those individuals inside and outside the class. The state's primary justification for prescribing differences in punishment between those persons who possess 3 grams of crack and less than 10 grams of cocaine came from the legislative testimony of one lone prosecutor. According to this prosecutor, these levels indicate whether one is using drugs or selling drugs. That is, a person who possesses 3 or more grams of drugs is a dealer, and a person who possesses 10 or more grams of cocaine powder is also a dealer. However, a report by the Minnesota Department of Public Safety Office of Drug Policy revealed that most prosecutors in Minnesota and other law enforcement officers did not accept the 3 and 10 distinction levels.

The second defect of the statute is that the defenders of it contended that the Minnesota legislature considered crack to be more addictive and dangerous than cocaine powder, and thus the legislature was justified in prescribing harsher penalties for crack possession. However, the majority, viewing this justification similar to the first, stated that the state had failed to establish a genuine and substantial difference between those inside and outside the class. The legislative view that crack is more addictive and dangerous than cocaine powder came from the testimony of a Minneapolis narcotic officer, who was not a trained chemist or scientist. But at the pretrial hearing, a certified chemist testified that crack and cocaine powder react differently on the central nervous and respiratory systems when crack is smoked and cocaine powder is inhaled. The primary difference is that a smaller amount of crack will produce the same effect as a slightly higher amount of cocaine powder. However, there is no difference in the two drugs' effect if cocaine powder is dissolved in water and injected. Thus, cocaine powder has the same effect as crack if it is injected rather than inhaled.

Third, the state contended that it was justified in prescribing higher penalties for crack because there is more violence associated with crack than with cocaine powder. The majority understood this justification to be the state's contention that crack had a pharmacological effect that leads to violence, but the majority rejected it. The majority, looking at sociological evidence, associated the violence surrounding crack to gang warfare and group dynamics, which do not justify distinguishing statutorily crack and cocaine powder.

The majority also considered the statute to be unconstitutional because the classification between the two drugs did not serve the statutory purpose. Indeed, the state has the right to try to eliminate drug problems by punishing individuals who possess drugs. However, without more substantial evidence, other than the anecdotal testimony, the statute failed to achieve its aims. A person who possesses 3 grams of crack may be a user rather than a dealer, and a person who possesses less than 10 grams of cocaine may be a dealer who intends to convert the drug into more than 3 grams of crack. Thus, the statute is arbitrary and unreasonable. Moreover, the majority considered the statute to be unconstitutional because it assumes that an individual intends to deal drugs, on the basis of the amount possessed, without proof and thus violates due process of law.

Federal Decisions Involving Differential Punishing

The U.S. Supreme Court has decided numerous cases that involve racial issues, such as deciding whether African American defendants were deprived of due process of law in the availability of persons for jury duty, and peripherally decided cases involving differential punishing of African Americans. For instance, in 1970, the Court reversed on procedural grounds a death sentence for an African American defendant who had been convicted of rape of a White female. However, in that same case in the court of appeals, the issue of discriminatory practices in rape cases was raised by the defendant's attorneys on the basis of a study by Marvin Wolfgang. Justice Blackmun wrote the majority decision by a three-judge panel and stated that statistical evidence resulting from a study of several states failed to provide convincing evidence of racial discrimination. Particularly, the study showed that the death penalty for rape was primarily given to African Americans who had been convicted of raping White females, but Justice Blackmun noted that the study did not involve the county in which the defendant was convicted (*Maxwell v. Bishop*, 1968).

Arguments continued to be presented to the Court about the racial effects in rape cases, and the Court decided eventually that the death penalty for rape was unconstitutional. In ruling as it did, the Court did not consider the equal protection argument or directly discuss the statistical evidence presented to them. Instead, it focused on the small number of states that retain the death penalty for rape and the seemingly consensus of society that the death penalty for rape was no longer a valid punishment. As a result, the death penalty for rape violated the Cruel and Unusual Punishment Clause of the Eighth Amendment (*Coker v. Georgia*, 1977). Observers speculated, however, that the Court was persuaded by the racial arguments but did not want to state that it had been influenced by the impact of the racial evidence and arguments (*McCleskey v. Kemp*, 1987).

However, the Court had considered several cases involving contentions that official actions were motivated by racial discrimination or had a discriminatory impact and thus violated the Equal Protection Clause of the Fourteenth Amendment. The effect of these decisions was the formulation of a legal framework for deciding cases involving violations of the Equal Protection Clause. In one case, the Court decided whether African American plaintiffs were denied the equal protection of the laws in a zoning case and as a result decided how courts should view officials' decisions that have been alleged to have had a discriminatory effect on African Americans.

The case involved a collaboration between a nonprofit corporation in partnership and a religious order to build low-income housing in Arlington Heights, Illinois, a suburb of Chicago. The area was zoned for detached family homes, and the proposed project required a zoning change to attached multifamily homes. The zoning commission, following heated input by residents, denied the request for a zoning change. The builder, along with several African Americans, filed a lawsuit, contending that the denial of the zoning change had a discriminatory effect on the plaintiffs in that they were more likely to need low-income housing. The U.S. district court ruled for the zoning commission, but the court of appeals reversed the lower court decision. By a 5 to 3 decision, the U.S. Supreme Court reversed the court of appeals and upheld the district court (*Arlington Heights v. Metropolitan Housing Corp.*, 1977).

Central to *Arlington Heights* was how courts should decide cases involving alleged discriminatory effects that result in a racially disproportionate impact. The Court stated that official action will not be held unconstitutional just because it results in a racially disproportionate impact. It is an issue to consider, but alone it does not rise to racial discrimination in violation of the Equal Protection Clause. Although the impact of official action and whether it bears more heavily on one race than another is an important starting point, a racially disparate outcome is not conclusive proof of official discrimination. A plaintiff, to establish a violation of the Equal Protection Clause, must establish proof of racially discriminatory intent or purpose. One evidentiary factor is the historical background of the

decision. Another is the sequence of events leading to the challenged decision, such as when the officials did have one policy and suddenly change
when learning that an integrated event had been proposed and is about to
be presented. Further, minutes, reports, and the testimony of officials may
provide evidence of purpose. Although these sources are not conclusive,
they are some of the sources that plaintiffs must present to the courts for
the determination of discrimination (*Arlington Heights v. Metropolitan Housing Corp.*, 1977).

A second prong in analyzing equal protection lawsuits was gleaned by
the Eleventh Circuit Court of Appeals (*Underwood v. Hunter*, 1984) and sec-
onded by the Court in *Hunter v. Underwood* (1985). The case involved an
African American and a White plaintiff. Both were convicted of passing
worthless checks, a misdemeanor in Alabama, and denied the right to vote
because such conviction indicated, according to the Alabama Constitution,
flaws in their moral turpitude. Both filed lawsuits against the Alabama registrars, contending that this law had a racist origin and violated the Equal
Protection Clause. All parties agreed that the Alabama Constitutional Convention that was called in 1901 had as its primary aim the disenfranchisement of African Americans and poor Whites so as to promote White
supremacy. The U.S. district court acknowledged that the 1901 convention
had a racist agenda, but the plaintiffs had failed to prove that the Alabama
registrars exemplified this same racism in disenfranchising them.

However, the Eleventh Circuit Court of Appeals reversed the U.S. district court. The court of appeals wrote that

> to establish a violation of the Fourteenth Amendment in the face of
> mixed motives, plaintiffs must prove by a preponderance of the evi-
> dence that racial discrimination was a substantial or motivating factor
> in the adoption of section 182 [Alabama Disenfranchisement Law].
> They shall then prevail unless the registrars prove by a preponderance
> of the evidence that the same decision would have resulted had the im-
> permissible purpose not been considered. (*Underwood v. Hunter*, 1984,
> p. 617)

Using this test, the court of appeals ruled that the plaintiffs had met this
burden and the registrars had not.

The court of appeals observed that before 1901, the Alabama Constitution denied persons who had been convicted of felonious crimes from voting. The conveners of the convention in 1901 were looking for legal reasons
to disenfranchise African Americans and poor Whites. They consulted the
Alabama justices of the peace, who had responsibility for trying African
Americans during and after slavery and learned what crimes African Americans were more likely to be accused of committing and brought to courts.
As a result, the 1901 delegates added to the list of disenfranchising offenses
those crimes that African Americans were more likely to commit. In addition, they added a catchall phrase, moral turpitude, to embrace behaviors

such as living in adultery. Enactment of this statute disenfranchised 10 times as many African Americans as Whites, and the effects of this law were still felt in the 1980s. The Alabama officials tried to defend this law by saying that it disenfranchised Whites and Blacks and, therefore, equal protection of the law was not violated. However, the court of appeals recognized the registrars' impartiality in administering the statute, but their impartiality could not cleanse a purposefully discriminatory law that had current effects.

Later, the Supreme Court examined an equal protection claim by a criminal defendant. The case involved Warren McCleskey, an African American, who was convicted in Atlanta, Georgia, of killing a White police officer and given the death penalty. On the basis of a study by Baldus, he argued that he was denied the equal protection of the law because African American defendants who have killed Whites were more likely to receive death sentences than were White defendants. The Court began its analysis of this equal protection claim by stating that a defendant alleging violation of equal protection shoulders the burden of proving the existence of purposeful discrimination. A corollary of this principle is that a criminal defendant also must prove that the purposeful discrimination had a discriminatory effect on *him or her*. Thus, McCleskey, to prevail in his equal protection argument, must show that the judicial officials in *his* case acted with discriminatory purpose. According to the majority, McCleskey did not and the Baldus study is insufficient. Also, McCleskey contended that the state of Georgia's capital punishment statute violated the Equal Protection Clause and allowed it to remain in force despite its discriminatory application. The Court stated that for McCleskey to prove this aspect, he must prove that the Georgia legislature enacted and maintained the death penalty statute *because* of an anticipatory racially discriminatory effect. However, the Court stated that he had failed to prove this claim, and as a result, his claim of a denial of equal protection must fail (*McCleskey v. Kemp*, 1987).

In sum, federal jurisprudence involving an equal protection claim in the criminal context requires a criminal defendant to prove that state officials acted specifically against him or her. This is a higher burden to overcome than the burden a person involved in a civil action must overcome. Moreover, although studies that show discriminatory racial effects are a starting point in determining a violation of equal protection in a civil matter, they have little effect in a criminal case, and a criminal defendant must show that state officials specifically behaved in a racially discriminatory manner toward him or her.

The federal legal test, applied to *Russell* and considered in federal courts, would result in upholding the constitutionality of Minnesota's statute and its penalties. Simply, African Americans would not be able to prove that Minnesota's legislators enacted the statute specifically for racial reasons. In addition, the federal legal test has been used to uphold differential punishing of persons convicted of the federal Anti-Drug Abuse Act of 1986. This act provides a 100-to-1 ratio, which means that for punishment purposes 100 grams of cocaine powder equal 1 gram of crack (*State v. Russell,* 1991).

Conclusion

Russell and *McCleskey* represent two divergent views on differential punishing of African Americans. The rationale adopted by the Minnesota Supreme Court clearly is the more enlightened approach and promotes social justice. Directly and indirectly targeting African Americans for differential punishing, as this article has discussed, has a long history in the United States and continues today. In the past, state legislatures were blatant in their racial intentions, knowing that African Americans did not have recourse in the courts. Now that African Americans' rights are more recognized, the discrimination is not as blatant and direct and has become more subtle and indirect. Whether blatant or subtle, the effect is the same. All courts, as a result, should look closely at the outcomes and adopt the standard used in Minnesota.

The effect of ensnaring more African Americans in the criminal justice system through drug laws is devastating and represents a major factor in their sharp increase in prisons across the country (Mauer, 1990; Miller, 1992). When vast numbers of middle-class Whites in the 1960s were being threatened with felony convictions for possessing marijuana, the response of policy makers and legislators was to make possession of small amounts a misdemeanor (Peterson & Hagan, 1984). Now, a similar response should be initiated for crack. Mere possession of crack should not be a crime, or if it is a crime, it should not be more than a misdemeanor. In this manner, African Americans will be treated with the same concern as Whites were in shaping social policy regarding marijuana.

References

Adamson, C. R. (1983). Punishment after slavery: southern state penal system, 1965–1980. *Social Problems, 30,* 555–569.

Anti-Drug Abuse Act of 1986, Pub. L. No. 104–316, 19 U.S.C. §2081 (1986).

Arlington Heights v. Metropolitan Housing Corp., 429 U.S. 252 (1977).

Blumstein, A. (1982). On the racial disproportionality of United States prison populations. *Journal of Criminal Law and Criminology, 73,* 1259–1281.

Bowers, W. J. (1984). *Legal homicide: Death as punishment in America, 1964–1982.* Boston: Northeastern University Press.

Christianson, S. (1991). Our Black prisons. In K. C. Haas & G. P. Albert (Eds.), *The dilemmas of corrections* (2nd ed., pp. 62–74). Prospect Heights, IL: Waveland. (Reprinted from *Crime and Delinquency,* 1981, *27,* 364–375).

Coker v. Georgia, 433 U.S. 584 (1977).

Dubois, W. E. B. (1970). The freedman's bureau. In L. J. Austin, L. H. Fenderson, & S. P. Nelson (Eds.), *The Black man and the promise of America* (pp. 112–124). Glenview, IL: Scott, Foresman.

Hart v. Commonwealth, 131 Va 726 (1921).

Haunton, R. H. (1992). Law and order in Savannah, 1850–1860. In P. Finkelman (Ed.), *Race, law, and American history 1700–1990* (pp. 189–212). New York: Garland. (Reprinted from *Georgia Historical Society, 1972, 56,* 1–24).

Herndon, A. (1937). *Let me live.* New York: Random House.

Hunter v. Underwood, 471 U.S. 222 (1985).

Johnson, J. B., & Secret, P. E. (1990). Race and juvenile court decision making revisited. *Criminal Justice Policy Review, 4,* 159–187.

Johnson, W. W. (1992, November). *Racial distribution and punishment: An analysis of state level data in the 1980s.* Paper presented at the annual meeting of the American Society of Criminology, New Orleans, LA.

Langan, P. A. (1985). Racism on trial: New evidence to explain the racial composition of prisons in the United States. *Journal of Criminal Law and Criminology, 76,* 666–683.

Levesque, G. A. (1992). Black political power and criminal justice: Washington county, Texas 1868–1884. In P. Finkelman (Ed.), *Race, law and American history 1700–1990* (pp. 268–279). New York: Garland. (Reprinted from *American Journal of Southern History,* 1989, *55,* 391–420).

Mauer, M. (1990). *Young Black men and the criminal justice system: A growing national problem.* Washington, DC: The Sentencing Project.

Maxwell v. Bishop, 398 F. 2d 138 (1968).

McCleskey v. Kemp, 481 U.S. 279 (1987).

Meier, A., & Rudwick, E. (1976). *From plantation to ghetto* (3rd ed). New York: Hill & Wang.

Meltsner, M. (1973). *Cruel and unusual: The supreme court and capital punishment.* New York: Random House.

Miller, J. G. (1991). *Last one over the wall.* Columbus: Ohio State University.

Miller, J. G. (1992). *Hobbling a generation: Young African-American males in D.C.'s criminal justice system.* Alexandria, VA: National Center on Institutions and Alternatives.

Minnesota Statute § 152.023 (1989).

Minnesota Statute § 152.025 (1990).

More Whites use drugs, more Blacks arrested. (1992, November). *Columbus Dispatch,* p. 14A.

Petersilia, J. (1983). *Racial disparities in the criminal justice system.* Washington, DC: National Institute of Corrections.

Peterson, R. D., & Hagan, J. (1984). Changing conceptions of race: Towards an account of anomalous findings of sentencing research. *American Sociological Review, 49,* 56–70.

Sellin, J. T. (1976). *Slavery and the penal system.* New York: Elsevier.

Sisk, G. S. (1992). Crime and justice in the Alabama Black belt, 1875–1917. In Finkelman (Ed.), *Race, law, and American history 1700–1990* (pp. 432–439). New York: Garland. (Reprinted from *Mid-America,* 1958, *40,* 106–113).

State v. Russell, 477 N. W. 2d 886 (Minn. 1991).

Underwood v. Hunter, 730 F. 2d 614 (1984).

Wilbanks, W. (1987). *The myth of a racist criminal justice system.* Monterey, CA: Brooks/Cole.

Wilson, W. J. (1980). *The declining significance of race: Black and changing American institutions* (2nd ed). Chicago: University of Chicago Press.

Cultural Transmission/Social Learning Theory

A central tenet underlying the cultural transmission model is the idea that one learns cultural traditions and values through symbolic communication with others. Two of the more famous representatives of this position are Gresham M. Sykes and David Matza.

In "Techniques of Neutralization: A Theory of Delinquency," Sykes and Matza argue that juveniles do not really reject middle-class values. Rather, because the existing normative structure has a certain flexibility, actors can "bend" the laws to fit their needs. Also basic to this thesis is the idea that when actors contemplate the commission of a delinquent or criminal act, they must come to grips with any immediate or potential threats to their identity. Developing an effective system of "neutralization" or rationalization is one way of accomplishing this. Sykes and Matza assert, moreover, that this attitude of self-justification is operative during and after the commission of an offense as well. The writers make the additional point that we all use rationalizations, whether we are involved in deviant activities or not.

Donald L. McCabe puts the "techniques of neutralization" to the test in an exploration of "The Influence of Situational Ethics on Cheating Among College Students." Situational ethics are guidelines for behavior or rules for behavior that are situationally determined. In short, students know how they should justify their cheating behavior in advance. It should be noticed here that Sykes and Matza argue for a similar temporal order—that rationalizations (typically thought to occur after deviant behavior) "may logically precede the deviant behavior." Of central concern for McCabe is whether techniques of neutralization, as described by Sykes and Matza, are actually used within typical social settings. What becomes clear in McCabe's research is that significant numbers of college students cheat and that these students use the rationalizations of Sykes and Matza to deflect attention onto external contextual factors. While the five techniques of neutralization were not reported equally, each was represented. Students deny responsibility ("it's the only way to keep up"), deny injury ("the grades aren't worth much," "no one gets hurt"), deny the victim (cheating was seen as "justified"), condemn the condemners (professors are more lenient on some), and appeal to higher loyalties (students shouldn't judge their peers).

Techniques of Neutralization: A Theory of Delinquency

12

Gresham M. Sykes
David Matza

As Morris Cohen once said, one of the most fascinating problems about human behavior is why men violate the laws in which they believe. This is the problem that confronts us when we attempt to explain why delinquency occurs despite a greater or lesser commitment to the usages of conformity. A basic clue is offered by the fact that social rules or norms calling for valued behavior seldom if ever take the form of categorical imperatives. Rather, values or norms appear as *qualified* guides for action, limited in their applicability in terms of time, place, persons, and social circumstances. The moral injunction against killing, for example, does not apply to the enemy during combat in time of war, although a captured enemy comes once again under the prohibition. Similarly, the taking and distributing of scarce goods in a time of acute social need is felt by many to be right, although under other circumstances private property is held inviolable. The normative system of a society, then, is marked by what Williams has termed *flexibility;* it does not consist of a body of rules held to be binding under all conditions.[1]

This flexibility is, in fact, an integral part of the criminal law in that measures for "defenses to crimes" are provided in pleas such as non-age, necessity, insanity, drunkenness, compulsion, self-defense, and so on. The individual can avoid moral culpability for his criminal action—and thus avoid the negative sanctions of society—if he can prove that criminal intent was lacking. *It is our argument that much delinquency is based on what is essentially an unrecognized extension of defenses to crimes, in the form of justifications for deviance that are seen as valid by the delinquent but not by the legal system or society at large.*

These justifications are commonly described as rationalizations. They are viewed as following deviant behavior and as protecting the individual from self-blame and the blame of others after the act. But there is also reason to believe that they precede deviant behavior and make deviant behavior possible. It is this possibility that Sutherland mentioned only in other writers have failed to exploit from the viewpoint of ry. Disapproval flowing from internalized norms and con- n the social environment is neutralized, turned back, or nce. Social controls that serve to check or inhibit deviant erns are rendered inoperative, and the individual is freed nquency without serious damage to his self-image. In this uent both has his cake and eats it too, for he remains com- ninant normative system and yet so qualifies its impera- tives that violations are "acceptable" if not "right." Thus the delinquent represents not a radical opposition to law-abiding society but something more like an apologetic failure, often more sinned against than sinning in his own eyes. We call these justifications of deviant behavior techniques of neutralization; and we believe these techniques make up a crucial com- ponent of Sutherland's "definitions favorable to the violation of law." It is by learning these techniques that the juvenile becomes delinquent, rather than by learning moral imperatives, values, or attitudes standing in direct contradiction to those of the dominant society. In analyzing these tech- niques, we have found it convenient to divide them into five major types.

1. The Denial of Responsibility

Insofar as the delinquent can define himself as lacking responsibility for his deviant actions, the disapproval of self or others is sharply reduced in effectiveness as a restraining influence. As Justice Holmes has said, even a dog distinguishes between being stumbled over and being kicked, and modern society is no less careful to draw a line between injuries that are unintentional, i.e., where responsibility is lacking, and those that are intentional. As a technique of neutralization, however, the denial of re- sponsibility extends much further than the claim that deviant acts are an "accident" or some similar negation of personal accountability. It may also be asserted that delinquent acts are due to forces outside of the individ- ual and beyond his control such as unloving parents, bad companions, or a slum neighborhood. In effect, the delinquent approaches a "billiard ball" conception of himself in which he sees himself as helplessly propelled into new situations. From a psychodynamic viewpoint, this orientation toward one's own actions may represent a profound alienation from self, but it is important to stress the fact that interpretations of responsibility are cultural constructs and not merely idiosyncratic beliefs. The similar- ity between this mode of justifying illegal behavior assumed by the delin- quent and the implications of a "sociological" frame of reference or a "humane" jurisprudence is readily apparent.[2] It is not the validity of this orientation that concerns us here, but its function of deflecting blame at- tached to violations of social norms and its relative independence of a particular personality structure.[3] By learning to view himself as more acted upon than acting, the delinquent prepares the way for deviance from the dominant normative system without the necessity of a frontal assault on the norms themselves.

2. The Denial of Injury

A second major technique of neutralization centers on the injury or harm involved in the delinquent act. The criminal law has long made a distinction between crimes which are *mala in se* and *mala prohibita*—that is, between acts that are wrong in themselves and acts that are illegal but not immoral—and the delinquent can make the same kind of distinction in evaluating the wrongfulness of his behavior. For the delinquent, however, wrongfulness may turn on the question of whether or not anyone has clearly been hurt by his deviance, and this matter is open to a variety of interpretations. Vandalism, for example, may be defined by the delinquent simply as "mischief"—after all, it may be claimed, the persons whose property has been destroyed can well afford it. Similarly, auto theft may be viewed as "borrowing," and gang fighting may be seen as a private quarrel, an agreed upon duel between two willing parties, and thus of no concern to the community at large. We are not suggesting that this technique of neutralization, labeled the denial of injury, involves an explicit dialectic. Rather, we are arguing that the delinquent frequently, and in a hazy fashion, feels that his behavior does not really cause any great harm despite the fact that it runs counter to law. Just as the link between the individual and his acts may be broken by the denial of responsibility, so may the link between acts and their consequences be broken by the denial of injury. Since society sometimes agrees with the delinquent, e.g., in matters such as truancy, "pranks," and so on, it merely reaffirms the idea that the delinquent's neutralization of social controls by means of qualifying the norms is an extension of common practice rather than a gesture of complete opposition.

3. The Denial of the Victim

Even if the delinquent accepts the responsibility for his deviant actions and is willing to admit that his deviant actions involve an injury or hurt, the moral indignation of self and others may be neutralized by an insistence that the injury is not wrong in light of the circumstances. The injury, it may be claimed, is not really an injury; rather, it is a form of rightful retaliation or punishment. By a subtle alchemy the delinquent moves himself into the position of an avenger and the victim is transformed into a wrong-doer. Assaults on homosexuals or suspected homosexuals, attacks on members of minority groups who are said to have gotten "out of place," vandalism as revenge on an unfair teacher or school official, thefts from a "crooked" store owner—all may be hurts inflicted on a transgressor, in the eyes of the delinquent. As Orwell has pointed out, the type of criminal admired by the general public has probably changed over the course of years and Raffles no longer serves as a hero;[4] but Robin Hood, and his latter-day derivatives such as the tough detective seeking justice outside the law, still capture the popular imagination, and the delinquent may view his acts as part of a similar role.

To deny the existence of the victim, then, by transforming him into a person deserving injury is an extreme form of a phenomenon we have mentioned before, namely, the delinquent's recognition of appropriate and inappropriate targets for his delinquent acts. In addition, however, the existence of the victim may be denied for the delinquent, in a somewhat different sense, by the circumstances of the delinquent act itself. Insofar as the victim is physically absent, unknown, or a vague abstraction (as is often the case in delinquent acts committed against property), the awareness of the victim's existence is weakened. Internalized norms and anticipations of the reactions of others must somehow be activated if they are to serve as guides for behavior; and it is possible that a diminished awareness of the victim plays an important part of determining whether or not this process is set in motion.

4. The Condemnation of the Condemners

A fourth technique of neutralization would appear to involve a condemnation of the condemners or, as McCorkle and Korn have phrased it, a rejection of the rejectors.[5] The delinquent shifts the focus of attention from his own deviant acts to the motives and behavior of those who disapprove of his violations. His condemners, he may claim, are hypocrites, deviants in disguise, or impelled by personal spite. This orientation toward the conforming world may be of particular importance when it hardens into a bitter cynicism directed against those assigned the task of enforcing or expressing the norms of the dominant society. Police, it may be said, are corrupt, stupid, and brutal. Teachers always show favoritism and parents always "take it out" on their children. By a slight extension, the rewards of conformity—such as material success—become a matter of pull or luck, thus decreasing still further the stature of those who stand on the side of the law-abiding. The validity of this jaundiced viewpoint is not so important as its function in turning back or deflecting the negative sanctions attached to violations of the norms. The delinquent, in effect, has changed the subject of the conversation in the dialogue between his own deviant impulses and the reactions of others; and by attacking others, the wrongfulness of his own behavior is more easily repressed or lost to view.

5. The Appeal to Higher Loyalties

Fifth, and last, internal and external social controls may be neutralized by sacrificing the demands of the larger society for the demands of the smaller social groups to which the delinquent belongs, such as the sibling pair, the gang, or the friendship clique. It is important to note that the delinquent does not necessarily repudiate the imperatives of the dominant normative system, despite his failure to follow them. Rather, the delinquent may see himself as caught up in a dilemma that must be resolved, unfortunately, at the cost of violating the law. One aspect of this situation has been studied by Stouffer and Toby in their research on the conflict between particularistic and universalistic demands, between the claims of friendship and general social obligations, and their results suggest that "it is possible to classify people according to a predisposition to select one or the other horn of a dilemma in role conflict."[6] For our purposes, however, the most important point is that deviation from certain norms may occur not because the norms are rejected but because others' norms, held to be more pressing or involving a higher loyalty, are accorded precedence. Indeed, it is the fact that both sets of norms are believed in that gives meaning to our concepts of dilemma and role conflict.

The conflict between the claims of friendship and the claims of law, or a similar dilemma, has of course long been recognized by the social scientist (and the novelist) as a common human problem. If the juvenile delinquent frequently resolves his dilemma by insisting that he must "always help a buddy" or "never squeal on a friend," even when it throws him into serious difficulties with the dominant social order, his choice remains familiar to the supposedly law-abiding. The delinquent is unusual, perhaps, in the extent to which he is able to see the fact that he acts in behalf of the smaller social groups to which he belongs as a justification for violations of society's norms, but it is a matter of degree rather than of kind.

"I didn't mean it." "I didn't really hurt anybody." "They had it coming to them." "Everybody's picking on me." "I didn't do it for myself." These slogans or their variants, we hypothesize, prepare the juvenile for delinquent acts. These "definitions of the situation" represent tangential or glancing blows at the dominant normative system rather than the creation of an opposing ideology; and they are extensions of patterns of thought prevalent in society rather than something created *de novo*.

Techniques of neutralization may not be powerful enough to fully shield the individual from the force of his own internalized values and the reactions of conforming others, for as we have pointed out, juvenile delinquents often appear to suffer from feelings of guilt and shame when called into account for their deviant behavior. And some delinquents may be so isolated from the world of conformity that techniques of neutralization need not be called into play. Nonetheless, we would argue that techniques of neutralization are critical in lessening the effectiveness of social controls and that they lie behind a large share of delinquent behavior. Empirical research in this area is scattered and fragmentary at the present time, but the work of Redl,[7] Cressey,[8] and others has supplied a body of significant data that has done much to clarify the theoretical issues and enlarge the fund of supporting evidence. Two lines of investigation seem to be critical at this stage. First, there is need for more knowledge concerning the differential distribution of techniques of neutralization, as operative patterns of thought, by age, sex, social class, ethnic group, etc. On a priori grounds it might be assumed that these justifications for deviance will be more readily seized by segments of society for whom a discrepancy between common social ideals and social practice is most apparent. It is also possible, however, that the habit of "bending" the dominant normative system—if not "breaking" it—cuts across our cruder social categories and is to be traced primarily to patterns of social interaction within the familial circle. Second, there is need for a greater understanding of the internal structure of techniques of neutralization, as a system of beliefs and attitudes, and its relationship to various types of delinquent behavior. Certain techniques of neutralization would appear to be better adapted to particular deviant acts than to others, as we have suggested, for example, in the case of offenses against property and the denial of the victim. But the issue remains far from clear and stands in need of more information.

In any case, techniques of neutralization appear to offer a promising line of research in enlarging and systematizing the theoretical grasp of juvenile delinquency. As more information is uncovered concerning techniques of neutralization, their origins, and their consequences, both juvenile delinquency in particular and deviation from normative systems in general may be illuminated.

Notes

1. Cf. Robin Williams, Jr., *American Society,* New York: Knopf, 1951, p. 28.

2. A number of observers have wryly noted that many delinquents seem to show a surprising awareness of sociological and psychological explanations for their behavior and are quick to point out the causal role of their poor environment.

3. It is possible, of course, that certain personality structures can accept some techniques of neutralization more readily than others, but this question remains largely unexplored.

4. George Orwell, *Dickens, Dali, and Others,* New York: Reynal, 1946.

5. Lloyd W. McCorkle and Richard Korn, "Resocialization Within Walls," *The Annals of the American Academy of Political and Social Science,* 293 (May, 1954), pp. 88–98.

6. See Samuel A. Stouffer and Jackson Toby, "Role Conflict and Personality," in *Toward a General Theory of Action,* edited by Talcott Parsons and Edward A. Shils, Cambridge, Mass.: Harvard University Press, 1951, p. 494.

7. See Fritz Redl and David Wineman, *Children Who Hate,* Glencoe, Ill.: The Free Press, 1956.

8. See D. R. Cressey, *Other People's Money,* Glencoe, Ill.: The Free Press, 1953.

The Influence of Situational Ethics on Cheating Among College Students

Donald L. McCabe

Introduction

Numerous studies have demonstrated the pervasive nature of cheating among college students (Baird 1980; Haines, Diekhoff, LaBeff, and Clark 1986; Michaels and Miethe 1989; Davis, et al. 1992). This research has examined a variety of factors that help explain cheating behavior, but the strength of the relationships between individual factors and cheating has varied considerably from study to study (Tittle and Rowe 1973; Baird 1980; Eisenberger and Shank 1985; Haines, et al. 1986; Ward 1986; Michaels and Miethe 1989; Perry, Kane, Bernesser, and Spicker 1990; Ward and Beck 1990).

Although the factors examined in these studies (for example, personal work ethic, gender, self-esteem, rational choice, social learning, deterrence) are clearly important, the work of LaBeff, Clark, Haines, and Diekhoff (1990) suggests that the concept of situational ethics may be particularly helpful in understanding student rationalizations for cheating. Extending the arguments of Norris and Dodder (1979), LaBeff et al. conclude

> that students hold qualified guidelines for behavior which are situationally determined. As such, the concept of situational ethics might well describe . . . college cheating [as] rules for behavior may not be considered rigid but depend on the circumstances involved. (1990, p. 191.)

LaBeff et al. believe a utilitarian calculus of "the ends justifies the means" underlies this reasoning process and "what is wrong in most situations might be considered right or acceptable if the end is defined as appropriate" (1990, p. 191). As argued by Edwards (1967), the situation determines what is right or wrong in this decision-making calculus and also dictates the appropriate principles to be used in guiding and judging behavior.

Sykes and Matza (1957) hypothesize that such rationalizations, that is, "justifications for deviance that are seen as valid by the delinquent but not by the legal system or society at large" (p. 666), are common. However, they challenge conventional wisdom that such rationalizations typically follow deviant behavior as a means of protecting "the individual from self-blame and the blame of others after the act" (p. 666). They develop convincing arguments that these rationalizations may logically precede the deviant behavior and "[d]isapproval from internalized norms and conforming others in the social environment is neutralized, turned back, or deflated in advance. Social controls that serve to check or inhibit deviant motivational patterns are rendered inoperative, and the individual is freed to engage in delinquency without serious damage to his self image" (pp. 666–667).

Using a sample of 380 undergraduate students at a small southwestern university, LaBeff et al. (1990) attempted to classify techniques employed by students in the neutralization of cheating behavior into the five categories of neutralization proposed by Sykes and Matza (1957): (1) denial of responsibility, (2) condemnation of condemners, (3) appeal to higher loyalties, (4) denial of victim, and (5) denial of injury. Although student responses could easily be classified into three of these techniques, denial of responsibility, appeal to higher loyalties, and condemnation of condemners, LaBeff et al. conclude that "[i]t is unlikely that students will either deny injury or deny the victim since there are no real targets in cheating" (1990, p. 196).

The research described here responds to LaBeff et al. in two ways; first, it answers their call to "test the salience of neutralization . . . in more diverse university environments" (p. 197) and second, it challenges their dismissal of denial of injury and denial of victim as neutralization techniques employed by students in their justification of cheating behavior.

Methodology

The data discussed here were gathered as part of a study of college cheating conducted during the 1990–1991 academic year. A seventy-two item questionnaire concerning cheating behavior was administered to students at thirty-one highly selective colleges across the country. Surveys were mailed to a minimum of five hundred students at each school and a total of 6,096 completed surveys were returned (38.3 percent response rate). Eighty-eight percent of the respondents were seniors, nine percent were juniors, and the remaining three percent could not be classified. Survey administration emphasized voluntary participation and assurances of anonymity to help combat issues of non-response bias and the need to accept responses without the chance to question or contest them.

The final sample included 61.2 percent females (which reflects the inclusion of five all female schools in the sample and a slightly higher return rate among female students) and 95.4 percent U.S. citizens. The sample paralleled the ethnic diversity of the participating schools (85.5 percent Anglo, 7.2 percent Asian, 2.6 percent African American, 2.2 percent Hispanic and 2.5 percent other); their religious diversity (including a large percentage of students who claimed no religious preference, 27.1 percent); and their mix of undergraduate majors (36.0 percent humanities, 28.8 percent social sciences, 26.8 percent natural sciences and engineering, 4.5 percent business, and 3.9 percent other).

Results

Of the 6,096 students participating in this research, over two-thirds (67.4 percent) indicated that they had cheated on a test or major assignment at least once while an undergraduate. This cheating took a variety of different forms, but among the most popular (listed in decreasing order of mention) were: (1) a failure to footnote sources in written work, (2) collaboration on assignments when the instructor specifically asked for individual work, (3) copying from other students on tests and examinations, (4) fabrication of bibliographies, (5) helping someone else cheat on a test, and (6) using unfair methods to learn the content of a test ahead of time. Almost one in five students (19.1 percent) could be classified as active-cheaters (five or more self-reported incidents of cheating). This is double the rate reported by LaBeff et al. (1990), but they asked students to report only cheating incidents that had taken place in the last six months. Students in this research were asked to report all cheating in which they had engaged while an undergraduate—a period of three years for most respondents at the time of this survey.

Students admitting to any cheating activity were asked to rate the importance of several specific factors that might have influenced their decisions to cheat. These data establish the importance of denial of responsibility and condemnation of condemners as neutralization techniques. For example, 52.4 percent of the respondents who admitted to cheating rated the pressure to get good grades as an important influence in their decision to cheat with parental pressures and competition to gain admission into professional schools singled out as the primary grade pressures. Forty-six percent of those who had engaged in cheating cited excessive workloads and an inability to keep up with assignments as important factors in their decisions to cheat.

In addition to rating the importance of such preselected factors, 426 respondents (11.0 percent of the admitted cheaters) offered their own justifications for cheating in response to an open-ended question on motivations for cheating. These responses confirm the importance of denial of responsibility and condemnation of condemners as neutralization techniques. They also support LaBeff et al.'s (1990) claim that appeal to higher loyalties is an important neutralization technique. However, these responses also suggest that LaBeff et al.'s dismissal of denial of injury as a justification for student cheating is arguable.

As shown in Table 1, denial of responsibility was the technique most frequently cited (216 responses, 61.0 percent of the total) in the 354 responses classified into one of Sykes and Matza's five categories of the neutralization. The most common responses in this category were mind block, no understanding of the material, a fear of failing, and unclear explanations of assignments. (Although it is possible that some instances of mind block and a fear of failing included in this summary would be more accurately classified as rationalization, the wording of all responses included here suggests that rationalization preceded the cheating incident. Responses that seem to involve post hoc rationalizations were excluded from this summary). Condemnation of condemners was the second most popular neutralization technique observed (99 responses, 28.0 percent) and included such explanations as pointless assignments, lack of respect for individual professors, unfair tests, parents' expectations, and unfair professors. Twenty-four respondents (6.8 percent) appealed to higher loyalties to explain their behavior. In particular, helping a friend and responding to peer pressures were influences some students could not ignore. Finally, fifteen students (4.2 percent) provided responses that clearly fit into the category of denial of injury. These students dismissed their cheating as harmless since it did not hurt anyone or they felt cheating did not matter

Table 1   Neutralization Strategies; Self-Admitted Cheaters

Strategy	Number	Percent
Denial of responsibility	216	61.0
Mind block	90	25.4
No understanding of material	31	8.8
Other	95	26.8
Condemnation of condemners	99	28.0
Pointless assignment	35	9.9
No respect for professor	28	7.9
Other	36	10.2
Appeal to higher loyalties	24	6.8
Help a friend	10	2.8
Peer pressure	9	2.5
Other	5	1.5
Denial of injury	15	4.2
Cheating is harmless	9	2.5
Does not matter	6	1.7

in some cases (for example, where an assignment counted for a small percentage of the total course grade).

Detailed examination of selected student responses provides additional insight into the neutralization strategies they employ.

The Denial of Responsibility

Denial of responsibility invokes the claim that the act was "due to forces outside of the individual and beyond his control such as unloving parents" (Sykes and Matza 1957, p. 667). For example, many students cite an unreasonable workload and the difficulty of keeping up as ample justification for cheating.

> Here at . . . , you must cheat to stay alive. There's so much work and the quality of materials from which to learn, books, professors, is so bad that there's no other choice.
>
> It's the only way to keep up.
>
> I couldn't do the work myself.

The following descriptions of students cheating confirm fear of failure is also an important form of denial of responsibility:

> . . . a take-home exam in a class I was failing.
>
> . . . was near failing.

Some justified their cheating by citing the behavior of peers:

> Everyone has test files in fraternities, etc. If you don't you're at a great disadvantage.
>
> When most of the class is cheating on a difficult exam and they will ruin the curve, it influences you to cheat so your grade won't be affected.

All of these responses contain the essence of denial of responsibility: the cheater has deflected blame to others or to a specific situational context.

The Denial of Injury

As noted in Table 1, denial of injury was identified as a neutralization technique employed by some respondents. A key element in denial of injury is whether one feels "anyone has clearly been hurt by (the) deviance." In invoking this defense, a cheater would argue "that his behavior does not really cause any great harm despite the fact that it runs counter to the law" (Sykes and Matza 1957, pp. 667–668). For example, a number of students argued that the assignment or test on which they cheated was so trivial that no one was really hurt by their cheating.

> These grades aren't worth much therefore my copying doesn't mean very much. I am ashamed, but I'd probably do it the same way again.

> If I extend the time on a take home it is because I feel everyone does and the teacher kind of expects it. No one gets hurt.

As suggested earlier, these responses suggest the conclusion of LaBeff et al. that "(i)t is unlikely that students will . . . deny injury" (1990, p. 196) must be re-evaluated.

The Denial of the Victim

LaBeff et al. failed to find any evidence of denial of the victim in their student accounts. Although the student motivations for cheating summarized in Table 1 support this conclusion, at least four students (0.1% of the self-admitted cheaters in this study) provided comments elsewhere on the survey instrument which involved denial of the victim. The common elements in these responses was a victim deserving of the consequences of the cheating behavior and cheating was viewed as "a form of rightful retaliation of punishment" (Sykes and Matza 1957, p. 668).

This feeling was extreme in one case, as suggested by the following student who felt her cheating was justified by the

> realization that this school is a manifestation of the bureaucratic capitalist system that systematically keeps the lower classes down, and that adhering to their rules was simply perpetuating this institution.

This "we" versus "they" mentality was raised by many students, but typically in comments about the policing of academic honesty rather than as justification for one's own cheating behavior. When used to justify cheating, the target was almost always an individual teacher rather than the institution and could be more accurately classified as a strategy of condemnation of condemners rather than denial of the victim.

The Condemnation of Condemners

Sykes and Matza describe the condemnation of condemners as an attempt to shift "the focus of attention from [one's] own deviant acts to the motives and behaviors of those who disapprove of [the] violations. [B]y attacking others, the wrongfulness of [one's] own behavior is more easily repressed or lost to view" (1957, p. 668). The logic of this strategy for student cheaters focused on issues of favoritism and fairness. Students invoking this rationale describe "uncaring, unprofessional instructors with negative attitudes who were negligent in their behavior" (LaBeff et al. 1990, p. 195). For example:

> In one instance, nothing was done by a professor because the student was a hockey player.

> The TAs who graded essays were unduly harsh.

> It is known by students that certain professors are more lenient to certain types, e.g., blondes or hockey players.
>
> I would guess that 90% of the students here have seen athletes and/or fraternity members cheating on an exam or papers. If you turn in one of these culprits, and I have, the penalty is a five-minute lecture from a coach and/or administrator. All these add up to a 'who cares, they'll never do anything to you anyway' attitude here about cheating.

Concerns about the larger society were an important issue for some students:

> When community frowns upon dishonesty, then people will change.
>
> If our leaders can commit heinous acts and then lie before Senate committees about their total ignorance and innocence, *then why can't I cheat a little?*
>
> In today's world you do anything to be above the competition.

In general, students found ready targets on which to blame their behavior and condemnation of the condemners was a popular neutralization strategy.

The Appeal to Higher Loyalties

The appeal to higher loyalties involves neutralizing "internal and external controls . . . by sacrificing the demands of the larger society for the demands of the smaller social groups to which the [offender] belongs. [D]eviation from certain norms may occur not because the norms are rejected but because other norms, held to be more pressing or involving a higher loyalty, are accorded precedence." (Sykes and Matza 1957, p. 669). For example, a difficult conflict for some students is balancing the desire to help a friend against the institution's rules on cheating. The student may not challenge the rules, but rather views the need to help a friend, fellow fraternity/sorority member, or roommate to be a greater obligation which justifies the cheating behavior.

Fraternities and sororities were singled out as a network where such behavior occurs with some frequency. For example, a female student at a small university in New England observed:

> There's a lot of cheating within the Greek system. Of all the cheating I've seen, it's often been men and women in fraternities & sororities who exchange information or cheat.

The appeal to higher loyalties was particularly evident in student reactions concerning the reporting of cheating violations. Although fourteen of the thirty-one schools participating in this research had explicit honor codes that generally require students to report cheating violations they observe, less than one-third (32.3 percent) indicated that they were likely to do so. When asked if they would report a friend, only four percent said they would and most students felt that they should not be expected to do so. Typical student comments included:

> Students should not be sitting in judgment of their own peers.
>
> The university is not a police state.

For some this decision was very practical.

> A lot of students, 50 percent, wouldn't because they know they will probably cheat at some point themselves.

For others, the decision would depend on the severity of the violation they observed and many would not report what they considered to be minor violations, even those explicitly covered by the school's honor code or policies on academic honesty. Explicit examination or test cheating was one of the few violations where students exhibited any consensus concerning the need to report violations. Yet even in this case many students felt other factors must be considered. For example, a senior at a women's college in the northeast commented:

> It would depend on the circumstances. If someone was hurt, *very likely.* If there was no single victim in the case, if the victim was [the] institution . . . , then *very unlikely.*

Additional evidence of the strength of the appeal to higher loyalties as a neutralization technique is found in the fact that almost one in five respondents (17.8 percent) reported that they had helped someone cheat on an examination or major test. The percentage who have helped others cheat on papers and other assignments is likely much higher. Twenty-six percent of those students who helped someone else cheat on a test reported that they had never cheated on a test themselves, adding support to the argument that peer pressure to help friends is quite strong.

Conclusions

From this research it is clear that college students use a variety of neutralization techniques to rationalize their cheating behavior, deflecting blame to others and/or the situational context, and the framework of Sykes and Matza (1957) seems well supported when student explanations of cheating behavior are analyzed. Unlike prior research (LaBeff et al. 1990), however, the present findings suggest that students employ all of the techniques described by Sykes and Matza, including denial of injury and denial of victim. Although there was very limited evidence of the use of denial of victim, denial of injury was not uncommon. Many students felt that some forms of cheating were victimless crimes, particularly on assignments that accounted for a small percentage of the total course grade. The present research does affirm LaBeff et al.'s finding that denial of responsibility and condemnation of condemners are the neutralization techniques most frequently utilized by college students. Appeal to higher loyalties is particularly evident in neutralizing institutional expectations that students report cheating violations they observe.

The present results clearly extend the findings of LaBeff et al. into a much wider range of contexts as this research ultimately involved 6,096 students at thirty-one geographically dispersed institutions ranging from small liberal arts colleges in the Northeast to nationally prominent research universities in the South and West. Fourteen of the thirty-one institutions have long standing honor-code traditions. The code tradition at five of these schools dates to the late 1800s and all fourteen have codes that survived the student unrest of the 1960s. In such a context, the strength of the appeal to higher loyalties and the denial of responsibility as justifications for cheating is a very persuasive argument that neutralization techniques are salient to today's college student. More importantly, it may suggest fruitful areas of future discourse between faculty, administrators, and students on the question of academic honesty.

References

Baird, John S. 1980. "Current Trends in College Cheating." *Psychology in Schools* 17:512–522.

Davis, Stephen F., Cathy A. Grover, Angela H. Becker, and Loretta N. McGregor. 1992. "Academic Dishonesty: Prevalence, Determinants, Techniques, and Punishments." *Teaching of Psychology.* In press.

Edwards, Paul. 1967. *The Encyclopedia of Philosophy,* no. 3, edited by Paul Edwards, New York: Macmillan Company and Free Press.

Eisenberger, Robert, and Dolores M. Shank. 1985. "Personal Work Ethic and Effort Training Affect Cheating." *Journal of Personality and Social Psychology* 49:520–528.

Haines, Valerie J., George Diekhoff, Emily LaBeff, and Robert Clark. 1986. "College Cheating: Immaturity, Lack of Commitment, and the Neutralizing Attitude." *Research in Higher Education* 25:342–354.

LaBeff, Emily E., Robert E. Clark, Valerie J. Haines and George M. Diekhoff. 1990. "Situational Ethics and College Student Cheating." *Sociological Inquiry* 60:190–198.

Michaels, James W., and Terance Miethe. 1989 "Applying Theories of Deviance to Academic Cheating." *Social Science Quarterly* 70:870–885.

Norris, Terry D., and Richard A. Dodder. 1979. "A Behavioral Continuum Synthesizing Neutralization Theory, Situational Ethics and Juvenile Delinquency." *Adolescence* 55:545–555.

Perry, Anthony R., Kevin M. Kane, Kevin J. Bernesser, and Paul T. Spicker. 1990. "Type A Behavior, Competitive Achievement-Striving, and Cheating Among College Students." *Psychological Reports* 66:459–465.

Sykes, Gresham M., and David Matza. 1957. "Techniques of Neutralization: A Theory of Delinquency." *American Sociological Review* 22:664–670.

Tittle, Charles, and Alan Rowe. 1973. "Moral Appeal, Sanction Threat, and Deviance: An Experimental Test." *Social Problems* 20:488–498.

Ward, David. 1986. "Self-Esteem and Dishonest Behavior Revisited." *Journal of Social Psychology* 123:709–713.

Ward, David, and Wendy L. Beck. 1990. "Gender and Dishonesty." *Journal of Social Psychology* 130:333–339.

Opportunity Theory

Those who subscribe to opportunity theory are concerned primarily with the social conditions that may produce a strain toward deviation. Of particular focus is the way actors posture themselves relative to the existing social structure. Robert K. Merton's article, "Social Structure and Anomie," represents what many consider the classic study, within anomie, or opportunity, theory, of the emergence of deviant behavior.

Basic to Merton's explanation is the contention that any society can be characterized in terms of its structure, particularly its goals and its means. A well-integrated society, he reasons, displays a balance between these elements. In such a society, when people want to obtain societal goals, they will use the appropriate institutionalized means for doing so. American society, according to Merton, does not maintain this sort of balance. It is a society in which emphasis is placed almost exclusively on the achievement of goals—regardless of the methods used to attain them. Those affected the most by the imbalance are the *lower classes*. Most members of the lower classes accept the American dream of attaining success; when they attempt to realize their goals through legitimate means, however, they find themselves blocked, mainly because they do not possess the necessary resources. They may substitute other means—for instance, stealing or robbing. Merton refers to these individuals as "innovators." He argues, further, that when there is a disjunction between goals and means, the result may be cultural chaos, or *anomie*. In this situation, the predictability and regulation of behavior become tenuous.

John M. Hagedorn, in "Homeboys, Dope Fiends, Legits, and New Jacks," offers an empirical account that has some relationship to opportunity theory, particularly those aspects that describe how subcultures may arise. The study also challenges some long-standing beliefs about the nature of gang involvement. The specific research questions addressed are two: (1) What happens as gang members age, and (2) are adult gang members typically the same kinds of people, or do gangs exhibit varying types? Hagedorn draws upon data obtained primarily from interviews with 101 members of some 18 gangs. He notes initially that, although more gang members appear to be working today, their overall involvement in the labor market is quite low. Perhaps most insightful and revealing is the fourfold typology of male adult gang membership that emerges from his data: (1) the *legits*, members who had left the gang; (2) the *homeboys*, members who worked alternatively at conventional jobs and drug sales; (3) the *dope fiends*, members who were addicted and participated in drug sales to maintain their source of drugs; and (4) the *new jacks*, members who pursued the drug game as a career. Hagedorn observes that mobility among the categories did occur. For example, some homeboys became legits, while others adopted the new jack role. Hagedorn continues his analysis by examining how his data compare with some of the major gang theories and studies that have been advanced, several of which are part of the anomie, or opportunity, tradition. He notes, for example, that the new jacks seem to mirror Cloward and Ohlin's conception of the criminal subculture, and most particularly their argument that not only must illegitimate opportunity structures exist but the novice must also learn the necessary skills associated with criminal activity; these contingencies seem to apply to the new jacks. Specifically, the existing cocaine economy and the large market for drugs provide the opportunities whereby the new jacks can, through a process of tutelage (i.e., given the opportunity to perform and learn the skills associated with various roles in the drug profession), become entrenched firmly within the drug world. In a sense, they become career deviants. Hagedorn concludes, in part, that although Cloward and Ohlin's opportunity theory seems to have some explanatory utility, it needs to be recast in light of the societal changes that have occurred over the past four decades.

14 Social Structure and Anomie

Robert K. Merton

There persists a notable tendency in sociological theory to attribute the malfunctioning of social structure primarily to those of man's imperious biological drives which are not adequately restrained by social control. In this view, the social order is solely a device for "impulse management" and the "social processing" of tensions. These impulses which break through social control, be it noted, are held to be biologically derived. Nonconformity is assumed to be rooted in original nature.[1] Conformity is by implication the result of a utilitarian calculus or unreasoned conditioning. This point of view, whatever its other deficiencies, clearly begs one question. It provides no basis for determining the nonbiological conditions which induce deviations from prescribed patterns of conduct. In this paper, it will be suggested that certain phases of social structure generate the circumstances in which infringement of social codes constitutes a "normal" response.[2]

The conceptual scheme to be outlined is designed to provide a coherent, systematic approach to the study of socio-cultural sources of deviate behavior. Our primary aim lies in discovering how some social structures *exert a definite pressure* upon certain persons in the society to engage in nonconformist rather than conformist conduct. The many ramifications of the scheme cannot all be discussed; the problems mentioned outnumber those explicitly treated.

Among the elements of social and cultural structure, two are important for our purposes. These are analytically separable although they merge imperceptibly in concrete situations. The first consists of culturally defined goals, purposes, and interests. It comprises a frame of aspirational reference. These goals are more or less integrated and involve varying degrees of prestige and sentiment. They constitute a basic, but not the exclusive, component of what Linton aptly has called "designs for group living." Some of these cultural aspirations are related to the original drives of man, but they are not determined by them. The second phase of the social structure defines, regulates, and controls the acceptable modes of achieving these goals. Every social group invariably couples its scale of desired ends with moral or institutional regulation of permissible and required procedures for attaining these ends. These regulatory norms and moral imperatives do not necessarily coincide with technical or efficiency norms. Many procedures which from the standpoint of *particular individuals* would be most efficient in securing desired values, e.g., illicit oil-stock schemes, theft, fraud, are ruled out of the institutional area of permitted conduct. The choice of expedients is limited by the institutional norms.

To say that these two elements, culture goals and institutional norms, operate jointly is not to say that the ranges of alternative behaviors and aims bear some constant relation to one another. The emphasis upon certain goals may vary independently of the degree of emphasis upon institutional means. There may develop a disproportionate, at times, a virtually exclusive, stress upon the value of specific goals, involving relatively slight concern with the institutionally appropriate modes of attaining these goals. The limiting case in this direction is reached when the range of alternative procedures is limited only by technical rather than institutional considerations. Any and all devices which promise attainment of the all important goal would be permitted in this hypothetical polar case.[3] This constitutes one type of cultural malintegration. A second polar type is found in groups where activities originally conceived as instrumental are transmuted into ends in themselves. The original purposes are forgotten, and ritualistic adherence to institutionally prescribed conduct becomes virtually obsessive.[4] Stability is largely ensured while change is flouted. The range of alternative behaviors is severely limited. There develops a tradition-bound, sacred society characterized by neophobia. The occupational psychosis of the bureaucrat may be cited as a case in point. Finally, there are the intermediate types of groups where a balance between culture goals and institutional means is maintained. These are the significantly integrated and relatively stable, though changing, groups.

An effective equilibrium between the two phases of the social structure is maintained as long as satisfactions accrue to individuals who conform to both constraints, viz., satisfactions from the achievement of the goals and satisfactions emerging directly from the institutionally canalized modes of striving to attain these ends. Success, in such equilibrated cases, is twofold. Success is reckoned in terms of the product and in terms of the process, in terms of the outcome and in terms of activities. Continuing satisfactions must derive from sheer *participation* in a competitive order as well as from eclipsing one's competitors if the order itself is to be sustained. The occasional sacrifices involved in institutionalized conduct must be compensated by socialized rewards. The distribution of statuses and roles through competition must be so organized that positive incentives for conformity to roles and adherence to status obligations are provided *for every position* within the distributive order. Aberrant conduct, therefore, may be viewed as a symptom of dissociation between culturally defined aspirations and socially structured means.

Of the types of groups which result from the independent variation of the two phases of the social structure, we shall be primarily concerned with the first, namely, that involving a disproportionate accent on goals. This statement must be recast in a proper perspective. In no group is there an absence of regulatory codes governing conduct, yet groups do vary in the degree to which these folkways, mores, and institutional controls are effectively integrated with the more diffuse goals which are part of the culture matrix. Emotional convictions may cluster about the complex of socially acclaimed ends, meanwhile shifting their support from the culturally defined implementation of these ends. As we shall see, certain aspects of the social structure may generate countermores and antisocial behavior precisely because of differential emphases on goals and regulations. In the extreme case, the latter may be so vitiated by the goal-emphasis that the range of behavior is limited only by considerations of technical expediency. The sole significant question then becomes, which available means is most efficient in netting the socially approved value.[5] The technically most feasible procedure, whether legitimate or not, is preferred to the institutionally prescribed conduct. As this process continues, the integration of the society becomes tenuous and anomie ensues.

Thus, in competitive athletics, when the aim of victory is shorn of its institutional trappings and success in contests becomes construed as "winning the game" rather than "winning through circumscribed modes of activity," a premium is implicitly set upon the use of illegitimate but technically efficient means. The star of the opposing football team is surreptitiously slugged; the wrestler furtively incapacitates his opponent through ingenious but illicit techniques; university alumni covertly subsidize "students" whose talents are largely confined to the athletic field. The emphasis on the goal has so attenuated the satisfactions deriving from sheer participation in the competitive activity that these satisfactions are virtually confined to a successful outcome. Through the same process, tension generated by the desire to win in a poker game is relieved by successfully dealing oneself four aces, or, when the cult of success has become completely dominant, by sagaciously shuffling the cards in a game of solitaire. The faint twinge of uneasiness in the last instance and the surreptitious nature of public delicts indicate clearly that the institutional rules of the game are *known* to those who evade them, but that the emotional supports of these rules are largely vitiated by cultural exaggeration of the success-goal.[6] They are microcosmic images of the social macrocosm.

Of course, this process is not restricted to the realm of sport. The process whereby exaltation of the end generates a *literal demoralization,* i.e., a de-institutionalization, of the means is one which characterizes many[7] groups in which the two phases of the social structure are not highly integrated. The extreme emphasis upon the accumulation of wealth as a symbol of success[8] in our own society militates against the completely effective control of institutionally regulated modes of acquiring of fortune.[9] Fraud, corruption, vice, crime, in short, the entire catalogue of proscribed behavior, becomes increasingly common when the emphasis on the *culturally induced* success-goal becomes divorced from a coordinated institutional emphasis. This observation is of crucial theoretical importance in examining the doctrine that antisocial behavior most frequently derives from biological drives breaking through the restraints imposed by society. The difference is one between a strictly utilitarian interpretation which conceives man's ends as random and an analysis which finds these ends deriving from the basic values of the culture.[10]

Our analysis can scarcely stop at this juncture. We must turn to other aspects of the social structure if we are to deal with the social genesis of the varying rates and types of deviate behavior characteristic of different societies. Thus far, we have sketched three ideal types of social orders constituted by distinctive patterns of relations between culture ends and means. Turning from these types of *culture patterning,* we find five logically possible, alternative modes of adjustment or adaptation *by individuals* within the culture-bearing society or group.[11] These are schematically presented in the following table, where (+) signifies "acceptance," (−) signifies "elimination," and (±) signifies "rejection and substitution of new goals and standards."

		Culture Goals	Institutional Means
I.	Conformity	1	1
II.	Innovation	1	2
III.	Ritualism	2	1
IV.	Retreatism	2	2
V.	Rebellion[12]	6	6

Our discussion of the relation between these alternative responses and other phases of the social structure must be prefaced by the observation that persons may shift from one alternative to another as they engage in different social activities. These categories refer to role adjustments in specific situations, not to personality *in toto.* To treat the development of this process in various spheres of conduct would introduce a complexity unmanageable within the confines of this paper. For this reason, we shall be concerned primarily with economic activity in the broad sense, "the production, exchange, distribution, and consumption of goods and services" in our competitive society, wherein wealth has taken on a highly symbolic cast. Our task is to search out some of the factors which exert pressure upon individuals to engage in certain of these logically possible alternative responses. This choice, as we shall see, is far from random.

In every society, Adaptation I (conformity to both culture goals and means) is the most common and widely diffused. Were this not so, the stability and continuity of the society could not be maintained. The mesh of expectancies which constitutes every social order is sustained by the modal behavior of its members falling within the first category. Conventional role behavior oriented toward the basic values of the group is the rule rather than the exception. It is this fact alone which permits us to speak of a human aggregate as comprising a group or society.

Conversely, Adaptation IV (rejection of goals and means) is the least common. Persons who "adjust" (or maladjust) in this fashion are, strictly speaking, *in* the society but not *of* it. Sociologically, these constitute the true "aliens." Not sharing the common frame of orientation, they can be included within the societal population merely in a fictional sense. In this category are *some* of the activities of psychotics, psychoneurotics, chronic autists, pariahs, outcasts, vagrants, vagabonds, tramps, chronic drunkards, and drug addicts.[13] These have relinquished, in certain spheres of activity, the culturally defined goals, involving complete aim-inhibition in the polar case, and their adjustments are not in accord with institutional norms. This is not to say that in some cases the source of their behavioral adjustments is not in part the very social structure which they have in effect repudiated nor that their very existence within a social area does not constitute a problem for the socialized population.

This mode of "adjustment" occurs, as far as structural sources are concerned, when both the culture goals and institutionalized procedures have been assimilated thoroughly by the individual and imbued with affect and high positive value, but where those institutionalized procedures which promise a measure of successful attainment of the goals are not available to the individual. In such instances, there results a two-fold mental conflict insofar as the moral obligation for adopting institutional means conflicts with the pressure to resort to illegitimate means (which may attain the goal) and inasmuch as the individual is shut off from means which are both legitimate *and* effective. The competitive order is maintained, but the frustrated and handicapped individual who cannot cope with this order drops out. Defeatism, quietism, and resignation are manifested in escape mechanisms which ultimately lead the individual to "escape" from the requirements of the society. It is an expedient which arises from continued failure to attain the goal by legitimate measures and from an inability to adopt the illegitimate route because of internalized prohibitions and institutionalized compulsives, *during which process the supreme value of the success-goal has as yet not been renounced.* The conflict is resolved by eliminating *both* precipitating elements, the goals and means. The escape is complete, the conflict is eliminated, and the individual is associated.

Be it noted that where frustration derives from the inaccessibility of effective institutional means for attaining economic or any other type of highly valued "success," that Adaptations II, III, and V (innovation, ritualism, and rebellion) are also possible. The result will be determined by the particular personality, and thus, the *particular* cultural background, involved. Inadequate socialization will result in the innovation response whereby the conflict and frustration are eliminated by relinquishing the institutional means and retaining the success-aspiration; an extreme assimilation of institutional demands will lead to ritualism wherein the goal is dropped as beyond one's reach but conformity to the mores persists; and rebellion occurs when emancipation from the reigning standards, due to frustration or to marginalist perspectives, leads to the attempt to introduce a "new social order."

Our major concern is with the illegitimacy adjustment. This involves the use of conventionally proscribed but frequently effective means of attaining at least the simulacrum of culturally defined success—wealth, power, and the like. As we have seen, this adjustment occurs when the individual has assimilated the cultural emphasis on success without equally internalizing the morally prescribed norms governing means for its attainment. The question arises, Which phases of our social structure predispose toward this mode of adjustment? We may examine a concrete instance, effectively analyzed by Lohman,[14] which provides a clue to the answer. Lohman has shown that specialized areas of vice in the near north side of Chicago constitute a "normal" response to a situation where the cultural emphasis upon pecuniary success has been absorbed, but where there is little access to conventional and legitimate means for attaining such success. The conventional occupational opportunities of persons in this area are almost completely limited to manual labor. Given our cultural stigmatization of manual labor, and its correlate, the prestige of white collar work, it is clear that the result is a strain toward innovational practices. The limitation of opportunity to unskilled labor and the resultant low income cannot compete *in terms of conventional standards of achievement* with the high income from organized vice.

For our purposes, this situation involves two important features. First, such antisocial behavior is in a sense "called forth" by certain conventional values of the culture *and* by the class structure involving differential access to the approved opportunities for legitimate, prestige-bearing pursuit of the culture goals. The lack of high integration between the means-and-end elements of the cultural pattern and the particular class structure combine to favor a heightened frequency of antisocial conduct in such groups. The second consideration is of equal significance. Recourse to the first of the alternative responses, legitimate effort, is limited by the fact that actual advance toward desired success-symbols through conventional channels is, despite our persisting open-class ideology,[15] relatively rare and difficult for those handicapped by little formal education and few economic resources. The dominant pressure of group standards of success is, therefore, on the gradual attenuation of legitimate, but by and large ineffective, strivings and the increasing use of illegitimate, but more or less effective, expedients of vice and crime. The cultural demands made on persons in this situation are incompatible. On the one hand, they are asked to orient their conduct toward the prospect of accumulating wealth and on the other, they are largely denied effective opportunities to do so institutionally. The consequences of such structural inconsistency are psychopathological personality, and/or antisocial conduct, and/or revolutionary activities. The equilibrium between culturally designated means and ends becomes highly unstable with the progressive emphasis on attaining the prestige-laden ends by any means whatsoever. Within this context, Capone represents the triumph of amoral intelligence over morally prescribed "failure," when the channels of vertical mobility are closed or narrowed[16] *in a society which places a high premium on economic affluence and social ascent for* all *its members.*[17]

This last qualification is of primary importance. It suggests that other phases of the social structure besides the extreme emphasis on pecuniary success must be considered if we are to understand the social sources of antisocial behavior. A high frequency of deviate behavior is not generated simply by "lack of opportunity" or by this exaggerated pecuniary emphasis. A comparatively rigidified class structure, a feudalistic or caste order, may limit such opportunities far beyond the point which obtains in our society today. It is only when a system of cultural values extols, virtually above all else, certain *common* symbols of success *for the population at large* while its social structure rigorously restricts or completely eliminates access to approved modes of acquiring these symbols *for a considerable part of the same population* that antisocial behavior ensues on a considerable scale. In other words, our egalitarian ideology denies by implication the existence of noncompeting groups and individuals in the pursuit of pecuniary success. The same body of success-symbols is held to be desirable for all. These goals are held to *transcend class lines,* not to be bounded by them, yet the actual social organization is such that there exist class differentials in the accessibility of these *common* success-symbols. Frustration and thwarted aspiration lead to the search for avenues of escape from a culturally induced intolerable situation; or unrelieved ambition may eventuate in illicit attempts to acquire the dominant values.[18] The American stress on pecuniary success and ambitiousness for all thus invites exaggerated anxieties, hostilities, neuroses, and antisocial behavior.

This theoretical analysis may go far toward explaining the varying correlations between crime and poverty.[19] Poverty is not an isolated variable. It is one in a complex of interdependent social and cultural variables. When viewed in such a context, it represents quite different states of affairs. Poverty as such, and consequent limitation of opportunity, are not sufficient to induce a conspicuously high rate of criminal behavior. Even the often mentioned "poverty in the midst of plenty" will not necessarily lead to this result. Only insofar as poverty and associated disadvantages in competition for the culture values approved for *all* members of the society are linked with the assimilation of a cultural emphasis on monetary accumulation as a symbol of success is antisocial conduct a "normal" outcome. Thus, poverty is less highly correlated with crime in southeastern Europe than in the United States. The possibilities of vertical mobility in these European areas would seem to be fewer than in this country, so that neither poverty *per se* nor its association with limited opportunity is sufficient to account for the varying correlations. It is only when the full configuration is considered, poverty, limited opportunity, and a commonly shared system of success-symbols, that we can explain the higher association between poverty and crime in our society than in others where rigidified class structure is coupled with *differential class symbols of achievement.*

In societies such as our own, then, the pressure of prestige-bearing success tends to eliminate the effective social constraint over means employed to this end. "The-end-justifies-the-means" doctrine becomes a guiding tenet for action when the cultural structure unduly exalts the end and the social organization unduly limits possible recourse to approved means. Otherwise put, this notion and associated behavior reflect a lack of cultural coordination. In international relations, the effects of this lack of integration are notoriously apparent. An emphasis upon national power is not readily coordinated with an inept organization of legitimate, i.e., internationally defined and accepted, means for attaining this goal. The result is a tendency toward the abrogation of international law, treaties become scraps of paper, "undeclared warfare" serves as a technical evasion, the bombing of civilian populations is rationalized,[20] just as the same societal situation induces the same sway of illegitimacy among individuals.

The social order we have described necessarily produces this "strain toward dissolution." The pressure of such an order is upon outdoing one's competitors. The choice of means within the ambit of institutional control will persist as long as the sentiments supporting a competitive system, i.e., deriving from the possibility of outranking competitors and hence enjoying the favorable response of others, are distributed throughout the entire system of activities and are not confined merely to the final result. A stable social structure demands a balanced distribution of affect among its various segments. When there occurs a shift of emphasis from the satisfactions deriving from competition itself to almost exclusive concern with successful competition, the resultant stress leads to the breakdown of the regulatory structure.[21] With the resulting attenuation of the institutional imperatives, there occurs an approximation of the situation erroneously held by utilitarians to be typical of society generally wherein calculations of advantage and fear of punishment are the sole regulating agencies. In such situations, as Hobbes observed, force and fraud come to constitute the sole virtues in view of their relative efficiency in attaining goals—which were for him, of course, not culturally derived.

It should be apparent that the foregoing discussion is not pitched on a moralistic plane. Whatever the sentiments of the writer or reader concerning the ethical desirability of coordinating the means-and-goals phases of the social structure, one must agree that lack of such coordination leads to anomie. Insofar as one of the most general functions of social organization is to provide a basis for calculability and regularity of behavior, it is increasingly limited in effectiveness as these elements of the structure become dissociated. At the extreme, predictability virtually disappears and what may be properly termed cultural chaos or anomie intervenes.

This statement, being brief, is also incomplete. It has not included an exhaustive treatment of the various structural elements which predispose toward one rather than another of the alternative responses open to individuals; it has neglected, but not denied the relevance of, the factors determining the specific incidence of these responses; it has not enumerated the various concrete responses which are constituted by combinations of specific values of the analytical variables; it has omitted, or included only by implication, any consideration of the social functions performed by illicit responses; it has not tested the full explanatory power of the analytical scheme by examining a large number of group variations in the frequency of deviate and conformist behavior; it has not adequately dealt with rebellious conduct which seeks to refashion the social framework radically; it has not examined the relevance of cultural conflict for an analysis of culture-goal and institutional-means malintegration. It is suggested that these and related problems may be profitably analyzed by this cheme.

Notes

1. E.g., Ernest Jones, *Social Aspects of Psychoanalysis,* 28, London, 1924. If the Freudian notion is a variety of the "original sin" dogma, then the interpretation advanced in this paper may be called the doctrine of "socially derived sin."

2. "Normal" in the sense of a culturally oriented, if not approved, response. This statement does not deny the relevance of biological and personality differences which may be significantly involved in the *incidence* of deviate conduct. Our focus of interest is the social and cultural matrix; hence we abstract from other factors. It is in this sense, I take it, that James S. Plant speaks of the "normal reaction of normal people to abnormal conditions." See his *Personality and the Cultural Pattern,* 248, New York, 1937.

3. Contemporary American culture has been said to tend in this direction. See André Siegfried, *America Comes of Age,* 26–37, New York, 1927. The alleged extreme(?) emphasis on the goals of monetary success and material prosperity leads to dominant concern with technological and social instruments designed to produce the desired result, inasmuch as institutional controls become of secondary importance. In such a situation, innovation flourishes as the *range of means* employed is broadened. In a sense, then, there occurs the paradoxical emergence of "materialists" from an "idealistic" orientation. Cf. Durkheim's analysis of the cultural conditions which predispose toward crime and innovation, both of which are aimed toward efficiency, not moral norms. Durkheim was one of the first to see that "contrairement aux idées courantes le criminel n'apparait plus comme un être radicalement insociable, comme une sorte d'element parasitaire, de corps étranger et inassimilable, introduit au sein de la société; c'est un agent régulier de la vie sociale." See *Les Règles de la Méthode Sociologique,* 86–89, Paris, 1927.

4. Such ritualism may be associated with a mythology which rationalizes these actions so that they appear to retain their status as means, but the dominant pressure is in the direction of strict ritualistic conformity, irrespective of such rationalizations. In this sense, ritual has proceeded farthest when such rationalizations are not even called forth.

5. In this connection, one may see the relevance of Elton Mayo's paraphrase of the title of Tawney's well-known book. "Actually the problem *is not that of the sickness of an acquisitive society; it is that of the acquisitiveness of a sick society." Human Problems of an Industrial Civilization,* 153, New York, 1933. Mayo deals with the process through which wealth comes to be a symbol of social achievement. He sees this as arising from a state of anomie. We are

considering the unintegrated monetary-success goal as an element in producing anomie. A complete analysis would involve both phases of this system of interdependent variables.

6. It is unlikely that interiorized norms are completely eliminated. Whatever residuum persists will induce personality tensions and conflict. The process involves a certain degree of ambivalence. A manifest rejection of the institutional norms is coupled with some latent retention of their emotional correlates. "Guilt feelings," "sense of sin," "pangs of conscience" are obvious manifestations of this unrelieved tension; symbolic adherence to the nominally repudiated values or rationalizations constitute a more subtle variety of tensional release.

7. "Many," and not all, unintegrated groups, for the reason already mentioned. In groups where the primary emphasis shifts to institutional means, i.e., when the range of alternatives is very limited, the outcome is a type of ritualism rather than anomie.

8. Money has several peculiarities which render it particularly apt to become a symbol of prestige divorced from institutional controls. As Simmel emphasized, money is highly abstract and impersonal. However acquired, through fraud or institutionally, it can be used to purchase the same goods and services. The anonymity of metropolitan culture, in conjunction with this peculiarity of money, permits wealth, the sources of which may be unknown to the community in which the plutocrat lives, to serve as a symbol of status.

9. The emphasis upon wealth as a success-symbol is possibly reflected in the use of the term "fortune" to refer to a stock of accumulated wealth. This meaning becomes common in the late sixteenth century (Spenser and Shakespeare). A similar usage of the Latin *fortuna* comes into prominence during the first century B.C. Both these periods were marked by the rise to prestige and power of the "bourgeoisie."

10. See Kingsley Davis, "Mental Hygiene and the Class Structure," *Psychiatry,* 1928, 1:esp. 62–63; Talcott Parsons, *The Structure of Social Action,* 59–60, New York, 1937.

11. This is a level intermediate between the two planes distinguished by Edward Sapir; namely, culture patterns and personal habit systems. See his "Contribution of Psychiatry to an Understanding of Behavior in Society," *Amer. J. Sociol.,* 1937, 42:862–870.

12. This fifth alternative is on a plane clearly different from that of the others. It represents a *transitional* response which seeks to *institutionalize* new procedures oriented toward revamped cultural goals shared by the members of the society. It thus involves efforts to *change* the existing structure rather than to perform accommodative actions *within* this structure, and introduces additional problems with which we are not at the moment concerned.

13. Obviously, this is an elliptical statement. These individuals may maintain some orientation to the values of their particular differentiated groupings within the larger society or, in part, of the conventional society itself. Insofar as they do so, their conduct cannot be classified in the "passive rejection" category (IV). Nels Anderson's description of the behavior and attitudes of the bum, for example, can readily be recast in terms of our analytical scheme. See *The Hobo,* 93–98, *et passim,* Chicago, 1923.

14. Joseph D. Lohman, "The Participant Observer in Community Studies," *Amer. Sociol. Rev.,* 1937, 2:890–898.

15. The shifting historical role of this ideology is a profitable subject for exploration. The "office-boy-to-president" stereotype was once in approximate accord with the facts. Such vertical mobility was probably more common then than now, when the class structure is more rigid. (See the following note.) The ideology largely persists, however, possibly because it still performs a useful function for maintaining the *status quo.* For insofar as it is accepted by the "masses," it constitutes a useful sop for those who might rebel against the entire structure, were this consoling hope removed. This ideology now serves to lessen the probability of Adaptation V. In short, the role of this notion has changed from that of an approximately valid empirical theorem to that of an ideology, in Mannheim's sense.

16. There is a growing body of evidence, though none of it is clearly conclusive, to the effect that our class structure is becoming rigidified and that vertical mobility is declining. Taussig and Joslyn found that American business leaders are being *increasingly* recruited from the upper ranks of our society. The Lynds have also found a "diminished chance to get ahead" for the working classes in Middletown. Manifestly, these objective changes are not alone significant; the individual's subjective evaluation of the situation is a major determinant of the response. The extent to which this change in opportunity for social mobility has been recognized by the least advantaged classes is still conjectural, although the Lynds present some suggestive materials. The writer suggests that a case in point is the increasing frequency of cartoons which observe in a tragi-comic vein that "my old man says everybody can't be President. He says if ya can get three days a week steady on W.P.A. work ya ain't doin' so bad either." See

F. W. Taussig and C. S. Joslyn, *American Business Leaders*, New York, 1932; R. S. and H. M. Lynd, *Middletown in Transition*, *67* ff., chap. 12, New York, 1937.

17. The role of the Negro in this respect is of considerable theoretical interest. Certain elements of the Negro population have assimilated the dominant caste's values of pecuniary success and social advancement, but they also recognize that social ascent is at present restricted to their own caste almost exclusively. The pressures upon the Negro which would otherwise derive from the structural inconsistencies we have noticed are hence not identical with those upon lower class whites. See Kingsley Davis, *op. cit.*, 63; John Dollard, *Caste and Class in a Southern Town*, 66 ff., New Haven, 1936; Donald Young, *American Minority Peoples*, 581, New York, 1932.

18. The psychical coordinates of these processes have been partly established by the experimental evidence concerning *Anspruchsniveaus* and levels of performance. See Kurt Lewin, *Vorsatz, Willie and Bedurfnis*, Berlin, 1926; N. F. Hoppe, "Erfolg und Misserfolg," *Psychol. Forschung*, 1930, 14:1–63; Jerome D. Frank, "Individual Differences in Certain Aspects of the Level of Aspiration," *Amer. J. Psychol.*, 1935, 47:119–128.

19. Standard criminology texts summarize the data in this field. Our scheme of analysis may serve to resolve some of the theoretical contradictions which P. A. Sorokin indicates. For example, "not everywhere nor always do the poor show a greater proportion of crime . . . many poorer countries have had less crime than the richer countries. . . . The [economic] improvement in the second half of the nineteenth century, and the beginning of the twentieth, has not been followed by a decrease of crime." See his *Contemporary Sociological Theories*, 560–561, New York, 1928. The crucial point is, however, that poverty has varying social significance in different social structures, as we shall see. Hence, one would not expect a linear correlation between crime and poverty.

20. See M. W. Royse, *Aerial Bombardment and the International Regulation of War*, New York, 1928.

21. Since our primary concern is with the socio-cultural aspects of this problem, the psychological correlates have been only implicitly considered. See Karen Horney, *The Neurotic Personality of Our Time*, New York, 1937, for a psychological discussion of this process.

15 Homeboys, Dope Fiends, Legits, and New Jacks

John M. Hagedorn

This paper addresses issues that are controversial in both social science and public policy. First, what happens to gang members as they age? Do most gang members graduate from gangbanging to drug sales, as popular stereotypes might suggest? Is drug dealing so lucrative that adult gang members eschew work and become committed to the drug economy? Have changes in economic conditions produced underclass gangs so deviant and so detached from the labor market that the only effective policies are more police and more prisons?

Second, and related to these questions, are male adult gang members basically similar kinds of people, or are gangs made up of different types? Might some gang members be more conventional, and others less so? What are the implications of this "continuum of conventionality" within drug-dealing gangs for public policy? Data from a Milwaukee study on gangs and drug dealing shed some light on these issues.

Gang Members, Drugs, and Work

An underlying question is whether the drug economy provides sufficient incentives to keep gang members away from legal work. If drug sales offer highly profitable opportunities for all who are willing to take the risks, we might expect many adult gang members to be committed firmly to the drug economy. On the other hand, if drug dealing entails many risks and produces few success stories, gang members might be expected to have a more variable relationship to illicit drug sales. In that case we could look at variation within the gang to explain different behaviors.

The research literature contains few empirical studies on the pull of the drug economy away from licit work. On the more general level, Carl Taylor (1990:120) asserts that "when drug distribution becomes the employer, $3.65 or $8.65 can't compare with drug business income." Martin Sanchez

Jankowski (1991:101), in his study of gangs in three cities, found an "entrepreneurial spirit" to be the "driving force in the world view and behavior of gang members." This "entrepreneurial spirit" pushes gang members to make rational decisions to engage in drug sales. Jerome Skolnick (1990) and his students argue that gangs are centrally involved with profitable mid-level drug distribution, although these findings have been challenged by researchers (Klein and Maxson, 1993; Waldorf, 1993).

Others have found that gang involvement in drug sales varies substantially (see Cummings and Monte, 1993; Huff, 1990). Klein et al. (1991) remind us that not all gangs are involved with drug sales, a point that is often overlooked in the discussion of an invariant gang/drug nexus. Among those who sell drugs, actual income varies. Fagan (1991) points out that earnings from drug dealing in two Manhattan neighborhoods ranged from about $1,000 to nearly $5,000 per month. Although most drug sellers had little involvement with the formal economy, 25% of Fagan's dealers also worked in conventional jobs, and most reported both illegal *and* legal income for each month. This finding suggests that incentives from drug sales were not always sufficient to make dealing a full-time job.

Similarly, a Rand Corporation study (MacCoun and Reuter, 1992:485) found that the typical Washington, D.C. small dealer made about $300 per month and the typical big dealer $3,700, with an average of about $1,300. Sullivan (1989) found illicit economic activities in Brooklyn to be a youthful enterprise, quickly outgrown when "real" jobs offered themselves. The seriousness of criminal activity varied with the intactness of networks providing access to legitimate work. Most of Williams's (1989) New York "cocaine kids" matured out of the drug business as they became young adults and their drug-dealing clique broke up. Padilla's (1992:162) "Diamonds" became "disillusioned" with the empty promises of street-level dealing and aspired to legitimate jobs.

These few studies suggest substantial variation in the degree and duration of gang involvement in drug dealing. The drug economy is not an unquestionably profitable opportunity for gang members; rather, its promise appears to be more ambiguous. If that conclusion is valid, research must examine both the actual amounts of money earned by adult gang drug dealers *and* variation within the gang to understand gang involvement in drug dealing. We have a few studies on how much money gang members make from selling drugs, but hardly any contemporary data on different types of gang members.

Variation Within the Gang

Some research has portrayed gang members as relatively invariant. Walter Miller (1969) viewed gang delinquents as representative of a lower-class cultural milieu; his six "focal concerns" are persistent and distinctive features of the entire American "lower class." Similarly, Jankowski (1991:26–28) said that male gang members were one-dimensional "tough nuts," defiant individuals with a rational "social Darwinist worldview" who displayed defiant individualism "more generally" than other people in low-income communities.

Other research, however, has suggested that gang members vary, particularly on their orientation toward conventionality. Whyte (1943) classified his Cornerville street corner men as either "college boys" or "corner boys," depending on their aspirations. Cloward and Ohlin (1960:95), applying Merton's (1957) earlier typology, categorized lower-class youths in four cells of a matrix, depending on their aspirations and "criteria for success." Many of their delinquents repudiated the legitimacy of conventional society and resorted to innovative solutions to attain success goals. Cloward and Ohlin took issue with Cohen (1955) and Matza (1964), whose delinquents were internally conflicted but, as a group, imputed legitimacy to the norms of the larger society.

Some more recent researchers also have found variation in conventionality within gangs. Klein (1971), echoing Thrasher (1927), differentiated between "core" and "fringe" members, a distinction that policy makers often use today as meaning more or less deviant. In the same view, Taylor (1990:8–9) saw gang members as "corporates," "scavengers," "emulators," "auxiliaries," or "adjuncts," mainly on the basis of their distance from gang membership. Fagan (1990:206), like Matza and Cohen, found that "conventional values may coexist with deviant behaviors for gang delinquents and other inner city youth." MacLeod (1987:124) observed surprising variation between ethnic groups. The white "hallway hangers" believed "stagnation at the bottom of the occupational structure to be almost inevitable" and were rebellious delinquents, whereas the African American "brothers" reacted to similar conditions by aspiring to middle-class status.

Joan Moore is one of the few researchers who have looked carefully at differentiation within gangs. In her early work (1978), she discovered both square and deviant career models among East Los Angeles gang members. In an impressive restudy (1991) she found that most adult gang members were working conventional jobs, but those who had been active in the gang in recent years had more difficulty finding employment as job networks collapsed. Many veteran gang members had been addicted to heroin for years, but by the 1990s few were dealing drugs to support themselves. Moore found that both male and female Chicano gang members could be categorized as "tecatos," "cholos," or "squares," a typology similar to those suggested for the nongang poor by Anderson (1978, 1990) and Hannerz (1969).

If gang members in fact vary on orientation to conventionality, and if the drug economy itself offers only an ambiguous lure, jobs and other programs that strengthen "social capital" (Coleman, 1988) might be effective means of integrating many adult gang members into the community (see Sampson and Laub, 1993). On the other hand, if adult gang members are look-alike criminals who are dazzled by the prospect of vast profits in the drug trade, jobs and social programs would have little effect, and our present incarceration strategy may be appropriate.

This paper provides quantitative and qualitative data on the conventional orientations of young adult gang members in Milwaukee. First we report on the licit work and illicit drug-dealing patterns of adult gang members. Then we offer a typology, drawn from Milwaukee data, that demonstrates a "continuum of conventionality" between core members of drug-dealing gangs. In conclusion, we discuss research and public policy consequences of the study.

Research Methods and Sources of Data

The interpretations presented here draw on observation and extensive fieldwork conducted over a number of years, specifically from two funded interview studies, in 1987 and in 1992. During the early 1980s I directed the first gang diversion program in the city and became acquainted with many leaders and other founders of Milwaukee's gangs. I have maintained a privileged relationship with many of these individuals.

In the 1987 study, we interviewed 47 members of 19 Milwaukee male and female gangs (Hagedorn, 1988). These "founders" were the core gang members who were present when their gangs took names. Founders are likely to be representative of hard-core gang members, not of peripheral members of "wannabes." As time has passed, the gang founders' exploits have been passed down, and younger Milwaukee gang members have looked up to them as street "role models." Our research design does not enable us to conclude how fully our sample represents subsequent groups of adult gang members.

As part of our current study, we conducted lengthy audiotaped interviews with 101 founding members of 18 gangs in the city; 90 were male and 11 female. Sixty percent were African American, 37% Latino, and 3% white. Their median age was 26 years, with 75% between 23 and 30. Twenty-three respondents also had been interviewed in the 1987 study; 78 were interviewed here for the first time. Members from two gangs interviewed in the earlier study could not be located. Each respondent was paid $50.

The interview picks up the lives of the founding members since 1987, when we conducted our original study, and asks them to recount their careers in the drug business, to discuss their pursuit of conventional employment, and to reflect on their personal lives. The respondents also were asked to describe the current status of their fellow gang members. In the 1987 study, we collected rosters of all members of each gang whose founders we interviewed. In the current study, we asked each respondent to double check the roster of his or her gang to make sure it was accurate. In both studies, we asked respondents to tell us whether the other members were still alive, had graduated from high school, were currently locked up, or were working. In the 1992 study, we also asked whether each of the founding members was selling or using dope (in our data "dope" means cocaine), had some other hustle, or was on the run, among other questions.

To understand more clearly the variation between and within the gangs, we interviewed nearly the entire rosters of three gangs and about half (64 of 152) of the original founding members from eight male gangs in three different types of neighborhoods. In each of these gangs, we interviewed some who still were involved with both the gang and the dope game and some who no longer were involved. This paper reports on data on all of the 90 males we interviewed and on their accounts of the present circumstances of 236 founders of 14 male gangs.

The interviews in this most recent study were conducted in late 1992 and early 1993.[1] As in the original study, the research follows an inductive and collaborative model (see Moore, 1978), in which gang members cooperate with the academic staff to focus the research design, construct interview schedules, conduct interviews, and interpret the findings.

Findings: Drug Dealing and Work

As expected, gang members appear to be working more today than five years ago, but participation in the formal labor market remains quite low (see Table 1).[2]

These low levels of labor market participation apply to more than gang members. A recent Milwaukee study revealed that in 1990, 51% of jobs held by *all* African American males age 20 to 24, slightly younger than our study population, lasted less than six weeks. The average *annual* income in retail trade, where most subjects held jobs, was $2,023; for jobs in service, $1,697; in education, $3,084 (Rose et al., 1992). African American young adults as a whole (and probably nongang Latinos) clearly were not working regularly and were not earning a living wage.

Table 1 1992 Status of Male Gang Founders, 236 Founding Members of 14 Male Groups

Predominant Activity/Status	African American	White	Latino	Total
Work: Part-Time or Full-Time	22.2%	68.8%	27.6%	30.5%
Hustling: Nearly All Selling Cocaine	50.4	15.4	56.3	47.9
Deceased	7.7	6.3	5.7	6.8
Whereabouts Unknown	19.7	9.4	10.3	14.8
Total $N = 100\%$	$N = 117$	$N = 32$	$N = 87$	$N = 236$

NOTE: Column percentages may not equal 100% because of rounding.

Selling cocaine seems to have filled the employment void. In 1987 only a few gang members dealt drugs, mainly marijuana. Within African American gangs, at least, cocaine dealing was not prevalent. By 1992, however, cocaine had become a major factor in Milwaukee's informal economy, evolving into widespread curbside sales and numerous drug houses (see Hamid, 1992). Of the 236 fellow gang founders, 72% reportedly had sold cocaine at some time in the last five years.[3]

That involvement has not been steady, however. We collected detailed data on the length of involvement in the drug economy and the amount of money made by those we interviewed. We asked our respondents to indicate how they had supported themselves in each month of the past three years, and then asked how much money they made in both legal and illegal employment. For most respondents, selling cocaine was an on-again, off-again proposition. About half (35) of those who had sold cocaine sold in no more than 12 months out of the past 36; only 12% (9) sold in more than 24 of the past 36 months. Latinos sold for slightly longer periods than African Americans, 17.7 months to 13.1 months ($p = .07$).

When gang members did sell dope, they made widely varying amounts of money. About one-third of those who sold reported that they made no more than they would have earned if they worked for minimum wage. Another one-third made the equivalent of $13 to $25 an hour. Only three of the 73 sellers ever made "crazy money," or more than $10,000 per month, at any time during their drug-selling careers. Mean monthly income from drug sales was approximately $2,400, or about $15 per hour for full-time work. By contrast, mean monthly income for legal work was only $677; Latinos made more than African Americans ($797 per month to $604 per month, $p = .08$; table not shown). The *maximum* amount of money earned monthly by any gang member from legal income was $2,400, the *mean* for gang drug sales (see Table 2).[4]

Qualitative data from our interviews support the view that for some respondents, the dope game indeed lives up to its stereotype. One dealer credibly reported income from his three drug houses at about $50,000 per month for several months in 1989. Another told how he felt about making so much money:

Q: Did you ever make crazy money?
R#220: Yeah . . . one time my hands had turned green from all that money, I couldn't wash it off, man, I loved it. Oh man, look at this . . . just holding all that money in my hand turned my hands green from just counting all that money. Sometimes I'd sit back and just count it maybe three, four times, for the hell of it.

Even for big dealers, however, that money didn't last. Some "players" were "rolling" for several years, but most took a fall within a year or so. As with Padilla's Diamonds, disappointments with the drug trade seemed to exceed its promise for most gang members. Prison and jail time frequently

Table 2 Mean Monthly Income from Drug Dealing: 1989–1991, 87 African American and Latino Respondents

Average Monthly Income from Drug Sales	African American	Latino[a]	Total
Never sold	15.8%	23.3%	18.4%
Less Than $1,000 Monthly (Equivalent to Less Than $6/Hour)	28.1	30.0	28.7
Between $1,000 and $2,000 Monthly (Equivalent to $7–$12/Hour)	28.1	6.7	20.7
Between $2,000 and $4,000 Monthly (Equivalent to $13–$25/Hour)	25.3	33.3	28.7
More Than $10,000 Monthly	1.8	6.7	3.4
Total N = 100%	N = 57	N = 30	N = 87

[a] Three whites were excluded from the analysis. One white founder never sold, and the other two made less than $2,000 monthly.
NOTE: Column percentages may not equal 100% because of rounding.

interrupted their lives. More than three-quarters of all gang founders on our rosters had spent some time in jail in the past five years, as had two-thirds of our respondents. Even so, our respondents had worked a mean of 14.5 months out of the last 36 in legitimate jobs, had worked 14.5 months selling dope, and had spent the remaining seven months in jail. Twenty-five percent of our respondents had worked legitimate jobs at least 24 of the past 36 months.

Yet an anomaly confronted us as we analyzed our data on work. As might be expected, nine out of 10 of those who were not working at the time of our interview had sold dope in the past three years. We also found, however, that three-quarters of those who *were* working in 1992 had sold dope as well within the previous five years (see Table 3).

Table 3 1992 Work Status by Involvement in Cocaine Sales, 220 Surviving Founding Members of 14 Male Gangs

Sold Dope Last Five Years?	Working Now	Not Working Now[a]	Work Status Unknown	Totals
Have Sold Dope	75.0%	91.2%	40.0%	77.7%
Have Not Sold Dope	16.7	5.3	2.9	8.6
Unknown	8.3	3.5	57.1	13.6
Total N = 100%	N = 72	N = 113	N = 35	N = 220

[a] Includes selling cocaine, being "on the run," being locked up, and being involved in other street hustles.

These findings lend themselves to alternative explanations. It may be that three-quarters of those who were working had sold cocaine in the past, but had stopped and were getting their lives together. A second interpretation is that full-time employment is nothing more than an income supplement or "front" for continuation in the drug game. Some gang founders indeed fit into one or the other of these categories.

A third interpretation evolved as we received reports from our staff and respondents about the current status of their fellow gang members. A few days after an interview with "Roger," one of our staff members would report that "Roger" was no longer working for a temporary agency, as he had reported, but was "back in the dope game." The next week "Roger" might call us from jail. A week or so later, we would learn that he was out on bail, his "lady" had put pressure on him, and he was now working full-time in construction with his brother-in-law. Our offices were flooded with similar reports about dozens of people on our rosters. Working and selling drugs were both part of the difficult, topsy-turvy lives led by our respondents. Elliot Liebow's (1967:219) colorful description of the confused lives on Tally's Corner also fits our data: "Traffic is heavy in all directions."

These vicissitudes became too complicated for us to track, so we "froze" the status of founders on our rosters at the time of the last and most reliable interview. Some of our founders seemed to be committed to the dope business and a few had "gone legit," but most of those we were trying to track appeared to be on an economic merry-go-round, with continual movement in and out of the secondary labor market. Although their average income from drug sales far surpassed their income from legal employment, most Milwaukee male gang members apparently kept trying to find licit work.

To help explain this movement in and out of the formal labor market, we created a typology of adult gang members, using constant comparisons (Strauss, 1987). This categorization has some similarities to earlier typologies, but it differs in that it intends to account for the different orientations of gang members in an era of decreased legitimate economic opportunities and increased drug-related, illicit opportunities.

A Typology of Male Adult Gang Members

We developed four ideal types on a continuum of conventional behaviors and values: (1) those few who had gone *legit*, or had matured out of the gang; (2) *homeboys*, a majority of both African American and Latino adult gang members, who alternately worked conventional jobs and took various roles in drug sales; (3) *dope fiends*, who were addicted to cocaine and participated in the dope business as a way to maintain access to the drug; and (4) *new jacks*, who regarded the dope game as a career.

Some gang members, we found, moved over time between categories, some had characteristics of more than one category, and others straddled the boundaries (see Hannerz, 1969:57). Thus a few homeboys were in the process of becoming legit, many moved into and out of cocaine addiction, and others gave up and adopted a new jack orientation. Some new jacks returned to conventional life; others received long prison terms or became addicted to dope. Our categories are not discrete, but our typology seemed to fit the population of gang members we were researching. Our "member checks" (Lincoln and Guba, 1985:314–316) of the constructs with gang members validated these categories for male gang members.

Legits

Legits were those young men who had walked away from the gang. They were working or may have gone on to school. Legits had not been involved in the dope game at all, or not for at least five years. They did not use cocaine heavily, though some may have done so in the past. Some had moved out of the old neighborhood; others, like our project staff, stayed to help out or "give back" to the community. These are prime examples of Whyte's "college boys" or Cloward and Ohlin's Type I, oriented to economic gain and class mobility. The following quote is an example of a young African American man who "went legit" and is now working and going to college.

> Q: Looking back over the past five years, what major changes took place in your life—things that happened that really made things different for you?
>
> R#105: I had got into a relationship with my girl, that's one thing. I just knew I couldn't be out on the streets trying to hustle all the time. That's what changed me, I just got a sense of responsibility.

Today's underclass gangs appear to be fundamentally different from those in Thrasher's or Cloward and Ohlin's time, when most gang members "matured out" of the gang. Of the 236 Milwaukee male founders, only 12 (5.1%) could be categorized as having matured out: that is, they were working full time *and* had not sold cocaine in the past five years. When these data are disaggregated by race, the reality of the situation becomes even clearer. We could verify only two of 117 African Americans and one of 87 Latino male gang founders who were currently working and had not sold dope in the past five years. One-third of the white members fell into this category.[5]

Few African American and Latino gang founders, however, were resigned to a life of crime, jail, and violence. After a period of rebellion and living the fast life, the majority of gang founders, or "homeboys," wanted to settle down and go legit, but the path proved to be very difficult.

Homeboys

"Homeboys" were the majority of all adult gang members. They were not firmly committed to the drug economy, especially after the early thrill of fast money and "easy women" wore off. They had reached an age, the mid-twenties, when criminal offenses normally decline (Gottfredson and Hirschi, 1990). Most of these men were unskilled, lacked education, and had had largely negative experiences in the secondary labor market. Some homeboys were committed more strongly to the streets, others to a more conventional life. Most had used cocaine, some heavily at times, but their use was largely in conjunction with selling from a house or corner with their gang "homies." Most homeboys either were married or had a "steady" lady. They also had strong feelings of loyalty to their fellow gang members.

Here, two different homeboys explain how they had changed, and how hard that change was:

Q: Looking back over the past five years, what major changes took place in your life—things that happened that really made things different for you?

R#211: The things that we went through wasn't worth it, and I had a family, you know, and kids, and I had to think about them first, and the thing with the drug game was, that money was quick, easy, and fast, and it went like that, the more money you make the more popular you was. You know, as I see it now it wasn't worth it because the time that I done in penitentiaries I lost my sanity. To me it feels like I lost a part of my kids, because, you know, I know they still care, and they know I'm daddy, but I just lost out. Somebody else won and I lost.

Q: Is she with somebody else now?

R#211: Yeah. She hung in there about four or five months after I went to jail.

Q: It must have been tough for her to be alone with all those kids.

R#211: Yeah.

Q: What kind of person are you?

R#217: Mad. I'm a mad young man. I'm a poor young man. I'm a good person to my kids and stuff, and given the opportunity to have something nice and stop working for this petty-ass money I would try to change a lot of things. . . .
. . . I feel I'm the type of person that given the opportunity to try to have something legit, I will take it, but I'm not going to go by the slow way, taking no four, five years working at no chicken job and trying to get up to a manager just to start making six, seven dollars. And then get fired when I come in high or drunk or something. Or miss a day or something because I got high smoking weed, drinking beer, and the next day come in and get fired; then I'm back in where I started from. So I'm just a cool person, and if I'm given the opportunity and if I can get a job making nine, ten dollars an hour, I'd let everything go; I'd just sit back and work my job and go home. That kind of money I can live with. But I'm not going to settle for no three, four dollars an hour, know what I'm saying?

Homeboys present a more confused theoretical picture than legits. Cloward and Ohlin's Type III delinquents were rebels, who had a "sense of injustice" or felt "unjust deprivation" at a failed system (1960:117). Their gang delinquency is a collective solution to the failure of institutional arrangements. They reject traditional societal norms; other, success-oriented illegitimate norms replace conventionality.

Others have questioned whether gang members' basic outlook actually rejects conventionality. Matza (1964) viewed delinquents' rationalizations of their conduct as evidence of techniques meant to "neutralize" deeply held conventional beliefs. Cohen (1955:129–137) regarded delinquency as a nonutilitarian "reaction formation" to middle-class standards, though middle-class morality lingers, repressed and unacknowledged. What appears to be gang "pathological" behavior, Cohen points out, is the result of the delinquent's striving to attain core values of "the American way of life." Short and Strodtbeck (1965), testing various gang theories, found that white and African American gang members, and lower- and middle-class youths, had similar conventional values.

Our homeboys are older versions of Cohen's and Matza's delinquents, and are even more similar to Short and Strodtbeck's study subjects. Milwaukee homeboys shared three basic characteristics: (1) They worked regularly at legitimate jobs, although they ventured into the drug economy when they believed it was necessary for survival. (2) They had very conventional aspirations; their core values centered on finding a secure place in the American way of life. (3) They had some surprisingly conventional ethical beliefs about the immorality of drug dealing. To a man, they justified their own involvement in drug sales by very Matza-like techniques of "neutralization."

Homeboys are defined by their in-and-out involvement in the legal and illegal economies. Recall that about half of our male respondents had sold drugs no more than 12 of the past 36 months. More than one-third never served any time in jail. Nearly 60% had worked legitimate jobs at least 12 months of the last 36, with a mean of 14.5 months. Homeboys' work patterns thus differed both from those of legits, who worked solely legal jobs, and new jacks who considered dope dealing a career.

To which goal did homeboys aspire, being big-time dope dealers or holding a legitimate job? Rather than having any expectations of staying in the dope game, homeboys aspired to settling down, getting married, and living at least a watered-down version of the American dream. Like Padilla's (1992:157) Diamonds, they strongly desired to "go legit." Although they may have enjoyed the fast life for a while, it soon went stale. Listen to this homeboy, the one who lost his lady when he went to jail:

Q: Five years from now, what would you want to be doing?
R#211: Five years from now? I want to have a steady job, I want to have been working that job for about five years, and just with a family somewhere.
Q: Do you think that's gonna come true?

R#211: Yeah, that's basically what I'm working on. I mean, this bullshit is over now, I'm twenty-five, I've played games long enough, it don't benefit nobody. If you fuck yourself away, all you gonna be is fucked, I see it now.

Others had more hopeful or wilder dreams, but a more sobering outlook on the future. The other homebody, who said he wouldn't settle for three or four dollars an hour, speaks as follows:

Q: Five years from now, what would you want to be doing?
R#217: Owning my own business. And rich. A billionaire.
Q: What do you realistically expect you'll be doing in five years?
R#217: Probably working at McDonald's. That's the truth.

Homeboys' aspirations were divided between finding a steady full-time job and setting up their own business. Their striving pertained less to being for or against "middle-class status" than to finding a practical, legitimate occupation that could support them (see Short and Strodtbeck, 1965). Many homeboys believed that using skills learned in selling drugs to set up a small business would give them a better chance at a decent life than trying to succeed as an employee.

Most important, homeboys "grew up" and were taking a realistic look at their life chances. This homeboy spoke for most:

Q: Looking back over the past five years, what major changes have taken place in your life—things that made a difference about where you are now?
R#220: I don't know, maybe maturity. . . . Just seeing life in a different perspective . . . realizing that from sixteen to twenty-three, man, just shot past. And just realizing that it did, shucks, you just realizing how quick it zoomed past me. And it really just passed me up without really having any enjoyment of a teenager. And hell, before I know it I'm going to hit thirty or forty, and I ain't going to have nothing to stand on. I don't want that shit. Because I see a lot of brothers out here now, that's forty-three, forty-four and ain't got shit. They's still standing out on the corner trying to make a hustle. Doing this, no family, no stable home and nothing. I don't want that shit. . . . I don't give a fuck about getting rich or nothing, but I want a comfortable life, a decent woman, a family to come home to. I mean, everybody needs somebody to care for. This ain't where it's at.

Finally, homeboys were characterized by their ethical views about selling dope. As a group, they believed dope selling was "unmoral"—wrong, but necessary for survival. Homeboys' values were conventional, but in keeping with Matza's findings, they justified their conduct by neutralizing their violation of norms. Homeboys believed that economic necessity was the overriding reason why they could not live up to their values (see Liebow, 1967:214). They were the epitome of ambivalence, ardently believing that dope selling was both wrong and absolutely necessary. One longtime dealer expressed this contradiction:

Q: Do you consider it wrong or immoral to sell dope?
R#129:   Um-hum, very wrong.
Q: Why?
R#129:   Why, because it's killing people.
Q: Well how come you do it?
R#129:   It's also a money maker.
Q: Well how do you balance those things out? I mean, here you're doing something that you think is wrong, making money. How does that make you feel when you're doing it, or don't you think about it when you're doing it?
R#129:   Once you get a (dollar) bill, once you look at, I say this a lot, once you look at those dead white men [*presidents' pictures on currency*], you care about nothing else, you don't care about nothing else. Once you see those famous dead white men. That's it.
Q: Do you ever feel bad about selling drugs, doing something that was wrong?
R#129:   How do I feel? Well a lady will come in and sell all the food stamps, all of them. When they're sold, what are the kids gonna eat? They can't eat the dope cause she's gonna go smoke that up, or do whatever with it. And then you feel like "wrong." But then, in the back of your mind, man, you just got a hundred dollars worth of food stamps for thirty dollars worth of dope, and you can sell them at the store for seven dollars on ten, so you got seventy coming. So you get seventy dollars for thirty dollars. It is not wrong to do this. It is not wrong to do this!

Homeboys also refused to sell to pregnant women or to juveniles. Contrary to Jankowski's (1991:102) assertion that in gangs "there is no ethical code that regulates business ventures," Milwaukee homeboys had some strong moral feelings about how they carried out their business:

R#109:   I won't sell to no little kids. And, ah, if he gonna get it, he gonna get it from someone else besides me. I won't sell to no pregnant woman. If she gonna kill her baby, I want to sleep not knowing that I had anything to do with it. Ah, for anybody else, hey, it's their life, you choose your life how you want.
Q: But how come—I want to challenge you. You know if kids are coming or a pregnant woman's coming, you know they're going to get it somewhere else, right? Someone else will make their money on it; why not you?
R#109:   'Cause the difference is I'll be able to sleep without a guilty conscience.

Homeboys were young adults living on the edge. On the one hand, like most Americans, they had relatively conservative views on social issues and wanted to settle down with a job, a wife, and children. On the other hand, they were afraid they would never succeed, and that long stays in prison would close doors and lock them out of a conventional life. They did not want to continue to live on the streets, but they feared that hustling might be the only way to survive.[6]

Dope Fiends

Dope fiends are gang members who are addicted to cocaine. Thirty-eight percent of all African American founders were using cocaine at the time of our interview, as were 55% of Latinos and 53% of whites. African Americans used cocaine at lower rates than white gang members, but went to jail twice as often. The main focus in a dope fiend's life is getting the drug. Asked what they regretted most about their life, dope fiends invariably said "drug use," whereas most homeboys said "dropping out of school."

Most Milwaukee gang dope fiends, or daily users of cocaine, smoked it as "rocks." More casual users, or reformed dope fiends, if they used cocaine at all, snorted it or sprinkled it on marijuana (called a "primo") to enhance the high. Injection was rare among African Americans but more common among Latinos. About one-quarter of those we interviewed, however, abstained totally from use of cocaine. A majority of the gang members on our rosters had used cocaine since its use escalated in Milwaukee in the late 1980s.

Of 110 gang founders who were reported to be currently using cocaine, 37% were reported to be using "heavily" (every day, in our data), 44% "moderately" (several times per week), and 19% "lightly" (sporadically). More than 70% of all founders on our rosters who were not locked up were currently using cocaine to some extent. More than one-third of our male respondents considered themselves, at some time in their lives, to be "heavy" cocaine users.

More than one-quarter of our respondents had used cocaine for seven years or more, roughly the total amount of time cocaine has dominated the illegal drug market in Milwaukee. Latinos had used cocaine slightly longer than African Americans, for a mean of 75 months compared with 65. Cocaine use followed a steady pattern in our respondents' lives; most homeboys had used cocaine as part of their day-to-day life, especially while in the dope business.

Dope fiends were quite unlike Cloward and Ohlin's "double failures," gang members who used drugs as part of a "retreatist subculture." Milwaukee dope fiends participated regularly in conventional labor markets. Of the 110 founders who were reported as currently using cocaine, slightly more were working legitimate jobs than were not working. Most dope fiends worked at some time in their homies' dope houses or were fronted an ounce or an "eightball" (3.5 grams) of cocaine to sell. Unlike Anderson's "wineheads," gang dope fiends were not predominantly "has-beens" and did not "lack the ability and motivation to hustle" (Anderson, 1978:96–97). Milwaukee cocaine users, like heroin users (Johnson et al., 1985; Moore, 1978; Preble and Casey, 1969), played an active role in the drug-selling business.

Rather than spending their income from drug dealing on family, clothes, or women, dope fiends smoked up their profits. Eventually many stole dope belonging to the boss or "dopeman" and got into trouble. At times their dope use made them so erratic that they were no longer trusted and were forced to leave the neighborhood. Often, however, the gang members who were selling took them back and fronted them cocaine to sell to put them back on their feet. Many had experienced problems in violating the cardinal rule, "Don't get high on your own supply," as in this typical story:

> R#131: . . . if you ain't the type that's a user, yeah, you'll make fabulous money but if you was the type that sells it and uses it and do it at the same time, you know, you get restless. Sometimes you get used to taking your own drugs. . . . I'll just use the profits and just do it . . . and then the next day if I get something again, I'd just take the money to pay up and keep the profits. . . . You sell a couple of hundred and you do a hundred. That's how I was doing it.

Cocaine use was a regular part of the lives of most Milwaukee gang members engaged in the drug economy. More than half of our respondents had never attended a treatment program; more than half of those who had been in treatment went through court-ordered programs. Few of our respondents stopped use by going to a treatment program. Even heavy cocaine use was an "on-again, off-again" situation in which most gang members alternately quit by themselves and started use again (Waldorf et al., 1991).

Alcohol use among dope fiends and homeboys (particularly 40-ounce bottles of Olde English 800 ale) appears to be even more of a problem than cocaine use. Like homeboys, however, most dope fiends aspired to have a family, to hold a steady job, and to find some peace. The wild life of the dope game had played itself out; the main problem was how to quit using.[7]

New Jacks

Whereas homeboys had a tentative relationship with conventional labor markets and held some strong moral beliefs, new jacks had chosen the dope game as a career. They were often loners, strong individualists like Jankowski's (1991) gang members, who cared little about group norms. Frequently they posed as the embodiment of media stereotypes. About one-quarter of our interview respondents could be described as new jacks: they had done nothing in the last 36 months except hustle or spend time in jail.

In some ways, new jacks mirror the criminal subculture described by Cloward and Ohlin. If a criminal subculture is to develop, Cloward and Ohlin argued, opportunities to learn a criminal career must be present, and close ties to conventional markets or customers must exist. This situation distinguishes the criminal from the violent and the retreatist subcultures. The emergence of the cocaine economy and a large market for illegal drugs provided precisely such an opportunity structure for this generation of gang members. New jacks are those who took advantage of the opportunities, and who, at least for the present, have committed themselves to a career in the dope game.

> Q: Do you consider it wrong or immoral to sell dope?
> R#203: I think it's right because can't no motherfucker live your life but you.
> Q: Why?
> R#203: Why? I'll put it this way . . . I love selling dope. I know there's other niggers out here love the money just like I do. And ain't no motherfucker gonna stop a nigger from selling dope . . . I'd sell to my own mother if she had the money.

New jacks, like other gang cocaine dealers, lived up to media stereotypes of the "drug dealer" role and often were emulated by impressionable youths. Some new jacks were homeboys from Milwaukee's original neighborhood gangs, who had given up their conventional dreams; others were members of gangs that were formed solely for drug dealing (see Klein and Maxson, 1993). A founder of one new jack gang described the scene as his gang set up shop in Milwaukee. Note the strong mimicking of media stereotypes:

> R#126: . . . it was crime and drug problems before we even came into the scene. It was just controlled by somebody else. We just came on with a whole new attitude, outlook, at the whole situation. It's like, have you ever seen the movie *New Jack City,* about the kid in New York? You see, they was already there. We just came out with a better idea, you know what I'm saying?

New jacks rejected the homeboys' moral outlook. Many were raised by families with long traditions of hustling or a generation of gang affiliations, and had few hopes of a conventional future. They are the voice of the desperate ghetto dweller, those who live in Carl Taylor's (1990:36) "third culture" made up of "underclass and urban gang members who exhibit signs of moral erosion and anarchy" or propagators of Bourgois's (1990:631) "culture of terror." New jacks fit the media stereotype of all gang members, even though they represent fewer than 25% of Milwaukee's adult gang members.

Discussion: Gangs, the Underclass, and Public Policy

Our study was conducted in one aging postindustrial city, with a population of 600,000. How much can be generalized from our findings can be determined only by researchers in other cities, looking at our categories and determining whether they are useful. Cloward and Ohlin's opportunity theory is a workable general theoretical framework, but more case studies are needed in order to recast their theory to reflect three decades of economic and social changes. We present our typology to encourage others to observe variation within and between gangs, and to assist in the creation of new taxonomies and new theory.

Our paper raises several empirical questions for researchers: Are the behavior patterns of the founding gang members in our sample representative of adult gang members in other cities? In larger cities, are most gang members now new jacks who have long given up the hope of a conventional life, or are most still homeboys? Are there "homeboy" gangs and "new jack" gangs, following the "street gang/drug gang" notion of Klein and Maxson (1993)? If so, what distinguishes one from the other? Does gang members' orientation to conventionality vary by ethnicity or by region? How does it change over time? Can this typology help account for variation in rates of violence between gang members? Can female gang members be typed in the same way as males?

Our data also support the life course perspective of Sampson and Laub (1993:255), who ask whether present criminal justice policies "are producing unintended criminogenic effects." Milwaukee gang members are like the persistent, serious offenders in the Gluecks' data (Glueck and Glueck, 1950). The key to their future lies in building social capital that comes from steady employment and a supportive relationship, without the constant threat of incarceration (Sampson and Laub, 1993:162–168). Homeboys largely had a wife or a steady lady, were unhappily enduring "the silent, subtle humiliations" of the secondary labor market (Bourgois, 1990:629), and lived in dread of prison. Incarceration for drug charges undercut their efforts to find steady work and led them almost inevitably back to the drug economy.

Long and mandatory prison terms for use and intent to sell cocaine lump those who are committed to the drug economy with those who are using or are selling in order to survive. Our prisons are filled disproportionately with minority drug offenders (Blumstein, 1993) like our homeboys, who in essence are being punished for the "crime" of not accepting poverty or of being addicted to cocaine. Our data suggest that jobs, more accessible drug treatment, alternative sentences, or even decriminalization of nonviolent drug offenses would be better approaches than the iron fist of the war on drugs (see Hagedorn, 1991; Reinarman and Levine, 1990; Spergel and Curry, 1990).

Finally, our typology raises ethical questions for researchers. Wilson (1987:8) called the underclass "collectively different" from the poor of the past, and many studies focus on underclass deviance. Our study found that some underclass gang members had embraced the drug economy and had forsaken conventionality, but we also found that the *majority* of adult gang members are still struggling to hold onto a conventional orientation to life.

Hannerz (1969:36) commented more than two decades ago that dichotomizing community residents into "respectables" and "disrespectables" "seems often to emerge from social science writing about poor black people or the lower classes in general." Social science that emphasizes differences within poor communities, without noting commonalities, is one-sided and often distorts and demonizes underclass life.

Our data emphasize that there is no Great Wall separating the underclass from the rest of the central-city poor and working class. Social research should not build one either. Researchers who describe violent and criminal gang actions without also addressing gang members' orientation to conventionality do a disservice to the public, to policy makers, and to social science.

Notes

1. This study was funded by NIDA Grant R01 DA 07218. The funding agency bears no responsibility for data or interpretations presented here.

2. Rosters of gangs in 1992 were refined and new gangs were added; thus it was difficult to make comparisons with 1987 rosters. In 1987, with $N = 225$, 20% of white male gang members, 10% of Latinos, and 27% of African Americans were working.

3. Selling cocaine is not only a gang-related phenomenon. Half of those who were reported as no longer involved with the gang also had sold cocaine within the last five years.

4. We asked respondents to report on the number of months they worked legitimate jobs, worked selling dope, and were in prison. We then asked them to tell us the average amount of money they made in those months working or selling dope. Hourly estimates are based on the monthly average divided by 160 hours. Most respondents reported that they worked selling dope "24/7," meaning full time.

5. About 15% of the founders whereabouts were not known by our informants, but "unknown" status was no guarantee that the missing member had gone legit. One founder of an African American gang was reported to us in a pretest as having "dropped from sight," but later we learned that he had been a victim of one of serial killer Jeffrey Dahmer's grisly murders. Others, with whom our respondents no longer have contact, may be heavy cocaine users who left the gang and the neighborhood because they were no longer trustworthy.

6. Homeboys varied as well. Some were entrepreneurs or players; typically they were the "dopemen" who started a "dopehouse" where other gang members could work. Others worked only sporadically in dopehouses as a supplement to legitimate work or during unemployment. Finally, some, often cocaine users, worked most of the time at the dopehouse and only sporadically at legitimate jobs. Although homeboys also varied over time in their aspirations to conventionality, as a group they believed that the lack of jobs and the prison time were testing their commitment to conventional values. We found no significant differences between Latino and African American homeboys.

7. It is too early to tell how many persons will succeed at freeing themselves from cocaine use. Ansley Hamid (1992) found that by the 1990s, most New York crack users were in their thirties and poor; their heavy drug involvement had ruined their chances for conventional careers.

References

Anderson, Elijah
    1978 A Place on the Corner. Chicago: University of Chicago Press.
    1990 Streetwise: Race, Class, and Change in an Urban Community. Chicago: University of Chicago Press.
Blumstein, Alfred
    1993 Making rationality relevant. Criminology 31:1–16.
Bourgois, Phillippe
    1990 In search of Horatio Alger: culture and ideology in the crack economy. Contemporary Drug Problems 16:619–649.
Cloward, Richard and Lloyd Ohlin
    1960 Delinquency and Opportunity. Glencoe, Ill.: Free Press.
Cohen, Albert
    1955 Delinquent Boys, Glencoe, Ill.: Free Press.

Coleman, James S.
1988 Social capital in the creation of human capital. American Journal of Sociology 94:S95–S120.
Cummings, Scott and Daniel J. Monte
1993 Gangs. Albany: State University of New York Press.
Fagan, Jeffrey
1990 Social processes of delinquency and drug use among urban gangs. In C. Ronald Huff (ed.), Gangs in America. Newbury Park: Sage.
1991 Drug selling and licit income in distressed neighborhoods: The economic lives of street-level drug users and dealers. In Adele V. Harrell and George E. Peterson (eds.), Drugs, Crime, and Social Isolation. Washington: Urban Institute Press.
Glueck, Sheldon and Eleanor Glueck
1950 Unraveling Juvenile Delinquency. New York: Commonwealth Fund.
Gottfredson, Michael and Travis Hirschi
1990 A General Theory of Crime. Stanford: Stanford University Press.
Hagedorn, John M.
1988 People and Folks: Gangs, Crime, and the Underclass in a Rustbelt City. Chicago: Lakeview.
1991 Gangs, neighborhoods, and public policy. Social Problems 38:529–542.
Hamid, Ansley
1992 The developmental cycle of a drug epidemic: the cocaine smoking epidemic of 1981–1991. Journal of Psychoactive Drugs 24:337–348.
Hannerz, Ulf
1969 Soulside: Inquiries into Ghetto Culture and Community. New York: Columbia University Press.
Huff, C. Ronald
1990 Gangs in America. Newbury Park: Sage.
Jankowski, Martin Sanchcz
1991 Islands in the Street: Gangs and American Urban Society. Berkeley: University of California Press.
Johnson, Bruce D., Terry Williams, Kojo Dei, and Harry Sanahria
1985 Taking Care of Business: The Economics of Crime by Heroin Abusers. Lexington, Mass.: Heath.
Klein, Malcolm W.
1971 Street Gangs and Street Workers. Englewood Cliffs, N.J.: Prentice Hall.
1992 The new street gang . . . or is it? Contemporary Sociology 21:80–82.
Klein, Malcolm W. and Cheryl L. Maxson
1993 Gangs and cocaine trafficking. In Craig Uchida and Doris Mackenzie (eds.), Drugs and the Criminal Justice System. Newbury Park: Sage.
Klein, Malcolm W., Cheryl L. Maxson, and Lea C. Cunningham
1991 Crack, street gangs, and violence. Criminology 29:623–650.
Liebow, Elliot
1967 Tally's Corner. Boston: Little, Brown.
Lincoln, Yvonna S. and Egon G. Guba
1985 Naturalistic Inquiry. Beverly Hills: Sage.
MacCoun, Robert and Peter Reuter
1992 Are the wages of sin $30 an hour? Economic aspects of street-level drug dealing. Crime and Delinquency 38:477–491.
MacLeod, Jay
1987 Ain't No Makin' It: Leveled Aspirations in a Low-Income Neighborhood. Boulder: Westview.
Matza, David
1964 Delinquency and Drift. New York: Wiley.
Merton, Robert K.
1957 Social Theory and Social Structure. 1968. New York: Free Press.

Miller, Walter B.
1969 Lower class culture as a generating milieu of gang delinquency. Journal of Social Issues 14:5–19.

Moore, Joan W.
1978 Homeboys: Gangs, Drugs, and Prison in the Barrios of Los Angeles. Philadelphia: Temple University Press.
1991 Going Down to the Barrio: Homeboys and Homegirls in Change. Philadelphia: Temple University Press.

Padilla, Felix
1992 The Gang as an American Enterprise. New Brunswick: Rutgers University Press.

Preble, Edward and John H. Casey
1969 Taking care of business: The heroin user's life on the street. International Journal of the Addictions 4:1–24.

Reinarman, Craig and Harry G. Levine
1990 Crack in context: politics and media in the making of a drug scare. Contemporary Drug Problems 16:535–577.

Rose, Harold M., Ronald S. Edari, Lois M. Quinn, and John Pawasrat
1992 The Labor Market Experience of Young African American Men from Low-Income Families in Wisconsin. Milwaukee: University of Wisconsin–Milwaukee Employment and Training Institute.

Sampson, Robert J. and John H. Laub
1993 Crime in the Making: Pathways and Turning Points through Life. Cambridge: Harvard University Press.

Short, James F. and Fred L. Strodtbeck
1965 Group Process and Gang Delinquency. Chicago: University of Chicago Press.

Skolnick, Jerome H.
1990 The social structure of street drug dealing. American Journal of Police 9:1–41.

Spergel, Irving A. and G. David Curry
1990 Strategies and perceived agency effectiveness in dealing with the youth gang problem. In C. Ronald Huff (ed.), Gangs in America. Beverly Hills: Sage.

Strauss, Anselm L.
1987 Qualitative Analysis for Social Scientists. Cambridge: Cambridge University Press.

Sullivan, Mercer L.
1989 Getting Paid: Youth Crime and Work in the Inner City. Ithaca: Cornell University Press.

Taylor, Carl
1990 Dangerous Society. East Lansing: Michigan State University Press.

Thrasher, Frederick
1927 The Gang. 1963. Chicago: University of Chicago Press.

Waldorf, Dan
1993 Final Report of the Crack Sales, Gangs, and Violence Study: NIDA Grant 5#R01DA06486. Alameda: Institute for Scientific Analysis.

Waldorf, Dan, Craig Reinarman, and Sheigla Murphy
1991 Cocaine Changes: The Experience of Using and Quitting. Philadelphia: Temple University Press.

Whyte, William Foote
1943 Street Corner Society. Chicago: University of Chicago Press.

Williams, Terry
1989 The Cocaine Kids. Reading, Mass.: Addison-Wesley.

Wilson, William Julius
1987 The Truly Disadvantaged. Chicago: University of Chicago.

Control Theory

A central feature of control theory is the view that various levels and types of societal commitment, when coupled with other factors, are often important precursors to the commission of deviant acts. Travis Hirschi offers a well-known statement of this position.

In "A Control Theory of Delinquency," he notes that control theorists assume that delinquency will result when an actor's bond to society is weakened or broken. He then proceeds to discuss and analyze the various elements that comprise the bond of society, particularly as they relate to the question of motivation. For example, the "commitment" element refers to the idea that most people invest a great deal of time and energy in conventional lines of activity (e.g., educational and occupational pursuits). When deviant behavior is contemplated, the risks of such deviation must be considered. The guiding assumption is that involvement in deviance or crime would jeopardize one's investments. Hirschi concludes with a section on "belief," another major element of the bond to society. The underlying premise is that society is characterized by a common value system. If this is correct—and if, further, one retains some type of allegiance to established values—then a basic question presents itself: "Why does a man violate the rules in which he believes?" Hirschi, in his attempt to answer this question, rejects the view that an actor must rationalize or neutralize his or her behavior. Hirschi prefers, instead, the notion that the weakness of one's beliefs can be used to explain motivation. When a person's belief in the validity of norms is weakened, the probability of delinquency and deviance increases.

Neal Shover and David Honaker, in "The Socially Bounded Decision Making of Persistent Property Offenders," offer another variant of this position. The researchers are concerned specifically with analyzing the criminal decision-making processes used by persistent property offenders. A central focus, then, becomes the matter of *choice*. Do, for example, prior offenders, in their pursuit of financial or criminal gain, actually "discount or ignore the formal risks of crime?" Shover and Honaker attempt to shed some light on this concern. They offer interview data obtained from 60 career criminals—all of whom had been out of prison at least seven months. The subjects were asked to recount the crimes they had committed subsequent to their release, as well as how the decision was made to commit the crime. Of concern were their assessments of the potential risks and awards associated with the commission of an illegal act. Some interesting findings emerged. For example, the majority gave little thought to the possibility of arrest or subsequent incarceration. The researchers go on to argue that it is useful to examine the decision-making process of offenders within the context of their lifestyle. A central characteristic of this process is referred to as the *life as party* syndrome—a lifestyle that in addition to promoting the notion of "good times," exhibits little concern for those commitments that go beyond one's present social setting. Shover and Honaker conclude by discussing various implications of their results. Risk perceptions, it is suggested, should be analyzed in terms of the various situations or contexts that affect people.

16 A Control Theory of Delinquency

Travis Hirschi

Control theories assume that delinquent acts result when an individual's bond to society is weak or broken. Since these theories embrace two highly complex concepts, the *bond* of the individual to *society,* it is not surprising that they have at one time or another formed the basis of explanations of most forms of aberrant or unusual behavior. It is also not surprising that control theories have described the elements of the bond to society in many ways, and that they have focused on a variety of units as the point of control. . . .

Elements of the Bond

Attachment

In explaining conforming behavior, sociologists justly emphasize sensitivity to the opinion of others.[1] Unfortunately, . . . they tend to suggest that man *is* sensitive to the opinion of others and thus exclude sensitivity from their explanations of deviant behavior. In explaining deviant behavior, psychologists, in contrast, emphasize insensitivity to the opinion of others.[2] Unfortunately, they too tend to ignore variation, and, in addition, they tend to tie sensitivity inextricably to other variables, to make it part of a syndrome or "type," and thus seriously to reduce its value as an explanatory concept. The psychopath is characterized only in part by "deficient attachment to or affection for others, a failure to respond to the ordinary motivations founded in respect or regard for one's fellow";[3] he is also characterized by such things as "excessive aggressiveness," "lack of superego control," and "an infantile level of response."[4] Unfortunately, too, the behavior that psychopathy is used to explain often becomes part of the *definition* of psychopathy. As a result, in Barbara Wootton's words: "[The psychopath] is . . . *par excellence,* and without shame or qualification, the model of the circular process by which mental abnormality is inferred

172

from anti-social behavior while anti-social behavior is explained by mental abnormality."[5]

The problems of diagnosis, tautology, and name-calling are avoided if the dimensions of psychopathy are treated as causally and therefore problematically interrelated, rather than as logically and therefore necessarily bound to each other. In fact, it can be argued that all of the characteristics attributed to the psychopath follow from, are effects of, his lack of attachment to others. To say that to lack attachment to others is to be free from moral restraints is to use lack of attachment to explain the guiltlessness of the psychopath, the fact that he apparently has no conscience or superego. In this view, lack of attachment to others is not merely a symptom of psychopathy, it *is* psychopathy; lack of conscience is just another way of saying the same thing; and the violation of norms is (or may be) a consequence.

For that matter, given that man is an animal, "impulsivity" and "aggressiveness" can also be seen as natural consequences of freedom from moral restraints. However, since the view of man as endowed with natural propensities and capacities like other animals is peculiarly unpalatable to sociologists, we need not fall back on such a view to explain the amoral man's aggressiveness.[6] The process of becoming alienated from others often involves or is based on active interpersonal conflict. Such conflict could easily supply a reservoir of *socially derived* hostility sufficient to account for the aggressiveness of those whose attachments to others have been weakened.

Durkheim said it many years ago: "We are moral beings to the extent that we are social beings."[7] This may be interpreted to mean that we are moral beings to the extent that we have "internalized the norms" of society. But what does it mean to say that a person has internalized the norms of society? The norms of society are by definition shared by the members of society. To violate a norm is, therefore, to act contrary to the wishes and expectations of other people. If a person does not care about the wishes and expectations of other people—that is, if he is insensitive to the opinion of others— then he is to that extent not bound by the norms. He is free to deviate.

The essence of internalization of norms, conscience, or superego thus lies in the attachment of the individual to others.[8] This view has several advantages over the concept of internalization. For one, explanations of deviant behavior based on attachment do not beg the question, since the extent to which a person is attached to others can be measured independently of his deviant behavior. Furthermore, change or variation in behavior is explainable in a way that it is not when notions of internalization or superego are used. For example, the divorced man is more likely after divorce to commit a number of deviant acts, such as suicide or forgery. If we explain these acts by reference to the superego (or internal control), we are forced to say that the man "lost his conscience" when he got a divorce; and, of course, if he remarries, we have to conclude that he gets his conscience back.

This dimension of the bond to conventional society is encountered in most social control-oriented research and theory. F. Ivan Nye's "internal control" and "indirect control" refer to the same element, although we avoid the problem of explaining changes over time by locating the "conscience" in the bond to others rather than making it part of the personality.[9] Attachment to others is just one aspect of Albert J. Reiss's "personal controls"; we avoid his problems of tautological empirical *observations* by making the relationship between attachment and delinquency problematic rather than definitional.[10] Finally, Scott Briar and Irving Piliavin's "commitment" or "stake in conformity" subsumes attachment, as their discussion illustrates, although the terms they use are more closely associated with the next element to be discussed.[11]

Commitment

"Of all passions, that which inclineth men least to break the laws, is fear. Nay, excepting some generous natures, it is the only thing, when there is the appearance of profit or pleasure by breaking the laws, that makes men keep them."[12] Few would deny that men on occasion obey the rules simply from fear of the consequences. This rational component in conformity we label commitment. What does it mean to say that a person is committed to conformity? In Howard S. Becker's formulation it means the following:

> First, the individual is in a position in which his decision with regard to some particular line of action has consequences for other interests and activities not necessarily [directly] related to it. Second, he has placed himself in that position by his own prior actions. A third element is present though so obvious as not to be apparent; the committed person must be aware [of these other interests] and must recognize that his decision in this case will have ramifications beyond it.[13]

The idea, then, is that the person invests time, energy, himself, in a certain line of activity—say, getting an education, building up a business, acquiring a reputation for virtue. When or whenever he considers deviant behavior, he must consider the costs of this deviant behavior, the risk he runs of losing the investment he has made in conventional behavior.

If attachment to others is the sociological counterpart of the superego or conscience, commitment is the counterpart of the ego or common sense. To the person committed to conventional lines of action, risking one to ten years in prison for a ten-dollar holdup is stupidity, because to the committed person the costs and risks obviously exceed ten dollars in value. (To the psychoanalyst, such an act exhibits failure to be governed by the "reality-principle.") In the sociological control theory, it can be and is generally assumed that the decision to commit a criminal act may well be rationally determined—that the actor's decision was not irrational given the risks and costs he faces. Of course, as Becker points out, if the actor is capable of in some sense calculating the costs of a line of action, he is also capable of calculational errors: ignorance and error return, in the control theory, as possible explanations of deviant behavior.

The concept of commitment assumes that the organization of society is such that the interest of most persons would be endangered if they were to engage in criminal acts. Most people, simply by the process of living in an organized society, acquire goods, reputations, prospects that they do not want to risk losing. These accumulations are society's insurance that they will abide by the rules. Many hypotheses about the antecedents of delinquent behavior are based on this premise. For example, Arthur L. Stinchcombe's hypothesis that "high school rebellion . . . occurs when future status is not clearly related to present performance"[14] suggests that one is committed to conformity not only by what one has but also by what one hoped to obtain. Thus "ambition" and/or "aspiration" play an important role in producing conformity. The person becomes committed to a conventional line of action, and he is therefore committed to conformity.

Most lines of action in a society are of course conventional. The clearest examples are educational and occupational careers. Actions thought to jeopardize one's chances in these areas are presumably avoided. Interestingly enough, even nonconventional commitments may operate to produce conventional conformity. We are told, at least, that boys aspiring to careers in the rackets or professional thievery are judged by their "honesty" and "reliability"—traits traditionally in demand among seekers of office boys.[15]

Involvement

Many persons undoubtedly owe a life of virtue to a lack of opportunity to do otherwise. Time and energy are inherently limited: "Not that I would not, if I could, be both handsome and fat and well dressed, and a great athlete, and make a million a year, be a wit, a bon vivant, and a lady killer, as well as a philosopher, a philanthropist, a statesman, warrior, and African explorer, as well as a 'tone-poet' and saint. But the thing is simply impossible."[16] The things that William James here says he would like to be or do are all, I suppose, within the realm of conventionality, but if he were to include illicit actions he would still have to eliminate some of them as simply impossible.

Involvement or engrossment in conventional activities is thus often part of a control theory. The assumption, widely shared, is that a person may be simply too busy doing conventional things to find time to engage in deviant behavior. The person involved in conventional activities is tied to appointments, deadlines, working hours, plans, and the like, so the opportunity to commit deviant acts rarely arises. To the extent that he is engrossed in conventional activities, he cannot even think about deviant acts, let alone act out his inclinations.[17]

This line of reasoning is responsible for the stress placed on recreational facilities in many programs to reduce delinquency, for much of the concern with the high school dropout, and for the idea that boys should be drafted into the army to keep them out of trouble. So obvious and persuasive is the idea that involvement in conventional activities is a major deterrent to delinquency that it was accepted even by Sutherland: "In the general area of juvenile delinquency it is probable that the most significant difference between juveniles who engage in delinquency and those who do not is that the latter are provided abundant opportunities of a conventional type for satisfying their recreational interests, while the former lack those opportunities or facilities."[18]

The view that "idle hands are the devil's workshop" has received more sophisticated treatment in recent sociological writings on delinquency. David Matza and Gresham M. Sykes, for example, suggest that delinquents have the values of a leisure class, the same values ascribed by Veblen to *the* leisure class: a search for kicks, disdain of work, a desire for the big score, and acceptance of aggressive toughness as proof of masculinity.[19] Matza and Sykes explain delinquency by reference to this system of values, but they note that adolescents at all class levels are "to some extent" members of a leisure class, that they "move in a limbo between earlier parental domination and future integration with the social structure through the bonds of work and marriage."[20] In the end, then, the leisure of the adolescent produces a set of values, which, in turn, leads to delinquency.

Belief

Unlike the cultural deviance theory, the control theory assumes the existence of a common value system within the society or group whose norms are being violated. If the deviant is committed to a value system different from that of conventional society, there is, within the context of the theory, nothing to explain. The question is, "Why does a man violate the rules in which he believes?" It is not, "Why do men differ in their beliefs about what constitutes good and desirable conduct?" The person is assumed to have been socialized (perhaps imperfectly) into the group whose rules he is violating; deviance is not a question of one group imposing its rules on the members of another group. In other words, we not only assume the deviant *has* believed the rules, we assume he believes the rules even as he violates them.

How can a person believe it is wrong to steal at the same time he is stealing? In the strain theory, this is not a difficult problem. (In fact, . . . the strain theory was devised specifically to deal with this question.) The motivation to deviance adduced by the strain theorist is so strong that we can well understand the deviant act even assuming the deviator believes strongly that it is wrong.[21] However, given the control theory's assumptions about motivation, if both the deviant and the nondeviant believe the deviant act is wrong, how do we account for the fact that one commits it and the other does not?

Control theories have taken two approaches to this problem. In one approach, beliefs are treated as mere words that mean little or nothing if the other forms of control are missing. "Semantic dementia," the dissociation between rational faculties and emotional control which is said to be characteristic of the psychopath, illustrates this way of handling the problem.[22] In short, beliefs, at least insofar as they are expressed in words, drop out of the picture; since they do not differentiate between deviants and non-deviants, they are in the same class as "language" or any other characteristic common to all members of the group. Since they represent no real obstacle to the commission of delinquent acts, nothing need be said about how they are handled by those committing such acts. The control theories that do not mention beliefs (or values), and many do not, may be assumed to take this approach to the problem.

The second approach argues that the deviant rationalizes his behavior so that he can at once violate the rule and maintain his belief in it. Donald R. Cressey had advanced this argument with respect to embezzlement,[23] and Sykes and Matza have advanced it with respect to delinquency.[24] In both Cressey's and Sykes and Matza's treatments, these rationalizations (Cressey calls them "verbalizations," Sykes and Matza term them "techniques of neutralization") occur prior to the commission of the deviant act. If the neutralization is successful, the person is free to commit the act(s) in question. Both in Cressey and in Sykes and Matza, the strain that prompts the effort at neutralization also provides the motive force that results in the subsequent deviant act. Their theories are thus, in this sense, strain theories. Neutralization is difficult to handle within the context of a theory that adheres closely to control theory assumptions, because in the control theory there is no special motivational force to account for the neutralization. This difficulty is especially noticeable in Matza's later treatment of this topic, where the motivational component, the "will to delinquency," appears *after* the moral vacuum has been created by the techniques of neutralization.[25] The question thus becomes: Why neutralize?

In attempting to solve a strain-theory problem with control-theory tools, the control theorist is thus led into a trap. He cannot answer the crucial question. The concept of neutralization assumes the existence of moral obstacles to the commission of deviant acts. In order plausibly to account for a deviant act, it is necessary to generate motivation to deviance that is at least equivalent in force to the resistance provided by these moral obstacles. However, if the moral obstacles are removed, neutralization and special motivation are no longer required. We therefore follow the implicit logic of control theory and remove these moral obstacles by hypothesis. Many persons do not have an attitude of respect toward the rules of society; many persons feel no moral obligation to conform regardless of personal advantage. Insofar as the values and beliefs of these persons are consistent with their feelings, and there should be a tendency toward consistency, neutralization is unnecessary; it has already occurred.

Does this merely push the question back a step and at the same time produce conflict with the assumption of a common value system? I think not.

In the first place, we do not assume, as does Cressey, that neutralization occurs in order to make a specific criminal act possible.[26] We do not assume, as do Sykes and Matza, that neutralization occurs to make many delinquent acts possible. We do not assume, in other words, that the person constructs a system of rationalizations in order to justify commission of acts he *wants* to commit. We assume, in contrast, that the beliefs that free a man to commit deviant acts are *unmotivated* in the sense that he does not construct or adopt them in order to facilitate the attainment of illicit ends. In the second place, we do not assume, as does Matza, that "delinquents concur in the conventional assessment of delinquency."[27] We assume, in contrast, that there is *variation* in the extent to which people believe they should obey the rules of society, and, furthermore, that the less a person believes he should obey the rules, the more likely he is to violate them.[28]

In chronological order, then, a person's beliefs in the moral validity of norms are, for no teleological reason, weakened. The probability that he will commit delinquent acts is therefore increased. When and if he commits a delinquent act, we may justifiably use the weakness of his beliefs in explaining it, but no special motivation is required to explain either the weakness of his beliefs or, perhaps, his delinquent act.

The keystone of this argument is of course the assumption that there is variation in belief in the moral validity of social rules. This assumption is amenable to direct empirical test and can thus survive at least until its first confrontation with data. For the present, we must return to the idea of a common value system with which this section was begun.

The idea of a common (or perhaps better, a single) value system is consistent with the fact, or presumption, of variation in the strength of moral beliefs. We have not suggested that delinquency is based on beliefs counter to conventional morality; we have not suggested that delinquents do not believe delinquent acts are wrong. They may well believe these acts are wrong, but the meaning and efficacy of such beliefs are contingent on other beliefs and, indeed, on the strength of other ties to the conventional order.[29]

Notes

1. Books have been written on the increasing importance of interpersonal sensitivity in modern life. According to this view, controls from within have become less important than controls from without in *producing* conformity. Whether or not this observation is true as a description of historical trends, it is true that interpersonal sensitivity has become more important in *explaining* conformity. Although logically it should also have become more important in explaining nonconformity, the opposite has been the case, once again showing that Cohen's observation that an explanation of conformity should be an explanation of deviance cannot be translated as "as explanation of conformity has to be an explanation of deviance." For the view that interpersonal sensitivity currently plays a greater role than formerly in producing conformity, see William J. Goode, "Norm Commitment and Conformity to Role-Status Obligations," *American Journal of Sociology,* LXVI (1960), 246–258. And, of course, also see David Riesman, Nathan Glazer, and Rouel Denney, *The Lonely Crowd* (Garden City, New York: Doubleday, 1950), especially Part I.

2. The literature on psychopathy is voluminous. See William McCord and Joan McCord, *The Psychopath* (Princeton: D. Van Nostrand, 1964).

3. John M. Martin and Joseph P. Fitzpatrick, *Delinquent Behavior* (New York: Random House, 1964), p. 130.

4. *Ibid.* For additional properties of the psychopath, see McCord and McCord, *The Psychopath*, pp. 1–2.

5. Barbara Wootton, *Social Science and Social Pathology* (New York: Macmillan, 1959), p. 250.

6. "The logical untenability [of the position that there are forces in man 'resistant to socialization'] was ably demonstrated by Parsons over 30 years ago, and it is widely recognized that the position is empirically unsound because it assumes [!] some universal biological drive system distinctly separate from socialization and social context—a basic and intransigent human nature" (Judith Blake and Kingsley Davis, "Norms, Values, and Sanctions," *Handbook of Modern Sociology,* ed. Robert E. L. Faris [Chicago: Rand McNally, 1964], p. 471).

7. Emile Durkheim, *Moral Education,* trans. Everett K. Wilson and Herman Schnurer (New York: The Free Press, 1961), p. 64.

8. Although attachment alone does not exhaust the meaning of internalization, attachments and beliefs combined would appear to leave only a small residue of "internal control" not susceptible in principle to direct measurement.

9. F. Ivan Nye, *Family Relationships and Delinquent Behavior* (New York: Wiley, 1958), pp. 5–7.

10. Albert J. Reiss, Jr., "Delinquency as the Failure of Personal and Social Controls," *American Sociological Review,* XVI (1951), 196–207. For example, "Our observations show . . . that delinquent recidivists are less often persons with mature ego ideals or non-delinquent social roles" (p. 204).

11. Scott Briar and Irving Piliavin, "Delinquency, Situational Inducements, and Commitment to Conformity," *Social Problems,* XIII (1965), 41–42. The concept "stake in conformity" was introduced by Jackson Toby in his "Social Disorganization and Stake in Conformity: Complementary Factors in the Predatory Behavior of Hoodlums," *Journal of Criminal Law, Criminology and Police Science,* XLVIII (1957), 12–17. See also his "Hoodlum or Business Man: An American Dilemma," *The Jews,* ed. Marshall Sklare (New York: The Free Press, 1958), pp. 542–550. Throughout the text, I occasionally use "stake in conformity" in speaking in general of the strength of the bond to conventional society. So used, the concept is somewhat broader than is true for either Toby or Briar and Piliavin, where the concept is roughly equivalent to what is here called "commitment."

12. Thomas Hobbes, *Leviathan* (Oxford: Basil Blackwell, 1957), p. 195.

13. Howard S. Becker, "Notes on the Concept of Commitment," *American Journal of Sociology,* LXVI (1960), 35–36.

14. Arthur L. Stinchcombe, *Rebellion in a High School* (Chicago: Quadrangle, 1964), p. 5.

15. Richard A. Cloward and Lloyd E. Ohlin, *Delinquency and Opportunity* (New York: The Free Press, 1960), p. 147, quoting Edwin H. Sutherland, ed., *The Professional Thief* (Chicago: University of Chicago Press, 1937), pp. 211–213.

16. William James, *Psychology* (Cleveland: World Publishing Co., 1948), p. 186.

17. Few activities appear to be so engrossing that they rule out contemplation of alternative lines of behavior, at least if estimates of the amount of time men spend plotting sexual deviations have any validity.

18. *The Sutherland Papers,* ed. Albert K. Cohen et al. (Bloomington: Indiana University Press, 1956), p. 37.

19. David Matza and Gresham M. Sykes, "Juvenile Delinquency and Subterranean Values," *American Sociological Review,* XXVI (1961), 712–719.

20. *Ibid.,* p. 718.

21. The starving man stealing the loaf of bread is the image evoked by most strain theories. In this image, the starving man's belief in the wrongness of his act is clearly not something that must be explained away. It can be assumed to be present without causing embarrassment to the explanation.

22. McCord and McCord, *The Psychopath,* pp. 12–15.

23. Donald R. Cressey, *Other People's Money* (New York: The Free Press, 1953).

24. Gresham M. Sykes and David Matza, "Techniques of Neutralization: A Theory of Delinquency," *American Sociological Review,* XXII (1957), 664–670.

25. David Matza, *Delinquency and Drift* (New York: Wiley, 1964), pp. 181–191.

26. In asserting that Cressey's assumption is invalid with respect to delinquency, I do not wish to suggest that it is invalid for the question of embezzlement, where the problem faced by the deviator is fairly specific and he can reasonably be assumed to be an upstanding citizen. (Although even here the fact that the embezzler's nonsharable financial problem often

results from some sort of hanky-panky suggests that "verbalizations" may be less necessary than might otherwise be assumed.)

27. *Delinquency and Drift*, p. 43.

28. This assumption is not, I think, contradicted by the evidence presented by Matza against the existence of a delinquent subculture. In comparing the attitudes and actions of delinquents with the picture painted by delinquent subculture theorists, Matza emphasizes—and perhaps exaggerates—the extent to which delinquents are tied to the conventional order. In implicitly comparing delinquents with a supermoral man, I emphasize—and perhaps exaggerate—the extent to which they are not tied to the conventional order.

29. The position taken here is therefore somewhere between the "semantic dementia" and the "neutralization" positions. Assuming variation, the delinquent is, at the extremes, freer than the neutralization argument assumes. Although the possibility of wide discrepancy between what the delinquent professes and what he practices still exists, it is presumably much rarer than is suggested by studies of articulate "psychopaths."

The Socially Bounded Decision Making of Persistent Property Offenders

Neal Shover
David Honaker

The 1970s were marked by the eclipse of labeling theory as the dominant individual-level criminological theory and by the reappearance of interest in approaches originally advanced by classical theorists. Economists and cognitive psychologists along with many in the criminological mainstream advanced an interpretation of crime as *choice*, offering models of criminal decision making grounded in the assumption that the decision to commit a criminal act springs from the offender's assessment of its anticipated net utilities (e.g., Becker 1968; Heineke 1978; Carroll 1978; Reynolds 1985). This movement in favor of rational-choice approaches to crime spurred empirical investigation of problems that previously were limited primarily to studies of the death penalty and its impact on the homicide rate.

Early investigations of a rational choice interpretation of crime reported a weak but persistent relationship between the certainty of punishment and rates of serious property crimes (Blumstein, Cohen, and Nagin 1978). It was recognized, however, that an understanding of criminal decision making also requires knowledge about individual perceptions and beliefs about legal threats and other constraints on decision making (e.g., Manski 1978). Investigators moved on two main fronts to meet this need. Some used survey methods to explore differential involvement in minor forms of deviance in samples of restricted age ranges, typically high school and college students (e.g., Waldo and Chiricos 1972). Alternatively they examined the link between risk assessments and criminal participation in samples more representative of the general population (e.g., Tittle 1980). Serious shortcomings of these studies are that most either ignore the potential rewards of crime entirely or they fail to examine its emotional and interpersonal utilities. Still other investigators turned attention to serious criminal offenders and began expanding the narrow existing knowledge base (e.g., Claster 1967), chiefly through the use of cross sectional research designs and survey methods.

For more than a decade now, investigators have studied offenders' attitudes toward legitimate and criminal pursuits, their perceptions of and beliefs about the risks of criminal behavior, and their estimates of the payoffs from conventional and criminal pursuits (e.g., Petersilia et al. 1978; Peterson & Braiker 1980). These studies raise serious questions about the fit between offenders' calculus and a priori assumptions about their utilities and criminal decision making. One investigation of 589 incarcerated property offenders concluded, for example, that the subjects apparently do not utilize "a sensible cost-benefit analysis" when weighing the utilities of crime (Figgie 1988, p. 25). They substantially underestimate the risk of arrest for most crimes, routinely overestimate the monetary benefit they expect, and seem to have "grossly inaccurate perceptions of the costs and benefits associated with property crime" (Figgie 1988, p. 81). Unfortunately, both design and conceptual problems undermine confidence in the findings of this and similar studies. Cross sectional survey methods, for example, are poorly suited for examining dynamic decision-making *processes*. Most such studies also fail to examine offenders' estimates of the likely payoffs from noncriminal alternatives or their non-monetary utilities, such as emotional satisfaction (Katz 1988).

As newer, empirically-based models of criminal decision making have been developed (e.g., Clarke and Cornish 1985; Cornish and Clarke 1986), a growing number of investigators are using ethnographic methods to examine the offender's criminal calculus, often in real or simulated natural settings (e.g., Carrol 1982; Carrol and Weaver 1986). The research reported here continues this line of ethnographic inquiry by using retrospective interviews to examine criminal decision making by serious and persistent property offenders. The focus of our attention is the decision to commit a crime rather than the target-selection decision that has received substantial attention elsewhere (e.g., Scar 1973; Repetto 1974; Maguire 1982; Bennett and Wright 1984a; Rengert and Wasilchick 1985; Cromwell, Olson, and Avary 1991). The first objective is to examine how closely the decision to commit crime conforms to a classical rational choice model in which decisions assumedly are based largely on an assessment of potential returns from alternative courses of action and the risk of legal sanctions. A second objective is to examine the influence of the lifestyle pursued by many persistent property offenders on the salience of their utilities and the risks they assess in criminal decision making.

Methods and Materials

The materials for analysis were collected during 1987–1988 as part of a larger study of crime desistance. From the population of all men incarcerated in Tennessee state prisons during 1987 we selected a sample of recidivists with a demonstrated preference for property crimes who were also nearing release from confinement. To select the sample, members of the research team first examined Tennessee Board of Paroles records to identify offenders incarcerated in Tennessee state prisons whose parole was imminent. We then used Department of Corrections records to cull the list of all but those (1) with at least one prior felony confinement, and (2) whose previous or current confinement was for serious property crime. Next the researchers visited prisons, primarily those located in the mid- and eastern areas of the state, and explained the study to and requested research participation from potential subjects. After meeting individually with approximately 75 inmates we reached our sample size objective of 60 subjects. Fifty-eight members of the sample had served at least one prior prison sentence and the remaining two had served one or more jail sentences. They had served time primarily for armed robbery, burglary, or theft. By limiting the sample as outlined we sought to approximate a population of career criminals, a type of offender that has received substantial attention from scholars and policy makers (Petersilia 1980; Blumstein et al. 1988). Subjects ranged from 23 to 70 years of age, with an average age of 34.1 years. In addition to the sample's adult criminal and incarceration profile, 47 percent ($n = 28$) of the men had also served one or more terms of juvenile confinement. Every member of the sample was interviewed approximately one month prior to release from prison. All data used in the present study, however, were collected in post-release interviews with the men.

Seven to 10 months after their release from prison we successfully traced, contacted, and interviewed 46 of the original sample of 60 men (76.7 percent). (In addition, we established contact with one subject who declined our request for an interview, and with close relatives of another who failed to respond to repeated requests that he contact us.) Semi-structured ethnographic interviews were the principal data-collection technique. The interview included questions about the former prisoner's activities and living arrangements following release, self-report items measuring postrelease criminal participation, and questions about the context of reinvolvement in crime. They were paid $100 for completing the interviews, all of which were audiotape recorded and transcribed for subsequent analysis. Fourteen subjects were in jail or prison again when interviewed, but most were interviewed in their former or newly established home communities.

Part of the interviews produced detailed descriptions of the most recent, easily recalled property crime that each subject had committed in the free world prior to the interview. They described either crimes they had committed prior to incarceration or, for those subjects who were locked up when interviewed, their return to jail or prison. Our objective was to gain through the repeat offender's eyes an understanding of the decision to commit specific criminal acts. We asked our subjects to focus their recollection on how the decision was made, and to provide a detailed account of the potential risks and rewards they assessed while doing so. The result was 40 usable descriptions of crimes and attempted crimes, which included 15 burglaries, 12 armed robberies, 5 grand larcenies, 4 unarmed robberies, 2 auto thefts, 1 series of check forgeries, and 1 case of receiving and concealing stolen property. Transcripts of the interviews were analyzed using *The Ethnograph,* a software package for use on text-based data (Seidel, Kjolseth, and Seymour 1988). Use of this software enabled us to code and to retrieve for analysis segments of interview text.

Findings

Analysis reveals the most striking aspect of the subject's decision making for the crimes they described is that a majority gave little or no thought to the possibility of arrest and confinement. Of 34 subjects who were asked specifically whether they considered the risk of arrest or who spontaneously indicated whether they did so, 21 (62 percent) said they did not. The comments of two subjects are typical:

Q: Did you think about . . . getting caught?
A: No.
Q: [H]ow did you manage to put that out of your mind?
A: [It] never did come into it.
Q: Never did come into it?
A: Never did, you know. It didn't bother me.

Q: Were you thinking about bad things that might happen to you?
A: None whatsoever.
Q: No?
A: I wasn't worried about getting caught or anything, you know. I was a positive thinker through everything, you know. I didn't have no negative thoughts about it whatsoever.

The 13 remaining subjects (38%) acknowledged they gave some thought to the possibility of arrest but most said they managed to dismiss it easily and to carry through with their plans:

Q: Did you worry much about getting caught? On a scale of one to ten, how would you rank your degree of worry that day?
A: [T]he worry was probably a one. You know what I mean? The worry was probably one. I didn't think about the consequences, you know. I know it's stupidity, but it didn't—that [I] might go to jail, I mean—it crossed my mind but it didn't make much difference.

Q: As you thought about doing that [armed robbery], were there things that you were worried about?

A: Well, the only thing that I was worried about was— . . . getting arrested didn't even cross my mind—just worrying about getting killed is the only thing, you know, getting shot. That's the only thing. . . . But, you know, . . . you'd have to be really crazy not to think about that . . . you could possibly get in trouble. It crossed my mind, but I didn't worry about it all that much.

Some members of our sample said they managed deliberately and consciously to put out of mind all thoughts of possible arrest:

When I went out to steal, I didn't think about the negative things. 'Cause if you think negative, negative things are going to happen. And that's the way I looked at it. . . . I done it just like it was a job or something. Go out and do it, don't think about getting caught, 'cause that would make you jumpy, edgy, nervous. If you looked like you were doing something wrong, then something wrong is gonna happen to you. . . . You just, you just put [the thought of arrest] out of your mind, you know.

Q: Did you think about [the possibility of getting caught] very much that night?

A: I didn't think about it that much, you know. . . . [I]t comes but, you know, you can wipe it away.

Q: How do you wipe it away?

A: You just blank it out. You blank it out.

Another subject said simply that "I try to put that [thought of arrest] the farthest thing from my mind that I can."

Many subjects attribute their ability to ignore or to dismiss all thought of possible arrest to a state of intoxication or drug-altered consciousness:

Q: You didn't think about going to prison?

A: Never did. I guess it was all that alcohol and stuff, and drugs. . . . The day I pulled that robbery?—no. I was so high I didn't think about nothing.

Another subject told us that he had been drinking the entire day that he committed the crime and, by the time it occurred, he was in "nightlight city."

While it is clear that the formal risks of crime were not considered carefully by most members of the sample, equally striking is the finding that very few thought about or assessed legitimate alternatives before opting to commit a criminal act. Of 22 subjects who were asked specifically whether they had done so, 16 indicated that they gave no thought whatsoever to legitimate alternatives. The six subjects who did either ignored or quickly dismissed them as inapplicable, given their immediate circumstances.

We recognize the methodological shortcomings of the descriptions of criminal decision making and behavior used as data for this study. Since the subjects were questioned in detail only about specific offenses they could remember well, the sample of descriptions may not be representative of the range of crimes they committed. By definition, they are memorable ones. Moreover, the recall period for these crimes ranged from one to 15 years, raising the possibility of errors caused by selective recall. Whether or not this could have produced systematic bias in the data is unknown. We cannot rule out the possibility that past crimes are remembered as being less rational than they actually were at the time of commission. Such a tendency could account in part for our interpretation of the data and our description of their style of decision making. The fact that we limited the sample to recidivists means also that we cannot determine how much their behavior may reflect either innate differences (Gottfredson and Hirschi 1990) or experimental effects, i.e., the effects of past success in committing crime and avoiding arrest (Nagin and Paternoster 1991). It could be argued that the behavior of our subjects, precisely because they had demonstrated a willingness to commit property crimes and had done so in the past, limits the external validity of their reports. Given sample selection criteria and these potential data problems, generalizations beyond the study population must be made with caution.

This said, we believe that the remarkable similarity between our findings and the picture of criminal decision making reported by others who have studied serious property offenders strengthens their credibility significantly. A study of 83 imprisoned burglars revealed that 49 percent did not think about the chances of getting caught for any particular offense during their last period of offending. While 37 percent of them did think about it, most thought there was little or no chance it would happen (Bennett and Wright 1984a, Table A14). Interviews with 113 men convicted of robbery or an offense related to robbery revealed that "over 60 percent . . . said they had not even thought about getting caught." Another 17 percent said that they had thought about the possibility but "did not believe it to be a problem" (Feeney 1986, p. 59–60). Analysis of prison interviews with 77 robbers and 45 burglars likewise revealed their "general obliviousness toward the consequences [of their crimes] and no thought of being caught" (Walsh 1986, p. 157). In sum, our findings along with the findings from other studies suggest strongly that many serious property offenders seem to be remarkably casual in weighing the formal risks of criminal participation. As one of our subjects put it, "you think about going to prison about like you think about dying, you know." The impact of alcohol and drug use in diminishing concern with possible penalties also has been reported by many others (e.g., Bennett and Wright 1984b; Cromwell, Olson, and Avary 1991).

If the potential legal consequences of crime do not figure prominently in crime commission decision making by persistent thieves, what *do* they think about when choosing to commit crime? Walsh (1980; 1986) shows that typically they focus their thoughts on the money that committing a crime may yield and the good times they expect to have with it when the crime is behind them. Carroll's data (1982) likewise indicate that the amount of gain offenders expect to receive is "the most important dimension" in their decision making, while the certainty of punishment is the least important of the four dimensions on which his subjects assessed crime opportunities. Our findings are consistent with these reports; our subjects said that they focused on the expected gains from their crimes:

> I didn't think about nothing but what I was going to do when I got that money, how I was going to spend it, what I was going to do with it, you know.

> See, you're not thinking about those things [possibility of being arrested]. You're thinking about that big paycheck at the end of thirty to forty-five minutes worth of work.

> [A]t the time [that you commit crime], you throw all your instincts out the window. . . . Because you're just thinking about money, and money only. That's all that's on your mind, because you want that money. And you throw, you block everything off until you get the money.

Although confidence in our findings is bolstered by the number of points on which they are similar to reports by others who have explored crime commission decision making, they do paint a picture of decision making that is different from what is known about the way at least some offenders make target selection decisions. Investigators (e.g., Cromwell, Olson, and Avary 1991) have shown that target decisions approximate simple commonsense conceptions of rational behavior (Shover 1991). A resolution of the problem presented by these contradictory findings is suggested by others (Cromwell, Olson, and Avary 1991) and is also apparent in our data: Criminal participation often results from a *sequence* of experientially and analytically discrete decisions, all of potentially varying degrees of intentional rationality. Thus, once a *motivational* crime commission decision has been made, offenders may move quickly to selecting, or to exploiting, an apparently suitable target. At this stage of the criminal participation process, offenders are preoccupied with the *technical* challenge of avoiding failure at what now is seen as a *practical task.* As one subject put it, "you don't think about getting caught, you think about how in hell you're going to do it *not* to get caught, you know." His comments were echoed by another man: "The only thing you're thinking about is looking and acting and trying *not* to get caught." Last, consider the comments of a third subject: "I wasn't afraid of getting caught, but I was cautious, you know. Like I said, I was thinking only in the way to prevent me from getting caught." Just as bricklayers do not visualize graphically or deliberate over the bodily carnage that could follow from a collapsed scaffold *once there is a job to be done,* many thieves apparently do not dwell at length on the likelihood of arrest or on the pains of imprisonment when proceeding to search out or exploit suitable criminal opportunities.

The accumulated evidence on crime commission decision making by persistent offenders is substantial and persuasive: the rationality they employ is limited or bounded severely (e.g., Carroll 1982; Cromwell, Olson, and Avary 1991). While unsuccessful persistent offenders may calculate potential benefits and costs before committing criminal acts, they apparently do so differently or weigh utilities differently than as sketched in a priori decision-making models. As Walsh (1980, p. 141) suggests, offenders' "definitions of costs and rewards seem to be at variance with society's estimates of them." This does not mean their decision making is *irrational,* but it does point to the difficulties of understanding it and then refining theoretical models of the process. Our objective in the remainder of this paper is an improved understanding of criminal decision making based on analysis of the socially anchored purposes, utilities, and risks of the acts that offenders commit. Put differently, we explore the contextual origins of their bounded rationality.

Lifestyle, Utilities, and Risk

It is instructive to examine the decision making of persistent property offenders in context of the lifestyle that is characteristic of many in their ranks: *life as party.* The hallmark of life as party is the enjoyment of "good times" with minimal concern for the obligations and commitments that are external to the person's immediate social setting. It is a lifestyle distinguished in many cases by two repetitively cyclical phases and correspondingly distinctive approaches to crime. When offenders' efforts to maintain the lifestyle (i.e., their party pursuits) are largely successful, crimes are committed in order to sustain circumstances or a pattern of activities they experience as pleasurable. As Walsh (1986, p. 15) puts it, crimes committed under these circumstances are "part of a continuing satisfactory way of life." By contrast, when offenders are less successful at party pursuits, their crimes are committed in order to avoid circumstances experienced as threatening, unpleasant, or precarious. Corresponding to each of these two phases of party pursuits is a distinctive set of utilities and stance toward legal risk.

Life as Party

Survey and ethnographic studies alike show that persistent property offenders spend much of their criminal gains on alcohol and other drugs (Petersilia et al. 1978; Maguire 1982; Gibbs and Shelley 1982; Figgie 1988; Cromwell, Olson, and Avary 1991). The proceeds of their crimes, as Walsh has noted (1986, p. 72), "typically [are] used for personal, non-essential consumption (e.g., 'nights out'), rather than, for example, to be given to family or used for basic needs." Thieves spend much of their leisure hours enjoying good times. Our subjects were no different in this regard. For example,

> I smoked an ounce of pot in a day, a day and a half. Every other day I
> had to go buy a bag of pot, at the least. And sometimes I've went two
> or three days in a row. . . . And there was never a day went by that I

didn't [drink] a case, case and a half of beer. And [I] did a 'script of pills every two days.

While much of their money is consumed by the high cost of drugs, a portion may be used for ostentatious enjoyment and display of luxury items and activities that probably would be unattainable on the returns from blue-collar employment:

[I]t was all just, it was all just a big money thing to me at the time, you know. Really, what it was was impressing everybody, you know. "Here Floyd is, and he's never had nothing in his life, and now look at him: he's driving new cars, and wearing jewelry," you know.

Life as party is enjoyed in the company of others. Typically it includes shared consumption of alcohol or other drugs in bars and lounges, on street corners, or while cruising in automobiles. In these venues, party pursuers celebrate and affirm values of spontaneity, autonomy, independence, and resourcefulness. Spontaneity means that rationality and long-range planning are eschewed in favor of enjoying the moment and permitting the day's activities and pleasures to develop in an unconstrained fashion. This may mean, for example, getting up late, usually after a night of partying, and then setting out to contact and enjoy the company of friends and associates who are known to be predisposed to partying:

I got up around about eight-thirty that morning. . . .
Q: Eight-thirty? Was that the usual time that you got up?
A: Yeah, if I didn't have a hangover from the night before. . . .
Q: What kind of drugs were you doing then?
A: I was doing . . . Percadans, Dilauds, taking Valiums, drinking. . . . [A]nyway, I got up that morning about eight-thirty, took me a bath, put on some clothes and . . . decided to walk [over to his mother's home]. [T]his particular day, . . . my nephew was over [there]. . . . We was just sitting in the yard and talking and drinking beer, you know. . . . It was me, him, and my sister. We was sitting out there in the yard talking. And this guy that we know, . . . he came up, he pulled up. So my nephew got in the car with him and they left. So, you know, I was sitting there talking to my sister. . . . And then, in the meantime, while we was talking, they come back, about thirty minutes later with a case of beer, some marijuana and everything, . . . and there was another one of my nephews in the car with them. So me, two of my sisters, and two of my nephews, we got in the car with this guy here and we just went riding. So we went to Hadley Park and . . . we stayed out there. There were so many people out there, they were parked on the grass and things, and the vice squad come and run everybody away. So when they done that, we left. . . . So we went back out [toward his mother's home] but instead of going over to my mother's house we went to this little joint [tavern]. Now we're steady drinking and smoking weed all during this day. So when we get there, we park and get out and see a few friends. We [were] talking and getting high, you know, blowing each other a shotgun [sharing marijuana].

Enjoyment of party pursuits in group context is enhanced through the collective emphasis on personal autonomy. Because it is understood by all that participants are free to leave if they no longer enjoy or do not support group activities, the continuing presence of each participant affirms for the remainder the pleasures of the lifestyle. Uncoerced participation thus reinforces the shared assumption that group activities are appropriate and enjoyable. The behavioral result of the emphasis on autonomy is acceptance of or acquiescence in group decisions and activities.

Party pursuits also appeal to offenders because they permit conspicuous display of independence (Persson 1981). This generally means avoidance of the world of routine work and freedom from being "under someone's thumb." It also may include being free to avoid or to escape from restrictive routines:

> I just wanted to be doing something. Instead of being at home, or something like that. I wanted to be running, I wanted to be going to clubs, and picking up women, and shooting pool. And I liked to go to [a nearby resort community] and just drive around over there. A lot of things like that. . . . I was drinking two pints or more a day. . . . I was doing Valiums and I was doing Demerol. . . . I didn't want to work.

The proper pursuit and enjoyment of life as party is expensive, due largely to the costs of drugs. As one of our subjects remarked: "We was doing a lot of cocaine, so cash didn't last long, you know. If we made $3,000, two thousand of it almost instantly went for cocaine." Some party pursuers must meet other expenses as well if the lifestyle is to be maintained:

> Believe it or not, I was spending [$700] a day.
> Q: On what?
> A: Pot, alcohol, women, gas, motel rooms, food.
> Q: You were living in hotels, motels?
> A: Yeah, a lot of times, I was. I'd take a woman to a motel. I bought a lot of clothes. I used to like to dress pretty nicely, I'd buy suits.

Party pursuits require continuous infusions of money, and no single method of generating funds allows enjoyment of it for more than a few days. Consequently, the emphasis on spontaneity, autonomy, and independence is matched by the importance attached to financial resourcefulness. This is evidenced by the ability to sustain the lifestyle over a period of time. Doing so earns for offenders a measure of respect from peers for their demonstrated ability to "get over." It translates into "self-esteem . . . as a folk hero beating the bureaucratic system of routinized dependence" (Walsh 1986, p. 16). The value of and respect for those who demonstrate resourcefulness means that criminal acts, as a means of sustaining life as party, generally are not condemned by the offender's peers.

The risks of employing criminal solutions to the need for funds are approached blithely but confidently in the same spontaneous and playful manner as are the rewards of life as party. In fact, avoidance of careful and detailed planning is a way of demonstrating possession of valued personal qualities and commitment to the lifestyle. Combined with the twin assumptions that peers have chosen freely and that one should not interfere with their autonomy, avoidance of rational planning finds expression in a reluctance to suggest that peers should weigh carefully the possible consequences of whatever they choose to do. Thus, the interaction that precedes criminal incidents is distinguished by circumspection and the use of linguistic devices that relegate risk and fear to the background of attention. The act of stealing, for example, is referred to obliquely but knowingly as "doing something" or as "making money":

> [After a day of partying,] I [got] to talking about making some money, because I didn't have no money. This guy that we were riding with, he had all the money. . . . So me and him and my nephew, we get together, talking about making some money. This guy tells me, he said, "man, I know where there's a good place at."
>
> Q: Okay, so you suggested you all go somewhere and rob?
> A: Yeah, "make some"—well, we called it "making money."
> Q: Okay. So, then you and this fellow met up in the bar. . . . Tell me about the conversation?
> A: Well, there wasn't much of a conversation to it, really. . . . I asked him if he was ready to go, if he wanted to go do something, you know. And he knew what I meant. He wanted to go make some money somehow, any way it took.

To the external observer, inattention to risk at the moment when it would seem most appropriate may seem to border on irrationality. For the offender engaged in party pursuits, however, it is but one aspect of behaviors that are rational in other respects. It opens up opportunities to enjoy life as party and to demonstrate commitment to values shared by peers. Resourcefulness and disdain for conventional rationality affirm individual character and style, both of which are important in the world of party pursuits (Goffman 1967).

Party Pursuits and Eroding Resources

Paradoxically, the pursuit of life as party can be appreciated and enjoyed to the fullest extent only if participants moderate their involvement in it while maintaining identities and routines in the straight world. Doing so maintains "escape value" but it also requires an uncommon measure of discipline and forbearance. The fact is that extended and enthusiastic enjoyment of life as party threatens constantly to deplete irrevocably the resources needed to sustain measured enjoyment of its pleasures. Three aspects of the life-as-party lifestyle can contribute to this end.

First, some offenders become ensnared increasingly by the chemical substances and drug using routines that are common there. In doing so, the meaning of drug consumption changes:

> See, I was doing drugs every day. It just wasn't every other day, it was to the point that, after the first few months doing drugs, I would have to do "X amount" of drugs, say, just for instance, just to feel like I do now. Which is normal.

Once the party pursuer's physical or psychological tolerance increases significantly, drugs are consumed not for the high they once produced but instead to maintain a sense of normality by avoiding sickness or withdrawal.

Second, party pursuits erode legitimate fiscal and social capital. They can not be sustained by legitimate employment and they may in fact undermine both one's ability and inclination to hold a job. Even if offenders are willing to work at the kinds of employment available to them, and evidence suggests that many are not (Cromwell, Olson, and Avary 1991), the time schedules of work and party pursuits conflict. The best times of the day for committing many property crimes are also the times the offender would be at work, and it is nearly impossible to do both consistently and well. For those who pursue life as a party, legitimate employment often is foregone or sacrificed (Rengert and Wasilchick 1985). The absence of income from noncriminal sources reinforces the need to find other sources of money.

Determined pursuit of life as party also may affect participants' relationships with legitimate significant others. Many offenders manage to enjoy the lifestyle successfully only by exploiting the concern and largesse of family and friends. This may take the form of repeated requests for and receipt of personal loans that go unreturned, occasional thefts, or other forms of exploitation:

> I lived well for awhile. I lived well . . . until I started shooting cocaine real bad, intravenously. . . . [A]nd then everything, you know, went up in smoke, you know. Up my arm. The watches, the rings, . . . the car, you know. I used to have a girl, man, and her daddy had two horses. I put them in my arm. You know what I mean? . . . I made her sell them horses. My clothes and all that stuff, a lot of it, they went up in smoke when I started messing with that cocaine.

Eventually, friends and even family members may come to believe that they have been exploited or that continued assistance will only prolong a process that must be terminated. As one subject told us, "Oh, I tried to borrow money, and borrow money and, you know, nobody would loan it to me. Because they knew what I was doing." After first refusing further assistance, acquaintances, friends, and even family members may avoid social contacts with the party pursuer or sever ties altogether. This dialogue occurred between the interviewer and one of our subjects.

Q: [B]esides doing something wrong, did you think of anything else that you could do to get money? . . . Borrow it?

A: No, I'd done run that in the ground. See, you burn that up. That's burned up, right there, borrowing, you know. . . . Once I borrow, you know, I might get $10 from you today and, see, I'll be expecting to be getting $10 tomorrow, if I could. And then, when I see you [and] you see me coming, you say, "no, I don't have none." . . . [A]s the guys in the penitentiary say, "you absorb all of your remedies," you see. And that's what I did: I burned my remedies up, you know.

Last, when party pursuits are not going well, feelings of shame and self-disgust are not uncommon (Frazier and Meisenhelder 1985). Unsuccessful party pursuers as a result may take steps to reduce these feelings by distancing themselves voluntarily from conventional others:

Q: You were married to your wife at that time?

A: Yeah, I was married . . .

Q: Where was she living then?

A: I finally forced her to go home, you know . . . I made her go home, you know. And it caused an argument, for her to go home to her mother's. I felt like that was the best thing I did for her, you know. She hated me . . . for it at the time, didn't understand none of it. But, really, I intentionally made her go. I really spared her the misery that we were going to have. And it came. It came in bundles.

When party pursuers sustain severe losses of legitimate income and social resources, regardless of how it occurs, they grow increasingly isolated from conventional significant others. The obvious consequence is that this reduces interpersonal constraints on their behavior.

As their pursuit of life as party increasingly assumes qualities of difficulty and struggle, offenders' utilities and risk perceptions also change. Increasingly, crimes are committed not to enhance or sustain the lifestyle so much as to forestall unpleasant circumstances. Those addicted to alcohol or other drugs, for example, must devote increasing time and energy to the quest for monies to purchase their chemicals of choice. Both their drug consumption and the frequency of their criminal acts increase (Ball et al. 1983; Johnson et al. 1985). For them, as for others, inability to draw on legitimate or low-risk resources may precipitate a crisis. One of our respondents retold how, facing a court appearance on a burglary charge, he needed funds to hire an attorney:

I needed some money bad or if I didn't, if I went to court the following day, I was going to be locked up. The judge was going to lock me up. Because I didn't have no lawyer. And I had went and talked to several lawyers and they told me . . . they wanted a thousand dollars, that if I couldn't come up with no thousand dollars, they couldn't come to court with me. . . . [S]o I went to my sister. I asked my sister, I said, "look here, what about letting me have seven or eight hundred dollars"—which I knowed she had the money because she . . . had been in a wreck and she had gotten some money out of a suit. And she said, "well, if I give you the money you won't do the right thing with it." And I was telling her, "no, no, I need a lawyer." But I couldn't convince her to let me have the money. So I left. . . . I said, shit, I'm fixin' to go back to jail. . . . [S]o as I left her house and was walking—I was going to catch the bus—the [convenience store] and bus stop was right there by each other. So, I said I'm going to buy me some gum. . . . [A]nd in the process of me buying the chewing gum, I seen two ladies, they was counting money. So I figured sooner or later one of them was going to come out with the money. . . . I waited on them until . . . one came out with the money, and I got it.

Confronted by crisis and preoccupied with relieving immediate distress, the offender eventually may experience and define himself as propelled by forces beyond his control. Behavioral options become dichotomized into those that hold out some possibility of relief, however risky, and those that promise little but continued pain. Legitimate options are few and are seen as unlikely solutions. A criminal act may offer some hope of relief, however temporary. The offender may imbue the criminal option with almost magical prospects for ending or reversing the state of discomfort:

I said, "well, look at it like this": If I don't do it, then tomorrow morning I've got the same [problems] that I've got right now. I could be hungry. I'm going to want food more. I'm going to want cigarettes more. I'm going to want everything more. [But] if I do it, and if I make it, then I've got all I want.

Acts that once were the result of blithe unconcern with risk can over time come to be based on a personal determination to master or reverse what is experienced as desperately unpleasant circumstances. As a result, inattention to risk in the offender's decision making may give way to the perception that he has *nothing to lose:*

It . . . gets to the point that you get into such a desperation. You're not working, you can't work. You're drunk as hell, been that way two or three weeks. You're no good to yourself, and you're no good to anybody else. Self-esteem is gone [and] spiritually, mentally, physically, financially bankrupt. You ain't got nothing to lose.

Desperate to maintain or reestablish a sense of normality, the offender pursues emotional relief with a decision to act decisively, albeit in the face of legal odds recognized as narrowing. By acting boldly and resolutely to make the best of a grim situation, one gains a measure of respect, if not from others, then at least from oneself.

I think, when you're doing . . . drugs like I was doing, I don't think you tend to rationalize much at all. I think it's just a decision you make. You don't weigh the consequences, the pros and the cons. You just do it.

> You know, all kinds of things started running through my mind. If I get caught, then there, there I am with another charge. Then I said, well if I don't do something, I'm going to be in jail. And I just said, "I'm going to do it."

The fact that sustained party pursuits often cause offenders to increase the number of offenses they commit and to exploit criminal opportunities that formerly were seen as risky should not be interpreted as meaning they believe they can continue committing crime with impunity. The opposite is true. Many offenders engaged in crimes intended to halt or reverse eroding fortunes are aware that eventually they will be arrested if they continue doing so:

Q: How did you manage not to think about, you know, that you could go to prison?
A: Well, you think about it afterwards. You think, "wow, boy, I got away with it again." But you know, sooner or later, the law of averages is gonna catch up with you. You just can't do it [commit crime] forever and ever and ever. And don't think you're not gonna get caught, cause you will.

Bennett and Wright (1984a) likewise show that a majority of persistent offenders endorse the statement that they will be caught "eventually." The cyclical transformation of party pursuits from pleasant and enjoyable to desperate and tenuous is one reason they are able to commit crimes despite awareness of inevitable and potentially severe legal penalties.

The threat posed by possible arrest and imprisonment, however, may not seem severe to some desperate offenders. As compared to their marginal and precarious existence, it may be seen as a form of relief:

> [When he was straight], I'd think about [getting caught]: I could get this, and that [penalties]. . . . [A]nd then I would think, well, I know this is going to end one day, you know. But, you know, you get so far out there, and get so far off into it that it really don't matter, you know. But you think about that. . . . I knew, eventually, I would get caught, you know. . . . I was off into drugs and I just didn't care if I got caught or not.

> When I [got] caught—and they caught me right at the house—it's kind of like, you feel good, because you're glad it's over, you know. I mean, a weight being lifted off your head. And you say, well, I don't have to worry about this shit no more, because they've caught me. And it's over, you know.

In sum, due to offenders' eroding acess to legitimately secured funds, their diminishing contact with and support from conventional significant others, and their efforts to maintain drug consumption habits, crimes that once were committed for recreational purposes increasingly become desperate attempts to forestall or reverse uncomfortable or frustrating situations. Pursuing the short term goal of maximizing enjoyment of life, legal threats can appear to the offender either as remote and improbable contingencies when party pursuits fulfill their recreational purposes or as an acceptable risk in the face of continued isolation, penury, and desperation.

We analyzed the descriptions of crime provided by our subjects, and their activities on the day the crime occurred. We focused specifically on: (1) the primary purpose of their crimes, i.e., whether they planned to use the proceeds of crime for pleasure or to cope with unpleasant contingencies, and (2) the extent and subjective meaning of their drug use at the time they decided to commit the crime in question. Based on the analysis, we classified the crimes of 15 subjects as behaviors committed in the enjoyment of life as party and 13 as behaviors committed in order to enhance or restore enjoyment of this lifestyle. The 12 remaining offenders could not be classified because of insufficient information in the crime descriptions or they are isolated criminal acts that do not represent a specific lifestyle. Two subjects, for example, described crimes that were acts of vengeance directed at the property of individuals who had treated them or their relatives improperly. One of the men related how he decided to burglarize a home for reasons of revenge:

> I was mad. . . . When I was in the penitentiary, my wife went to his house for a party and he give her a bunch of cocaine. . . . It happened, I think, about a week before I got out. . . . I just had it in my mind what I wanted to do: I wanted to hurt him like I was hurt. . . . I was pretty drunk, when I went by [his home], and I saw there wasn't no car there. So, I just pulled my car in.

The other subject told how an acquaintance had stolen drugs and other possessions from his automobile. In response the subject "staked out the places where he would be for several days before I caught him, at gun point, [and] made him take me to his home, [which] I ransacked, and found some of the narcotics that he had stolen from me." Although neither of these crimes was committed in pursuit of life as party, other crimes committed by both these subjects during their criminal careers did occur as part of that lifestyle. Other investigators have similarly reported that revenge is the dominant motive in a minority of property offenses (e.g., Cromwell, Olson, and Avary 1991, p. 22).

Implications

We have suggested that daily routines characteristic of the partying lifestyle of persistent and unsuccessful offenders may modify both the salience of their various decision utilities and their perceptions of legal risk in the process of their crime commission decisions. This is not to say that these decisions are irrational, only that they do not conform to decision making as sketched by rational choice theories. Our objective was not to falsify the rational choice approach to criminal decision making, for we know of no way this could be accomplished. Whatever it is, moreover, rationality is not a dichotomous variable. Indeed, offenders' target selection decision making appears more rational in the conventional sense than do crime commission decisions.

The lesson here for theories of criminal decision making is that while utilities and risk assessment may be properties of individuals, they are also shaped by the social and personal contexts in which decisions are made. Whether their pursuit of life as party is interpreted theoretically as the product of structural strain, choice, or even happenstance is of limited importance to an understanding of offenders' discrete criminal forays. What is important is that their lifestyle places them in situations that may facilitate important transformations in the utilities of prospective actions. If nothing else, this means that some situations more than others make it possible to discount or ignore risk. We are not the first to call attention to this phenomenon:

> [The] situational nature of sanction properties has escaped the scales and indicators employed in official record and self-report survey research. In this body of research an arrest and a year in prison are generally assumed to have the same meaning for all persons and across all situations. The situational grounding of sanction properties suggests[, however,] that we look beyond official definitions of sanctions and the attitudinal structure of individuals to the properties of situations (Ekland-Olson et al. 1984, p. 174).

Along the same line, the longitudinal survey of adult offenders concludes that decision making "may be conditioned by elements within the immediate situation confronting the individual . . . [such that] perceptions of the opportunity, returns, and support for crime within a given situation may influence . . . perceptions of risks and the extent to which those risks are discounted" (Piliavin et al. 1986, p. 115). The same interpretation has been suggested by Shover and Thompson (1992) for their failure to find an expected positive relationship between risk estimates and crime desistance among former prison inmates.

In light of the sample and data limitations of this study we cannot and have not argued that the lifestyle we described *generates* or *produces* the characteristic decision-making behaviors of persistent property offenders. The evidence does not permit such interpretive liberties. It does seem reasonable to suggest, however, that the focal concerns and shared perspectives of those who pursue life as party may function to *sustain* offenders' freewheeling, but purposeful, decision-making style. Without question there is a close *correspondence* between the two. Our ability to explain and predict decision making requires that we gain a better understanding of how utilities and risk perceptions are constrained by the properties of situations encountered typically by persons in their daily rounds. In other words, we must learn more about the daily worlds that comprise the immediate contexts of criminal decision-making behavior.

Note

This research was supported by grant #86-IJ-CX-0068 from the U.S. Department of Justice, National Institute of Justice (Principal Investigator: Neal Shover). Points of view or opinions expressed here do not necessarily reflect the official position or policies of the Department of Justice. For their critical comments while the paper was in gestation we are grateful to Derek Cornish and to participants in a March 1991 colloquium at the Centre for Socio-Legal Studies, Wolfson College, University of Oxford. Werner Einstadter, Michael Levi, Mike Maguire, and anonymous reviewers also provided helpful comments.

References

Ball J. C., Shaffer, J. W. and Nurco, D. N. (1983) "The day-to-day criminality of heroin addicts in Baltimore: A study in the continuity of offense rates," *Drug and Alcohol Dependence, 12,* 119–142.

Becker, G. (1968) "Crime and punishment: An economic approach," *Journal of Political Economy, 76,* 169–217.

Bennett, T. and Wright, R. (1984a) *Burglars on Burglary,* Hampshire, U.K.: Gower.

—— (1984b) "The relationship between alcohol use and burglary," *British Journal of Addiction, 79,* 431–437.

Blumstein, A., Cohen, J. and Nagin, D., editors (1978) *Deterrence and Incapacitation: Estimating the Effects of Criminal Sanctions on Crime Rates,* Washington, D.C.: National Academy of Sciences.

Carroll, J. S. (1978) "A psychological approach to deterrence: The evaluation of crime opportunities," *Journal of Personality and Social Psychology, 36,* 1512–1520.

—— (1982) "Committing a crime: The offender's decision," in: J. Konecni and E. B. Ebbesen (Eds.), *The Criminal Justice System: A Social-Psychological Analysis,* San Francisco: W. H. Freeman.

Carroll, J. S. and Weaver, F. (1986) "Shoplifters' perceptions of crime opportunities: A process-tracing study," in: D. B. Cornish and R. V. Clarke (Eds.), *The Reasoning Criminal: Rational Choice Perspectives on Offending,* New York: Springer-Verlag.

Clarke, R. V. and Cornish, D. B. (1985) "Modeling offenders' decisions: A framework for research and policy," in: M. Tonry and N. Morris (Eds.), *Crime and Justice: A Review of Research,* Vol. 4, Chicago: University of Chicago Press.

Claster, D. S. (1967) "Comparison of risk perception between delinquents and nondelinquents," *Journal of Criminal Law, Criminology, and Police Science, 58,* 80–86.

Cornish, D. B. and Clarke, R. V., editors (1986) *The Reasoning Criminal: Rational Choice Perspectives on Offending,* New York: Springer-Verlag.

Cromwell, P. F., Olson, J. N. and Avary, D. W. (1991) *Breaking and Entering: An Ethnographic Analysis of Burglary,* Newbury Park, Calif.: Sage.

Ekland-Olson, S., Lieb, J. and Zurcher, L. (1984) "The paradoxical impact of criminal sanctions: Some microstructural findings," *Law & Society Review, 18,* 159–178.

Feeney, F. (1986) "Robbers as decision-makers," in: D. B. Cornish and R. V. Clarke (Eds.), *The Reasoning Criminal: Rational Choice Perspectives on Offending,* New York: Springer-Verlag.

Figgie International (1988) *The Figgie Report Part VI—The Business of Crime: The Criminal Perspective,* Richmond, Va.: Figgie International, Inc.

Frazier, C. E. and Meisenholder, T. (1985) "Criminality and emotional ambivalence: Exploratory notes on an overlooked dimension," *Qualitative Sociology,* 8, 266–284.

Gibbs, J. J. and Shelley, P. L. (1982) "Life in the fast lane: A retrospective view by commercial thieves," *Journal of Research in Crime and Delinquency,* 19, 299–330.

Goffman, E. (1967) *Interaction Ritual,* Garden City, N.Y.: Anchor.

Gottfredson, M. R. and Hirschi, T. (1990) *A General Theory of Crime,* Stanford, Calif.: Stanford University Press.

Heineke, J. M., editor (1978) *Economic Models of Criminal Behavior,* Amsterdam: North-Holland.

Johnson, B. D., Goldstein, P. J., Preble, E., Schmeidler, J., Lipton, D. D., Spunt, B. and Miller, T. (1985) *Taking Care of Business: The Economics of Crime by Heroin Addicts,* Lexington, Mass.: D.C. Heath.

Katz, J. (1988) *Seductions of Crime,* New York: Basic Books.

Maguire, M. in collaboration with T. Bennett (1982) *Burglary in a Dwelling,* London: Heinemann.

Manski, C. F. (1978) "Prospects for inference on deterrence through empirical analysis of individual criminal behavior," in: A. Blumstein, J. Cohen, and D. Nagin (Eds.), *Deterrence and Incapacitation: Estimating the Effects of Criminal Sanctions on Crime Rates,* Washington, D.C.: National Academy of Sciences.

Nagin, D. S. and Paternoster, R. (1991) "On the relationship of past to future participation in delinquency," *Criminology,* 29, 163–189.

Persson, M. (1981) "Time-perspectives amongst criminals," *Acta Sociologica,* 24, 149–165.

Petersilia, J. (1980) "Criminal career research: A review of recent evidence," in: N. Morris and M. Tonry (Eds.), *Crime and Justice: An Annual Review of Research,* Vol. 2, Chicago: University of Chicago Press.

—— Greenwood, P. W. and Lavin, M. (1978) *Criminal Careers of Habitual Felons,* Washington, D.C.: U.S. Department of Justice, National Institute of Law Enforcement and Criminal Justice.

Peterson, M. A. and Braiker, H. B. (1980) *Doing Crime: A Survey of California Prison Inmates,* Santa Monica, Calif.: Rand Corporation.

Piliavin, I., Gartner, R. and Matsueda, R. (1986) "Crime, deterrence, and rational choice," *American Sociological Review,* 51, 101–119.

Rengert, G. F. and Wasilchick, J. (1985) *Suburban Burglary,* Springfield, Ill.: Charles C. Thomas.

Repetto, T. A. (1974) *Residential Crime,* Cambridge, Mass.: Ballinger.

Reynolds, M. O. (1985) *Crime by Choice: An Economic Analysis,* Dallas: Fisher Institute.

Scarr, H. A. (1973) *Patterns of Burglary* (second edition), Washington, D.C.: U.S. Department of Justice, National Institute of Law Enforcement and Criminal Justice.

Seidel, J. V., Kjolseth, R. and Seymour, E. (1988) *The Ethnograph: A User's Guide* (Version 3.0), Littleton, Col.: Qualis Research Associates.

Shover, N. (1991) "Burglary," in: M. Tonry (Ed.), *Crime and Justice: An Annual Review of Research,* Vol. 14, Chicago: University of Chicago Press.

Shover, N. and Thompson, C. Y. (1992) "Age, differential expectations, and crime desistance," *Criminology,* 30, 89–109.

Tittle, C. R. (1980) *Sanctions and Deviance: The Question of Deterrence,* New York: Praeger.

Waldo, G. P. and Chiricos, T. G. (1972) "Perceived penal sanction and self-reported criminality: A neglected approach to deterrence research," *Social Problems,* 19, 522–540.

Walsh, D. (1980) *Break-Ins: Burglary from Private Houses,* London: Constable.

—— (1986) *Heavy Business,* London: Routledge & Kegan Paul.

The Interactionist, Societal Reactions, or Labeling Perspective

Individuals who subscribe to the interactionist, or labeling, school examine those social and psychological, or interactional, processes that take place among actors, audiences, and third parties, particularly in terms of their impact on the personal and social-public identity of the actor. The production of a range of deviant careers and identities is also given focus. The main concern, then, is definitional processes and products, and their effects.

Howard S. Becker has explored the concept of *career*, the major orienting focus of this volume, in some depth. He also introduces some important analytical distinctions. In "Career Deviance," he argues that public labeling is generally the most crucial step in building a long-term deviant career. Not only does being branded a deviant affect one's continued social participation, but it frequently produces notable changes in the actor's self-image. The most drastic change, however, seems to occur with respect to the actor's public identity—that is, how others view him or her. Suddenly, in the eyes of others he or she has become a different person; this new status can be effectively referred to as a *master status*. In offering an important distinction between master and subordinate statuses, Becker argues that master statuses assume a certain priority and appear to override most other status considerations.

The status of a deviant is one such status. In relating to a deviant, people will frequently respond to the label and not to the individual. Treatment of an actor in this fashion—as if he or she is generally deviant and not specifically deviant—can serve as a self-fulfilling prophecy whereby attempts are made to mold the actor into the image others have of him or her. Deliberate attempts may be made, for example, to exclude the deviant from any meaningful social intercourse. The actor may respond negatively to such treatment, and, over time, exclusion and its associated reactions can actually give rise to more deviance. The treatment situation, Becker claims, is especially likely to produce such a result.

The statement by Frank Tannenbaum, "Definition and the Dramatization of Evil," represents one of the earliest attempts at describing how individuals may be singled out for special treatment by the community. His basic thesis is that two opposing definitions of the situation may arise. For example, what may be viewed as play or fun by the young actor may be seen as a form of evil or delinquency by community members. Gradually there may occur a shift "from definition of the specific acts as evil to a definition of the individual as evil." This defining process is not without its effects. To the community, the individual has become a bad or evil person. To the individual, a sense of injustice emerges; this forces him to realize that he is different from other boys in the neighborhood, school, street, and community. Tannenbaum suggests further that such a person may not only change his personal identity—that is, come to view himself as a young criminal or delinquent—but may become part of a group or subculture that shares his activities. Primarily as a result of the self-fulfilling prophecy, then, he may begin to act in accordance with the expectations associated with his label. He may, moreover, move into a pattern of career deviance or crime.

18 Career Deviance

Howard S. Becker

One of the most crucial steps in the process of building a stable pattern of deviant behavior is likely to be the experience of being caught and publicly labeled as a deviant. Whether a person takes this step or not depends not so much on what he does as on what other people do, on whether or not they enforce the rule he has violated. . . . First of all, even though no one else discovers the nonconformity or enforces the rules against it, the individual who has committed the impropriety may himself act as an enforcer. He may brand himself as deviant because of what he has done and punish himself in one way or another for his behavior. This is not always or necessarily the case, but may occur. Second, there may be cases like those described by psychoanalysts in which the individual really wants to get caught and perpetrates his deviant act in such a way that it is almost sure he will be.

In any case, being caught and branded as deviant has important consequences for one's further social participation and self-image. The most important consequence is a drastic change in the individual's public identity. Committing the improper act and being publicly caught at it place him in a new status. He has been revealed as a different kind of person from the kind he was supposed to be. He is labeled a "fairy," "dope fiend," "nut," or "lunatic," and treated accordingly.

In analyzing the consequences of assuming a deviant identity let us make use of Hughes' distinction between master and auxiliary status traits.[1] Hughes notes that most statuses have one key trait which serves to distinguish those who belong from those who do not. Thus the doctor, whatever else he may be, is a person who has a certificate stating that he has fulfilled certain requirements and is licensed to practice medicine; this is the master trait. As Hughes points out, in our society a doctor is also informally expected to have a number of auxiliary traits: most people expect him to be upper middle class, white, male, and Protestant. When he is not there is a sense that he has in some way failed to fill the bill. Similarly, though skin color is the master status trait determining who is Negro and who is white, Negroes are informally expected to have certain status traits and not to have others; people are surprised and find it anomalous if a Negro turns out to be a doctor or a college professor. People often have the master status trait but lack some of the auxiliary, informally expected characteristics; for example, one may be a doctor but be female or Negro.

Hughes deals with this phenomenon in regard to statuses that are well thought of, desired and desirable (noting that one may have the formal qualifications for entry into a status but be denied full entry because of lack of the proper auxiliary traits), but the same process occurs in the case of deviant statuses. Possession of one deviant trait may have a generalized symbolic value, so that people automatically assume that its bearer possesses other undesirable traits allegedly associated with it.

To be labeled a criminal one need only commit a single criminal offense, and this is all the term formally refers to. Yet the word carries a number of connotations specifying auxiliary traits characteristic of anyone bearing the label. A man who has been convicted of housebreaking and thereby labeled criminal is presumed to be a person likely to break into other houses; the police, in rounding up known offenders for investigation after a crime has been committed, operate on this premise. Further, he is considered likely to commit other kinds of crimes as well, because he has shown himself to be a person without "respect for the law." Thus, apprehension for one deviant act exposes a person to the likelihood that he will be regarded as deviant or undesirable in other respects.

There is one other element in Hughes' analysis we can borrow with profit: the distinction between master and subordinate statuses.[2] Some statuses, in our society as in others, override all other statuses and have a certain priority. Race is one of these. Membership in the Negro race, as socially defined, will override most other status considerations in most other situations; the fact that one is a physician or middle-class or female will not protect one from being treated as a Negro first and any of these other things second. The status of deviant (depending on this kind of deviance) is this kind of master status. One receives the status as a result of breaking a rule, and the identification proves to be more important than most others. One will be identified as a deviant first, before other identifications are made. The question is raised: "What kind of person would break such an important rule?" And the answer is given: "One who is different from the rest of us, who cannot or will not act as a moral human being and therefore might break other important rules." The deviant identification becomes the controlling one.

Treating a person as though he were generally rather than specifically deviant produces a self-fulfilling prophecy. It sets in motion several mechanisms which conspire to shape the person in the image people have of him.[3] In the first place, one tends to be cut off, after being identified as deviant, from participation in more conventional groups, even though the specific consequences of the particular deviant activity might never of themselves have caused the isolation had there not also been the public knowledge and reaction to it. For example, being a homosexual may not affect one's ability to do office work, but to be known as a homosexual in an office may make it impossible to continue working there. Similarly, though the effects of opiate drugs may not impair one's working ability, to be known as an addict will probably lead to losing one's job. In such cases, the individual finds it difficult to conform to other rules which he had no intention or desire to break, and perforce finds himself deviant in these areas as well. The homosexual who is deprived of a "respectable" job by the discovery of his deviance may drift into unconventional, marginal occupations where it does not make so much difference. The drug addict finds himself forced into other illegitimate kinds of activity, such as robbery and theft, by the refusal of respectable employers to have him around.

When the deviant is caught, he is treated in accordance with the popular diagnosis of why he is that way, and the treatment itself may likewise produce increasing deviance. The drug addict, popularly considered to be a weak-willed individual who cannot forego the indecent pleasures afforded him by opiates, is treated repressively. He is forbidden to use drugs. Since he cannot get drugs legally, he must get them illegally. This forces the market underground and pushes the price of drugs up far beyond the current legitimate market price into a bracket that few can afford on an ordinary salary. Hence the treatment of the addict's deviance places him in a position where it will probably be necessary to resort to deceit and crime in order to support his habit.[4] The behavior is a consequence of the public reaction to the deviance rather than a consequence of the inherent qualities of the deviant act.

Notes

1. Everett C. Hughes, "Dilemmas and Contradictions of Status," *American Journal of Sociology,* L (March, 1945), 353–359.
2. *Ibid.*
3. See Marsh Ray, "The Cycle of Abstinence and Relapse Among Heroin Addicts," *Social Problems, 9* (Fall, 1961), 132–140.
4. See *Drug Addiction: Crime or Disease?* Interim and Final Reports of the Joint Committee of the American Bar Association and the American Medical Association on Narcotic Drugs (Bloomington, Indiana: Indiana University Press, 1961).

19 Definition and the Dramatization of Evil

Frank Tannenbaum

In the conflict between the young delinquent and the community there develop two opposing definitions of the situation. In the beginning the definition of the situation by the young delinquent may be in the form of play, adventure, excitement, interest, mischief, fun. Breaking windows, annoying people, running around porches, climbing over roofs, stealing from pushcarts, playing truant—all are items of play, adventure, excitement. To the community, however, these activities may and often do take on the form of a nuisance, evil, delinquency, with the demand for control, admonition, chastisement, punishment, police court, truant school. This conflict over the situation is one that arises out of a divergence of values. As the problem develops, the situation gradually becomes redefined. The attitude of the community hardens definitely into a demand for suppression. There is a gradual shift from the definition of the specific acts as evil to a definition of the individual as evil, so that all his acts come to be looked upon with suspicion. In the process of identification his companions, hang-outs, play, speech, income, all his conduct, the personality itself, become subject to scrutiny and question. From the community's point of view, the individual who used to do bad and mischievous things has now become a bad and unredeemable human being. From the individual's point of view there has taken place a similar change. He has gone slowly from a sense of grievance and injustice, of being unduly mistreated and punished, to a recognition that the definition of him as a human being is different from that of other boys in his neighborhood, his school, street, community. This recognition on his part becomes a process of self-identification and integration with the group which shares his activities. It becomes, in part, a process of rationalization; in part, a simple response to a specialized type of stimulus. The young delinquent becomes bad because he is defined as bad and because he is not believed if he is good. There is a persistent demand for consistency in character. The community cannot deal with people whom it cannot define. Reputation is this sort of public definition. Once it is established, then unconsciously all agencies combine to maintain this definition even when they apparently and consciously attempt to deny their own implicit judgment.

Early in his career, then, the incipient professional criminal develops an attitude of antagonism to the regulated orderly life that he is required to lead. This attitude is hardened and crystallized by opposition. The conflict becomes a clash of wills. And experience too often has proved that threats, punishments, beatings, commitments to institutions, abuse and defamation of one sort or another, are of no avail. Punishment breaks down against the child's stubbornness. What has happened is that the child has been defined as an "incorrigible" both by his contacts and by himself, and an attempt at a direct breaking down of will generally fails.

The child meets the situation in the only way he can, by defiance and escape—physical escape if possible, or emotional escape by derision, anger, contempt, hatred, disgust, tantrums, destructiveness, and physical violence. The response of the child is just as intelligent and intelligible as that of the schools, of the authorities. They have taken a simple problem, the lack of fitness of an institution to a particular child's needs, and have made a moral issue out of it with values outside the child's ken. It takes on the form of war between two wills, and the longer the war lasts, the more certainly does the child become incorrigible. The child will not yield because he cannot yield—his nature requires other channels for pleasant growth; the school system or society will not yield because it does not see the issues involved as between the incompatibility of an institution and a child's needs, sometimes physical needs, and will instead attempt to twist the child's nature to the institution with that consequent distortion of the child which makes an unsocial career inevitable. The verbalization of the conflict in terms of evil, delinquency, incorrigibility, badness, arrest, force, punishment, stupidity, lack of intelligence, truancy, criminality, gives the innocent divergence of the child from the straight road a meaning that it did not have in the beginning and makes its continuance in these same terms by so much the more inevitable.

The only important fact, when the issue arises of the boy's inability to acquire the specific habits which organized institutions attempt to impose upon him, is that this conflict becomes the occasion for him to acquire another series of habits, interests, and attitudes as a substitute. These habits become as effective in motivating and guiding conduct as would have been those which the orderly routine social institutions attempted to impose had they been acquired.

This conflict gives the gang its hold, because the gang provides escape, security, pleasure, and peace. The gang also gives room for the motor activity which plays a large role in a child's life. The attempt to break up the gang by force merely strengthens it. The arrest of the children has consequences undreamed-of, for several reasons.

First, only some of the children are caught though all may be equally guilty. There is a great deal more delinquency practiced and committed by the young groups than comes to the attention of the police. The boy arrested, therefore, is singled out in specialized treatment. This boy, no more guilty than the other members of his group, discovers a world of which he knew little. His arrest suddenly precipitates a series of institutions, attitudes, and experiences which the other children do not share. For this boy there suddenly appear the police, the patrol wagon, the police station, the other delinquents and criminals found in the police lock-ups, the court with all its agencies such as bailiffs, clerks, bondsmen, lawyers, probation officers. There are bars, cells, handcuffs, criminals. He is questioned, examined, tested, investigated. His history is gone into, his family is brought into court. Witnesses make their appearance. The boy, no different from the rest of his gang, suddenly becomes the center of a major drama in which all sorts of unexpected characters play important roles. And what is it all about? about the accustomed things his gang has done and has been doing for a long time. In this entirely new world he is made conscious of himself as a different human being than he was before his arrest. He becomes classified as a thief, perhaps, and the entire world about him has suddenly become a different place for him and will remain different for the rest of his life. . . .

The first dramatization of the "evil" which separates the child out of his group for specialized treatment plays a greater role in making the criminal than perhaps any other experience. It cannot be too often emphasized that for the child the whole situation has become different. He now lives in a different world. He has been tagged. A new and hitherto non-existent environment has been precipitated out for him.

The process of making the criminal, therefore, is a process of tagging, defining, identifying, segregating, describing, emphasizing, making conscious and self-conscious; it becomes a way of stimulating, suggesting, emphasizing, and evoking the very traits that are complained of. If the theory of relation of response to stimulus has any meaning, the entire process of dealing with the young delinquent is mischievous in so far as it identifies him to himself or to the environment as a delinquent person.

The person becomes the thing he is described as being. Nor does it seem to matter whether the valuation is made by those who would punish or by those who would reform. In either case the emphasis is upon the conduct that is disapproved of. The parents or the policeman, the older brother or the court, the probation officer or the juvenile institution, in so far as they rest upon the thing complained of, rest upon a false ground. Their very enthusiasm defeats their aim. The harder they work to reform the evil, the greater the evil grows under their hands. The persistent suggestion, with whatever good intentions, works mischief, because it leads to bringing out the bad behavior that it would suppress. The way out is through a refusal to dramatize the evil. The less said about it the better. The more said about something else, still better.

> The hard-drinker who keeps thinking of not drinking is doing what he can to initiate the acts which lead to drinking. He is starting with the stimulus to his habit. To succeed he must find some positive interest or line of action which will inhibit the drinking series and which by instituting another course of action will bring him to his desired end.[1]

The dramatization of the evil therefore tends to precipitate the conflict situation which was first created through some innocent maladjustment. The child's isolation forces him into companionship with other children similarly defined, and the gang becomes his means of escape, his security. The life of the gang gives it special mores, and the attack by the community upon these mores merely overemphasizes the conflict already in existence, and makes it the source of a new series of experiences that lead directly to a criminal career.

In dealing with the delinquent, the criminal, therefore, the important thing to remember is that we are dealing with a human being who is responding normally to the demands, stimuli, approval, expectancy, of the group with whom he is associated. We are dealing not with an individual but with a group.

> In a study of 6,000 instances of stealing, with reference to the number of boys involved, it was found that in 90.4 per cent of the cases two or more boys were known to have been involved in the act and were consequently brought to court. Only 9.6 per cent of all the cases were acts of single individuals. Since this study was based upon the number of boys brought to court, and since in many cases not all of the boys involved were caught and brought to court, it is certain that the percentage of group stealing is therefore even greater than 90.4 per cent. It cannot be doubted that delinquency, particularly stealing, almost invariably involves two or more persons.[2]

That group may be a small gang, a gang of children just growing up, a gang of young "toughs" of nineteen or twenty, or a gang of older criminals of thirty. If we are not dealing with a gang we may be dealing with a family. And if we are not dealing with either of these especially we may be dealing with a community. In practice all these factors—the family, the gang, and the community—may be important in the development and the maintenance of that attitude towards the world which makes a criminal career a normal, an accepted and approved way of life.

Direct attack upon the individual in these circumstances is a dubious undertaking. By the time the individual has become a criminal his habits have been so shaped that we have a fairly integrated character whose whole career is in tune with the peculiar bit of the environment for which he has developed the behavior and habits that cause him to be apprehended. In theory isolation from that group ought to provide occasion for change in the individual's habit structure. It might, if the individual were transplanted to a group whose values and activities had the approval of the wider community, and in which the newcomer might hope to gain full acceptance eventually. But until now isolation has meant the grouping in close confinement of persons whose strongest common bond has been their socially disapproved delinquent conduct. Thus the attack cannot be made without reference to group life.

The attack must be on the whole group; for only by changing its attitudes and ideals, interests and habits, can the stimuli which it exerts upon the individual be changed. Punishment as retribution has failed to reform, that is, to change character. If the individual can be made aware of a different set of values for which he may receive approval, then we may be on the road to a change in his character. But such a change of values involves a change in stimuli, which means that the criminal's social world must be changed before he can be changed.

The point of view here developed rejects all assumptions that would impute crime to the individual in the sense that a personal shortcoming of the offender is the cause of the unsocial behavior. The assumption that crime is caused by any sort of inferiority, physiological or psychological, is here completely and unequivocally repudiated.

This of course does not mean that morphological or psychological techniques do not have value in dealing with the individual. It merely means that they have no greater value in the study of criminology than they would have in the study of any profession. If a poor IQ is a bad beginning for a career in medicine, it is also a poor beginning for a career in crime. If the psychiatrist can testify that a psychopath will make an irritable doctor he can prove the same for the criminal. But he can prove no more. The criminal differs from the rest of his fellows only in the sense that he has learned to respond to the stimuli of a very small and specialized group; but that group must exist or the criminal could not exist. In that he is like the mass of men, living a certain kind of life with the kind of companions that make that life possible.

This explanation of criminal behavior is meant to apply to those who more or less consistently pursue the criminal career. It does not necessarily presume to describe the accidental criminal or the man who commits a crime of passion. Here perhaps the theories that would seek the cause of crime in the individual may have greater application than in attempting to deal with those who follow a life of crime. But even in the accidental criminal there is a strong presumption that the accident is the outcome of a habit situation. Any habit tends to have a background of social conditioning.

> A man with the habit of giving way to anger may show his habit by a murderous attack upon some one who has offended. His act is nonetheless due to habit because it occurs only once in his life. The essence of

habit is an acquired predisposition to *ways* or modes of response, not to particular acts except as, under special conditions, these express a way of behaving. Habit means special sensitiveness or accessibility to certain classes of stimuli, standing predilections and aversions, rather than bare recurrence of specific acts. It means will.[3]

In other words, perhaps the accidental criminal also is to be explained in terms such as we use in discussing the professional criminal.

Notes

1. John Dewey, *Human Nature and Conduct,* p. 35. New York, 1922.
2. Clifford R. Shaw and Earl D. Myers, "The Juvenile Delinquent," *The Illinois Crime Survey,* pp. 662–663. Chicago, 1929.
3. Dewey, op. cit., p. 42.

An Integrated Approach

As we suggested earlier, explanations often implicitly overlap or directly share common themes, concepts, or processes. For Merton, identifying these overlaps and underlying similarities should be of central concern to sociology. The following article contributes to the sociology of deviance by integrating three different perspectives. Jeffery T. Ulmer, in "Commitment, Deviance, and Social Control," addresses a current debate in the sociology of deviance by arguing that the "opposing positions share a common sociological goal—the explanation of continuity and change in lines of action." On one side of the debate are perspectives suggesting that individuals may be socialized into traditions favorable to deviance. These perspectives include differential association and social learning approaches which emphasize personal relationships and definitions of self that may lead to commitment to deviant behaviors and identities. Others argue that deviance is the expression of the lack of commitment to conventional traditions.

Ulmer is concerned with going beyond the debate to provide tools to address questions related to the different positions. Suggesting that the notion of commitment is central to the projects of differential association, social learning, and social control perspectives, Ulmer argues that a threefold framework of commitment (including structural, personal, and moral commitment) and their sources should be used. This and other attempts to integrate theories represent important steps toward a more complete understanding of deviance in society.

20 Commitment, Deviance, and Social Control

Jeffery T. Ulmer

The dialectics of structural constraint and agency, continuity and change, and self and social organization are fundamental sociological issues (Giddens 1984; Westby 1991; Shalin 1986; Mead 1934). The concept of commitment occupies a central conceptual space where these issues intersect (Katz 1994; Strauss 1993). I apply a commitment framework, created by Michael Johnson (1991), to deviance and conformity as types of situational action embedded in the contexts of corporal and phantom communities (Athens 1998). Developed in Johnson's (1991) research on personal relationships, this framework identifies three conceptually distinct types of commitment (structural, personal, and moral), each with its own particular sources. Each type depicts selves choosing between lines of action, sometimes in the face of internal or external constraints, and thus negotiating continuity and change in lines of action and biography.

The study of deviance and social control has been a core area of sociological concern since the work of Marx, Durkheim, and Weber. An important debate currently exists between prominent control theorists and proponents of differential association and social learning approaches. The latter emphasize socialization favorable to deviance, as well as personal relationships between deviant peers and definition of self in terms of deviant identities (Akers 1996; 1998; Heimer and Matsueda 1994; Warr 1993). On the other hand, Kornhauser (1978), Hirschi (1996), and Gottfredson (1999) sharply criticize what they derisively call "cultural deviance" theories as contrary to human nature and the nature of social organization. They argue instead that commitment to deviance is a contradiction in terms (Hirschi 1996), that "crime represents the antithesis of culture and that it necessarily spoils rather than enhances interpersonal relations" (Gottfredson 1999, p. 284).

The conceptualization of commitment I apply here transcends this debate by illustrating that these opposing positions share a common sociological goal—the explanation of continuity and change in lines of action. I argue that commitment is central to the projects of both differential

212

association/social learning and social control perspectives. However, despite Howard Becker's (1960) call for a more systematic conceptualization of commitment, most scholars of deviance—as well as scholars working in other substantive areas—use the term in a simplistic, undifferentiated manner (see reviews by Johnson 1991; Bernard 1987; Ulmer 1994).

In an earlier article (Ulmer 1994) I applied Johnson's (1991) threefold commitment framework to labeling theory, arguing that structural, moral, and personal commitment contingencies were the mechanisms by which sanctions may entrench people further into deviance careers. This article goes beyond that to make two contributions. First, if commitment is an important concept for deviance and social control, then it is critical to inquire into the possibility of different types of commitment and determine whether distinct sources produce them. This article presents a theoretical framework with which to investigate such questions for the field of deviance. I argue that any time deviance scholars investigate commitment, we should rely on the threefold framework.

Second, Makkai and Braithwaite (1991, p. 213) argue that future work needs to "explore new strategies of theoretical integration that transcend the existing criminological frameworks" (see also Matsueda 1988; 1992; Agnew 1995; Tittle 1989). The threefold commitment framework is a useful tool for such integration, as well as new insights, because it accomplishes three tasks that Merton (1997, p. 520) identified as essential for sociology: (1) conceptual clarification, (2) synthesis and integration of different theories by identifying underlying complementarities, and (3) "explicit identification of theoretical problems and the emergence of consequential concepts that [have] remained implicit in prior formulations."

Some of this framework's types and sources of commitment are explicitly recognized in differential association, opportunity, labeling, or social control theories. Others are merely implied, and some are unique to the commitment framework itself. Furthermore, none of the major deviance theories, by themselves, encompass or incorporate all of the types and sources of continuity in deviance or conventionality recognized by the threefold commitment framework, nor do other efforts at theoretical integration encompass such breadth (e.g., Braithwaite 1989; Tittle 1995).

A Threefold Commitment Typology

Several general conceptualizations and typologies of commitment have been developed (Becker 1960; Kanter 1972; Etzioni 1964; Stryker 1980; Burke and Reitzes 1991). The concept has proved particularly useful in research on close relationships (Johnson 1973; 1991), social movements (Walsh and Warland 1983; McAdam 1989; Hirsch 1990; Klandermans 1997), and organizations and work (Selznick 1969; Etzioni 1964; Faulkner 1974; Kanter 1977; Clarke 1991).

Michael Johnson developed the threefold commitment typology as a framework for explaining continuity in personal relationships. He has written extensively about the framework, its advantages compared to other commitment conceptualizations, and its potential for application beyond the topic of close relationships (Johnson 1973; 1976; 1982; 1991). I have also applied it to the relationship between labeling contingencies and entrenched commitment to deviant activity (Ulmer 1994). The framework extends and refines Becker's (1960; 1964) and Strauss's (1969) treatments of commitment (see also Gerson 1976). Becker (1960; 1964) described adjustment (change in lines of action in order to adapt to problematic situations or life course transitions) and commitment (continuity in lines of action produced by temporally prior lines of action by self and others) as twin, mutually reinforcing social processes in that, for example, the situational adjustments of the present can become the commitments of the future. Strauss (1969) later expanded on Becker's treatment of commitment by emphasizing the self and identity in commitment processes (see also Burke and Reitzes 1991) and by distinguishing between the development of commitments and the experience or awareness of them at problematic life course "turning points" (see also Bolton 1961). As in Becker's and Strauss's work, Johnson's threefold framework focuses on people making decisions and acting within situational opportunities and constraints, that are in turn shaped by larger scale structural arrangements.

Table 1 summarizes the three commitment types and their sources. Each type is defined in terms of a dialectic of constraint and desired choice.[1] The framework further distinguishes between external and internal constraints. Each commitment type is also defined by a distinct experience and definition of the situation.

Johnson (1991) defines the three types primarily in terms of phenomenological experiences. While I certainly do not disagree with Johnson's original formulation, I note that each commitment type also corresponds to a distinct kind of situational definition. To define the three types of commitment in terms of distinct situational definitions is to say that they represent three distinct sets of causes of continuity in action. I am using the term "cause" in the same sense as Blumer (1969; 1990; see also Maines and Morrione 1990, p. xx; Athens 1993) and Strauss (1993). That is, causes of action lie in how actors (both individual and collective ones) interpret and define their situations.[2]

Structural commitment is characterized by external constraints of two kinds: (1) the external constraints that structure and influence choices between lines of action and (2) the external constraints that restrict the termination of a given line of action. Structural commitment is defined by the situational definition that one "has to" pursue a line of action; it has four sources: (1) the availability and attractiveness of alternative lines of action, (2) irretrievable investments in lines of action, (3) difficulty of processes necessary to terminate a line of action, and (4) social reaction to

Table 1   Three Types of Commitment and Their Sources

Structural commitment (external constraint)

  1. Alternative lines of action

      a. availability of alternatives

      b. relative attractiveness of available alternatives

  2. Irretrievable investments

  3. Difficulty of terminating lines of action once they are started

  4. Social reactions to terminating lines of action once they are started

Personal commitment (internal choice)

  1. Attitudes toward lines of action

  2. Attitudes toward others with whom one participates in lines of action

  3. Definitions of self in terms of identities mobilized by lines of action

Moral commitment (internal constraint)

  1. Sense of moral obligation to others with whom one participates in lines of action

  2. Internalization of action-specific norms that discourage termination of specific lines of action once they are started

  3. Internalization of general norms of consistency in lines of action

termination of a line of action. Structural commitment is focused on the level at which larger scale structural arrangements shape situations within which individuals make decisions, act, and interact. This is the meso-level that symbolic interactionists emphasize as crucial to sociological analysis (Maines 1982; Blumer 1990; Couch 1995; Hall 1997); McCarthy and Hagan (1992) call this level a fundamental but underemphasized one in contemporary studies of deviance.

Personal commitment is defined by choice driven by internal desire to continue a line of action. In other words, personal commitment refers to individuals continuing a line of action because they define it as desirable, something they *want* to do. As shown in Table 1, personal commitment flows from three sources: (1) positive attitudes toward lines of action, (2) positive attitudes toward others with whom one engages in a line of action, and (3) self-definitions in terms of identities mobilized by lines of action.

Sociologists have long recognized internal as well as external constraints as important influences on decisions and action (Durkheim [1897]1951) and as potential factors producing continuity in deviance or conventionality (Lemert 1951; Lofland 1969; Reckless 1973). Moral commitment involves this kind of internal constraint.[3] It is characterized by the situational definition that one "ought to" continue a line of action regardless of whether one wants to or has to. Moral commitment has three sources: (1) perceived moral obligations to others with whom one participates in a line of action, (2) internalization of action-specific norms discouraging termination of a line of action once one has already gotten involved in it, and (3) internalization of general cultural values that encourage consistency in lines of action.

Contexts of Commitment: Corporal and Phantom Communities

Commitment processes are embedded in two dialectically related communities, one external, one internal. "Corporal communities" refer to the external, corporal social environment (Athens 1998, p. 677). These communities are the arena in which larger-scale social organization and structure enter group life and shape situational action (Blumer 1990; Giddens 1984). Examples include neighborhoods, workplaces, organizations, networks, and race or ethnic communities. Especially important are corporal communities' power relations and dominance orders, because these most immediately shape situational contexts (Hall 1997; Athens 1998). Situational contexts set parameters for decisions, actions, and interactions. Action and interaction, in turn, react back on situations and corporal communities (Giddens 1984).

Modifying Mead's (1934) conception of the self, Athens (1994, p. 526; see also 1997; 1998) depicts the self as a ongoing soliloquy with phantom others: "The phantom other is both a single and multiple entity because the individual phantom companions, when taken together, comprise a *phantom community*, which provides people with a multi but unified voice and sounding board for making sense of their varied social experiences." "Through soliloquizing, [actors] interpret the situations that confront them daily in their corporal communities, and, on the basis of their interpretations, assemble their actions" (Athens 1998, p. 676).

Commitment processes are embedded in and occur through actors engaging, confronting, and participating in corporal and phantom communities. The corporal community presents and shapes situations in which actors make choices as well as the available lines of action to which actors can become committed or to which they can commit themselves. The situational definitions and sources of all three types of commitment engage the corporal community and represent lines along which that community enters individual decisions and actions—corporal communities present the objects and events that actors define and the potential actions from which they choose (Blumer 1990, p. 152). Structural commitment focuses especially on the definitions of situations and decisions as actors confront their corporal communities in the situations, rules and resources, and social reactions they present. Actors form the distinctive definitions of situations that characterize structural, personal, and moral commitment through soliloquies with their phantom communities. Each source of each commitment type works through—and actors assess each source through—dialogue with their phantom communities.

Continuity in both deviant and conventional behavior represents two sides of the same coin (see also Athens 1985). That is, both involve generic social processes of structural, personal, or moral commitment to lines of action. Some lines of action are defined as deviant and some are defined as conventional within particular structures of power relations, cultures, subcultures, or historical periods, but the commitment processes are the same. Also, the threefold commitment framework does not imply any particular overarching societal consensus on deviance definitions and norms, as some other treatments of commitment and social control do (Kornhauser 1978; Hirschi 1969; 1996, p. 255). Rather, the framework recognizes that deviance definitions are inextricably intertwined with politics and power (Quinney 1970; Hagan 1992) as well as cultural and media processes (Altheide 1997). Further, it is congruent with "Chicago School" symbolic interactionism's assumption that collectivities of all kinds are as likely—perhaps more likely— to be characterized by normative conflicts as by normative consensus (Maines, Bridger, and Ulmer, 1996; Park 1926; 1938).

Johnson's commitment framework is not limited in scope to one gender. For example, Johnson (1982; 1991) has forcefully argued that the framework is crucial to understanding why women exit or stay in unsatisfying marriages or partnerships, including abusive ones. Rachel Einwohner (1999) has recently applied the framework in research on both male and female targets of social protest, and their commitment to engaging in the protested-against activities. Likewise, my use of the framework here applies to deviance careers of both males and females. In fact, the sources of each type of commitment are highly likely to condition gender variation in the amount and qualitative nature of deviance.

Commitment to Deviance

Opportunity, differential association/social learning (along with neutralizations and accounts), and labeling theories provide a set of concepts and propositions that are compatible with one another and are recognized by many as central to any theoretical discussion of continuity in deviant behavior. Each of these theories implies processes and contingencies by which actors develop, maintain, and change sources of structural, personal, and moral commitment to deviance. More importantly, the commitment framework specifies potential factors that these theories either merely imply or fail to recognize.

Structural Commitment

Larger scale structures and culture shape situations, and actors make decisions, act, and interact within those situations (Blumer 1962; Maines 1982; Hall 1997). In crime and deviance, this situational level of analysis is undertheorized and underresearched (McCarthy and Hagan 1992; Matsueda

1992; Matsueda and Heimer 1997). This level is exactly what structural commitment is all about.

Structural commitment has four sources. First, actors are structurally committed to lines of action to the extent that alternatives are either unavailable or to the extent that available alternatives are unacceptable. Actors' assessments of the *availability and attractiveness of alternatives* implies the process by which actors face and interpret opportunity structures. The causal mechanism linking opportunity structures (Cloward and Ohlin 1960; Steffensmeier 1983) and action is actors' definitions of alternatives according to their availability and attractiveness. Thus, opportunity structures do not determine action but set constraints within which actors make choices on the basis of their definitions of situations (Blumer 1969; Maines 1977).

This first source of structural commitment thus constitutes a crucial link between the individual and larger scale social structural arrangements. Broader structural contexts within which actors' lives are embedded condition the situational alternatives they confront. For example, Shover's (1996) study of persistent property offenders and Baron and Hartnagel's (1997) study of street youth both depict actors who actively choose between the situated conventional and criminal alternatives they see as being realistically available and attractive. Excellent ethnographies of the heavily gender-stratified worlds of crack dealing (Maher and Daly 1996) and street robbery (Miller 1998) provide further examples. The female crack dealers described by Maher and Daly (1996) and street robbers described by Miller (1998) skillfully find gender-specific niches within these male-dominated criminal activities, in the face of severely restricted conventional *and* criminal alternatives.

Further, this source of structural commitment is not static. People's choices and adjustments to present problematic situations, social positions, or roles can restrict the availability and/or attractiveness of their future alternatives, a process Becker (1960) called "unfitting." A person's adjustment to deviant roles through learning skills, attitudes, and motives favorable to given forms of deviance may restrict his/her opportunity to enact conventional roles in the future, or may render such conventional roles unattractive.[4]

A second source of structural commitment involves the extent to which actors perceive that they have *irretrievable investments* in a line of action. Action consumes resources, which are perceived as investments when made in anticipation of future returns that are not yet realized and the expenditures are not seen as returnable (Johnson 1991; Glaser and Strauss 1971). Pursuing deviant learning and performance opportunities can potentially foster structural commitment through irretrievable investments. The learning necessary for successful performance of deviant activities and the cultivation of relationships with networks of deviant others may entail the investment of considerable personal resources such as time, energy, or money (Steffensmeier 1986). To the extent that one later defines such investments as irretrievable, this may lead to an experience of structural commitment to deviant lines of action (e.g., "I can't back out now, I'm committed"). For example, one may spend a great deal of time and energy learning the necessary skills for manufacturing, smuggling, or marketing illegal drugs in pursuit of a lucrative career in upper-level drug trafficking (Adler and Adler 1983). Since many such skills are not readily transferable to more conventional lines of action, the investments made in learning them may become a source of structural commitment to obtaining income through such drug trafficking activities.

The third source of structural commitment involves the *difficulty of termination procedures*. The difficulty of terminating different lines of action varies greatly. For example, casual involvement in shoplifting is relatively simple to quit, compared to ceasing involvement in an organized crime network, which could require a set of complex, costly, and potentially hazardous actions. Variations in the degree of difficulty in terminating a line of action therefore present structural constraints of varying strength, depending on the organizational characteristics of deviant activities and networks (Best and Luckenbill 1994; Steffensmeier 1983).

The strength of ties (Granovetter 1973), the emotional intensity of relationships with deviant others (which is also related to a source of personal commitment to deviance, as discussed below), the complexity of deviant networks, and one's centrality to those networks potentially influence the level of difficulty of terminating involvement in those networks (Adler and Adler 1983). Extensive participation in deviant activities, networks, and relationships may make later termination very difficult indeed (Best and Luckenbill 1994). For example, complex, organized criminal activities that require special skills or integration into supportive networks may require complex and costly processes for termination, or at least termination procedures that are structured and governed by certain informal norms (e.g., on termination of membership in outlaw biker gangs, see Ulmer 1994; Abadinsky 1994; Wolf 1991). As another example, anecdotal accounts describe how some street gangs will allow members to quit, but they must be "beaten out." The member can quit but must submit to a beating at the hands of other gang members first. On the other hand, for some forms of deviance, this source of structural commitment would be irrelevant. Some deviant activities (e.g., casual petty theft, surfing the Internet for pornography) may require little integration into supporting networks, few strong ties to deviant others, and few or no structured procedures for termination. For such forms of deviance, termination procedures would be relatively simple. Thus, the key empirical question posed by this source of structural commitment is, how difficult, in a practical sense, is it to exit a given line of deviant behavior?

The final source of structural commitment involves *contingencies of social reaction* that involve potential concrete rewards or penalties. Obviously, this source may often be interrelated with difficulty of termination procedures, but it is conceptually distinct. With the source involving difficulty of termination procedures, individuals may be allowed to quit the activity or relationship as long as they "jump through the hoops" that others may expect (by analogy, a person is allowed to end a marriage, but must go through a number of complex and costly social and legal procedures first [Johnson 1991]). This final source of structural commitment, however, involves social reactions from others that actually *hamper or prevent* quitting (by analogy, an oppressive boss may threaten to sabotage an employee's future job prospects if the employee quits).

If social reactions in the conventional world can foster continuity in conventional lines of action, might social reactions from deviant others foster continuity in deviance? Evidence indicates that this can sometimes be the case. For example, when female offenders are involved in criminal activity in the service of male partners, the fear of violent reaction from those male partners is a very real, salient barrier to the women's quitting. Also, involvement in some types of crime (e.g., organized, lucrative crime in the underworld) entails immersion in networks of interdependence and exchange (Steffensmeier 1983; 1986; Best and Luckenbill 1994). Ceasing involvement in such networks can entail penalties or retaliation, since quitting can threaten either the material interests or the "cover" of associates.[5]

In sum, the concept of structural commitment would first direct researchers to the processes by which actors become aware of and interpret deviant opportunity structures in terms of availability and attractiveness and to key decision processes between deviant and conventional lines of action. Second, research could investigate how actors interpret investments of resources in the onset of deviant careers and how expectations of future returns on these resources affect the continuation, frequency, and termination of offending. Third, studies could also explore variations in the difficulty of concrete procedures required to terminate deviant activities, how these might vary according to different forms of deviance social organization (Best and Luckenbill 1994), and how actors' awareness and definitions of these procedures fosters continuity in deviant activities, networks of relationships, and subcultures. Research could explore potential similarities and differences in structural commitment contingencies between "street crime" and white-collar crime or between "underworld" and "upperworld" crime (to use Steffensmeier's [1983] terminology). Finally, research could focus on ways in which social reactions from either deviant networks or labeling from conventional authorities produce or exacerbate sources of structural commitment to deviant careers and how these contingencies might vary according to gender, age, race, class, resources, the actor's position in deviant networks (if any), and other factors (see Ulmer 1994; Heimer and Staffen 1995; Stebbins, 1971).

Personal Commitment

Socialization favorable to deviance involves learning definitions, attitudes, behaviors, skills, and vocabularies of motive favorable to given forms of deviance (Sutherland 1947; Akers et al. 1979; Sykes and Matza 1957), as well as forming relationships with deviant others (Warr 1993) and self-definitions in terms of deviant identities (Glaser 1956; Matsueda 1992). Three sources of personal commitment encompass these process of deviant socialization as they produce continuity in deviant lines of action based on individuals' personal desires or "tastes" (Steffensmeier 1986, p. 231) for that activity. For example, Heimer and Matsueda (1994, p. 368) propose that "the likelihood of delinquency should be increased by delinquent views of the self from the standpoint of others, attitudes favorable to delinquency, perceptions that others would approve of delinquency, friendships with delinquent peers, and histories of delinquent habit." All of these factors involve sources of personal commitment.

First, personal commitment flows from one's attitudes toward specific lines of action. Personal commitment to deviance can result from the development of favorable attitudes toward given lines of deviant activity. This source of personal commitment to deviance focuses on the subjective rewards of the deviant activity itself, which of course sometimes necessitate learning to perceive the activity and its consequences as rewarding (Becker 1960). For example, a skilled burglar may continue to steal because he/she feels it is lucrative, may enjoy the thrills and risks entailed, and may develop the "larceny sense" that is crucial to continued participation in serious and lucrative property crime (Steffensmeier 1986). Katz's (1988) discussion of the "thrills and seductions" of certain kinds of deviant activity provides another example of this source of personal commitment (though a limited one, see McCarthy 1995). Adler and Adler (1983) show that one significant obstacle to the termination of careers in upper-level drug smuggling was participants' enjoyment of the lifestyle and rewards. Plus, neutralizations and accounts (Sykes and Matza 1957; Benson 1985) may foster this source of personal commitment by providing a vocabulary of motive and rhetoric of justification for continuing a given type of deviant activity.

The second source of personal commitment is positive attitudes toward others with whom one acts in a given line of action. Involvement in relationships with deviant others and deviant networks can be another source of personal commitment to deviance in that such relationships may foster the development of favorable attitudes toward deviant others (Schur 1969, p. 316). Contrary to depictions of "cold and brittle" relationships between deviants (Hirschi 1969; Gottfredson and Hirschi 1990), considerable support exists for the notion of close relationships between individuals involved in a variety of forms of deviance. These relationships and attitudes can certainly be a factor that keeps such individuals participating in deviance. For example, recovering alcoholics often say that one key difficulty in quitting drinking is that everything and *everyone* they enjoy is connected to alcohol (Denzin 1987). To list just a few among many other examples, Giordano et al.'s (1986) findings regarding delinquent peer groups and Adler and Adler's (1983) research on upper-level drug traffickers have shown how friendship bonds in deviant networks can foster continuity in deviant activities. Further, Kandel and Davies (1991) found that gang members' friendships with and positive sentiments toward fellow members were key factors in keeping them involved in crime and delinquency. Studies by Warr (1996), Warr and Stafford (1991), and Zhang and Messner (1995) also illustrate a variety of ways in which delinquent peer friendships sustain and channel careers in juvenile delinquency. Finally, deviant role modeling (Akers 1998) is a process by which actors emulate the deviant behavior of role models toward whom they have positive attitudes.

The third source of personal commitment involves the definition of self in terms of identities mobilized by lines of action—a dimension of commitment also noted by Burke and Reitzes (1991). The importance of identity and self-definition in producing continuity in deviance has been recognized for decades (Lemert 1951; Becker 1963; Lofland 1969). The development of deviant self-definitions can occur through differential identification (Glaser 1956), implicating personal commitment through the definition of self in terms of identities mobilized by deviant lines of action. Adler and Adler's (1983, p. 611) work on upper-level drug traffickers implies how personal commitment to deviance can come from the definition of self in terms of criminal activities: "Dealers and smugglers identified with . . . the occupation of drug trafficking. Their self-images were tied to that role and could not be easily disengaged." More recently, Ross Matsueda (1992) has emphasized the important part that identities and reflected appraisals of self can play in producing and sustaining deviant behavior.

The concept of personal commitment can help future researchers conceptually to distinguish and organize sources of continuity in crime derived from attitudes and self-definitions learned through association with deviant definitions, deviant others, and participation in deviant activities. Too often, we gloss over these factors or lump them all together as deviant socialization or differential association, without careful analytical distinctions (but see Akers 1998). While existing research implies ways in which sources of personal commitment to crime are developed, there is less research on how actors experience such commitments in situational decisions. For example, how do problematic situations and turning points mobilize attitudes and self-definitions favorable to continued involvement in deviance? How do actors' awareness and experience of these sources translate into continuity in crime through concrete decisions? Future research into such questions would greatly improve our understanding of personal, interpretive sources of continuity and change in deviant activity (Matsueda 1988, pp. 351–353).

Moral Commitment

Moral commitment derives from three sources. First, it flows from actors' normative values governing the termination of specific lines of action in specific contexts. This source does not refer to individuals' attitudes or beliefs about the moral rightness or wrongness of a given line of action per se (a source of personal commitment). Rather, moral commitment refers to moral beliefs that discourage terminating a given line of action after becoming involved in it (Johnson 1991). For example, one may stay in an unhappy marriage because he/she believes that divorce is immoral. The second source of moral commitment has to do with the extent to which actors define themselves as incurring moral obligations to specific others with whom they are involved in lines of action. The final source of moral commitment involves the extent to which one generally values consistency in one's own action. For example, sayings such as "stick to your guns," or "quitters never win" embody such general consistency values in contemporary U.S. culture (Johnson 1991, p. 121).

Moral commitment to deviance—as well as personal commitment—might develop through deviant socialization as well. The possibility of moral commitment to crime is undertheorized and underresearched. But involvement in some kinds of organized deviant networks can entail learning action-specific norms, such as those emphasizing dependability, trustworthiness, loyalty, and a sense of moral obligation to other members (Best and Luckenbill 1994). These norms and obligations sometimes foster consistency in relations between members of deviant networks and can discourage unexpected termination of involvement in violation of those norms and obligations (Luckenbill and Best 1981). For example, such personal codes of conduct and informal rules of obligations are especially important in coordinating and safeguarding activities among networks of relatively skilled, successful thieves and fences (Steffensmeier 1983; 1986; Klockars 1974). Furthermore, a reputation for dependability, for recognizing obligations to associates by keeping one's mouth shut when one gets in trouble, and an ability to keep one's word are all prized attributes in the realm of organized, lucrative, underworld crime (Steffensmeier 1983). Steffensmeier's subject in *The Fence* (1986, p. 58) captures the importance of this kind of dependability and trustworthiness, which can be seen as involving moral commitment to deviance through action-specific norms and perceived obligations to others:

> Thieves have to have confidence in each other. That's where heart comes in, too. . . . That's when you're going to have to depend on a person. Not have a guy that's going to get all shitty and run out, and he gets away and you get popped. That's part of being trustworthy, too. Being dependable. You got to know the man's on your back all the time. . . . Another thing, if the good thief is caught and has to do time, you will not hear a peep out of him. As long as the cops didn't set him up, fuck him over, you'd hear no peep out of him.

A sense of moral obligation to specific deviant others, as well as general consistency values, might also be used as a neutralization of conventional moral codes to self and as an account to agents of social control, such as "appeals to higher loyalties" or "a defense of necessity" (Sykes and Matza 1957; Klockars 1974). These neutralizations and accounts can then foster continuity in deviance by justifying continued involvement. Thus, the concept of moral commitment suggests that entrenchment in deviant networks and internalization of their normative codes (if any) may produce continuity in deviant lines of action. Moral commitment to deviance might develop to the extent that differential association processes produce a sense of moral obligation to other members of interdependent deviant networks and foster learning and applying norms emphasizing consistency in deviant action.

The term "moral commitment to crime" might seem like an oxymoron, and some would see it as a conceptual impossibility (e.g., Kornhauser 1978; Gottfredson and Hirschi 1990). I suspect this is why the study of deviance has paid comparatively little explicit attention to what this framework identifies as sources of moral commitment to crime. Such lack of attention leaves several interesting questions about deviance unanswered. For example, how might informal rules of obligation and action-specific norms vary in degree and importance in relation to social organizational differences in deviant networks and subcultures (Best and Luckenbill 1994; Steffensmeier 1983)? How might such informal rules and norms be learned and interpreted by participants in such networks and subcultures, and how much importance do members attach to them as constraints? If participants internalize a deviant group's rules and norms that foster moral commitment to crime, can these be neutralized by the same kinds of techniques that are used to neutralize conventional moral beliefs (Jacobs 1992)? How do specific situations and contexts mobilize sources of moral commitment in actors' awareness, and how do these moral commitments figure into concrete decisions to produce continuity in deviant lines of action?

Moral commitment would also have particular relevance for certain kinds of female crime. Women's criminal activity is often embedded in relationships with men in that such women often serve as accomplices to male partners or even directly "work for" male partners (e.g., selling drugs, prostitution, theft, see Steffensmeier 1983; Steffensmeier and Allan 1995). A sense of obligation to these male partners might be an important source of moral commitment to deviance for such women.

Commitment to Conformity

The importance of commitment in conventional social control is well established (Reckless 1973; Hirschi 1969; Bernard 1987). Thus, I argue that the threefold framework provides a more analytically precise conceptualization of commitment than that found in the social control literature. At the same time, the framework specifies how deviance theories that many treat as competitors (e.g., Hirschi 1996; Gottfredson 1999) are complimentary.

A tension has traditionally existed between social control theory and differential association, opportunity, and labeling theories. In fact, Hirschi (1969) and Kornhauser (1978) argued for the outright rejection of other theories in favor of social control theory. More recently, Sampson and Laub (1993) have recognized the importance of opportunity structures and associations with deviant peers, but argued that their age-graded social control theory yields the most explanatory power (but see Warr 1998). In spite of surface differences, however, all these theories implicitly share a common underlying goal: the explanation of continuity (and discontinuity) in lines of action. Debates about whether one or another of these theories is "better" are unnecessary and unproductive, *since both represent two sides of a generic social process.* Only a handful of deviance scholars have explicitly recognized this point (e.g., Athens 1985; Matsueda and Heimer 1997),[6] while others deny the possibility of commitment to deviance (Goffman 1967; Kornhauser 1978; Gottfredson and Hirschi 1990; Hirschi 1996). The commitment framework therefore integrates insights from control, opportunity, differential association, and labeling theories in order to explain continuity in deviant and conventional activity.

This integration, however, hinges on revising Hirschi's (1969) and Kornhauser's (1978) social control theory assumption of the constancy of deviant motivation, replacing it with both differential association theory's assumption that the motivations for different types of crime are learned, and opportunity theory's assumption that the opportunity to learn them is differentially distributed throughout society (see also Athens 1985). Further, the development and strength of stakes in conformity are themselves conditioned by the relative availability and attractiveness of conventional and deviant alternatives and by actors' choices on the basis of these alternatives.

Such integration would also call for revising Hirschi's (1969; Gottfredson and Hirschi 1990) argument that commitment to deviance is a nonsensical concept, recognizing instead (as Athens [1985] and Matsueda and Heimer [1997] do) that commitment to deviant lines of action and relationships with deviant others is an empirical possibility. In this view, deviant and conventional careers are twin, intertwined aspects of the same generic process—the development and experience of commitments that produce continuity in lines of action. Plus, the threefold commitment framework does not imply an overarching normative consensus in society, as do Hirschi (1969) and Kornhauser (1978) (for treatments of social control that do not rely on an assumption of societal normative consensus, see Heimer and Matsueda 1994; Matsueda and Heimer 1997). Instead, this framework simply describes different types of commitment to lines of action of any kind. Some lines of action are defined as deviant at particular times and places by particular groups, with particular interests and power (Quinney 1970; Schur 1980).

The threefold commitment framework could make several specific contributions to explaining continuity in conventional action and would provide social control researchers with more refined tools for investigating commitment to conformity. First, the framework would be a valuable tool for developmental and life course research in deviance (Thornberry 1995; Agnew 1997; Sampson and Laub 1997). For example, Agnew (1997) and Sampson and Laub (1997) argue that variation in (and disruption of) commitments to conventional activity and conventional adult roles account for variation in the onset, persistence, and termination of criminal careers throughout the life course. The commitment framework could help specify exactly what kinds of commitments to conventional activity (and their sources) are developed or disrupted over the life course, and allow more refined studies of the development and experience of these commitments at key life-course turning points in which decisions are made. In addition, Sampson and Laub (1997, p. 138) call for deviance concepts and theories that are processual rather than static. The processual nature of the threefold commitment framework and its interactionist assumptions would seem to make it (like labeling theory, see Sampson and Laub 1997, p. 138) an especially attractive conceptual tool for research on deviance and the life course, since it is sensitive to intraindividual differences in the types of commitment and their sources over time.

Sampson and Laub's (1993; Laub, Nagin, and Sampson 1998) age-graded social control theory is loaded with implications for the utility of the threefold commitment framework in explaining continuity in both deviant and conventional lines of action. Their work argues that both stability and change in deviant career trajectories throughout life are systematically produced by social bonds to conventional adult institutions of informal social control, particularly bonds to work and family. Arguably, their analysis could just as easily be framed as a study of structural, personal, and perhaps even moral commitments to deviant versus conventional activities, as well as continuity and change in those commitments over the life course. While their interpretations emphasize the ways in which their data support their age-graded social control theory, their findings also show that factors such as associations with deviant peers and contact with the criminal justice system produce continuity in deviant careers (see also Warr 1998). Within the threefold commitment framework, such findings are not surprising, and in fact they illustrate twin sides of a generic set of commitment processes to deviant and conventional lines of action and transitions between them throughout the life course. Regarding the effects of formal criminal justice sanctions on later criminal behavior, for example, the sources of each type of commitment specify intervening mechanisms by which labeling effects produce future stability or entrenchment in deviant behavior (see also Ulmer 1994).[7] In fact,

interrelated chains of commitment processes may produce what Sampson and Laub (1997, p. 144) describe as cumulative disadvantages over
time in terms of conventional adult social bonds and conventional controls. Structural, personal, and/or moral commitment processes may be
the mechanisms behind the long-term labeling consequences and effects
of conventional social bonds, including cumulative disadvantages, found
in Sampson and Laub's body of life course research. The types of commitment and their sources may therefore be intervening mechanisms between labeling processes, the disruption of conventional adult social
bonds, and entrenched deviant careers.

In addition, Warr's (1998) study of life course transitions and crime finds
that marriage contributes to desistance from crime by producing a shift
away from relations with deviant peers in favor of spouse and children.
Warr (1998, p. 209) states that this finding "offers preliminary evidence for
a general mechanism of desistance that may explain the links between life-
course transitions and crime" (my emphasis added). The commitment
processes described here, especially the potential interplay of structural
and personal commitment, specify this general mechanism in life course
transitions from deviant peer relations to conventional ties. Further, as implied above, the commitment framework would also suggest the opposite
possibility—that negative life events (e.g., divorce, arrest, job loss, etc.) can
disrupt conventional commitment processes and foster deviant ones.
Again, the sources of the different types of commitment—especially structural and personal commitment sources—may be *intervening factors* in the
relationship between life-course events and conventional or deviant behavior and therefore worthy of further study.

The threefold commitment framework would also extend Matsueda and
Heimer's (1997; Heimer and Matsueda 1994; Matsueda 1992) theory of differential social control. They rely heavily on Becker's (1960), Stryker's
(1980), and Burke and Reitzes's (1991) conceptualizations of commitment,
which are extended and refined by the threefold framework (Johnson 1991;
Ulmer 1994). Matsueda and Heimer (1997, p. 174) identify two general
mechanisms that produce continuity in either deviant or conventional behavior over the life course: (1) the "endogenous" or "subjective" process "in
which actors consider aspects of the life course in carrying out meaningful, self-conscious behavior" and (2) the "exogenous social structuring that
may or may not condition the consciousness of actors." Clearly, the sources
of personal and moral commitment specify the former processes in greater
detail, while structural commitment sources specify the latter processes.
Plus, the concept of structural commitment specifies sources of what
Heimer and Matsueda (1994, p. 369) call "differential organizational control," that is, social organizational arrangements within which processes of
differential social control are embedded. The four structural commitment
sources would each be important social organizational factors that produce
more or less conventional control. Finally, the threefold commitment

framework answers Heimer and Matsueda's (1994, p. 384) call for a greater conceptual focus on individual motivations in problematic situations, and how these situations are lodged in "contexts of structural locations, commitment to social roles, and institutional arrangements." Such a focus, after all, is at the heart of the threefold commitment framework.

Conclusion

Since commitment is central to the study of deviance and social control, it makes sense to conceptualize it in all its variation, complexity, and implications. In addition to the more specific research directions involving the source of commitment discussed above, the threefold commitment framework as a whole has broader implications for deviance research. First, class, race, ethnicity, and gender are key social statuses correlated with the distribution of resources, power, and life chances and are likely to be associated with different contingencies of structural, personal, and moral commitment to deviance and conformity. To take just one example, the contingencies of structural commitment to deviance and conformity would likely be very different for a seventeen-year-old black male from a poor family in an inner city neighborhood compared to an affluent thirty-five-year-old white woman in a small town. These two individuals would also likely be enmeshed in different personal relationships and socialization processes; they would transact different identities and hold different self-definitions, and these would be all differentially favorable to different kinds of deviance or conformity. The framework directs attention to the ways in which larger scale patterns of social structure (e.g., race, class, and gender stratification, the social organization of aging, and the life course) operate in people's lives by shaping situational alternatives and constraints within which actors make decisions, act, and interact. The commitment framework may be especially relevant for examining aspects of certain kinds of careers in crime and deviance among women. Many women often stay involved in crime (Steffensmeier and Allan 1995; Maher and Daly 1996) or some types of deviance (e.g., Thio 1988) through either: (1) restricted and unattractive alternatives (invoking the first source of structural commitment from Table 1) or (2) enmeshment in relationships with men involved in crime (invoking, at the very least, the third source of structural commitment, the second source of personal commitment, and/or the first source of moral commitment).

Second, future research could investigate ways in which types of commitment and their sources might mutually interrelate and interact. For example, Hagan's (1991) finding that the effects of adolescent participation in "partying" or "delinquent" subcultures were class-specific implies that the effect of personal commitment to deviant activity is contingent on class-based structural commitment contingencies now and later in the life course, such as the availability and attractiveness of alternatives. Hagedorn's (1994) typology of adult gang members' careers also suggests the interactive nature of sources of structural, personal, and perhaps moral commitment to crime and conventionality.[8]

Furthermore, Matsueda and Anderson (1998) note the need for theories of crime and deviance to incorporate theories of peer relations and friendship networks. Johnson (1991) developed the threefold commitment framework through research on personal relationship dynamics. Its concepts of personal commitment, and the conditioning influences of structural commitment, have a great deal to offer in understanding peer selection processes, friendship networks, and their reciprocal relation to deviance and conventional social control.

Third, one exciting research direction would involve the commitment framework's potential use in analyzing the social organization of deviant activity. Commitments are the "glue" of conventional organizations (Gerson 1976; Clarke 1991). The threefold commitment framework suggests that organized groups centered around deviant activity may be held together by the glue of structural, personal, or moral commitment to deviant activities and relationships. Just as the framework challenges Gottfredson and Hirschi's (1990) notion that relationships between deviant peers are cold and brittle, the framework likewise questions their notion that organized deviant or criminal activity is an illusion. In both cases, the commitment framework recognizes deviant peer relations and organized deviant activities as lines of action for which structural, personal, or moral commitments may potentially be developed. In fact, it is probable that moral commitment to deviance is *most* likely to be found in the context of organized deviant groups.

Variations in the types and strength of commitments between members of deviant groups to each other, to the group, and to its activities are likely a measure of the degree of deviant groups' organizational complexity, and vice versa. The commitment framework could be used to study the structure and relationships of organized deviant groups and how these affect the careers of the individuals within them. For example, commitment types and sources would likely vary a great deal in relevance, importance, and consequences along Best and Luckenbill's (1994) continuum of the organizational complexity of deviant activity. The strength and consequences of different types of commitment would likely vary between groups that differ in organizational sophistication, from small delinquent groups to large-scale "formal organizations" that persist in time and space. On one hand, organizationally sophisticated groups like La Cosa Nostra in the United States, or the Japanese Yakusa are likely held together by complex webs of personal, structural, and moral commitments. On the other hand, Warr (1996, pp. 13, 26) found that preexisting friendship ties and peer pressure (a possible combination of personal commitment and structural commitment) fostered continuity in delinquent activities and groups, but also shaped the social organization (however primitive) of small, transitory delinquent groups and roles within those groups. Thus, preexisting personal and structural commitments affected the social organization of even small, short-lived delinquent groups, which in turn affected delinquent career contingencies such as length of participation and specialization.

Other Applications

The threefold commitment framework is relevant not just to personal relationships (as Johnson's work shows) or to deviance and social control (as I have argued here), but to a wide variety of substantive areas of sociological inquiry. I close by briefly suggesting some of the framework's potential contributions to the topics of social movements and the sociology of organizations as further examples.

The threefold commitment framework would be potentially useful for analyzing continuity in participation in social movement activities. For example, factors that may discourage termination of participation include fear of negative social reaction from one's network of movement associates (a source of structural commitment), a sense of moral obligation to movement associates or to social movement goals (moral commitment), or the definition of self in terms of identities invoked by movement participation (personal commitment) (McAdam 1986; 1989; Walsh and Warland 1983). Furthermore, Einwohner (1999) examines how the three types of commitment and their sources help to explain variation in the willingness or ability of *targets* of protest (in this case hunters versus circus patrons, two targets of animal rights protesters) to change behavior against which others have grievances. In other words, the commitments of targeted actors or audiences to the activities that are the object of protest vary not only in strength, but also in type. Since protest "success" is often measured as getting targets to stop or change what they are doing, it follows that the chances for protest success in part depend on such targets' structural, personal, or moral commitments to the protested activity (Einwohner 1999).

Commitments are the "glue" of conventional as well as deviant organizations (Gerson 1976; Clarke 1991). I suggest that variations in the types, degrees, and objects of organizational members' commitment strongly influence organizational structuration, culture, and politics. For example, members' structural, personal, and moral commitments to organizations and relational networks within them will likely influence the manner in which organizations mobilize and coordinate joint actions in pursuit of formal goals. Also, complex and conflicting webs of personal, structural, and moral commitments between organizational actors probably shape and are shaped by organizational negotiations, politics, and conflicts (Clarke 1991; Couch 1986; Couch and Weiland 1986; Hall and McGinty 1997).

Commitment stands at the intersection of at least three of sociology's core dialectics: continuity and change, agency and constraint, and self and society. It is hard to think of a substantive area of sociology in which commitment is not relevant. It also makes sense to push the concept further, so that it can sensitize researchers to the differences in situational definitions, experiences, and processes of development that we have typically lumped under the general heading of commitment. That is what the Johnson commitment framework does, and I think our empirical inquiries into any area of group life will be the richer for using it.

Notes

1. This framework's interactionist conception of a dialectical relationship between choice and constraint, or agency and structure, is compatible with Giddens's (1984) theory of structuration and notion of "duality of structure." As Hall (1997) describes, both interactionism and structuration theory view structure (whether at the micro-, meso-, or macrolevels) as both constraining and enabling. Furthermore, both theories hold that actors' situational decisions and actions are shaped and channeled by external structures, but also always reproduce, modify, and even sometimes radically change those structures.

2. This interpretive conception of causal processes is certainly congruent with, but more basic than, the idea of vocabularies of motive and the derivative concepts of accounts (Scott and Lyman 1968) and disclaimers and neutralizations (Hewitt and Stokes 1975; Sykes and Matza 1957). Such vocabularies of motive are, of course, definitions of situations themselves, and actors use them rhetorically to explain their conduct to themselves and others (Mills 1940). In particular, actors use such vocabularies of motive to excuse or justify deviant conduct to self and others retrospectively (accounts) or prospectively (disclaimers, neutralizations).

The situational definitions characteristic of the three types of commitment can certainly be articulated as general vocabularies of motive, as well as accounts and neutralizations. In addition, each of the sources of structural, personal, and moral commitment could provide actors with potential accounts, disclaimers, or neutralizations for deviant activity, or even for articulating the reasons for conformity to deviant audiences (Jacobs 1992). A full exploration of how actors might draw on the situational definitions characteristic of each type of commitment as vocabularies of motive is beyond the scope of this article, but would be an excellent and novel line of empirical inquiry.

3. Moral commitment "is not to be confused with moral aspects of social reaction, a source of structural commitment, which has its locus outside the individual" (Johnson 1991, p. 121).

4. As an extreme example, a career as a professional "hitter" requires complicated opportunity structures and learning elaborate skills, attitudes, and neutralizations favorable to murder for profit (Levi 1989), yet a career in murder-for-hire hardly opens up conventional job opportunities.

5. "Made members" of La Cosa Nostra cannot terminate their involvement without risk of severe and violent reactions from other members of their La Cosa Nostra families (Abadinsky 1994). As another example, members of outlaw biker clubs who fail to participate in club functions, such as meetings, road runs, or fights, face violent punishments from club leaders (Ulmer 1994).

6. For example, in his critique of Goffman's (1967) idea of violent crimes as "character contests," Athens (1985) argues that people may have commitments to (or "stakes in") deviant as well as conventional social worlds. The threefold framework extends this idea, enabling investigations into what *kinds* of commitment, and what distinct sources produce them.

7. For example, criminal justice sanctions may, under certain circumstances, reduce the availability and attractiveness of conventional alternatives and increase the availability and attractiveness of deviant alternatives. This source of structural commitment, in turn, can set in motion chains of processes that foster the development of other structural and personal commitment sources, such as irretrievable investments in further pursuit of deviant activities, relationships with deviant peers, further socialization processes that foster positive attitudes toward deviant lines of action, and engulfment in deviant identities (Stebbins 1971; Ulmer 1994).

8. Hagedorn (1994) distinguishes between "legits," "homeboys," "dope fiends," and "new jacks." In terms of the threefold commitment framework, legits exited gang life by developing personal and structural commitment to conventionality through conventional work and family. Homeboys had little personal commitment to gang life but faced few available and attractive conventional alternatives. Dope fiends "unfitted" themselves for conventional work

and relationships through continued drug use and immersion in the practical constraints of heroin or cocaine addiction. Finally, new jacks were structurally embedded in gang activities and had significant personal commitment to gang life and money.

References

Abadinsky, Howard. 1994. *Organized Crime.* Chicago: Nelson-Hall.

Adler, Patricia, and Peter Adler. 1983. "Relations Between Dealers: The Social Organization of Illicit Drug Transactions." *Sociology and Social Research* 67:260–278.

Agnew, Robert. 1995. "Determinism, Indeterminism, and Crime: An Empirical Exploration." *Criminology* 33:83–110.

——. 1997. "Stability and Change in Crime over the Life Course: A Strain Theory Explanation." Pp. 101–131 in *Developmental Theories of Crime and Delinquency,* edited by Thornberry.

Akers, Ronald. 1996. "Is Differential Association/Social Learning Cultural Deviance Theory?" *Criminology* 34:229–248.

——. 1998, *Social Learning and Social Structure: A General Theory of Crime and Deviance.* Boston: Northeastern University Press.

Akers, Ronald, Marvin Krohn, Lonn Lanza-Kaduce, and Maria Radosevich. 1979. "Social Learning and Deviant Behavior: A Specific Test of a General Theory." *American Sociological Review* 44:635–655.

Altheide, David. 1997. "Crime, Media, and the Production of Fear." *The Sociological Quarterly* 38:645–666.

Athens, Lonnie. 1985. "Character Contests and Violent Criminal Conduct: A Critique." *The Sociological Quarterly* 26:419–432.

——. 1993. "Blumer's Advanced Course on Social Psychology." *Studies in Symbolic Interaction* 18:245–261.

——. 1994. "The Self as a Soliloquy." *The Sociological Quarterly* 35:521–532.

——. 1997. *Violent Criminal Acts and Actors Revisited.* Urbana: University of Illinois Press.

——. 1998. "Dominance, Ghettos, and Violent Crime." *The Sociological Quarterly* 39:673–691.

Baron, Stephen, and Timothy Hartnagel. 1997. "Attributions, Affect, and Crime: Street Youths' Reactions to Unemployment." *Criminology* 35:409–434.

Becker, Howard. 1960. "Notes on the Concept of Commitment," *American Journal of Sociology* 66:32–40.

——. 1963. *Outsiders.* New York: Macmillan.

——. 1964. "Personal Change in Adult Life." *Sociometry* 27(1):40–53.

Benson, Michael. 1985. "Denying the Guilty Mind: Accounting for Involvement in White Collar Crime." *Criminology* 23:583–607.

Bernard, Thomas. 1987. "Structure and Control: Reconsidering Hirschi's Concept of Commitment." *Justice Quarterly* 4:409–424.

Best, Joel, and David Luckenbill. 1994. *Organizing Deviance.* Englewood Cliffs, NJ: Prentice-Hall.

Blumer, Herbert. 1962. "Society as Symbolic Interaction," in *Human Behavior and Social Processes,* edited by A. Rose. Boston: Houghton-Mifflin.

——. 1969. *Symbolic Interactionism.* Englewood Cliffs, NJ: Prentice-Hall.

——. 1990. *Industrialization as an Agent of Social Change.* New York: Aldine de Gruyter.

Bolton, Charles. 1961. "Mate Selection as the Development of a Relationship." *Marriage and Family Living* 23:234–240.

Braithwaite, John. 1989. *Crime, Shame, and Reintegration.* Cambridge: Cambridge University Press.

Burke, Peter, and Donald Reitzes, 1991. "An Identity Theory Approach to Commitment." *Social Psychology Quarterly* 54:239–251.

Clarke, Adele. 1991. "Social Worlds/Arenas Theory as Organizational Theory." Pp. 119–158 in *Social Organization and Social Process: Essays in Honor of Anselm Strauss,* edited by David Maines. New York: Aldine de Gruyter.

Cloward, Richard, and Lloyd Ohlin. 1960. *Delinquency and Opportunity.* Glencoe, IL: Free Press.

Couch, Carl. 1986. "Structural Conditions of Intergroup Negotiations." *Studies in Symbolic Interaction.* Supplement 2:353–364.

———. 1995. "Let Us Rekindle the Passion by Constructing a Robust Science of the Social." *The Sociological Quarterly* 36:1–14.

Couch, Carl, and Marion Weiland. 1986. "A Study of the Representative-Constituent Relationship," in *Studies in Symbolic Interaction: The Iowa School,* Supplement 2:375–392.

Denzin, Norman. 1987. *The Alcoholic Self.* Newbury Park, CA: Sage.

Durkheim, Emile. [1897] 1951. *Suicide.* Glencoe, IL: The Free Press.

Einwohner, Rachel. 1999. "Practices, Opportunity, and Protest Effectiveness: Illustrations from Four Animal Rights Campaigns." *Social Problems* 46:169–188.

Etzioni, Amitai. 1964. *Modern Organizations.* Englewood Cliffs, NJ: Prentice-Hall.

Faulkner, Robert. 1974. "Coming of Age in Organizations: A Comparative Study of Career Contingencies and Adult Socialization." *Sociology of Work and Occupations* 1:131–173.

Gerson, Elihu M. 1976. "On 'Quality of Life.'" *American Sociological Review* 41:793–806.

Giddens, Anthony. 1984. *The Constitution of Society.* Berkeley: University of California Press.

Giordano, Peggy, Stephen Cernovich, and M.D. Pugh. 1986. "Friendships and Delinquency." *American Journal of Sociology* 91:1170–1202.

Glaser, Barney, and Anselm Strauss. 1971. *Status Passage.* Chicago: Aldine de Gruyter.

Glaser, Daniel. 1956. "Criminality Theories and Behavioral Images." *American Journal of Sociology* 61:440–441.

Goffman, Erving. 1967. *Interaction Ritual.* New York: Doubleday.

Gottfredson, Michael. 1999. Review of *Social Learning and Social Structure,* by Ronald Akers. *American Journal of Sociology* 105:283–284.

Gottfredson, Michael, and Travis Hirschi. 1990. *A General Theory of Crime.* Stanford, CA: Stanford University Press.

Granovetter, Mark. 1973. "The Strength of Weak Ties." *American Journal of Sociology* 78:1360–1380.

Hagan, John. 1991. "Destiny and Drift: Subcultural Preferences, Status Attainments, and the Risks and Rewards of Youth." *American Sociological Review* 56:567–581.

———. 1992. "The Poverty of a Classless Criminology." *Criminology* 30:1–20.

Hagedorn, John. 1994. "Home Boys, Dope Fiends, Legits, and New Jacks." *Criminology* 32:197–220.

Hall, Peter. 1997. "Meta-Power, Social Organization, and the Shaping of Social Action." *Symbolic Interaction* 20:397–418.

Hall, Peter, and Peter McGinty. 1997. "Policy as the Transformation of Intentions: Producing Program from Statute." *The Sociological Quarterly* 38:439–468.

Heimer, Carol, and Lisa Staffen. 1995. "Interdependence and Reintegrative Social Control." *American Sociological Review* 60:635–654.

Heimer, Karen, and Ross Matsueda. 1994. "Role Taking, Role Commitment, and Delinquency: A Theory of Differential Social Control." *American Sociological Review* 59(3):365–390.

Hewitt, John, and Randall Stokes. 1975. "Disclaimers." *American Sociological Review* 40:1–11.

Hirsch, Eric. 1990. "Sacrifice for the Cause: Group Processes, Recruitment, and Commitment in a Student Social Movement." *American Sociological Review* 55:243–254.

Hirschi, Travis. 1969. *Causes of Delinquency.* Berkeley, CA: Free Press.

———. 1996. "Theory without Ideas: Reply to Akers." *Criminology* 34(2):249–256.

Jacobs, Bruce. 1992. "Undercover Drug Use and Evasion Tactics: Excuses and Neutralizations." *Symbolic Interaction* 15:435–454.

Johnson, Michael. 1973. "Commitment: A Conceptual Structure and Empirical Application." *The Sociological Quarterly* 14:395–406.

———. 1976. "The Role of Commitment in Social Problems Theory." Paper presented at the annual meetings of the Society for the Study of Social Problems, New York, NY.

———. 1982. "Social and Cognitive Features of the Dissolution of Commitment to Relationships." Pp. 51–73 in *Personal Relationships 4: Dissolving Personal Relationships,* edited by Steven Duck. New York: Academic Press.

———. 1991. "Commitment to Personal Relationships." Pp. 117–143 in *Advance in Personal Relationships,* Vol. 3, edited by William Jones and Dan Perlman. London: Jessica Kingsley Publishers.

Kandel, Denise, and Mark Davies. 1991. "Friendship Networks, Intimacy, and Illicit Drug Use in Young Adulthood: A Comparison of Two Theories." *Criminology* 29:441–470.

Kanter, Rosabeth Moss. 1972. *Commitment and Community.* Cambridge, MA: Harvard University Press.

———. 1977. *Men and Women of the Corporation.* New York: Basic Books.

Katz, Jack. 1988. *Seductions of Crime: Moral and Sensual Attractions of Doing Evil.* New York: Basic Books.

———. 1994. "Jazz in Social Interaction: Personal Creativity, Collective Constraint, and Motivational Explanation in the Social Thought of Howard S. Becker." *Symbolic Interaction* 17:253–280.

Klandermans, Bert. 1997. *The Social Psychology of Protest.* Cambridge, MA: Blackwell.

Klockars, Carl. 1974. *The Professional Fence.* New York: Free Press.

Kornhauser, Ruth. 1978. *Social Sources of Delinquency.* Chicago: University of Chicago Press.

Laub, John, Daniel Nagin, and Robert Sampson. 1998. "Trajectories of Change in Criminal Offending: Good Marriages and the Desistance Process." *American Sociological Review* 63:225–238.

Lemert, Edwin. 1951. *Social Pathology.* New York: McGraw-Hill.

Levi, Ken. 1989. "Neutralizations in a Very Deviant Career: The Case of Professional Hit-Men." Pp. 447–458 in *Deviant Behavior,* edited by Delos Kelly. New York: St. Martin's Press.

Lofland, John. 1969. *Deviance and Identity.* Englewood Cliffs, NJ: Prentice-Hall.

Luckenbill, David F., and Joel Best. 1981. "Careers in Deviance and Respectability: The Analogy's Limitations." *Social Problems* 29:197–206.

Maher, Lisa, and Kathleen Daly. 1996. "Women in the Street Level Drug Economy: Continuity or Change." *Criminology* 34:465–492.

Maines, David R. 1977. "Social Organization and Social Structure in Symbolic Interactionist Thought." *Annual Review of Sociology* 3:235–259.

———. 1982. "In Search of Mesostructure: Studies in the Negotiated Order." *Urban Life* 11:267–279.

Maines, David R., and Thomas Morrione. 1990. "On the Breadth and Relevance of Blumer's Perspective." Pp. xi–xxiv in *Industrialization as an Agent of Social Change,* by Herbert Blumer. New York: Aldine.

Maines, David R., Jeffrey Bridger, and Jeffrey Ulmer. 1996. "Mythic Facts and Park's Pragmatism: On Predecessor Selection and Theorizing in Human Ecology." *The Sociological Quarterly* 37:521–549.

Makkai, Toni, and John Braithwaite. 1991. "Criminological Theories and Regulatory Compliance." *Criminology* 29:191–220.

Matsueda, Ross. 1982. "Testing Control Theory and Differential Association: A Causal Modeling Approach." *American Sociological Review* 47:489–504.

———. 1988. "The Current State of Differential Association Theory." *Crime and Delinquency* 34:277–306.

———. 1992. "Reflected Appraisals, Parental Labeling, and Delinquency: Specifying a Symbolic Interactionist Theory." *American Journal of Sociology* 97:1577–1611.

Matsueda, Ross, and Karen Heimer. 1997. "Developmental Theories of Crime." Pp. 174–186 in *Advances in Criminological Theory*, edited by Terence Thornberry. New Brunswick, NJ: Transaction.

Matsueda, Ross, and Kathleen Anderson. 1998. "The Dynamics of Delinquent Peers and Delinquent Behavior." *Criminology* 36:269–308.

McAdam, Douglas. 1986. "Recruitment to High-Risk Activism: The Case of Freedom Summer." *American Journal of Sociology* 94:64–90.

———. 1989. "The Biographical Consequences of Activism." *American Sociological Review* 54:744–760.

McCarthy, Bill. 1995. "Not Just 'for the Thrill of It': An Instrumentalist Elaboration of Katz's Explanation of Sneaky Thrill Property Crimes." *Criminology* 33:519–538.

McCarthy, Bill, and John Hagan. 1992. "Mean Streets: The Theoretical Significance of Situational Delinquency among Homeless Youths." *American Journal of Sociology* 98:597–627.

Mead, George Herbert. 1934. *Mind, Self, and Society.* Chicago: University of Chicago Press.

Merton, Robert. 1997. "On the Evolving Synthesis of Differential Association and Anomie Theory: A Perspective from the Sociology of Science." *Criminology* 35:517–525.

Miller, Jody. 1998. "Up It Up: Gender and the Accomplishment of Street Robbery." *Criminology* 36:37–66.

Mills, C. Wright. 1940. "Situated Actions and Vocabularies of Motive." *American Sociological Review* 5:904–913.

Park, Robert. 1926. "The Urban Community as a Spatial and Moral Order." Pp. 3–18 in *The Urban Community*, edited by Ernest Burgess. Chicago: University of Chicago Press.

———. 1938. "Reflections on Communication and Culture." *American Journal of Sociology* 44:187–205.

Quinney, Richard. 1970. *The Social Reality of Crime.* Boston: Little, Brown.

Reckless, Walter. 1973. *The Crime Problem*, 5th ed. Englewood Cliffs, NJ: Prentice-Hall.

Sampson, Robert, and John Laub. 1993. *Crime in the Making: Pathways and Turning Points through Life.* Cambridge, MA: Harvard University Press.

———. 1997. "A Life-Course Theory of Cumulative Disadvantage and the Stability of Delinquency." Pp. 133–161 in *Developmental Theories of Crime and Delinquency*, edited by Terence Thornberry. New Brunswick, NJ: Transaction.

Schur, Edwin. 1969. "Reactions to Deviance: A Critical Assessment." *American Journal of Sociology* 75:309–322.

———. 1980. *The Politics of Deviance: Stigma Contests and the Uses of Power.* Englewood Cliffs, NJ: Prentice-Hall.

Scott, Marvin, and Stanford Lyman. 1968. "Accounts." *American Sociological Review* 33:46–62.

Selznick, Philip. 1969. *TVA and the Grass Roots*. Los Angeles: University of California Press.

Shalin, Dmitri. 1986. "Pragmatism and Social Interactionism." *American Sociological Review* 51:9–27.

Shover, Neal. 1996. *Great Pretenders: Pursuits and Careers of Persistent Thieves*. Boulder, CO: Westview Press.

Stebbins, Robert A. 1971. *Commitment to Deviance*. Westport, CT: Greenwood.

Steffensmeier, Darrell. 1983. "Organization Properties and Sex-Segregation in the Underworld: Building a Sociological Theory of Sex Differences in Crime." *Social Forces* 6:1010–1032.

———. 1986. *The Fence: In the Shadow of Two Worlds*. Totowa, NJ: Rowman and Littlefield.

Steffensmeier, Darrell, and Emilie Allan. 1995. "Gender, Age, and Crime." Pp. 67–94 in *Criminology*, edited by Joseph Sheley. Belmont, CA: Sage.

Strauss, Anselm. 1969. *Mirrors and Masks*. San Francisco: Sociology Press.

———. 1993. *Continual Permutations of Action*. New York: Aldine de Gruyter.

Stryker, Sheldon. 1980. *Symbolic Interaction: A Social Structural Version*. Menlo Park, CA: Benjamin/Cummings.

Sutherland, Edwin. 1947. *Principles of Criminology*. Philadelphia: Lippincott.

Sykes, Gresham, and David Matza. 1957. "Techniques of Neutralization: A Theory of Delinquency." *American Sociological Review* 22:664–670.

Thio, Alex. 1988. *Deviant Behavior*. New York: Harper and Row.

Thornberry, Terence. 1995. *Developmental Theories of Crime and Delinquency*. New Brunswick, NJ: Transaction.

Tittle, Charles. 1989. "Prospects for Synthetic Theory." Pp. 161–178 in *Theoretical Integration in the Study of Deviance and Crime*, edited by Steven Messner, Marvin Krohn, and Allen Liska. Albany, NY: State University of New York Press.

———. 1995. *Control Balance: Toward a General Theory of Deviance*. Boulder, CO: Westview Press.

Ulmer, Jeffery T. 1994. "Revisiting Stebbins: Labeling and Commitment to Deviance." *The Sociological Quarterly* 35:135–157.

Wallerstein, Immanuel. 1997. "Social Science and the Quest for a Just Society." *American Journal of Sociology* 102:1241–1257.

Walsh, Edward, and Rex Warland. 1983. "Social Movement Involvement in the Wake of a Nuclear Accident: Activists and Free Riders in the Three Mile Island Area." *American Sociological Review* 48:764–781.

Warr, Mark. 1993. "Age, Peers, and Delinquency." *Criminology* 31:17–40.

———. 1996. "Organization and Instigation in Delinquent Groups." *Criminology* 34:11–37.

———. 1998. "Life-Course Transitions and Desistance from Crime." *Criminology* 36:183–216.

Warr, Mark, and Mark Stafford. 1991. "The Influence of Delinquent Peers: What They Think or What They Do?" *Criminology* 29:851–866.

Westby, David. 1991. *The Growth of Sociological Theory: Human Nature, Knowledge, and Social Change*. Englewood Cliffs, NJ: Prentice-Hall.

Wolf, Daniel. 1991. *The Rebels: A Brotherhood of Outlaw Bikers*. Toronto: University of Toronto Press.

Zhang, Lening, and Steven Messner. 1995. "Family Deviance and Delinquency in China." *Criminology* 33:359–388.

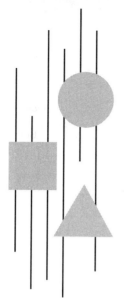

Becoming Deviant

Private Domains, Information Control, and Accommodation

In Part I, we made some general statements about the way deviant categories arise and the way violators of these categories may be reacted to. In Part II, we explored some of the major theories and perspectives that serve to explain why actors may commit deviant acts. In this part of the book, we will deal more systematically with reactions that may bring about early stages of deviant careers—careers which may ultimately become subject to institutional control and regulation (Part IV).

In the General Introduction, a distinction was made between the initiation of the labeling ceremony in a private domain and initiation in the public domain. We also noted how those engaged in deviant pursuits attempt to manage their behavior and attitudes in such a way as to avoid detection by socially significant "straights," especially formal agents of social control. This avoidance clearly indicates both the existence of some potentially stigmatizing or discreditable feature of their biography and the knowledge that detection is frequently associated with a range of personal and social costs. As an example, the drug pusher runs the risk of being sanctioned by the courts. It is conceivable, of course, that the pusher may never experience any direct contact with the social-control apparatus. In such a case he or she would remain what we have termed a noninstitutional deviant. Still, the pusher is aware of the potentially damaging nature of his or her activities and realizes that if authorities became aware of those activities, that knowledge could be used to initiate some type of institutional career.

In the analysis of strategies for information control and management, it is useful, therefore, to think in terms of actor *and* audience response. The pusher, in an effort to protect his or her self-image and identity cluster, as well as to reduce the odds of being officially designated as a deviant, may employ certain strategies (e.g., denying to self and others that he or she is a pusher). Similarly, those who must deal with actual or potential deviance often invoke various types of coping or accommodative strategies. A wife, for example, may try to accommodate herself to her husband's increasingly violent behavior. If she is successful, the deviance will remain primarily a matter of private knowledge, regulation, and management—although the wife herself may consider her husband to be deviant. If, on the other hand, the wife's accommodative strategies (e.g., attempts at neutralization or rationalization) fail, she may find it necessary to bring in third parties (e.g., social-control agents such as the police) to regulate her husband's behavior. Not only have the wife's "tolerance limits" been exceeded in this case, but behavior that had been managed in the private setting now becomes subject to institutional control. And the husband may be typed, processed, and responded to as an involuntary mental patient.

The selections that follow explore some of the ways in which strategies for management and accommodation operate in private settings. The lead article introduces an important analytical distinction concerning public and personal identity, while the remaining pieces illustrate how audiences may not only help in the production of deviant behavior or beginning deviant careers, but also how audiences may respond to deviance on the part of significant or generalized others. These pieces also provide excellent illustrations of the usefulness of many of the basic concepts and processes introduced in Parts I and II. For example, McCabe specifically tests the techniques of neutralization presented by Sykes and Matza (selection 12 in this book). Although some attention is placed on an actor's behavior, it should be emphasized that the primary focus in this part is given to audience response to perceived or actual deviance on the part of others.

Erving Goffman, in "Information Control and Personal Identity: The Discredited and the Discreditable," draws an important distinction between the *discredited* and the *discreditable*. He notes that when there is a discrepancy between an actor's actual social identity and his or her virtual one, it is possible that this information, if it is stigmatizing, will become known to us before we interact with the actor. A stigmatizing feature or, as Goffman prefers, a "spoiled identity," can affect how we actually relate to the stigmatized. We may, for example, recognize a discrediting feature or make no notice of it. The actor is, however, often viewed as a discredited person. When the "known differentness" or stigmatizing feature of an actor's biography is not known, he or she must be viewed, conceptually, as potentially discreditable. This situation, Goffman argues, presents the actor with a dilemma. Does one tell or not tell? Does one lie or not lie? Or, does one release the potentially discrediting and stigmatizing information to selected individuals in specific settings or domains? Goffman reasons that the release of stigmatizing information can produce certain effects. For example, the release of information can help to confirm or round out the image one may have of an actor. At this point, Goffman introduces a useful distinction among *prestige symbols, stigma symbols,* and *disidentifiers.* A prestige symbol (e.g., a wedding band or a badge) often draws attention to a positive aspect of one's identity, while a stigma symbol (e.g., a conviction for rape or child molestation) causes focus on a discrediting or debasing feature of identity. A disidentifier (e.g., an advanced education of a street person) can be a sign that may disrupt or cast doubt on the validity of an actor's virtual identity. Goffman cautions that not only do signs vary in their reliability, but they can be used as a source of information about the identity of others. He cites, as an example, how anyone who associates with a known criminal or person wanted for arrest can be contaminated.

Patricia A. Adler and Peter Adler, in "Tinydopers: A Case Study of Deviant Socialization," focus on the phenomenon of *tinydoping* or, in this case, the practice of marijuana smoking on the part of young children. This activity, the researchers suggest, raises some interesting questions about changing societal mores and parental socialization. Adler and Adler give specific attention to marijuana-smoking children under the age of nine. Of particular focus is the way in which parents actually influence and socialize their children with respect to the use of marijuana. They present case materials on four children they feel to be typical of other children and adults. After describing various patterns and stages of development, the researchers move to an analysis of how parents instruct their children in the ways of dealing with the outside world. And while the use of marijuana may be open and direct in the privacy of one's own confines, parents are aware that by allowing marijuana use on the part of their young children, they are frequently taking on "an extra social and legal stigma." The motivation for doing so seems to be the desire on the part of the parents to have their children view marijuana smoking in a positive light and not as an evil or unnatural thing. In the words of Adler and Adler, "thus, to destigmatize marijuana they stigmatize themselves in the face of society." The researchers conclude by offering additional insight into the "moral passage" or transformation of marijuana's social and legal status from criminalization to relative legitimization. They demonstrate what is likely to happen when smoking spreads to one of society's sacred groups—children. Adler and Adler present a five-stage of model of social change that they feel captures the diffusion and legitimization of marijuana. For example, during Stage I (the 1940s), the "carriers" or users were what the authors term "stigmatized outgroups" (blacks). By Stage II (the 1950s), usage had spread to "ingroup deviants" (e.g., jazz musicians) who identified with stigmatized outgroups. From there, usage spread to such "avant-garde ingroup members" as college students (Stage III, the 1960s), to such "normal ingroup members" as the middle class (Stage IV, the 1970s), and finally to such "sacred groups" as children (Stage V, from 1975 on). Adler and Adler maintain that the spread of deviance to Stage V can produce social revulsion and trigger attempts to ban the behavior by children; this appears to be the case with respect to tinydopers. This analysis of the moral passage of marijuana has direct relevance for the discussion in Part VI on the transformation of deviant categories.

Karolynn Siegel, Howard Lune, and Ilan H. Meyer provide an interesting account of how people attempt to manage discreditable information about themselves in their article "Stigma Management Among Gay/Bisexual Men with HIV/AIDS." Of particular importance is recasting some stigmatized groups, traditionally seen as simply reacting to the negative effects of stigma, into groups that are proactive and successful in managing the negative effects of stigma. That is to say, stigma management strategies may be offensive as well as defensive in nature. The purpose of the study was to catalog the various stigma management strategies used by HIV-infected gay/bisexual men and to organize the strategies into a classification scheme representing a continuum from reactive (defensive) to proactive (offensive).

Regulating the availability of information (e.g., concealment or selective disclosure) is a common reactive strategy regarding stigma management. Active or offensive responses may include preemptive disclosure, attempts to confront stigma, or molding one's own identity through public education or social activism. Intermediate strategies include gradual disclosure, selective affiliation, discrediting one's discreditors, and challenging moral attributes.

The advent of the Internet has stimulated much sociological research. Chat rooms and chat room cultures have been of particular interest. For example, how is it that norms emerge and particular behaviors are selected as deviant? Further, how are these deviations from the norm managed within "virtual communities"? Audience response is at the center of Rhonda D. Evans' article "Examining the Informal Sanctioning of Deviance in a Chat Room Culture." Of interest to her are the following questions: (1) How are behaviors judged to be deviant? (2) What are the probable origins of deviance in the chat room setting? and (3) What are the likely consequences—how is deviance sanctioned?

Considering informal sanctioning reveals many important elements central to the study of deviance in society. What becomes apparent is that mechanisms that function to identify and manage deviance at the formal, societal level are built into and operate within informal settings as well. The first mechanism is to directly confront the deviance. Virtual communities have developed unique mechanisms because of the limitations of the technology and those resulting from propinquity. The second mechanism allows members of the virtual community to limit access to communal activities. Here again, unique mechanisms have been built in (e.g., members can simply ignore the violating individual). Penetrating the barriers of acceptable behaviors defines the boundaries of group norms, as well as reinforcing the norms through collective response.

Information Control and Personal Identity: The Discredited and the Discreditable

Erving Goffman

When there is a discrepancy between an individual's actual social identity and his virtual one, it is possible for this fact to be known to us before we normals contact him, or to be quite evident when he presents himself before us. He is a discredited person, and it is mainly he I have been dealing with until now. As suggested, we are likely to give no open recognition to what is discrediting of him, and while this work of careful disattention is being done, the situation can become tense, uncertain, and ambiguous for all participants, especially the stigmatized one.

The cooperation of a stigmatized person with normals in acting as if his known differentness were irrelevant and not attended to is one main possibility in the life of such a person. However, when his differentness is not immediately apparent, and is not known beforehand (or at least known by him to be known to the others), when in fact his is a discreditable, not a discredited, person, then the second main possibility in his life is to be found. The issue is not that of managing tension generated during social contacts, but rather that of managing information about his failing. To display or not to display; to tell or not to tell; to let on or not to let on; to lie or not to lie; and in each case, to whom, how, when, and where. For example, while the mental patient is in the hospital, and when he is with adult members of his own family, he is faced with being treated tactfully as if he were sane when there is known to be some doubt, even though he may not have any; or he is treated as insane, when he knows this is not just. But for the ex-mental patient the problem can be quite different; it is not that he must face prejudice against himself, but rather that he must face unwitting acceptance of himself by individuals who are prejudiced against persons of the kind he can be revealed to be. Wherever he goes his behavior will falsely confirm for the other that they are in the company of what in effect they demand but may discover they haven't obtained, namely, a mentally untainted person like themselves. By intention or in effect the ex-mental patient conceals information about his real social identity, receiving and accepting treatment based on false suppositions concerning himself. It is this second general issue, the management of undisclosed discrediting information about self, that I am focusing on in these notes, in brief, "passing." The concealment of creditable facts—reverse passing—of course occurs, but is not relevant here.[1]

The information of most relevance in the study of stigma has certain properties. It is information about an individual. It is about his more or less abiding characteristics, as opposed to the moods, feelings, or intents that he might have at a particular moment.[2] The information as well as the sign through which it is conveyed, is reflexive and embodied; that is, it is conveyed by the very person it is about, and conveyed through bodily expression in the immediate presence of those who receive the expression. Information possessing all of these properties I will here call "social." Some signs that convey social information may be frequently and steadily available, and routinely sought and received; these signs may be called "symbols."

The social information conveyed by any particular symbol may merely confirm what other signs tell us about the individual, filling out our image of him in a redundant and unproblematic way. Some lapel buttons, attesting to social club membership, are examples, as are male wedding rings in some contexts. However, the social information conveyed by a symbol can establish a special claim to prestige, honor, or desirable class position—a claim that might not otherwise be presented or, if otherwise presented, then not automatically granted. Such a sign is popularly called a "status symbol," although the term "prestige symbol" might be more accurate, the former term being more suitably employed when a well-organized social position of some kind is the referent. Prestige symbols can be contrasted to *stigma symbols,* namely, signs which are essentially effective in drawing attention to a debasing identity discrepancy, breaking up what would otherwise be a coherent overall picture, with a consequent reduction in our valuation of the individual. The shaved head of female collaborators in World War II is an example, as is an habitual solecism through which someone affecting middle class manner and dress repeatedly employs a word incorrectly or repeatedly mispronounces it.

In addition to prestige symbols and stigma symbols, one further possibility is to be found, namely, a sign that tends—in fact or hope—to break up an otherwise coherent picture but in this case in a positive direction desired by the actor, not so much establishing a new claim as throwing severe doubt on the validity of the virtual one. I shall refer here to disidentifiers. One example is the "good English" of an educated northern Negro visiting the South[3]; another is the turban and mustache affected by some urban lower class Negroes.[4] A study of illiterates provides another illustration:

> Therefore, when goal orientation is pronounced or imperative and there
> exists a high probability that definition as illiterate is a bar to the

achievement of the goal, the illiterate is likely to try to "pass" as liter-
ate. . . . The popularity in the group studied of windowpane lenses with
heavy horn frames ("bop glasses") may be viewed as an attempt to emulate the stereotype of the businessman-teacher-young intellectual and
especially the high status jazz musician.[5]

A New York specialist in the arts of vagrancy provides still another illustration:

> After seven-thirty in the evening, in order to read a book in Grand Cen-
> tral or Penn Station, a person either has to wear horn-rimmed glasses
> or look exceptionally prosperous. Anyone else is apt to come under sur-
> veillance. On the other hand, newspaper readers never seem to attract
> attention and even the seediest vagrant can sit in Grand Central all
> night without being molested if he continues to read a paper.[6]

Note that in this discussion of prestige symbols, stigma symbols, and
disidentifiers, signs have been considered which routinely convey social information. These symbols must be distinguished from fugitive signs that
have not been institutionalized as information carriers. When such signs
make claims to prestige, one can call them points; when they discredit tacit
claims, one can call them slips.

Some signs carrying social information, being present, first of all, for
other reasons, have only an overlay of informational function. There are
stigma symbols that provide examples: the wrist markings which disclose
that an individual has attempted suicide; the arm pock marks of drug addicts; the handcuffed wrists of convicts in transit;[7] or black eyes when
worn in public by females, as a writer on prostitution suggests:

> Outside [the prison where she now is] I'd be in the soup with it. Well,
> you know how it is: the law sees a chick with a shiner figures she's up
> to something. Bull figures maybe in the life. Next thing trails her
> around. Then maybe bang! busted.[8]

Other signs are designed by man solely for the purpose of conveying social
information, as in the case of insignia of military rank. It should be added
that the significance of the underlay of a sign can become reduced over
time, becoming, at the extreme, merely vestigial, even while the informational function of the activity remains constant or increases in importance.
Further, a sign that appears to be present for non-informational reasons
may sometimes be manufactured with malice aforethought solely because
of its informing function, as when dueling scars were carefully planned
and inflicted.

Signs conveying social information vary according to whether or not
they are congenital, and, if not, whether, once employed, they become a
permanent part of the person. (Skin color is congenital; a brand mark or
maiming is permanent but not congenital; a convict's head-shave is neither

congenital nor permanent.) More important, impermanent signs solely employed to convey social information may or may not be employed against the will of the informant; when they are, they tend to be stigma symbols.[9] Later it will be necessary to consider stigma symbols that are voluntarily employed.

It is possible for signs which mean one thing to one group to mean something else to another group, the same category being designated but differently characterized. For example, the shoulder patches that prison officials require escape-prone prisoners to wear[10] can come to mean one thing to guards, in general negative, while being a mark of pride for the wearer relative to his fellow prisoners. The uniform of an officer may be a matter of pride to some, to be worn on every possible occasion; for other officers, weekends may represent a time when they can exercise their choice and wear mufti, passing as civilians. Similarly, while the obligation to wear the school cap in town may be seen as a privilege by some boys, as will the obligation to wear a uniform on leave by "other ranks," still there will be wearers who feel that the social information conveyed thereby is a means of ensuring control and discipline over them when they are off duty and off the premises.[11] So, too, during the eighteen hundreds in California, the absence of a pigtail (queue) on a Chinese man signified for Occidentals a degree of acculturation, but to fellow-Chinese a question would be raised as to respectability—specifically, whether or not the individual had served a term in prison where cutting off of the queue was obligatory; loss of queue was for a time, then, very strongly resisted.[12]

Signs carrying social information vary of course as to reliability. Distended capillaries on the cheek and nose, sometimes called "venous stigmata" with more aptness than meant, can be and are taken as indicating alcoholic excess. However, teetotalers can exhibit the same symbol for other physiological reasons, thereby giving rise to suspicions about themselves which aren't justified, but with which they must deal nonetheless.

A final point about social information must be raised; it has to do with the informing character of the "with" relationship in our society. To be "with" someone is to arrive at a social occasion in his company, walk with him down a street, be a member of his party in a restaurant, and so forth. The issue is that in certain circumstances the social identity of those an individual is with can be used as a source of information concerning his own social identity, the assumption being that he is what the others are. The extreme, perhaps, is the situation in criminal circles: a person wanted for arrest can legally contaminate anyone he is seen with, subjecting them to arrest on suspicion. (A person for whom there is a warrant is therefore said "to have smallpox," and his criminal disease is said to be "catching.")[13] In any case, an analysis of how people manage the information they convey about themselves will have to consider how they deal with the contingencies of being seen "with" particular others.

Notes

1. For one instance of reverse passing, see "H.E.R. Cules" and "Ghost-Writer and Failure," in P. Toynbee, ed., *Underdogs* (London: Weidenfeld, and Nicolson, 1961), Chap. 2, pp. 30–39. There are many other examples. I knew a physician who was careful to refrain from using external symbols of her status, such as car-license tags, her only evidence of profession being an identification carried in her wallet. When faced with a public accident in which medical service was already being rendered the victim, or in which the victim was past helping, she would, upon examining the victim at a distance from the circle around him, quietly go her way without announcing her competence. In these situations she was what might be called a female impersonator.

2. The difference between mood information and other kinds of information is treated in G. Stone, "Appearance and the Self," in A. Rose, *Human Behavior and Social Processes* (Boston: Houghton Mifflin, 1962), pp. 86–118. See also E. Goffman, *The Presentation of Self in Everyday Life* (New York: Doubleday & Co., Anchor Books, 1959), pp. 24–25.

3. G. J. Fleming, "My Most Humiliating Jim Crow Experience," *Negro Digest* (June 1954), 67–68.

4. B. Wolfe, "Ecstatic in Blackface," *Modern Review*, III (1950), 204.

5. Freeman and Kasenbaum, *op. cit.,* p. 372.

6. E. Love, *Subways Are for Sleeping* (New York: Harcourt, Brace & World, 1957), p. 28.

7. A. Heckstall-Smith, *Eighteen Months* (London: Allan Wingate, 1954), p. 43.

8. T. Rubin, *In the Life* (New York: The Macmillan Company, 1961), p. 69.

9. In his *American Notes,* written on the basis of his 1842 trip, Dickens records in his chapter on slavery some pages of quotations from local newspapers regarding lost and found slaves. The identifications contained in these advertisements provide a full range of identifying signs. First, there are relatively stable features of the body that in context can incidentally provide partial or full positive identification: age, sex, and scarrings (these resulting from shot and knife wounds, from accidents, and from lashings). Self-admitted name is also provided, though usually, of course, only the first name. Finally, stigma symbols are often cited, notably branded initials and cropped ears. These symbols communicate the social identity of slave but, unlike iron bands around the neck or leg, also communicate something more narrow than that, namely, ownership by a particular master. Authorities then had two concerns about an apprehended Negro: whether or not he was a runaway slave, and, if he was, to whom did he belong.

10. See G. Dendrickson and F. Thomas, *The Truth About Dartmoor* (London: Victor Gollancz, 1954), p. 55, and F. Norman, *Bang to Rights* (London: Secker and Warburg, 1958), p. 125. The use of this type of symbol is well presented in E. Kogon, *The Theory and Practice of Hell* (New York: Berkley Publishing Corp., n.d.), pp. 41–42, where he specifies the markings used in concentration camps to identify differentially political prisoners, second offenders, criminals, Jehovah's Witnesses, "shiftless elements," Gypsies, Jews, "race defilers," foreign nationals (according to nation), feeble-minded, and so forth. Slaves on the Roman slave market also were often labeled as to nationality; see M. Gordon, "The Nationality of Slaves Under the Early Roman Empire," in M. I. Finley, ed., *Slavery in Classical Antiquity* (Cambridge: Heffer, 1960), p. 171.

11. T. H. Pear, *Personality, Appearance and Speech* (London: George Allen and Unwin, 1957), p. 58.

12. A. McLeod, *Pigtails and Gold Dust* (Caldwel, Idaho: Caxton Printers, 1947), p. 28. At times religious-historical significance was also attached to wearing this queue; see *ibid.,* p. 204.

13. See D. Maurer, *The Big Con* (New York: Pocket Books, 1949), p. 298.

Tinydopers:
A Case Study
of Deviant Socialization

Patricia A. Adler
Peter Adler

Marijuana smoking is now filtering down to our youngest generation; a number of children from 0 to 8 years old are participating in this practice under the influence and supervision of their parents. This phenomenon, *tinydoping*, raises interesting questions about changes in societal mores and patterns of socialization. We are not concerned here with the desirability or morality of the activity. Instead, we will discuss the phenomenon, elucidating the diverse range of attitudes, stratagems and procedures held and exercised by parents and children.

An examination of the history and cultural evolution of marijuana over the last several decades illuminates the atmosphere in which tinydoping arose. Marijuana use, first located chiefly among jazz musicians and ghetto communities, eventually expanded to "the highly alienated young in flight from families, schools and conventional communities" (Simon and Gagnon, 1968:60. See also Goode, 1970; Carey, 1968; Kaplan, 1971; and Grinspoon, 1971). Blossoming in the mid-1960s, this youth scene formed an estranged and deviant subculture offsetting the dominant culture's work ethic and instrumental success orientation. Society reacted as an angry parent, enforcing legal, social and moral penalties against its rebellious children. Today, however, the pothead subculture has eroded and the population of smokers has broadened to include large numbers of middle-class and establishment-oriented people.

Marijuana, then, may soon take its place with alcohol, its "prohibition" a thing of the past. These two changes can be considered movements of moral passage:

> Movements to redefine behavior may eventuate in a moral passage, a transition of the behavior from one moral status to another. . . . What is attacked as criminal today may be seen as sick next year and fought over as possibly legitimate by the next generation. (Gusfield, 1967:187. See also Matza, 1969; Kitsuse, 1962; Douglas, 1970; and Becker, 1963 for further discussions of the social creation of deviance.)

Profound metamorphoses testify to this redefinition: frequency and severity of arrest is proportionately down from a decade ago; the stigma of a marijuana-related arrest is no longer as personally and occupationally ostracizing; and the fear that using grass will press the individual into close contact with hardened criminals and cause him to adopt a deviant self-identity or take up criminal ways has also largely passed.

The transformation in marijuana's social and legal status is not intrinsic to its own characteristics or those of mood-altering drugs in general. Rather, it illustrates a process of becoming socially accepted many deviant activities or substances may go through. This research suggests a more generic model of social change, a sequential development characteristic of the diffusion and legitimation of a formerly unconventional practice. Five stages identify the spread of such activities from small isolated outgroups, through increasing levels of mainstream society, and finally to such sacred groups as children.[1] Often, however, as with the case of pornography, the appearance of this quasi-sanctioned conduct among juveniles elicits moral outrage and a social backlash designed to prevent such behavior in the sacred population, while leaving it more open to the remainder of society.

Most treatments of pot smoking in the sociological literature have been historically and subculturally specific (see Carey, 1968; Goode, 1970; Grupp, 1971; Hochman, 1972; Kaplan, 1971; and Simon and Gagnon, 1968), swiftly dated by our rapidly changing society. Only Becker's (1953) work is comparable to our research since it offers a general sequential model of the process for becoming a marijuana user.

The data in this paper show an alternate route to marijuana smoking. Two developments necessitate a modification of Becker's conceptualization. First, there have been many changes in norms, traditions and patterns of use since the time he wrote. Second, the age of this new category of smokers is cause for reformulation. Theories of child development proposed by Mead (1934), Erikson (1968), and Piaget (1948) agree that prior to a certain age children are unable to comprehend subtle transformations and perceptions. As we will see, the full effects and symbolic meanings of marijuana are partially lost to them due to their inability to differentiate between altered states of consciousness and to connect this with the smoking experience. Yet this does not preclude their becoming avid pot users and joining in the smoking group as accepted members.

Socialization practices are the final concern of this research. The existence of tinydoping both illustrates and contradicts several established norms of traditional childrearing. Imitative behavior (see Piaget, 1962), for instance, is integral to tinydoping since the children's desire to copy the actions of parents and other adults is a primary motivation. Boundary maintenance also arises as a consideration: as soon as their offspring can communicate, parents must instruct them in the perception of social borders and the need for guarding group activities as secret. In contrast, refutations of convention include the introduction of mood-altering drugs into the sacred childhood period and, even more unusual, parents and children get high together. This bridges, often to the point of eradication, the intergenerational gap firmly entrenched in most societies. Thus, although parents view their actions as normal, tinydoping must presently be considered as deviant socialization.

Methods

Collected over the course of 18 months, our data include observations of two dozen youngsters between the ages of birth and eight, and a similar number of parents, aged 21 to 32, all in middle-class households. To obtain a complete image of this practice we talked with parents, kids and other involved observers (the "multiperspectival" approach, Douglas, 1976). Many of our conversations with adults were taped but our discussions with the children took the form of informal, extemporaneous dialogue, since the tape recorder distracts and diverts their attention. Finally, our study is exploratory and suggestive; we make no claim to all-inclusiveness in the cases or categories below.

The Kids

The following four individuals, each uniquely interesting, represent many common characteristics of other children and adults we observed.

"Big Ed": The Diaperdoper

Big Ed derives his name from his miniature size. Born three months prematurely, now three years old, he resembles a toy human being. Beneath his near-white wispy hair and toddling diapered bottom, he packs a punch of childish energy. Big Ed's mother and older siblings take care of him although he often sees his father who lives in a neighboring California town. Laxity and permissiveness characterize his upbringing, as he freely roams the neighborhood under his own and other children's supervision. Exposure to marijuana has prevailed since birth and in the last year he advanced from passive inhalation (smoke blown in his direction) to active puffing on joints. Still in the learning stage, most of his power is expended blowing air into the reefer instead of inhaling. He prefers to suck on a "bong" (a specially designed waterpipe), delighting in the gurgling sound the water makes. A breast fed baby, he will go to the bong for oral satisfaction, whether it is filled or not. He does not actively seek joints, but Big Ed never refuses one when offered. After a few puffs, however, he usually winds up with smoke in his eyes and tearfully retreats to a glass of water. Actual marijuana inhalation is minimal; his size renders it potent. Big Ed has not absorbed any social restrictions related to pot use or any awareness of its illegality, but is still too young to make a blooper as his speech is limited.

Stephanie: The Social Smoker

Stephanie is a dreamy four-year old with quite good manners, calm assurance, sweet disposition and a ladylike personality and appearance. Although her brothers are rough and tumble, Stephanie can play with the boys or amuse herself sedately alone or in the company of adults. Attendance at a progressive school for the last two years has developed her natural curiosity and intelligence. Stephanie's mother and father both work, but still find enough recreational time to raise their children with love and care and to engage in frequent marijuana smoking. Accordingly, Stephanie has seen grass since infancy and accepted it as a natural part of life. Unlike the diaperdoper, she has mastered the art of inhalation and can breathe the smoke out through her nose. Never grasping or grubbing for pot, she has advanced from a preference for bongs or pipes and now enjoys joints when offered. She revels in being part of a crowd of smokers and passes the reefer immediately after each puff, and never holding it for an unsociable amount of time. Her treasure box contains a handful of roaches (marijuana butts) and seeds (she delights in munching them as snacks) that she keeps as mementos of social occasions with (adult) "friends." After smoking, Stephanie becomes more bubbly and outgoing. Dancing to records, she turns in circles as she jogs from one foot to the other, releasing her body to the rhythm. She then eats everything in sight and falls asleep—roughly the same cycle as adults, but faster.

When interviewed, Stephanie clearly recognized the difference between a cigarette and a joint (both parents use tobacco), defining the effects of the latter as good but still being unsure of what the former did and how the contents of each varied. She also responded with some confusion about social boundaries separating pot users from non-users, speculating that perhaps her grandmother did smoke it but her grandfather certainly did not (neither do). In the words of her father: "She knows not to tell people about it but she just probably wouldn't anyway."

Josh: The Self-Gratifier

Everyone in the neighborhood knows Josh. Vociferous and outgoing, at age five he has a decidedly Dennis-the-Menace quality in both looks and personality. Neither timid nor reserved, he boasts to total strangers of his fantastic exploits and talents. Yet behind his bravado swagger lies a seeming insecurity and need for acceptance, coupled with a difficulty in accepting authority, which has led him into squabbles with peers, teachers, siblings and parents.

Josh's home shows the traditional division of labor. His mother stays home to cook and care for the children while his father works long hours. The mother is always calm and tolerant about her youngster's smart-alec ways, but his escapades may provoke an explosive tirade from his father. Yet this male parent is clearly the dominating force in Josh's life. Singling

Josh out from his younger sister and brother, the father has chosen him as his successor in the male tradition. The parent had himself begun drinking and smoking cigarettes in his early formative years, commencing pot use as a teenager, and now has a favorable attitude toward the early use of stimulants which he is actively passing on to Josh.

According to his parents, his smoking has had several beneficial effects. Considering Josh a "hyper" child, they claim that it calms him down to a more normal speed, often permitting him to engage in activities which would otherwise be too difficult for his powers of concentration. He also appears to become more sedate and less prone to temper tantrums, sleeping longer and more deeply. But Josh's smoking patterns differ significantly from our last two subjects. He does not enjoy social smoking, preferring for his father to roll him "pinners" (thin joints) to smoke by himself. Unlike many other tinydopers, Josh frequently refuses the offer of a joint saying, "Oh that! I gave up smoking that stuff." At age five he claims to have already quit and gone back several times. His mother backs this assertion as valid; his father brushes it off as merely a ploy to shock and gain attention. Here, the especially close male parent recognizes the behavior as imitative and accepts it as normal. To others, however, it appears strange and suggests surprising sophistication.

Josh's perception of social boundaries is also mature. Only a year older than Stephanie, Josh has made some mistakes but his awareness of the necessity for secrecy is complete; he differentiates those people with whom he may and may not discuss the subject by the experience of actually smoking with them. He knows individuals but cannot yet socially categorize the boundaries. Josh also realizes the contrast between joints and cigarettes down to the marijuana and tobacco they contain. Interestingly, he is aggressively opposed to tobacco while favoring pot use (this may be the result of anti-tobacco cancer propaganda from kindergarten).

Kyra: The Bohemian

A worldly but curiously childlike girl is seven-year-old Kyra. Her wavy brown hair falls to her shoulders and her sun-tanned body testifies to many hours at the beach in winter and summer. Of average height for her age, she dresses with a maturity beyond her years. Friendly and sociable, she has few reservations about what she says to people. Kyra lives with her youthful mother and whatever boyfriend her mother fancies at the moment. Their basic family unit consists of two (mother and daughter), and they have travelled together living a free life all along the West Coast and Hawaii. While Josh's family was male dominated, this is clearly female centered, all of Kyra's close relatives being women. They are a bohemian group, generation after generation following a hip, up-to-the-moment, unshackled lifestyle. The house is often filled with people, but when the visitors clear out, a youthful, thrillseeking mother remains, who raises this daughter by treating her like a sister or friend. This demand on Kyra to be-have as an adult may produce some internal strain, but she seems to have grown accustomed to it. Placed in situations others might find awkward, she handles them with precocity. Like her mother, she is being reared for a life of independence and freedom.

Pot smoking is an integral part of this picture. To Kyra it is another sym-bol for her adulthood; she enjoys it and wants to do it a lot. At seven she is an accomplished smoker; her challenge right now lies in the mastery of rolling joints. Of our four examples, social boundaries are clearest to Kyra. Not only is she aware of the necessary secrecy surrounding pot use, but she is able to socially categorize types of people into marijuana smokers and straights. She may err in her judgment occasionally, but no more so than any adult.

Stages of Development

These four and other cases suggest a continuum of reactions to marijuana that is loosely followed by most tinydopers.

From birth to around 18 months a child's involvement is passive. Most parents keep their infants nearby at all times and if pot is smoked the room becomes filled with potent clouds. At this age just a little marijuana smoke can be very powerful and these infants, the youngest diaperdopers, mani-fest noticeable effects. The drug usually has a calming influence, putting the infant into a less cranky mood and extending the depth and duration of sleep.

After the first one and a half years, the children are more attuned to what is going on around them: they begin to desire participation in a "mon-key see, monkey do" fashion. During the second year, a fascination with paraphernalia generally develops, as they play with it and try to figure it out. Eager to smoke with the adults and older children, they are soon dis-couraged after a toke (puff) or two. They find smoking difficult and painful (particularly to the eyes and throat)—after all, it is not easy to inhale burn-ing hot air and hold it in your lungs.

But continual practice eventually produces results, and inhalation seems to be achieved somewhere during the third or fourth year. This brings con-siderable pride and makes the kids feel they have attained semi-adult sta-tus. Now they can put the paraphernalia to work. Most tinydopers of this age are wild about "roach clips," itching to put their joints into them as soon as possible after lighting.

Ages four and five bring the first social sense of the nature of pot and who should know about it. This begins as a vague idea, becoming further refined with age and sophistication. Finally, by age seven or eight kids have a clear concept of where the lines can be drawn between those who are and aren't "cool," and can make these distinctions on their own. No child we interviewed, however, could verbalize about any specific effects felt after smoking marijuana. Ironically, although they participate in smoking and actually manifest clear physical symptoms of the effects, tinydopers are rationally and intellectually unaware of how the drug is acting upon them. They are too young to notice a change in their behavior or to make the symbolic leap and associate this transformation with having smoked pot previously. The effects of marijuana must be socially and consensually delineated from non-high sensations for the user to fully appreciate the often subtle perceptual and physiological changes that have occurred. To the youngster the benefits of pot smoking are not at all subtle: he is permitted to imitate his elders by engaging in a social ritual they view as pleasurable and important; the status of adulthood is partially conferred on him by allowing this act; and his desire for acceptance is fulfilled through inclusion in his parents' peer group. This constitutes the major difference in appreciation between the child and adult smoker.

Parents' Strategies

The youth of the sixties made some forceful statements through their actions about how they evaluated the Establishment and the conventional American lifestyle. While their political activism has faded, many former members of this group still feel a strong commitment to smoking pot and attach a measure of symbolic significance to it. When they had children the question then arose of how to handle the drug vis-à-vis their offspring. The continuum of responses they developed ranges from total openness and permissiveness to various measures of secrecy.

Smoking Regularly Permitted

Some parents give their children marijuana whenever it is requested. They may wait until the child reaches a certain age, but most parents in this category started their kids on pot from infancy. These parents may be "worried" or "unconcerned."

Worried: Ken and Deedy are moderate pot smokers, getting high a few times a week. Both had been regular users for several years prior to having children. When Deedy was pregnant she absolutely refused to continue her smoking pattern.

> I didn't know what effect it could have on the unborn child. I tried to read and find out, but there's very little written on that. But in the *Playboy* Advisor there was an article: they said we advise you to stay away from all drugs when you're pregnant. That was sort of my proof. I figured they don't bullshit about these types of things. I sort of said now at least somebody stands behind me because people were saying, "You can get high, it's not going to hurt the baby."

This abstinence satisfied them and once the child was born they resumed getting high as before. Frequently smoking in the same room as the baby, they began to worry about the possible harmful effects this exposure might have on his physical, psychological and mental development. After some discussion, they consulted the family pediatrician, a prominent doctor in the city.

> I was really embarrassed, but I said, "Doctor, we get high, we smoke pot, and sometimes the kid's in the room. If he's in the room can this hurt him? I don't want him to be mentally retarded." He said, "Don't worry about it, they're going to be legalizing it any day now—this was three years ago—it's harmless and a great sedative."

This reassured them on two counts: they no longer were fearful in their own minds, and they had a legitimate answer when questioned by their friends.[2]

Ken and Deedy were particularly sensitive about peer reactions:

> Some people say, "You let your children get high?!" They really act with disgust. Or they'll say, "Oh you let your kids get high," and then they kind of look at you like, "That's neat, I think." And it's just nice to be able to back it up.

Ken and Deedy were further nonplussed about the problem of teaching their children boundary maintenance. Recognizing the need to prevent their offspring from saying things to the wrong people, they were unsure how to approach this subject properly.

> How can you tell a kid, how can you go up to him and say, "Well you want to get high, but don't tell anybody you're doing it"? You can't. We didn't really know how to tell them. You don't want to bring the attention, you don't want to tell your children not to say anything about it because that's a sure way to get them to do it. We just never said anything about it.

They hope this philosophy of openness and permissiveness will forestall the need to limit their children's marijuana consumption. Limits, for them, resemble prohibitions and interdictions against discussing grass: they make transgressions attractive. Both parents believe strongly in presenting marijuana as an everyday occurrence, definitely not as an undercover affair. When asked how they thought this upbringing might affect their kids, Deedy offered a fearful but doubtful speculation that her children might one day reject the drug.

> I don't imagine they'd try to abuse it. Maybe they won't even smoke pot when they get older. That's a big possibility. I doubt it, but hopefully they won't be that way. They've got potheads for parents.

Unconcerned: Alan and Anna make use of a variety of stimulants—pot, alcohol, cocaine—to enrich their lives. Considered heavy users, they consume marijuana and alcohol daily. Alan became acquainted with drugs, particularly alcohol, at a very early age and Anna first tried them in her teens. When they decided to have children the question of whether they would permit the youngsters to partake in their mood-altering experiences never arose. Anna didn't curtail her drug intake during pregnancy; her offspring were conceived, formed and weaned on this steady diet. When queried about their motivations, Alan volunteered:

> What the hell! It grows in the ground, it's a weed. I can't see anything wrong with doing anything, inducing any part of it into your body anyway that you possibly could eat it, smoke it, intravenously, or whatever, that it would ever harm you because it grows in the ground. It's a natural thing. It's one of God's treats.

All of their children have been surrounded by marijuana's aromatic vapor since the day they returned from the hospital. Alan and Anna were pleased with the effect pot had on their infants; the relaxed, sleepy and happy qualities achieved after inhaling pot smoke made childrearing an easier task. As the little ones grew older they naturally wanted to share in their parents' activities. Alan viewed this as the children's desire to imitate rather than true enjoyment of any effects:

> Emily used to drink Jack Daniels straight and like it. I don't think it was taste, I think it was more of an acceptance thing because that's what I was drinking. She was also puffing on joints at six months.

This mimicking, coupled with a craving for acceptance, although recognized by Alan in his kids, was not repeated in his own feelings toward friends or relatives. At no time during the course of our interview or acquaintance did he show any concern with what others thought of his behavior; rather, his convictions dominated, and his wife passively followed his lead.

In contrast to the last couple, Alan was not reluctant to address the problem of boundary maintenance. A situation arose when Emily was three, where she was forced to learn rapidly:

> One time we were stopped by the police while driving drunk. I said to Emily—we haven't been smoking marijuana. We all acted quiet and Emily realized there was something going on and she delved into it. I explained that some people are stupid and they'll harm you very badly if you smoke marijuana. To this day I haven't heard her mention it to anyone she hasn't smoked with.

As each new child came along, Alan saw to it that they learned the essential facts of life.

Neither Alan nor Anna saw any moral distinction between marijuana smoking and other, more accepted pastimes. They heartily endorsed marijuana as something to indulge in like "tobacco, alcohol, sex, breathing or anything else that brings pleasure to the senses." Alan and Anna hope their children will continue to smoke grass in their later lives. It has had beneficial effects for them and they believe it can do the same for their kids:

> I smoked marijuana for a long time, stopped and developed two ulcers; and smoked again and the two ulcers went away. It has great medicinal value.

Smoking Occasionally Permitted

In contrast to uninterrupted permissiveness, other parents restrict marijuana use among their children to specific occasions. A plethora of reasons and rationalizations lie behind this behavior, some openly avowed by parents and others not. Several people believe it is okay to let the kids get high as long as it isn't done too often. Many other people do not have any carefully thought-out notion of what they want, tending to make spur-of-the-moment decisions. As a result, they allow occasional but largely undefined smoking in a sporadic and irregular manner. Particular reasons for this inconsistency can be illustrated by three examples from our research:

1. *Conflicts between parents* can confuse the situation. While Stella had always planned to bring her children up with pot, Burt did not like the idea. Consequently, the household rule on this matter varied according to the unpredictable moods of the adults and which parent was in the house.
2. Mike and Gwen had trouble *making up their minds*. At one time they thought it probably couldn't harm the child, only to decide the next day they shouldn't take chances and rescind that decision.
3. Lois and David didn't waver hourly but had *changing ideas over time*. At first they were against it, but then met a group of friends who liked to party and approved of tinydoping. After a few years they moved to a new neighborhood and changed their lifestyle, again prohibiting pot smoking for the kids.

These are just a few of the many situations in which parents allow children an occasional opportunity to smoke grass. They use various criteria to decide when those permissible instances ought to be, most families subscribing to several of the following patterns:

Reward: The child receives pot as a bonus for good behavior in the past, present or future. This may serve as an incentive: "If you're a good boy today, Johnny, I may let you smoke with us tonight," or to celebrate an achievement already completed like "going potty" or reciting the alphabet.

Guilt: Marijuana can be another way of compensating children for what they aren't getting. Historically, parents have tried to buy their kids off or make themselves loved through gifts of money or toys but pot can also be suitable here. This is utilized both by couples with busy schedules who don't have time for the children ("We're going out again tonight so we'll give you this special treat to make it up to you") and by separated parents who are trying to compete with the former spouse for the child's love ("I know Mommy doesn't let you do this but you can do special things when you're with me").

Cuteness: To please themselves parents may occasionally let the children smoke pot because it's cute. Younger children look especially funny because they cannot inhale, yet in their eagerness to be like Mommy and Daddy they make a hilarious effort and still have a good time themselves. Often this will originate as amusement for the parents and then spread to include cuteness in front of friends. Carrying this trend further, friends may roll joints for the little ones or turn them on when the parents are away. This still precludes regular use.

Purposive: Giving marijuana to kids often carries a specific anticipated goal for the parents. The known effects of pot are occasionally desired and actively sought. They may want to calm the child down because of the necessities of a special setting or company. Sleep is another pursued end, as in "Thank you for taking Billy for the night; if he gives you any trouble just let him smoke this and he'll go right to bed." They may also give it to the children medicinally. Users believe marijuana soothes the upset stomach and alleviates the symptoms of the common cold better than any other drug. As a mood elevator, many parents have given pot to alleviate the crankiness young children develop from a general illness, specific pain or injury. One couple used it experimentally as a treatment for hyperactivity (see Josh).

Abstention

Our last category of marijuana-smoking parents contains those who do not permit their children any direct involvement with illegal drugs. This leaves several possible ways to treat the topic of the adults' own involvement with drugs and how open they are about it. Do they let the kids know they smoke pot? Moreover, do they do it in the children's presence?

Overt: The great majority of our subjects openly smoked in front of their children, defining marijuana as an accepted and natural pastime. Even parents who withhold it from their young children hope that the kids will someday grow up to be like themselves. Thus, they smoke pot overtly. These marijuana smokers are divided on the issue of other drugs, such as pills and cocaine.

a. *permissive*—One group considers it acceptable to use any drug in front of the children. Either they believe in what they are doing and consider it right for the kids to observe their actions, or they don't worry about it and just do it.

b. *pragmatic*—A larger, practically oriented group differentiated between "smokable" drugs (pot and hashish) and the others (cocaine and pills), finding it acceptable to let children view consumption of the former group, but not the latter. Rationales varied for this, ranging from safety to morality:

> Well, we have smoked hashish around them but we absolutely never ever do coke in front of them because it's a white powder and if they saw us snorting a white powder there goes the drain cleaner, there goes baby powder. Anything white, they'll try it; and that goes for pills too. The only thing they have free rein of is popping vitamins.

Fred expressed his concern over problems this might engender in the preservation of his children's moral fiber:

> If he sees me snorting coke, how is he going to differentiate that from heroin? He gets all this anti-drug education from school and they tell him that heroin is bad. How can I explain to him that doing coke is okay and it's fun and doesn't hurt you but heroin is something else, so different and bad? How could I teach right from wrong?

c. *capricious*—A third group is irregular in its handling of multiple drug viewing and their offspring. Jon and Linda, for instance, claim that they don't mind smoking before their child but absolutely won't permit other drugs to be used in his presence. Yet in fact they often use almost any intoxicant in front of him, depending on their mood and how high they have already become.

In our observations we have never seen any parent give a child in the tinydoper range any kind of illegal drug other than marijuana and, extremely rarely, hashish. Moreover, the treatment of pot has been above all direct and open: even those parents who don't permit their children to join have rejected the clandestine secrecy of the behind-closed-doors approach. Ironically, however, they must often adopt this strategy toward the outside world; those parents who let it be known that they permit tinydoping frequently take on an extra social and legal stigma. Their motivation for doing so stems from a desire to avoid having the children view pot and their smoking it as evil or unnatural. Thus, to destigmatize marijuana they stigmatize themselves in the face of society.

Conclusions

Tinydoping, with its combined aspects of understandably innovative social development and surprising challenges to convention, is a fruitful subject for sociological analysis. A review of historical and cultural forces leading to the present offers insight into how and why this phenomenon came to arise. Essentially, we are witnessing the moral passage of marijuana, its transformation from an isolated and taboo drug surrounded by connotations of fear and danger, into an increasingly accepted form of social relaxation, similar to alcohol. The continuing destigmatization of pot fosters an atmosphere in which parents are willing to let their children smoke.

Marijuana's social transition is not an isolated occurrence, however. Many formerly deviant activities have gradually become acceptable forms of behavior. Table 1 presents a general model of social change which outlines the sequential development and spread of a conduct undergoing legitimization.

Particular behaviors which first occur only among relatively small and stigmatized outgroups are frequently picked up by ingroup deviants who identify with the stigmatized outgroup. In an attempt to be cool and avant-garde, larger clusters of ingroup members adopt this deviant practice, often for the sake of nonconformity as well as its own merits. By this time the deviant activity is gaining exposure as well as momentum and may spread to normal ingroup members. The final step is its eventual introduction to sacred groups in the society, such as children.

Becker's (1953) research and theory are pertinent to historical stages I and II. More recently, Carey (1968) and Goode (1970) have depicted stage III. To date, sociologists have not described stage IV and we are the first to portray stage V.

The general value of this model can be further illustrated by showing its application to another deviant activity which has followed a similar progression—pornography. Initially a highly stigmatized practice engaged in by people largely hidden from public view, it slowly became incorporated into a wider cross-section of the population. With the advent of *Playboy*, mainstream media entered the scene, resulting in the present proliferation of sexually-oriented magazines and tabloids. Recently, however, this practice passed into stage V; a violent societal reaction ensued, with moralist

Table 1   Sequential Model of Social Change: The Diffusion and Legitimization of Marijuana

Stage		Carriers	
I	1940s	Stigmatized outgroup	Blacks
II	1950s	Ingroup deviants who identify with stigmatized outgroup	Jazz musicians
III	1960s	Avant-garde ingroup members	College students and counterculture
IV	1970s	Normal ingroup members	Middle class
V	1975+	Sacred group	Children

groups crusading to hold the sacred period of childhood free from such deviant intrusions.

Tinydoping has not become broadly publicly recognized but, as with pornography, the widespread (collective) softening of attitudes has not extended to youngsters. Rather, a backlash effect stemming from conventional morality condemns such "intrusions and violations of childhood" as repulsive. Thus, the spread of deviance to Group V prompts social revulsion and renewed effort to ban the behavior by children while allowing it to adults.

These data also recommend a re-examination of sociological theories about marijuana use. Becker's (1953) theory is in some ways timeless, illuminating a model of the actor which encompasses a dynamic processual development. It proposes an initiation process that precedes bona fide membership in a pot smoking milieu. Minimally, this includes: learning the proper techniques to ensure adequate consumption; perception of the drug's unique effects; association of these effects with the smoking experience; and the conceptualization of these effects as pleasurable. Symbolic *meaning* is crucial to this schema: through a "sequence of social experiences" the individual continually reformulates his attitudes, eventually learning to view marijuana smoking as desirable. The formation of this conception is the key to understanding the motivations and actions of users.

Accepting this model for the adult initiate, the present research has explored an historically novel group (tinydopers), describing a new route to becoming a marijuana user taken by these children. As has been shown, tinydopers are unable to recognize the psychological and physiological effects of pot or to connect them with having smoked. This effectively precludes their following Becker's model which accords full user status to the individual only after he has successfully perceived the effects of the drug and marked them as pleasurable. Our research into child perception relied mostly on observation and inference since, as Piaget (1948) noted, it is nearly impossible to discover this from children; the conceptual categories are too sophisticated for their grasp. That the marijuana affects them is certain: giddy, they laugh, dance and run to the refrigerator, talking excitedly and happily until they suddenly fall asleep. But through observations and conversations before, during and after the intoxicated periods, tinydopers were found to be unaware of any changes in themselves.

Their incomplete development, perceptually, cognitively and interactionally, is the cause of this ignorance. According to the socialization theories of Mead (1934), Erikson (1968), and Piaget (1948), children of eight and under are still psychologically forming, gradually learning to function. Piaget particularly notes definitive cognitive stages, asserting that conservation, transformation and classification are all too advanced for the tinydoper age bracket. According to Mead (see also Adler and Adler, 1979), the essence lies in their lack of mature selves, without which they cannot fully act and interact competently. The ages 8–9 seem to be a decisive turning point as youngsters change in internal psychological composition and become capable of *reflecting* on themselves, both through their own eyes and those of the other. (Mead argues that this is possible only after the child has completed the play, game and generalized other stages and can competently engage in roletaking.) Hence, before that time they cannot genuinely recognize their "normal selves" or differentiate them from their "high selves." Without this perception, the effects of marijuana are held to those created by the parents, who frame the experience with their own intentional and unintentional definitions of the situation. Thus, tinydopers become marijuana users almost unconsciously, based on a decision made by others. Moreover, the social meanings they associate with its use are very different than those experienced by adult initiates.

How does this new practice correspond to conventional modes of child rearing? One traditional procedure we see reaffirmed is imitative behavior (see Piaget, 1962), through which the child learns and matures by copying the actions of significant adult models. Several of the illustrative cases chosen show particularly how directly the youngsters are influenced by their desire to behave and be like older family members and friends. They have two aspirations: wanting to be accorded quasi-adult status and longing for acceptance as members of the social group. Parents have corresponding and natural positive feelings about inculcating meaningful beliefs and values into their offspring. Teaching boundary maintenance is also a necessary adjunct to allowing tinydoping. Marijuana's continued illegality and social unacceptability for juveniles necessitate parents ensuring that information about pot smoking is neither intentionally nor accidentally revealed by youngsters. Children must early learn to differentiate between members of various social groups and to judge who are and are not appropriate to be told. This is difficult because it involves mixing positive and negative connotations of the drug in a complex manner. Valuable parallels for this contradictory socialization can be found in child use of alcohol and tobacco, as well as to families of persecuted religious groups (i.e., Marrano Jews in 15th century Spain, covert Jews in Nazi Germany and possibly Mormons in the 19th century). Members of these enclaves believed that what they were teaching their offspring was fundamentally honorable, but still had to communicate to the younger generation their social ostracization and the need to maintain some barriers of secrecy.

Juxtaposed to those aspects which reproduce regular features of socialization are the contradictory procedures. One such departure is the introduction of mood-altering intoxicants into the sacred childhood period. Tinydoping violates the barriers created by most societies to reserve various types of responsibilities, dangers and special pleasures (such as drugs and sex) for adults only. Yet perhaps the most unusual and unprecedented facet of tinydoping socialization observed is the intergenerational bridging that occurs between parent and child. By introducing youngsters into the adult social group and having them participate as peers, parents permit generational boundaries to become extremely vague, often to the point of nonexistence. Several cases show how children have come to look at parents and other adults as friends. This embodies extreme variance from cultures and situations where parents love and treasure their children yet still treat them unequally.

How then can tinydoping be compared to traditional childrearing practices and habits? Existing indicators suggest both similarity and divergence. The parents in this study consider marijuana a substance they overwhelmingly feel comfortable with, regard as something "natural" (i.e., Alan and Anna), and would like their progeny to be exposed to in a favorable light. To them, tinydoping represents a form of normal socialization within the context of their subcultural value system. From the greater society's perspective, however, the illegality of the behavior, aberration from conventional child rearing norms and uncertain implications for futurity combine to define tinydoping as deviant socialization.

Notes

1. The period of childhood has traditionally been a special time in which developing adults were given special treatment to ensure their growing up to be capable and responsible members of society. Throughout history and in most cultures children have been kept apart from adults and sheltered in protective isolation from certain knowledge and practices (see Aries, 1965).

2. Particularly relevant to these "justifications" is Lyman and Scott's (1968) analysis of accounts, as statements made to relieve one of culpability. Specifically, they can be seen as "denial of injury" (Sykes and Matza, 1957) as they assert the innocuousness of giving marijuana to their child. An "excuse" is further employed, "scapegoating" the doctor as the one really responsible for this aberration. Also, the appeal to science has been made.

References

Adler, Peter and Patricia A. Adler
    1979 "Symbolic Interactionism," in Patricia A. Adler, Peter Adler, Jack D. Douglas, Andrea Fontana, C. Robert Freeman and Joseph Kotarba, An Introduction to the Sociologies of Everyday Life, Boston: Allyn and Bacon.
Aries, Phillipe
    1965 Centuries of Childhood: A Social History of Family Life, New York: Vintage.
Becker, Howard S.
    1953 "Becoming a Marijuana User," American Journal of Sociology, 59, November.
    1963 Outsiders, New York: Free Press.
Carey, James T.
    1968 The College Drug Scene, Englewood Cliffs: Prentice Hall.
Douglas, Jack D.
    1970 "Deviance and Respectability: The Social Construction of Moral Meanings," in Jack D. Douglas (ed.), Deviance and Respectability, New York: Basic Books.
Douglas, Jack D.
    1976 Investigative Social Research, Beverly Hills: Sage.
Erikson, Erik
    1968 Identity, Youth and Crisis, New York: Norton.
Goode, Erich
    1970 The Marijuana Smokers, New York: Basic Books.
Grinspoon, Lester
    1971 Marihuana Reconsidered, Cambridge: Harvard University Press.

Grupp, Stanley E. (ed.)
    1971 Marihuana, Columbus, Ohio: Charles E. Merrill.
Gusfield, Joseph R.
    1967 "Moral Passage: The Symbolic Process in Public Designations of Deviance,"
    Social Problems, 15, II, Fall.
Hochman, Joel S.
    1972 Marijuana and Social Evolution, Englewood Cliffs: Prentice Hall.
Kaplan, John
    1971 Marihuana: The New Prohibition, New York: Pocket.
Kitsuse, John I.
    1962 "Societal Reactions to Deviant Behavior," Social Problems, 9, 3, Winter.
Lyman, Stanford and Marvin B. Scott
    1968 "Accounts," American Sociological Review, 33, 1.
Matza, David
    1969 Becoming Deviant, Englewood Cliffs: Prentice Hall.
Mead, George H.
    1934 Mind, Self and Society, Chicago: The University of Chicago Press.
Piaget, Jean
    1948 The Moral Judgment of the Child, New York: Free Press.
    1962 Play, Dreams and Imitation in Childhood, New York: Norton.
Simon, William and John H. Gagnon
    1968 "Children of the Drug Age," Saturday Review, September 21.
Sykes, Gresham and David Matza
    1957 "Techniques of Neutralization," American Sociological Review, 22, December.

Stigma Management Among Gay/Bisexual Men with HIV/AIDS

Karolynn Siegel
Howard Lune
Ilan H. Meyer

Since its inception, the AIDS epidemic has evoked widespread public fear and condemnation both of the disease and those afflicted by it. The stigmatization of AIDS derives in large part from a dread of the illness as one that is still poorly understood, highly debilitating and usually fatal, as well as a threat to the larger community because of its communicable nature (Alonzo & Reynolds 1995). Also at the root of AIDS stigma is its association with socially disapproved behaviors, especially homosexuality, and illicit drug use (Jones et al. 1984; Alonzo & Reynolds 1995; Crandall & Coleman 1992; Herek & Glunt 1988; Herek & Capitanio 1993). Further, because these behaviors are popularly viewed as voluntary 'life-style choices,' AIDS has been construed as a self-inflicted disease for which the infected individual must assume personal responsibility (Weitz 1990). This construction has legitimized viewing most infected individuals as culpable for their plight and depriving them of the compassion normatively accorded seriously ill individuals (Weiner, Perry, & Magnusson 1988).

Stigmatized persons have been described as experiencing a number of negative sequelae including social exclusion, anxiety, alienation, loss of self-esteem, discrimination, and social disenfranchisement (Allport 1954; Goffman 1963; Rosenberg 1979; Jones et al. 1984; Alonzo & Reynolds 1995; Whiteford & Gonzalez 1995). The anticipated liabilities of being labeled as deviant create sufficient motivation for most potentially discreditable individuals to try to manage (i.e., avoid or minimize) stigmatization.

Goffman's (1963) seminal work on stigma is almost certainly the most important contribution to this field of inquiry to date and has strongly influenced much of the subsequent writing in this field. Yet his writings, and much derivative work, can and has been criticized as heavily biased toward seeing individual responses to stigma as primarily defensive and aimed at reducing or avoiding the private experience of stigmatization (Anspach 1979; Gussow & Tracey 1968). Gussow and Tracey (1968: 317), for example, contend that "Goffman's people are both other- and self-stigmatized and forever doomed" to feeling discredited because ultimately they "concur with the norms and therefore view themselves as failures." Similarly, Anspach (1979) points out that while Goffman (1963: 767–8) sees stigmatized persons as "strategists and con artists" rather than merely passive victims, he nevertheless depicts them as ultimately accepting the prevailing definitions of normals and thus "deriving their identity reactively, in response to the imputations of the wider society." Anspach's (1979: 767) criticism, however, is not limited to Goffman. She writes, "most studies of deviance generated by the labeling perspective portray the deviant as powerless, passive and relatively uninvolved in the labeling process." Fine and Asch (1988) have also noted that much social psychological work on disability has inadvertently fostered stigmatizing views of disabled individuals, including that they are victims who cope through self-blame, reinterpretation of their suffering or denial.

More recently, scholars studying AIDS have also confronted the limitations of the traditional perspectives on stigma. Crandall and Coleman's (1992: 172) questionnaire study identified a significant "group of people infected with HIV who do not feel much stigma and do not show the effects of stigmatization." Alonzo and Reynolds (1995: 305) attempt to explain the "differentials in stigma experience," found in the literature on people living with HIV, with reference to "variation in individual social identities and attitudes confronted in one's social networks and reference groups." And Crawford's (1996) "meta-analysis" of AIDS-related stigma suggested that the interactions among numerous moderating variables make it particularly difficult to apply familiar conceptions of stigma processes to AIDS without a much deeper analysis of the many different experiences and social settings of people living with HIV. Thus while classic approaches to stigma establish the framework, they do not address the unique aspects of HIV-related stigma.

Among the most commonly written about defensive strategies are those aimed at regulating the availability of information about the discreditable trait and those that regulate contact with "normals" in an effort to minimize opportunities for enacted stigma. The latter class of strategies, which includes self-segregation, is more commonly applied when the individual's discreditable trait is known or easily discerned. Examples of such defensive strategies include Goffman's (1963) "passing" and "covering," Jones et al.'s (1984) descriptions of "withdrawal" and "concealment," Anspach's (1979) discussions of "dissociation" and "retreatism," and Hughes and Degher's (1993) descriptions of "avoidance." As would be expected, these strategies have been identified as frequently enacted by HIV-infected individuals. Alonzo and Reynolds (1995) described the life of HIV-infected persons as a constant struggle to manage a stigma. Along with the increasing effort these individuals must undertake to conceal their illness as their disease advances, they suffer greater and greater social isolation. Similarly, Weitz (1990: 25) noted that "PWAs [persons with AIDS] avoid or reduce stigma by concealing their illnesses, learning when and to whom they should reveal their illnesses, changing their social networks. . . . "

While early sociological writing may have been biased toward emphasizing the passivity of deviants in the face of societal stigmatization, more recent work has emphasized that stigmatized individuals are not passive recipients of stigma and prejudice, but rather may reject prevalent constructions and seek to influence "normals" to do so as well. Gussow and Tracey (1968: 317), for example, discussed attempts by stigmatized groups to develop theories or ideologies "to counter the ones that discredit them" and "disavow their imputed inferiority or danger." Weitz (1990) described the use of the same strategy among people with AIDS.

In reviewing the dominant theoretical orientations to stigma, Anspach (1979: 768) contended that "the sociology of deviance must revise its conceptions to account for active attempts on the part of those labeled as deviant to mold their own identities." As an example, she described how handicapped individuals and former mental patients used political activism to counter the prevailing negative societal beliefs and assumptions about them, and in so doing enhanced their own self-conceptions. Jones et al. (1984: 153) wrote that such collective action by stigmatized groups to repudiate the norms that render them discreditable "may take the form of banding together with fellow targets, . . . withdrawing from one social environment and embracing another, and redefining an attribute of the self that was previously considered to be negative as positive." Crocker and Major (1989) noted that by uniting, stigmatized individuals may be able to affirm and validate their minority culture and values, and to discredit stigmatizing norms and values of the dominant culture. Active responses to managing stigma often involve attempts to confront stigma in the hope of "breaking through" societal prejudice (c.f., Jones et al. 1984, Crocker & Major 1989) and altering the assumptions by which a condition is treated as discrediting. As an example, with the "Black is Beautiful" campaigns of the 1960s African Americans challenged stigma by reappropriating the discrediting trait as a source of pride. Whittaker (1992), studying "resistance by [HIV] positive people" in Australia, identified similar reappropriation processes as "the inversion of AIDS metaphors."

Yet for people with a shared illness, especially a stigmatized one, there are impediments to adopting strategies that require collective action. Usually a sick person becomes labeled upon diagnosis and begins to cope with the stigma attached to his or her new condition alone. It is usually only after a considerable period of time, if at all, that he or she may seek a "community" of others with the same illness to help in coping with the stigma. If this occurs at all, the sick person may then become a part of a loosely defined group of similarly afflicted individuals. However, this process is often hindered by the desire to conceal one's condition in an effort to reduce or avoid stigmatization. Thus, persons with stigmatizing illnesses may remain isolated from one another. For example, Schneider and Conrad

(1980) found that regarding epilepsy, where "there is no illness subculture [patients] are separate, alone, and unconnected with others sharing the same problems." Similarly, Link and colleagues noted that stigmatized mentally ill individuals are not likely to band together in fighting stigma because they typically "avoid collective settings for fear of being associated with a stigmatized group" (Link et al. 1987: 25).

While there has been considerable discussion in the literature on AIDS about the strong stigma associated with the disease, there has been surprising little empirical investigation to date on how infected individuals cope with this problem. In this paper, we describe a variety of stigma management strategies that were discerned from unstructured interviews with 139 HIV-infected gay/bisexual men who provided narrative accounts of their experiences living with HIV infection. In so doing, we explicitly seek to incorporate the full range of responses and to consider both the reactive strategies and the "fighting back" strategies, which we define as proactive. Finally, we propose a provisional classification scheme for ordering these strategies along a continuum based on the degree to which individuals accepted or rejected the values, norms, or assumptions that underpin the stigma.

Methods

The qualitative study from which the data presented below are drawn was designed to examine gay men's experiences of living with HIV infection as a chronic illness. Specifically, we were interested in the adaptational tasks their HIV-infection posed for them (e.g., developing strategies for maintaining health and preserving functioning, confronting existential/spiritual issues, making treatment decisions under conditions of uncertainty) and the coping strategies they invoked to meet these challenges. The "representative case" sampling method (Shontz 1965) was used in which cases are not chosen at random, but rather are selected because they are judged to be representative examples with respect to the phenomenon under investigation. Through selecting cases with maximal theoretical relevance, the representative case method seeks to learn about a general class of individuals by studying representative members. The emphasis of these methods is not on statistical generalizability, but on the analytical generalization of issues and problems that may provide insight into the study topic.

One-hundred and forty-four men were accrued. These men had been identified through self-referral in response to advertisements, flyers and community outreach efforts. Eligible were HIV-positive gay and bisexual men between the ages of 20–45 who lived in the greater New York metropolitan area and who had not injected drugs within the past two years. Cases were quota sampled to provide approximately equal numbers of African Americans ($N = 46$), Puerto Ricans ($N = 47$), and non-Hispanic whites ($N = 46$). These three ethnic groups were chosen because available epidemiologic data indicated that they accounted for the large majority of AIDS cases in New York City (and therefore also presumably the large majority of infected cases, although infection is not a reportable condition). Within each ethnic group an approximately equal number of men were sampled who were asymptomatic, were symptomatic but not qualifying for a diagnosis of AIDS, and who had a diagnosis of AIDS. This assured that there was adequate representation of cases across the full range of the disease spectrum since it was felt that this variable might be a significant factor in understanding adaptational patterns. Those with a history of intravenous drug use in the past two years were excluded because we felt such use would complicate the problems of adaptation (e.g., through requiring disclosure of an illegal activity, of managing treatment around current drug use) and distract from the discovery of more usual patterns of adjustment among gay and bisexual men. From among men who met the criteria for eligibility, we selected cases based on theoretical considerations. For example, in the present study, we attempted to include men who were and were not in stable relationships, who had been aware of the infected status for varying periods of time and who varied on how widely they had disclosed their status to others. While we did not impose formal sampling quotas on these criteria because practically it would have created too many cells, we did make deliberate efforts to ensure variability on such factors.

The men had a mean age of 36 years ($SD = 6$). About a third (32%) had 12 or less years of education, 39% had some college education, and 28% had graduated college or received a postgraduate degree. At the time of interview, 33% were employed full- or part-time, and 67% were unemployed (mostly due to disability).

Participants were asked to participate in three research meetings with a mental health clinician, typically spaced about two weeks apart. They completed an extensive battery of standardized measures at the initial meeting. At the second and third meetings a clinician interviewer conducted an unstructured focus interview to elicit respondents' own perspectives on their experiences living with HIV infection. Whereas structured interviews reflect the investigators' frame of reference in choosing the domains of the investigation, the use of unstructured interviews allows discovery of each respondent's perspective by allowing him to define the situation by choosing the topics of his narratives and identifying his own issues, emphases, and categories (Merton, Fiske, & Kendall 1956).

Each unstructured interview lasted approximately two hours and covered a wide variety of issues in the respondent's life. The interview was initiated with a very general question as a stimulus. Respondents were asked to talk about what it has been like living with the knowledge that they are HIV-infected. The interviewed followed the respondent's lead and, when possible, used his material to introduce natural bridges to other topics. For example, "In talking about how you have changed your daily routines since learning about your infection, you mentioned that you spend more time alone at home now and less time with your friends. Can you tell me more about how your condition has changed your relationship with your friends, as well as your family, or other people?" The interviewer had only a set of topic areas that were assumed to be of theoretical relevance based on a prior review of the literature on illness behavior. Respondents typically addressed most of these issues spontaneously over the four hours of interviewing. However, if they did not, the interviewer introduced the topic again with a general question that allowed the respondent to address the issue in any of a number of ways that seemed relevant to his own experiences. The interviewer used questioning and prompting only to clarify issues raised by the respondent and to encourage elaboration of themes that had been raised in the respondent's narrative. In most cases, the interviewer and respondents were matched on ethnic background to facilitate establishing rapport. Spanish speaking respondents had the option of using Spanish for both the standardized questionnaires and the interview.

The unstructured interviews were audiotaped and transcribed verbatim. From the content analysis of subsets of the interviews, the authors developed a list of search terms to help identify any textual material from the interviews that might bear on feared or experienced stigmatization and attempts to avoid or manage such occurrences. An extensive list was developed which included, for example, the terms stigma, discriminate, fag, shame, contaminated, reject, avoid, disgrace, disapprove, ashamed, discredit, hide. Relevant text was excerpted through ZY-Index, a text-based software program designed to aid in qualitative analysis. From the narrative material we identified the array of stigma management strategies used by study participants across a variety of situations.

Results

The stigma management strategies discerned in the men's narratives can be arranged along a continuum from reactive to proactive. We derived this distinction, in part, from Charles Tilly's studies of social movement activism (Tilly 1978; Tilly, Tilly, & Tilly 1975). He distinguishes different forms of collective action in terms of claims made against the State. Reactive actions address some tangible claim, some desired change in law, or protection against these events. A campaign to lower property taxes, or repeal Jim Crow legislation, or strike down the Colorado gay-discrimination laws, are reactive efforts. Such strategies implicitly or explicitly accept the state's procedures and authority to enact judgements on the matter under question, while challenging particular decisions, events, or applications. Proactive movements, by contrast, seek greater empowerment. They "assert group claims which have not previously been exercised" (Tilly 1978: 147). Proactive strategies question the legitimacy of state actions and implicitly challenge the authority underlying them. Reactive strategies to cope with stigma involve defensive attempts to avoid or mitigate the impact of stigma, but imply acceptance of the underlying social norms and values that construct the stigma. In reactively coping with stigma, individuals attempt to avoid its impact but they do not challenge it. Proactive strategies involve confronting the stigma. They challenge the validity of the stigma and imply disavowal of the social norms and values underlying the stigma, and represent an effort to redefine them.

Table 1 displays the strategies we identified along the reactive-proactive continuum. We use the categorization proposed—*reactive, intermediate,* and *proactive* strategies[1]—heuristically in an effort to make the discussion more manageable. While some strategies may be defined as essentially purely proactive or reactive, most involve a mixture of these elements. For example, those who participate in collective efforts to alter societal attitudes about a stigmatized condition usually recognize that their efforts, if successful, will ultimately also reduce the personal stigma they experience. Virtually all of the men relied on a combination of strategies.

A. Reactive Strategies

Using reactive strategies, respondents sought to avoid being discredited by hiding their HIV seropositive status, by disclosing selectively under "safe" conditions, and by creating distinctions between themselves and "other" people living with HIV. Concealing and disclosing strategies were aimed at controlling information about HIV/AIDS within one's close social network. When disclosing, respondents typically employed a complex set of strategies to control the content and timing of information released about themselves, how information about their condition would be presented, and, where possible, how it would be received.

I. Concealment Strategies Concealment strategies, perhaps the most commonly invoked response to the fear of stigmatization, aim at avoiding being discredited by hiding the discreditable attribute. Men who attempted to conceal their HIV/AIDS status used varied strategies depending on the stage of their HIV disease, whether they had visible signs or symptoms of

Table 1   Stigma Management Strategies Along the Reactive-Proactive Continuum

Reactive	Intermediate	Proactive
I. Concealment	IV. Gradual Disclosure	VIII. Preemptive Disclosure
II. Selective Disclosure	V. Selective Affiliation	IX. Public Education
III. Personal Attributional Style	VI. Discrediting One's Discreditors	X. Social Activism
	VII. Challenging Moral Attributions	

HIV infection, and the extent to which social withdrawal was possible. In concealing, they attempted to represent themselves as healthy. Or, if visibly ill, they presented themselves as having a less stigmatizing condition.

When possible, before symptoms of HIV appeared, some respondents chose to conceal their HIV status altogether. The strategy, which Goffman (1963) referred to as "passing," aims at maintaining and protecting normal social relations. The decision to conceal was often painful. Respondents felt that they needed to hide the truth to protect themselves, but still viewed that choice as requiring them to "live a lie," and "live a double life." Many men spoke of the strain of excluding family and intimates from the most significant aspects of their lives, cutting themselves off from possible sources of support, and distancing themselves from the communities of other people living with HIV.

One man reported that he had not divulged his HIV infected status to his family because of the "mixed signals" he perceived from them. While on the one hand he felt they would want to support him, he added, "I also have the fear that they would desert me . . . And it's much easier for me to go through my life not telling them." Another respondent struggled with the decision of whether or not to disclose his status to his family:

> I'm weighing the pros and the cons. The pros are that, you know, [my mother] shouldn't know because the cons are that she doesn't accept me for being gay. So if you don't accept me for being gay then I don't think you could . . . accept the fact that I'm HIV.

Passing required men to conceal their illness by hiding or disguising symptoms that they thought could evoke AIDS-stigma. Wasting syndrome and Kaposi's Sarcoma were the two conditions most often mentioned as strongly evocative of AIDS stigma. As one respondent said, "Just by looking at me, you could tell something wasn't right because of my face." Passing sometimes involved concealing evidence of the use of medications associated with AIDS (e.g., AZT or Bactrim). To hide their use of such medication some respondents were even willing to relinquish insurance reimbursement.

> I wouldn't even write a check for them, because I think—I think it was because I was trying to change my insurance policy, and I didn't want any record of any, you know, treatment for HIV.

> I don't want anybody to see me on medication, either. . . . because [if] they see [me, they'd say], "Oh, this is a gay person. Oh, he's taking medication. Oh, he's got AIDS." You know. "Oh, you're losing a lot of weight. Oh, you look sick. Are you alright?" You know, they see, gay, and they immediately associate you with being sick. And it's so ridiculous.

If what the men regarded as telling symptoms could not be concealed, they might withdraw from all but the most essential social encounters in an attempt to completely hide themselves. This response inevitably led to a disruption of normal social encounters and isolation from family, friends and neighbors. One man who described himself as unable to "deal with leaving my house with all these black blotches all over my body, and everybody looking at me as if I'm some ugly duckling" said that he would "seriously consider suicide" rather than live with such marks permanently. A sense of alienation and hopelessness was often associated with this response.

When respondents could not conceal that they were ill (e.g., because of functional limitations), but their symptoms were not unequivocally HIV-related, some chose to conceal or misrepresent the true nature of their illness, usually preferring to report they had cancer. This subterfuge seemed to convey the seriousness of their illness, while avoiding strong censure. Goffman conceptualized such behavior as "covering."

> I tell them it's, it's, it's a bone cancer. And I feel bad lying, but, you know, why should everybody know? I mean, because discrimination is almost—to me, discrimination ranks up there with racism. . . . Because you see people going around talking to other people with leukemia. You see them going talking around to people who have one leg, one arm, you know. To them that's horrible. But having HIV or AIDS isn't. So, I tell them it's cancer. Having cancer is normal.

II. Selective Disclosure   In deciding who to tell about their HIV status, respondents considered the strength of the relationship, its ability to withstand a challenge, the potential for support and intimacy, the other's need to know, and the other person's ability to understand the disease. One respondent said that he only disclosed to "those that are HIV themselves," describing it as "like a death sentence" to tell others. Another simply said "I only tell people that I have it in common with." Some could only tell those closest to them, while others were most afraid of hurting those to whom they were closest.

The perception that a gay identity and having AIDS were two negatively viewed statuses led to the expectation of understanding and acceptance from gay or bisexual people who did not have HIV/AIDS. When gay/bisexual people proved intolerant, respondents seem to experience great disappointment, anger and frustration. One man related:

> I remember being on a phone once with somebody who had answered an ad that I had in a magazine or I had answered his ad. I don't remember which was which. . . . And he said, he made the comment that he wouldn't want to get to know anybody who was HIV positive because they might not be around. And I was furious. I, you know, I got—started ranting and raving at him over the phone. Consequently we never got together.

III. Personal Attribution Strategies   Some respondents attempted to defend themselves against stigmatization by attributing the cause of their HIV infection to a more socially acceptable source than homosexual behavior or drug use (e.g., blood transfusion) or by distancing themselves from other infected individuals. In doing so, they did not challenge the stigma or guilt ascribed to infected people, but rather attempted to expand the category of "innocent victims" to include themselves. One man contended:

> Well, they—it could be, um, I'm from New Jersey and they say, like 90% of all hemophiliacs in New Jersey have gotten it, so it's in like one batch of blood. But I also got a operation on my elbow, four months prior to that, . . . , so it could have been from that, too. So I really didn't know. And also, I think a lot of it, um, has to do with that it really wasn't my fault.

Other respondents while accepting responsibility for their infection, attempted to distance themselves from infected individuals they felt were viewed most negatively. Thus, respondents asserted that they were not like "most" gay men who were infected in that they had never been promiscuous or gone to bath houses or engaged in anonymous sex. Others offered ignorance as an "excuse" (Scott & Lyman 1968) and defense against blame. They asserted that they were quite certain that they had become infected before much was known about AIDS since they had adopted safer-sex guidelines as soon as they had been identified. One man said:

> So I can hold my head up because . . . [i]t really wasn't my fault that I got it, 'cause I didn't know [about the risk from sex] at the time. . . . I really started taking precautions as soon as I started reading about everything that was going on.

Some men who accepted personal responsibility for their infection tried to reduce the application of stigma against them by openly and voluntarily admitting the "error of their ways." The men we interviewed condemned their own past behavior and seemed to hope that a public confession and display of contrition would soften their discreditors' negative attitudes toward them. Goffman (1971) termed such actions "apologies." Weitz (1981) also observed this strategy among the HIV-infected men and women she interviewed. It is an exemplary reactive approach, in that it protects the individual in their personal encounters while internalizing the stigmatizing discourse about HIV.

> I'm not too proud of this. I'm not, it's not the greatest thing in my life. I feel ashamed at times for not being more, more precautious [sic], but something that I just didn't think I would get. And I got it, so I deal with it.

B. Intermediate Strategies

Each of the approaches described below is potentially empowering, but they do not provide a fully-formed challenge to the dominant ideology. In other words, each is potentially proactive, but also somewhat reactive.

Gradual disclosure helps to diminish the stigmatizing attitudes of small numbers of people in private settings, but the lasting influence may be minimal. *Selective affiliation* brings respondents into self-help groups and empowering actions but may also be a form of hiding. *Discrediting the discreditors* usually takes place in isolated encounters and has little impact in a larger social arena. Lastly, *challenging moral attributions* questions the basis for some of the most significant forms of discrediting, but, unlike the activism and education strategies discussed later, it rejects the source of the stigma without substituting something more constructive for it proactively.

IV. Gradual Disclosure

Some men disclosed information about the disease and their own HIV status in a controlled incremental manner that allowed them to "test the waters" (Schneider & Conrad 1980) and, if necessary, adjust the future release of information. For example, in preparation for disclosing their status to others, they might raise the topic of AIDS in a general way in order to have an opportunity to assess both the other people's attitudes and their knowledge about HIV/AIDS. If when they did so, they encountered negative attitudes, stereotypes or misinformation, they sought to modify these through education and emotional support. In this way, they attempted to create a situation that would permit a more favorable reception to their ultimate disclosure of their own infection.

> Ah, my parents sort of—I don't want to say, "they knew," but I tried to prepare them. So when I went and took the test, you know, like I sat down with both of them on separate occasions and told them that ah, that I think that I—there's a good possibility that I, you know, have been exposed to AIDS or whatever. . . . And we went through a whole kind of, I guess, growth process because I had to sort of educate them and still be the person that I always was, without all the stereotypical images of AIDS patients and what not.

Placing themselves in the role of educator and leader may also have enhanced respondents' own sense of worth and allowed for a more favorable presentation of the self.

> I sat my father down, my ex-lover down. I said, "oh I want to watch this program. It's all about HIV positive people." . . . And they all, we all sat and looked at it. I started to cry a little bit. And then my father said ah, "oh is that person on the film straight or gay?" I said, "they're straight." He said, "Oh you can get AIDS from being straight?" I said, "yeah." So and then that's probably all the comment he—my ex-lover didn't make any comment. And that was all. Just, I'm slowly trying to indoctrinate them, and through that process. That's why I have them watch it. So I guess I'm not ready to actually tell them, but I'm working on it. The first step was to have them watch a program about it.

V. Selective Affiliation Strategies   Many men described a preference for largely restricting their social contacts to "the own and the wise" (Goffman 1963: 19 fn.)—other infected people or those who held favorable attitudes toward infected individuals—among whom they felt accepted and supported. They emphasized the psychological distance between themselves and others who lacked their experience and understanding. As one man commented about dealing with HIV-negative people: "[It is] frustrating, so I keep away, I stay away, I don't talk to them no more . . . fuck them, even my family."

Often, the men's affiliative strategies of coping with AIDS-related stigma were borrowed from previous experiences of coping with stigma, especially regarding homosexuality. In many instances, social networks that provided support regarding HIV/AIDS overlapped with those that provided support for respondents' gay identity, ethnic identity or those relating to treatment of addictions (e.g., twelve-step programs). This provided access to resources and opportunities to learn from others facing the same stigmas.

By restricting their social contacts as much as possible to supportive networks, respondents accomplished two tasks. First, they reduced the opportunity for enacted stigma by avoiding potentially troublesome encounters. Equally important, they exposed themselves to supportive encounters which might facilitate the development of alternative ideologies about HIV/AIDS. The communities of HIV-positive people or sympathetic others they joined shared many common constructions of the experience from which new values and attitudes were derived. This shared value system allowed respondents to adopt a construction of HIV that contrasted with prevalent social stereotypes. Supportive encounters thus reinforced the collective identity of PWA/HIV providing a source of strength and self-enhancement.

VI. Discrediting the Discreditors   Discrediting those who sought to discredit them was another strategy men used for defending themselves against stigmatization. They raised questions about the real motivations of those who condemned or rejected them. For example, they contended that religious leaders were compelled to support negative beliefs towards HIV/AIDS and to view the epidemic as divine retribution in order to uphold church doctrine condemning homosexuality. Medical practitioners who displayed AIDS-phobic attitudes were described as ignorant. In discrediting their detractors, respondents undermined the legitimacy of the stigma.

Many respondents interpreted their experiences of prejudice as evidence of ignorance. They saw themselves as having been educated by their illness experience so that they could now teach others. Respondents often expressed understanding, patience, and even sympathy for the ignorance of others, a position that also allowed them to morally elevate themselves above their intolerant and sometime malicious discreditors. One man whose sister no longer allowed him to hug her daughters because of fear of AIDS said:

> And she's trying to keep them distant from me. But I saw it at first as her sort of punishing me for having, for being HIV positive. But, and

then I realized it's just due to her ignorance. . . . It just has to deal with her being ignorant and just the type of person she is. . . . So I just tack it up to sheer ignorance. Ah, and I just pray that she wakes up one day, you know, and realizes that ah, life is too short and that you shouldn't turn your back on anyone.

VII. Challenging Moral Attributions Respondents were particularly plagued by the public's distinction between the innocent (i.e., blood transfusion recipients, babies) and the guilty (i.e., gay men, drug users) "victims" of AIDS. Such attitudes were often associated with religious groups. One way in which respondents combated these attitudes was by denying the legitimacy of religious values in HIV/AIDS discourse and advocating a countervailing secular explanation for the epidemic. This achieved two functions. It both helped to normalize HIV by associating it with familiar medical conditions and it emphasized the humane obligation of society towards the sick. As one respondent said: "This is just a virus, the virus doesn't have a morality." Another concurred: "It's not like God's punishment, no. And it's not a disease that only affects gay people, no. It's not a gay disease. No. It's a disease. It's like lung cancer."

Some men employed a different attributional approach in which they constructed HIV infection as a source of moral enhancement rather than a moral stigma. These men spoke of their diagnosis as having galvanized them to reprioritize their lives and transforming them morally. Several contended that while before their diagnosis they were exploitative of others or narcissistic, they now derived great satisfaction from volunteering their time to help other less fortunate infected individuals. They saw themselves as more mature and socially responsible now, and as having adopted a more authentic, spiritually informed approach to life because of their illness.

One man who described his experience as "torturous" added "I thank God it happened because it forced me to wake up and realize that the things that I had been taught and so many ideas I held near and dear were wrong."

> I used to tell people, in actuality it was a blessing. That may seem funny, but when you're living and you don't care, and if you die it's all right. And if you live, it's a blessing. It gave me motivation, a point of reference, something to work from. Okay, I'm HIV positive. Now what am I going to do?

C. Proactive Strategies

Proactive strategies were used by men in an effort to construct and promote alternative views of AIDS that undermine societal stigma. The responses that we identified as most proactive address the meaning, values, beliefs, practices and power imbalances behind the stigma rather than the situations in which stigma might be encountered. Respondents use preemptive disclosure to present a positive framing of the illness to those close to them, ignoring and replacing the negative images found in the popular discourse of AIDS. Public education strategies attempt to do the same for a larger audience, while social activist strategies seek to bring their more positive framing of the disease into the popular discourse.

VIII. Preemptive Disclosure   In the most proactive form of disclosure, some respondents chose to take charge of the timing and manner of their disclosure. Respondents who adopted the preemptive approach disclosed their HIV status widely and voluntarily. Men used this approach to control the exchange of information and to bring about a discussion of the illness on their own terms.

Preemptive disclosure protected respondents from the risk of being exposed and accused of hiding. By choosing to volunteer this information they hoped to create the impression that it was not shameful and did not need to be concealed. This strategy forced others to confront their own assumptions that the illness should be hidden. Preemptive disclosure protected respondents from unexpected questions about HIV that might be provoked by changes in their appearance for example.

As one respondent who had disclosed his condition on national television explained: "It only gives you strength, because if you hide it's because you're ashamed of something, and I'm not ashamed of having HIV." Others found that hiding their condition was counterproductive. One man said:

> The more you talk about it, the less stigmatized you feel. And the more people you tell, the more people are on your side. The more love and understanding and comprehension you get from everyone, and the less ostracized you feel.

IX. Public Education Strategies   By attempting to alter the discourse on AIDS and the prejudices and misperceptions that contribute to the stigmatization of PWA/HIV, respondents acted publicly on behalf of all people living with HIV and AIDS. Proactive strategies could potentially improve conditions for the individual invoking them, but typically only indirectly and in the long term. Most often the immediate effects to the individual would be increased stress, stigma, and discrimination in their private lives, since coming out as a PWA/HIV often carried great personal risk. Still, some chose to disclose their HIV status in order to refute negative social attitudes related to AIDS. Those who chose to do so expressed a sense of social responsibility that prompted them to come out. As one man said, "I could just say nothing or I could do what I believed in, which was to come forward and I did that."

Men cited the ignorance of HIV-negative people as the primary cause of their discrediting attitudes and discriminatory behavior. In confronting stigma, they sought to alter public attitudes by providing information and offering themselves as examples that defied stereotypes about PWA/HIV.

They hoped, for example, that their life as functional, capable individuals with HIV would serve as a model to challenge the stereotypical image of PWA/HIV as diseased and disabled. Weitz (1981) similarly observed that some of the HIV-infected individuals she studied attempted to reduce stigma through the use of a kind of "bravado" in which they tried to refute negative stereotypes and convince others of their continued normalcy by offering themselves as examples of normal functioning individuals.

In taking active, socially valued roles as HIV educators, for example, they strove to offer a positive image which could supplant the popular negative image associated with being a PWA/HIV. The education that respondents provided commonly centered on risk prevention. The underlying message they sought to convey was that despite the public perception that susceptibility to HIV is virtually limited to marginalized groups, the risk for HIV infection is universal. By universalizing the risk for HIV, men attempted to break through the stigma of PWA/HIV as "other," confronting the "we-they" distinction that allowed some uninfected individuals to define themselves as both safe and morally superior to PWA/HIV. Many men expressed a keen awareness of their public roles.

> Yeah I've spoken, especially if they tell me they're bisexual or they're . . . straight, and they think that they're okay or that . . . it's not going to happen to them. I spill the beans and just tell them, that's not the way to think, you know. . . . They learn a little bit, and then they start to, then they talk differently.

Speaking on behalf of all PWA/HIV helped them to make proactive identity claims in opposition to the notion of a "spoiled identity."

> Something I've realized about being HIV positive, . . . I became more out, more vocal, and more defensive but also willing to help other people to deal with it, as opposed to just, you know "it's not my problem." Whereas, you know, people would make homophobic remarks before, you just let them pass, now, I like stop and try to find out, you know, it's like "OK if, why does it bother you so?" . . . look, people need to be educated. I think for me, being able to be this open, out and honest, is one of the most important things, I think, that has come out of my being HIV positive and diagnosed with AIDS.

X. Social Activism   Social activism was the most proactive strategy identified used to manage stigma. By demanding policy changes and increased funding for HIV-related research, activists protested discrimination. By asserting the right to inclusion in the policies that affected their lives (e.g., FDA approval of experimental treatments), rather than hiding, activists resisted marginalization. Defying stigma, activists asserted the right to define their own identities. While most of the benefits of social activism are long-term, activism also offers immediate gains. In having chosen to participate in social activism, men attached themselves to an empowerment movement. This allowed them to identify with a community of strength and often provided an accepting and supportive social network. But some activists demonstrated an altruistic concern for the gay community that went beyond personal gain.

> Of course I'm gonna fight it until the last day, the last breath of mine I'm gonna fight any way I can by writing letters, phoning Senators, phoning Congressmen.

> Now I'm even active in voicing help for this for all peoples. Especially in Harlem . . . No one cares about people, what happens to the people in Harlem.

Discussion

We have provided, we believe, the most extensive discussion to date of strategies used by individuals to manage the stigma of HIV-infection. In addition, we have offered a heuristic scheme for classifying these strategies along a continuum based on the degree to which they challenge or implicitly acquiesce to existing social norms and values which support the discrediting of infected individuals.

In coping with HIV-related stigma, individuals face conflicting needs. To avoid personal liabilities related to stigma, they may need to conceal their illness. However, to maintain a positive sense of self, to preserve their social standing, and to live a full and meaningful life, they may need to challenge societal reactions to their illness. Using reactive strategies, such as concealment, individuals may avoid enacted stigma. However, there may be significant psychological costs associated with the burden of having to always be vigilant about maintaining "the secret." Additionally, such strategies implicitly reinforce the norms by which they are discredited. Prior work on the effectiveness of reactive coping (when compared to no coping) among former mental patients showed it to be ineffective in reducing the negative effects of stigma on mental health and employment problems (Link et al. 1987). Using proactive strategies, such as social protest, stigmatized individuals may expose themselves to greater risks of discrimination and social rejection, but may ultimately help to bring about modified norms and beliefs that could help to improve their social standing.

We found that men often used proactive and reactive strategies in different parts of their social networks. For example, some engaged in public education efforts which required publicly disclosing their HIV-status, yet concealed it from family. Others covered their illness publicly while disclosing to their families. The use of strategies seemed also to be in part related to how long men had been living with awareness of their infection. Typically, men's initial response to diagnosis and the accompanying threat of stigmatization was to adopt reactive strategies. Movement toward the incorporation of intermediate or proactive strategies often came later as they either achieved greater self-acceptance as an infected person or felt that they had adequate support to risk more public exposure of their discreditable trait.

Charmaz (1987) has argued that the struggle to define one's identity is the central task facing chronically ill persons. She defined this struggle as "a quest for control and self-esteem." In adjusting to illness, Charmaz (p. 289) noted, "some persons aim for high identity levels, requiring much effort to *overcome* stigmatizing identifications and to live autonomous lives. Others aim for lower identity levels to *avoid* stigmatizing identifications, rather than risk more attention focused on themselves. . . . [The latter] simply fade into quiet lives, largely anonymous except to those who reside with them" (emphasis in original). Higher identity levels include restoration of premorbid identity or aspiration to "supernormal" identity and functioning, lower identity levels include a "salvaged self," in which individuals "hold little hope of realizing typical adult identities" (p. 287).

The classification scheme of stigma management strategies we propose supports Charmaz's conceptualization. Men who routinely adopted proactive strategies may be seen as striving for higher identity levels by directly confronting threats to maintaining a valued identity by, for example, attempting to promote alternative constructions of HIV or by challenging the values and norms that underpin the stigmatization of the illness. These individuals wished to avoid restrictions on their social activities and interactions (i.e., social control) that those who discredited them would seek to impose. Men who relied on reactive strategies could be said to be willing to accept lower identity levels. They chose to acquiesce to the prevailing norms and values and accept a life in the shadows, out of public scrutiny. Withdrawal into a more protected, but limited, social world was an acceptable solution to the problem of minimizing or avoiding being stigmatized.

It is plausible, as Link et al. (1993) have suggested, that a proactive approach to stigma is superior to reactive strategies because it involves rejection and disavowal of the stigma and replacing it with self-enhancing attitudes and attributions. Research is needed to determine to what extent the strategies we describe help protect individuals from the negative effects of stigma, and what are the costs and benefits of the different strategies. For example, by employing primarily concealing strategies individuals may protect themselves from the negative impact of stigma, but this may lead to poor self-esteem, social isolation, and lack of support. In contrast, engaging in proactive strategies may lead to an increase in exposure to stigma and discrimination, but it may bring about secondary gains including a sense of control over one's life, self-fulfillment that comes from commitment to the cause, an improved sense of self and community, and social support. The costs and the benefits of each of the strategies depend greatly upon the social conditions under which one seeks to enact them and on the social resources available to the individual making this decision.

A number of limitations of the study should be noted. While we have described the varied stigma management strategies used by HIV-infected individuals, we have not addressed to what extent, if at all, engaging in these strategies promotes or impedes adaptation to the illness in a broader sense. Nor do we know the relative value of one style of coping over another in any given context.

Further, our sample was entirely composed of gay/bisexual men in a concentrated urban setting. It must be recognized that the experiences of gay men dealing with the disease seem unique in that they were an already discredited group with experience in collectively fighting stigma related to their sexuality. AIDS initially affected gay men who were strongly identified with the gay community (Shilts 1987). For them, the gay community has provided the opportunity and means to develop proactive strategies to manage stigma that could be utilized by gay/bisexual men with AIDS. The gay community had ideologies, values, and institutions in place that were ready to confront the newly defined AIDS-related stigma. They had access to resources such as communications networks and community-based organizations which facilitated their mobilization against AIDS-related stigma. As Schneider and Conrad (1980) observed in their study of epileptics, the "link between the closet metaphor and the development of identity is premised . . . on the assumption that in 'coming out' there is indeed something to come out to: that there are some developed or developing social definitions that provide the core of this new, open and proud self."

It remains unclear to what extent the example of gay/bisexual men confronting AIDS-related stigma can serve the self-protective and identity-reconstructive needs of others groups (e.g., women, socioeconomically disadvantaged minorities) facing HIV/AIDS. Future work is necessary to consider the role of proactive coping strategies among resource-poor communities of persons coping with AIDS-related or other stigmas.

Endnote

1. These categories in many ways parallel Schneider and Conrad's (1980: 214) three subtypes of adjusted epileptics—secret, pragmatic, and quasi-liberated—their typology attempts to characterize broad adaptational styles to living with the disease "as a personal, physical and social object." While stigma management is clearly the central motivational force in such adaptational choices, their typology nevertheless has a broader conceptual focus than our own.

References

Allport G. W. (1954). *The Nature of Prejudice.* Addison-Wesley Publishing Company: Reading, MA.

Alonzo A. and Reynolds N. (1995). An exploration and elaboration of a stigma trajectory. *Social Science & Medicine,* 41, 303–315.

Anspach R. (1979). From stigma to identity politics: political activism among the physically disabled and former mental patients. *Social Science & Medicine,* 13A, 765–773.

Charmaz K. (1987). Struggling for a self: Identity levels among the chronically ill. In Roth J. and Conrad P. (eds.) *Research in the Sociology of Health Care,* 6, 283–321. JAI Press: Greenwich, CT.

Crandall C. S. and Coleman R. (1992). AIDS-related stigmatization and the disruption of social relationships. *Journal of Social and Personal Relationships*, 9, 163–177.

Crocker J. and Major B. (1989). Social stigma and self-esteem: the self protective properties of stigma. *Psychological Review*, 96, 608–630.

Farina A., Allen J. G., Saul B. (1968) The role of the stigmatized in affecting social relationships. *Journal of Personality*, 36, 169–182.

Fine M., Asch A. (1988). Disability beyond stigma: Discrimination and activism. *Journal of Social Issues*, 44, 3–21.

Goffman E. (1961). *Asylums*. Doubleday and Company: Garden City, New York.

Goffman E. (1963). *Stigma: Notes on the Management of Spoiled Identity*. Prentice-Hall: Englewood Cliffs, New Jersey.

Gussow Z., Tracey G. S. (1968). Status, ideology and adaption to stigmatized illness: a study of leprosy. *Human Organization*, 27, 316–325.

Herek G., Capitanio J. (1993). Public reaction to AIDS in the United States: a second decade of stigma. *American Journal of Public Health*, 83, 574–577.

Herek G. M., Glunt E. K. (1988). An epidemic of stigma: public reactions to AIDS. *American Psychologist*, 43, 886–891.

Hughes G., Degher D. (1993). Coping with a deviant identity. *Deviant Behavior: An Interdisciplinary Journal*, 14, 297–315.

Jones E., Farina, A., Hastorf, A., Markus, H., Miller, D., and Scott, R. (1984). *Social Stigma: The Psychology of Marked Relationships*. W.H. Freeman: New York.

Link B. G. (1987). Understanding labeling effects in the area of mental disorders: an assessment of the effects of expectations of rejection. *American Sociological Review*, 52, 96–112.

Link, B. G., Mirotznik, J., Cullen, F. T. (1991). The effectiveness of stigma coping orientations: can negative consequences of mental illness labeling be avoided? *Journal of Health and Social Behavior*, 32, 302–320.

Merton R. K., Fiske M., Kendall, P. (1956). *The Focused Interview: A Manual and Procedures*. Free Press: Glencoe, IL.

Rosenberg M. (1979). *Conceiving the Self*. Basic Books: New York.

Schneider J., Conrad P. (1980). In the closet with illness: epilepsy, stigma potential and information control. *Social Problems*, 28, 32–44.

Schur E. (1971). *Labeling Deviant Behavior*. Harper and Row: New York.

Scott, M. B., Lyman, S. M. (1968). Accounts. *American Sociological Review*, 33, 46–62.

Shilts, Randy (1987). *And the Band Played On: Politics, People, and the AIDS Epidemic*. New York: St. Martin's Press.

Shontz F. (1965) *Research Methods in Personality*. Appleton Crafts: New York.

Sontag, S. (1977). *Illness as Metaphor*. Farrar, Strauss & Giroux: New York.

Tilly, C., Tilly, L., Tilly, R. (1975). *The Rebellious Century, 1830–1930*. Harvard University Press: Cambridge.

Tilly, C. (1978). *From Mobilization to Revolution*. Addison-Wesley Publishing Company: Reading, MA.

Weiner, B., Perry, R. P., Magnusson, J. (1988). An attributional analysis of reactions to stigmas. *Journal of Personality and Social Psychology*, 55, 738–748.

Weitz R. (1990) Living with the Stigma of AIDS. *Qualitative Sociology*, 13, 23–38.

Weitz R. (1991) *Life with AIDS*. Rutgers University Press: New Brunswick, NJ.

Whiteford L. M., Gonzalez L. (1995). Stigma: The hidden burden of infertility. *Social Science and Medicine*, 40, 27–36.

Whittaker, Andrea M. (1992). Living with HIV: resistance by positive people. *Medical Anthropology Quarterly*, 6(4), 385–390.

Examining the Informal Sanctioning of Deviance in a Chat Room Culture

24

Rhonda D. Evans

Introduction

With the advent of computer technology, and more specifically the Internet, as a mode of communication and a virtual place in which to engage in social interaction, a plethora of social science research studies have erupted. Multiple issues concerning cyberspace communication have been explored. Some scholars have focused attention of the issues of identity formation within cyberspace communications (Zizek 1998; Bromberg 1996; Turkle 1996, 1997; Poster 1995). Other researchers have focused on the possibility of forming transcultural global communities via the Internet (Levalley 1997) as well as the possibility of promoting egalitarian transnational global communities (Ribeiro 1997). Feminist scholars have explored the possibility of transforming gender relations through cyberspace and the impediments to such transformation (Cushing 1996; Morse 1997; Plant 1996; Wise 1997). An abundance of research has been conducted on sexual and intimate relationships formed through cyberspace communications (Cooper and Sportolari 1997; Lieblum 1997; Mills 1998; Schnarch 1997; and Zizek 1996). However, the study of deviant behavior on the Internet has been largely confined to the examination of chat communities as a social space for engaging in forms of sexual deviance (Durkin and Bryant 1995, 1999; Lamb 1998) and the opportunity for promoting such behavior through the distribution of pornographic materials (Barak and Safir 1997).

This study explores the nature of everyday deviance at the micro level, within the context of a Married Life (ML) chat room culture. It focuses on the normative structure of the ML chat culture through examination of the process of informal social sanctioning of behavior that is defined as deviant within the culture. It also examines this particular culture in order to identify the mechanisms of sanctioning deviance within cyber cultures in general. Several main questions are addressed. First, how are particular behaviors judged to be deviant in chat cultures? Second, what are the probable causes of deviance within the culture? And third, what are the likely consequences of the deviant behavior for the individual that has transgressed the norms and the cultural system of which the person is a part? Also, the relevance of contemporary sociological theories of deviance for explaining these processes is explored.

Methodology

The data for this study were collected via participant observation within the ML chat room over the course of several months. This researcher initially participated as a guest within the culture and later became a member. It is necessary, due to the nature of chat rooms, to participate as a full member in order to truly understand the normative system of the culture and the defining and sanctioning processes of deviance within the culture. Observations and interactions took place at various times of the day. The nature of cyberspace communication creates difficulties in the study of deviance, due to the lack of human bodies and, more specifically, body language. It is only through understanding written communications that take the form of visible gestures and symbols within the culture that the norms of the culture become apparent.

The Nature of the Married Life Chat Room

The particular chat room where observations and participation were conducted for the purpose of this study is part of the larger social system of Virtual Places (VP). VP is a software program that offers various chat rooms in which to interact through typed messages. However, it also offers graphic images and gestures that serve as symbols of communication within the chat cultures as well as avatars, which serve as visual representations of the individual chatter. Because communications and interactions within VP are limited to typed messages, various forms of emotional symbolic expression have developed to take the place of the invisible body. For example, the symbol :) represents a smile and :(a frown. While such symbols can take various forms, it is important to note that chatters have developed symbols with which to express their emotional reactions to behaviors, and these symbols can function as sanctioning mechanisms within the culture.

The language used within the cultures relies heavily on abbreviations to cut back on the amount of time it takes to communicate typed messages. The following are common abbreviations that are used within the Married Life chat room: lol = laughing out loud; lmao = laughing my ass off; wb = welcome back; ty = thank you; yw = you're welcome; sis = sister; Reg = regular member of the VP culture in general and within the context of the current culture of Married Life in particular; and Mug = a person that chats as a guest. It is necessary to be familiar with these abbreviations in order to understand the interaction between chatters within the culture. Also, capitalization of typed messages can serve as either an expression of anger or excitement or as an indicator that an individual is screaming.

Much of the communication between chatters takes the form of gestures that are generic typed messages. This research[1] identified four main types of gestures within the chat room culture that are differentiated by their prospective functions. The first type will be termed "solidarity gestures" because they serve the function of promoting cohesiveness within the chat culture. The following are examples of solidarity gestures:

> Married Life . . . sometimes you wanna go where everybody knows your name.
>
> Hubby said if I come to VP one more time he leavin!!!! Man I am Gonna Miss Him!!!
>
> ML REGS . . . Thank you for being a friend . . . 1999
>
> A Salute to the REGS
>
> True friendship is seen through the heart, not the eyes.

These gestures serve the purpose of declaring a commitment to the ML culture and comembers and also offer an indication as to the purpose of the culture. The married life culture exists for the purpose of allowing individuals with the common characteristic of being married to interact and make friends. As many of the members have suggested it is the perfect place to visit with friends for people that lead busy lives. Over and over again they comment that they do not have to leave their homes in order to interact with other adults and make good friends from all over the world. These solidarity gestures serve to promote the cohesiveness of the group members. They also make the relationships seem more "real" in the context of cyberspace.

The second type of gestures function as markers of status and therefore are termed "symbolic status gestures." These take the form of gestures for individual members that promote the status of the individual member. The Regulars have access to their fellow reg's gestures. These gestures are played when a member arrives in the room to mark their entrance and serve as symbols of their status within the culture room. Persons that are not of a high status within the culture do not have personal gestures. The written message that is played by members of the culture is visible to all, letting others know that this person is of a higher and more accepted status within the culture. However, the visual dimension of the gesture is only available to those that have access to the gesture, thus excluding lesser members from partaking in

---

[1] Virtual Places installed voice chat shortly after this research was conducted.

the privilege of sharing the total experience of the symbol. The visual dimension usually takes the form of graphic images of the person's avatar with music playing. It is similar to a clip from a movie. The following are some of the status gestures of individual members within the Married Life culture:

~Jill is here . . . Ready to put some spice in your LIFE~~

Big Mom . . . Protector of the Innocent, washer of the dirty shorts

Jake has arrived . . . Who's First!?

Dallaste is here . . . Watch him work his magic!!!

~~Stephanie is here time to grab your boots the shit's getting deep~~

~~~Sand Man . . . He's an . . . All Nite Man~~~ Sand Man . . . He's gonna keep u up all nite . . . such a smoothie

~~~Love is . . . What Letty is all about~~~

Trisha is here and she is so Yummy for your Tummy!!!!

Little is HERE to THRILL YOUR SOUL . . . so LET the GOOD TIMES ROLL!!!!

~~~Sexy is now OFFDUTY . . . and READY to PLAY~~~

Jim's Here For Some R & R

~~~Just being here with Slide is . . . HOT

Jim might be CHEAP but he's not EASY

The third type of gestures are used largely for the purpose of facilitating interaction of various kinds within the culture, thus they are termed "facilitative gestures." These gestures most commonly take the form of music, sexually flirtatious comments, or humorous comments. The most common form of facilitating gesture is sexually flirtatious in nature. These gestures also function as a socializing mechanism for new members of the culture in that they allow new members to quickly become familiar with the type of interactions that are prescribed within the culture. All regs are expected to engage in this type of interaction with their fellow regs. The following are just a few examples of such gestures:

I don't cyber, but DAMN I love to tease

Give White Rose

smooch I wuv you

The fourth, and most important type of gesture for the purposes of the current study are "sanctioning gestures." These are gestures that are used to sanction deviant behavior within the chat culture. However, many of these are also indicative of the low status of mugs within the culture. The following are examples of such gestures:

Mugg Toss!!! . . . (CRASH!!!!!)

I don't cyber mugs!!!!!!!!!

I drink from mugs, I don't talk to them

Lord be with our guest, and prepare them for the butt whoopin they're about to receive!!

What do you mean you're a GUEST? I never fuckin invited ya

MUG stands for Mother Fuckin Uninvited Guest

Hello mug suicide hotline . . . yes sir, put your face right up to the barrel and PULL THE TRIGGER! /// MUG KILL

CALL THE COPS, I'VE BEEN MUGGED!!!!

Damn Mugs! Why must you needlessly complicate everything?

VP REGS PISS ON MUGS!!!!!!!!!

Mug hunting season is declared OPEN!!

Excuse me? Do you see the word guest by your name and not mine? Know your place

Forgive them Father, for they are mugs and know not how to download

Horny Mug ALERT!!!!

Attention K-Mart shoppers, an asshole just entered the room!

Just because I wear a sexy AV [avatar] doesn't mean I want to cyber every loser in the room

We have Attitude in MARRIED LIFE . . . So Bite US!!!!

<<<<Go check your ATTITUDE at the door!!!>>>>

I can go from 0 to bitch in 1.2 secs., Don't Push Me!!!

Will the owner of the GREAT BIG BUTT, please move it out of my face!

As is evident in the above gestures the most common form of sanctioning is in reaction to mugs. This demonstrates that to be a mug is considered deviant in and of itself. The social context of Virtual Places does not distinguish between VP users and Java users. Java users are forced to sign on as guests in VP, but they chat in the same rooms as the Virtual Places users. These two groups of users are distinguished by whether or not they have access to the VP software and therefore the status symbols that are valued within the culture, such as avatars and gestures. Because the environment does not have different rooms for mugs and regs to chat it creates a conflict between the two groups.

The structure of the cyberspace can be likened to the geographical characteristics of inner city areas that were studied by the Chicago theorists in the first half of the 20th century (Park et al. 1925 and Shaw and McKay 1931). Many of the elements of social disorganization that were conducive to increasing crime rates are an inherent part of cyberspace of which the ML culture is a part. Like the zone of transition (Faris and Dunham 1999) in Chicago, cyberspace is set up in such a way that heterogeneity and transiency are central features, as is anonymity. The VP community is set up so that people can quickly move in and out of chat rooms, and the community is available to anyone with access to a computer. Because the individual has the option of changing their identity once they have been sanctioned for deviant behavior and reentering the community incognito, the structure of cyberspace offers anonymity to the people using it, which creates an increased willingness to engage in deviant behavior. These combined features of the social structure, in which ML culture is embedded, result in an increase in the frequency of occurrences of deviant acts and the need to sanction these behaviors in order to maintain the boundaries and normative structure of the culture. These characteristics of cyberspace in general and VP and ML in particular combine to influence the nature of deviant behavior and the form of sanctioning that arises in response to deviant acts within the married life culture.

Sanctioning Mechanisms of Chat Room Cultures

As in all cultures, an act can be judged to be deviant by examining the negative responses to the act and the sanctioning that follows. Conversely, identification of what is deviant within a culture also serves to define the normative boundaries of that particular culture. There are two general types of sanctioning mechanisms within the context of the ML culture and VP more generally. The first and most obvious is the use of gestures or typed text as written symbols of sanctioning. The second is the use of the ignore button which puts a person that is engaging in rude or inappropriate behavior on ignore. One also can choose to ignore an individual's avatar. More often than not, the ignore sanction is used only as a last resort when someone is behaving in a manner that is disruptive to the communication of the other chat members. When this happens all of the other members will place the person on ignore. This results in the person being excluded from communication and interaction within the culture.

Social Positioning, Roles, and Normative Expectations

While all of the participants in the culture share the common social position of "chatter" within chat rooms, there is a hierarchy of social status within the Married Life culture. Observations revealed that a large part of the sanctioning that occurs within the Married Life culture serves as a socializing mechanism designed to teach new and potential members both the values and norms of the society as well as new members' proper position within the culture. This demonstrates that individuals occupying certain social positions are expected to behave in certain ways within the culture. This form of sanctioning is most acutely demonstrated in the course of interaction between mugs and regs. Mugs are considered lower class members of the culture, because they lack certain attributes. First, they have not downloaded the VP software and therefore show up as a visual image of a coffee cup in the chat room environment. They also lack access to gestures, which are a key component to extensive participation in the culture, through witty generic remarks, that are often sexual in content. Regs are those members that have been a part of the culture for an extensive period of time, have access to the valued avatars and gestures and are most thoroughly skilled in the valued attributes within the culture, being humorous and flirtatious.

Occupying the status of mug within the culture does not preclude interaction with other members. However, this researcher's observations of incidents of sanctioning within the culture indicate that there are certain expectations concerning how a mug should behave. The first expectation is that you will not challenge the authority of regs. The second expectation is that mugs will follow the conversation set up by the regs and refrain from expressing their disagreement with the regs' choice of social interaction. If mugs deviate from these prescribed behaviors they are likely to be sanctioned with gestures that express anti-mug sentiments by all of the regs in the room. Also, to the extent that the culture is largely based on flirtatious behavior, this largely takes place between regs. When mugs flirt with regs it is considered disrespectful and sanctioning follows. Thus, they are sanctioned for engaging in the same behaviors that regs engage in due to their social status. A mug identity is in essence a negative ascriptive characteristic. However, it is not completely ascribed; part of the negative evaluation of mugs is due to the nature of their participation in the culture. Because many of the individuals that chat as mugs often consider themselves transitory within the culture, they are much more likely to engage in explicit solicitation of sexual interaction, which is a proscribed behavior within the culture. It is typically believed that they are there to seek out cyber sex, not to participate in the culture. This negative stereotype results in a need for mugs to prove their commitment to the culture in order to be accepted. Once this is done they are then accepted as honorary members of the culture and regs will try to encourage them to download the VP software in order to enjoy the full privileges of membership. By doing so the mug expresses his or her commitment to the values within the culture.

The Nature of Deviance in the Married Life Culture

Much of the deviance within this culture seems to result from improper socialization, due to the nature of cyberspace. Because there aren't firm boundaries within cyberspace people can move with ease from one chat room to another. Thus, many people that enter the cultural milieu are not familiar with the cultural practices and norms or the positions of the members within the culture. In such a context, communication with gestures serves as a mechanism for quick socialization, but the heterogeneity and quick turnover of the population within the culture creates a sort of social disorganization within.

In the case of men overtly asking for sex in the ML chat room, there appears to be a complex of intertwining reasons. First these men are typically not aware of the normative expectations of the particular culture as is evident in the reactions of some men to these sanctions. For example, it is common for them to respond that they thought all chat rooms were for the purpose of sex talk. Some will apologize and choose to join the ML culture because they like the interaction that takes place within it. Others will exit the room once they have been sanctioned as outsiders and search for cybersex in some other room. This suggests that the nature of the broader VP environment indeed motivates some individuals to engage in sexual behaviors that might be considered deviant in the more inclusive culture of ML. The overarching belief that chat rooms are for the purpose of sex chat or cybersex leads people to discount the normative system of the particular chat room. Such individuals can be assumed to be abiding by the normative structure of VP and therefore the norms of ML are not relevant to them. They are outsiders that are being sanctioned according to the normative structure of the more inclusive married life culture.

Although far less frequent, another form of deviance observed within the culture appears to take the form of occupying conflicting roles. For example, some individuals are more committed to their role as a religious member of their church in their real lives than they are to their role in the ML culture. To the extent that the ML culture promotes overt sexually flirtatious behavior, these members react negatively to such behavior. In turn the more committed members of the culture will sanction the negative reactions because this type of interaction is highly valued as a form of fun within the culture. If the person doesn't apologize and refrain from making comments regarding the nature of the behavior within the chat room, they will be sanctioned with comments suggesting that they are in the wrong chat room and that they should try a religious one. This same process of sanctioning occurs when men come into the room and overtly suggest engaging in sexual relations with others. They are told to go to a sex chat room.

The most disruptive form of deviance seems to stem from bad or negative experiences within the ML cultural milieu. This type of deviance is far less frequent than the other types previously mentioned. This usually takes the form of an individual entering the chat room with the sole purpose of being disruptive because they have previously been rejected or sanctioned for not acting appropriately in the culture. They will type messages that are crude and aimed at challenging the norms of the culture or play nonsense gestures over and over, so as to impede the communication and interaction of the cultural members. The sanctioning of such incidents depends highly on the length of duration of the deviant behavior. Typically the individual will first be sanctioned with gestures, then if that doesn't work the entire group will resort to putting the individual on ignore. When individual members of the group put an individual on ignore, the person's typed communication no longer shows up on the screen. Essentially, the offending individual has been excluded from the conversation and interaction within the culture.

A form of deviance that is more likely to be displayed by members of the culture than by outsiders is that of improper avatar etiquette. The married life culture has a range of avatars that are considered appropriate for the room. This can range from those that have no sexually explicit symbolic value to those that are provocative. However, avatars that are considered vulgar are unacceptable within the culture. If an individual wears an avatar that is considered inappropriate to the culture the person will be sanctioned through comments that may or may not take on a humorous nature. For example, a.male member of the culture came in with an avatar that was completely nude and the other members expressed their disapproval with comments like "OMG!!" (oh my God!!) and requested that he put clothing back on. The person did as he was asked and joked about the incident as a form of reaffirming his commitment to the culture.

Another incident in which avatar etiquette was violated was when one of the women that participates in the culture put up an avatar with her real picture. The picture was of her dancing in a strip club with no top on. She was proud of this avatar and said, "look everyone this is me!" The room responded in silence and pretended that they didn't see her statement. Meanwhile numerous private instant messages were popping up on my screen from both male and female fellow chatters with derogatory comments expressing their disapproval of her behavior. From that time on she was ostracized from the group and limited in her social interactions. She eventually quit coming to ML.

Although infrequent, a form of deviance considered serious by members of the culture is what they refer to as "stalking." This refers to any unwanted advances that occur or harassment of one member by another. Typically this takes the form of one individual interpreting his or her relationship with another individual as more intimate or serious than it is. Generally, the member that is being stalked will discuss it with other members when the person accused of stalking is not present. It is generally known among the central members of the culture that a person is engaging in stalking behavior, and members will avoid any private conversations with that person. Members also avoid engaging in flirtatious communication within the chat room with this person. He or she is thus excluded from any type of intimate relationships with others in the ML culture because he or she has been labeled a "stalker." Once this has occurred the person is limited in the types of interaction that he or she can engage in with other members. Stalking is sanctioned rather harshly because the nature of the behavior is threatening to the anonymity of the member the individual is stalking and there is a potential for the stalker to interfere with the other member's real life, and his or her marriage. The stalker has been defined as breaking the informal rule of not getting too close to other members. While relationships with other members are highly valued within the culture, it is understood that there is a boundary that relationships will not cross. Because all of the members are identified as married people, the flirtatious behavior is regarded as harmless and fun, and is expected to stay at that level. This is not to say that some members may not engage in serious relationships with one another that spill over into their personal lives, but such behavior is not overtly condoned within the culture.

Members are sometimes sanctioned for the failure to meet proscribed expectations of humorous and flirtatious behavior in the context of the culture. This is seen when people come into the room and talk about heavy topics such as financial problems or marital problems. Although members of the culture may listen briefly to such accounts, if the individual continues to talk about such incidents they will be sanctioned. This can take the form of being ignored, having other members change the topic, or receiving direct verbal sanctions that tell the person that he or she is ruining the fun in the room.

Observation suggests that individual instances of deviance are most likely to be committed by those persons that do not share or value the norms of the culture (mugs), those who participate less often in the culture, and those that occupy a position of lesser status within the culture. Most of the deviant acts that occur are committed by persons that are not actual members of the culture (mugs) or by those individuals that are in the process of being socialized within the culture. Although less frequent, deviance also can occur when a person occupies conflicting social roles or has a commitment to another culture that he or she values more highly than their participation in the ML culture.

The examination of sanctioning suggests that a functional analysis is fitting to the study of deviance within the Married Life Chat Culture. The sanctioning of mugs as outsiders in particular serves to strengthen the moral fabric of the culture and creates group cohesion as does the sanctioning of individuals that openly solicit sex within the chat room (Coser 1956). The sanctioning of such behavior reaffirms the commitment of the group members to both the value they place on the interaction offered by access to the VP software and their commitment to the norm that defines the boundaries of interaction and innocent flirtation. To the extent that members talk about sex, it is in a light and humorous manner between fellow members and all members understand that humor is the purpose of such interaction. Also the instances in which group members are sanctioned for engaging in serious conversations reaffirm the commitment of the group to a norm of humorous and fun interaction. Deviance within this culture appears to serve the function of boundary maintenance as articulated by Kai Erikson (1999) and Joseph Gusfield (1963). In essence, deviance serves the purpose of identifying the normative boundaries of the culture for its members.

Consequences of Deviant Behavior for the Individual Deviant

For those persons that are not a part of the culture, to be labeled deviant has no negative consequences, other than possibly the realization that they will have to search for another chat room. Some of the obvious consequences of being labeled deviant within the context of the ML chat culture for members is that it restricts interactions with other members of the culture and therefore limits the positive value of engaging in the culture. While the psychological consequences of deviant behavior for the individual cannot be ascertained in the course of the current analysis, it can be assumed that the consequences will be more negative for those who identify most strongly with the norms of the culture and value the positive social interactions they receive by being members of the culture (Gusfield 1963). However, the context of cyberspace also makes it possible for individuals that have been ostracized from the culture to change their identity and reemerge as an unidentified member. However, for individuals that valued the friendships they made and invested much time in creating an identity within the culture, this would not be a desirable option.

Consequences of Deviance for the Married Life Culture

As functionalist theorists have asserted, deviant incidents serve both positive and negative functions for the functioning of the cultural system. Within the context of the Married Life Culture, the sanctioning of deviance in general and that of mugs in particular serves the function of creating cohesiveness among the group members. When mugs are sanctioned for who they are, the value of being a member of VP and the status and prestige that come with such membership is reaffirmed. When individuals are sanctioned for soliciting cybersex in ML, this affirms the commitment to the norm that such behavior is inappropriate. When members are sanctioned for engaging in conversation that is too serious this reaffirms the commitment of the members to the value of having fun within the culture. All these instances of deviance function to reaffirm the group's values.

However, there are also negative social consequences for the functioning of the social system that stem from deviance. The most obvious negative consequence is that it impedes the proper functioning of the system. When people engage in behaviors that are disruptive to the culture it impedes the interaction and communication of other members within the culture. Time is wasted on responding to and sanctioning deviance that could be otherwise spent engaging in positive social interaction within the culture. Also, deviant occurrences impede the socialization process of the person committing the deviant act.

Conclusion

This paper demonstrates that the nature of deviance can be studied within the context of cyberspace and offers insight into the forms sanctioning will take within the context of cyberspace chat cultures. The observations suggest that incidents of deviance occur within the context of chat rooms for various reasons, ranging from improper socialization to rejection of the cultural norms. It is argued that the structure of cyberspace contributes to the frequency and the nature of deviance within chat rooms by creating a perpetual state of social disorganization within chat rooms. Future research should examine other cultures to see if the same factors influence the nature of deviance. Researchers also should examine the possible effects that sanctioning may have on the individual on a psychological level through interviews with people that engage in deviant behavior and have been sanctioned within a chat room culture. Another important avenue for research is to explore the extent to which the identity and self-esteem of individuals within chat room cultures are dependent upon their participation in such cultures. In essence, researchers need to ask if this culture is influential in the participant's life and to their identity, and if so how this affects the nature of deviance. While one would assume that the nature of cyberspace would make participation in such cultures somehow less than real, observation suggests that for some of the members in the ML culture participation was extensive, often occupying a central place in their lives.

References

Barak, Azy and Marilyn P. Safir. 1997. "Sex and the Internet: An Israeli Perspective." *Journal of Sex Education & Therapy* 22(1):67–73.

Bromberg, Heather. 1996. "Are MUDs Communities? Identity, Belonging and Consciousness in Virtual Worlds." Pp. 143–152 in *Cultures of Internet: Virtual Spaces, Real Histories, and Living Bodies,* edited by Rob Shields. London, England: Sage.

Coser, Lewis A. 1956. *The Functions of Social Conflict.* New York: Free Press.

Cushing, Pamala J. 1996. "Gendered Conversational Rituals on the Internet: An Effective Voice Is Based on More than Simply What One Is Saying." *Anthropologica* 38(1):47–80.

Durkin, Keith F. and Clifton D. Bryant. 1995. "Log on to Sex: Some Notes on the Carnal Computer and Erotic Cyberspace as an Emerging Research Frontier." *Deviant Behavior* 16(3):179–200.

Durkin, Keith F. and Clifton D. Bryant. 1999. "Propagandizing Pederasty: A Thematic Analysis of the On-Line Exculpatory Accounts of Unrepentant Pedophiles." *Deviant Behavior* 20(2):103–127.

Erikson, Kai T. 1999. "On the Sociology of Deviance." Pp. 22–30 in *Theories of Deviance,* edited by Stuart H. Traub and Craig B. Little. Itasca, IL: F. E. Peacock.

Faris, Robert E. L. and H. Warren Dunham. 1999. "Natural Areas of the City." Pp. 74–82 in *Theories of Deviance,* edited by Stuart H. Traub and Craig B. Little. Itasca, IL: F. E. Peacock.

Gusfield, Joseph R. 1963. *Symbolic Crusade: Status Politics and the American Temperance Movement.* Urbana, IL: University of Illinois Press.

Lamb, Michael. 1998. "Cybersex: Research Notes on the Characteristics of the Visitors to Online Chat Rooms." *Deviant Behavior* 19(2):121–135.

Levalley, Janet. 1997. "Doing it in Cyberspace: Cultural Sensitivity in Applied Anthropology." *Anthropology of Consciousness* 8(4): 113–132.

Lieblum, Sandra Risa. 1997. "Sex and the Net: Clinical Implications." *Journal of Sex Education & Therapy* 22(1):21–27.

Mills, Russell. 1998. "Cyber: Sexual Chat on the Internet." *Journal of Popular Culture* 32(3):31–46.

Morse, Margaret. 1997. "Virtually Female: Body and Code." Pp. 23–35 in *Processed Lives: Gender and Technology in Everyday Life,* edited by Jennifer Terry and Melodie Calvert. London, England: Routledge.

Park, Robert E., Ernest W. Burgess, and Roderick D. McKenzie. 1925. The City. Chicago, IL: University of Chicago Press.

Plant, Sadie. 1996. "On the Matrix: Cyberfeminist Simulations." Pp. 170–183 in *Cultures of Internet: Virtual Spaces, Real Histories, and Living Bodies,* edited by Rob Shields. London, England: Sage.

Poster, Mark. 1995. "Postmodern Virtualities." *Body and Society* 1(3–4): 79–95.

Ribeiro, Gustavo Lins. 1997. "Transnational Virtual Community? Exploring Implications for Culture, Power and Language." *Organization* 4(4):496–505.

Schnarch, David. 1997. "Sex, Intimacy, and the Internet." *Journal of Sex Education & Therapy* 22(1):15–20.

Shaw, Clifford R. and Henry D. McKay. 1931. "Formal Characteristics of Delinquency Areas." Pp. 60–108 in National Commission of Law Observance and Enforcement Report on the Causes of Crime, Vol II. United States Government Printing Office.

Turkle, Sherry. 1996. "Parallel Lives: Working on Identity in Virtual Space." Pp. 156–175 in *Constructing the Self in a Mediated World,* edited by Debra Grodin and Thomas R. Lindlof. Thousand Oaks, CA: Sage.

Turkle, Sherry. 1997. "Multiple Subjectivity and Virtual Community at the End of the Freudian Century." *Sociological Inquiry* 67(1):72–84.

Wise, Patricia. 1997. "Always Already Virtual: Feminist Politics in Cyberspace." Pp. 179–196 in *Virtual Politics: Identity and Community in Cyberspace,* edited by David Holmes. London, England: Sage.

Zizek, Slavoj. 1996. "Sex in the Age of Virtual Reality." *Science as Culture* 4(25):506–525.

Zizek, Slavoj. 1998. "Cyberspace, or, How to Transverse the Fantasy in the Age of the Retreat of the Big Other." *Public Culture* 10(3):483–513.

The Production of Institutional Careers and Identities

Part III described how deviant behavior may initially be managed in a private setting. The material that was presented demonstrated how such behavior may become subject to regulation by a social-control agent or agency. When such regulation occurs, the actor's behavior is screened by the institution and its staff, and a label may be placed on him or her. The individual then becomes an institutional deviant, expected thereafter to conform to the institution's definition of the label. Some people will accept this labeling. In this event, the person's public identity (how others view him or her) meshes with personal identity (how the person views himself or herself), so that we can speak of the secondary, or career, deviant. Other deviants, however, will reject the label and attempt to structure and present to others a nondeviant image of self. The selections in this part explore such possibilities as these; they also illustrate clearly how institutional careers are initiated, perpetuated, and transformed. Throughout the following discussion of the various articles, the "organizational paradigm," which was presented in the general introduction, is applied.

Organizational Structures, Ideologies, Social-Control Agents, and Recruitment: The Institutional Backdrop

It is difficult to understand the processes behind the production of deviance and deviants unless we first analyze the institution out of which a specific social-control agent operates. It is particularly important to know how the prevailing theory of the office, existing deviant categories, and diagnostic stereotypes are applied to clients. The first selection, "Bureaucratic Slots and Client Processing," from Delos H. Kelly's book *Creating School Failure, Youth Crime, and Deviance*, not only elaborates on these ideas but presents an in-depth analysis of how the "organizational paradigm" can be applied to the study of social deviance. Kelly initially stresses the importance of analyzing how social institutions are structured. Here, by drawing particularly upon the works of Cicourel and Kitsuse, and Hargreaves, he describes the origin of a range of school career lines (e.g., ability groups and track systems). He notes, for example, in terms of actor selection and placement, that students who give teachers a hard time or are perceived as troublemakers often land in the low, basic, or non-college-prep tracks. After describing selected organizational structures and components, he moves to a general discussion of how clients are identified, selected, sorted, and processed by bureaucrats. Critical to an understanding of this process is the *content* of an agency's existing theory of the office and associated working ideology. Not only is the theory of the office embedded within an agency's organizational fabric (see Part I), but it becomes, through socializing experiences in formal and informal settings, inculcated within relevant actors, audiences, and third parties.

Kelly uses certain aspects of the structure and process of schooling to underscore the importance of locating, describing, and characterizing the content of an agency's theory of the office. If, as argued, society and its educational institutions are predicated firmly on an ideology that *presumes differential ability*, then we can expect to obtain outcomes commensurate with that view. Hence, some students will be destined to fail while others will be programmed for success. Ability groups, track systems, and other means for stratifying students offer graphic representations of how a society's educational philosophy becomes translated into bureaucratic entities. Actually predicting who will succeed or fail requires an analysis of how existing student stratification systems articulate with student attributes. For example, is the person of color more likely, independent of demonstrated academic success and competence, to be relegated to a low or basic track? If this happens (and there is increasing evidence that it does), then what can we say about the educational decision maker? Is he or she, either advertently or inadvertently, acting in a discriminatory or bigoted fashion? After addressing questions such as these, Kelly provides additional observations on what he terms the *bureaucratic matching game*, the decision-making process whereby a bureaucrat or decision maker assesses a client's attributes or traits and then renders an assignment decision. Kelly concludes by offering an overview of how client processing can destroy an actor's personal and public identity, as well as produce an erosion of self-image. He also comments on how institutions create, use, and misuse records.

Ideologies that orient social systems, and individuals within them, exist at many levels. Ideas that support the privatization of public services, for example, have resulted in the privatization of correctional facilities and a subsequent "correctional industry." While privatization of prisons promised greater efficiency, according to the driving ideology, there are also several important issues to consider. David Shichor, in "The Corporate Context of Private Prisons," addresses the privatization of correctional institutions. Shichor's concerns revolve around the "corporate nature of the private providers," a context that may easily result in exploitation and various forms of corporate deviance.

As explained by Shichor, free competition in the pursuit of profit is at the core of the privatization movement and is also at the heart of potential problems. In fact, when a profit motive is added to the correctional system, the "customer" is at greatest risk. Corporations can use their political power to encourage a "tough on crime" policy that, in effect, insures a more durable clientele. If profits fail to meet expectations, costs, in particular any remunerations for "clients," are easily altered. The primary concern here is that in a privatized system of corrections, it is possible to increase the costs to the government through contracts in a number of ways, while reducing the "quality of care" that is characteristic of for-profit firms.

Social-control agents, both formal (e.g., the police) and semi-formal (e.g., the school administrator), must become familiar with and act according to the agency's theory of the office. This socialization takes place within formal and informal domains. We have police academies and we have on-the-job training. We have teacher education programs and we have teacher lounges. Regardless of the specific institution or interactional context considered, however, a novice must "learn the ropes." And what he or she is taught in a formal setting (e.g., the police academy) may not mesh with what is expected in an informal context (e.g., the streets). The official mandate or theory of the office might be "to protect and serve all" or "to provide equal access for all to educational opportunities." An important question arises: How is an agency's theory of the office or official perspective translated into action? Are all citizens actually accorded equal protection under the law? Are all students provided equal access to educational opportunities? We need to examine how the theory of the office actually becomes translated into action. Is there a direct correspondence between an agency's official perspective and its actual working ideology? Answering these questions requires an ongoing examination of how social-control agents go about processing clients. In a very real sense, we need to get inside the minds of the bureaucrats and examine their decision-making processes. For example, what can we say about the content and range of diagnostic stereotypes that are used to identify, select, sort, process, sanction, and treat clients? Is one hiding under the cloak of bureaucratic competence?

The selection by Jennifer Hunt and Peter K. Manning, "The Social Context of Police Lying," provides an account of how social-control agents become familiar with an agency's theory of the office and working ideology, in both formal and informal settings. Hunt and Manning use as their source of data an eighteen-month field study of a large urban police force, and they operate on the assumption that police, like many people in official positions, lie. Hunt and Manning analyze the types of lies police tell and the ways in which they lie. They note initially that instructors in the police academy not only often encourage recruits to lie but tell the recruits that lying is an element of "good police work." During classes on the law and courts, however, recruits receive a different message; they are taught that the best way to win in court is by presenting a factual account of an event. Once the rookie is on the job the situation changes, and he or she is taught when it is appropriate to lie. In fact, learning to lie is a prerequisite to gaining membership on the force. This is particularly important in view of the observation that the police in Metro City routinely engage in a range of illicit activities such as drinking and sleeping on the job. And those rookies who show little skill in constructing or using lies are often subject to criticism. Associated with lies is a range of acceptable justifications and excuses which the officers can use. Accounts, however, are often audience-specific. For example, a story directed at an "external" audience such as an attorney or the media is often viewed as more problematic than one directed at a supervisor. Hunt and Manning offer various illustrations of how case lies are used in court to obtain a conviction. For example, "probable cause" can be constructed in numerous ways (e.g., by adding to the facts). The researchers also report how the court can be manipulated to gain a conviction. The case of the boy who "hung out" with a corner group offers an excellent example. Throughout this specific analysis, the involved officer, who believes the boy is guilty, constructs and presents an account consisting of a combination of excuses and justifications. The researchers then describe cover stories, or those lies that officers tell in an attempt to shield themselves against disciplinary action. For example, one who does not respond to a radio call may claim that his or her radio was dead. Similarly, an officer who uses brutal force is often expected to lie to protect himself or herself. Hunt and Manning conclude by noting that the extent to which an organization uses lies varies across selected dimensions.

25 Bureaucratic Slots and Client Processing

Delos H. Kelly

I have illustrated how actors may become progressively defined by a range of others as societal misfits. Understanding this process, I have argued, requires a preliminary consideration of how, over time, individual traits, features, and biographies articulate with organizational components and processes to produce selected organizational products (e.g., the academic failure, troublemaker, or school dropout). Even more basic than this, I have argued that one must initially describe, as well as dissect, an institution's underlying organizational structure; this need was documented most graphically by Cicourel and Kitsuse's (1963) research on the origin of school career lines. They, it may be recalled, were able to locate three distinct career lines (i.e., the academic, clinical, and delinquent). These career lines not only composed an integral element of the school's organizational structure but they also provided the molds for student placement. Another significant finding of the Cicourel-Kitsuse (1963) study that should be made note of, once again, is the fact that the career lines could be characterized by a set of deviant and non-deviant labels. Teachers, for example, referred to those who gave them trouble or who were late as delinquents or pre-delinquents. The significance of this observation becomes especially meaningful when we find these same labels being invoked in the student selection and assignment processes. Thus, students who were late, did not work, or gave the teachers difficulty were more apt to be relegated to the delinquent career line. Thereafter, they became subject to the values associated with their low or deviant school status. The research by Hargreaves (1967) was used to buttress this observation, as well as claim.

Like the Cicourel-Kitsuse (1963) evidence, Hargreaves' (1967) observations point to the need for dissecting and understanding organizational structures. At Lumley, not only were student and teacher attitudes, reactions, and behaviors stream-specific, but the streaming system itself operated in such a fashion as to cut off effectively interaction between the lowest and highest streams; this organizational impediment to communication was also linked to subcultural differentiation. Hence, Lumley came to be characterized by two basic subcultures (i.e., the academic and the delinquescent), each possessing a set of dominant values. Low-stream students, it may be remembered, received positive sanctions by teachers and peers when they acted in accordance with the reigning values. The content of some of these values was such that misbehavior, even petty delinquency, was encouraged and supported by group members.

In effect, then, approaching a feeling for the structural roots or origins of school crime requires a basic and initial examination and documentation of the school's underlying organizational structure. Not only must the career lines and their labels be noted, but the corresponding value systems must also be mapped out; these comprise the basic structures to which individuals become molded.

Once the basic structural features of the educational system have been fixed, one can begin to examine student identifying, selecting, sorting, and processing. In this respect, I have argued that teachers-educators play a critical role in the initiation of a range of deviant careers; they are what I have termed "initiators of status degradation ceremonies." Several works were offered to support the fact that many teachers do invoke non-academic criteria (e.g., class, color, stigma symbols) in deciding which students will occupy the deviant, delinquent, or non-academic career lines. The importance of these observations, however, is found in the fact that once a pupil is assigned to a low school status or deviant career line, then that student must become subject to and be influenced by the prevailing value system, the general content of which is frequently non-academic in nature. It is in this way that a deviant, delinquent, and, perhaps ultimately, a criminal career is launched. The impact of the school experience and associated deviant labels is frequently more critical and wide-ranging than this. The efforts by Cicourel and Kitsuse (1963), and Polk (1975) were used to underscore this point.

As Cicourel and Kitsuse (1963) acknowledge, the school actually serves as a clearing house, and in this capacity it both sends and receives information about its students. Selected bits of biographical or stigmatizing material, however, seem especially vulnerable to dissemination and particularly that which evolves out of what I have termed "the success-fail philosophy" that permeates our society and its basic institutions. Thus, to fail academically, most assuredly, foretells of failure in other domains. In this regard, Polk (1975) noted that students who had been formally tagged as an academic failure by the school (i.e., a socializing institution) *and* who also had been adjudicated as a delinquent by the court (i.e., a social control institution) were more likely to possess an adult criminal record. Specific labels, or combinations of labels, thus assume a certain priority in our society, most notably those associated with the educational and social control apparatus. In fact, such labels have common meanings and are used interchangeably by institutions.

The Organizational Paradigm
and Institutional Processing

. . . Most interactions or status degradation ceremonies become eminently more meaningful when examined within an institutional context. Once we understand, for example, how the school is structured (i.e., the type and range of career lines), then the exchanges between teachers and pupils, or between students, make more sense. Similarly, after one becomes familiar with and understands how a law enforcement agency is structured in terms of its available career lines, then citizen-agent encounters take on added meaning and significance. Thus, the institutional fabric provides the backdrop against which interactions must be evaluated.

Elsewhere, in my studies of deviance (Kelly, 1979) and crime (Kelly, 1980), I have developed an analytical tool that can be used to gain an understanding of how organizations, in general, are structured and function. I have termed this the *organizational paradigm;* this basic paradigm or tool can be applied to the study of school crime.

What must be recognized initially is that the educational system has been given the major task of socializing or educating our youth. In this capacity, the educational decision makers must, as the major differentiators of academic talent, decide which students possess ability and which do not; this task, however, is not especially difficult, nor is it, necessarily, left to chance, primarily because the educators operate on the basis of a theory of the office which is, as I have stressed, predicated fundamentally upon the presumption of differential ability—a working ideology that guarantees the continued production of winners and losers. Not only have educators, parents, students, and others been effectively socialized into this dominant, all-pervading educational philosophy but, and upon closer examination, it becomes obvious that the success-fail philosophy can be characterized by a range of school labels (i.e., diagnostic stereotypes) and associated career lines. The career lines, however, become the most objective, bureaucratic representation of this ideology; they can, as Cicourel and Kitsuse (1963) demonstrated, be located and described. Moreover, the career lines or organizational entities constitute the molds into which students, once identified and tagged by the authorized school personnel, are placed. The paradigm illuminates this process very nicely.

The Organizational Paradigm and Client
Processing: A Brief Overview

Conceptually, the major audience in the case of the school is usually the counselor; this institutional representative or agent has, during the course of formal and informal socializing experiences and influences, been indoctrinated with the school's theory of the office and associated elements (i.e., the diagnostic stereotypes and career lines). . . . The diagnostic stereotypes, once mastered, serve as the criteria by which actors (i.e., students) are selected out and placed into the existing career lines. . . . If, for example, and to sketch a brief scenario, an actor (i.e., student) violates a school rule, regulation, or expectation (i.e., this is the act in terms of the paradigm), and is observed doing so by the primary audience (i.e., the counselor), this violation may, and depending upon the content of the audience's diagnostic stereotypes (e.g., the counselor may, and probably does, feel that problem or difficult students belong in the non-academic career lines), be enough to result in placement in a deviant or delinquent career line. In this event, not only has the status degradation ceremony been initiated, but the student may, by virtue of his or her implication in a deviant status, be on the road to the development of a delinquent career and identity. Quite obviously, a single act of defiance, deviance, or misconduct may not constitute sufficient grounds for such treatment.

The probability, however, increases with repeated violations, and particularly so if the acts are observed by others (i.e., third parties or witnesses in terms of my paradigm); this, it may be recalled, is one of the major messages offered by the works of Tannenbaum (1938), Becker (1963), and Lemert (1951). Stated somewhat more directly, if others report acts of misbehavior to the counselor, then a conception of an individual may evolve to the effect that he or she is truly an academic misfit and should be processed and treated accordingly. Thus, third parties or witnesses are often important in structuring a degree of *consensus* about an actor (e.g., that he or she is evil, a troublemaker, a gang member, an academic failure, and the like).

As I indicated previously, the organizational paradigm can be used to refine Polk's (1975) "status flow chart." . . . Specifically, the paradigm can be applied in such a way as to *flesh out* the underlying organizational structure. For example, and in looking at the school—the domain Polk (1975) considers critical in the generation of delinquent careers and identities, his conceptualization of the role and significance of academic performance could be easily recast into a discussion of career lines. Thus, and similar to Cicourel and Kitsuse (1963), we can speak of deviant and non-deviant career lines, as well as the dominant value systems that, according to Hargreaves' (1967) research, characterize a school's career lines. Also evident in Polk's (1975) analysis of status flows is the idea that certain students, by virtue of their status origins (e.g., low social class or minority status), are more apt to land in a low school status or deviant career line; this notion, too, can be handled very easily by the paradigm, particularly if we incorporate a concern for the role that the educational decision maker (i.e., the school's primary audience) plays. In effect, and as the evidence by Schafer and Olexa (1971), Pink and Sweeney (1978), Kelly (1976), Kelly and Grove (1981), and others indicates clearly, decision makers often apply non-academic criteria (i.e., class and race) in the selection and assignment processes, and, accordingly, students who fit the diagnostic stereotypes are selected out to play the role of the deviant, delinquent, or academic misfit. Polk's (1975) treatment of the interconnections between the educational system (i.e., a major socializing institution) and other social control institutions (i.e., police units, courts, and training schools) can also benefit from this type of refinement.

Not only do social control institutions become attuned to and act on the basis of a selected range of institutional labels (i.e., diagnostic stereotypes) but they, like the educational system, can also be described in terms of their underlying organizational structure. Thus, each agency can be analyzed relative to its prevailing theory of the office, diagnostic stereotypes, career lines, staff socializing procedures (both the formal and informal aspects), client selection and assignment routines (i.e., the application of diagnostic stereotypes to actors), and the like.

The police, by way of illustration, are expected to maintain peace and enforce the law. In this capacity, they are generally guided and constrained by what I would term a "good guy-bad guy" philosophy or, perhaps more generally, a "we-they" working ideology. Rookies, as do any other novices (Scheff, 1966), become socialized into this ideology, and they soon learn how to recognize the good guys from the bad guys; this is accomplished through familiarity with and application of a department's diagnostic stereotypes to clients or suspected clients. Officers, for example, develop conceptions of the "typical" features of the burglar, how the act of burglary is apt to be committed, where the event is likely to occur, and the range of possible victims. Similarly, the officer is taught how to spot, classify, and handle suspected cases of rape, homicide, spouse abuse, child molestation, and the like; these typical cases, or "normal crimes" in Sudnow's (1965) usage, are extremely important in the initiation of a *public* deviant identity and career, primarily because the initial classification of an actor (e.g., police labeling as a drunk driver or suspected rapist) has a direct bearing upon how that individual will be processed. Stated somewhat differently, the law enforcement apparatus contains a set of career lines commensurate with the diagnostic stereotypes or normal crimes; therefore, if a person is tagged as a child molester, murderer, or rapist, then he or she will be treated as such throughout the system. Not only this but what is often lost sight of is the fact that the suspected or adjudicated criminal, delinquent, or deviant is expected to act in accordance with the new public identity, status and associated roles. In effect, then, clients are examined with an eye toward seeing if they match the organization's selection criteria or standards.

Diagnostic Stereotypes and Client Processing: The Matching Game

One of the best illustrations of this matching process is found in Wiseman's (1970) research on skid row alcoholics, particularly her description of the judicial screening process. By using various combinations of physical appearance, past performance, and social position, she was able to produce a paradigm of expected social types and matching sentences. . . .

Of significance is the observation that there was an excellent fit between the derived social types and actual sentencing. Derelicts, for example, who looked rough, as well as men who were repeaters, were more apt to serve time and receive the longest sentences. Similarly, derelicts who appeared rough were "the least likely of any social type to escape jail" (Wiseman, 1970:93).

Even though the judge must, according to my paradigm, be conceptualized as occupying the position as major audience in the court, it must be recognized that, in the determination of a sentence, he or she often relies heavily on the inputs from others. In Pacific City, two court helpers—"the Rapper" and "the Knocker"—assumed a major role in the sentencing process. Specifically, the Rapper, an ex-alcoholic himself, not only claimed intimate knowledge of the skid row alcoholics and their life style, but he acted as the major advisor to the judge. Thus, and as each case passed before the judge, the Rapper would offer a recommended case disposition and the judge then passed sentence (Wiseman, 1970:94). The Knocker, operating in his capacity as record keeper, also supplied information to the judge. In fact, and according to Wiseman (1970:95–96), it was often difficult to distinguish the Knocker's role (i.e., supplier of information to the judge) from the Rapper's (i.e., recommender of sentence to the judge). A major conclusion Wiseman (1970:97) offers is that:

> Far from freeing the judge to make idiosyncratic personalized decisions, the result of the drunk court system is to *standardize drunks on the basis of social types* and then with the *assistance of court aides objectify them in such a way as to fit the predetermined types.* Thus the decision of the patrolman in typification of the Skid Row Drinker is not only accepted in the court without question—it is reinforced and embellished. [Italics mine]

Thus, and as I have argued, the initial typification or labeling of an actor contains certain consequences for subsequent processing and treatment. In the case of the public drunk, the police type this person in a specified way (e.g., as a derelict, young repeater, or out-of-towner) and this designation then determines how the individual will be handled. Emerson's (1969) research on the court processing of juveniles also illustrates very nicely how clients are identified and processed in accordance with existing organizational categories or career lines and associated diagnostic stereotypes.

Emerson (1969:83) makes a beginning statement to the effect that juveniles appearing before the court have created problems for some institution:

> . . . youths brought before the juvenile court generally represent "trouble" for some caretaking or control institution. In this sense every delinquent is "trouble" for someone. It may be added here that every delinquency complaint represents a plea that the court "do something"

to remedy or alleviate that "trouble." Hence, one fundamental set of problems and demands confronting the juvenile court arises from the pressures and expectations of those initiating court action that "something be done." In this sense the court must work out practical solutions to cases that satisfy, or at least take some cognizance of, the concerns of complainants.

Diagnostic Stereotypes and Client Processing: The Destruction of Identity

Not all cases, however, represent "trouble" in the eyes of the court. Rather, cases are subjected to two rather distinct phases of organizational screening or sorting. During phase one, troubled cases are separated from the untroubled or, more specifically, attempts are made to distinguish between cases requiring special handling as opposed to those that can be released. Assessing a juvenile's moral character triggers the subsequent, second phase of screening. At this juncture, the court specifies how the case is to be processed. If a decision is reached that no trouble exists, then the assumption is the delinquent's moral character is *normal.* If, by contrast, trouble is found to exist, then one's moral character is viewed as being *problematic* in nature; this latter decision brings about additional scrutiny by court personnel. Emerson (1969:90–91) maintains that, during the decision-making process, court staff endeavor to fit the juvenile into one of three kinds of moral character:

> . . . First, a youth may be *normal,* i.e., basically like most children, acting for basically normal and conventional reasons, despite some delinquent behavior. Second, a youth may be regarded as a *hard-core* or *criminal-like* delinquent, maliciously or hostilely motivated, consciously pursuing illegal ends. Third, a youth may be *disturbed,* driven to acting in senseless and irrational ways by obscure motives or inner compulsions. [Italics his]

Emerson (1969:91) goes on to say that the existing categories of moral character not only "provide institutionally relevant means for 'explaining' or 'accounting for' the patterns of behavior that led to the identification of 'trouble'" but placement in a category "both suggests and justifies particular court actions to deal with it." To determine that a person is "disturbed" explains or accounts for one's "bizarre" behavior. Such a finding would indicate a need for psychiatric treatment. It would also justify such care or institutionalization. Categories of moral character are thus associated with rather specific courses of action. In Emerson's (1969:91) words:

> . . . The three classes of moral character recognized by the court—normal, criminal, and disturbed—correspond to the following general reactions which the court may try to implement: (a) routine handling of

the case: generally probation and the relatively minor obligations and checks accompanying it; (b) incarceration in reform school or some other institution of that nature; and (c) special care and treatment, especially in a psychiatric setting.

Even though the court looks for trouble and then assesses moral character, this does not mean that a decision relative to character will be linked to a specific outcome or disposition. Rather, and as Emerson (1969:96–97) points out, an initial decision often represents nothing more than a recommendation, primarily because the court must deal with several practical considerations (e.g., those of placement and treatment). As an illustration, he cites the case of the "disturbed" delinquent. Specifically, the decision makers may decide that such an individual needs hospitalization, yet the youth may never be institutionalized. To obtain the desired recommendation (i.e., institutionalization), psychiatrists must validate the "disturbed" or "sick" diagnosis, and the court must convince the mental hospital to accept the case. If these contingencies are not met, the youth's case will be disposed of differently.

> . . . Contingencies surrounding the actual "solution" of a case may lead to different case outcomes despite common assessments of moral character. For example, the juvenile court may come to classify a boy as a dangerous, criminally motivated person, in which case some penal sanction such as commitment to reform school would seem indicated. But the decision actually to invoke this sanction is influenced by factors such as the boy's home situation and the availability of alternatives to reform school. Thus a boy who is a state ward is more likely to be committed to reform school than a boy judged just as criminally inclined but from a stable home. Commitment follows for the first case because there is no other place to put the public ward. [Emerson, 1969:97]

The Destruction of Identity: The Role of Witnesses

Once a youth has been initially typed (e.g., by a police officer) relative to moral character, efforts must be made, thereafter, to convince others (e.g., the probation officer), and even the actor, of the correctness of the decision. As Emerson (1969:101) stresses:

> Moral character is not passively established. It is the product of interaction and communicative work involving the delinquent, his family, enforcers, complainants generally, and the court itself. *Specific versions of moral character must be successfully presented if they are to be adopted by others* (Garfinkel, 1956). Officials, who play the dominant role in this process, both directly communicate their opinions of the moral character of the youth involved and more indirectly make selective reports of incidents and information pertinent to the court's evaluation of this

character. In general, *the version of moral character finally established is negotiated from among these presented "facts," opinions, and reports.* [Italics mine]

In effect, then, competing versions of moral character are presented to the court, and the judge, acting in his or her capacity as the major audience or decision maker, must decide ultimately which version of moral character will prevail; this, according to Emerson (1969:102), often leads to contests over moral character:

> Character-related presentations are inextricably linked to issues of disposition. For moral character is established in the process of negotiating a disposition of a case among the various expectations and demands of the parties involved. In this process, the court determines an outcome not by balancing the relative merits and demerits of possible disposition alternatives, but by attempting to establish a correspondence between a youth's moral character and a particular alternative. As a result, issues of disposition lead to contests over moral character, and parties to these contests, who seek to influence the outcome of a particular case, have to marshal and present evidence to establish a version of moral character appropriate to their desired outcome.

Not only is the court concerned with establishing a linkage between a juvenile's moral character and a particular disposition but the success of this process depends heavily upon inputs from other third parties or witnesses. In this respect, the probation officer frequently plays a central role in the construction of one's moral character. Similar to the Knocker and the Rapper in Wiseman's research, he or she attempts to convey a specific image of character to the judge; this is especially evident in the following case reported in Emerson's (1969:102–103) research:

> Rodney Knight, a 16-year-old Negro boy, was accused of stealing a handbag from a woman in a subway station. The police told of the arrest, and complained that the boy had given them "difficulties," particularly by using false names, address, and age. The probation officer recommended that Knight be held in county jail under $1,000 bail until the hearing. The judge reacted: "My only problem is the county jail. I can understand the $1,000 bail for this crime—it's serious enough to warrant it. But I'm curious about the recommendation of county jail." Probation officer replied that the boy had a previous record for use without authority at the municipal court. In addition he had been "uncooperative-information limited" with the police. Judge: "Let me put it this way: Is this something that in your opinion could not be handled at the YCA [Detention Center]?" Probation Officer (hesitating): "It's a problem of either the one or the other. (pause) I think that possibly the YCA is more of a picnic grounds." Judge: "Are you making this recommendation because of uncooperativeness, or because of some knowledge you have of his previous conduct?" Probation officer replied that he knew nothing about the boy's prior life and conduct. But another

probation officer reported that the municipal court had told him that Knight had not done well while on probation there. The arresting policeman again told of how much trouble the boy had given them. The judge finally agreed to county jail, but with considerable reluctance.

In the preceding case, the probation officer obviously tries to convince the judge that the youth's moral character is criminal in nature. The judge initially balks at this suggestion; however, additional witnesses (i.e., the second probation officer and policeman) are brought into the picture, and they testify in such a manner as to corroborate or validate the probation officer's image of Knight. Thus consensus is reached (i.e., that the youth is criminal) and the judge uses this information as a basis for sentencing to jail. At this point, a beginning delinquent career becomes solidified, at least in terms of the individual's public identity.

What the research by Emerson (1969) and others (e.g., Wiseman, 1970) indicates very clearly is that organizational personnel are interested in matching clients with the existing organizational categories or career lines. And if the efforts in this direction are successful, then the actor does, at least in the eyes of the institution, become effectively molded to the category or line he or she has been cast into. Emerson's (1969) observations also provide additional substance to my claim that there is often a high degree of correspondence between one social control agency's diagnostic stereotypes and another's; this is probably most apparent in Emerson's discussion of how the first probation officer used statements by the policeman—the actual initiator of the status degradation ceremony—and another probation officer to convince the judge that the court was dealing with a young criminal. What should be noted, however, is the fact that processes and associated outcomes such as these are not only routine and recurring features of the court but they become eminently more meaningful once we realize that the underlying organizational structure of the judicial system guarantees this kind of handling. Stated very simply, the court does not deal in individuals per se. It deals in social types, categories, and labels. Thus, and similar to the statements and research by Wiseman, court personnel, and especially the probation officer, are concerned primarily with the "typicalness" of their cases. Can, for example, a delinquent act be classified and processed in accordance with any of the court's existing categories of "typical delinquencies?" This is the basic question.

Organizational Slots and Processing: Further Observations on Becoming a Client

Organizational constructs (e.g., categories of typical academic types or delinquencies), once mastered, provide for the smooth and efficient processing of clients; this was pointed out by Scheff (1966). In effect, once a staff member has been effectively inculcated with the current diagnostic stereotypes, he or she becomes more proficient in the screening and processing of prospective clients (i.e., in the application of diagnostic stereotypes). Unfortunately, and as also suggested by Scheff's (1966) comments, the perceptions of many staff members seem to be locked in at the stereotypic level. Hence, the individual merits or demerits of a case are often lost sight of or else ignored. Of major concern to the staff member or social control agent is whether or not there are enough typical features of an event or case to allow for classification in terms of reigning categories. Emerson (1969), in drawing upon the work by Sudnow, stresses the important role that "typical delinquencies" play in the structuring of a successful degradation ceremony.

> Court personnel regularly deal with a recurring sequence of delinquent acts. In this activity, they come to make certain characterizations about routinely encountered delinquencies and delinquents. *A given delinquent act is understood in terms of these characterizations; that is, its organizationally relevant meaning derives from its membership in a known class of "typical delinquencies."* Typical delinquencies are constructs of the typical features of regularly encountered delinquent acts, embodying the court staff's previous experience with and common-sense knowledge of the situations and setting of delinquent acts. . . . [Emerson, 1969:106–107] [Italics mine]

To illustrate the substantive nature of typical delinquencies, Emerson (1969:107) offers some comments made by probation officers:

> *Boy shoplifters:* "Usually it's very mild type of boy. There are not many seriously delinquent boys." Generally no previous record. Often from "well-to-do families" and taking goods "for kicks." "Usually they're pretty nice children. They give you no trouble." Seldom in court again. "Usually they're not thieves at heart. They're in the store and they succumb to a beautiful display or something that looks good to them."

Typical delinquencies, according to Emerson (1969:107), actually "indicate *the kind of actor* typically involved." Similar to Sudnow's usage, typical delinquencies (1) "identify typical actors in terms of such *social characteristics* as age, sex, class, and residence," (2) "provide explanations or 'reasons' for the particular delinquent act, including but not limited to the actor's *immediate motives;*" and (3) "identify the kind of typical actor in terms of *moral character*" (Emerson, 1969:107–108) [italics his].

Throughout court processing or, for that matter, any status degradation ceremony, an actor's public identity is under attack. And if the assault is successful, an individual becomes viewed, at least in the eyes of others, as a new or different person; this, it may be recalled, is one of the basic messages contained in the works by Werthman (1967), Tannenbaum (1938), Garfinkel (1956), Becker (1963), Hughes (1945), and Lemert (1951). I argued subsequently, however, that prior to making any statements or conducting any analysis relative to status denunciation ceremonies or institutional handling, one must see the underlying organizational structure. The research by especially Wiseman and Emerson illustrates the need for doing so. Evidence of this type also indicates that potential clients are processed in accordance with the existing organizational categories or career lines. Not only this, but fitting a candidate to a particular career line often involves various stages of screening. For example, Emerson's juveniles were subjected to two distinct stages of screening. Another excellent illustration of this process is contained in McCleary's (1978) research with parolees, particularly his discussion of those stages involved in becoming a client. . . .

McCleary (1978:124–127) points out that parole officers work with a set of social types. Thus when a prisoner's dossier is received, the officer must decide how to classify the individual; this is an important decision, primarily because, and as illustrated by the efforts of Wiseman and Emerson, each decision and corresponding type or organizational category is associated with a specific line of action. In terms of actual typing, the officer must decide initially whether the prisoner should be typed as a criminal or non-criminal. If the decision is to the effect that the person is a non-criminal, the decision-making process moves to stage four where the individual will be labeled subsequently as a client or paper man. If, by contrast, the parole officer decides that the parolee is a criminal, then another decision must be made: Is the parolee controllable? This is determined during the site visit. For example, if selected environmental factors exist (e.g., a good job or stable family) as potential controls, then, and similar to the non-criminal's processing, the prisoner will be designated as a client or paper man. Some parolees, however, are not only viewed as criminals and uncontrollable but they are perceived as dangerous; these men are kept under surveillance and returned to prison at the first sign of trouble. A parolee who is judged as sincere becomes transformed into a client; this person interacts frequently with the officer and if problems develop, attempts will be made to "save" the client. The paper man category or type comprises those who have been judged as insincere, yet controllable, and those who have not been judged; these men remain on the books, however, they experience very little interaction with the parole officer. Most see the officer a couple of times a year. Clients and dangerous men usually see the officer once a week. In fact, McCleary (1978) characterizes the interaction between the officer and the paper man as being one of "mutual disinterested toleration."

Institutional Records: Their Creation, Use, and Misuse

Even though it may be assumed that parole records accurately describe a parolee's behavior relative to the classification criteria, this is often not the case. Rather, McCleary (1978:129) maintains that "parole records are more likely to reflect the needs and problems of the POs [parole officers];" this produces a bureaucratic dysfunction, one that can be related directly to the discretionary license allowed the officer, particularly in the creation or production of parole records. In McCleary's (1978:129) words:

> . . . [the] bureaucratic dysfunction can be attributed to the great discretion allowed POs in the gathering and reporting of information. In most cases, the PO himself decides what portion of the information he has gathered will actually go into the official record. By exercising editorial discretion in this area, the PO can suppress information that might make his job more difficult or complex and can include information that might facilitate work goals or objectives. This is how POs "use" their records.

Although rarely acknowledged, the parole officer, like any other bureaucrat, must come to grips with several bureaucratic demands—considerations that have a significant impact upon the production of records. In fact, and according to McCleary (1978:129), the parole officer's work environment consists of two distinct halves: PO-parolee interaction and PO-bureaucracy interaction. McCleary (1978:129–130) points out that successful parole officers must not only control their clients but they must satisfy the bureaucracy's explicit and implicit demands. A feature common to both halves, however, is record-keeping and successful POs know how to "use" their records. Record-keeping is not necessarily a simple or straightforward task, primarily because the officers must weigh the costs or benefits that may ensue from "using" their records. McCleary's (1978:130) major argument is that, other things being equal,

> . . . a PO will not report any of the minor crimes, incidents, or violations he observes in his caseload. When a PO does report an incident, he is creating records that will accomplish some end, the benefits of which are expected to outweigh the practical costs of reporting the incident. The implication of this argument is that parole records do not accurately reflect the behavior of parolees, but rather, reflect the many problems that arise in the PO's work environment. Three general problems . . . lead to the three most common "uses" of records: (1) records created to threaten parolees, (2) records created to get rid of troublesome parolees, and (3) records created to protect the PO and his superiors.

Not only is the creation of a record associated with potential costs but organizational incentives exist for underreporting. McCleary (1978:131–136) lists and describes several practical considerations a parole officer must deal with. For example, the complete or full reporting of each event may cut into the parole officer's "free" time (e.g., many of them moonlight) or place the officer in jeopardy (e.g., a lengthy hearing may result). Full reporting may also create a great deal of "busy work" for the officer, as well as restrict his or her options (e.g., most feel that their job is to counsel and not catch clients).

The significance of the preceding observations can be found in the fact that not only do bureaucratic factors affect the production of records but they must also impact significantly on client processing. Teachers, I might add, are not immune from these influences; they, too, must come to grips with demands of their profession, as well as the bureaucracy they are immersed in.

References

Becker, H. S. (1963) *Outsiders: Studies in the Sociology of Deviance.* New York: Free Press.

Cicourel, A. V. and J. I. Kitsuse (1963) *The Educational Decision Makers.* New York: Free Press.

Emerson, R. M. (1969) *Judging Delinquents.* Chicago: Aldine.

Garfinkel, H. (1956) "Conditions of successful degradation ceremonies." *The American Journal of Sociology* 61:420–424.

Hargreaves, D. (1967) *Social Relations in a Secondary School.* New York: Humanities Press.

Hughes, E. C. (1945) "Dilemmas and contradictions of status." *The American Journal of Sociology* 50:353–359.

Kelly, D. H. (1976) "The role of teachers' nominations in the perpetuation of deviant adolescent careers." *Education* 96:209–217.

Kelly, D. H., Ed. (1979) *Deviant Behavior.* New York: St. Martin's.

Kelly, D. H., Ed. (1980) *Criminal Behavior.* New York: St. Martin's.

Kelly, D. H. and W. D. Grove (1981) "Teachers' nominations and the production of academic 'misfits'." *Education* 101:246–263.

Lemert, E. M. (1951) *Social Pathology.* New York: McGraw-Hill.

McCleary, R. (1978) *Dangerous Men.* Beverly Hills: Sage.

Pink, W. T. and M. E. Sweeney (1978) "Teacher nomination, deviant career lines and the management of stigma in the junior high school." *Urban Education* 13:361–380.

Polk, K. (1975) "Schools and the delinquency experience." *Criminal Justice and Behavior* 2:315–338.

Schafer, W. E. and C. Olexa (1971) *Tracking and Opportunity.* Scranton: Chandler.

Scheff, T. J. (1966) "Typification in the diagnostic practices of rehabilitation agencies." In M. B. Sussman, Ed., *Sociology and Rehabilitation.* Washington, D.C.: American Sociological Association.

Sudnow, D. (1965) "Normal crimes: sociological features of the penal code in a public defender office." *Social Problems* 12:255–276.

Tannenbaum, F. (1938) *Crime and Community.* New York: Ginn and Company.

Werthman, C. (1967) "The function of social definitions in the development of delinquent careers." In the President's Commission on Law Enforcement and Administration of Justice, *Task Force Report: Juvenile Delinquency and Youth Crime.* Washington, D.C.: U.S. Government Printing Office.

Wiseman, J. P. (1970) *Stations of the Lost.* Chicago: University of Chicago Press.

26   The Corporate Context of Private Prisons

David Shichor

Introduction

Since the 1970s there has been a growing interest in Western countries in the privatization of public services. This interest increased considerably during the 1980s when conservative social philosophy and political climate proved favorable to the curtailment of the functions of government and the financing and management of social programs became a major issue. This development was also felt in the field of corrections. Such a trend is not a new phenomenon in the United States and Western Europe. During the 19th century there was extensive private involvement in U.S. corrections (see, for instance, Adamson, 1983; Ayers, 1984; Sellin, 1976; Rothman, 1980; Walker, 1988; McAfee and Shichor, 1990; Cody and Bennett, 1987) and on the continent (e.g., O'Brien, 1982; Babington, 1971). However, for various reasons privatization in corrections had declined in the first part of the 20th century.

The revival of the interest in privatization of corrections contains some distinctive features: (a) It includes the privatization of the management of entire prisons. This was only seldom advocated in the past and is different from the privatization of prison industries and various services (medical treatment, laundry, etc.) which has been in practice for some time. (b) Modern correctional privatization is being done by firms which have been formed specifically for this purpose (e.g. Corrections Corporation of America, Buckingham) or are specialized subsidiaries of large corporations (e.g., RCA, Westinghouse, General Electric Wackenhut). Usually the stocks of these corporations are publicly traded. This development also has some historical precedents, since during the 19th century there were numerous prisons in the U.S. that were leased out in their entirety to commercial companies (Sellin, 1976; Ayers, 1984; Carleton, 1971; Cody and Bennett, 1987; Walker, 1988).

The involvement of corporations in the privatization of prisons was undoubtedly propelled by the immense amount of money spent on corrections in Western Societies, especially in the United States. There exists today, according to Lilly (1991) an international "correctional industry" which remains to be studied. The present paper reviews some of the major issues involved in the private management of entire correctional facilities with a special emphasis on the corporate context of this trend and the possible ramifications of it for corrections.

Privatization of Correctional Facilities: Theoretical Premises

The current interest in the privatization of entire prisons for profit stems from several interrelated sources: First, the Reagan and Thatcher administrations favored private involvement in the management of social and public services which until recently were considered to be the exclusive domain of the public sector.[1] This trend was influenced by libertarian arguments and reflected a basic distrust of the state and of "big" government and a conviction that the private sector would be more efficient than government agencies in providing public services. Second, the unprecedented growth in prison population during the 1980s, due to the "get tough" criminal justice policies that emphasize retribution, deterrence, and incapacitation, rather than rehabilitation. Third, the public inability and reluctance to pay the increased cost of corrections involved with the overcrowding of prisons. In this trend it was very tempting to launch an attempt to divest the state of the "expensive crime-control functions by allowing private enterprise to process deviant populations for profit" (Cohen, 1985:63). Fourth, the slow bureaucratic process of siting and building of new government-run correctional facilities. Fifth, the generally accepted perception that existing public prisons are mismanaged and prison conditions are so bad that no change can worsen the prevailing situation.

As mentioned, there is an increasing trend toward using private providers for the provision of various public services. Many consider the private sector to be more efficient because it is driven by the profit motive, thus it has an incentive to do better, it is more flexible and less encumbered by restrictions than the public sector. Therefore, it is suggested that the private sector will provide public services cheaper and better than public agencies do, and it will be more flexible to add services or to answer new demands (e.g., Savas, 1982).

On the ideological level, the privatization trend is greatly influenced by the neoclassical economic theory promoted by the "public choice" approach. It claims that "the competitive marketplace produces goods and services efficiently, whereas monopolies, whether public or private, tend toward both inefficiency and unresponsiveness" (De Hoog, 1984:4). Basic to this argument are the principles of classical economy focusing on the free enterprise system, free competition, and profit maximization. According to the classical approach, "'profit-and-loss' incentives are superior to bureaucratic, or 'budget-based', incentives in the delivery of public services; the quest for profit makes private operators efficient" (Weiss, 1989:31). Profit seeking, following the classical-liberal model, should take place through free competition, which will lead to maximum productivity. The best way to achieve this is by reducing state intervention into the economic marketplace. This principle is the cornerstone of the laissez-faire socioeconomic theory.

The Reagan administration followed this philosophy by easing regulations and by abolishing government regulatory agencies or severely diminishing their activities and effectiveness (e.g. Calavita, 1983). Critics of these policies claim that regulations provide protection against the avarice of the marketplace and that deregulation played down the importance of protecting the public (Tolchin and Tolchin, 1983). To a large degree it brought back the "caveat emptor" philosophy as a driving force of American economy. In several deregulated industries the free competition is eroding because of mergers and bankruptcies (see Dempsey, 1991). In the case of private correctional institutions, one of the major questions is to what degree the free competition model applies?

Theoretically, economic competition is considered to work for the general social good. It is assumed that customers shop around and choose needed merchandise or services according to their best judgment and interest. However, in corrections there are some problems in applying this economic model. First, in corrections and in other human service organizations for profit into which government agencies place clients, the customers (the government agencies which pay for the services) are not identical with the people who are the direct recipients of the services. Client relationship assumes a long-term, mutually dependent interaction between the provider of a service and the recipient of it, while a customer relationship is based on economic exchange of money for goods and services (Parsons, 1970). Besides that, there is another client relationship (dependence) between the service recipients and the government agency which is paying for the services. Thus, in the case of prisons, immates have a more complex web of relationships in which they are dependent on the government agency, the official representative of the entity which has the legal authority to punish and the "hired hand" company which executes the punishment. In this web of relationships, recipients of services do not have the same direct control over services as the customers have; they cannot pick and choose, "take it or leave it." It is problematic to establish the nature of relations in this triad: who is responsible for what, who handles complaints, who evaluates the services and on what basis, who makes final decisions regarding institutional conditions, who is monitoring and "judging" inmate behavior?

Another question in this vein is: Whose interest should be the determining one regarding the nature, the quality, and the cost of the services? Garsombke and Garsombke (1987) make the distinction between "customers" who pay for the services and "users" who receive the services and show the complexities of this relationship in public services provided by private for-profit corporations. The needs and wants of these two groups do not always coincide. In the case of private prisons, this problem is even more pointed because the "users" are usually politically, economically and socially powerless, stigmatized, and unwanted people. In this conjunction, Jayewardene and Talbot (1983:184) state that: "One of the main problems that must be faced in a situation where services are rendered by one party to a second party with payment made by a third party is the fraud that the system can generate." For instance, doctors often submit bills to Medicare, or other government programs, for services that they did not provide for patients on these programs (e.g., Pontell et al., 1982). Private correctional companies may be tempted to overcharge the government for services not rendered, or rendered through unqualified personnel.[2] In this case, there is an organizational blurring of the "cui bono"—who benefits[3]—principle, since the primary beneficiaries are the owners and managers of the organization ("business concerns") rather than the clients ("service organizations") or the public-at-large ("commonwealth organizations") as is the case, at least in theory, in public prisons (Blau and Scott, 1962).

Second, as implied, inmates are not free to seek out the "best" services, products and deals for themselves, and they cannot change facilities if they are not satisfied with the one into which they are placed (e.g., Palumbo, 1986). According to Hasenfeld and English (1974:468), in human service organizations clients ". . . potentially have little or no control over their fate in the organization. This is particularly the case whenever the client is involuntarily committed to the organization." Thus, the free-market model of private corrections seems to be overstated. If any "shopping around" would occur it would be done by the customer (government) rather than by the users (inmates). If that would occur, it is likely that the major concern would be cost, rather than quality of services, since in the case of businesses "the ultimate profit is the bottom line. There are no exceptions, for business does nothing unless it can see some benefit for itself or its investors" (Carroll and Easton, 1987:20).

Third is the issue of the profit motive. The major motivation of private corporations, according to the classical model, is the maximization of profit (e.g. Garsombke and Garsombke, 1987). Although there are claims that corporations seek a "satisfactory" level of profits rather than "maximization" of profits (e.g., Stone, 1975) the definition of what is satisfactory remains in the hands of the management of corporations vis à vis the shareholders. Since organizations are formally rational, the congruence between their procedures and their substantive goals is closer than that of most other social groups (Sutton and Wild, 1978). This means that profit-making can be rigorously and systematically pursued by private corporations.

The introduction of the principle of profit-making to corrections is controversial. Advocates of privatization point out that nothing is wrong with having this motive in corrections. They argue that in the application of punishment the motivation of those who apply is not relevant; the important thing is that the criminal procedure will follow due process requirements, and that the sentence will be meted out "for the right reasons" (Logan, 1987:38). Second, it is maintained that profit motives already exist in the punishment process because prison officials and employees earn their livelihood from the penal system. Following this argument, the profit motive in corrections is universal; thus objecting to the "profit motive" in the private sector alone is discriminatory and prejudicial (Logan, 1990). However, some critics categorically object to the idea that profit should be pursued through the deliberate imposition of suffering on other people. It can also be argued that to work for a salary as a prison employee is not exactly the same profit motive as that of the management of a corporation (Rutherford, 1990) that has to produce a profit for its stockholders and can increase personal benefits by increasing the income and/or decreasing costs. Ryan and Ward (1989:61) claim in this regard that ". . . to equate these wage earners with those who wish to exploit the penal system for corporate gain is quite simply wrong. . . ." They continue their statement using Marxist concepts to counter the above pro-privatization argument by pointing out that: "it fails to make the obvious distinction between those who sell their labor and those who own and control capital." As implied earlier, the privatization of prisons is a part of the conservative agenda. It is ideologically justified by libertarian principles according to which the state should be ultimately dispensed with or there should be "a 'minimal' state in which political coercion is strictly confined to the task of protecting property and enforcing contracts" (Hoffman, 1988). In this kind of state private organizations are supposed to fulfill most of the government functions including punishment. Paradoxically, Feeley (1991:5) in his historical analysis of the privatization of prisons demonstrated that ". . . the reliance on private contractors facilitated the expansion of the capacity of the criminal justice system. . . ." Thus, instead of reducing the state's coercive power, privatization of prisons helped to expand it.

Issues of Organizational Deviance

There are other issues, beyond the moral principle, which are of concern. The centrality of the free competition in the privatization movement was mentioned earlier. Some critics point out that often the pursuit of profit seeking and free competition are conflicting (Conklin, 1977). As known, the profit motive in corporate America became so prevalent that it was often used to justify questionable business practices, especially through the embracement of the "caveat emptor" doctrine (Hamilton, 1931; Shichor, 1989). While, as mentioned, some scholars question the "maximum profit seeking" nature of corporations (e.g., Stone, 1975), it seems that their "paramount objectives" remain maximum profit and financial success (Clinard, 1990).

A corporation can increase its profit and market share by limiting free competition (Conklin, 1977; Vaughan, 1980). Sutherland (1956:90) pointed out that "big business does not like competition, and it makes careful arrangements to reduce it and even eliminate it." Indeed, large corporations tend to engage in various strategies to limit competition in order to reduce uncertainty that can obstruct their goal attainment (Thompson, 1967). In several major industries (e.g., car manufacturing, defense, oil), a handful of large corporations dominate the market (Mills, 1956). Certain kinds of accommodations and market sharing among these companies are likely to develop (Moore, 1962). Thus a symbiosis among corporations rather than a genuine competition becomes a reality (Blau and Scott, 1962). This often leads to unlawful practices such as antitrust violations and price fixing (Geis, 1967). An oligopolic trend among private firms contracting in corrections was found by Camp and Camp (1985), who reported that a few companies account for a large portion of private contracting.

In an emerging field of enterprise, such as the private management of correctional facilities, the oligopolic trend issue is even more critical, because a few dominant corporations can have a strong influence in setting standards for the evolving marketplace, a fact which may have far-reaching consequences.[4]

The pursuance of profit has other ramifications as well. Corporations, by setting performance standards often tied to income goals, can "indirectly initiate deviant actions by establishing particular norms, rewards, and punishments for people occupying lower-level positions" (Ermann and Lundman, 1982:7). Executives frequently realize that the violation of laws, regulations, or norms are the shortest way for higher profits, and such violations can be mandated through policy directives to lower echelon workers and mid-level managers (Meyer, 1972). The corporate culture often generates a crimogenic atmosphere which in a private correctional institution may influence lower echelon employees (guards) who are usually underpaid, have few opportunities to advance, and lack job security. Those who want to keep their jobs and advance in the corporation may feel a pressure to follow deviant practices to further organizational goals (e.g., cut corners to increase profits, write reports that are favorable for the prison, etc.) or not to report violations of procedures or inmates' rights. Clinard (1983) found that financially oriented top executives, as opposed to the professionally oriented ones, were primarily concerned with short-term profits and were more inclined to resort to deviance. Because most corporations have shareholders seeking short-term profits and there is a trend in American business to place financial experts in top management positions, there is considerable possibility of the emergence of an organizational climate in the private correctional industry which may be conducive to follow certain deviant practices.

Legal Issues

A central question of privatization is to what degree will a balance be maintained between the corporate economic concerns on the one hand, and accountability for the correctional services rendered and for the maintenance of human rights of the clientele on the other (Bozeman, 1988). Several students of privatization have raised this issue, pointing out, among other things, that

> the public and private sectors have distinctive characters and that these distinctions are premised on legal principles, not economic or social science theories . . . the public sector is being profoundly altered, and ultimately harmed by the deliberate blurring of these public and private characteristics (Moe, 1988:674).

One of the major problems with the diminishing public and private distinction is that the government delegates some of its powers and functions to a party whose legitimacy is not always clear (Moe, 1988).

Another important issue having legal ramifications is involved in economic strategies for revamping corporations to make them more profitable. During the 1980s there was an unprecedented trend for corporate takeovers (friendly and hostile), "reorganizations" resulting in the "spinning off" of companies and divisions from a corporation which was losing money or making less profit than anticipated. It is a major question how the government's reliance on private prison management would fare in this kind of situation. What are the legal guarantees to the government if a correctional corporation is bought out or sold out by its parent company? What happens if a corporation is taken over by a foreign company, a situation which occurs quite frequently? Is it acceptable that a foreign corporation will handle American prisoners and will make profit on it?

Furthermore, what would happen if a private prison corporation would declare bankruptcy? What would be the legal obligations of the government vis à vis the creditors of the prison corporation (American Bar Association, 1986)? How would it affect the legal and other obligations of the private corporations themselves toward the government, and how would it affect the government agencies? How will it be ensured that the prison will continue to operate? Holley (1988) deals with the legal complexities of this problem, but the potential operational complexities are even greater, e.g., who will step in to continue the operations of a facility.

The problematic nature of this issue should be seen in light of the complexities[5] of corporate bankruptcies which can be used as business strategies, such as the alteration of bargaining positions, renegotiation of debts and contracts, stalling for time, and shifting the financial risk to other parties (Delaney, 1990) not to mention the increasing number of fraudulent bankruptcies. Many corporations become dependent on financial institutions which control their capital flow (Glasberg, 1981). Most businesses raise their money for the start up from these institutions. They also need financial institutions in the case of expansion, mergers, takeovers, or in other occasions when they get into a difficult economic situation. Banks, because of their lending power often are able to gain a seat on the recipients' board of directors. Also they are usually the major holders of bonds which are longer-term loans. In the case of bankruptcy of a company, bondholders' claims have a precedence over stockholders' claims (Glasberg, 1989). Thus other corporate entities, which do not have any experience in prison management and do not have a direct contract with the government, may become involved in the running of a private facility. This underlines the potentially strong influence and interest of financial institutions in the privatization of prisons even though they do not get involved in the hands on management of the facility.

As an example, we can mention the E.F. Hutton brokerage company which intended to move into the private prison business during the early 1980s. Later, this firm was found to be involved in illegally using its clients' money without interest through check kiting and it had to pay two million dollars in fines. Shortly after, Hutton merged with Shearson and Lehman, which owns American Express. These possibilities underline the problem of stability and continuity of private enterprise in the correctional business, a field in which it is not likely that many corporations will be available to step in and take over companies that get into financial or legal troubles.

Robbins (1986; 1989), a student of the legal aspects of correctional privatization, shows that privatization will not reduce government liability for the handling of prisoners. For instance, under 42 U.S.C. Sec. 1983, the government will be liable for any civil rights violations against inmates in a private prison (Thomas and Hanson, 1989; Pellicciotti, 1987). A major problem will be the inability to use the sovereign-immunity defense in a civil rights violation lawsuit (Robbins, 1989). Several writers mention that this problem should be dealt with by making certain that the private corporation carries a high liability insurance contract (e.g., Thomas, 1987; Robbins, 1989). In third party suits against the government ("deep pocket"), when privately operated correctional institutions are sued for civil rights violations, government agencies will have less control to avoid such cases than they had before when the prisons were run by public agencies.

Monitoring Correctional Corporations and Evaluating Performance

The previous deliberation leads to the issue of the monitoring and regulation of the private prison "industry." This is important because "corporations have become powerful, autonomous institutions, largely independent of external influence of control" (Mizruchi, 1982:15).

Several scholars have pointed out that often the cost of monitoring is not calculated into the economic analysis of prison privatization (e.g., Gentry,

1986). To maintain meaningful supervision over private corporations delivering human services, especially in corrections, a rigorous monitoring mechanism has to be established. The extra expenses involved with monitoring will influence the cost effectiveness of private prisons. However, McDonald (1990) estimates the monitoring cost only to be about one percent of the total contract. Oversight must be especially rigorous, since as seen, the usual control mechanism of the free marketplace, exercised by customers and clients, may have only a limited role in the prison business. A clearly written and detailed contract is a key element in the success of correctional privatization (e.g., Woolley, 1985; Mullen, 1985; McAfee, 1987). Effective monitoring mechanisms are needed to determine whether the contractor meets the standards laid down in the contract (Keating, 1990).

A related issue is that it is hard to evaluate correctional performance. If we accept that the prison, which is a total institution (Goffman, 1961) based on coercive compliance (Etzioni, 1961), has only one major task (e.g., incapacitation—locking people away to protect society), then probably measuring effectiveness is manageable. But currently, even with the decline of the ideal of rehabilitation, we expect the attainment of multiple goals by the prison (Cressey, 1965) which makes evaluation much more complex. Also, since for-profit private correctional institutions run by corporations are relatively new, there is very little collected data available that could serve as evaluative benchmarks. Similarly, there may be some reluctance from the management and staff to fully cooperate with the researchers (Durham, 1988), although Roberts and Powers (1985) claim that the evaluation of private prisons is not much different from that of other prisons. Nevertheless, there is a lack of adequate evaluation of the performance of private prisons (Durham, 1989).

Close monitoring may raise similar problems as the regulation of private industry does. Regulations, as mentioned, are vigorously objected to by the proponents of laissez-faire economy who claim that it distorts the meaning of a free marketplace. While contract monitoring and legal regulations are not the same, some of their problems are similar. One concern is the "revolving door" syndrome. There are privatized correctional institutions (prisons, detention camps, facilities for parole violators) in which State officials monitor the operations, but at the same time a job is waiting for them at the corporation that runs the facility upon their retirement.[6]

The experience of government agencies with private contractors indicates that even when contracts are clearly written, there are problems with securing adherence to them. Critics of privatization of human services or, as some refer to them, "soft services . . . performed for or on people" (Nelson 1980:431) point out that standards set for regulations are being reduced by the (for profit) propriety lobby.[7]

Private corporations contracting with government agencies often know from the beginning that there is a good chance that they will not be able to deliver the promised product or services for the price indicated in their bid. They bank on the dependency of the government agency on their services that is going to make it hard to terminate a contract (e.g., Keating, 1990). Thus, not only is the way the contract is written important, but also that there will be alternative private prison companies available. Ring (1987:25) underscores this problem in the following:

> Cost will increase, according to opponents, because private operators will engage in low-balling: intentionally underestimating costs in their initial bids in the hope that the government will become dependent upon their services over time. Once this occurs, the contractor will raise his fees or allow conditions to deteriorate, gambling that the government will accept the charges rather than risk losing his services.

Contract violations by companies dealing with the government is a common occurrence; various types of violations in the defense industry are well documented (e.g., Goodwin, 1985; Glazer and Glazer, 1989). For example, Northrop Corporation in 1990 pleaded guilty to 34 criminal fraud charges and was fined 17 million dollars; 141 other charges were dropped in a plea bargain agreement. One of the main charges was the falsification of tests on the components for nuclear-armed cruise missiles (Weinstein, 1990). It can be assumed that if in the field of national defense, a major concern of government, there are serious corporate violations, then in the provision of human services, which have a politically powerless and socially neglected clientele, the likelihood of corporate violations will be greater. Thus, the rational nature of organizations, which is harnessed to achieve profits, opens ample opportunities for corporate violations, especially in the case of human services provided for undesired populations. The legal enforcement of the contract and the provision of proof that there was an intent to deceive the government is also a complex drawn-out process requiring time and allocation of resources (e.g., Goodwin, 1985).

Another contention by critics is that many companies prefer contracts which detail only the most essential services that will be provided; anything beyond that will become an "extra" service, charged for separately, or the contract will have to be renegotiated for a higher price.

The corporation's risk of being penalized for contract violations is minimized by factors such as (1) reduced competition, since only a few companies are active in a limited market; (2) the lack of state ability to take over the facilities; (3) lack of adequate monitoring;[8] (4) the lack of deterrent effect, since penalties assessed against corporations are usually fines that are far below the gains derived from illegal activities or from regulation violations (e.g., Fisse, 1985; Stone, 1975); (5) the shielding of top decision-makers from individual criminal liability: since the decision-making in corporations is diffused, there is an opportunity to abdicate personal responsibility (Clinard and Yeager, 1980; Kramer, 1982); (6) corporations have access to expert legal services[9] and, if there is a court case, they often have more resources to outlast government prosecutors, as the well-known Pinto case demonstrated (Cullen et al., 1987).

This discussion indicates that it is feasible that under certain conditions private corporations contracted to serve government's functions may have an incentive to carry out their state's function imperfectly since their major concern is to serve their own interest (Gentry, 1986).

Political Influence

Another relevant issue concerns the political influence of corporations moving into the prison business. Large corporate interests often organize in political action committees (PACs) through which they can make substantial contributions to political candidates. Those contributions are given, even so that it is often denied, with the intent to influence legislation favorable to the PACs' interests. It is feasible that corporations involved in corrections for profit will form their own PACs and organize other lobbying efforts. The development of PACs in the U.S. during the 1970s and 1980s has demonstrated the growing political and social influence of corporations in America. A major aim of this political involvement has been the neutralization of "government regulation of business practices and to obtain government assistance for business activities" (Ryan et al., 1987:105). PACs are well organized and are using the most modern management skills to raise money and the latest computer methods to evaluate political candidates' standings on issues of interest to them (Fraser/Associates, 1980). Political activity of corporations that operate prisons may be very rigorous since it is suggested that those companies which are more dependent on the government for the sale of their products or services display more intense political activity than corporations which depend less on government contracts (Jacobs et al., 1991).

Conceivably, private correction PACs will seek to influence issues that are of importance to the industry. At the same time, they also may collaborate with other PACs to form a political force in contributing to "candidates whose ideology is perceived as compatible with free enterprise values and business positions on public policy issues" (Ryan et al., 1987:119). As Kamerman and Kahn (1989) note, privatization is basically a political act aimed at diminishing the social role of government.

These features of corporate political activity should be seen in light of the fact that there are no comparable PACs or lobbying organizations dedicated for the sole purpose of representing the inmates. The ACLU and other civil rights organizations which often take up the interests of inmates are not geared to put all their efforts and resources into this one issue. Prisoners constitute a "throw away" population which is ignored by most "decent" people. While there is lately more emphasis on the formal legal rights of prisoners (Alpert, 1980), they are not able to command a widespread public concern for their interests. Basically, "prisoners are declasse, they are the outcasts of society, exercising virtually no suasion upon public policy" (Geis, 1987:78). They cannot even vote, and there should be a continuous concern that privatization may have a negative impact on their rights (Sullivan, 1989).

Regarding the public's concern with the handling of convicts, Donahue (1988:21) comments that:

> One might legitimately wonder whether a public that has refused to put up the resources to bring public prisons up to minimal standards will resist the temptation to turn a blind eye on the conditions of confinement in bargain-rate private prisons.

Thus, there may not be a balance between the corporate private prison lobby's influence and organizations that are likely to be concerned with prisoners' rights.

Management Issues

The privatization trend is based on the belief that innovations and flexibility to attack problems will come only from private initiatives (Greenwood, 1981; McConville, 1987). There is a great emphasis on the importance of effective management. In this regard, DiIulio (1988:75) states:

> Most claims that private corrections firms can outperform public corrections agencies rest on two assumptions. The first is that there are significant differences between public and private management, that business firms are necessarily more "efficient," "effective," and "innovative" than government agencies, and that these advantages of private management are universal: they obtain whether the task is picking up garbage or locking up prisoners. The second assumption is that the public sector's administrative experience in corrections has been an unmitigated disaster: prisons and jails have been, and continue to be, horrible places that are horribly run.

Several works underline the crucial role of executive leadership in correctional institutions (e.g., Street et al., 1966; Morris, 1974; Jacobs, 1977; DiIulio, 1988, 1990). This role includes the setting of specific goals and policies for the institution, the maintenance of communication with the outside community, and the definition of roles and responsibilities inside the organization.

One of the interesting features of corporations which manage private prisons is that, among the managers they employ, former administrators of state departments of corrections and prisons are prominent. Some of these managers had legal and disciplinary problems during their tenure in public institutions (Becker and Stanley, 1985; McShane and Williams, 1989). The question is how these administrators, some of whom did not show much creativity and efficiency in the public sector, will be able to run a new, more effective private correctional institution. They will have to perform under different circumstances than before. In the private corporate sector "profit, not morality, is the ultimate test of effectiveness" (Clinard and Yeager, 1980:273). Their performance, corporate status, and monetary compensation will be determined mainly on the basis of the economic balance sheet of the corporation.

Research on corporations indicates that managers can be pressured by profit standards set too high to resort to questionable, sometimes even illegal practices to attain these goals (Clinard and Yeager, 1980). Similarly, corporate crime literature suggests that executives have a special responsibility for setting the tone of corporate cultures including the readiness to violate rules (Braithwaite, 1989).

DiIulio (1988) points out that the quality of life in prisons and jails depends mainly on the quality of management. Thus the issue of management of private prisons is an area which has to be a major concern for policy makers and for everyone who has a genuine interest in corrections.

There are some additional factors that raise concern regarding corporate managers of private institutions. Managers in corporations seem to have a very wide range of discretion; in effect, they have more actual power than the legal owners, the shareholders have (e.g., Ermann and Lundman, 1982). Therefore, they may be freer to resort to unethical or deviant practices to manage the institution. As Clinard (1983) has shown, corporate managers with financial backgrounds more readily "cut corners" to achieve performance goals than technologically oriented managers. Also, corporations tend to "shield" their top managers from personal liability by delegation of responsibility to various departments and middle-range managers (e.g., Braithwaite, 1989; Conklin, 1977; Vaughan, 1980) who are judged by how close they come to their set target of profits (Gross, 1980). The risk of penalty for corporate executives who violate rules is relatively minor (Clinard and Yeager, 1980), a fact which may mitigate the preventive effect of deterrence which otherwise may well be strong with corporate crime because of its national nature (Braithwaite and Geis, 1982).

Labor Related Issues

One of the controversies regarding the privatization of prisons is related to the labor force in these institutions. Several issues recur: (a) the quality of the work force; (b) labor relations; (c) the authority of the officers in a private prison.

Corrections is a labor intensive industry; between 60–80 percent of the correctional cost is labor related (Donahue, 1988; McDonald, 1990). As seen, private corporations claim that they can deliver the same or better correctional services at a lower cost than the government does. This implies that they will be able to reduce their labor cost, which can be achieved in several ways: (1) cutting salaries or the pay scale of employees, (2) providing less or no fringe benefits and pension funds, (3) economizing on the screening procedures, (4) hiring fewer employees, (5) providing less training, (6) combination of any of the above.

Paying lower salaries to correctional employees, whose income is not considered to be very lucrative to begin with, may result in the reduction of the quality of lower echelon employees in private prisons. Private prison guards usually come from the unskilled labor force, many of them working only part-time (Weiss, 1989). Referring to private security guards as one likely pool for private prison employees, Donahue (1988) indicates that public employees are more likely to be high school graduates, full-time workers, and to be in the prime working age than the pool of private security employees. A lower-paid labor force usually means a lower-quality labor force. Schuman (1989) found an unusually high staff turnover in privately run correctional facilities. Many staff members eventually applied for the better paid and more secure public sector positions. High turnover rate may influence the quality of services because of lack of stability in the institutions. A similar situation occurs in the private police organizations. Often individuals who, for various reasons, are not hired as law enforcement agents get jobs as private police officers. Generally, private security companies have a high turnover rate. Relying on information from the 1970s, Lipson (1975) concludes that private security firms did not have minimum standards for physical or mental fitness or for educational or literacy levels. Similarly, the job training of the officers was minimal. South (1988) indicates similar trends in the British private security industry. He points to low wages, low standards, little training, and high turnover in this industry. He also found that private security companies try to cut corners in their contract in order to be able to make profit.

Dissatisfaction with low pay and difficult working conditions may lead to many employee strikes in private prisons if and when employees unionize (although private correctional companies make every effort not to employ unionized workers and not to let their workforce unionize). There also may be employee refusal to work with certain kinds of inmates (e.g., AIDS patients). As Novey (1985:8) points out: "Being in the private sector, employees will have the legal right to organize a union and conduct slow downs with potential strikes as an end result." If this problem arises government authorities may have to intervene by manning the facility until the strike is over or the correctional corporation is able to hire strike breakers, who probably will be less qualified than the striking workers, and because of the emergency situation will not have even the minimal training that the permanent officers had. If the correctional officers in private prisons will not be able to unionize, which is clearly an aim of the corporations, the question will be raised whether the government should work with companies that make their profits because their workers do not have civil service and union protections. Some critics of privatization of prisons refer to these practices as a form of union-busting (e.g., Geis, 1987). On the other hand, avid supporters of privatization go out of their way to attack public workers' unions by accusing them of involvement in various kinds of corruption (see Logan, 1990). Any problems emanating from the labor disputes, such as labor violence or mishandling of inmates by inexperienced personnel, still will be the government's liability.

Punishment is a public function supposedly executed by government authorities. The question is how much authority can be delegated to the staff in a private facility who are hired to fulfill the public function of executing punishment. The interaction between correctional staff and inmates in a private facility often affects the extent and nature of punishment. A disciplinary write up by a private correctional officer may cause the loss of "good time" or may have other punishment consequences.

One of the questions in this regard is whether a private corporation should be involved in the adjudication of disciplinary charges. The issue is that the maintenance of discipline is an integral part of management of a correctional facility. Punishment of inmates is a part of this task. Even if the final judgment of a disciplinary case were determined by an officer of the State Department of Corrections, the disciplinary write-up would be done by private employees and the investigation might be seriously influenced by them (Press, 1990). Besides, to fulfill the disciplinary function itself will cost money for the Department of Corrections, an expense which will have to be calculated into the cost of private corrections. Disciplinary practices have a direct influence on the duration of the stay of a prisoner in the facility and may have other direct punitive implications, such as spending time in segregation cells and losing various privileges. This means that the government function of punishment is contracted away (Elvin, 1985) and introduces a private discretionary element into the system.

Direct or indirect influence by corporate staff on the length of stay of inmates has economic implications as well; it may result in more expanded periods of incarceration, thus it can contribute to the occupancy level of the facility, which is a major corporate concern when per-diem payment is involved. In the current situation when an overabundance of convicts is the case, this does not seem to be a problem; presently the replacement of released inmates is secured (Logan, 1990). However, when far-reaching, long-term policies are contemplated, such factors have to be taken into consideration. There are also indications that the "flow" of new inmates is slowing down (Hurst, 1991).

Economic Issues

The major argument for privatization is economic. It is said to save money. So far, available assessments of the economic results of privatization of correctional management tends to be favorable. Most reports indicate real or potential savings by private correctional facilities (e.g., Sellers, 1989; Logan and Rausch, 1985; Camp and Camp, 1985; Logan and McGriff, 1989; Mc-Donald, 1990); others report no substantial difference in cost between private and public institutions (e.g., Urban Institute, 1989; Levinson, 1985). McDonald (1990) in a detailed analysis of the various problems entailed in trying to entangle the most correct ways of cost comparison did not come to a clear conclusion in establishing whether private corrections is cheaper than public corrections, although he lent some support to the claims of the proponents of privatization.

Several hidden and not so hidden problems exist concerning the cost of private corrections. One of the controversial issues is the "marginal cost" of institutionalization (McDonald, 1989). Almost all private corporations that manage correctional facilities are paid on a per-diem per capita basis. While at a certain capacity level a private prison can cost less per inmate, increasing population may decrease the expenses in a public institution vis à vis a private facility "because so many of the costs of imprisonment are relatively fixed, the cost of adding additional prisoners is actually much less than the average cost per prisoner in a facility" (McDonald, 1989:20). In this respect, publicly managed institutions can be more flexible in handling a growing inmate population without increasing substantially the cost, while in private prisons each new prisoner will add to the budget an equal amount. On the other hand, this feature of public facilities may contribute to the increased number of prison sentences and to prison overcrowding.

There are additional issues that may have economic implications. One of them concerns the possible dependence of government agencies on private corporations after the initial contract is in effect. It is likely that competition will be limited in the prison industry, since the only customers are government agencies and, therefore, only a few companies will compete for contracts. The latest private facility census conducted by Thomas and Foard (1991) found 14 private companies operating 44 facilities. Two companies, CCA (14) and Wackenhut (8) operate 22 (50 percent) of the facilities, handling 56.6 percent (7,559) of the total number of inmates (13,348) in private facilities. This can result in a situation in which criminal justice agencies will be at the mercy of a few corporations, which may try and succeed to raise prices, lower standards, and violate some contract clauses. In addition, when the current contract expires and a new one is negotiated, the bargaining position of the government may become weaker because of its growing reliance on private corporations, the lack of competition, the lack of alternative public facilities, and the lack of available management and staff personnel. Thus the option of reopening government institutions or reorganizing private facilities by government agencies would not be an easy one to take. Also, to change private contractors may be problematic because the changeover from one company to another having different policies, management styles, staffing practices, etc., may cause disruptions and disturbances.

It is reasonable to assume that private corporations, by using their political influence and public relation abilities, will be able to push legislation for longer prison sentences, thus making sure that their "occupancy rate" will be at the maximum. In that way, they also may impact penal policies in favor of extension of incarceration and away from alternatives to imprisonment (Anderson et al., 1985).[10] Government agencies usually have to guarantee a certain level of occupation rate, below which the per diem rate goes up in order to reimburse the contractors for their investments and for their income loss. Thus, there is a built in incentive to continue a high level of incarceration rate (State of California, 1985). Therefore, if government becomes dependent on private corporations for incarceration, it will either be compelled to keep people imprisoned who otherwise would be released, or will have to agree to price adjustments. Common sense would suggest that government agencies will keep the prison population at a certain level rather than pay the same sum of money for the incarceration of fewer inmates.

Borna (1986) mentions the hidden cost of the interest payments and tax breaks which would come out of taxpayers' money and would go to private developers or finance corporations and their investors involved in the construction of private prisons. Private corporations also use consultants for various services (e.g., drawing up the lease agreements). Consulting costs are included in the lease payments. In addition, facility and equipment depreciations will be reimbursed. The government also reimburses corporations for changes in variable interest rates if they are used for the construction or other financing of a facility.

Another issue connected with the hidden cost of private corrections is that private corporations would still rely on certain public services, especially in the case of emergencies such as prison riots, public health problems, employee strikes, and bankruptcy (Bowditch and Everett, 1987). The cost of these services cannot be estimated currently because of the lack of benchmark data.

Conclusions

This paper has reviewed some of the major issues concerning the privatization of management of correctional facilities with special attention to the corporate nature of the private providers. In this analysis certain problems are general to corrections but exacerbated by the corporate involvement; others are unique to the corporate context of private corrections.

The corporate involvement in correctional privatization amplifies the political influence of the private sector upon correctional public policy-making. Through political lobbying, PACs, and campaign contributions, corporations are likely to continue and even to accelerate incapacitation oriented policies by which more people spend longer periods of time in correctional institutions. Conversely, this trend will diminish the emphasis on alternative programs that emphasize rehabilitation and will result in the pursuance of the "Hilton Inn mentality," i.e., trying to maintain high occupancy rates for profit purposes.

There is also a concern that by using their political influence, corporations will be able to "cream the crop," meaning that they will be able either to deal with inmates classified as lower security risks—which allows the institution to hire fewer custody personnel and operate without major disturbances avoiding adverse public reaction, or to manage institutions with specified clientele (e.g., drug addicts), since higher profits can be made when "specific" or "professional" services are provided. In this situation, the most violent inmates and career criminals would have to be handled by the public institutions while the private corporations could demonstrate a better performance record, working with less hard core offenders, on top of their higher profits.

The issue of profit-making in human services in general and in corrections in particular is a controversial one. Is it proper to make profits by causing deliberate suffering to others? Profit-making will be rationally and systematically pursued by a corporation which will have to show profits to its investors. Some of the profit-making rigor may lead to unethical or even illegal practices. Even so that contracts will be carefully written, they will be closely scrutinized by the legal departments of the corporations to minimize corporate risks. Rigorous monitoring of compliance with the contract will cost extra money for the government; these costs are often not calculated fully into the budget. Since only a limited number of corporations will offer complete facility management services, the government may have a difficult time replacing companies which do not abide by the contracts and/or will not perform according to the expectations. Meanwhile, government agencies may lose their organizational structure and resources to take over management. This can be a major problem with the increased number of corporate bankruptcies, mergers, takeovers, and "spin-offs."

There may be problems with waging legal cases against private corporations since they can afford high quality legal defense and their resources for long-term litigations may be greater than those of local governments. Also the risk of penalties for corporate wrong-doings is minimized since usually the corporations are punished rather than the corporate decision makers. In general, punishments are monetary and not substantial. Because of the uniqueness of the "correctional marketplace," adverse publicity, which is suggested as an option for corporate punishment (e.g., Fisse, 1985), will be minimized as a deterrent.

The fact that corporations often violate legal or at least moral and ethical codes is underscored by the extensive scholarly literature on corporate ethics (e.g., Donaldson, 1982; Bradshaw and Vogel, 1981; Anderson, 1989). Thus it is recognized that large corporations often do not act according to the highest moral standards or the law. This can be particularly disturbing in the case of human services provided to groups that are politically powerless and do not attract much public interest and support. Robbins (1989: 542) expresses this concern by stating: "privatization is not a panacea; the private sector is more interested in doing well than in doing good."

The credibility of corporations became particularly shaky during the 1980s and early 1990s during the savings and loans crisis, with the bankruptcy of large insurance companies and with the revelation of constant overcharging of government agencies, cost overruns on government contracts and corruption of inspectors. And as Sagarin and Maghan (1985:E4) pointed out concerning E.F. Hutton's intent to enter into the private prison business: "It is only an added irony that E.F. Hutton itself became involved in one of the largest white collar frauds in American history. Is this the company to which we are going to turn over the prisons?"

Involvement of corporations in the private management of correctional facilities is often held out as a panacea, or at least a major step forward and a way out of the shameful conditions that generally mark the operation of correctional facilities today. This opinion is buttressed by some scholarly works with conservative leanings that in the current political context are appealing. But, as this paper implies, in many instances the privatization of corrections may further aggravate an already malignant condition. It seems that a revamping and upgrading of the public prisons could be an alternative venue in corrections which would eliminate at least the problem of private "greed" from the administration of punishment. One core problem of corrections seems to be that the government does not fulfill sufficiently its "duty to govern" (DiIulio, 1990).

Keeping governmental inefficiency and negligence in the management of correctional institutions in mind, Wecht's concern should be taken seriously: "While state prison authorities may be inept or worse, they lack the incentives to raise prices and reduce quality which characterize a for-profit firm" (Wecht, 1987:829). This situation may become more a reality after the initial "honeymoon" period—in which the private corporation will make efforts to live up to all standards and to perform exceptionally—will be over (Wecht, 1987).

Notes

1. For British sources, see Papadakis and Taylor-Gosby (1987), Riddel (1989), Ryan and Ward (1989), etc. In Britain the government policies toward privatized institutions are not very clear. While ideologically the conservative government supports privatization of corrections in 1989 the plan to establish private jails was abandoned (Cowdry, 1989). On the other hand, the Home Office Secretary Kenneth Baker announced on the 5th of December, 1991, that half of Britain's prisons are to be privatized (Daily Mail, 1991). Also there is an interest in privately managed prisons in Australia and the Correctional Corporation of America has opened a facility with Australian partners in Queensland.

2. In their study of placements of juveniles in public and private institutions, Shichor and Bartollas (1990) found that a number of private institutions that were supposedly providing psychological treatment for juveniles (and charging the county accordingly) did not have the fully qualified staff, and/or did not have the professionals on the premises for the required number of hours per day.

3. Blau and Scott (1962:43) suggest using this principle in organizational analysis. According to this scheme, four types of organizations can be distinguished: (1) "mutual benefit associations," where the prime beneficiary is the membership, (2) "business concerns," where the owners are the prime beneficiary; (3) "service organizations," where the client group is the prime beneficiary; and (4) "commonwealth organizations," where the prime beneficiary is the public-at-large.

4. The tendency for reduced competition in the privatization of public services other than correction is mentioned by Starr (1987).

5. Some of the problems that government may face in the case of bankruptcy of a private company with which it has contracts are analyzed by Flener (1989).

6. In one case known to the author, the wife of the official responsible for the monitoring was working for the private facility supervised by him while he was getting ready to retire and to assume a position at the same facility. Thus, there has to be more sensitivity to "conflict of interest". This case is only one example and should only be seen as an illustration of an issue.

7. In January 1991 Wackenhut Corrections Corporation, the private contractor of Monroe County jail in Florida broke its contract and returned control of the jail to the Sheriff. The company asked for $2.6 million extra for the four-year contract because it planned to staff the jail with six guards per shift; however, state standards require 11 guards per shift. The corporation claimed that it was unaware of this requirement. The county commissioners accepted Wackenhut's proposal for a settlement that included a $300,000 payment to the company to settle its claims over the staffing issue, utility bills and transportation costs. The county also agreed to pay $206,000 for equipment at the jail that the corporation purchased (Keating, 1991).

8. This may include the purposeful corruption of government inspectors by corporations (Coleman, 1989), and the lack of resources to upgrade monitoring by the inability to train inspectors that would gain high level of expertise (e.g. Lynxwiler et al., 1984).

9. Mann (1985) in his book "Defending White-Collar Crime" describes the strategies and complexities of legal counsel that may go into white collar and corporate law cases and the expertise of these highly paid lawyers.

10. So far, available accounts on private facilities do not indicate such practices (e.g., Brakel, 1988).

References

Adamson, Christopher R., "Punishment after Slavery: Southern State Penal Systems, 1865–1890," *Social Problems,* 1983 (30), 555–569.

Alpert, Geoffrey P., (ed.), *Legal Rights of Prisoners* (Beverly Hills, CA: Sage, 1980).

American Bar Association, *Section of Criminal Justice,* Report to the House of Delegates (Chicago: American Bar Association Division for Communications and Public Affairs, 1986).

Anderson, Jr., Jerry W., *Corporate Social Responsibility* (Westport, CT: Quorum Books, 1989).

Anderson, Patrick, Charles R. Davoli and Laura J. Moriarity, "Private Corrections: Feast or Fiasco?", *The Prison Journal,* 1985 (452), 32–41.

Ayers, Edward L., *Vengeance and Justice: Crime and Punishment in the 19th-Century American South* (New York: Oxford University Press, 1984).

Babington, Anthony, *The English Bastille: A History of Newgate Gaol and Prison Conditions in Britain, 1188–1902* (London: MacDonald, 1971).

Becker, Craig and Amy Dru Stanley, "The Downside of Private Prisons," *The Nation* (June 15, 1985): 728–730.

Blau, Peter M. and W. Richard Scott. *Formal Organizations* (San Francisco: Chandler, 1962).

Borna, Shaheen. "Free Enterprise Goes to Prison," *The British Journal of Criminology* 1986 (26), 321–334.

Bowditch, Christine and Ronald S. Everett, "Private Prisons: Problems within the Solution," *Justice Quarterly* 1987 (3), 441–453.

Bozeman, Barry, "Exploring the Limits of Public and Private Sectors: Sector Boundaries as Maginot Line," *Public Administration Review*, 1988 (March–April): 672–674.

Bradshaw, Thorton and David Vogel (eds.), *Corporations and Their Critics* (New York: McGraw-Hill, 1981).

Braithwaite, John, "Criminological Theory and Organizational Crime," *Justice Quarterly*, 1989(6), 333–358.

Braithwaite, John and Gilbert Geis, "On Theory and Action for Corporate Crime Control," *Crime and Delinquency*, 1982 (28), 292–314.

Brakel, Samuel J., "Prison Management, Private Enterprise Style: The Inmate's Evaluation." *The New England Journal on Criminal and Civil Confinement*, 1988 (14): 175–244.

Calavita, Kitty, "The Demise of the Occupational Safety and Health Administration: A Case Study in Symbolic Action," *Social Problems*, 1983 (30), 437–448.

Camp, Camille and George Camp, "Correctional Privatization in Perspective," *The Prison Journal*, 1985 (45(2)): 14–31.

Carleton, Mark T., *Politics and Punishment* (Baton Rouge, LA: Louisiana University Press, 1971).

Carroll, Barry J., and Thomas A. Easton, "Motivating the Private Sector: What Role for Public Policy," in Barry J. Carroll, Ralph W. Conant, and Thomas A. Easton (eds.), *Private Means—Public Ends: Private Business in Social Service Delivery* (New York: Praeger, 1987).

Clinard, Marshall B., *Corporate Corruption: The Abuse of Power* (New York, NY: Praeger, 1990).

Clinard, Marshall B., *Corporate Ethics and Crime* (Beverly Hills, CA: Sage, 1983).

Clinard, Marshall B. and Peter C. Yeager, *Corporate Crime* (New York: The Free Press, 1980).

Cody, W. J. Michael and Andy D. Bennett, "The Privatization of Correctional Institutions: The Tennessee Experience," *Vanderbilt Law Review*, 1987 (40): 829–849.

Cohen, Stanley, *Visions of Social Control* (Cambridge [Eng]: Polity Press, 1985).

Coleman, James W., *The Criminal Elite: The Sociology of White Collar Crime* (New York: St. Martin's Press, 1989).

Conklin, John E., "Illegal But Not Criminal": *Business Crime in America* (Englewood-Cliffs, NJ: Prentice-Hall, 1977).

Cowdry, Quentin, "Tories to Abandon Private Jails Plan," *Times of London*, 1989 (November 24).

Cressey, Donald R., "Prison Organizations," In James G. March (ed.), *Handbook of Organizations* (Chicago: Rand McNally, 1965).

Cullen, Francis T., William J. Maakestad and Gray Cavender, *Corporate Crime Under Attack: The Ford Pinto Case and Beyond* (Cincinnati: Anderson, 1987).

Daily Mail, "Speeding to Private Jails: Baker Aims to Contract Out Half the Prisons," 1991, December 5.

De Hoog, Ruth Hoogland, *Contracting Out for Human Services* (Albany: State University of New York Press, 1984).

Delaney, Kevin J., "Power, Intercorporate Networks, and 'Strategic Bankruptcy'," *Law and Society Review*, 1990 (23): 643–666.

Dempsey, Paul S., "Perspective on Airline Deregulation. Successful Reform? Horrid Results," *Los Angeles Times*, 1991 (April 8).

DiIulio, Jr., John J., "What Is Wrong With Private Prisons," *The Public Interest*, 1988 (92): 66–83.

DiIulio, Jr., John J., "A Critical Perspective on the Private Management of Prisons and Jails," in Douglas C. McDonald (ed.), *Private Prisons and the Public Interest* (New Brunswick, NJ: Rutgers University Press, 1990).

Donahue, John D., *Prisons for Profit: Public Justice, Private Interests* (Washington, DC: Economic Policy Institute, 1988).

Donaldson, Thomas, *Corporations and Morality* (Englewood Cliffs, NJ: Prentice Hall, 1982).

Durham, III, Alexis M., "Evaluating Privatized Correctional Institutions: Obstacles to Effective Assessment," *Federal Probation,* 1988 (52(2)): 65–71.

Durham, III, Alexis M., "Origins of Interest in the Privatization of Punishment: The Nineteenth and Twentieth Century American Experience," *Criminology,* 1989 (27): 107–139.

Elvin, John, "A Civil Liberties View of Private Prisons," *The Prison Journal,* 1985 (45(2)): 48–52.

Ermann, M. David and Richard J. Lundman, *Corporate Deviance* (New York: Holt. Rinehart and Winston, 1982).

Etzioni, Amitai, *A Comparative Analysis of Complex Organizations* (New York: Free Press, 1961).

Feeley, Malcolm M., "The Privatization of Prisons in Historical Perspective," *Criminal Justice Research Bulletin,* 1991 (6(2)): 1–10.

Fisse, Brent, "New Penal Sanctions Against Corporations," Paper Presented at the Annual Meeting of the Pacific Sociological Association, 1981.

Fisse, Brent, "Sanctions Against Corporations: The Limitations of Fines and the Enterprise of Creating Alternatives," in Brent Fisse and Peter A. French (eds.), *Corrigible Corporations and Unruly Law* (San Antonio, TX: Trinity University Press, 1985).

Flener, Mark H., "Legal Considerations in Privatization and the Role of Legal Counsel," in Lawrence K. Finley (ed.), *Public Sector Privatization* (Westport, CT: Quorum, 1989).

Fraser/Associates, *Political Action for Business: The PAC Handbook* (Cambridge, MA: Ballinger, 1980).

Garsombke, Diane J. and Thomas W. Garsombke, "Strategic Marketing of Social Services," in Barry J. Carroll, Ralph W. Conant and Thomas A. Easton (eds.), *Private Means—Public Ends: Private Business in Social Service Delivery* (New York: Praeger, 1987).

Geis, Gilbert, "The Heavy Electrical Equipment Antitrust Cases of 1961," in Marshall B. Clinard and Richard Quinney (eds.), *Criminal Behavior Systems* (New York: Holt, Rinehart and Winston, 1967).

Geis, Gilbert, "The Privatization of Prisons: Panacea or Placebo?", in Barry J. Carroll, Ralph W. Conant and Thomas A. Easton (eds.), *Private Means—Public Ends: Private Business in Social Service Delivery* (New York: Praeger, 1987).

Gentry, James T., "The Panopticon Revisited: The Problem of Monitoring Private Prisons," *Yale Law Journal,* 1986 (96): 353–375.

Glasberg, Davita Silfen, "Corporate Power and Control: The Case of Leasco Corporation Versus Chemical Bank" *Social Problems,* 1982 (29): 104–116.

Glasberg, Davita S., *The Power of Collective Purse Strings: The Effect of Bank Hegemony on Corporations and the State* (Berkeley, CA: University of California Press, 1989).

Glazer, Myron P. and Penina Migdal Glazer, *The Whistleblowers: Exposing Corruption in Government and Industry* (New York: Basic Books, 1989).

Goffman, Erving, *Asylums* (Garden City, NY: Doubleday, Anchor Books, 1961).

Goodwin, Jacob, *Brotherhood of Arms* (New York: Times Books, 1985).

Greenwood, Peter, *Private Enterprise Prisons? Why Not? The Job Would Be Done and at Less Cost* (Santa Monica, CA: The Rand Corporation, 1981).

Gross, Edward, "Organization Structure and Organizational Crime," in Gilbert Geis and Ezra Stotland (eds.), *White-Collar Crime: Theory and Research* (Beverly Hills, CA: Sage, 1980).

Hamilton, Walton H., "The Ancient Maxim Caveat Emptor," *Yale Law Review,* 1931 (40): 1133–1187.

Hasenfeld, Yeheskel and Richard A. English (eds.), *Human Service Organizations* (Ann Arbor: The University of Michigan Press, 1974).

Hoffman, John, *State, Power and Democracy* (Sussex: Delinquency Books, 1988).

Holley, Cathy E., "Privatization of Corrections: Is the State out on a Limb When the Company Goes Bankrupt?," *Vanderbilt Law Review,* 1988 (41): 317–339.

Hurst, John, "$1.5 Billion Savings Seen as Prison Admissions Drop," *Los Angeles Times,* 1991 (October 8), p. A3.

Jacobs, David, Michael Useem and Mayer N. Zald, "Firms, Industries and Politics," *Research in Political Sociology,* 1991 (5):141–165.

Jacobs, James B., *Stateville* (Chicago: University of Chicago Press, 1977).

Jayewardene, C. H. S. and C. K. Talbot, "Entrusting Corrections to the Private Sector," *International Journal of Offender Therapy and Comparative Criminology,* 1983 (26): 177–187.

Kamerman, Sheila B. and Alfred J. Kahn, "Conclusion: Continuing the Discussion and Taking a Stand," in Sheila B. Kamerman and Alfred J. Kahn (eds.), *Privatization and the Welfare State* (Princeton, NJ: Princeton University Press, 1989).

Keating, Dan, "Monroe County Sheriff Gets Back Control of Jail from Wackenhut," *The Miami Herald,* 1991, January 30, 4B.

Keating, Jr., J. Michael, "Public on Private: Monitoring the Performance of Privately Operated Prisons and Jails," in Douglas C. McDonald (ed.), *Private Prisons and the Public Interest* (New Brunswick, NJ: Rutgers University Press, 1990).

Kramer, Ronald C., "Corporate Crime: An Organizational Perspective," in Peter Wickman and Timothy Dailey (eds.), *White Collar Crime and Economic Crime* (Lexington, MA: D.C. Heath, 1982).

Levinson, Robert B., "Okeechobee: An Evaluation of Privatization in Corrections," *The Prison Journal,* 1985 (45(2)): 75–94.

Lilly, J. Robert, "Power, Profit, and Penality: A Beginning." Paper Presented at the Annual Meeting of the American Society of Criminology (San Francisco, November, 1991).

Lipson, Milton, *On Guard: The Business of Private Security* (New York: Quadrangle, 1975).

Logan, Charles H., "The Propriety of Proprietary Prisons," *Federal Probation,* 1987 (51(3)): 35–40.

Logan, Charles H., *Private Prisons: Cons and Pros* (New York: Oxford University Press, 1990).

Logan, Charles H. and Bill W. McGrift, *Comparing Cost of Public and Private Prisons: A Case Study. National Institute of Justice Research in Action* (Washington, DC: Department of Justice, 1989).

Logan, Charles H. and Sharla P. Rausch, "Punish and Profit: The Emergence of Private Enterprise Prisons," *Justice Quarterly,* 1985 (2): 303–318.

Lynxwiler, John, Neal Shover and Donald Clelland, "Determinants of Sanction Severity in a Regulatory Bureaucracy," in Ellen Hochstedler (ed.), *Corporations as Criminals* (Beverly Hills, CA: Sage, 1984).

McAfee, Ward M., "Tennessee's Private Prison Act of 1986: An Historical Perspective with Special Attention to California's Experience," *Vanderbilt Law Review,* 1987 (40): 851–865.

McAfee, Ward M. and David Shichor, "A Historical-Sociological Analysis of California's Private Prison Experience in the 1850s: Some Modern Implications," *Criminal Justice History,* 1990 (11): 89–103.

McConville, Sean, "Aid from Industry? Private Corrections and Prison Crowding," in Stephen D. Gottfredson and Sean McConville (eds.), *America's Correctional Crisis* (Westport, CT: Greenwood Press, 1987).

McDonald, Douglas C., "The Cost of Corrections: In Search of the Bottom Line," *Research in Corrections,* 1989 (2): 1–25.

McDonald, Douglas C., "The Cost of Operating Public and Private Correctional Facilities," in Douglas C. McDonald (ed.), *Private Prisons and the Public Interest* (New Brunswick, NJ: Rutgers University Press, 1990).

McKanna, Clare V., "1851–1880: The Origins of San Quentin," *California History,* 1987 (March): 49–54.

McShane, Marilyn D. and Frank P. William, III, "Running on Empty: Creativity and the Correctional Agenda," *Crime and Delinquency,* 1989 (35): 562–576.

Mann, Kenneth, *Defending White-Collar Crime* (New Haven: Yale University Press, 1985).

Meyer, Jr., John C., "An Action-Orientation Approach to the Study of Occupational Crime," *Australian and New Zealand Journal of Criminology,* 1972 (5): 35–48.

Mills, C. Wright, *The Power Elite* (New York: Oxford University Press, 1956).

Mizruchi, Mark S., *The American Corporate Network* (Beverly Hills, CA: Sage, 1982).

Moe, Ronald C., "'Law' versus 'Performance' as Objective Standard," *Public Administration Review,* 1988 (March–April): 674–675.

Moore, Wilbert E., *The Conduct of the Corporation* (New York: Vintage Books, 1962).

Morris, Norval, *The Future of Imprisonment* (Chicago: University of Chicago Press, 1974).

Mullen, Joan, "Corrections and the Private Sector," *The Prison Journal,* 1985 (45(2)):1–13.

Nelson, B. J., "Purchase of Service," in G. J. Washnis (ed.), *Productivity Improvement Handbook for State and Local Government* (New York: John Wiley, 1980).

Novey, Donald L., "Privatization in Prisons: A Potential Forest Fire Across the USA," *Correctional Peacekeeper,* 1985 (3):8.

O'Brien, Patricia., *The Promise of Punishment: Prisons in Nineteenth-Century France* (Princeton NJ: Princeton University Press, 1982).

Palumbo, Dennis J., "Privatization and Corrections Policy," *Policy Studies Review,* 1986 (5): 598–605.

Papadakis, Elim and Peter Taylor-Gosby, *The Private Provision of Public Welfare* (New York: St. Martin's Press, 1987).

Parsons, Talcott, "How Are Clients Integrated into Service Organizations?," in William R. Rosengreen and Mark Lefton (eds.), *Organizations and Clients: Essays in the Sociology of Service* (Columbus, OH: Charles E. Merrill, 1970).

Pellicciotti, Joseph M., "42 U.S.C. Sec. 1983 Correctional Officials Liability: A Look to the New Century," *Journal of Contemporary Criminal Justice,* 1987 (3): 1–9.

Pontell, Henry N., Paul D. Jesilow and Gilbert Geis, "Policing Physicians: Practitioner Fraud and Abuse in a Government Medical Program," *Social Problems,* 1982 (30): 117–125.

Press, Aric, "The Good, the Bad, and the Ugly: Private Prisons in the 1980s," in Douglas McDonald (ed.), *Private Prisons and the Public Interest* (New Brunswick, NJ: Rutgers University Press, 1990).

Riddell, Peter, *The Thatcher Decade* (Oxford: Basil Blackwell, 1989).

Ring, Charles, *Contracting for the Operation of Private Prisons* (College Park, MD: The American Correctional Association, 1987).

Robbins, Ira P., "Privatization of Corrections: Defining the Issues," *Federal Probation,* 1986 (50) (September): 24–30.

Robbins, Ira P., "The Legal Dimensions of Private Incarceration," *The American University Law Review,* 1989 (3): 531–854.

Roberts, Albert R. and Gerald T. Powers, "The Privatization of Corrections: Methodological Issues and Dilemmas Involved in Evaluative Research," *The Prison Journal,* 1985 (45(2)): 95–107.

Rothman, David J., *Conscience and Convenience: The Asylum and Its Alternatives in Progressive America* (Boston: Little, Brown, 1980).

Rutherford, Andrew, "Prison Privatization in Britain," in Douglas C. McDonald (ed.), *Private Prisons and the Public Interest* (New Brunswick, NJ: Rutgers University Press, 1990).

Ryan, Mick and Tony Ward, "Privatization and Penal Politics," in Roger Matthews (ed.), *Privatizing Criminal Justice* (London: Sage, 1989).

Ryan, Mike H., Carl L. Swanson and Rogene A. Buchholz, *Corporate Strategy, Public Policy and the Fortune 500: How America's Major Corporations Influence Government* (Oxford: Basil Blackwell, 1987).

Sagarin, Edward and Jess Maghen, "Should States Opt for Private Prisons? No," *The Hartford (CT) Journal*, 1986 (January 12): E1–E4.

Savas, E. S., *Privatizing the Public Sector* (Chatham, NJ: Chatham House, 1982).

Schuman, Alan M., "The Cost of Correctional Services: Exploring a Poorly Chartered Terrain," *Research in Corrections*, 1989 (2): 27–33.

Sellers, Martin P., "Private and Public Prisons: A Comparison of Costs, Programs and Facilities," *International Journal of Offender Therapy and Comparative Criminology*, 1989 (33): 241–256.

Sellin, J. Thorsten, *Slavery and the Penal System* (New York: Elsevier, 1976).

Shichor, David, "On Corporate Deviance and Corporate Victimization: A Review and Some Elaborations," *International Review of Victimology*, 1989 (1): 67–88.

Shichor, David and Clemens Bartollas, "Private and Public Placements: Is There a Difference?," *Crime and Delinquency*, 1990 (36): 296–299.

South, Nigel, *Policing for Profit* (London: Sage, 1988).

Starr, Paul, "The Limits of Privatization," *Proceedings of the Academy of Political Science*, 1987 (3/3): 124–137.

State of California, *Financial Management Handbook for Private Return-to-Custody Facilities* (Sacramento: Department of Corrections, 1985).

Stone, Christopher D., *Where the Law Ends* (New York: Harper and Row, 1975).

Street, David, Robert D. Vinter and Charles Perrow, *Organization for Treatment* (New York: The Free Press, 1966).

Sullivan, Harold J., "Privatization of Corrections and the Constitutional Rights of Prisoners," *Federal Probation*, 1989 (53(2)): 36–42.

Sutherland, Edwin H., "Crime of Corporations," in Albert Cohen, Alfred Lindesmith and Karl Schuessler (eds.), *The Sutherland Papers* (Bloomington: Indiana University Press, 1956).

Sutton, Adam and Ron Wild, "Corporate Crime and Social Structure," in Paul R. Wilson and John Braithwaite (eds.), *Two Faces of Deviance: Crimes of the Powerless and the Powerful* (Brisbane, Queensland, Australia: University of Queensland Press, 1978).

Thomas, Charles W. and Suzanne L. Foard, *Private Correctional Facility Census*. Gainesville, FL: Private Corrections Project, Center for Studies in Criminology and Law (University of Florida, 1991).

Thomas, Charles W. and Linda S. Calvert Hanson, "The Implications of 42 U.S.C. § 1983 for the Privatization of Prisons," *Florida State University Law Review*, 1989 (16): 933–962.

Thomas, John C., "Privatization of Prisons: A New Breed of Liability," *Journal of Security Administration*, 1987 (10): 27–34.

Thompson, James D., *Organizations in Action* (New York: McGraw-Hill, 1967).

Tolchin, Susan J. and Martin Tolchin, *Dismantling America: The Rush to Deregulate* (Boston: Houghton Mifflin Company, 1983).

United States Committee on Education and Labor, *Private Police Systems* (Washington, DC: U.S. Government Printing Office, 1939).

Urban Institute, *Comparison of Privately and Publicly Operated Corrections Facilities in Kentucky and Massachusetts* (Washington, DC: The Urban Institute, 1989).

Vaughan, Diane, "Crime Between Organizations: Implications for Victimology," in Gilbert Geis and Ezra Stotland (eds.), *White Collar Crime: Theory and Research* (Beverly Hills, CA: Sage, 1980).

Walker, Donald R., *Penology for Profit: A History of the Texas Prison System 1867–1912* (College Station, TX: Texas A&M University Press, 1988).

Wecht, David N., "Breaking the Code of Deference: Judicial Review of Private Prisons," *The Yale Law Journal,* 1987 (96): 815–837.

Weinstein, Henry, "Northrop, Guilty in Fraud Case, Is Fined $17 Million," *Los Angeles Times,* 1990 (February 28).

Weiss, Robert P., "Private Prisons and the State," in Roger Matthews (ed.), *Privatizing Criminal Justice* (London: Sage, 1989).

Woolley, Mary R., "Prisons for Profit: Policy Considerations for Government Officials," *Dickinson Law Review,* 1985 (90): 307–331.

The Social Context of Police Lying

27

Jennifer Hunt
Peter K. Manning

Introduction

Police, like many people in official capacities, lie. We intend here to examine the culturally grounded bases for police lying using ethnographic materials.[1] Following the earlier work of Manning (1974), we define lies as speech acts which the speaker knows are misleading or false, and are intended to deceive. Evidence that proves the contrary must be known to the observer.[2] Lying is not an obvious matter: it is always socially and contextually defined with reference to what an audience will credit; thus, its meaning changes and its effects are often ambiguous (Goffman 1959, pp. 58–66). The moral context of lying is very important insofar as its definition may be relative to membership status. The outsider may not appreciate distinctions held scrupulously within a group; indeed, differences between what is and is not said may constitute a lie to an outsider, but these distinctions may not be so easily made by an insider. In a sense, lies do not exist in the abstract; rather they are objects within a negotiated occupational order (Maines 1982). In analytic terms, acceptable or normal lies become one criteria for membership within a group, and inappropriate lying, contextually defined, sets a person on the margins of that order.

The structural sources of police lying are several. Lying is a useful way to manipulate the public when the applying of the law and other threats are of little use (see Bittner 1970; Westley 1970; Skolnick 1966; Klockars 1983, 1984; Wilson 1968; Stinchcombe 1964). The police serve as gatherers and screeners of facts, shaping them within the legal realities and routines of court settings (Buckner 1978). The risks involved in establishing often problematic facts and the adversarial context of court narratives increases the value of secrecy and of concealing and controlling information generally (Reiss 1974). Police are protected for their lies by law under stipulated circumstances (see McBarnett 1981; Ericson and Shearing 1986).[3] The internal organization of policing as well as the occupational culture

339

emphasize control, punishment, and secrecy (Westley 1970; Manning 1977). Some police tasks, especially those in specialized police units such as vice, narcotics and internal affairs, clearly require and reward lying skills more than others, and such units may be subject to periodic scandals and public outcry (Manning 1980). The unfilled and perhaps impossible expectations in drug enforcement may escalate the use of lies in the "war on drugs," further reducing public trust when officers' lies are exposed. Most police officers in large forces at one time or another participate in some form of illicit or illegal activity, from the violation of departmental morals codes to the use of extra-legal force. Perhaps more importantly, there is an accepted view that it is impossible to "police by the book;" that any good officer, in the course of a given day, will violate at least one of the myriad rules and regulations governing police conduct. This is certain; what is seen as contingent is when, how and where detection by whom will take place.

Lying is a sanctioned practice, differentially rewarded and performed, judged by local occupationally-grounded standards of competence.[4] However, it is likely that these standards are changing; as police claims to professional competence and capacity to control crime and incivilities in cities are validated, and absent any changes in internal or external sources of control and accountability (cf. Reiss 1974), police may encounter less external pressure and public support in routine tasks and are less likely to be called into account. Policing has emerged as a more "professional" occupation and may be less at risk generally to public outcry. One inference of this line of conjecture is that lying is perceived as less risky by police. The occupational culture in departments studied by researchers contains a rich set of stories told to both colleagues and criminals. However, like the routinely required application of violence, some lies are "normal," and acceptable to audiences, especially colleagues, whereas others are not.

Given the pervasiveness of police lies, it is surprising that no research has identified and provided examples of types of lies viewed from the officers' perspective. We focus here on patrol officers' lies and note the skill with which they cope with situations in which lies are produced. Some officers are more frequently in trouble than others, and some more inclined to lie. We suggest a distinction between lies that excuse from those that justify an action, between troublesome and non-troublesome lies, and between case and cover lies. Lies are troublesome when they arise in a context such as a courtroom or a report in which the individual is sworn to uphold the truth. In such a context, lying may risk legal and/or moral sanctions, resulting in punishment and a loss in status. *Case lies* and *cover stories* are routinely told types of troublesome lies. Case lies are stories an officer utilizes systematically in a courtroom or on paper to facilitate the conviction of a suspect. Cover stories are lies an officer tells in court, to supervisors, and to colleagues in order to provide a verbal shield or mitigation in the event of anticipated discipline.

Methodology

The senior author was funded to study police training in a large Metropolitan police department ("Metro City"). Continuous fieldwork, undertaken as a known observer-participant for eighteen months, focused on the differences and similarities in the socialization experiences of young female and male officers.[5] The fieldwork included observation, participation in training with an incoming class in the policy academy, tape-recording interviews in relaxing informal settings with key informants selected for their verbal skills and willingness to give lengthy interviews. The social milieu encouraged them to provide detailed and detached stories. The observer had access to the personnel files of the two hundred officers who entered the force during the research period. She attended a variety of off-duty events and activities ranging from meetings of the Fraternal Order of the Police, sporting events, parties, and funerals (for further details see Hunt 1984). The data presented here are drawn primarily from tape recorded interviews.

Learning to Lie

In the police academy, instructors encouraged recruits to lie in some situations, while strongly discouraging it in others. Officers are told it is "good police work," and encouraged to lie, to substitute guile for force, in situations of crisis intervention, investigation and interrogation, and especially with the mentally ill (Harris 1973).[6] During classes on law and court testimony, on the other hand, students were taught that the use of deception in court was illegal, morally wrong, and unacceptable and would subject the officer to legal and departmental sanctions. Through films and discussions, recruits learned that the only appropriate means to win court cases was to undertake and complete a "solid," "by the books" investigation including displaying a professional demeanor while delivering a succinct but "factual" narrative in court testimony.

Job experience changes the rookies' beliefs about the circumstances under which it is appropriate to lie. Learning to lie is a key to membership. Rookies in Metro City learn on the job, for example, that police routinely participate in a variety of illicit activities which reduce the discomfort of the job such as drinking, sleeping on duty, and staying inside during inclement weather. As these patterns of work avoidance may result in discovery, they demand the learning of explanatory stories which rationalize informal behavior in ways that jeopardize neither colleagues nor supervisors (Cain 1973; Chatterton 1975). Rookies and veteran police who demonstrate little skill in constructing these routine lies were informally criticized. For example, veteran officers in Metro City commented sympathetically about rookies who froze on footbeats because they were too green to know that "a good cop never gets cold or wet . . . " and too new to have attained expertise in explaining their whereabouts if they were to leave their beats. After a few months in the district, several veteran officers approvingly noted that most of the rookies had learned not only where to hide but what to say if questioned by supervisors.

Rookies also learn the situational utility of lying when they observe detectives changing reports to avoid unnecessary paperwork and maintain the clearance rate. In the Metro City police department, some cases defined initially as robberies, assaults, and burglaries were later reduced to less serious offenses (cf. Sudnow 1965). Police argued that this practice reduced the time and effort spent on "bullshit jobs" little likely to be cleared. Rookies who opposed this practice and insisted on filing cases as they saw fit were ridiculed and labeled troublemakers. As a result, most division detectives provided minimal cooperation to these "troublemakers." This added the task of reworking already time-consuming and tedious reports to the workload of young officers who were already given little prospective guidance and routine assistance in completing their paperwork.

Young police also observe veterans lying in court testimony regarding, for example, the presence of probable cause in situations of search, seizure and arrest (see, for example, McClure 1986, pp. 230–232).

There are also counter-pressures. While learning to lie, rookies also recognize that the public and court officials disapprove of lying, and that if caught in a serious lie, they may be subject to either legal sanctioning and/or departmental punishment. But recognizing external standards and their relevance does not exhaust the learning required. There are also relevant tacit rules within the occupational culture about what constitutes a normal lie. Complexity and guile, and agile verbal construction are appreciated, while lying that enmeshes or makes colleagues vulnerable or is "sloppy" is condemned. Lying is judged largely in pragmatic terms otherwise. Soon, some rookies are as skillful as veterans at lying.[7]

Police Accounts of Lying

Lies are made normal or acceptable by means of socially approved vocabularies for relieving responsibility or neutralizing the consequences of an event. These accounts are provided *after* an act if and when conduct is called into question (see the classic, Mills 1940; Sykes and Matza 1957; Scott and Lyman 1968). Police routinely normalize lying by two types of accounts, excuses and justifications (Van Maanen 1980; Hunt 1985; Waegel 1984). These accounts are not mutually exclusive, and a combination is typically employed in practice. The greater the number of excuses and justifications condensed in a given account, the more the police officer is able to reduce personal and peer related conflicts. These accounts are typically tailored to an audience. A cover story directed to an "external" audience such as the district attorneys, courts, or the media is considered more problematic than a lie directed to supervisors or peers (Manning 1974). Lies are more troublesome also when the audience is perceived as less trustworthy (Goffman 1959, p. 58).

Excuses deny full responsibility for an act of lying but acknowledge its inappropriateness. Police distinguish passive lies which involve omission, or covering oneself, from active lies such as a "frame" of a person for a crime by, for example, planting a gun, or the construction of a sophisticated story. The latter are more often viewed as morally problematic.

Justifications accept responsibility for the illegal lie in question but deny that the act is wrongful or blameworthy. They socially construct a set of justifications, used with both public and other police, according to a number of principles (These are analogous to the neutralizations found by Sykes and Matza 1957 in another context). When lying, police may appeal to "higher" loyalties that justify the means used, deny that anyone is truly hurt or a victim of the lies. Police may also deny injury by claiming that court testimony has little consequence as it is merely an extension of the "cops and robbers" game. It is simply a tool in one's repertoire that requires a modicum of verbal skill (see Sudnow 1965; Blumberg 1967). Finally, as seen in "cover stories," officers justify lies instrumentally and pragmatically (see Van Maanen 1980; Waegel 1984).

Lying in Action

Case Stories and the Construction of Probable Cause

The most common form of case lying, used to gain a conviction in court, involves the construction of probable cause for arrest, or search and seizure in situations where the legally required basis in the street encounter is weak or absent.[8] Probable cause can be constructed by reorganizing the sequence of events, "shading" or adding to the facts, omitting embarrassing facts, or entering facts into a testimony that were not considered at the time of arrest or while writing the report.

The following is a typical case story-account chosen from a taped interview in which probable cause was socially constructed. The officer was called to a "burglary in progress" with no further details included and found a door forced open at the back of the factory.

> So I arrive at the scene, and I say, I know: I do have an open property and I'm going in to search it. And I'm looking around, and I hear noise. Then, I hear glass break. And I run to the window, and obviously something just jumped out the window and is running and I hear skirmishing. So I run, and I still don't see anyone yet. I just hear something. I still haven't seen anyone. You hear a window, you see a window and you hear footsteps running. Then you don't hear it anymore. I don't

find anybody. So I say to myself "whoever it is is around here some-where." So, fifteen minutes go by, twenty go by. The job resumes.

One cop stays in the front and about a half an hour or forty-five min-utes later, low and behold, I see someone half a block away coming out of a field. Now, the field is on the other side of the factory. It's the same field that I chased this noise into. So a half hour later I see this guy at quarter to four in the morning just happened to be walking out of this field. So I grab him. "Who are you? What are you doing?" Bla bla bla. . . . And I see that he has flour on him, like flour which is what's inside of this factory. So I say to myself, "you're the suspect under ar-rest for burglary." Well, I really, at this point it was iffy if I had proba-ble cause or not. . . . A very conservative judge would say that that was enough. . . . But probably not, because the courts are so jammed that that weak probable cause would be enough to have it thrown out. So in order to make it stick, what I said was "As I went to the factory and I noticed the door open and I entered the factory to search to see if there was anybody inside. Inside, by the other side of the wall, I see a young black male, approximately twenty two years old, wearing a blue shirt and khaki pants, jump out of the window, and I chase him and I lost him in the bushes. An hour later I saw this very same black male walk-ing out of the field and I arrested him. He was the same one I saw in-side." O.K.? . . .

What I did was to construct probable cause that would definitely stick in court and I knew he was guilty. So in order to make it stick. . . . That's the kind of lies that happen all the time. I would de-fend that.[9]

The officer's account of his activity during the arrest of a suspect and sub-sequent testimony in court reveals a combination of excuses and justifica-tions which rationalize perjury. He clearly distinguishes the story he tells the interviewer from the lie he told in court. Near the end of the vignette, by saying "O.K.?," he seeks to emphasize phatic contact as well to estab-lish whether the interviewer understood how and why he lied and how he justified it. Within the account, he excuses his lies with reference to or-ganizational factors ("conservative judges"—those who adhere to proce-dural guarantees—and "overcrowded courts"), and implies that these are responsible for releasing guilty suspects who should be jailed. These fac-tors force the officer to lie in court in order to sustain an ambiguous and weak probable cause. The officer further justifies his lies by claiming that he believes the suspect to be guilty and responsible for perpetrating crime more serious than the lie used to convict him. He ends by claiming that such lies are acceptable to his peers—they "happen all the time"—and im-plicitly appeals to the higher goal of justice. As in this case, officers can shape and combine observed and invented facts to form a complex, elab-orate yet coherent, picture which may help solve a crime, clear a case, or convict a criminal.

Case Stories and the Manipulation of the Court as an Informal Entity

As a result of community pressure in Metro City, a specialized unit was created to arrest juveniles who "hung out" on street corners and disturbed neighborhoods. The unit was considered a desirable assignment because officers worked steady shifts and were paid overtime for court appearances. They were to be judged by convictions obtained, not solely upon their arrests. An officer in this unit explains some of the enforcement constraints produced by the law and how they can be circumvented:

> Legally . . . when there's any amount of kids over five there is noise, but it's not really defined legally being unruly even though the community complains that they are drunk and noisy. Anyway, you get there, you see five kids and there's noise. It's not really criminal, but you gotta lock them up, particularly if someone had called and complained. So you lock them up for disorderly conduct and you tell your story. If they plead not guilty then you have to actually tell a story.
>
> . . . It's almost like a game. The kids know that they can plead guilty and get a $12.50 fine or a harder judge will give them a $30.50 fine or they can plead not guilty and have the officer tell their story of what occurred which lead to the arrest.
>
> . . . The game is who manipulates better, the kid or the cop? The one who lies better wins.
>
> Well, the kids are really cocky. I had arrested this group of kids, and when we went to court the defense attorney for the kids was arguing that all of the kids, who I claimed were there the first time that I warned them to get offa the corner, weren't there at all. Now, you don't really have to warn them to get offa the corner before you arrest them, but the judge likes it if you warn them once.
>
> Meanwhile, one of the kids is laughing in the courtroom, and the judge asks why he's laughing in her courtroom and showing disrespect.
>
> At this point, the kid's attorney asks me what the kid was wearing when I arrested him. I couldn't remember exactly what he had on so I just gave the standard uniform; dungarees, shirt, sneakers. . . . Then, the defense attorney turns around and asks the kid what he was wearing and he gives this description of white pants with a white sports jacket. Now, you just know the kid is lying because there ain't a kid in that neighborhood who dresses like that. But, anyway, I figure they got me on this one.
>
> But then I signal the District Attorney to ask me how I remembered this kid outta the whole bunch who was on the corner. So the District Attorney asks me, "Officer, what was it that made you remember this male the first time?" And I said, "Well, your honor, I referred this one here because the first time that I warned the group to get off the corner, this male was the one that laughed the hardest." I know this would get the Judge because the kid has pissed her off in the first place by

> laughing in the courtroom. Well, the judge's eyes lit up like she knew what I was talking about.
> "Found guilty. . . . 60 dollars." (The Judge ruled).

In this case, the officer believed the boy was guilty because he "hung out" regularly with the juvenile corner group. Although the officer forgot the boy's dress on the day he was arrested, he testifies in court that it was the "standard [juvenile] uniform." The boy, however, claims he wore pants and a sports jacket. The officer was in a potentially embarrassing and awkward spot. In order to affirm the identification of the suspect and win the case, the officer constructs another lie using the District Attorney's question. He manipulates the emotions of the judge whose authority was previously threatened by the boy's disrespectful courtroom demeanor. He claims that he knows this was the boy because he displayed arrogance by laughing when arrested just as he had in court.

The officer's account of the unit's organization, the arrest, and his courtroom testimony reveals a combination of excuses and justifications. He justifies his lie to make the arrest without probable cause and to gain a conviction citing the organizational and community pressures. He also justifies perjury by denying the reality and potential injury to the suspect caused by his actions. He sees courtroom communications as a game, and argues that the penalty is minor in view of the offense and the age of the suspect. The officer argues instrumentally that the lie was a means to gain or regain control as well as a means to punish an offender who has not accepted the police definition of the situation. The latter is evident in the officer's assertion that the boys are "really cocky." Their attempts to question the police version of the story by presenting themselves as clean cut children with good families is apparently viewed as a demonstration of deliberate arrogance deserving of retaliation in the form of a lie which facilitates their conviction.

Another officer from the same unit describes a similar example of case construction to gain a conviction. The clumsy character of the lie suggests that the officer believes he is at little risk of perjury. According to a colleague's account:

> We arrested a group of kids in a park right across from the hospital. They all know us and we know them, so they are getting as good as we are at knowing which stories go over better on the judge. So the kids in this instance plead not guilty which is a real slap in the face because you know that they are going to come up with a story that you are going to have to top [That is, the case will go to court and require testimony].
>
> So, the kids' story was that they were just sitting in the park and waiting for someone and that they were only having a conversation. [The police officer's testimony was]: "The kids were making so much noise, the kids were so loud. . . . They had this enormous radio blasting and the people in the hospital were so disturbed that they were just hanging outta the windows. And some nuns, some of the nuns that

work in the hospital, they were coming outside because it was so loud." And the thing that appalled the officer the most was that this was going on right in front of the entrance to the hospital. The kids were acting in such a manner that the officer immediately arrested them without even a warning.

Well, the kid, when he hears this, likely drops dead. He kept saying "what radio, what radio?" The funny part of it was that the other police officers who were in the back of the courtroom watching the cop testify kept rolling their eyes at him. First of all, because when he said that the people were hanging outta the hospital windows, the windows in the hospital don't open. They're sealed. Another thing was that the cop said this occurred at the entrance of the hospital. Two years ago this was the entrance to the hospital. But it's not the entrance now. Another thing was that there never was a radio. But when the officer testified regarding the radio, he got confused. He actually did think there was one but in fact, the radio blasting was from another job. The cop realized after he testified that the kid didn't have a radio blasting.

The lies are described as instrumental: they are designed to regain control in court and to punish the offender for violating the officer's authority by verbally "slapping him in the face." In addition, the court-as-a-game-metaphor is evident in the notion that each participant must top the other's story in court. The amused reaction evidenced by peers listening to what they viewed as absurd testimony, rolling their eyes, also suggests their bemused approval. The informant's ironic identification of his colleague's factual errors points out the recognized and displayed limits and constraints upon lying. The officers recognized the difference between a rather sloppy or merely effective lie and an admired lie that artfully combines facts, observations, and subtle inferences. Perhaps it is not unimportant to note that the police engaged in the first instance in a kind of social construction of the required social order. The police lied in virtually every key facet of this situation because they believed that the juveniles should be controlled. What might be called the police ordering of a situation was the precondition for both of these court lies. Such decisions are potentially a factor in community policing when police define and then defend in court with lies their notions of public order (see Wilson and Kelling 1982).

Cover Stories

A cover story is the second kind of legal lie that police routinely tell on paper, in court, and to colleagues. Like most case stories, cover stories are constructed using sub-cultural nuances to make retelling the dynamics of encounters legally rational. Maintaining the capacity to produce a cover story is viewed as an essential skill required to protect against disciplinary action.

A cover story may involve the manipulation of legal and departmental rules, or taken-for-granted-knowledge regarding a neighborhood, actions of people and things. A common cover story involves failure to respond to a radio call. Every officer knows, for example, that some districts have radio "dead spots" where radio transmissions do not reach. If "radio" (central communications) calls an officer who doesn't respond or accept, "pick up the job," radio will usually recall. If he still doesn't respond, another officer typically takes the job to cover for him, or a friendly dispatcher may assign the job to another unit. However, if radio assigns the same job to the same car a third time and the unit still doesn't accept the job, the officer may be subject to formal disciplinary action. One acceptable account for temporary unavailability (for whatever reason) is to claim that one's radio malfunctioned or that one was in a "dead spot" (see Rubinstein 1973; Manning 1988).

The most common cover stories involving criminal matters are constructed to protect the officer against charges of brutality or homicide. Such cover stories serve to bridge the gap between the normal use of force which characterizes the informal world of the street and its legal use as defined by the court.

Self-protection is the presumed justification for cover stories. Since officers often equate verbal challenges with actual physical violence, both of which are grounds for retaliatory violence, either may underlie a story.[10] Threats of harm to self, partner, or citizens, are especially powerful bases for rationalizations. Even an officer who is believed by colleagues to use brutal force and seen as a poor partner as a result, is expected to lie to protect himself (see Hunt 1985; Waegel 1984). He or she would be considered odd, or even untrustworthy, if he or she did not. There is an interaction between violence and lying understood by police standards.

In the following account, the officer who fired his weapon exceeded "normal" force and committed a "bad shooting" (see Van Maanen 1980). Few officers would condone the shooting of an unarmed boy who they did not see commit a crime. Nevertheless, the officers participate in the construction of a cover story to protect their colleague against disciplinary action and justify it on the basis of self-defense and loyalty. Officers arrived at a scene that had been described mistakenly in a radio call as a "burglary in progress" (in fact, boys were stripping a previously stolen car). Since this is a call with arrest potential, it drew several police vehicles and officers soon began to chase the suspect(s):

> Then they get into a back yard chasing one kid. The kid starts running up a rain spout like he's a spider man, and one of the cops took a shot at him. So now they're all panicky because the kid made it to the roof and he let out a scream and the cops thought that they hit him. And that was a bad shooting! What would you think if you was that kid's mother? Not only did they not have an open property, but they don't

know if it's a stolen car at all. Well, when they shot the kid I gave them an excuse by mistake, inadvertently. I was on the other side of the place with my partner when I heard the one shot. [The officer telling the story is on one side of an iron gate, and another officer J.J. was on the other side. He kicks open the gate, thinking it is locked. It is not locked and swings wildly open, striking J.J. in the head] . . .

J.J. keeps stepping backward like he wanted to cry . . . like he was in a daze. "It's all right, it's not bleeding." I says to him . . . like he was stunned.

So then the Sergeant gets to the scene and asks what happened, cause this shot has been fired, and the kid screamed, and you figure some kid's been hit and he's up on the roof.

They gotta explain this dead kid and the shot to the sergeant when he gets there. So J.J. and Eddy discuss this. Eddy was the cop who'd fired the shot at the kid climbing up the rain spout, and all of a sudden they decide to claim he got hit with something in the head, and J.J. yells, "I'm hit, I'm hit." Then Eddy, thinking his partner's been shot, fires a shot at the kid. So they reported this all to the Captain and J.J. gets reprimanded for yelling "I'm shot" when he said, "I'm hit."

J.J. was never involved at all, but he just says this to cover for Eddy.

Meanwhile, the fire department is out there looking on the roof for the kid and they never found him so you figure he never got hit.

Here, the officer telling the story demonstrates his solidarity with colleagues by passively validating (refusing to discredit) the construction of an episode created by collusion between two other officers. The moral ambiguity of participation in such a troublesome lie is recognized and indicated by the interviewed officer. He disclaims responsibility for his involvement in the lie by insisting that he was not at the scene of the shooting and only "by mistake . . . inadvertently . . . gave them [the other officers] an excuse" used to create the cover story. In such morally ambiguous situations, individual officers remain in some moral tension. Note the officers' role-taking capacity, empathy, and concern for the generalized other when he asks in the vignette what the interviewer's thoughts would be if ". . . you was that kid's mother?" Such views may conflict with those of peers and supervisors. Moral tensions also arise in situations producing case stories.

The Morally Ambiguous Lie in a Case Story

Occasionally, officers cannot fully neutralize their sense of self-responsibility in the context of the police role. Their lies remain troubling in a moral sense. Such lies suggest the moral limits of pragmatism within the police, but in this case, the lie may be also a sign of the youth and gender of the officer involved. In the following example, a five-year veteran police officer experiences a profound moral dilemma as a result of pressures to frame a boy for a burglary she did not see him commit and did not believe he had committed. She refuses, even under peer and supervisory officers' pressure to do so, to produce a case story lie. Refusing to lie in this instance does not constitute a violation of police officers' sense of mutual obligation since she does not jeopardize peers. She sets the scene by noting that she and her partner are talking to John near his butcher shop when Frankie, a powerful and well-connected community member, approaches her and wants her to watch his shop. He claims a guy is trying to pass a bad check. She continues:

> Well, Frankie's a close friend of the Police Commissioner and his sister's married to the owner of a drug manufacturing company. He donated a lot of money to the mayor's political campaign. . . . The police commissioner vacations at Frankie's sister's summer home in [an elite resort location]. . . . Frankie has "a lot of pull" and we [the police] sometimes call ourselves "Frankie's private little army."
>
> Anyway, I tell Frankie, "O.K. I'll watch the store." But I don't think anything's really gonna happen. Frankie's just jealous because I'm spending more time with John than with him. Anyway, I go in the butcher shop and talk to John and when I come out, I hear Frankie screaming, "Stop him, stop him!" I respond, "Stop who?" Frankie says, "Stop the guy walking with the bag." I see a black kid walking away from the store with a bag in his hand and I call him over. I ask Frankie, "What's going on?" He responds, "Something's fishy, something fishy's going on." At this point, the kid opens the bag in front of me and there's nothing in it and I search the kid. . . . The so called bad check that the kid was trying to cash at Frankie's store turned out to be a valid money order. I ask the kid to come over to the car and make out a ped stop. Thank God, I made up a good ped stop. . . . I got all the information on the kid.
>
> At this point a "man with a gun" [call] comes over the radio. As no one else picks up the job, we take it. It was unfounded and I tell my partner that we'd better go back and check on Frankie because there might be trouble. When we return I ask Frankie, "Is everything all right?" He responds, "No it isn't." I say, "What's wrong?" Frankie says, "I told you he took something." I say, "That's not good enough, you have to tell me what he took . . . not that 'something's fishy and he must have taken something.' . . . Did you see him take anything?" Frankie responds, "Three radios."
>
> I go inside the appliance store to see the missing radios and there are a number of radios on a shelf way above the counter where it would be difficult for anyone to reach them, particularly a kid. I ask Frankie if he wants me to take the report or if he would prefer a regular district car to do it. He tells me, "You take it!" I take a report and right away call a 43rd district car to take it into the detectives.
>
> An hour later, I got a call to go to the district. The captain asks me again, "What did you do to Frankie?" I tell him, "nothing." The captain

asks me again, "What did you do to Frankie?" I say "nothing," and tell him exactly what had occurred at the incident. The captain says, "Did you run him [the suspect] through the computer?" I say, "No, I didn't . . . because he had legitimate identification." The captain then tells me, "Well, you better get your story together because Frankie's going before the Board of Inquiry. You fucked up. Now, tomorrow you're gonna apologize!" I say, "But if I apologize, it makes it seem like I did something wrong. I did nothing wrong." The captain adds, "Don't argue with me, I told you what you're gonna do."

An hour later, I receive a call from the Division detective and he wants to know my side of the story. I tell him what happened. The detective says, "Well, we have to put out a warrant for the kid's arrest." I say, "For what?" The detective explains, "Believe me, the only reason this kid is getting locked up is because it's Frankie. . . . Have you ever been burnt by Frankie? Do you know who Frankie is?"

The detective then asks, "Will you go to court?" I say, "Why should I go to court, I didn't make the arrest." The detective says, "Well, you're the key to the identification of the kid." I respond, "O.K. you send me to court and I'll make the asshole out of him that he is." The detective then says, "O.K. if I'm not man enough to stand this up in court, then I won't ask you to do it. . . . Let the old bastard do it himself."

Later, I'm called back into the Captain's office . . . and he tells me that "You're in for it now . . . the detectives have put out a warrant for the kid's arrest and that makes you look foolish. . . . " He then orders me to tell my story again. I tell it again. Finally, I say, "I didn't lock the kid up because I had no probable cause and to this day, I have no probable cause." The Captain warns me, "Well, you're going to the Board of Inquiry and there's nothing you can say that will get you out of this one. . . . I hope your partner's a good front man." I told him, "My partner don't need to lie."

In this incident, the officer is unwilling, in spite of quite direct threats and pressures, to neutralize her felt responsibility by constructing a case story lie. She believed that the boy was innocent and did not believe that "higher truth" was served by participating in a lie that would have framed the boy and saved Frankie's face. She also thought her lie would facilitate the conviction of the boy for burglary, an offense that was so serious that injury to him could not be denied. The officer not only refused to lie but agreed to testify for the boy if subpoenaed to appear in court.

This ambiguous lie highlights several important subpoints. The officer clung to a version of the situation that denied the relevance of lying, and featured her view of the facts, her duty and her distrust of Frankie. The pressure to lie illustrated here makes evident some divergence of opinions about what is acceptable practice by rank and function. She refuses to lie in part because neither she nor her partner were at fault in her eyes (in contrast to the other examples in this article in which officers understood

that both the public and themselves viewed a story as a lie), and her refusal does not jeopardize other officers. The officer first is confronted by
her Captain who tells her she "fucked up" and should apologize. He implies
that she should agree with Frankie's view (which she, in turn, views as a
lie), be prepared to apologize, and to go before a Board of Inquiry. The division detective is ambivalent and unsure of what to do, and passes responsibility on to her. He asks her if she will go to court. The Captain again
calls her in and by telling her that a warrant has been issued by detectives,
i.e., that there is probable cause in the case, and that she will look foolish
for persisting in her story. He does not go into the details of the case with
her, just listens to her story and then implies that she is lying and that her
partner will have to lie for her before the Board of Inquiry.

While officers are oriented to peers and their sergeants and are sensitive to those loyalties (Cain 1973), administrative officers may justify their
actions with regard to higher political obligations, organizational pressures
or even loyalty to the Police Commissioner or the Mayor (even though
such politicians may have no direct involvement in the case). If a case involves for an officer such higher loyalties and patronage as well as political corruption, there is more to be lost by *not* lying.[11] Detectives are more
cynical and view their role as mediating between the street realities and
those of the courtroom. Their standards for judging normal lies differ from
those of uniformed officers. This patrol officer, however, defined her loyalties in terms of her immediate peers and the public rather than officials
whom she viewed as corrupt. Rank, age, and other factors not explored
here may mediate an officer's relationship with the community, his/her allegiance to the police department, and sense of right and wrong.

Conclusion

This ethnographic analysis relies principally upon the perspective of the officers observed and interviewed. It draws, however, on broad ethnographic
accounts or general formulations of the police mandate and tasks. We attempt to integrate the pressures inherent in the inevitable negotiation
within hierarchical systems between official expectations and roles, and
one's individual sense of self. Officers learn how to define and control the
public and other officers, and to negotiate meanings. The social constructions or lies which arise result from situational integration of organizational,
political and moral pressures. These are not easily captured in rules, norms,
or values. Repeatedly, officers must negotiate organizational realities *and*
maintain self-worth. Police lies, serving in part to maintain a viable self, are
surrounded by cultural assumptions and designations, a social context
which defines normal or acceptable lies and distinguishes them from those
deviant or marginal to good practice. The meanings imputed to the concepts
"lie," "lying," and "truth" are negotiated and indicate or connote subtle

intergroup relationships. In a crisis, ability to display solidarity by telling a proper and effective lie is highly valued and rewarded. The ironic epithet "police liar" is neutralized. Subtle redefinition of truth includes forms of group-based honesty that are unrecognized by legal standards or by the standards of outsiders. These findings have implications that might be further researched.

Lying is a feature of everyday life found in a variety of personal, occupational and political interactions. Although telling the full truth may be formally encouraged throughout life, it is not always admired or rewarded. Neither truth nor lies are simple and uniform; cultural variation exists in the idea of normal lying and its contrast conception. Those who continue to tell the truth and do not understand communications as complex negotiations of formal and informal behavioral norms, find themselves in social dilemmas, and are vulnerable to the variety of labels used in everyday life like "tactless," "undersocialized," "deviant," or "mentally ill." The application of the label is contingent upon taken-for-granted modes of deception that structure interpersonal relations. As the last few years have shown, given the impossible mandate of the police, certain police tasks are more highly visible, e.g., drug enforcement, and even greater pressure to lie may emerge. Thus, the mandate is shaped and patterned by tasks as well as general social expectations; the sources of lying may differ as well.

The cultural grounds explored here are features of any organization which lies as a part of its routine activities, such as government agencies carrying out domestic intelligence operations and covert foreign activities. Standards of truth and falsehood drawn from everyday life do not hold here, and this shifting ground of fact and reality is often difficult to grasp and hold for both insiders and outsiders. As a result, organization members, like the police, develop sophisticated and culturally sanctioned mechanisms for neutralizing the guilt and responsibility that troublesome and even morally ambiguous lying may often entail. In time, accounts which retrospectively justify and excuse a lie may become techniques of neutralization which prospectively facilitate the construction of new lies with ready-made justifications. When grounds for lying are well-known in advance, it takes a self-reflective act to tell the truth, rather than to passively accept and use lies when they are taken-for-granted and expected. Police, like politicians, look to "internal standards" and practices to pin down the meaning of events that resonate with questions of public morality and propriety (Katz 1977). When closely examined in a public inquiry, the foreground of everyday internal standards may become merely the background for a public scandal. Normal lies, when revealed and subjected to public standards, can become the basis for scandals. This may be the first occasion on which members of the organization recognize their potential to be seen in such a fashion.

Finally, the extent to which an organization utilizing lies or heavily dependent upon them perceives that it is "under siege" varies. In attempts to shore up their mandate, organizations may tacitly justify lying. As a result, the organization may increase its isolation, lose public trust and credibility, and begin to believe its own lies. This differentially occurs within policing, across departments, and in agencies of control generally. Such dynamics are suggested by this analysis.

Acknowledgment

20 June 89. Revision of a paper presented by the senior author to The Society for the Study of Social Problems, New York, 1986. We acknowledge the very useful comments from this journal's reviewers as well as from Betsy Cullum-Swan, and Peter and Patti Adler.

Notes

1. The many social functions of lying, a necessary correlate of trust and symbolic communication generally, are noted elsewhere (Ekman 1985; Simmel 1954; Manning 1977). Our focus is restricted. We do not discuss varieties of concealment, falsification and leakage (Ekman 1985, pp. 28–29), nor interpersonal dynamics, such as the consequence of a sequence of lies and cover lies that often occur. We omit the case in which the target, such as a theater audience or someone conned, is prepared in advance to accept lies (Ekman 1985, p. 28). Nor do we discuss in detail horizontal or vertical collusions within organizations that generate and sustain lying (e.g., Honeycombe 1974).

2. We do not distinguish "the lie" from the original event, since we are concerned with verbal rationalizations in the sense employed by Mills (1940), Lindesmith and Strauss (1956) and Scott and Lyman (1969). We cluster what might be called accounts for lies (lies about lies found in the interview material included here) with lies, and argue that the complexity of the formulations, and their embeddedness in any instance (the fact that a story may include several excuses, and justifications, and may include how these, in turn, were presented to a judge) makes it misleading to adhere to a strict typology of lies such as routine vs. non-routine, case lies (both justifications and excuses) vs. cover stories (both justifications and excuses), and troublesome vs. not troublesome lies. If each distinction were worked out in a table, as one reader noted, omitting ambiguous lies, at least 16 categories of lies would result. After considering internal distinctions among lies in policing, we concluded that a typology would suggest a misleading degree of certainty and clarity. More ethnographic material is required to refine the categories outlined here.

3. Police organization, courts, and the law permit sanctioned freedom to redefine the facts of a case, the origins of the case, the bases of the arrest and the charge, the number of offenders and the number of violations. Like many public officials, they are allowed to lie when public well-being is at issue (for example, posing as drug dealers, buying and selling drugs, lying about their personal biographies and so on. See Manning 1980). Officers are protected if they lie in order to enter homes, to encourage people to confess, and to facilitate people who would otherwise be committing crimes to commit them. They have warrant to misrepresent, dissemble, conceal, and reveal as routine aspects of an investigation.

4. Evidence further suggests, in a point we do not examine here, that departments differ in the support given for lies. This may be related to legalistic aspects of the social organization of police departments (cf. Wilson 1968, Ch. 6). Ironically, for members of specialized units like "sting operations" or narcotics, the line between truth and lies becomes so blurred that according to Ekman's definition (the liar must know the truth and intend to lie), they are virtually always "telling the truth." Furthermore, as noted above, such units are more vulnerable to public criticism because they are held to unrealistic standards, and feel greater pressure to achieve illegally what cannot be accomplished legally. Marx (1988) argues that increased use of covert deceptive operations leads to further penetration of private life, confusion of public standards, and reduced expectations of police morality.

5. She spent some 12 weeks in recruit classes at the academy. For fifteen months, she rode as a non-uniformed research observer, usually in the front seat of a one officer car, from 4–midnight and occasionally on midnight to eight shifts. Although she rode with veteran

officers for the first few weeks in order to learn official procedures, the remainder of the time was spent with rookie officers. Follow-up interviews were conducted several years after the completion of the initial 18 months of observation.

6. Typically, recruits were successful in calming the "psychotic" actor when they demonstrated convincingly that they shared the psychotic's delusion and would rescue him/her from his/her persecutors by, for instance, threatening to shoot them. Such techniques were justified scientifically by trained psychologists who also stressed their practical use to avoid violence in potentially volatile situations.

7. Previous research has shown how detailed the knowledge is of officers of how and why to lie, and it demonstrates that trainees are taught to lie by specific instructions and examples (see Harris 1973; McClure 1986; Fielding 1988).

8. Technically, adding facts one recalls later, even in court, are not the basis for lies. Lies, in our view, must be intended.

9. This is taken verbatim from an interview, and thus several rather interesting linguistic turns (especially changes in perspective) are evidenced. Analysis of this sociolinguistically might suggest how this quote replicates in microcosm the problem officers have in maintaining a moral self. They dance repeatedly along the edges of at least two versions of the truth.

10. Waegel (1984) explores the retrospective and prospective accounts police use to excuse and justify the use of force. However, he does not distinguish accounts told by colleagues which are viewed as true by the speaker and those told to representatives of the legal order which are viewed as lies and fit the description of a cover story. For example, the account of accidental discharge which Waegel perceives as a denial of responsibility may also be a cover story which itself is justified as "self defense" against formal reprimand. In contrast, other police excuses and justifications invoked to account for the use of force are often renditions of events that present the officer in the morally favorable light rather than actual lies (see Van Maanen 1980; Hunt 1985; Waegel 1984). Whether the police categorize their use of force as "normal" or "brutal" (Hunt 1985) also structures the moral assessment of a lie, a point which Waegel also overlooks. Thus, acts of normal force which can be excused or justified with reference to routine accounting practices may necessitate the construction of cover stories which became morally neutral by virtue of the act the disguise. Other acts of violence viewed as demonstrating incompetence or brutality may not be excused or justified according to routine accounting practices. Although cover stories in such cases are perceived as rational, they may not provide moral protection for the officer because the lie takes on aspects of moral stigma associated with the act of violence which it conceals.

11. Supervisors and higher administrators, of course, collude in maintaining the viability of lies because they *share* the beliefs of officers that it is not possible to police by the book, and that one should not rock the boat and should keep your head down (Van Maanen 1975). It is viewed as impossible to manage routine tasks without lying both to colleagues and supervisors (Punch 1985). The working bases of corruption are thus laid, as well as the potential seen in so many corruption scandals of cover-ups, lies about lies, and vertical and horizontal collusion in lying as seen in both the Watergate and the Iran-Contra affairs.

References

Bittner, E. 1970. *Functions of the Police in an Urban Society.* Bethesda: NIMH.

——. 1974. "A Theory of Police: Florence Nightingale in Pursuit of Willie Sutton." In *The Potential for Reform of Criminal Justice,* edited by H. Jacob. Beverly Hills: Sage.

Blumberg, A. 1967. *Criminal Justice.* Chicago: Quadrangle Books.

Buckner, H. T. 1978. "Transformations of Reality in the Legal Process," *Social Research* 37:88–101.

Cain, M. 1973. *Society and the Policeman's Role.* London: Routledge & Kegan Paul.

Chatterton, M. 1975. "Organizational Relationships and Processes in Police Work: A Case Study of Urban Policing." Unpublished Ph.D. thesis, University of Manchester.

———. 1979. "The Supervision of Patrol Work Under the Fixed Points System." In *The British Police,* edited by S. Holdaway. London: Edward Arnold.

Ekman, P. 1985. *Telling Lies.* New York: W.W. Norton.

Ericson, R. and C. Shearing. 1986. "The Scientification of the Police." In *The Knowledge Society,* edited by G. Bohme and N. Stehr. Dordrecht and Boston: D. Reidel.

Fielding, N. 1988. *Joining Forces.* London: Tavistock.

Goffman, E. 1959. *The Presentation of Self in Everyday Life.* New York: Doubleday Anchor Books.

Harris, R. 1973. *The Police Academy.* New York: Wiley.

Honeycombe, G. 1974. *Adam's Tale.* London: Arrow Books.

Hunt, J. C. 1984. "The Development of Rapport Through the Negotiation of Gender in Fieldwork Among the Police." *Human Organization.*

———. 1985. "Police Accounts of Normal Force." *Urban Life* 13:315–342.

Katz, J. 1977. "Cover-up and Collective Integrity: On the Natural Antagonisms of Authority Internal and External to Organizations." *Social Problems* 25:3–17.

Klockars, C. 1983. "The Dirty Harry Problem." *Annals of the American Academy of Political and Social Science* 452 (November):33–47.

———. 1984. "Blue Lies and Police Placebos." *American Behavioral Scientist* 27:529–544.

Lindesmith, A. and A. Strauss. 1956. *Social Psychology.* New York: Holt, Dryden.

McBarnett, D. 1981. *Conviction.* London: Macmillan.

McClure, J. 1986. *Cop World.* New York: Laurel/Dell.

Maines, D. 1982. "In Search of Mesostructure: Studies in the Negotiated Order." *Urban Life* 11:267–279.

Manning, P. K. 1974. "Police Lying." *Urban Life* 3:283–306.

———. 1977. *Police Work.* Cambridge, MA: M.I.T. Press.

———. 1980. *Narc's Game.* Cambridge, MA: M.I.T. Press.

———. 1988. *Symbolic Communication: Signifying Calls and the Police Response.* Cambridge, MA: M.I.T. Press.

Marx, G. 1988. *Undercover. Policework in America: Problems and Paradoxes of a Necessary Evil.* Berkeley: University of California Press.

Mills, C. W. 1940. "Situated Actions and Vocabularies of Motive." *ASR* 6 (December): 904–913.

Punch, M. 1985. *Conduct Unbecoming.* London: Tavistock.

Reiss, A. J., Jr. 1971. *The Police and the Public.* New Haven: Yale University Press.

———. 1974. "Discretionary Justice." Pp. 679–699 in *The Handbook of Criminal Justice,* edited by Daniel Glaser. Chicago: Rand McNally.

Rubinstein, J. 1973. *City Police.* New York: Farrar, Straus and Giroux.

Scott, M. B. and S. Lyman. 1968. "Accounts." *American Sociological Review* 33:46–62.

Simmel, G. 1954. *The Society of Georg Simmel,* edited by Kurt Wolff. Glencoe: Free Press.

Skolnick, J. 1966. *Justice Without Trial.* New York: Wiley.

Stinchcombe, A. 1964. "Institutions of Privacy in the Determination of Police Administrative Practice." *American Journal of Sociology* 69:150–160.

Sudnow, D. 1965. "Normal Crimes: Sociological Features of the Penal Code in a Public Defender Office." *Social Problems* 12:255–276.

Sykes, G. M. and D. Matza. 1957. "Techniques of Neutralization: A Theory of Delinquency." *American Sociological Review* 22:664–670.

Van Maanen, J. 1974. "Working the Street . . . " in *Prospects for Reform in Criminal Justice,* edited by H. Jacob. Newbury Park, CA: Sage.

———. 1975. "Police Socialization: A Longitudinal Examination of Job Attitudes in an Urban Police Department." *Administrative Science Quarterly* 20 (June): 207–228.

———. 1980. "Beyond Account: The Personal Impact of Police Shootings." *Annals of the American Academy of Political and Social Science* 342:145–156.

Waegel, W. 1984. "How Police Justify the Use of Deadly Force." *Social Problems* 32: 144–155.

Westley, W. 1970. *Violence and the Police.* Cambridge, MA: M.I.T. Press.

Wilson, J. Q. 1968. *Varieties of Police Behavior.* Cambridge: Harvard University Press.

Wilson, J. Q. and G. Kelling. 1982. "The Police and Neighborhood Safety: Broken Windows." *Atlantic* 127 (March):29–38.

Social-Control Agents and the Application of Diagnostic Stereotypes: The Beginning Destruction of Public Identity

Quite clearly, social-control agents must become familiar with an agency's theory of the office, its working ideology, associated diagnostic stereotypes, and the like. Once we have located and described an institution's underlying formal and informal organizational structures, components, and decision-making processes, much more attention and research must be focused on the decision makers themselves; this is one of the messages of Hunt and Manning's research, discussed in the preceding selection. We can ask: Are the decision makers rendering decisions on the basis of organizational and/or individual stereotypes? Stated differently, are selected bureaucrats applying a range of gender, racial, and class stereotypes in the identifying, processing, and sanctioning of clients? Evidence suggests that some agents may very well be doing this.

In "The Epistemological Challenge of the Early Attack on 'Rate Construction,'" Troy Duster addresses the issue of "how we know what we know" about crime and deviance. Duster provides a brief history of the alternative approaches to the study of deviance (e.g., using official data versus field studies). Previous approaches to the study of deviance are compared to the new approach, which asks "What are the social processes that explain why some get classified and others don't—even though both are engaged in the same or similar behavior?" Duster's answers are unsettling, to some extent, because they point to systematic selection processes that emerge from organizational operating strategies. These issues are echoed and further expanded upon in the following work by Albert J. Meehan.

Meehan, in "The Organizational Career of Gang Statistics: The Politics of Policing Gangs" reminds us that "all statistics have an organizational career." Meehan recognizes that gangs are real—not simply the creation of the police. However, what is clear is that the record keeping practices and the statistics that they create contribute, in a significant way, to the perception and interpretation of gangs and gang activities. Further, record keeping practices of police are shaped to meet the requirements of political and organizational leaders, as well as the community that they serve. In the end, the gang problem, and the problem of deviance more generally, must be understood in the overall context of community, organizational, and political exigencies—the expressions of the theory of the office.

Meehan's work helps to demonstrate, once again, the way in which the theory of the office generates organizational procedures, processes, and protocol by directing attention to how these organizational elements shape the construction of reality. The article also focuses on the interdependent relationships that exist among police records, the statistics that are generated by the records, and the subsequent legitimation of any social-control activity that may result. We argue that the theory of the office lies at that core of these relationships. It is the theory of the office that shapes the bureaucratic slots generated for categorizing deviance and establishes a set of exigencies/responsibilities. One can also notice in the article the importance of accountability and how such accountability is satisfied by social-control agents. Satisfying accountability creates a statistical reality that supports the social-control activities or the expansion of them.

In his article, "The Medicalisation of Deviance," Richard Gosden observes an expanding application of diagnostic stereotypes. The medicalization of deviance produces a unique set of concerns where human variability is concerned. Issues of human variation (e.g., physiology, cognitive abilities, mental states, and so on) are not violations of law and are generally managed differently than criminal deviance. For example, mental health professionals have generally not taken a proactive approach to managing individuals who are experiencing mental disorders. The role of mental health professionals as agents of social control is normally initiated when an individual seeks assistance or is presented by another as needing care. Significant concerns for proactive, or "preventive," treatment should be considered, including reducing community tolerance for individual variations, a greater use of pharmaceutical therapies, and the expanded use of medicalization to manage specific populations.

Gosden makes several important observations concerning diagnostic stereotypes and/or categories, the data that they generate, and how these data are used. More importantly, perhaps, is the way in which social-control agents "think" about the existing diagnostic criteria and the agency's efficacy in managing the deviance. Sufficient faith in psychometric measures and the diagnostic criteria may well stimulate action. We agree with Gosden that "[t]he medical profession seems to be exacerbating [the] situation by disguising the essential subjectivity of psychiatric diagnosis with rhetorical claims that the DSM diagnostic system is now a branch of medical science."

The Epistemological Challenge of the Early Attack on "Rate Construction"

28

Troy Duster

The philosopher Alisdair McIntyre calls it an "epistemological crisis" when something that we acknowledge has just happened forces us to question the very foundation of what we otherwise have accepted as a truism. In its crispest form, that would be: "If what I am seeing is true, then other things that I thought were true are no longer certain. How can I now have confidence in my capacity—or confidence in the tools I have been using to assess what I thought I knew?"

At mid-century, in the period when the Society for the Study of Social Problems was just coming off the starting blocks, there were two major competing sociological approaches to the study of deviance, law, and the criminal justice system in the United States. The first was centered at Columbia and could be described, grossly, as that dominated by Merton and functionalist theory. Drawing from both Durkheim and Parsons, Merton and his students and colleagues approached the study of deviance by exploring (a) the theoretical relationship between "the deviant world" and "the normal world" through (b) an empirical strategy relying on statistical aggregates of deviant and criminal behavior as reflected in local police records and the Uniform Crime Reports of the FBI. While there was an occasional foray into field site investigations, the overwhelming tendency of this approach assumed that the data from official statistics sufficiently reflected the phenomenal world that theorizing from these databases warranted little (theoretically consequential) concern.

Chicago was the alternative and competitive approach, with a long tradition of field site investigations of particular forms of "deviance"—from "the gang" to "the hobo" to the prostitute, gambler, and other vice sets and settings. The Chicago tradition assumed the stance of "the natural world" of common-sense actors. Their practitioners *literally* went to those places in the society that any competent actor would presume to be the site of deviance. Folklore has it that one of the most celebrated sociologists of the era got "caught with his pants down" in an up-close ethnography of prostitution—

and that both the *Chicago Tribune* and the University of Chicago joined in the demand that his head roll. This tale is not so much a digression, but rather one of the more colorful remembrances of the extent of Chicago's commitment to the study of deviance in its natural setting. Yet, as Martin Nicolas would point out years later, Chicago was not doing fieldwork on white-collar crimes such as the Great Electrical Conspiracy. In short "Chicago" most generally accepted the domain assumptions about the taxonomies of the deviant world, even when challenging and correcting the accuracy of the most popular representations.

While there were significant differences between Chicago and the Columbia rendering of deviance, in very important ways, both adopted a "taken-for-granted" empirical world.

As the Sixties dawned, a third set of key players would quickly shift the focus to challenge the epistemological foundations of the whole playing field, and not just of theory and research on deviance. Egon Bittner, Aaron Cicourel, and Joseph Gusfield would ride around in police cars and see just how and when police used discretion in their arrest procedures. David Sudnow would go to the Public Defender's office and record the way in which the Public Defender and the Prosecuting Attorney worked in concert to secure guilty pleas from "certain suspects," but let others bargain "harder" when their legal representation took a private turn. Erving Goffman would even venture into mental hospital wards and break the path for the next generation that would study intake decisions for mental institutions.

When Kitsuse and Cicourel tried to publish their now classic article on the use and misuse of official statistics in the *American Sociological Review, Social Forces,* and the *American Journal of Sociology,* they ran headfirst into a brick wall with patterns and predictable grooves. Reviewers from both traditions (noted above) wrote critiques that explicitly acknowledged, "if this were true, we would have to go back to the drawing board and reorient research and theory." (Kitsuse would later write about how the "social reaction" approach to deviance required that the investigator go out into the field and study the social responses to deviance in its natural setting. So, while this approach affirmed the "natural setting" methodology of the Chicago School, it asked the investigator to look at the social patterns in the discretions and strategies of sorting and naming and classifying.) After those many tries in which they could not get the article published, Cicourel and Kitsuse told the story to Howie Becker. Just at that time, Becker had become the editor of *Social Problems.* He published it. Indeed, the new journal began to publish a series of articles that would later dominate the literature and push the other schools to the back burner. It was *Social Problems* that opened the door that led the other journals to incorporate a much richer theoretical dialogue. The Sixties later exploded with a host of competing paradigms—from Marxist theory to ethnomethodology—each with its own challenge of how to approach control and deviance. The border did not end with the sub-field of deviance. For example, in medical sociology, Irving Zola would observe and analyze how medical doctors read and interpreted the symptoms of Jewish, Italian, and Irish patients—how their presenting symptoms for the same medical condition were dramatically different. The implications for medical diagnosis and practice are deeply consequential, and Zola's work is frequently incorporated in medical training.

In some ways, the methodology of this new breed of work seemed parallel to the earlier field research traditions. However, in fundamental ways, the domain assumptions were strikingly different. Chicago was mainly trying to find out and explain what "the deviants were really like" in their natural setting. The new approach, appearing in the first decade of *Social Problems*, was to raise a different order of question: "What are the social processes that explain why some get classified and others don't—*even though both are engaged in the same or similar behavior?*" When Cicourel and Bittner were riding around in police cars observing and recording how official statistics are compiled, they were asserting that the point at which rate construction occurs is the preferred site for an investigation of those "taken for granted" statistics that had been the structural underpinning database for theorizing about deviance and crime. It would not be much of a leap to conclude that, if the site of rate construction was the preferred focal point for inquiry and theorizing about these data, then surely it would have bearing and impact on all manners of rate construction, from epidemiological work in public health to coroner's collective accounts of the causes of death.

On a personal note, I should say why this was so appealing to me as a fledgling would-be sociologist trying to make sense of the remarkably divergent police behavior that I had both witnessed and experienced. I grew up for the first 17 years on the streets near the South Side of Chicago, in an overwhelmingly black community. For example, my high school, with nearly 2,400 students, had only one student who was not black. He was the son of Chinese immigrants who owned a restaurant in the area. Then, I traveled about twenty miles north (and 10,000 light years away) to Northwestern University as an undergraduate, which, at that time, was 98 percent white. In short, from the spring of my last year in high school to the fall of my first semester of college, I went from the nearly all-black scene I just described to a college in which I was one of seven blacks on a campus of more than 7,000 whites. I did not have to earn a doctorate to discern the strikingly different police behavior in the two settings. I had not changed any of my behavior. Set and setting had changed—and so would the nature of my contact with the police.

This was long before the drug war—long before systematic racial profiling and before incarceration rates had reached our current obscene levels, with an eight to one ratio of race differences we are now witnessing across the nation. But even back in those years, the only way one could believe that real behavioral differences were reflected in those official statistics was if one never had to deal with rate construction at the site in which actors make decisions about what to sort and classify. If sociology was a behavioral science, I reasoned, it was the behavior that should be the focal point, not the already-collected statistics where the behavior was assumed to be reflected in the numbers. Many of my peers and most of the profession did not see it that way. Or at least, even if they acknowledged "a problem," for the purposes of getting on with publishing, one must act as if it is not true. No crisis of epistemology for them.

But as the Ramparts police scandal surfaces in Los Angeles, some of my colleagues in sociology come by my office, scratching their heads and struggling to make sense of it. They have to "exceptionalize it" as "bad apples" because to accept the systematic focus on young people of color as patterned practice (with occasional planting of drugs and other contraband—with false testimony in courts), would be to force a whole new way of thinking about the use of official statistics. No matter that similar police scandals have surfaced in New Orleans, Philadelphia, Chicago, Newark, and New York City in the last two decades. In the tradition of McIntyre's "epistemological crisis," if they are to believe that happens routinely, they would have to "go back to the drawing boards." An audience of members of the Society for the Study of Social Problems knows that this field went back to that drawing board forty years ago. The rich tradition of theory and research that it spawned and fostered has enhanced our understandings of many forms of behavior.

The Organizational Career of Gang Statistics: The Politics of Policing Gangs

Albert J. Meehan

How social problems are constructed by those claims makers with the power to do so is a critical sociological issue (Spector and Kitsuse 1977; Best 1995). The emergence of gangs as a social problem is arguably as much a product of the various interactional and recordkeeping practices of the police that have developed in response to the problem as it is to "labeling" in a broader sense. The daily work practices of persons working in organizations are responsive not only to public and media pressure but also to internal recordkeeping procedures and the various legal and political bodies to which they are accountable (Emerson 1991; Bowditch 1993; Margolin 1992; Meehan 1986). This means that interactional and recordkeeping practices, in essential ways, create and reproduce reality (Garfinkel 1967; Collins 1981, 1987; Rawls 1987; Fine 1991) and make an important contribution to the construction of social problems. Consequently, an understanding of these interactional and recordkeeping practices is indispensable to the study of social problems (Maynard 1988).

In the late 1970s I conducted research in a large urban East Coast police department (Bigcity) during a time when a special gang program was developed by the incumbent mayor (in an election year) to rid the city's neighborhoods of gangs. During the 1990s I collected data on the emerging response to gangs from a Midwestern police department (Plantville). Then, as now, such programs make use of the police and their recordkeeping practices in the construction of a "reality" that legitimates the political agendas of those in a position to influence matters in a police department. All statistics have an organizational career. The significance of recordwork in creating the statistics with which gangs and other social problems are measured and organizational effectiveness assessed is the subject of this article.

Throughout the twentieth century, Americans have had a recurring concern with "gangs" of young people inhabiting their streets and committing disorderly and illegal behaviors. Efforts to prevent the formation of gangs and to control their behaviors have preoccupied law enforcement and social work personnel, researchers and lawmakers alike. Indeed, in the past ten years, interest in the gang issue has intensified and shows little sign of abatement. Legislators and criminal justice officials continue to develop laws, such as the Federal Gang Violence Act (U.S. Senate 1997), and implement model strategies for Urban Street Gang Enforcement (U.S.BJA 1997). Concurrently, efforts by social scientists to integrate community-wide approaches to gang problems within the current law enforcement suppression strategy are reflected in, for example, the National Youth Gang Suppression and Intervention Program (Spergel 1994; 1995). Despite such efforts, however, the prevalent view is that, if anything, gangs have become more widespread (Klein 1995; Curry, Ball, and Decker 1996), their behaviors more violent and lethal (Fagan 1996), and their criminal behavior more highly organized (Padilla 1992; Skolnick, Bluthenthal, and Correl 1993; Taylor 1990; Sanchez-Jankowski 1991), although these last two trends are much debated (Klein 1995; Short 1997).

There is an important question, however, as to whether the increase in "gang" statistics reflects an actual increase in serious or "real" gang activity or a complex social construction. Police officers frequently express opinions that accord with a social constructionist view:

Author: Does your community have a gang problem?
Officer: When you take two officers from patrol division and put them together with two undercover detectives from special investigations for intelligence purposes to form a gang unit, I *guarantee* you that they will find gangs in the city; there will be a gang problem. This is an issue for the mayor not a real problem for the police. (Plantville PD field notes, March 15, 1998)[1]

For the officer in this exchange, "gangs" in his city are a *political* problem not a crime problem; one that the police socially construct in response to political pressure, as the officer puts it "not a real problem for the police." The officer's view accords with that of Richard C. McCorkle and Terence D. Miethe (1998) who argue that a socially constructed "fear" of "gangs" (or moral panic) has been used strategically by politicians and criminal justice officials to increase budgets and gain support for legislation that increases the powers of the police. Given the national focus of personnel and resources on gangs, combined with a response that is primarily punitive, the question of the degree to which gang problems are an artifact of political interests and their effect on police practices is an important one.

This article focuses on the relationships between police records, the statistics they generate, and the local exigencies of police work during the critical period when gangs were becoming recognized as a widespread national problem. At one point during a two-year field study in Bigcity, in 1979, youth gangs were identified as a significant problem and a special "gang" car program was instituted for dealing with it. These cars were special units specifically designated to handle "gang problems." The institution of the gang car facilitated the categorization of problems as "gang" relevant as well as heightening the visibility of a gang problem for the public. Using data from citizens' calls for service, the police response, and corresponding records generated by the police, I argue that the category "gang" became a resource for citizens and police personnel (e.g., police operators, dispatchers, and responding officers) to categorize a variety of problems with young people—usually not gangs—as "gang" problems.

The daily work practices of persons working in organizations are accountable to a variety of different internal organizational and external (e.g., political, legal, and normative) expectations (Emerson 1991; Margolin 1992). The details of those practices are organized to satisfy the demands of that accountability in ways that affect how records are constructed and maintained and the view of reality it produces (Mills 1940; Garfinkel 1967). This means not only that interactional practices reproduce and create reality in essential ways, but that this micro production always occurs within a context of accountability that shapes it in essential ways (Gill and Maynard 1995; Manning 1997; Meehan 1986). In practical organizational terms, this means that if those with political power (e.g., strong mayors) view gangs as a problem, then the police will legitimate this view and, in doing so, create its statistical reality. In this way, political interests can make use of the police and their recordkeeping practices in the construction of a "reality" that legitimates the political agendas of those in a position to influence matters in a police department. The significance of police recordkeeping and its responsiveness to political contexts of accountability is generally overlooked in contemporary discussions of America's street gang problems (for an exception to this point, see Klein 1995).

The definition of what constitutes a "gang" is generally assumed to determine what will be measured as gang activity. If definitions vary—and there is considerable debate and discussion about the definition of a gang (Klein 1995; Huff 1996; Short 1997)—most researchers believe that the activities measured and classified as gang activities would necessarily vary as well. For example, Cheryl Maxson and Malcolm Klein (1996) have demonstrated that police adoption of a member versus motive conception of gang-related homicide affects the rate of reported gang-related homicides in a jurisdiction. Confounding this issue is the widespread diffusion of gang culture that has spawned behaviors by small, highly transitory groups that "pass" as gang behavior in suburban communities and smaller cities (Short 1996).

More important than the official definitions, however, are the working practices used by the police in recording their activities as gang related. The application of definitions in practice is not necessarily affected by official or even informal definitions of gangs. If a practice develops in a particular department, that certain sorts of incidents can most efficiently be labeled as gang incidents, or, if there is a unit designated to take care of gangs, or if citizens for some reason begin to refer to certain problems as related to gangs, then those activities are more likely to be recorded as gang activities and consequently produce gang statistics in that department, regardless of the existence of an official definition of gangs.[2]

Crime statistics have often been created and manipulated by political pressure to accomplish a variety of ends (McCorkle and Miethe 1998, pp. 54–56; Chambliss 1994; Zatz 1987; Seidman and Couzens 1974). In Bigcity, the "problem" with youth gangs was identified during an election year and consequently had political implications. In such a context, the claimed presence of gangs allowed the Bigcity police organization to enhance and reinforce the mayor's claim that he was doing something "for the neighborhoods" by bringing the youth gangs under control. Such external political pressures constitute an important context of accountability for the police, and the police as an organization tend to manage such pressures through the manipulation of their records (Seidman and Couzens 1973; Manning 1997; Meehan 1993).[3]

This article illustrates how this management of political and organizational accountability is achieved at the local interactional level across the various layers of the police response. The context of accountability has a political and organizational dimension but the police practices that satisfy the demands of accountability and create the statistical reality that supports organizational and political accountability are *interactional*. An analysis of the documentary reality (Smith 1974; Wheeler 1969) created by the organization through local interactional practices is particularly relevant to understanding how the police "solve" a problem, in this case creating, maintaining, and controlling the appearance of the street gang problem. I am not suggesting that there are no street gangs in Bigcity. In "Corktown," the district I studied, officers thought there were one, maybe two identifiable street gangs, but they felt that most of the so-called "gang calls" they were assigned to handle were unrelated to "real" gang activity. By "real," the police refer to activities that *they* believed to be gang activities, as opposed to the way the police organization expected them to report gang activities. Both are social constructions, but at different levels. When asked what a "real" gang was, officers utilized a classic "social science" definition: an organized group of young people (typically teenagers) with a leadership structure, who wore common identifiable clothing and who committed serious and/or violent crime. Yet officers and dispatchers routinely and unproblematically interchanged "gang" and "group" when referring to young people. The issue here is not whether there are real gang problems but rather to analyze how an increased awareness of a public problem places particular kinds of constraints upon the police as an organization to show itself as accountable and as solving that problem. In doing so, we can see how groups of ordinary young people were constituted as gangs at various points in the course of citizen complaints and police responses to incidents during a time when gangs have been publicly designated as a problem.

I refer to the various stages at which such constitutive formulations of activities into "gang" activities occur as the organizational career of a statistic. This career involves:

1. Citizens' formulation of a problem to the police operator in a call for service and how such formulations are understood by operators as constituting a gang/group problem and subsequently encoded into an organizationally relevant and actionable category;

2. Dispatchers' formulation of the problem to the patrol officers assigned to respond to a call;

3. Patrol officers' understanding of the dispatchers' formulation of the problem to which they are responding;

4. Patrol officers' location and assessment of the "problem";

5. Patrol officers' response to the "problem";

6. The various records produced by patrol officers regarding their response and the gang statistics that result from those records.

Methods and Data

Whereas other researchers have used surveys and vignette scenarios (Decker and Kempf-Leonard 1991) or a combination of media reports, statistics, and legislative responses (McCorkle and Miethe 1998) to document the social construction of gang problems, I focus on the various stages and practices through which activities are transformed officially into gang activities by the police and the context of accountability within the police organization. This allows the formulation of an organizational "career" for statistics. Examining the organizational career of statistics necessarily involves utilizing a multimethod approach, and I draw upon several types of data.

The first data set consists of a sample of telephone calls to the Bigcity 911 emergency number that were categorized as gang calls by the police operators and dispatchers and subsequently assigned to the gang car in Bigcity's Corktown police district. The organizational career of most police patrol work begins with the citizen's call for service (Reiss 1971; Skogan 1975; Lundman 1980; Maxfield, Lewis and Szoc 1980; Manning 1988; 1992). Consequently, the citizens' calls to the police analyzed below can be treated as constituting the first step in the organizational career of most statistics. The calls were identified by obtaining gang car patrol logs ($N = 34$) from the Corktown police district for a twelve-week period in the fall, which is the height of the political campaign season. The gang car was fielded three evenings (Thursday–Saturday) per week in two, four-hour shifts. Thus, there are two patrol logs generated each evening. Three of the six logs produced each week were randomly selected for this analysis. In patrol logs, officers record all calls for service assigned to the car in

addition to other activities undertaken on a given evening (e.g., routine patrol of parks, and field interrogations). Seventeen logs, which reflected the
most active shifts, were then chosen; and recordings of the seventy-three
citizens' calls for service assigned to the gang car on those shifts were obtained from the communications division. These seventy-three calls represent 70 percent of all citizen calls assigned to the gang car during this
twelve-week period.[4]

The focus of the analysis will be upon the relationship of the call to the
subsequent gang categorization. A conversational or interactional analysis
(Sacks, Schegloff, and Jefferson 1974) of the calls affords a view of the citizens' own formulations of their problems and how these formulations are
constituted and negotiated by operators and citizens as a "gang" problem
(see Sasson 1995 for a different use of citizen formulations). Further, they
illustrate how police operators encode such problems, a process, that is sensitive to the interactional organization of the call, the political context to
which the operator/dispatcher and the police are accountable, and the organization's current solution: namely, the availability of a "gang" car to handle such problems.

The second data set consists of all available records and recordings for
one evening's work in the gang car in the same district and includes the
transcripts of citizens' calls, dispatchers' assignments of the calls, transcripts of the police response (tape-recorded), the author's field notes from
the car, and the corresponding records (e.g., patrol logs) of the police response for that evening.[5] These data allow an examination of how the police assess and respond to the "problem" they have been assigned by the
dispatcher, as well as those which problems they initiate on their own
(i.e., "on view"), and how these activities are utilized by officers to construct their recordwork (e.g., patrol logs) for the evening. These materials illustrate how the responding officers constitute the activities of
persons as a "gang," to use Harold Garfinkel's (1967) term, "for all practical purposes."

The logs for this one evening are also compared with the thirty-four gang
car patrol logs in the first data set in order to assess the representativeness
of that night's work. The analysis shows that, if anything, the officers responded to my presence with a more conservative use of the gang designation. That is, the logs from the other thirty-four shifts show a
significantly greater proportion of gang designations. Therefore, generalizing from that night's work does not overestimate the effect.

In addition to my data set of actual calls for service, I utilize a statistical
data set developed by Glenn Pierce (personal communication) that aggregates the department's categorizations of all citizen calls for service to Bigcity emergency 911 during a six-year period (3.2 million calls). This allowed
for a comparison of statistics on gangs for the period covered by my research with statistics for prior and subsequent years. The analysis shows

that significantly more calls received a gang designation during the election year than calls in the years immediately before or after.

The variety of records available allows for a consideration of whether and how the police interpretation and transformation of an incident into a gang problem is preserved in a documentary form. I argue that police recordkeeping is geared toward external accountability and is only a gloss for "what happened." To the patrol officer, recordwork is secondary in importance to the job of policing the streets. That job consists of managing the continual problematic contingencies created by the ambiguities inherent in social interaction in such a way as to render nonproblematic the meaning of the task at hand (Meehan 1986).

Therefore, the officers' organization and use of the category "gang" is responsive not only to the immediate problems of achieving the police relevance of a citizen's complaint (i.e., within a call for service) but also to the organization's work relevancies (i.e., generating "activity") and the larger political framework to which the police are held accountable (e.g., "solving" a problem in an election year to make the incumbent mayor look good). In this fashion, "solutions" to problems may in fact produce the records that are used to constitute the statistical existence of a problem in the first place. The statistic represents the organizational response under specific conditions of accountability. It does not represent what the police consider to be real gang activity. Research results based upon such records are as much out of step with the "reality" behind the documents as the political action that created them and which they sustain.

The Political Context of the Gang Problem

In May 1979, a mayoral election year in Bigcity, the Corktown police district, along with other police districts throughout the city, initiated a supplemental weekend patrol, as they had for several previous summers, to help control teen behavior on the streets. Corktown is a predominantly white (99.5 percent), Irish, working-class area of Bigcity with approximately twenty thousand residents. It is one square mile in size and contains two housing projects, although most of the residents live in one- and two-family dwellings. The gang car was a supplemental unit to the regularly assigned patrol cars for Corktown. In previous years, these supplemental units had been fielded at the discretion of the district captain, and were called the "drinking" car by the police (taking care of public drinking in the district), not the "gang" car. This supplemental unit was an overtime assignment for district officers who drew double pay for each four-hour shift. Two shifts, back to back (7:45 P.M.–11:45 P.M. and 11:45 P.M.–3:45 A.M.), were assigned each evening from Thursday through Saturday. In 1979, they became "gang" cars for the first time. More significantly, until the summer before the election, this effort had not been a media event.

Statistically, gangs appeared to be a big problem for Corktown[6] as well as for Bigcity as a whole. For example, an aggregate analysis of the 3.2 million calls for police service to Bigcity's 911 emergency number during the years 1977–1982 reveals that gang calls were one of the most prominent categories of problem reported to the police and handled by officers. In 6.4 percent ($N = 206,101$) of these 3.2 million calls for service, it was the 911 *police operators* who initially classified a call as a "gang" call. The gang category was the third most frequent category used by 911 operators, following the categories "investigate" (10.6 percent) and "internal assistance" (8.3 percent), which do not identify any specific type of problem. Thus, gang activities would appear to figure prominently in the police operators' categorization of a reported problem into a police relevant category.[7]

In June, the police chief announced a citywide program to curtail street gangs. The primary component was a citywide gang squad, not controlled by the district captain, that would patrol the various districts throughout the city. At the onset of this citywide program there was considerable media coverage of the gang cars. One Bigcity newspaper reported: "The Bigcity police began what they termed 'an all out war' on teenage gangs across the city last night." Newspapers reported that the police program included a unit of men, dubbed the "G-Squad," who would patrol selected areas of the city. One report also announced that each of the districts would field a car to curb the behavior of "gangs" in the neighborhoods. In addition, a newspaper reported that officers would file Field Interrogation/Observation (FIO) reports with headquarters downtown for youths who are seen in groups, even when they are not causing trouble. The information would be entered into a computerized database, and if a name showed up more than one time the police would send a letter to the parents to alert them that their child was part of a neighborhood gang.

Ten days after the beginning of the citywide gang patrols, Bigcity's mayor and police chief announced that the gang program was a *success*. Citing statistics based upon officers' responses to calls for service, they claimed that throughout the city, and in Corktown, the gang squads were effective. While the unit generated increased statistics documenting gang activities, calls for service regarding "gangs" were reportedly declining as the police announced that the message had gone out to the youth gangs. The mayor announced in a newspaper report: "The added police presence in the neighborhoods is just what is needed to convey to young people we are serious about controlling and eventually eradicating youth gangs in this city. The destruction and disruptiveness youth gangs represent can no longer be tolerated." The police chief, in an interview with one of Corktown's community newspapers, commented:

> When the people of Corktown begin to notice our prompt response, I think you'll find more residents willing to call 911 when local gangs begin to cause problems for neighborhood residents. I'm quite sure that

the Anti-Gang patrol will prove a very successful component of our overall gang prevention effort.

Perhaps the best explanation of the "gang squad" came from some of the officers during the ride-alongs who simply said: "It's an election year, time for the mayor to show something's being done for the neighborhoods." This view was shared by a youth who, when asked what he thought of the use of dogs by the gang squad, was quoted in the newspaper saying: "It's election year, the dogs will be around until the election is over and then you won't see them any more."[8] As predicted, the gang program ended approximately fifteen days after the November election, which the incumbent mayor won.

Monitoring newspaper reports in the year following the election showed that the city had no "gang problem" that year. Over the next two years, the Bigcity police, due to layoffs in the department and city budget problems, announced that the police would no longer respond to calls about groups "bothering the neighborhood" because there were more pressing crime problems and not enough police personnel. This was, in some sense, more consistent with police experience on the street than the original formulation of and response to the "gang" problem. Further, there were no supplemental overtime units fielded during the summer months. Bigcity also closed a number of district stations during this time period and attempted to consolidate its police force. As the next election year approached, however, Bigcity finally managed to overcome the many political problems that they faced in funding additional police. As the summer prior to the election approached, the mayor and police chief unveiled a new neighborhood patrol in each precinct to supplement existing units to help stop the underage drinking and vandalism. The program, they said, was not like the "gang" units during the last election. However, by all the accounts of their activities reported in the newspaper, they sounded extremely similar.

Table 1 provides aggregate data on gang calls before and after the election year, data that support the "election year" interpretation of the gang problem and illustrate how the number of gang calls changed over the course of the six-year period. These data show that, during the election year, the number of gang calls, as classified by the 911 operator, increased by 12.8 percent (4,982 calls) from the previous year. Gang calls represented 9.8 percent of all dispatched calls to the 911 operator during the election year, the highest during the six-year period. After the election year, the total number and percentage of gang calls declined. As expected during the election year, the number of calls categorized by responding officers with a gang designation also increased, although slightly, from the previous year. After the election year, both the number of gang calls and the number confirmed by responding officers progressively declined, reaching its low point some three years later.[9]

**Table 1   Operator and Officer Categorization
of Gang Calls by Year**

Year	911 Calls Dispatched[a]	Categorized Gang by 911 Operator		Confirmed Gang by Officer	
		Number	Percentage	Number	Percentage
2 yrs. before	384,807	34,715	9.0 %	56,976	14.8 %
1 yr. before	427,749	38,901	9.0	52,681	12.3
Election	446,171	43,883	9.8	56,094	12.5
1 yr. after	436,523	38,905	8.9	49,152	11.2
2 yrs. after	393,934	28,914	7.3	37,136	9.4
3 yrs. after	333,955	20,783	6.2	26,096	7.8

[a] This number reflects the total number of 911 calls that resulted in the dispatch of a patrol unit. It excludes internal or administrative calls made to the 911 number.

While the social construction of a gang problem offered obvious benefits to both the police and the mayor, the question remains how such a complex process is managed and what role individual citizens, 911 police operators, dispatchers, and officers played in generating the statistics on which the appearance of the problem depends.

911 Calls Reporting "Gang" Activity

The calls analyzed in this section are from Corktown residents to Bigcity's 911 emergency number.[10] These calls report incidents that operators categorized as "gang incidents." The gang car for the Corktown section of the city was then dispatched to respond to the citizen's call. Moreover, the categorization of these calls as involving "gang" problems was entered on the computer records of calls for service retained by the department. Subsequently, the official department records of these calls became part of the official police statistics on the gang problem in Bigcity and Corktown.

Some Conversational Features of "Gang Calls"

The analysis of actual calls to the police, categorized by the police operator as "gang calls," indicates that what constitutes a gang problem is equivocal in a number of ways. The phenomenon, a gang problem, and how it comes to be seen as a problem, is an issue. Increased attention to gangs as a "problem" (e.g., via media attention) may itself constitute and produce the visibility and problematic character of groups of youths for citizens and police alike. Consequently, any next incident involving young persons can be inspected for its gang relatedness. The use of a categorization device (Sacks 1972) such as "gang" can be said to be in vogue given this newfound relevance and possible remedy (that is, a gang car will be sent). If attention to the gang problem and the availability of an official categorization increases the percentage of calls recorded as gang calls, then a statistical increase in gang problems may be due to the various ways in which police, media, and citizens come to use the term "gang" to refer to some activity, or collection of activities, rather than representing a real increase in what was formerly considered to be gang activity.

For example, in the call below, *playing tag football* under the new lights is formulated by the caller, and accepted by the operator, as a gang-related activity. (Note: **Boldface** print highlights the features of the call discussed in the text. Timed pauses are in parentheses. Double slashes // indicate overlapped talk. PD represents the police operator, CA represents the citizen caller.)[11]

[Call 32: Tape 1]

PD: Bigcity police three eight five
CA: In Corktown
PD: Yes
CA: **In front of ninety eight Bedford Street there's a gang of teenagers playing tag football under these new lights (.5) can you get them out of here please?**
PD: Yes, ma'am

In the following call, no activities of the persons being reported are described by the citizen, and nothing is revealed about the nature of the incident except the label "gang":

[Call 10: Tape 2]

PD: Bigcity Police
CA: Yeah you wanna send a car down to twenty seven Parton Street in Corktown//**for the gang of ki-**
PD: What's the prob-(1.0)
PD: What's the address again sir?

Indeed, no activities are described, and it appears that the use of the term "gang" suffices for a description of the problem. However, the use of the term gang to describe the persons being reported to the police is not a necessary feature of calls that were categorized as "gang" calls, either. One notable observation about the vast majority of citizen reports in the collection of "gang" calls under consideration here is that the term "gang" is rarely used. Yet the calls are designated "gang" calls by the police operator and dispatched to the "gang car" for the district. The category has organizational accountability for the police operator which enhances its use. Indeed, various types of activity (not necessarily involving legal violations) appear in these calls as if they were categorically tied to "gangs" and seem to be usable by both caller and operator as a resource for constituting the "gangness" of the incident.

Such gang-associated activities include drinking, fighting, smoking pot, throwing rocks or beer bottles, banging on doors, being in the hallways, hanging out on corners, "pissing on the steps of the rectory," or any combination of the above. The term "gang," and those activities associated with it, are clearly interchangeable with "kids," "group," and "youths," and these terms were typically found in calls subsequently categorized as "gang" calls. Indeed, descriptions of "rowdy" behavior were, in these calls, presumed by police operators to be categorically tied to any gathering of young people and officially categorized as "gang" behavior.

For example, in the following call, the use of "gang" by the police *operator* indicates that the term is not necessarily tied to particular people or identifiable groups per se but rather to the types of activities *expected* from groups of young people in general:

[Call 16: Tape 2]

PD: Bigcity Police
CA: Yeah, I'd like to report a disturbance on the corner of Shakerhill and Alton Street in Corktown (.5)
PD: Shakerhill and Alton?
CA: That's right
PD: And what's the problem? (.5)
CA: **They're throwing beer bottles and uh//**
PD: **What's this a gang?**
CA: Yeah

The caller's description "They're throwing beer bottles" is formulated by the operator in next turn as "What's this a gang?" This formulation solicits and receives an agreement from the caller. Thus, in this call, it is the activity of "throwing beer bottles" that is treated as "gang" behavior.

In the following call, where the report is about "some boys," it is not immediately clear how the operator arrives at the categorization of the problem as a "gang" problem:

[Call 40: Tape 2]

CA: Hi **I'd like to report some boys** right now there on Masters Street, somebody has to call the cops right?
PD: Alright, what number Masters?
CA: It's right down from the (.5) one twenty nine Bastille Way (.5)
PD: What number are you at now?
CA: One twenty nine (.5)
PD: You're at one twenty nine Bastille Way?
CA: Yes
PD: **And the gang is out there?**
CA: **The gang is out there yeah they gotta go home and go to bed**
PD: All right we'll be down

The caller begins the call by stating what they want to do in the call (report some boys) rather than report what the "boys" are actually doing. After determining a location for the complaint, the operator formulates a description of the problem in the form of a question: "And the gang is out there?" In this utterance, some "boys" have now been constituted by the police operator as a "gang," a categorization the caller agrees with in their next turn. How the "boys" become the "gang" cannot be inferred from any activities reported by caller, as in the previous cases, because no such activities are reported. Nor does the caller offer the category themselves. But *it doesn't really matter.* The operator's candidate categorization, "gang," is "police relevant" and provides for police intervention, whereas exploring the caller's reason for "reporting some boys" would require more time on the call, which has already been occupied with some difficulties in establishing the location. Further exploration might also turn up the police *irrelevance* of "they gotta go home and go to bed." The caller concludes by agreeing with the operator's categorization.

In calls 16 and 40 above, the operator clearly selects the category "gang" and then solicits an agreement for the proposed categorization of the problem. These dispatcher formulations "And the gang is out there?" (call 40) and "What's this a gang?" (call 16) are themselves distinctive interactional practice in calls to the police (see Meehan 1989), and illustrate the negotiated character of these reports which are then produced as *"facts" for all practical purposes* (Garfinkel 1967). The calls make it clear that many different types of activities are classifiable within the calls themselves, as gang related. There are some calls where the categorization of the problem as a "gang" problem is explicitly formulated in the complaint by the caller or operator, that is, where the caller and/or operator utilize the categorization "gang" to formulate the problem. In other calls, the designation of the problem as a "gang problem" is an achievement arrived at by the operator only *over the course of the call.* Sometimes the designation "gang" does not appear in the call at all. But the "gang car" is dispatched, and the call results in a gang statistic nevertheless. Therefore, it is misleading to search for explicit uses of the term "gang" by the operator or caller, simply because all of the calls have resulted in a "gang" statistic. The operator's categorization of the call as an official "gang" statistic obviously does not depend upon such initial displays, but rather, relies on how, for all practical purposes, what is being produced by the caller in the complaint can be heard for its "gang" relevance.

There are several points raised by this analysis of citizens' calls with respect to police records, and the statistics generated from them. First, the fact that each call resulted in a statistic regarding youth gangs cannot be overlooked. Calls such as the "gang playing tag football under the new lights" are a clear case for arguing that taking the "outcome" of the call to represent the problem as reported by the caller creates misinterpretations of police problems regarding gangs. Second, by analyzing calls for service, we can see that problems are often constituted as "gang" problems, not at the beginning of the call, but only over its course. The negotiations between the police operator and caller generate the record and project a particular organizational career for the reported problem. The response by the police patrol, and the records generated therein, constitute further categorizations, negotiations, and interpretations of the incident. How this response contributes to the "facts" about the gang problem is the focus of the remaining sections of this article.

The Police Response: An Evening's Work in the Gang Car

Calls to the 911 number that report "gangs" suggest that a wide variety of activities are labeled as gang activities by callers, operators, and dispatchers. The police officers' role in this labeling process begins when a car is dispatched. The following discussion of the organizational career of incidents is based upon data collected during one evening (2 four-hour shifts) in the Corktown gang car. Although I rode along in the gang car on other evenings, I chose this evening's work for analysis because of the detailed interactional data available for this particular evening, including audio-taped citizens' calls, audiotapes of both the dispatchers and the police response in the car, and my field notes. My goal is to compare the actual police response to the evening's events to both the reported problem in the original citizen's call and with the officer's actual patrol logs that report and document the "official" record of the incident.

In comparing the actual police responses at various levels of the organization to the problem as reported by the citizen, this analysis is not a comparison of facts with social constructions. Rather, I treat all of these as levels of socially constructed activity. The police response is one level of socially constructed activity. The problem as reported in the original citizen's call is another level of socially constructed activity. Finally, the resulting official record is a social construction comprised of a complex combination of the other levels.

This following discussion is divided into five key areas:

1. Keeping the patrol log and its relationship to the documentary reality of the police organization;
2. Citizens' complaints as a source of ambiguity for the responding patrol officers;
3. The most typical police response to citizens' calls (brooming);
4. On-view, or proactive, responses that are *recorded* in the patrol logs;
5. Incidents that are *not* recorded in the patrol logs.

Keeping-the-Patrol-Log

The patrol logs are part of the work relevancies of officers, where maintaining a record of their response is a part of the context of accountability operating within the police organization. That is, officers can be held accountable for what they do and don't do and for how they do it. The hyphenated term, keeping-the-log, is used to indicate that this is not just a task or an instance of an action, but rather a set of practices officers have created that display their orientation to organizational accountability. From the patrol officer's viewpoint, keeping-the-patrol log is, first and foremost, displaying police "activity" *for the record.* As Jonathan Rubenstein (1973 p. 44) observes: "'Activity' is the internal product of police work. It is the statistical measure which the sergeant uses to judge the productivity of his men, the lieutenant uses to assure himself that the sergeant is properly directing his men, the captain to assure his superiors that he is capably administering his district, and the department administrators to assure the public that their tax dollars are not being squandered."

For example, in Corktown, patrol logs were often reviewed by the precinct captain and lieutenants prior to attending community meetings with residents, so that they would have a sense of what had been happening in the district. Or, when citizens complained about a specific problem or the lack of patrol in their neighborhood, the logs would be consulted to determine how often officers had been in a specific area, neighborhood, or address. At roll call, officers would be instructed about those areas or addresses where the "brass" (supervisory police officers above the rank of sergeant) or citizens had requested extra patrols. Such areas would typically receive additional attention throughout the shift, but most important, whether the officers actually patrolled that area or not, those areas or addresses would be reported in the logs as having received extra patrols. Thus, the logs do not necessarily reflect "what happened" but rather a version of "what happened" created by the work demands and relevancies entailed in keeping-the-log and its accountability to organizational expectations (McCleary 1977; Meehan 1986).[12]

The patrol logs consist of a sheet filled out by officers during the course of a shift. These logs figure prominently in the recordwork for the shift, as they are the primary documents that officers produce to account for their time. In patrol logs, officers record how they received an incident (BC = Bigcity central dispatch; OS = on-view); the times of dispatch, arrival, and clearance of the incident; the location of the incident (using street address or common landmark) and sector location (an organizational designation); the nature of the incident; and a disposition code. Figures 1, 2, and 3 below replicate the logs for the two shifts discussed and the accompanying coding instructions for filling them out.[13]

The description of an incident is initially shaped by the dispatcher's description of the problem when a call is dispatched to a car. Although such

Figure 1 ● Gang Car Patrol Log (Shift 1).
(All hand printed entries made by officers are in italics.)

BIGCITY POLICE OFFICERS' LOG STATION: *9* DATE: *8-12-79*

Odometer 15825 22 mi. *7:45 p.m.–11:45 p.m.*

OFFICER'S NAME	BADGE #	PARTNER'S NAME	BADGE #	TOUR	CAR
Sgt. Rossi	*0321*	*Ptlm. Alpen*	*2931*	*B*	*290 Gang Car*

Assigned by	Dispatch Time	Time of Arrival	Time Cleared	Location of Incident	Sector	Nature of Incident	Disp.
BC	*7:45 pm*	*7:45 pm*	*7:45 pm*	*Station*	*C*	*Log on*	*O-N*
BC	*7:59 pm*	*7:59 pm*	*8:10 pm*	*Station garage*	*C*	*Gas 19 gals.*	*C.R.*
	8:10 pm	*8:13 pm*	*8:18 pm*	*Mountain Square*	*C*	*Assist k-9 group*	
BC	*8:18 pm*	*8:21 pm*	*8:33 pm*	*Peters School*	*C*	*Group disturbing*	*7-B*
OS	*9:15 pm*	*9:15 pm*	*9:25 pm*	*Rainey Field*	*C*	*Disbursed group*	*NA*
BC	*9:25 pm*	*9:27 pm*	*9:35 pm*	*1 O'Malley Way*	*B*	*Loud Music*	*12-P*
OS	*9:45 pm*	*9:45 pm*	*10:05 pm*	*Peters School*	*C*	*Kids disturbing neighbors*	*NA*
OS	*10:07 pm*	*10:07 pm*	*10:15 pm*	*Murtry Playground*	*C*	*Area check*	*NEG*
OS	*10:30 pm*	*10:30 pm*	*10:50 pm*	*Davis Playground*	*C*	*Area check*	*NEG*
BC	*10:55 pm*	*10:55 pm*	*11:05 pm*	*1 Barker St.*	*C*	*Disbursed group*	*7-P*
OS	*11:07 pm*	*11:07 pm*	*11:12 pm*	*Wolcott School*	*C*	*Disbursed group*	*NA*
BC	*11:12 pm*	*11:15 pm*	*11:20 pm*	*52 Corsant St.*	*C*	*Group disturbance*	*9-C*
OS	*11:35 pm*	*11:35 pm*	*11:40 pm*	*31 Salk St. area*	*B*	*Area check*	*NEG*
BC			*11:45 pm*	*Station (5 FIOs)*	*C*	*Logoff*	*O-F*

formulations are generally considered "imprecise" characterizations by the responding officers (Manning 1988, p. 21), when reporting the disposition of the call they must confirm or disconfirm the initial characterization of the "nature of the incident" through a disposition code. The disposition code contains two designations: a number that indicates the type of incident and a phonetic designation that indicates the type of police action taken (Figure 3). For example, in Figure 2 the dispatcher reports a "gang" at 74 Alcon Street, and this is entered in the log. After the incident is handled, the officer will radio the dispatcher a disposition code. The disposition code, 7-Paul (or 7-P in the logs) would be read as "gathering causing annoyance (outside) and services were rendered" (i.e., group dispersed). Even though not obviously a "gang" designation, the disposition confirms the original report and the dispatch categorization of the incident as a gang incident stands for the record.

Figure 2 ● Gang Car Patrol Log (Shift 2).
(All hand printed entries made by officers are in italics.)

BIGCITY POLICE   OFFICERS' LOG   STATION: *9*   DATE: *8-12/13-79*

11:45 p.m.–3:45 p.m.

OFFICER'S NAME	BADGE #	PARTNER'S NAME	BADGE #	TOUR	CAR
Sgt. Rossi	*0321*	*Ptlm. Cramer*	*1345*	*A*	*290 Gang Car*

Assigned by	Dispatch Time	Time of Arrival	Time Cleared	Location of Incident	Sector	Nature of Incident	Disp.
BC	*11:45 pm*			*Station*		*Log on*	*C-R*
BC	*11:50 pm*	*11:55 pm*	*12:00 am*	*74 Alcon*	*C*	*Gang*	*7-P*
BC	*12:00 am*	*12:05 am*	*12:10 am*	*65 Salk*	*C*	*Gang on roof*	*7-P*
BC	*12:15 am*	*12:17 am*	*12:20 am*	*Manelt & Mountainhill*	*C*	*Gang on roof*	*7-P*
BC	*12:30 am*	*12:35 am*	*12:40 am*	*65 Salk*	*C*	*Gang*	*8-P*
BC	*1:45 am*	*1:50 am*	*1:55 am*	*Mtain & Mountainhill*	*C*	*Gang*	*8-P*
BC	*2:00 am*	*2:10 am*	*2:15 am*	*Kane Crt.*	*C*	*Gang*	*7-P*
BC	*2:30 am*	*2:35 am*	*2:40 am*	*Battlehill & Mountain*	*C*	*Disturbance*	*7-B*
BC	*2:45 am*	*2:50 am*	*2:55 am*	*50 Walters Way*	*C*	*Disturbance*	*7-P*
BC	*3:00 am*	*3:05 am*	*3:10 am*	*127 Redfern St.*	*C*	*Log off*	*O-F*
BC	*3:45 am*			*Station*	*C*		

In the logs for the two shifts discussed here (Figures 1 and 2), thirteen calls for service were handled, four on the first shift and nine on the second shift. The 7-Paul disposition code (gathering causing annoyance and services rendered) was used in six out of the thirteen calls. The 7-Boy code (gathering causing annoyance and no person can be found) was used in three calls; the 8-Paul code (investigate persons and services rendered) was used in two calls. The 9-Charles code (investigate premises and no such address) and 12-Paul code (loud music and services rendered) were each used once. No arrests were made by the officers on these two shifts.

I compared the log sheets for this evening with thirty-four other gang car log sheets. A total of 103 citizens' calls for service were handled for an average of three calls per four-hour shift. So this particular evening was busier in terms of handling citizen calls for service. For the 34 tours, only one arrest was made by the gang car, and three drunks were taken to the station. In spite of the obvious lack of serious problems handled, however, the Adam disposition code, which indicates that an incident was "not a bona fide" police matter was only used once over this three-month period.[14]

Figure 3 ● Bigcity Log Disposition Codes Used on These Shifts

Procedure Codes:
  O-N = unit logging on
  O-F = unit logging off
  C-R = unit clearing from assignment not requiring code

Reporting Codes for Disposition:

No.	*Incident*
7	Gathering causing annoyance (outside)
8	Investigation persons (routine)
9	Investigation premises (routine)
12	Noisy Party-Radio, T.V., etc.

Phonetic	*Police Action*
A-Adam	Not a bona fide incident
B-Boy	No person can be found
C-Charles	No such address
P-Paul	Services rendered

The logs are a type of *pre-structured observation schedule,* and the task of the responding officers is to *fit* the behaviors they encounter (e.g., gathering causing annoyance; disturbance) and their response (e.g., service rendered; peace restored) into one of the available categories. This involves making sense of the scenic unfolding of behaviors they observe, and finding in that process, some feature that is usable in determining a category code for the record (i.e., the patrol logs). In short, the keeping-of-the-log requires making the codes appear to be a sensible and rational procedure by formulating how, in some way, the codes correspond to "what happened" for all practical purposes.

The correspondence of the written log to "what happened" (i.e., what the officers in the car observed, and their interpretation of it, and their actions) is, in an important sense, irrelevant. Formulating the night's work in police relevant terms is much more important. That is, *it is the appearance of orderliness that is necessary* for the log to do its work. For example, Figure 1 shows that the car began the shift at 7:45 P.M. and ended at 11:45 P.M. While this shows that the time the car was in service corresponds to the time it was supposed to be in service (according to the organization schedule), this does not correspond to when the car actually left and returned. In fact, there was about a five to ten minute difference between the actual and recorded times. The reported times on the log correspond to scheduled organizational shift changes and display organizationally ordered time not the time as experienced in the car. If the sequence of events, as the officers experienced it, was entered in the log it would be problematic from both a practical point of view (i.e., not enough space) as well as from an organizational standpoint. Practical problems, such as checking out the portable radios, and remembering a flashlight or ticket book, are part of routine shift changes. Yet, for purposes of keeping the log, noting those routine checks, or the consequences of their occurrence (i.e., forgetting to log on), would not provide a display of an "efficient" organization. By contrast, recording that the shift began and ended on time *is* a display of efficiency, thus making the "organization" appear as though it is working as planned.

The keeping-of-the-log, by its very format and use, exhibits in documentary form, for any next reader, the "rational procedures" for responding to incidents. "Rule following" and "hierarchy" are clear via the proper entries. When dispatched to a location, officers record they went there, announced their arrival to dispatch, and informed them when matters were under control (even if that is not what happened, i.e., the police don't see anyone but record that they do so as to confirm the dispatch code). "Technical skills" and "competency" are evidenced in the learning of and application of special codes that provide an "organization" for the meaning of an incident and the corresponding actions of the officers. By encoding events that are initially understood through commonsense knowledge of "policing the streets" into a technical or analytical format, the officer creates a record of the incident that only has meaning in the context of the practice. It is through the keeping-of-the-log that the "formal organization" is created and sustained. The encoding procedure and the document it produces provide no insight into the discovery procedures (commonsense practices) that officers use in policing the streets. It is that social "organization" of discovery which is the focus of the remaining analysis.

Citizens' Calls as a Source of Ambiguity

Patrol officers often encounter considerable ambiguity in determining the nature of the problem they are dispatched to handle. The citizen's description of the problem, which is encoded into some organizationally actionable, yet cryptic category by the operator (e.g., "gang"), requires officers to interpret what the category "means" in the context of the actual police response. The police task when responding to a call such as the "gangs" or groups disturbing the neighborhood is threefold: (1) if possible, approach the area without being seen and "find" and "see for oneself" the reported problem, (2) determine if the behavior constitutes a problem that requires police action, and (3) take some action. Police consider the second task as the most critical and, as the next two examples illustrate, it entails important interpretive work.

In the first example which occurred at 74 Alcon (Shift 2: 11:50 P.M.), we observe how the citizen's call initially creates considerable ambiguity about *both* the problem and location, due to the lack of specific information provided by the caller. In the call, the citizen requests police presence because of a bottle-throwing incident that occurred the night before by "people" who caused recurring problems in the neighborhood. The operator's attempt to provide an excuse for the lack of police presence is met with a sharp reply by the citizen ("I don't want another bottle through my window").

[Call 7: Tape 1 (11:42 P.M.)]

PD: What's the problem?

CA: Well, we had an incident last night where **someone threw a bottle through our window at twelve o'clock and the police said that they would patrol now at night. Now these people are out on the street again and screaming and just carrying on the same** and I would just appreciate it if—I don't want anyone to come to the house, but if they could please patrol the street as they said they were going to

PD: If they could what?

CA: Patrol Battlehill Street between Prince and Alcon, this goes on every single night

PD: Okay, but this is Friday night ma'am there's a lot of crime in the city and we're short on police everywhere I guess. But I'll put the call in

CA: Well, ya know I don't wanna have another bottle through our window, this happened last night (1 .0)

PD: Okay we'll put the call in. They're on the corner of Prince and Battlehill? [caller's address given earlier in call]

CA: No, right now they're down on Alcon, which is just two streets down **but they're screaming and there's a whole bunch of them together tonight.**

The lack of a specific location is relevant to the dispatch and response of the gang car, as the problem reported is essentially a "bunch of them screaming" (note that there is no mention of youths, a group, or gang). The officers received the assignment over the telephone at the station house, instead of in the car, because they were ten minutes late beginning the shift (which of course is not noted in the logs). Central dispatch had called to inquire about the availability of the district's gang car. The dispatcher's formulation of the problem to the officer over the telephone was "a gang in the area," not "a group of them screaming."

The call presents a twofold task for the police responding to the call: to find *both* the location and the problem. After several minutes of driving around the block, the officers located a group of four to six youths (age fifteen to seventeen), described by the police as "troublemakers." They were hanging out in a doorway leading to some project apartments. Although there was no noticeable legal violation, when they saw the car, they gestured in a taunting manner, as if to say "come and get us," which generated a discussion in the car that illustrates the trivial nature of the officer's prior contacts with this "gang":

[Field tape number one]

Off1: **There's the crew, that's the crew**
Off2: **They're going into Debbie's house**
Off1: Yep
　　　　(10.0) ((still driving))
Off2: My patience is about run out with them
Off1: It doesn't do any good, Bob
Off2: No, it doesn't do any good at all
Off1: Give them a break, you give them another break (2.0) you give them a shake, is that what they call it? [referring to kids' term for letting them off this time] come back the next day and they shit all over you. That's it. What's the sense of it? Then you're back with them again. (4.0) You can't be nice to them.
Off2: Yeah
Off1: **Let me go in there and let me see (inaudible) we'll check around the side.**
Off2: **No, they're all gone, John, I'm sure.**
Off1: They might be upstairs
Off2: They're all gone, they sit in that hallway, they go in and out of the street.
Off1: All right.
　　　　(3.0)
Off1: **Should we give them an adam robert? ((tell dispatch the car has arrived at the call))**
Off2: **Yeah, did we go out ocean nora? ((code to dispatch that unit is logged on for the tour))**
Off1: **David two-ninety (.) give us a 7-Paul ((disposition code for the call))**
Disp: **David two-ninety. 7-Paul. You going out car two-ninety?**
Off1: **Give us ocean nora ((code for logged on))**
Disp: **All right** ((we continue driving slowly turn car around and view the same hallway))
Off2: They're all in the hallway there
Off1: Yeah they're in Debbie's there, they go in and out of Debbie's. They just want a chase see//they just want a chase.
Off2: Yeah

　　The disposition of the call 7-Paul indicates *for the record* that there was a "gathering causing annoyance (outside)" and that a service was rendered.[15] This disposition confirms the dispatcher's original designation of the call as a gang call. Was the group causing an annoyance that could constitute some legal violation? No. Was the group outside? No. Were they screaming? No. Was the group a "gang?" No. At the time the group was located, they were in the hallway, and *presumed* to be moving from this semi-private space to a public space (outside) and to a private space (Debbie's apartment). What service was rendered? The police showed up. Did they have verbal contact with the group? No. In fact, the suggestion that contact be made was considered to be of "no use." Yet, for the keeping-of-the-log, the officers have constituted *this* group as the "gang" and have coded the relevant police response and disposition.

A second example illustrating the ambiguity of the process is O'Malley Way (Shift 1: 9:25). The caller reported a party of people "sitting on the stairs(.) they have the radio kinda real loud and they're kinda loud themselves they just woke up my kids(.) I was wondering could you do anything about it?" The call was dispatched to the gang car as a "group playing loud music on the steps." On the way to the location, one officer (who regularly walks a beat in that neighborhood) commented, "we *never* get a gang call for this address." Upon arrival, three local residents in their early thirties, who were known to the officer, were sitting on the stairs playing a radio that was audible from our vantage point of twenty-five yards. The following conversation between the officers (Off1, Off2) and myself (AJM) occurred in the car:

[Field tape number one]

Off1: Loud music coming from over there

Off2: Let me go talk to them

Off1: (said to author) That's loud music that's why, I knew, I knew I figured it would be loud music here that's just what it was here because we never get no calls for here

AJM: Right

Off1: Very, very seldom get a call here. I walk through here and never get it—people in front talk—they're adults

AJM: So this is a music call?

Off1: This is just loud music, sure, that's what it is just, that's exactly ((laughing)) what it is. They didn't say ((referring to radio dispatch)), they take—they figured a group or we got the group there but then you've got to evaluate what you're up against when you get here

AJM: Right. Have you had any really tough gang calls this summer though or has it been a lot of this routine stuff?

Off1: That's it, routine stuff, that's all. Loud music and loud music. Hey what are you gonna do, hit them with the city ordinance? They got so many. I've never *yet* really got a call where there's destruction. We do get a lot of stolen cars and they strip them. It's not gangs, it's two or three kids doing it.

At this call, the music was turned down and the entry in the log reflected the officer's assessment above. It read "Loud Music 12-P" (services rendered).[16] The officer's assessment is interesting and reflects the interpretive work entailed in policing. The dispatch to that location for a "group" was incongruous with the officer's knowledge and experience of the location and his assumptions about the behavior of the people who typically occupy that place. Thus, he concluded that he "knew," prior to actual arrival on the scene, that it had to be a loud music call and *not* a group or gang call. He refers to the dispatcher who "figured" a group was responsible (hence, send the gang car), but then notes, "We got the group but then you have to evaluate what you're up against" (i.e., not a gang). Distinctions between types of groups are quite evident; adult groups are treated differently from youth groups. In fact, adults routinely sat out on their front steps on warm summer evenings in Corktown, playing music and cards and talking with neighbors without being harassed.

Furthermore, when asked about the types of gang calls he had responded to, the officer answered that he has yet to have a call (this summer) where there is "destruction." This provides some insight into how gang calls were evaluated in Corktown that summer. In the officer's view, a "real" gang call involves some destruction or serious criminal problem. Routine music calls and other violations that entail enforcement of city ordinances (e.g., with respect to hanging out, drinking, etc.) would seem to be the appropriate legal designation for most of the problems handled by the gang car. Nevertheless, many calls that officers do not believe involve gangs, like this one, receive service as a gang problem and end up in both the logs and calls database confirmed as gang calls.

Reactive Policing: Brooming the Gang

As noted earlier, over this three-month period, the gang car made only one arrest and brought three drunks to the station house for protective custody. While the gang car was generating substantial statistics on gang activities, the police were in most cases doing nothing more than "brooming," a term they used to refer to simply moving a group. Usually, a brooming results in the group moving to another corner. The police consider this a legitimate, if only a temporary solution, hoping that the next corner chosen by the group will not house a citizen who will call in a complaint. The problem from the police standpoint is that standing on the corner is *not* illegal and, while citizens frequently call to complain about it, there is very little the police can actually do. Yet, if the calls continue they can create problems for the officer (Meehan 1992). Therefore, citizen calls about this "problem" often result in the dispatch of the gang car. One example from the shift I observed illustrates a typical problem the police have in evaluating "what the citizen has called about" and then deciding what the police can, or should do about it.

In this call (Mountain and Mountain Hill, Shift 2: 1:45), the caller reported that there was a "noisy gang playing a radio on top of the car which woke me up." The records at communications show that the caller had called *three times* within *fourteen minutes.* The officers approached the scene of the call unobtrusively and upon arrival could *not* "hear" *loud* music. Three people (about eighteen to twenty years old) were observed sitting on the hood of their car with a (boombox) radio on the roof. The radio was playing but not loudly. The officers had the following discussion between themselves and then spoke to the group:

[Field tape number one]

Off1: Should I broom them or just let them
Off2: I don't know what do you think you wanna do anything?
Off1: They're not doing anything

(3.0)
Off2: They're not doing anything ((we drive the car over to the group))
Off2: Somebody just called I don't know who it was but if we have to—if they call again, we'll have to make you move all right?
Cit: Okay

The officers stopped no more than fifty yards away from this corner to speak to a friend of one of the officers. We were there for five minutes when the dispatcher radioed to the car that the "gang had returned to the corner playing their radio." However, the group had never left the corner and neither had the police. The volume of the radio was not turned up (as the caller had reported in their second call). The officer informed the dispatcher that the matter was handled: the officer backed up the car and told the group that if they just moved somewhere else, this caller would stop calling. They readily complied.

This example highlights a major problem for the police. As long as there are calls about a group, the police have to take some action, even if they can see for themselves that there is no problem. The key here is that the police can exert some control over the group but not over the caller's behavior. Callers often ask the police to solve problems they have no legal jurisdiction over. If the police do not do something, the caller will continue to call, and complaints may find their way to the precinct captain, or worse, city hall and/or the media.

In brooming the group, the police make it clear that they don't hold the group accountable or responsible for the problem. They tell the group that it is the caller's problem. Yet, the log entry for the call (7-P) read as "gathering causing annoyance and services rendered," and the gang car was dispatched. The resulting gang designation is interesting in light of the officer's obvious judgment that the caller, not the group, is the problem. They could have reported the disposition under the "Adam" code: not a bona fide incident. Given the comparison between the caller's report of a gang playing loud music and the police assessment of the situation at the scene, the "Adam" code would seem to have been appropriate in this case. By reporting services rendered and not using the Adam code, the police create a statistical database representing "gang" problems that do not, in their own assessment, exist.

By contrast, even when there were problems (e.g., loud, disturbing behavior) being caused by groups that involve illegal activities (such as drinking and/or smoking pot), the police would still "broom" the group in an effort to displace the problem from the caller. For example, two calls to the Salk Street public housing projects within twenty minutes resulted in "brooming" a group the officers knew were responsible for making noise and drinking. In the first call to 65 Salk (Shift 2: 12:00 A.M.), the caller reported a "noisy gang on the roof drinking with a loud radio." When we arrived, there was a group of five teenagers (ages fifteen to seventeen) in the courtyard area with a radio playing loudly. One officer went up to the roof, the other went over and had the kids shut off the radio. The group was told to keep their radio off because it was bothering people in the apartments. When we returned the second time (65 Salk, Shift 2: 12:35 A.M.) because the caller reported the "gang" was still there playing its radio, the radio had in fact been turned off and the youths were milling about the courtyard. The following discussion occurred between the group and the police:

[Field tape number one]

Off2: Hey, somebody keeps—somebody's calling on you guys what's the story?
Kid1: huh?
Off2: Somebody's calling. Were you making a lot of noise here or what?
Kid1: Nope!
Off2: Why don't you guys move okay so we don't have to come back here again, all right?
Kid2: Yeah
Off2: Go around to the other corner ((kids begin to leave))
Off2: They must be smoking ((dope)), there's no bottles around
Off1: They had some beer earlier I broke some upstairs
Off2: Was there?
Off1: I broke some on the roof—they had some Michelob—Lowenbrau, looked like I'm not sure maybe a six pack.

Proactive Responses and Recorded Log Entries

Accounting for how time is spent on patrol is an age-old problem because a complete accounting for time spent on activities other than dispatched calls is impossible (Rubenstein 1973; Fogelson 1977). When officers spend less time on calls, they report other activity so as to look "busy." But they can never report everything. For example, the on-view activities of officers during the first gang car shift are quite extensively reported in the logs (six OS or "on view" entries), whereas there are no on-view entries for the second, much busier shift. The first shift had four calls, whereas the second shift had nine and therefore no extra time needed to be accounted for.

During the course of a shift, only certain activities are selected for recording in the log, not because they merit police attention but because *recording* their occurrence can fill the spaces of time between calls to show that *initiative is being undertaken by officers*. With the gang car, there are particular on-view entries that are likely to be recorded. There are certain areas that the captain requests the gang car to check throughout the evening. These are areas from which the captain has received citizen complaints; his solution is to designate these places for "patrol." Officers know that the logs are inspected by their supervisors to see that these areas are indeed being checked, especially when the place has achieved a reputation for direct complaints to the captain. Thus, these are "ready-made" on-view entries. The entries for the first shift indicate that these areas were checked, and indeed they were checked. During the second shift, however, even though these areas were checked, no log entries were made because the officers already had enough "call" activity to fill the log and account for their time. When areas are designated to be checked, however, the question "are they doing anything illegal?" is irrelevant. The area has achieved a reputation, and people occupying that place are presumed to be responsible for both the place and the behaviors that occur there.

Three of the area checks for the first shift showed "negative": no one was there. The other three indicate that officers found a "group" and in two cases dispersed them (at Rainey Field and the Walcott school). At Rainey Field, which borders a playground, the car pulled in and was immediately approached by ten young children (approximately eight to ten years old) checking out "who's working" in the police car tonight. One of the officers was well known and quite popular with young children in Corktown, and he was recognized immediately. While this was happening, the other officer noticed that a group of older teenagers were hastily leaving the area and that they had beer bottles. After a minute of talking with these younger children, the officer pulled the car down to the area where these older youths were seen leaving. That was the extent of our contact with the group that was, according to the log, "dispersed."

At the Walcott school, a group of about seven to ten youths was drinking on the steps of the school and playing music on a boom box. As we approached the schoolyard, the regular patrol unit dispersed the group (their car had been parked where we could not see it). These other officers yelled "get the hell out of here," and the kids scattered. One officer then smashed two six-packs of beer and picked up the boom box while the other picked up two other six-packs. On seeing us, one of the officers came over to our car and gave us two six-packs of beer saying they already had too much in their car (we returned directly to the station and placed the beer in the departmental refrigerator). However, if you look at the log entry, it indicates that we dispersed the group at the Walcott school, which of course we did not.

The last on-view incident I discuss occurred during the first shift: the Peter's School entry. There are two points of analytic interest about this on-view incident: (1) it is not really an on-view incident, and (2) it is a follow-up action from an earlier dispatched call. To simplify matters, I will first discuss the earlier call and police response.

In the earlier call, the citizen asked the 911 operator if the police could move a gang of kids out of the play area in the schoolyard: "They're lighting fireworks and putting them in cans and everything else." We were dispatched to the schoolyard for a "group of kids disturbing the neighbors" with no mention made of the fireworks. Upon arrival, we could not see any "disturbance." However, a woman (the one who, it turned out, had made the call) standing on the curb waved to us to come over. She reported that a group of thirteen- to fourteen-year-old "little punks" who had "split the scene" just before the police arrived had a "big fire" burning in the doorway and that they were exploding firecrackers.

The officer then drove the car to the front of the school where there were four girls sitting on the steps. He asked them if they were with the ones who lit the firecrackers, to which they replied, "No." The log entry read 7-Boy (gathering causing annoyance and no person can be found). This means that the officer's log entry verifies that the reported problem of firecrackers occurred and that the person(s) responsible could not be located. Yet there was no attempt to see if there was any evidence of a "big fire" in the alleyway, and the officers had not seen any firecrackers. This example contrasts with the earlier example on Alcon (call seven, tape I) where the problem was formulated as a "gang" of young males on the basis of the officer's prior knowledge of them and their presence within a two-block area of the call. Here, the young females are not similarly perceived. Even though they are at the location of the problem, they do not "fit" the officer's conception of a group or gang and their demeanor is appropriately respectful as opposed to the "taunting" gestures of the males. The treatment of their account by the police is very restrained, and the police do not challenge their claim when they deny being involved with the kids lighting fireworks.

The officer told the citizen that they would keep an eye on the area, to which the citizen delivered a sarcastic but realistic appraisal of the problem: "You'll be here every five minutes" and "You don't have enough gas." Approximately an hour later, we were returning to the schoolyard (at the suggestion of one of the officers) when the dispatcher reported "a gang of kids back in the schoolyard again." The word "again" indicated the dispatcher's awareness that this was a repeat call. Having promised to keep an eye on the situation, being "on-view" at just that moment, and having intended to be there at the time anyway, *the call was entered into the log as an on-view incident* even though it came in as a call from dispatch.

When we arrived at the school, a group of about thirty kids was in the alleyway. The officers went into the alleyway to investigate. As this was happening, two youths approached me, asking questions about who I was and what I was doing. I asked them what had been happening:

[Field tape number one]

Kid1: Nothing much, some girls wrote something about this one girl and then their sisters came down and made them erase it
Kid2: Oh Magoo, that lady's over there talking to the cop
Kid1: The lady next door talking to them now, drop the dime this lady always calls the cops ((referring to lady we spoke to earlier)) we call her a dime dropper she always calls—drops the dime on us calls the cops you know you don't even do nothing, you sit in the pit and she'll call the cops [the pit is the kids' term for the alleyway between the school building and the fence]

The youths did not mention firecrackers or fires. The officers, upon returning to the car, reported that there was a verbal dispute about some writing on the wall, but it was "nothing major." They concluded that the woman who called was upset about having all the kids down in the alley-way. Thus, their assessment essentially corroborated the kids' version as reported to me independently and not the caller's.

The call for this incident, which was the citizen's second call, differs both from what the officers observed and what they entered into their log as an on-view entry. The citizen's second call reported a complaint about kids drinking, although no evidence of this was found at the scene by the officers:

[Call 3: Tape 1]

CA: Yes could you do me a favor put a call into the Corktown Police and **tell them to do their jobs**
PD: What job, ma'am?
CA: **Getting the kids off the corner drinking**
PD: What corner, ma'am? What corner?
CA: It's the Peter's School (gives address) right there in the schoolyard right in front of everything.
((police and citizen have interchange to confirm address))
CA: I called earlier// for
PD: Okay we'll send someone over

Citizens will often upgrade the seriousness of the problem they report to police operators in order to increase the probability that the police will respond (Meehan 1989). By reporting "drinking" as the problem, the citizen provides a specific legal violation to mobilize the police rather than what apparently is her "real" problem, which was "kids" in the alleyway. The former requires no justification, whereas the latter may require more elaboration. Further, beginning the call with a complaint about the police (tell them to "do their jobs"), the "job" of controlling drinking (whether it is really the case or not), is more "police relevant" than complaining about kids hanging around. When the police arrive, the complaint from the caller is the "kids." The complaint from the kids is the "lady." The job for the police is to check out the complaint from the caller, which is considered "minor" (i.e., there was a verbal dispute, no fighting). But there is one other matter.

A repeat call, by the same person, may lead to a specific complaint to the precinct captain that the police weren't doing their jobs as promised. *Solution:* Show this incident as one's own initiative. *Procedure:* Log it as on-view and as a minor problem, "group of kids disturbing neighbors." Characterizing the nature of the incident in this manner ("group of kids disturbing neighbors") as opposed to reporting what they did on-view ("dispersed group") suggests that the disturbance may not have been legitimate police business even though the police did indeed disperse the group. Usually, officers would use the log entry "dispersed group" even when they didn't. Therefore, the log can be read by the police or their supervisors as the *neighbor's* problem, not a police matter, and therefore not a problem for which the police should take action. By officially recording it as on-view, the officers can claim they were doing their job as promised, that there was not a problem requiring the notation of a police disposition, as there is with calls for service, and that the "proof" is in the log.

These matters of internal accountability provide the police with good reasons for recording a "gang" problem as on-view, when they actually did not locate any police relevant business. Thus, the generation of a gang statistic shows that they responded to the caller's demands, not that there was a gang in the area.

Unrecorded Proactive Incidents

In this section, I discuss one encounter during the first shift that could have been logged as an on-view incident but was not entered at all. This police mobilization was initiated by a citizen on the street, not a phone call. So it was not assigned by dispatch and did not result in a dispatch statistic. This encounter is selected for analysis due both to its serious nature and to the amount of time spent on the incident (both initially and subsequently in talking to the youths observed), all of which would seem to have warranted an entry into the log. The incident did result in the writing of FIO cards, an informal, internal record that police officers treat more seriously than the official log (Meehan 1986; 1993). But it did not generate a gang statistic.

A citizen informed the officers on patrol that several kids, who were in an alley across the street, might be trying to break into the window of a second floor apartment. We immediately pulled over and found several kids in the alley whom the officers believed had been trying to open the window of an apartment. The kids told the officers they were in the alley "taking a piss," which the officers skeptically characterized as the "taking a piss routine." The officers treated this routine as a cover for, as they put it, "breaking in a house right in their own back yard" (said in a disgusted tone of voice).

This incident was never recorded in the log, although clearly the officers "believed" that the youths were attempting to break into the apartment. As we drove away, one officer began filling out FIO cards on each youth that was in the alley. The first officer to go into the alley said, "One was trying the window," *as if* he had seen it occurring. But he didn't. However, the officers did not arrest. Instead, they chose to question the youths, who were known to them, regarding their activity. I was told by the officers that each youth in this group had a record for breaking and entering. In situations where it appears that an arrest could have been made and wasn't, the "legal elements" for a prosecution to hold up in a court of law may not be present, or the officers have chosen not to create the "legal elements" by lying in their arrest report (see Manning 1997; Meehan 1986). The absence of a call leaves it to the discretion of the police whether or not to log it in. Responses to calls, on the other hand, must be logged in because the police organization is accountable to the caller.

Thus, this incident, which involved considerable time and interaction between police and juveniles, and was far more serious than other calls labeled as gang calls, was preserved "for the record" elsewhere (i.e., on FIO cards) but not entered on the log.[17] Therefore, it did not generate a "gang" statistic, even though the activities of these youths (who, according to the police, each had "records" and were in a group) represent, in the officer's view, the closest approximation to serious criminal activity observed during that evening.

Conclusion

The police are responsive to the political and organizational contexts that selected "gangs" as a problem for the community. Certainly, the people of Corktown, as well as Bigcity, had their share of problems with young people who hang out on corners, make noise, drink, harass neighbors, and engage in some criminal activity. "Gangs" are real and not themselves an artifact of organizational recordkeeping practices. On the other hand, activities by groups that the police considered to be "real gangs" did not constitute a significant proportion of the incidents handled by the gang car that resulted, nonetheless, in official "gang" statistics. Treating these gang statistics as reflecting actual gang activity reifies gangs to the point where a fiction *is* created: "gangs" and their activities are the primary source of trouble for the community that the political organization can "solve." Indeed, it is *this* fiction that the recordkeeping practices can effectively create and manage. In this sense, the popularized conception of the gang problem is a complex artifact; it is the consequence of increasing police attention to the activities of young people in the community and of shifting definitions and perceptions of gangs in the community. As such, the "gang" problem can only be examined through the various interactional and recordkeeping practices that create this version of reality.

In Plantville in 1999, the development of this process continues. The identification of gangs as an important problem facing the city, and specifically using the term "gangs" as a frame for the city's problem with its young people, shapes political discourse and organizational action. One officer observed:

> Hey if you're the mayor of Plantville and you say hey we're gonna get a group of six–eight guys together and we're gonna handle these youth problems, that ain't shit. But you say gangs, everybody looks and goes, "Gangs! What the hell, we got gangs in Plantville. Now we're dedicating six officers to a gang problem? We got a gang problem!" If you say that we're gonna do a youth intervention program, nobody gives a shit. Because it's not politically correct. Politically correct is to say, "We got a gang problem and we got six guys on it." And that's how it is. (Plantville Focus Group, February 4, 1998)

This officer's comments capture the sort of moral panic (McCorkle and Miethe 1998) that can be created by framing troubles with young people as gang problems. Using the term "gang" has an important symbolic meaning and conveys a sense of threat and urgency to the community. The community perceives that the threat posed by gangs requires drastic action of the sort not captured by "youth intervention programs." It is precisely this meaning of "gangs" that is used to justify the creation of gang units. Some have observed that the initial response to claims of gang activity is often denial, in large part due to the negative public relations impact such an admission might generate (Klein 1995, p. 87). However, in both Bigcity and Plantville, the gang issue provided a convenient political opportunity sufficient to overcome such considerations.

The connection between the gang problem, the gang unit, and winning votes is not lost on police officers in Plantville either. One officer commented (while his fellow officers nodded their heads in agreement and chuckled throughout):

> He's [the mayor] a year and a half away from getting reelected. Most likely he's gonna be reelected, but he sure has to score points. He says, "I gotta a gang unit, I live on the east side, I gotta gang unit over there and they are taking care of problems." If he said, "Hey we've put six officers for youth intervention," people would look at him like, "What are they crazy, they aren't doing nothing. Youth intervention, what are they gonna do with that?" But you say, "I got a gang squad. Man, that's politically correct." (Plantville Focus Group, February 4, 1998)

As Plantville's newly formed "gang unit" approaches its task of responding to gangs in the community, no doubt there will be a need for constructing a corresponding documentary reality to satisfy the politicians and the department's brass that the "gang" problem not only exist, but that the police have it under control.

One important implication of police recordkeeping practices is that research measuring the extent of the gang problem, while relying upon police estimates of the number of gangs, or on records generated by patrol and specialized gang units, without understanding how such records are generated and what their internal uses are, is problematic. It is critical to examine how these organizational efforts are affected by the political process that uses the "gang problem." The consequences of the gang label can be serious for individuals who find their names in gang databases, as legislators are stiffening penalties for offenses that are deemed "gang related" or committed by "known" gang members (Spergel 1995; Klein 1996). Currently, gang intelligence databases are being generated and shared by criminal justice officials on local, regional, and national levels (Klein 1995; Spergel 1995; U.S.BJA 1997). Malcolm Klein (1995, p. 189) notes that, while such increased information sharing has increased police cohesiveness, it may just be "disseminating, reifying and distorting the general image of street gangs."

In addition, the proliferation of gang databases has the consequence of labeling individuals as gang members who do not meet specified criteria. Klein (1995, p. 193) observes, "We stand, it seems on the threshold of a

national gang roster system . . . without anything approaching an evaluation of its utility to enforcement or its endangerment of civil liberties. Even
careful assessment of system errors—false positives and negatives—has yet
to be undertaken." No matter how strict the definitional criteria for inclusion in these databases are, it is how these criteria are actually applied that
is at issue. As one officer from New York commented, "I don't really have
any great problem with the definition, how we are going to use it is another story" (Spergel and Bobrowski 1989, p. 51).

The recordkeeping practices of the police easily accommodate and manage the various political and organizational pressures brought to bear upon
them. The management of documentary reality is an important competency and resource for any individual who is accountable to a bureaucracy.
Social scientists tend to ignore this process and often approach the matter
of their use of official statistics and police records with a "caveat emptor"
warning to readers that a certain amount of "measurement error" is attributable to organizational processes. But this is not enough. It is not solely
an issue of measurement error but rather that organizational features of
policing, and other organizations, which can change from year to year, determine the incident count and records from which those statistics are derived. Social science research must focus on those interactional and
recordkeeping processes that constitute the careers of organizational statistics rather than treat statistics as standing in a correspondence relationship to the incidents they purport to represent.

Research is needed that focuses on the process through which statistics
are generated. This entails a multilevel approach to the social construction
of statistics that would examine the various levels of organizational practices and the corresponding member's competencies, which together result
in the statistic. Statistics generated by organizational personnel, for their
own "good" organizational reasons (Garfinkel 1967), should never be
treated as an indicator of events as they would appear to an observer. This
means they are not intended as an interpretation of events. They are intended to represent organizational work as rational and orderly. Consequently, they are a direct indicator of the organization's priorities, that is,
of its context of accountability and how its members orient to and develop
competencies to produce "facts" that are relevant within this context.

Acknowledgments

I would like to thank the anonymous *TSQ* reviewers and Norman Denzin,
editor, for their helpful comments. Harold Garfinkel, Doug Maynard, and
Peter Manning read this article in various drafts, and I have benefitted from
their suggestions and encouragement. I also thank the Department of Sociology and Anthropology Faculty Workshop, organized by David Maines, for
their comments and support. Finally, I owe my deepest gratitude to Anne

Warfield Rawls, my staunchest critic, editor, and supporter, whose guidance has been immeasurable and persistence endless despite my shortcomings.

Notes

1. Plantville is a Midwestern city with a population of 170,000. Its police force is comprised of 265 officers. I have been conducting field research in this department for four years (1996–1999), studying how the organization utilizes information technologies. My research includes extensive ride-alongs with patrol officers (two hundred hours), twenty-five formal interviews with all levels of the command staff and specialized units (e.g., detective bureau, internal affairs, community policing unit), focus groups drawing upon officers from different units as well as a specialized community policing unit, and analysis of department records (e.g., calls for service data in computer-aided dispatch). Plantville's emerging construction of its gang problem and response are similar to what I observed in Bigcity and report on in this article. I juxtapose relevant data from Plantville to illustrate the similar underlying political and organizational processes involved in the social construction of a gang problem.

2. Even within a given department, reaching agreement about the criteria used to define a gang in practice can be problematic. This is illustrated by the following exchange among officers in a focus group discussion of various problems (including troubled youths/gangs) that the Plantville police face on the east side, a high crime area:

> *Gang Unit Officer:* Throughout the country there is no set criteria, no set definition of what a gang is. [Referring to officers around the table] He's got a different definition than he does and he does and he does and he does. So you ask all of us and we'll all give different reasons. "He's not a gang banger he's just a troubled kid. But yeah here's a gang banger because you know he looks like he's from LA." There's different reasons for that throughout the department
>
> *Patrol Officer 1:* I don't view most of them as gangs. If you go by his [the gang unit officer's] criteria, the whole east side is a gang.
>
> *Patrol Officer 2:* [to gang officer] All you're doing is labeling. (Plantville Focus Group, February 4, 1998)

As this discussion illustrates, the conflict between definition and practice is not easily resolved. The patrol officers disagree with the gang unit officer's criteria for applying the term "gang." Accounting for these differences is beyond the scope of the present article. However, it is important to consider that gang unit officers receive specialized "gang" training at regional seminars and return to their departments armed with new beliefs about gangs, including issues such as the problem of definition, which is nicely articulated in the above exchange. The skepticism of their fellow officers does not deter them. In fact, gang unit officers are told that "denial" is the typical response of the community (and fellow officers) when gangs first make their presence felt in communities. As one ranking officer observed, there is definitely a "true believer quality to the gang squad members" that suggests a sort of conversion process at work in transforming them to the view that "gangs" are an important threat to communities. As Klein (1995) notes, one of the consequences of gang training for law enforcement has been to increase their group cohesion.

3. The use of official agency statistics for doing social science research has been the subject of considerable discussion (Merton 1957; Kitsuse and Cicourel 1963; Skogan 1975; McCleary, Nienstedt, and Erven 1982). Yet there are few studies of the actual practices for producing the records from which those statistics are derived. Specifically, how an interactional event is reduced to some written form, whether that form is an extended report, or as in the case of calls for service, a simple category designation such as "gang," raises important issues. For example, the transformation of some "interactional" fact into a written format presupposes a "correct" correspondence between the two. However, the initial problem posed by such a process is achieving the interactional "facticity" of an event in the first place. Thus, analyzing the interactions which constitute the organizational career of a record from which statistics are derived is essential.

4. Combining these seventy-three calls with the thirteen calls from the two shifts I discuss in the article, a total of eighty-six gang calls were collected. Locating the actual calls on stored tapes was a very tedious, time-consuming process as the calls are not stored by district but by their time of occurrence. A technician assisted me over two full days. I am grateful to command staff who generously aided me in this process.

5. I also spent time in the gang car on four other evenings (eight shifts) and, in terms of type of calls and police response, the evening analyzed in this article was representative of these other gang car shifts I observed. The research project during which these data were collected spanned a two-year period and required considerable time in the field (on average, one to two days a week). I also conducted other ride-alongs and semistructured interviews with patrol officers, youth officer detectives, and command staff officers in the district. These data were gathered as part of a policy-making project on the police handling of juveniles in two urban police departments. As one of three sociologists and two lawyers who worked full time on the project, I was primarily responsible for coordinating research on the police. This included collecting and analyzing police and court records, conducting surveys of the police and citizenry, coordinating ride-alongs for project staff, attending community meetings, and working closely with a police and citizen task force on the development of policies related to the police handling of juveniles.

6. This claim is supported by the following data. All patrol officers' logs from Corktown for a two-month period were examined to see what types of activities and problems officers encountered on patrol. A winter month (December) and a summer month (June) were selected to observe seasonal variation. For this sixty-one-day period, officers' log entries for all three shifts per day totaled 3,079, with June (1,664 entries) a slightly more active month than December (1,415 entries). In June, patrol officers' responses to gangs and groups ranked first, constituting 23 percent of all activities listed in their logs. This was followed by patrol and area checks (15.2 percent) and traffic offenses (10.7 percent). During December, traffic ranked first (20.7 percent), patrol and area checks were second (19.3 percent), and gangs and groups ranked third (14.0 percent) despite the cold weather. In addition, thirty-nine of the sixty patrol officers in the Corktown district also completed a questionnaire that asked them to rate the seriousness and troublesomeness of juvenile-related problems in the district. Police officers rank-ordered street gangs second in terms of seriousness (surpassed only by auto theft) and first in terms of troublesomeness. Clearly, from data gathered from official sources (patrol logs) as well as the questionnaire, street gangs and groups were considered a significant problem in Corktown. A questionnaire similar to the one for patrol officers was distributed to a group of Corktown teenagers. While they reported hanging out in groups on street corners with high frequency, they rated this problem as one of the least serious (ranked 29). Thus, for police, street gangs and groups were a serious and troublesome problem although more as a nuisance than a crime problem, whereas for teenagers they were not.

7. When the gang category was analyzed by looking at how *responding officers* categorize the problem *after* their response, gang calls represented 8.7 percent ($N = 278,135$) of all calls, a 2.3 percent difference. When compared with other categories, gang calls still ranked third, preceded only by "services rendered" (29.6 percent) and "investigation" (21.2 percent). *More calls are subsequently recategorized as a gang problem by the responding officers* than are initially dispatched as gang calls. The following list identifies the initially reported problems and the percentage from each category that are recategorized as "gang" problems by responding officers: disturbances (22.1 percent), fights (21.5 percent), public nuisance (12.8 percent), argument (12.1 percent), crime in progress (10.3 percent) and loud party (8.8 percent). If officers use the category to gloss the range of problems they confront on the streets, this expands the use of the term "gang" to cover many problems having nothing to do with gangs. This analysis suggests that the "gang" designation is a label that officers often find useful and at times politically advantageous. Thus, the resulting gang statistics generated by the police in this sort of political and organizational environment report a much higher rate of problems caused by gangs than the police actually assess as gang problems during the encounter.

8. In one letter to the editor of a Bigcity newspaper, a youth complained that the gang units were indiscriminately moving groups of people even when they were doing nothing wrong. Some Corktown residents reported in community meetings that the citywide gang units were just brooming everybody, even though the Corktown gang car passed by and said nothing in many cases. My observations in the field confirmed this view as well. Some Corktown officers complained that they were taking a lot of the heat for the actions of these other officers

who did not "know who the good kids are." In newspaper reports of the effectiveness of the "gang patrols," however, no distinction was made between the activities of the Corktown unit and the citywide unit.

9. These data lend support to the election year interpretation and they also raise some other interesting issues that cannot be fully addressed here. First, it is clear that responding officers were categorizing more calls into gang calls than the police operators or dispatchers over the total six-year period, although the differential between operators' categorizations and officers' categorizations is smaller for each successive year. The first year of data represented in Table 1 was also the first full year after the department employed civilian operators and the computer-aided dispatch system was installed. The convergence of categorization between operator and officer over the six-year period may reflect this adjustment to some degree. Second, although calls classified by the operators as gang problems also increased for the two years prior to the election year, these two years also coincide with the use of "drinking cars" by district captains to control rowdy youth behavior and drinking (noted earlier). Thus, the gang category was in all likelihood a global, catchall category for both operators and officers. However, it did not have the same significance for purposes of public-political discourse until the election year. The dramatic decline in the number of gang calls in the subsequent years illustrates the malleability of the category and the importance of the categorization process.

10. In Bigcity, the 911 emergency number handles between 500,000 and 600,000 calls per year; an average of about 1,600 calls on any given day (in a twenty-four-hour period). The 911 emergency number receives calls from all parts of the city. Thus, there is no special operator for a particular section of the city, such as Corktown. Each call is automatically routed into a queuing system and the call is handled on a "first-come-first-served" basis by the next available operator. The police telephone operators in Bigcity are trained civilians, whereas the dispatchers are sworn officers. All transcription symbols are taken from the transcription system developed by Jefferson (in Schenkein 1978). All references to individuals and places have been changed to preserve the anonymity of speakers.

11. The argument is not citizens use the category "gang" in a naive or incorrect manner. Rather, the point is that there is a utility to the use of the category. Police operators formulate the caller's problem into a category that reflects organizational utility and priorities. Through this process, callers learn that certain categories are more useful than others in generating a police response.

12. One reviewer requestioned the significance of calling attention to various department log-keeping "practices" given the fact that "everyone including supervisors knows that they are actually estimations." My point is that the relationship between practice and recordwork is not a relationship of correspondence, whether imprecise or otherwise. The log is a very complex, patterned social construction, not an estimation. The police have a vested interest in constructing a record that displays their organizational accountability. Further, when statistics derived from those records are utilized to define a problem without an understanding of and appreciation for this accountability, the claims based upon those "facts" are further distortions. The fact that any competent member of a police organization "knows" this suggests that when they utilize data like these in the public arena to defend police actions or to solicit additional funding for personnel, equipment, and budgets to staff programs like "gang" cars, their uses are politically motivated.

13. From an organizational standpoint, the logs should indicate all calls that officers respond to as well as other activities performed during the shift (e.g., on-view encounters, traffic stops, etc.). Elsewhere, I argue that these types of records have important actuarial uses within the organization, for purposes of accountability, and are therefore subject to considerable manipulation by patrol officers. This is one reason why the logs are often called the "cheat sheets" or "my lies" (Meehan 1986). This article, however, illustrates in detail, just how these logs are managed by officers and their role in keeping the visibility of gangs prominent for the record. I have only reproduced the logs and log codes used for this one evening (the log code sheet is quite extensive, with numerous codes). The logs are not corrected for spelling errors.

14. On the other thirty-four shifts, 7-Paul was the disposition code in 75 percent ($N = 77$) of the calls. This differs from the two shifts I observed where 7-Paul was used for only 46 percent ($N = 6$) of the calls. On the other thirty-four shifts, the 7-Boy code (gathering causing annoyance–no person can be found) was used in only 8 percent ($N = 8$) of all calls, while on my two shifts 7-Boy was used 23 percent ($N = 4$) of the time. Three other codes also showed differences. For the other thirty-four shifts, the 8-Paul code (investigate persons–services ren-

dered) was used in only 2 percent of all calls ($N = 2$) and the 12-Paul (loud music–services rendered) and 9-Charles (investigate persons–no such address) were not used at all. During the two shifts discussed here, these designations appeared four times. This suggests that the presence of a researcher in the car prompted the officers to use their codes more carefully. In all likelihood, my presence in the car made them more conscious of their work (including paperwork) and instead of using 7-P for all sorts of calls, they used other appropriate designations. So we need to consider that what was observed was a "good" recordkeeping performance.

15. In this example, the officers do not report their arrival on the scene to dispatch, which is required of all patrol cars responding to calls. This omission is recognized and discussed by the officers after the work of responding to the call has begun and their course of action has already been decided. When the officer finally does contact dispatch, he provides the disposition (7-Paul), for the call upon which the failure to log on is raised by the dispatcher. The two omissions (i.e., logging on and reporting arrival to the call) have already been a topic in the car *prior* to contacting dispatch. Thus, we can see how both the officers and the dispatcher orient to organizational accountability and actually produce it. But this orientation is of secondary importance to the in situ work of policing the streets.

16. This entry was the *only* use of this code (12-Paul) not only in this evening's log but also in the thirty-four other gang car logs. Indeed, the disposition code here is not 7-Paul, which as will be shown later, is used in the other music calls (examples 3 and 4 in the text). The primary difference between this call and these other music calls is that at the other calls the presence of juveniles, or teenagers, was observed. When adults are observed doing the same thing, the designation is different.

17. FIO records are discussed in a separate article (Meehan 1992). It is important to note here, however, that retaining this type of information on an FIO form indicates the officer's assessment of the situation as "more serious," because FIOs are considered more useful as internal records, particularly for intelligence or surveillance purposes, whereas the patrol logs are viewed more as "administrative tools," to force officers to account for their time spent in the field. Thus, the officer's recordkeeping here is quite consistent with their action of not making this an on-view log entry but preserving the information elsewhere in a more useful form. While the officer writes in their last entry *"Station (5 FIOs)"* at the end of the shift, this is not linked to any particular log entry, because no entry has been made for this incident.

References

Alexander, Jeffrey, Bernhard Geisen, Richard Munch, and Neil Smelser, eds. 1987. *The Micro-Macro Link*. Berkeley: University of California Press.

Best, Joel. 1995. Images of Issues: *Typifying Contemporary Social Problems*. New York: Aldinede Gruyter

Bowditch, Christine. 1993. "Getting Rid of Troublemakers: High School Disciplinary Procedures and the Production of Dropouts." *Social Problems*. 40(4): 493–509.

Chambliss, William J. 1994. "Policing the Ghetto Underclass: The Politics of Law and Law Enforcement." *Social Problems*, 41:177–195.

Collins, Randall. 1981. "The Microfoundations of Macrosociology." *American Journal of Sociology*, 86:984–1014.

———. 1987. "Interaction Ritual Chains, Power and Property: The Micro-Macro Connection as an Empirically Based Theoretical Problem." Pp. 193–206 in *The Micro-Macro Link*, edited by Alexander, Geisen, Munch, and Smelser.

Curry, G. David, Richard A. Ball, and Scott H. Decker. 1996. "Estimating the National Scope of Gang Crime from Law Enforcement Data." Pp. 21–38 in *Gangs in America*, edited by Huff.

Decker, Scott, and Kimberly Kempf-Leonard. 1991. "Constructing Gangs: The Social Definition of Youth Activities." *Criminal Justice Policy Review* 5(4):271–291.

Emerson, Robert. 1991. "Case Processing and Interorganizational Knowledge: Detecting the 'Real Reasons' for Referrals." *Social Problems* 38:198–212.

Fagan, Jeffrey. 1996. "Gangs, Drugs and Neighborhood Change." Pp. 39–74 in *Gangs in America,* edited by Huff.

Fine, Gary Alan. 1991. "On the Macrofoundations of Microsociology: Constraint and the Exterior Reality of Structure." *The Sociological Quarterly* 32:161–177.

Fogelson, Robert. 1977. *Big City Police.* Cambridge, MA: Harvard University Press.

Garfinkel, Harold. 1967. *Studies in Ethnomethodology.* Englewood Cliffs, NJ: Prentice-Hall.

Gill, Virginia, and Douglas Maynard. 1995. "On Labeling in Actual Interaction: Delivering and Receiving Diagnoses of Developmental Disabilities." *Social Problems* 42(1):11–37.

Huff. C. Ronald, ed. 1996. *Gangs in America.* 2nd ed. Thousand Oaks, CA: Sage.

Kitsuse, John, and Aaron Cicourel. 1963. "A Note on the Use of Official Statistics." *Social Problems* 11:131–139.

Klein, Malcolm. 1995. *The American Street Gang.* New York: Oxford University Press.

——. 1996. "Street Gangs and Deterrence Legislation." Pp. 203–321 in *Three Strikes and You're Out: Vengeance as Public Policy,* edited by David Shichor and Dale Sechrist. Thousand Oaks, CA: Sage.

Lundman, Richard. 1980. *Policing: An Introduction.* New York: Holt, Reinhart, and Winston.

Manning, Peter K. 1988. *Symbolic Communication: Signifying Calls and the Police Response.* Cambridge, MA: MIT Press.

——. 1992. "Technological Dramas and the Police: Statement and Counterstatement in Organizational Analysis." *Criminology* 30:327–346.

——. 1997. *Police Work: The Social Organization of Policing.* 2nd ed. Prospect Heights. IL: Westview Press.

Margolin, Leslie. 1992. "Deviance on Record: Techniques for Labeling Child Abusers in Official Documents." *Social Problems* 39:58–70.

Maxfield, Michael, D. Lewis, and Ron Szoc. 1980. "Producing Official Crimes: Verified Crime Reports as Measures of Police Output." *Social Science Quarterly* 61:221–236.

Maxson, Cheryl, and Malcolm Klein. 1996. "Defining Gang Homicide: An Updated Look at Member Versus Motive Approaches." Pp. 3–20 in *Gangs in America,* edited by Huff.

Maynard, Douglas W. 1988. "Language, Interaction and Social Problems." *Social Problems* 35:311–334.

McCleary, Richard. 1977. "How Parole Officers Use Records." *Social Problems* 24:576–589.

McCleary, Richard, Barbara C. Nienstedt, and James M. Erven. 1982. "Uniform Crime Reports as Organizational Outcomes: Three Time Series Experiments." *Social Problems* 29:361–372.

McCorkle, Richard C., and Terance D. Miethe. 1998. "The Political and Organizational Response to Gangs: An Examination of a 'Moral Panic' in Nevada." *Justice Quarterly* 15(1):50–64.

Meehan, Albert J. 1986. "Recordkeeping Practices in the Policing of Juveniles." *Urban Life* 15(1):70–102.

——. 1989. "Assessing the Police Worthiness of a Citizen's Call to the Police: Accountability and the Negotiation of 'Facts.'" Pp. 116–40 in *The Interactional Order: New Directions in the Study of Social Order,* edited by D. Helm, T. Anderson, A. J. Meehan, and A. W. Rawls. New York: Irvington Press.

——. 1992. "'I Don't Prevent Crime, I Prevent Calls': Policing as Negotiated Order." *Symbolic Interaction* 15:455–80.

——. 1993. "Internal Police Records and the Control of Juveniles: Politics and Policing in a Suburban Town." *British Journal of Criminology* 33:504–524.

Merton, Robert. 1957. *Social Theory and Social Structure*. Glencoe, IL: Free Press.

Mills, C. Wright. 1940. "Situated Action and Vocabularies of Motives." *American Journal of Sociology* 5:315–357.

Padilla, Felix. 1992. *The Gang as an American Enterprise*. New Brunswick, NJ: Rutgers University Press.

Rawls, Anne. 1987. "The Interaction Order Sui Generis: Goffman's Contribution to Social Theory." *Sociological Theory* 5(2):136–149.

Reiss, Albert. 1971. *The Police and the Public*. New Haven, CT: Yale University Press.

Rubenstein, Jonathan. 1973. *City Police*. New York: Farrar, Strauss and Giroux.

Sacks, Harvey. 1972. "An Initial Investigation of the Usability of Conversational Data for Doing Sociology." Pp. 31–74 in *Studies in Social Interaction*, edited by David Sudnow. New York: Free Press.

Sacks, Harvey, and Emmanuel Jefferson Schegloff. 1974. "A Simplest Systematics for the Organization of Turn-Taking in Conversation." *Language* 50(4):696–735.

Sanchez-Jankowski, Martin. 1991. *Islands in the Street: Gangs in American Urban Society*. Stanford, CA: Stanford University Press.

Sasson, Theodore. 1995. *Crime Talk: How Citizens Construct a Social Problem*. Hawthorne, NY: Aldine de Gruyter.

Schegloff, Emanuel. 1987. "Between Micro and Macro: Contexts and Other Connections." Pp. 207–34 in *The Micro-Macro Link*, edited by Alexander, Geisen, Munch, and Smelser. University of California Press.

Schenkein, James. 1978. *Studies in the Organization of Conversational Interaction*. New York: Academic Press.

Seidman, Darryl, and Michael Couzens. 1974. "Getting the Crime Rate Down: Political Pressure and Crime Reporting." *Law and Society Review* 8:457–493.

Short, James. 1996. "Preface." Pp. 21–38 in *Gangs in America*, edited by Huff.

———. 1997. *Poverty, Ethnicity and Violent Crime*. Boulder, CO: Westview Press.

Skogan, Wesley. 1975. "Measurement Problems in Official and Survey Crime Rates." *Journal of Criminal Justice* 3:17–32.

Skolnick, Jerome H., Ricky Bluthenthal, and Theodore Correl. 1993. "Gang Organization and Migration." Pp. 193–218 in *Gangs: The Origins and Impact of Contemporary Youth Gangs in the United States*, edited by Scott Cummings and Daniel Monti. Albany, NY: State University of New York Press.

Smith, Dorothy. 1974. "The Social Construction of Documentary Reality." *Sociological Inquiry* 44:257–268.

Spector, Malcolm, and John Kitsuse. 1977. *Constructing Social Problems*. Menlo Park, CA: Cummings Publishing Company.

Spergel, Irving A. 1994. *Gang Suppression and Intervention: Problem and Response. Research Summary*. Washington, DC: Office of Juvenile Justice and Delinquency Prevention.

———. 1995. *The Youth Gang Problem: A Community Approach*. New York: Oxford University Press.

Spergel, Irving A., and Lawrence Bobrowski. 1989. "Law Enforcement Definitional Conference" (Transcript). Rockville, MD: Juvenile Justice Clearinghouse. http://www.ncjrs.org.txtfiles/ d0030.txt

Taylor, Carl. 1990. *Dangerous Society*. East Lansing: Michigan State University Press.

U.S. Bureau of Justice Assistance (U.S.BJA). 1997. *Urban Street Gang Enforcement*. Washington, DC.

U.S. Senate. 1997. *Gangs: A National Crisis. Hearing Before the Committee on the Judiciary*. 105th Cong. Washington, DC: GPO.

Wheeler, Stanton. 1969. *On Record: Files and Dossiers in American Life*. New York: Russell Sage Foundation.

Zatz, M. 1987. "Chicago Youth Gangs and Crime: The Creation of a Moral Panic." *Contemporary Crises* 11:129–158.

30 The Medicalisation of Deviance

Richard Gosden

Scattered throughout a recently published Annual Report of the NSW [New South Wales, Australia] Mental Health Review Tribunal are repeated references to a perception by members of the Tribunal that involuntary commitment to mental hospitals is being erroneously restricted. The Mental Health Review Tribunal is a quasi-judicial body constituted under the NSW Mental Health Act with some 29 designated responsibilities for hearing appeals and reviewing the cases of detained mental patients. As the Act currently stands people who are judged to be mentally ill or mentally disordered by a medical practitioner can only be 'scheduled' into a mental hospital against their will if there is a risk they might cause serious physical harm to themselves or other people. This requirement of dangerousness can only be downgraded when the symptoms of mental illness concern disorders of mood in which case serious risk to the person's finances or reputation can also be considered.

The Mental Health Review Tribunal appears to be of the opinion that the current interpretations of these requirements are too strict and that a much wider net should be cast for coercive psychiatric practice. One of the Tribunal's statements even goes so far as to appeal for involuntary commitment to be expanded to include people with personality disorders "who would benefit from behavioural modification, rehabilitation, or drug and alcohol programmes".

Yet, despite these repeated appeals to widen the criteria for involuntary commitment, the Tribunal, in the same report, has ironically also drawn attention to the way the numbers of involuntary patients are steadily increasing under the existing criteria. The total number of involuntary admissions in NSW has risen from 5499 in 1992, to 6403 in 1993, to 7190 in 1994.

This has been accompanied by an even more accelerated rise in the numbers of Community Counselling Orders (CCOs) and Community Treatment Orders (CTOs). CCOs and CTOs are legal devices in NSW which facilitate the involuntary medication of a person for psychiatric reasons outside of an institution. A CCO achieves this under threat of arrest for non-compliance. A CTO provides for arrest and incarceration for non-compliance. There has been a lot of opposition to the concept of CCOs and CTOs, particularly in the United States where variants are currently being introduced state by state. One NSW community mental health nurse has criticised them because "they offer too many avenues for abuse by punitive and anxious staff." The NSW Minister for Health, however, is currently proposing to amend the Mental Health Act so that the maximum period for CTOs can be extended from three months to six months. The combined total in NSW of CCOs and CTOs for 1992 was 510; for 1993 it was 782; and for 1994 it was 1233.

Apart from drawing attention to the increase in the numbers of involuntary patients, the Tribunal has also reported declining numbers of voluntary patients. According to the Tribunal, the combination indicates a developing "trend towards coercive, as opposed to consensual, treatment." But the Tribunal does not indicate any disapproval of this trend and it is difficult to avoid the conclusion that it is deliberately encouraging the trend by arguing for a relaxation of the criteria for involuntary commitment.

Expanding the Diagnostic Net

The significance of a trend towards coercive psychiatry can perhaps be brought into focus by reference to a recent survey published in *The Medical Journal of Australia*. Using the standard DSM diagnostic system the South Australian study found that 26.4% of 1009 ordinary rural adults had mental illnesses. 11% were found to have two or more disorders. This compared to a similar study undertaken in Christchurch NZ which found that 20.6% of the general population had mental illnesses and two studies in the United States which found rates of 20% and 29%.

The South Australian study found that only 4.2% of the people with mental illnesses had seen a psychiatrist or psychologist in the previous 12 months and it agreed with U.S. researchers that "most community residents are not treated for their psychiatric problems." Blame for this was directed towards GPs: "the ability of GPs to identify psychiatric problems and to provide an accurate diagnosis, particularly of depression, has been questioned."

These findings can be expected to encourage the medical profession in the belief that they are underdiagnosing mental illness and that more effort should be put into early diagnosis and treatment. Yet there is an altogether different way of interpreting these findings. Of 1009 people there were 11 people (4.2% of 26.4%) who acknowledged they had mental problems and who sought specialist treatment for them. A further 255 people (26.4% minus 11) were diagnosed with mental illnesses but were not receiving treatment.

From the medical point of view these 255 people should receive treatment and if they are unwilling to volunteer for it then coercion might be necessary. But at the same time most of these 255 people must be coping with life in their untreated state—otherwise they would have already come into contact with psychiatry as either voluntary or involuntary patients.

What is apparent from this interpretation of the survey is the huge gap that exists between the psychiatric profession's view of the community's state of mental health and the community's own view of itself. This confirms sociological research which has found that "lay beliefs are often quite distinctive in form and content" to clinical medicine. By finding about a quarter of the population to be mentally ill, when these same people seem to be willing to carry on with life as they are, the psychiatric researchers have raised very interesting questions: Are we living in a society that is quite literally partly mad, where a quarter of the population seem to be unaware that they have already developed mental illnesses, and where the rest of us appear unwilling to acknowledge that soon it might be our turn? Or is there something wrong with the diagnostic techniques used by the researchers? Is there something about the way psychiatry is practised that predisposes psychiatrists to find pathology where ordinary lay people might find foolishness, stupidity, aggression, laziness, drunkenness, boorishness, unhappiness, self doubt and numerous other character faults that affect most people at some time or another, making them unpleasant company, but which do not really distinguish people as having sick minds?

The DSM Diagnostic System

The Diagnostic and Statistical Manual of Mental Disorders (DSM) used in the South Australian survey was devised and published by the American Psychiatric Association (APA). The APA is the main professional organisation of psychiatrists in the United States and their diagnostic manual has become a de facto international standard for psychiatric diagnosis. The DSM system is deeply entrenched in Australian medical practice, and codes from the manual are required for lodging medicare claims for psychiatric expenses.

Early versions of the DSM had little pretence of being scientific and were largely heuristic guide books that incorporated much of the psychiatric lore derived from Freudian psychoanalytical techniques. But with the third revision in 1980, a "fateful point in the history of the American psychiatric profession was reached. . . . The decision of the APA first to develop DSM III and then to promulgate its use represents a significant reaffirmation on the part of American psychiatry to its medical identity and its commitment to scientific medicine." Scientific pretensions have been a central feature of the hyperbole surrounding the use of subsequent revisions of the manual.

The recent editions of DSM attempt to classify all deviant personality types in such a way as to provide a universal reference for aspects of human expression and identity that the APA thinks require modification. The preparation of the most recent edition, DSM IV, was a "team effort" involving more than a thousand people. Codes and descriptions are supplied for a total of 390 separate mental disorders. They range in scope from "Disorders Usually First Diagnosed in Infancy, Childhood or Adolescence" like the learning disorders—315.00 Reading Disorder and 315.1 Mathematics Disorder—and the disruptive behaviour disorder—313.81 Oppositional Defiant Disorder—through to a whole range of adult forms of deviancy including substance abuse of various kinds, sexual dysfunctions, personality disorders, and psychoses.

There are obvious dangers to human rights arising from the empowerment of medical practitioners to use the DSM system as a template for dividing the general population into a 75% portion of normal people and a 25% portion of people who are unfit in their present condition. Even if the alienation of a quarter of the population were acceptable in human rights terms, why should a conservative American professional organisation be allowed to specify the types of people that are unacceptable to Australian society? Consider some of the features of 301.7.

Antisocial Personality Disorder for Instance

"Irresponsible work behaviour may be indicated by significant periods of unemployment . . . or by the abandonment of several jobs without a realistic plan for getting another job. There may be a pattern of repeated absences from work. . . . They may have an inflated and arrogant self-appraisal (e.g. feel that ordinary work is beneath them or lack a realistic concern about their current problems or their future) and may be excessively opinionated, self-assured or cocky."

This type of person may be unattractive to employers in the United States, and indeed to Australian employers as well, but do most Australians really believe that these character traits are manifestations of a sick mind? Some Australian psychiatrists have argued, apparently with little success, against the respect given to the DSM system in Australia, particularly by courts of law:

"When a sceptical psychiatrist points out that the DSM is no more than a distillate of the prejudices and power plays of a group of aging American academics, of no interest to most Europeans and only passing relevance to some Australasians, this carries no weight."

Doubts about whether a U.S.-devised classification system for mental *deviance* has validity in Australia are further compounded by doubts about whether diagnosticians can even be consistent in their identification of the forms of *deviance* that the manual describes. The diagnostic system largely deals with manifestations of mind and personality and requires subjective value judgements that have to be made without the assistance of definitive methods of measurement or laboratory tests. What is "excessively opinion-ated, self-assured and cocky" to one diagnostician might be "well-informed, confident and amusing" to another.

In extensive surveys of psychiatric diagnosis, where two psychiatrists were required to interview the same patients on admission to psychiatric hospitals, it has been repeatedly found that agreement between the psy-chiatrists is often little better than mere chance. Using a statistical system called Kappa, which is designed to determine the diagnostic agreement be-tween psychiatrists which is over and above chance, researchers found in six studies conducted in the U.S. and the UK that the diagnostic agreement for schizophrenia, for instance, was "no better than fair." When the Kappa figure for chance is .46, the average of the six tests was found to be .57, with a low range in New York well below chance of .32.

This critical weakness in psychiatric practice was exposed over 20 years ago by the much-cited Rosenhan experiment. In 1973 an American profes-sor of psychology enlisted eight volunteers to act as pseudo-patients. Over a period of time they presented themselves at 12 psychiatric hospitals and complained of hearing voices saying the words "empty," "hollow" and "thud." These words had been chosen because of their existential connota-tions suggesting the emptiness of life and because they had never appeared in psychiatric literature as being symptoms of mental illness.

On each occasion the pseudo-patients were admitted to the hospitals and on all but one occasion they were diagnosed as having schizophrenia. After the initial interview the volunteers did not mention the voices again and acted their normal sane selves. The agreement they had made with the co-ordinator of the experiment was that they would each have to gain their own release without any outside assistance. This had to be done by con-vincing the hospital staff they were sane. The length of hospitalisation ranged from 7 to 52 days with an average of 19 days. All those originally diagnosed as having schizophrenia were released with the diagnosis of "schizophrenia in remission." One conclusion made by the coordinator of the experiment was that "Psychiatric diagnoses . . . are in the minds of the observers and are not valid summaries of the characteristics displayed by the observed."

Despite these known shortcomings of psychiatric diagnosis the mental health industry continues to expand with the assistance of the DSM diag-nostic system which provides psychiatrists with a 'scientific' justification for "the *medicalisation* of *deviance.*" In the United States between 1975 and 1990, "the number of psychiatrists increased from 26,000 to 36,000, clini-cal psychologists 15,000 to 42,000, and clinical social workers from 25,000 to 80,000" while the total cost of mental health care rose between 1980 and 1990 from about $20 billion to about $55 billion.

This '*medicalisation* of *deviance*' is even becoming apparent in the so-cialisation of children. Social commentators are beginning to observe a growing tendency amongst parents and schoolteachers to rely on drugs like

Ritalin to "suppress the passion of children" and to assist in the correction of perceived behavioural problems.

Early detection of supposedly serious psychiatric problems in children is also becoming a widely discussed imperative. For instance, in NSW the Schizophrenia Information Centre warns parents to be watchful for early signs of insanity in their children, advising that treatment should be given immediately if any symptoms are observed. One of the signs they advise parents to look for is a child who is observed to "say or do things most people find socially embarrassing—like telling someone they're ugly or their nose is a funny shape. . . . It is as if their brain disorder involves some damage to the internal 'filter' which helps people sort out what's appropriate from what's not."

A recent paper on childhood schizophrenia in the U.S. gives a number of examples of supposedly psychotic symptoms that have been observed in child patients. Its observations include: "An 8-year-old girl reported hearing multiple voices including the voice of a dead baby brother saying—'I love you sister, sister I'm going to miss you.' An 11-year-old boy heard God's voice saying, 'Sorry D., but I can't come now, I'm helping someone else.' An 8-year-old girl reported an angel saying things like, 'You didn't cry today' and 'You've been a very nice girl today.' An 8-year-old boy stated, 'I can hear the devil talk—God interrupts him and the devil says 'shut up God.' God and the devil are always fighting.' A boy described monsters calling him 'Stupid F . . . ' and say they will hurt him."

The researcher reports that the mean age of the onset of Nonpsychotic Symptoms in these children was 4.6 years; the mean age of the onset of Psychotic Symptoms was 6.9 years; and the mean age at diagnosis of schizophrenia was 9.5 years.

It is worth noting that this particular study was conducted in Los Angeles on 38 children, 17 of whom were black, 16 Hispanic, 4 white and 1 Asian. All the children had been screened to ensure their symptoms met "strict DSM III criteria for schizophrenia." The DSM description of schizophrenia is normally used to determine abnormality in adults and it seems extraordinary to read a paper like this, published in a prestigious journal of the U.S. National Institute of Mental Health, reporting research that has adapted the diagnostic criteria for use on children without any explanation or equivocation. The implication is that the researcher believes that children should meet the same standards of conformity in their thoughts, beliefs and expression as are expected of adults. Perhaps the racial mix of the sample can explain why the researcher might hold such an intolerant view.

Observers of psychiatric trends in the U.S. have become concerned about a tendency to fund research into a perceived link between inner-city street crime and an assumed imbalance of brain chemistry in the perpetrators. A part of this line of research involves the development of new psychiatric drugs which it is hoped will pacify aggressive people by increasing the availability of serotonin in their brains. Young black males are seen as the prime targets for this type of therapy and the accompanying debate has inspired the headline in at least one black newspaper, "PLOT TO SEDATE BLACK YOUTH."

Unfortunately, the Australian Human Rights and Equal Opportunity Commission seems to be unaware of the harm that might be done to human rights by encouraging the early diagnosis and treatment of mental illness. The Burdekin Report, for instance, claimed that:

"Conduct disorder and other disruptive behaviours are a source of considerable morbidity in child and adolescent mental health with problems occurring in 3.2–6.9 percent of young people. . . . Prevention of conduct disorders in childhood and adolescence, or their early and effective treatment, is of special significance given the great personal, social and economic costs produced by antisocial behaviour and other disorders."

Conduct disorder is specifically confined to children and adolescents. According to the DSM IV, "The essential feature of Conduct Disorder is a repetitive and persistent pattern of behaviour in which the basic rights of others or major age-appropriate societal norms or rules are violated. . . . Children with this disorder often have a pattern of staying out late at night despite parental prohibitions." The text-book recommendation for treating this kind of waywardness, as well as for treating other social imperfections in children like Tourette's Disorder, characterised by the blurting out of obscene expletives, is dosing with haliperidol, one of the high-strength neuroleptics.

The Burdekin Report was particularly enthusiastic about the early diagnosis and treatment of schizophrenia:

"Psychiatrists working with general practitioners in an English community have been able to detect the earliest signs of schizophrenia—and with education, supportive interventions and short-term psychotropic medication—prevent the onset of an episode. . . . Obviously this research must be repeated and tested in different settings, including Australia, but these early findings are encouraging and warrant urgent attention."

The Human Rights Commission apparently had not considered the potential threat which this line of research might pose to basic human rights like those specified in Article 18 of the International Covenant on Civil and Political Rights concerned with the freedom of thought and belief. The implication of the Burdekin Report is that it might be useful to screen the general population for the "earliest signs of schizophrenia." If this screening were to be carried out in Australia, and people with the "earliest signs" were then coerced into preventative psychiatric programmes, the effect would be to lower the community's tolerance level for individual deviancy in thoughts and beliefs.

The current tolerance level is only crossed when a person manifests the symptoms of full-blown psychosis. But if the "earliest signs of schizophrenia" were used to lower the tolerance level this aspect of Western psychiatry might begin to look suspiciously like the type of psychiatry that was practised in the Soviet Union.

As early as 1974, psychiatrists in the West had become curious about reports of the high prevalence of schizophrenia in the Soviet Union—5–7 per 1,000 population compared to 3–4 per 1,000 in the UK. In due course it was revealed that Soviet psychiatrists had discovered a unique form of mental disease to fit the profile of political dissidents. They called the condition "sluggish schizophrenia, a form of schizophrenia where the symptoms are subtle, latent or only apparent to the skilled eye of the psychiatrist." Soviet dissidents who "wanted to reform the system and claimed that they had the personal vision to do it . . . were exhibiting the text-book symptoms of sluggish schizophrenia." Soviet psychiatrists became so deeply involved in the control of political dissidents that a whole system of special mental hospitals was established which they ran in co-operation with the KGB.

Conclusion

The Mental Health Review Tribunal in NSW has identified a growing trend towards coercive psychiatric practice and away from consensual treatment. A widening gap seems to be developing between the psychiatric profession's perception of the general community's state of mental health and the community's own view of itself. The medical profession seems to be exacerbating this situation by disguising the essential subjectivity of psychiatric diagnosis with rhetorical claims that the DSM diagnostic system is now a branch of medical science. The DSM system further promotes the "*medicalisation* of *deviance*" by continually expanding the number of abnormal thinking and behavioural patterns which it defines as varieties of mental disorder. In this way the net of coercive psychiatry is rapidly expanding, but strangely this expansion appears to have been endorsed by the recent human rights inquiry into mental illness. The only reasonable conclusion that can be drawn is that psychiatry is set to play a growing role in social control.

Ronald Leifer has argued that the prevailing conditions in modern industrial societies have given rise to "the therapeutic state." This is a form of social organisation in which the law still respects the right to individual autonomy and where people are not criminalised for being different, but where there is also a large class of non-criminal people, with undesirable attitudes and beliefs, who are medically controlled by forcing them into the role of patients.

Social-Control Agents, Sanctioning, and the Production of Institutional Careers and Identities

In this section we take a much closer look at how the process of identifying and sanctioning produces institutional careers and identities. We do so by focusing on how individuals are recruited into their institutional careers and on how clients' "bodies or selves" become the embodiment of deviancy and therefore the focus of change. The first selection provides some insight into the sanctioning process and how it actually contributes to institutional careers. One important observation that should be made at this point is that selected moral campaigns may expand to include new agencies as managers or identifiers of deviance. Such is the case of medicalization, discussed earlier, and the point of this article.

In "Criminalizing Women's Behavior," Nora S. Gustavsson and Ann E. MacEachron show how moral campaigns can coopt other agencies into their struggle and create new paths of entry into institutional careers. The drug war in the United states has cost billions of dollars a year for more than a decade, with the bulk of the war on drugs being waged against major suppliers and distributors, and managed for the most part by the criminal justice system. More recently, the drug war has been expanded to include pursuit of individuals who use illegal substances as well as those who supply the drug. And by coopting the medical establishment it is possible to monitor drug use in a vast number of individuals, in this case, childbearing women.

The authors carefully dismantle the notion that potential fetal harm is either the reason for punitive policies against drug-using pregnant women or legitimation for the sexist policies that victimize poor women. It becomes clear that illicit drug use by women is the concern and the focus of management, since fetal harm is caused by many factors that remain unregulated (e.g., the harm to the reproductive process and fetal development that may occur as a result of drug use by fathers). In the end, this type of state intervention results in the "manufacture" and introduction of two sets of misfits: mothers (the fastest growing population in the criminal justice system) and children (taxing an already stressed and often inadequate child welfare agency). Once shunted into an institutional career, the process of detecting, diagnosing, and treating the deviancy—thought to lie within the person—is initiated.

Vincent Lyon-Callo, in "Medicalizing Homelessness: The Production of Self-Blame and Self-Governing within Homeless Shelters," draws on three years of ethnographic research in an emergency homeless shelter and reveals important issues relating to the medicalized treatment of the homeless. One aspect of the medicalization of deviance is that it places the origins of the deviance within the individual, and hence absolves society of any real responsibility. As Lyon-Callo observes "[w]hen homelessness is individualized and medicalized, those concerns remain peripheral to the central work of normalizing perceived shortcomings or deviance within homeless people." The end result of this process is that the individual must accept the diagnosis and then accept the responsibility for his or her deviance.

As noted throughout, agencies' theory of the office remains central, since the diagnostic categories emerge or flow from this guiding ideology. In this specific case, medicalized conceptions—the theory of the office—guide institutional responses. But there is more of interest here. The behavior of social control agents that is designed to resolve the "disease" actually helps to reproduce and to reinforce the dominant images of homelessness within the institution and the larger society, and of homeless people, and contribute to producing particular states among the homeless. These states can be viewed as iatrogenic subjectivities, experiences, self-images, and behavior. If individuals are resistant to treatment, they may be identified or categorized as being troublemakers and then released from the program, or an additional label may be applied—such as "the person is in denial." What is interesting about this particular label is that any resistance to the label is perceived as evidence that the diagnosis is, in fact, correct. And in a very real sense, the individual becomes mired in an "institutional catch-22" situation—he or she becomes locked in.

31 Criminalizing Women's Behavior

Nora S. Gustavsson
Ann E. MacEachron

Introduction

Criminalizing the behavior of drug-using pregnant and parenting women is a policy fraught with contradictions and helps to perpetuate actions that can harm women and their children. The assumptions used to support these punitive policies are based upon suspect evidence and questionable data. We critically examine the evidence as well as the policies and suggest an alternative policy approach to dealing with families in which parental drug use may be an issue.

Incidence of Drug Use

The seemingly simple task of identifying the number of pregnant women using drugs presents serious challenges. Estimates of drug use vary widely. Some estimates are inferred from estimates of drug use by all women of child bearing age. Other estimates are drawn from incidence studies at hospitals and clinics. Variability among estimates is influenced by the nature, location, and size of the sample; the definition of drugs; and the methods used for drug identification. Moreover, after reviewing these studies it becomes clear that we do not know how many pregnant women are using drugs, what drugs they are using, in what quantities and with what frequency, and during which stages of pregnancy.

The National Institute on Drug Abuse (NIDA) is a commonly cited source of data. The Institute's (1993b) data suggest that illicit drug use has been declining. In 1985 the household survey reported 22.3 million current users of illicit drugs. This dropped to 11.7 million in 1993. Cocaine use dropped during the same period from 4.2 million to 1.3 million. Drug use by adolescents, however, is on the increase, as is the use of heroin. Chronic or hard core drug users represent one fifth of the drug-using population and consume two thirds of the cocaine (Office of National Drug Control Policy 1995).

Estimating the number of women of child bearing age using both licit and illicit drugs can be complex. For example, there are a reported 100 million users of alcohol (NIDA 1989). If 30% of these users are women of child bearing age, then a large number of infants could be at risk for prenatal alcohol exposure.

Studies conducted at hospitals report different incidence rates. A Miami study reported a 12% perinatal cocaine exposure rate (Bandstra et al. 1989). A study at a Detroit public hospital revealed that 27% of delivering women tested positive for one or more drugs, with marijuana the most common (Land and Kushner 1990). A study at Boston City Hospital reported that 18% of mothers had used cocaine and 27% had used marijuana (Zuckerman et al. 1989). Another study at an urban hospital of women using prenatal services reported that 17% of the women had used cocaine (Frank et al. 1988). The Federal government estimates that 100,000 infants are exposed prenatally to cocaine (U.S. General Accounting Office 1990). Another study of 36 hospitals in urban areas found an average incidence rate of illicit drugs of 11% with a range of 0.4 to 27% (Chasnoff 1989). Hospitals that intensively screened for drugs reported a higher incidence rate.

These studies were conducted at public hospitals that serve primarily poor and minority women. A Florida study of 715 pregnant women attempted to address the class and race bias. Women using both public and private obstetrical offices were screened. More than 14% tested positive for one or more drugs. There was little difference in the rates between public and private patients and between white and African-American women. Florida has legislation requiring mandated health workers, educational staff, and many human resources workers to notify the state of pregnant, drug-using women. African-American women in the study were 10 times more likely to be reported to state officials than were white women (Chasnoff et al. 1990).

Using data from a number of sources, Gomby and Shiono (1991) estimate that 2% to 3% of newborns were exposed prenatally to cocaine and 3% to 12% were exposed to marijuana. They also suggest that a large number of pregnant women drank alcohol (73%) during their pregnancies and that 37.6% smoked cigarettes. Based on these percentages, approximately 158,000 infants were prenatally exposed to cocaine, 611,000 to marijuana, 2.6 million to alcohol, and 1.3 million to cigarettes. A few million infants may thus be exposed prenatally to licit and illicit drugs annually. However, the consequences of this exposure have yet to be understood.

Effects of Prenatal Exposure

Consistent with the lack of knowledge about the actual incidence of drug use among pregnant women, there is inconsistent and contradictory evidence about the effects of prenatal drug exposure. The drugs with well established and documented negative consequences for fetal well being are two legal drugs—alcohol and tobacco. The consequences of illicit drug exposure for the fetus are unclear.

The effects of alcohol on the fetus have been studied for decades, especially since Fetal Alcohol Syndrome (FAS) was identified (Jones and Smith 1973). The syndrome is characterized by growth deficiency and central nervous system impairments. Fetal Alcohol Effect (FAE) is a more common condition in which the infant suffers some but not all of the characteristics of FAS. FAE is estimated to occur at 10 times the frequency of FAS (Rosengren 1990), and FAS is estimated to occur at the rate of 1.9 births per thousand (Abel and Sokel 1987). What remains unclear are the mechanisms of interaction, contributions of other factors, how much alcohol is used and how frequently, and during which phase of fetal development its use results in fetal harm.

Low birth weight, sudden infant death syndrome, spontaneous abortion, premature rupture of the membranes, and abnormal placentation are associated with maternal tobacco use (Li and Daling 1991; Office on Smoking and Health 1988; Williams et al. 1991). More recent studies are suggesting a relationship between maternal smoking and increased systolic and diastolic blood pressure in the infants of women who smoked during pregnancy (Beratis et al. 1996). Intrauterine growth retardation, and the incidence of both orofacial clefts and congenital urinary tract anomalies are associated with maternal cigarette smoking (Nordentoft et al. 1996; Shaw et al. 1996; Li et al. 1996). The mechanisms of harm are poorly understood due in part to the large number of chemicals found in cigarette smoke. It seems clear that there are significant risks associated with cigarette smoking (Benowitz 1991).

Unlike alcohol and tobacco, the consequences of illicit drugs such as cocaine have only recently been studied in depth. Early studies reported a number of negative consequences including preterm birth, small head circumference, and genitourinary malformations (Bingol et al. 1987; Cordero and Custard 1990; Chasnoff et al. 1987; McGregor et al. 1987; and Zuckerman et al. 1989). Other studies have reported few differences between cocaine and non-cocaine exposed infants (Woods et al. 1993). There is some evidence to suggest that infants exposed prenatally to cocaine may have more difficulty with habilitation (reduced response to repeated stimuli) and experience more stress behaviors (Eisen et al. 1991).

Studies of maternal marijuana use suggest an association with impaired fetal growth, exaggerated startles, an increase in fine tremors and tremors associated with the Moro reflex (Fried and Makin 1987; and Zuckerman et al. 1989). Long-term consequences have been studied and suggest that few differences exist until age 48 months, when memory and verbal measures were negatively affected in children prenatally exposed to heavy marijuana use. Another study suggests that attentional behaviors of 6-year-olds are also negatively affected (Fried and Watkinson 1990; Fried et al. 1992).

Consequences of opioid exposure include the risk of preterm birth, low birth weight, small head circumference, and a neonatal abstinence syndrome (Wilson 1989). The syndrome is characterized by high pitched crying, exaggerated reflexes, sneezing, restlessness, and diarrhea. Longitudinal studies indicate these children may suffer difficulties with visual-motor-perception skills and poor school performance (Wilson 1989).

Analysis of the Research

Generalizing the results of these studies is problematic. The samples are often small, composed primarily of poor women with an over-representation of minority women, and the studies do not separate out the effects of other variables. Samples with an $n = 1$ have been reported (Telsey et al. 1988). Poor women are likely to face additional challenges to successful reproductive outcomes such as lack of access to early, consistent, and quality prenatal care (Burns et al. 1985). Negative environmental factors such as poor housing and nutrition, living in neighborhoods that experience violence and lack social supports and services, depression, histories of abuse and neglect, as well as involvement with male partners who may be drug involved and violent are not conducive to positive infant and maternal outcomes (Amaro et al. 1990; Regan et al. 1987).

Research designs often have difficulty controlling for the effects of other variables. Polydrug use, particularly the use of tobacco and alcohol, is common (Hutchings 1990). These two legal drugs have clearly established negative consequences for the fetus. If a woman is using marijuana and/or cocaine along with legal drugs, attributing fetal harm to any one drug becomes difficult. An experimental design, for example, in which there is random assignment of pregnant women to a cocaine group or a control group is not ethically or legally feasible.

Caution must be exercised in attributing negative fetal outcomes to drug use. It is estimated that 10% to 15% of congenital malformations are due to environmental agents, 10 to 15% are due to hereditary factors, and the rest are a result of multiple or unknown factors (Hutchings 1985). Prescription medications such as diethystilbestrol (DES), Accutane, lithium, and anticonvulsants are particularly toxic to the fetus.

Reproductive outcomes are influenced by multiple variables. The small, non-representative samples and the inability to control for all variables that can influence reproductive outcomes compromise the conclusions of many of the medical studies. Of particular interest is the political ideology such research represents. Not only is this reproductive research focused exclusively on only one party (the female), but studies that report minimal or no negative consequences of drug use have little visibility in the professional literature.

The exclusion of men from studies on the influence of drugs on the fetus lends credence to the notion that research serves the purposes of power elites who want to police women and control their behavior. The dearth of research on the effects of drugs on male reproduction is striking. There are a few studies that offer preliminary evidence to suggest that chemically abusing men face an elevated risk of infertility and chromosome damage (Close et al. 1990; Shafer et al. 1990). Licit drugs are also reported to adversely impact the morphology of sperm (Office of Technology Assessment 1985). A recent study reported the presence of tobacco residue in semen (Davis et al. 1992).

Tobacco may provide a vehicle for including the contributions of men to fetal and infant health. It has become more commonplace to see reports on the relationship between smoking and health. There was a period in which the medical community and tobacco companies were allies. The medical organizations discounted studies which reported negative consequences of smoking and tobacco companies opposed federal legislation that would regulate physicians, their services, and their fees. Today, respected medical journals publish studies that indicate children are at risk from the adults in their environments who use tobacco and advocate for new laws to protect children from the harm attributable to the use of tobacco products by others (DiFranza and Lew 1996).

In addition to the role of damaged sperm, men contribute to fetal outcomes by their abuse of the mother. This is another understudied area. Estimates on the number of women battered during pregnancy vary from 4% to 8% (Helton 1987). A more recent study at public prenatal clinics, which served primarily poor women, found an exceedingly high rate of physical abuse. Only 17% of the patients had *not* been physically abused during their current pregnancy (McFarlane et al. 1992).

Another disturbing factor in the research on drug-using, pregnant women is the reluctance to acknowledge that much of what has passed for fact is more accurately described as myth. Even the medical establishment is beginning to recognize the role of political ideology in their research. In a recent article a physician suggested that the desire to exert control over women, and identifying black women in particular for criminal prosecution and child protection referrals, meets political goals but ignores the social factors in women's lives such as family dysfunction, untreated addiction, and persistent poverty (Neuspiel 1993).

The medical community has added to the myth of maternal illicit drug use and severe fetal harm by its hesitancy to provide a forum for research that suggests that the association between maternal drug behavior and fetal harm is tangential. Studies that showed a negative association between maternal cocaine use and fetal outcome were significantly more likely to be accepted for presentation by the Society for Pediatric Research than studies showing no association, even though they were more methodologically sound. These studies had a negligible chance for acceptance (Koren et al. 1989).

The difficulty in establishing causal links between drug use and fetal harm is beginning to be reported in the professional literature. Measures of overall competence do not show any difference between cocaine exposed and non-cocaine exposed infants. Some of the difficulties observed in drug exposed infants attenuate with age (Chasnoff et al. 1992; Zuckerman and Frank 1992). There are questions about the later developmental problem experienced by drug exposed children (Day et al. 1994; Fried et al. 1992). However, the contributions of illicit drugs to these problems is not clear. Poverty seems to be a major contributor to the problems experienced by these children (NIDA 1993a).

The unwillingness to evaluate commonly accepted myths about the frequency and extent of fetal harm due to maternal behavior leads inexorably to the conclusion that the attempts to control women in their reproductive role is due to factors other than concern for the well being of infants.

Elevating Fetal Rights

Criminalizing the behavior of pregnant women results, in part, from perceiving the fetus as a person with enforceable rights. This is a new development made possible through advances in medical science. The technology of the 20th century has made it commonplace to monitor and even see the developing fetus. There are a number of serious consequences of making the fetus a person.

The resolution of potential conflicts between the developing fetus and the mother is complicated by viewing the fetus as a person. The state has intervened in the lives of pregnant women in an attempt to protect the fetus. It is important to note that the State is protecting the fetus *against* the mother. An adversarial relationship between mother and fetus is thus established by State intervention. These political intrusions are supported by the medical industry. This raises another set of questions that are beyond the scope of this paper about the omniscience of medical science and the price a woman can pay for failing to do what she is told.

Precedents for State intervention in cases in which the fetus was assumed to be at risk and the mother was assumed to be recalcitrant for not following the advice of medical providers can be found in many jurisdictions. The State has forced blood transfusions on pregnant women, even when the women object on religious grounds. The State argues that the viable fetus must be protected and its welfare takes precedence over the mother's wishes (*in re Jamaica Hospital* 1985).

Forced cesareans are even more invasive medical procedures and courts have been willing to order them against the wishes of the mother. In one especially sad case, the court ordered a cesarean section over the objections of a terminally ill woman (*in re A.C.* 1990). The court decided that because the mother was going to die anyway, her wishes need not be respected. Saving the fetus was deemed more important. The 26-week-old fetus died 3 hours after the surgery. The mother died the next day.

Pregnant women bear an obligation, which can carry the weight of law, to place the needs and welfare of the fetus above their own. No other group of Americans are expected to sacrifice their individual rights to autonomy, privacy, or even health, to enhance the viability of another person, much less a developing fetus. Whether this is an unintended consequence of biology and anatomy is open to debate. It is a gender specific duty. Only women, at least at this time, can sustain a fetus.

The State's interest in fetal well being is highly specific and appears limited to monitoring maternal behavior. Yet the State is reluctant to provide other services that could enhance fetal well being such as accessible and affordable prenatal care, nutrition, housing, and environments free from hazards.

Intrusive medical procedures assumed to benefit the fetus provide the base for extending the interests of the State into maternal behaviors. If the State can force unwanted procedures onto pregnant women, then the next step of proscribing acceptable behaviors follows easily.

Criminalizing Maternal Conduct

There are a number of major assumptions in the policy of criminalizing maternal behaviors in addition to the belief that the fetus is a person. There is the belief that women have an affirmative duty to refrain from activities that medical practitioners say are harmful and if they do not, then prosecution is an appropriate response. One justification for this policy is the belief that fetal outcomes will be improved by criminalizing maternal behavior. Pregnancy has become the basis for determining criminal behavior. A biologically based temporary condition is a sufficient condition for the determination of criminal action.

One example of the criminalization approach occurred in California (*People v. Stewart* 1987). The case involved a woman who gave birth to a severely damaged preterm infant who died a few weeks after birth. Blood tests revealed amphetamines in the baby's blood. The mother was arrested and charged with failing to provide medical care to her fetus under a child support statute. The mother had been told to stop using drugs and not to have intercourse. She allegedly engaged in both of the forbidden activities. The charges were eventually dismissed. But the policy precedent of trying to force pregnant women to behave in acceptable ways by relying on prosecution was established.

Another California case occurred a decade earlier and involved trying to prosecute a woman addicted to heroin for felony endangerment (*Reyes v. Superior Court* 1977). The case was dismissed because the action occurred before the birth of the twins and the statute was intended to cover harm to already born children.

Other states have used existing laws to prosecute women such as those that prohibit manslaughter and the delivery of drugs, especially to a minor.

The state of Illinois charged a woman with both manslaughter and delivering drugs to a minor when her child died shortly after birth and cocaine was found in the infant's urine and the mother's blood (American Bar Association 1989).

Florida convicted a woman for giving birth to two children, both of whom tested positive for drugs, under a statute used to prosecute drug dealers (*Johnson v. State* 1991). She was sentenced to 15 years probation and 200 hours of community service for delivering drugs through the umbilical cord to her children. The conviction was later overturned by the Florida Supreme Court. Yet this case was important because the umbilical cord had been redefined as a piece of drug paraphernalia, a method for the delivery of contraband. There are no other human organs so viewed.

Texas prosecuted a woman for possession of a controlled substance when she gave birth to a stillborn premature infant (*Jackson v. State* 1992). The prosecution argued that because a high level of cocaine was found in the infant's blood, it had to have passed to the infant from the mother. The conviction was later overturned.

In addition to criminal prosecution, pregnant, drug-using women are at an elevated risk for "protective" incarceration. A judge in the District of Columbia sentenced a pregnant cocaine-using woman convicted of forgery to jail to protect her fetus from further illicit drug exposure (McNulty 1990). The benevolent, paternalistic concern of the judge for the health of the fetus might be more commendable if jails provided high quality prenatal care and were, indeed, drug-free environments. Miscarriage rates in jails and prisons are disturbingly high. The miscarriage rate in California's prisons is 33% and in some county jails, this rate is 50 times higher than the State rate (Barry 1985).

Examples from these States demonstrate a disturbing policy response to criminalize the behavior of woman. Although there have been few successful criminal prosecutions, the trend is clearly established that some women will be punished for drug use during pregnancy. Another State system that can be used to hurt women and their children is the child welfare system, and although the motivations of child welfare agencies may be less punitive, the ramifications of child welfare involvement can have dire consequences for families.

The Child Welfare Response

Child maltreatment has become increasingly visible. Legislative initiatives at the State and Federal level designed to address the complexities associated with child abuse are common. The 1980s were marked by significant increases in the number of children reported as abused and neglected. In addition, the number of children entering substitute care began to increase and issues associated with maternal drug use became another rallying point for new legislation and expansion of the child welfare system.

The problems in public child welfare have been subject to extensive study and have resulted in congressional hearings. Large numbers of children drifting through the foster care system, receiving few if any services and without a plan for stability, were not uncommon. The Federal government enacted major child welfare legislation in 1980 that was supposed to reduce the number of children in foster care and help the children find secure living arrangements (Gustavsson and Segal 1994). The legislation appeared to be successful—for a while. By 1986 the number of children in care had dropped to 280,000. However, 3 years later the number had jumped to 360,000, a 27% increase (Subcommittee on Human Resources 1990). By the end of 1993, an estimated 450,000 children were in foster care (U.S. General Accounting Office 1995a).

These increases in the incidence of foster care placement paralleled increases in the number of children reported as abused or neglected. Maternal drug use was identified as the major contributor to these increases. Between 1983 and 1993 reports of child abuse and neglect doubled to 2.3 million, the foster care caseload grew by two thirds, and in 1991 in four large cities, 62% of preschool-age foster children were at risk of health problems due to prenatal drug exposure compared to just 21% 5 years earlier (U.S. General Accounting Office 1995a). During a 6-year period in the early 1980s, Los Angeles County experienced a 500% increase in the number of children placed in foster care due to parental drug use, and in some California counties, drug-exposed children comprised two thirds of the foster care population (Select Committee on Children, Youth, and Families 1989). Child welfare agencies began, in the 1980s, to actively assess for drug use in referred families. As many as 80% of the families substantiated for child maltreatment are affected by drug use (Child Welfare League of America 1990).

Minority children fare poorly in the foster care system. In 1990, 40% of the children in foster care were African-American, 11% were Hispanic, and 39% were white (U.S. General Accounting Office 1995b). Not only do minority children enter foster care more frequently, but they stay longer. More than half of the children leaving care in 1987 were white and 26% were African-American (Committee on Ways and Means 1991). Foster care has become a major form of family life for increasing numbers of minority children.

The median age of children entering care has been dropping since the late 1980s, and the number of infants entering care increased by two thirds between 1983 and 1990 (U.S. General Accounting Office 1995b). This is consistent with the increased recognition afforded poor, pregnant drug-using women. As these woman became identified, their children became subject to State child welfare intervention.

The precedent for considering an infant maltreated and in need of protection due to maternal drug use was clearly established as early as 1980 (*in re Baby X*). This was a Michigan case in which an infant suffering from a drug withdrawal syndrome was considered neglected and removed from the custody of the parent. Most States have amended their child abuse reporting statutes to include drug use by pregnant women and/or positive toxicology screens of an infant or a mother as a reportable offense (Gustavsson 1991a). This change in policy had both anticipated and unanticipated consequences.

By increasing the number of reportable offenses, child welfare agencies received more referrals. More resources were needed to investigate these referrals and then to provide services to the families. Unfortunately, few child welfare agencies had the resources to help families dealing with drug abuse issues, especially when the mother was drug-involved. Child welfare agencies were now faced with trying to provide services to an increasingly large population for which few resources existed.

Child welfare agencies were forced to develop strategies for helping drug-using women. The traditional drug treatment system had little to offer the child welfare agency. The proprietary sector served primarily white affluent men with health insurance (Wesson and Smith 1985). Public facilities faced a high demand for their services and often had waiting lists. It misses the point to ask a pregnant drug user to wait 6 months for a drug rehabilitation program. To further complicate the delivery of services, slots for pregnant drug users were few.

More than half of the drug treatment facilities in New York City refuse to admit pregnant drug users, and Massachusetts allocated only 15 residential treatment slots, statewide, to pregnant women (U.S. General Accounting Office 1990). Child welfare agencies would have to develop partnerships with the drug treatment sector to offer services to an increasingly large percentage of their case load.

The priorities of drug treatment centers and child welfare agencies differ. Issues associated with abuse, neglect, and parenting are priorities for child welfare. These are also issues women bring with them to drug-treatment settings. The traditional drug treatment agency is male oriented. It reflects the paths men take into treatment as well as the needs of men and has not served women, especially pregnant women, well (Center for Substance Abuse Treatment 1993; Kumpfer 1991). Child welfare agencies continue to experiment with gender sensitive programs (Carten 1996).

Mixed Messages and the Drug War

Systems that come into contact with the drug-using pregnant woman, such as health care, criminal justice, child welfare, education, and drug treatment, have failed to serve her well. There are a number of factors that may account for this lack of quality service. A major contributor to the lack of comprehensive services is that we do not know how to view this woman. Is she a criminal, who inflicts harm on her fetus, or is she someone with a problem who needs assistance?

The attempt to use the force of law to compel women to behave in a proscribed fashion is doomed to failure (Hawk 1994). Criminalizing maternal conduct may also have unintended consequences such as discouraging women from seeking health care. Prenatal care is essential if fetal and maternal outcomes are to be improved. Of particular concern is the latent gender, social class, and racial bias in the criminal justice approach.

Criminalizing behavior for only one group of citizens, based solely on their gender and a temporary biological condition, establishes a worrisome precedent. There may be other maternal behaviors which could be harmful to the fetus. Homelessness, not obtaining prenatal care, poor eating habits, failure to follow a physician's orders, working in a setting with hazardous chemicals, being abused, and being poor are also associated with negative fetal outcomes. However, there has not yet been a suggestion to criminalize these behaviors.

Drug behavior is subject to sanction because it is assumed to indicate a character flaw. Drug users are seen as defective people who deliberately engage in harmful behavior. In a recent Arizona case in which a woman was indicted for child abuse because she allegedly gave birth to a heroin-addicted baby, the judge explained that the woman made a choice to engage in sexual conduct and also chose to take heroin (*Reinesto v. Superior Court of the State of Arizona* 1994). The degree of choice that the drug dependent person can exercise, or that women can exercise in both the sexual and drug areas, is unclear. It may soon be argued that women chose to be poor, homeless, or involved with a violent partner.

Women have become the latest casualties in the war on drugs (Gustavsson 1991b). Pregnant drug users are viewed unsympathetically and are easy to want to punish. Saving children who are being deliberately harmed by the actions of the drug-using mothers can serve as a rallying point in the drug war. The lack of gender-sensitive drug treatment has not impeded the development of punitive responses.

The drug war has increased the prison population. The percentage of State prisoners serving a drug sentence tripled from 1980 to 1993 (6% to 22%) and the number of Federal prisoners serving a drug sentence more than doubled from 25% in 1983 to 60% in 1993 (Bureau of Justice Statistics 1995a). There has been a ninefold increase (19,000 to 172,300) in the number of convicted drug offenders (Bureau of Justice Statistics 1995b). Between 1982 and 1991, the number of women arrested for drug offenses increased by 89% (National Institute of Justice 1994). Women constitute the fastest growing population in the criminal justice system.

The political realities of drug importation and use in America should not be ignored. Cocaine and heroin, for example, are derived from plants that are not indigenous to the United States. These products must be imported and questions arise about how so many drugs are able to enter the country and find their way to poor inner city neighborhoods. There have been allegations that suggest a link between the importation of cocaine and the Central Intelligence Agency (Webb 1996). Recent congressional hearings did not find any evidence to support these allegations.

The criminal justice approach to drug use is expensive. For fiscal year 1996, President Clinton requested $14.6 billion for the drug war, a 9.7% increase over the 1995 budget of $13.3 billion (Office of National Drug Control Policy 1995). Almost $3 billion would be used for drug treatment. The rest of the money is allocated for reducing the drug supply. The results of these efforts to reduce the supply of drugs are mixed (U.S. General Accounting Office 1995c). There is also funding for the drug war in Title V of the Violent Crime Control and Law Enforcement Act of 1994. This act created drug courts whose effectiveness is unknown (U.S. General Accounting Office 1995b). The Crime Control Act also allocates funds for more law enforcement officers.

Criminalizing illicit drug use for pregnant women ignores the most serious threats to fetal well being—tobacco and alcohol. With a current prison population of over one million, it may not be practical to incarcerate all pregnant women who smoke. There also is a tobacco lobby that can be counted on to advocate on behalf of women and their fundamental right to smoke.

The more appropriate response to maternal drug use is to place it in an ecological context and see it as one of many factors that can negatively influence both maternal and fetal outcomes. The billions spent in the drug war and for incarceration could do much to bring prenatal care, nutrition programs, counseling, parenting classes, housing assistance, and income support programs to pregnant women. These programs would do more to ensure infant health than maternal prosecution and incarceration strategies.

The cost effectiveness of these supportive strategies are well established. Helping pregnant women, for example, deliver full-term babies is much less costly than caring for a premature infant. (Children's Defense Fund 1989). The fact that there are still many women in America who do not get prenatal care or receive it late in their pregnancy suggests that concern for fetal well being may not be the real reason behind the trend toward criminalization.

References

Abel, E. L., and R. J. Sokel
1987 Incidence of fetal alcohol syndrome and economic impact of FAS related anomalies. *Drug and Alcohol Dependence* 19:51–70.
Amaro, H., L. Fried, and H. Cabral
1990 Violence during pregnancy and substance abuse. *American Journal of Public Health* 80:5.
American Bar Association
1989 Crime and Pregnancy. *American Bar Journal* 14–16.
Bandstra, E., B. Steele, G. Burkette, D. Paltrow, N. Levandowski, and B. Rodriguez
1989 Prevalence of perinatal exposure in an urban multi-ethnic population (Summary). *Program Issues of Pediatric Research* 25(2):247.
Barry, E.
1985 Quality of prenatal care for incarcerated women challenged. *Youth Law News* 6(6):1–4.

Benowitz, N. L.
1991 Nicotine replacement therapy during pregnancy. *Journal of the American Medical Association* 266(22):3174–3177.
Beratis, N. G., D. Panagoulias, and A. Varvarigou
1996 Increased blood pressure in neonates and infants whose mothers smoked during pregnancy. *Journal of Pediatrics* 128(6):806–812.
Bureau of Justice Statistics
1995a *Prisoners in 1994.* Washington, DC: U.S. Department of Justice.
Bureau of Justice Statistics
1995b *Correctional populations in the United States.* Washington, DC: U.S. Department of Justice.
Burns, K., M. Melamed, W. Burns, I. Chasnoff, and R. Hatcher
1985 Chemical dependency and clinical depression in pregnancy. *Journal of Clinical Psychology* 41(6):851–854.
Carten, A. J.
1996 Mothers in recovery: Rebuilding families in the aftermath of addiction. *Social Work* 41:214–223.
Center for Substance Abuse Treatment
1993 *Pregnant, substance-using women.* Rockville, MD: U.S. Department of Health and Human Services.
Chasnoff, I. J.
1989 Drug use and women: Establishing a standard of care. *Annals of New York Academy of Sciences* 562:2008–10.
Chasnoff, I. J., D. Griffith, C. Freier, and J. Murray
1992 Cocaine/polydrug use in pregnancy: Two year followup. *Pediatrics* 89:284–289.
Chasnoff, I. J., H. J. Landress, and M. E. Barrett
1990 The prevalence of illicit drug or alcohol use during pregnancy and the discrepancies in mandatory reporting in Pinellas County, Florida. *New England Journal of Medicine* 322(17):1202–1206.
Child Welfare League of America
1990 *Crack and other addictions: Old realities and new challenges.* Washington, DC: Author.
Children's Defense Fund
1989 *A vision for America's future.* Washington, DC: Children's Defense Fund.
Close, C., P. Roberts, and R. Berger
1990 Cigarettes, alcohol and marijuana are related to pyospermia in infertile men. *Journal of Urology* 144(4):900–903.
Committee on Ways and Means
1991 *Background material and data on programs within the jurisdiction of the Committee on Ways and Means.* Washington, DC: U.S. Government Printing Office.
Cordero, L. and M. Custard
1990 Effects of maternal cocaine abuse on perinatal and infant outcomes. *Ohio Medicine* 86(5):410–412.
Davis, D. L., G. Friedler, R. Mattison, and R. Morris
1992 Male-mediated teratogenesis and other reproductive effects: Biologic and epidemiologic findings and a plea for clinical research. *Reproductive Toxicology* 6:289–292.
Day, N. L., G. A. Richardson, L. Goldschmidt, N. Robles, P. M. Taylor, D. S. Stoffer, M. D. Cornelius, and D. Geva
1994 Effect of prenatal marijuana exposure on the cognitive development of offspring at age three. *Neurotoxicology and Teratology* 16(2):169–175.
DiFranza, J. R., and R. A. Lew
1996 Morbidity and mortality in children associated with the use of tobacco products by other people. *Pediatrics* 97(4):560–568.

Eisen, L. N., T. M. Field, E. S. Bandstra, J. P. Roberts, C. Morrow, S. K. Larson, and B. M. Steele
1991 Perinatal cocaine effects on neonatal stress behavior and performance on the Brazelton scale. *Pediatrics* 88:477–480.

Fried, P. A. and J. E. Makin
1987 Neonatal behavioral correlates of prenatal exposure to marijuana, cigarettes, and alcohol in a low risk population. *Neurotoxicology and Teratology* 9:1–7.

Fried, P. A., B. Watkinson, and R. Gray
1992 A follow-up study of attentional behavior in 6 year old children exposed prenatally to marijuana, cigarettes, and alcohol. *Neurotoxicology and Teratology* 14:299–311.

Gomby, D. S., and P. H. Shiono
1991 Estimating the number of substance-exposed infants. *The Future of Children* 1(1):17–25.

Gustavsson, N. S.
1991a Chemically exposed children: The child welfare response. *Child and Adolescent Social Work Journal* 8(4):297–307.

Gustavsson, N. S.
1991b The war metaphor: A threat to vulnerable populations. *Social Work* 36:277–278.

Gustavsson, N. S.
1992 Drug exposed children and their mothers: Facts, myths, and needs. *Social Work in Health Care* 16(4):87–100.

Gustavsson, N. S. and E. A. Segal
1994 *Critical issues in child welfare.* California: Sage.

Hawk, M. A.
1994 How social policies make matters worse: The case of maternal substance abuse. *Journal of Drug Issues* 24(3):517–526.

Hutchings, D.
1985 Prenatal opioid exposure and the problem and casual inference. In *Current research on the consequences of maternal drug abuse,* ed. T. Pinkert, 6–19. Maryland: National Institute on Drug Abuse.

Hutchings, D.
1990 Issues of risk assessment: Lessons from the use and abuse of drugs during pregnancy. *Neurotoxicology and Teratology* 12(3):183–189.

Jones, K. and D. Smith
1973 Recognition of fetal alcohol syndrome in early infancy. *Lancet* II(7836):999–1001.

Koren, G., H. Shear, K. Graham, and T. Einarson
1989 Bias against the null hypothesis: The reproductive hazardous of cocaine. *Lancet* 2(December 16):1440–1442.

Kumpfer, K.
1991 Treatment programs for drug abusing women. *The Future of Children* 1(1):50–60.

Land, D., and R. Kushner
1991 Drug abuse during pregnancy in an inner-city hospital: Prevalence and patterns. *Journal of the American Osteopathic Association* 90(5):421–426.

Li, D. K., and J. R. Daling
1991 Maternal smoking, low birth weight, and ethnicity in relation to sudden infant death syndrome. *American Journal of Epidemiology* 134:958–964.

Li, D. K., Mueller, B. A., Hickok, D. E., Daling, J. R., Fantel, A. G., Checkoway, H., and N. S. Weiss
1996 Maternal smoking during pregnancy and the risk of congenital urinary tract anomalies. *American Journal of Public Health* 86(2):249–253.

McFarlane, J., B. Parker, K. Soeken, and L. Bullock
1992 Assessing for abuse during pregnancy. *Journal of the American Medical Association* 267(23):3176–3178.
McNulty, M.
1990 Pregnancy police: Implications of criminalizing fetal abuse. *Youth Law News* 11(1):33–37.
National Institute of Justice
1994 *Drug-abusing women offenders: Results of a national survey.* Washington, DC: U.S. Department of Justice.
National Institute on Drug Abuse
1993a *Conference Highlights from the 2nd National Conference on Drug Abuse Research and Practice.* Rockville, MD: National Institute on Drug Abuse.
1993b *National household survey on drug abuse.* Rockville, MD: National Institute on Drug Abuse.
Neuspiel, D. R.
1993 Cocaine and the fetus: Mythology of severe risk. *Neurotoxicology and Teratology* 15:305–306.
Nordentoft, M., Lou, H. C., Hansen, D., Nim, J., Pryds, O., Rubin, P., and R. Hemmingsen
1996 Intrauterine growth retardation and premature delivery: The influence of maternal smoking and psychosocial factors. *American Journal of Public Health* 86(3):347–354.
Office of National Drug Control Policy
1995 *National drug control strategy.* Washington, DC: Executive Office of the President.
Office on Smoking and Health
1988 *The health consequences of smoking: Nicotine addiction.* Washington, DC: U.S. Government Printing Office.
Office of Technology Assessment
1985 *Reproductive health hazards in the workplace.* Washington, DC: U.S. Government Printing Office.
Regan, D., S. Ehrlich, and L. Finnegan.
1987 Infants of drug addicts: At risk for child abuse, neglect, and placement in foster care. *Neurotoxicology and Teratology* 9:315–319.
Rosengren, J.
1990 Alcohol: A bigger drug problem? *Minnesota Medicine* 73:33–34.
Select Committee on Children, Youth, and Families
1989 *Born hooked: Confronting the impact of perinatal substance abuse.* Washington, DC: U.S. Government Printing Office.
Shafer, D., V. Dunbar, A. Falek, R. Donahoe, R. Madden, and P. Bokos
1990 Enhanced assays detect increased chromosome damage and sister-chromatid exchanges in heroin addicts. *Mutation Research* 234(5):327–336.
Shaw, G. M., Wasserman, C. R., Lammer, E. J., O'Malley, C. D., Murra, J. C., Bassart, A. M., and M. M. Tolarova
1996 Craniofacial clefts, parental cigarette smoking, and transforming growth factor-alpha gene variants. *American Journal of Human Genetics* 58(3):551–561.
Subcommittee on Human Resources
1990 The impact of crack cocaine on the child welfare system. Hearing held in Washington, DC.
Telsey, A., A. Merrit, and S. Dixon
1988 Cocaine exposure in a term neonate: Necrotizing enterocolitis as a complication. *Clinical Pediatrics* 258(11):547–550.
U.S. General Accounting Office
1990 *Drug exposed infants: A generation at risk.* Washington, DC: U.S. Government Printing Office.

1995a *Child welfare: Complex needs strain capacity to provide services.* Washington, DC: U.S. Government Printing Office.

1995b *Drug courts: Information on a new approach to address drug-related crime.* Washington, DC: U.S. Government Printing Office.

1995c *Drug war: Observations on the U.S. international drug control strategy.* Washington, DC: U.S. Government Printing Office.

Webb, G.

1996 Drug network linked street gangs, contras. *The Arizona Republic,* August 25, A23.

Williams, M. A., R. Mittendorf, E. Leiberman, R. R. Monson, S. C. Schoenbaum, and D. R. Genest

1991 Cigarette smoking during pregnancy in relation to placenta previa. *American Journal of Obstetrics and Gynecology* 165:28–32.

Wilson, G.

1989 Clinical studies of infants and children prenatally exposed to heroin. In *Prenatal abuse of licit and illicit drugs,* ed. D. E. Hutchings, 183–194. New York: New York Academy of Sciences.

Woods, N. S., F. D. Eyler, M. Behnke, and M. Conlon

1993 Cocaine use during pregnancy: Maternal depressive symptoms and infant neurobehavior over the first month. *Infant Behavior Development* 16:83–98.

Zuckerman, B., and D. Frank

1992 Crack kids not broken. *Pediatrics* 89:337–339.

Zuckerman, B., D. Frank, R. Hingson, H. Amaro, S. Levenson, H. Kayne, S. Parker, R. Vinci, K. Aboagye, L. Fried, H. Cabral, R. Timperi, and H. Bauchner

1989 Effect of maternal marijuana and cocaine use on fetal growth. *New England Journal of Medicine* 320(12):762–767.

Cases Cited

In re A.C., 573 A.2d 1235 (D.C. App. 199 0).

In re Baby X, 293 N.W. 2d 736, 739 (Mich. Ct. App. 1980).

In re Jamaica Hospital, 491 N.Y.S. 2d at 900 (N.Y. 1985).

Jackson v. State, 833 S.W. 2d 220, 221 (Tex. 1992)

Johnson v. State, 578 So. 2d 419, 419 (Fla. 1991).

People v. Stewart, No. M508097 (San Diego County Court, February 23, 1987).

Reinesto v. Superior Court of the State of Arizona (ICA-SA 94-0348 1994).

Reyes v. Superior Court 141 Cal. Rptr. 912 (Cal. Ct. App. 1977).

Medicalizing Homelessness: The Production of Self-Blame and Self-Governing within Homeless Shelters

Vincent Lyon-Callo

> Sometimes I just can't believe how stupid people here are. They know they're being oppressed, but they won't say anything about it.

Raymond, a homeless African American man in his late forties, spoke those words to me one evening in 1996 as we sat in the living room of an emergency homeless shelter in Northampton, Massachusetts.[1] We had just left another in a long series of shelter meetings where many staff and guests advocated increased staff surveillance of homeless people's individual behaviors as the most reasonable means for responding to increasing local homelessness. They appeared to be suggesting that surveillance was a key tool for uncovering "causes" of homelessness that need to be treated if we hoped to decrease homelessness.

Raymond, a man with a long history of social activism focused on racism and poverty, was one of the few people at the shelter to openly question routine shelter practices. Many guests complained about shelter rules, but Raymond was nearly alone in characterizing the staff counseling and training efforts as misplaced, insofar as they did not work against systemic inequities in the community. Consequently, Raymond spent much time arguing against staff "helping" practices, which he characterized as inhumane for misplacing attention on individual homeless people. At the meeting we had just left, Raymond had been the only person staying at the shelter to argue against a proposal to initiate drug testing of shelter residents and another to begin using "workfare" recipients as "volunteers" within the shelter. He could not understand why he and I were the only people at the meeting voicing opposition to those policies. He read the compliance of other homeless people as the result of their being too stupid or uninformed to know any better.

I told Raymond I shared his sentiment that efforts to resolve homelessness through disciplining homeless people and reforming their perceived deviancy were misplaced. We both interpreted such practices as ignoring increasing structural violence as well as the historical and political-economic context within which homelessness has become a "normal" feature of life in the United States. But I also suggested an alternative interpretation to Raymond. I asserted that it doesn't really help us either understand or work against consent to domination if we simply think of people who disagree with us as lacking the intelligence to see "the truth" about homelessness and inequality. Instead, we need to analyze how particular understandings and practices are constituted and come to make sense to those embracing and enacting them. This article is a part of that effort.

As recent work by Susan Ruddick (1995), David Wagner (1993), and Talmadge Wright (1997) makes clear, homeless people are active social agents who respond to homelessness in a variety of ways. Wright and Wagner document how responses sometimes take the form of open defiance. But I have observed that many people who find themselves homeless often engage in more individualized strategies of coping and accommodating. This article analyzes these strategies and the seeming acquiescence to the systemic conditions of homelessness they represent by ethnographically exploring how homelessness is medicalized through the discourses surrounding it. I accomplish this by examining the everyday practices of staff and guests within one homeless shelter.

Medicalizing Social Inequity

Scholarship has demonstrated clear links between tactical business and governmental decisions and the recent production of homelessness in the United States. The increasing globalization of capital, deindustrialization (Hopper et al. 1985), the growth of temporary labor, altered tax policies, declining union membership, the growth of non-unionized service sector employment, institutionalized racism, gentrification in the name of community development (Marcuse 1989; Williams 1996), and a changing political landscape all have contributed to the production of increased economic inequality and homelessness during the past 20 years. In addition, neither the public nor private housing markets have managed to keep up with the growing demand for affordable housing (Burt 1992). In short, homelessness has become routine during a two-decade period characterized by growing inequality in wealth and income in the United States.

Despite these clear connections, very few practices aimed at resolving homelessness have specifically addressed such conditions. The implementation of emergency shelters was the initial dominant response, as homelessness first became widespread in the 1970s and 1980s. These shelters simply provided a "safe" place to sleep, often a meal, and sometimes a shower and place to store one's belongings.[2] However, large emergency shelters did little to address homelessness and were often unsafe, inhumane, and degrading places that warehoused poor people (Dordick 1997;

Gounis 1992; Liebow 1993). Often shelter rules even made it nearly impossible for a person to maintain employment and still reside at the shelter (Roofless Women's Action Research Mobilization 1996).

As the limitations and abuses of the emergency shelter approach have been documented in recent years, advocates and policy makers have searched for more effective methods of addressing the homelessness crisis. While many cities have opted to criminalize homelessness, federal agencies and some local communities have responded by advocating a "continuum of care" approach. Under this model, communities develop programs and services to treat the myriad symptoms thought to create homelessness, and shelters offer the services understood to be needed to help people obtain (and maintain) housing.[3] The move toward this model is part of a broader effort undertaken by some advocates and policy makers to reframe homelessness as a condition afflicting those victimized by disease and dysfunction rather than the result of bad individual choices. For example, efforts have been made to publicly represent people who find themselves homeless as suffering from the effects of traumatic episodes in their youth or during military service, a poorly functioning foster care system, depression or schizophrenia, the disease of alcoholism and substance abuse, domestic abuse, or similar ailments that restrict their capacity to remain employed and housed. The goal is a more effective and caring response to homelessness.

However, the move toward a disease model often has ambiguous and conflicting impacts (Singer et al. 1992). On the one hand, recent efforts may have facilitated increased services to reform, treat, and retrain individualized homeless people, and such efforts do improve the lives of some individuals who are homeless. On the other hand, however, the "continuum of care" approach also does not fundamentally address questions of access to and distribution of resources in the community. In fact, I argue here that the focus on "disease" within the discourses of "helping" actually obliterates discussion of alternative explanations and thus hinders developments aimed at resolving homelessness through altering class, race, or gender dynamics. When homelessness is individualized and medicalized, those concerns remain peripheral to the central work of normalizing perceived shortcomings or deviancy within homeless people.

Undoubtedly, this outcome is partly the result of a combination of both dominant imaginings and stigmatized perceptions about homeless people (Dear and Gleeson 1991) and the impact that federal funding concerns and religious organizations have on influencing public priorities and sheltering industry practices (Lyon-Callo 1998). Yet these are only small pieces needed to understand the complex puzzle of social processes and social relations that produce widespread homelessness. What is also needed is an understanding of how such understandings and practices have come to be so common. One small part of that larger project involves examining how medicalized and individualized understandings about homeless people as deviant are constituted, reproduced, and reinforced through discourses and practices.

It is hardly surprising that a medicalized conceptual framework guides responses to homelessness at this moment in history. Homelessness is just one social condition among many that have been medicalized in recent years. Conditions and behaviors ranging from sexual decision-making, depression, credit card debt, sexuality, drug use, gambling, weight problems, and teen pregnancy are increasingly portrayed in popular and scientific discourses as the results of pathology or disorders within particular bodies or the bodies of groups of people. One effect of conceptualizing social problems through a lens of diseased bodies is often a neglect of systemic inequality. Consideration of the material and historical conditions that might contribute to the production of problems is silenced or marginalized by a focus on individual traits and habits.

As Vicente Navarro describes it, the medicalization of social problems plays the ideological function of legitimizing existing class relations and serves to "depoliticize what is intrinsically a political problem. Thus, within a medical framework, what requires a collective answer is presented as an individual problem, demanding an individual response" (1986:40). Navarro argues that much of what is thought of as illness is in fact the result of a fundamentally disproportionate distribution of resources. Yet, rather than working collectively to alter class relations and the distribution of health services, many health care and social service efforts focus on treating perceived disorders within individual bodies.

Critical medical anthropologists writing from the perspective of political economy have produced much work related to Navarro's arguments. Paul Farmer et al. (1996) stress the degree to which AIDS research and social policy efforts focus on discovering and treating behaviors. They argue that such practices have the effect of silencing work against the class and gender processes that also contribute to illness. Other scholars have analyzed how racial, class, and gender inequities are often manifested in terms of alcohol abuse, AIDS, poverty, physical illness, mental illness, and homelessness (Morsy 1990; Singer and Baer 1996). Merrill Singer, for example, argues that to understand a "disorder" such as alcohol abuse, one needs to consider the broader historical and material conditions that produce the behavior (Singer et al. 1992).

Similar dynamics apply to homelessness. In her study of the medicalization of homelessness in New York City during the 1980s, Arline Mathieu (1993) discusses how representations of "the homeless" by government officials as mentally ill served to marginalize the political-economic context of homeless people. She details how press releases from the mayor's office in support of a policy of randomly taking homeless people off the streets by force emphasized that the people still living on the streets were homeless due to mental illness. Mathieu argues that as long as homeless people were biomedically represented as deviant, their living on the streets could be "solved" by housing them in shelters and forcing them into treatment programs. Attention to systemic inequities that contribute to producing widespread homelessness was thus deemed unnecessary.

Through my work on homelessness, I have come to agree that systemic inequities contribute to the production of many behaviors that are commonly read as pathological disorders in people without permanent shelter.[4] Reading these behaviors as individual disorders certainly plays a role in silencing work against exploitative social conditions and in limiting our ability as medical anthropologists to work more effectively against the conditions the work documents (Hopper 1988; Singer 1995). However, there is another component that deserves analytical attention. Something much more subtle and insidious than simply mystification takes place when homelessness is medicalized. It is my contention that routine, everyday practices undertaken by shelter staff and guests to resolve "diseases" actually reproduce and reinforce dominant imaginings about homelessness and homeless people and, thus, contribute to producing particular subjectivities, experiences, self-images, and behaviors among homeless people.

To make this argument, I draw upon insights coming out of the critical-interpretive approach in medical anthropology represented by Robert Desjarlais (1997), Margaret Lock and Nancy Scheper-Hughes (1990), and Alan Young (1995), as well as by scholars outside of anthropology writing on the production of medicalized knowledge (Hacking 1986, 1995), governmentality, and the practices of self-making (Rose 1990, 1996). These scholars demonstrate how all knowledge of society, normality, illness, and self is socially produced and determined and that all knowledge about the body, health, and illness is constituted through historically situated cultural negotiations (Scheper-Hughes and Lock 1990). To analyze that process it is imperative to examine the techniques and practices through which people who are without a permanent place of residence are made into subjects to be governed by their selves, social workers, social planners, and medical experts. In this article, therefore, I outline a strategy for considering the ways in which the homeless body (the social body and the body politic regarding homelessness, as well as individualized homeless bodies) is, in part, produced and reproduced by social practices within homeless shelters.[5]

Even prior to being connected with the facility, many of the people who volunteered, worked, or lived at the shelter I observed articulated understandings supporting the dominant conceptual framework in which homelessness is viewed as embodied deviance. This is hardly surprising given the preponderance of public discourses that pathologize poor people as well as dominant stigmatized images of homeless people as deviants. Yet, in analyzing precise practices in the shelter setting, I uncover how the well-intentioned efforts within the shelter actually work to reproduce and reinforce the image of homelessness as a social problem with an origin in individual deviancy. Reformative efforts often focus on "treatments" that fit within constructed views of "normal" and "deviant." These practices produce subjects who come to understand reform of the individualized self as the most "reasonable" and "realistic" ways of resolving homelessness. Through their experiences in the shelters, many homeless people are thus produced (and reproduced) as political subjects who are more likely to engage in self-blame and self-governing than in collective work against structural violence.

Producing Homeless Subjects: An Exploration of Routine Shelter Practices

From 1993 through 1997, I conducted activist ethnographic research at a 20-bed emergency homeless shelter in Northampton, Massachusetts, where I was also employed as a staff member.[6]

This setting was an ideal location for investigating the effects of the "continuum of care" and disease model for at least two reasons. First, Northampton, like much of the northeastern United States, has undergone vast economic changes in the past two decades. Lost manufacturing jobs have been replaced by low-wage, often part-time employment in food services, social services, and retail trade. Recent gentrification and redevelopment of the downtown area has created a bustling urban core but has led to the loss of one-half of the city's single-room-occupancy units. Housing costs are out of reach of many citizens, while waiting lists for housing assistance are closed for years at a time.

Northampton was also an ideal setting for the study because local shelter providers and policy makers strongly embraced the "continuum of care" concept. As a result, staff members at the shelter counseled people on a wide range of issues as well as referring "guests" to outside experts. Likewise, community planners and policy makers developed a broad array of "helping" services in the community. Such services included increased substance abuse treatment programs, enhanced access to mental health services, veteran's services, job training, increased shelter beds, and an assortment of counseling options and workshops within shelters. Consequently, the city and the shelter were both often described by guests as the best place in the entire state to try to resolve one's homelessness.

In this setting, I conducted archival research on economic and housing conditions at the local level, which provided a systemic context within which I could better contemplate local responses to homelessness. I also spent over 6,000 hours ethnographically detailing how homeless people, shelter staff, local advocates, and local policy makers responded to homelessness. I observed and participated in a broad range of shelter activities, including weekly staff meetings, case management efforts, the daily enforcement of shelter rules, statistical record keeping, the development of shelter policies, intake interviews, staff hiring, efforts to locate housing and income, the development of grant applications, and staff training. Data from these activities were supplemented by a series of open-ended interviews with nine staff members, several dozen homeless people, shelter administrators, local advocates, and local policy makers.[7]

I employed an explicitly activist position while conducting this research. By activist ethnographic research I do not mean a simple stance of advocacy for a particular position or understanding. Rather, I engaged in a constantly evolving dialogue with the community members with whom I worked. The goal was not simply to find data to support my views, nor was it my intention to impose my views or visions upon these people, as if I had "the solution" to homelessness.[8] Homelessness is much too complex for any simple social policy change to "solve." By activist research, what I am referring to is an ethnographic method of openly challenging each other's ideas in an effort to think more critically about all of our views and practices. My intention was to facilitate our learning from each other through engaging in debate and dialogue regarding the effects of our routine, well-meaning practices and by asking how to understand homelessness in as comprehensive and complex a fashion as possible. It was my hope that this engagement might stretch the parameters of what was thinkable and doable and, thus, create the possibility for new discourses, new practices, and new subjectivities to emerge.[9]

Through engagement of this sort, I uncovered and challenged an underlying hegemonic hypothesis of deviancy functioning within the local sheltering industry. I found that routine practices focus primary attention on developing techniques for detecting, diagnosing, and treating pathological disorders within individual homeless people.

Detecting and diagnosing disorders begins the moment a homeless person first enters the shelter. The new shelter guest is quickly directed into the staff office for an intake interview. The intake interview serves several functions. On one level, it is simply an opportunity for the staff to compile basic statistical and demographic data while detailing the shelter rules and procedures. A case history, used to guide case management, is also started. Of paramount importance, though, is that the intake interview is the first opportunity for the staff and guest to diagnose the disorder(s) of the self that caused the person to be homeless.

In addition to the required components of the intake, the staff member works to comfort the recently homeless person, who is often quite nervous about being in a shelter. A caring staff member uses this opportunity to develop a sense of rapport with the new guest. Through this more informal discussion and from the homeless person's mannerisms and articulations, the staff member attempts to gather additional data on possible disorders within the person. If, for example, the staff member detects what he or she perceives to be possible mental illness or substance abuse, these observations are noted in the person's case folder and in the staff log. Other staff can thus be made aware of the diagnosis and look for possible supporting symptoms.

Staff gathers this information in a variety of ways. One specific question during the intake asks the recently homeless person to state his or her "reason for homelessness." The intake form includes a number of suggested reasons, each particular to that individual. As most homeless people have already learned a great deal of self-blame prior to entering the shelter, many guests will respond by disclosing a behavioral or training problem as the cause of their homelessness. For example, 39 percent of the people at this shelter during 1995 stated that they were homeless due to "substance abuse." Thus, overcoming that individualized problem became the focus of their subsequent efforts to become housed.

Formal efforts to diagnose possible causes of homelessness continue throughout the person's stay at the shelter. Within one week, a case management meeting is scheduled for the new arrival to meet with staff for a second intake. This setting is more clearly defined as establishing a counseling relationship. Here, the staff and guest meet privately for a prolonged discussion about the "issues" that brought the person to the shelter and the resources available to help with those needs. A more detailed case management intake form asks about the level of education, employment history, medical history, past therapy or counseling experiences, and any background with substance abuse or mental health treatment programs. This information is used to determine what issues the homeless person should "work on" while at the shelter. Detected problems range from mental illness to a need for employment training, but all are understood as situated within the homeless person.

With the initial diagnosis in hand, the shelter staff and homeless person proceed to look for evidence to support, refute, or augment the initial diagnosis. This evidence is gathered through both formal case management meetings and less formal surveillance mechanisms. Surveillance takes place while monitoring the guest's obedience to shelter rules, counseling guests, resolving conflicts, and engaging in informal discussions in the shelter. As Ann, an ex-staff member, summed it up, "Whenever you are at the shelter, you are supposed to be monitoring the guests."

The monitoring is understood as a vital function through which the staff and guests can garner information for diagnosing the disorder needing treatment. For example, when staff monitoring or guest disclosure reveals an infraction of the rules, the offending person is called into the staff office to discuss the incident. A written warning describing the transgression is placed in the guest's case file. More importantly, a conversation follows wherein the staff member uses the violation of shelter policies as evidence of an issue the homeless person needs to resolve if he or she hopes to become housed. This is portrayed as a mechanism by which homeless people can be made to come to grips with the issues (always disorders within their selves) causing their unstable lives and homelessness.

These practices initially seemed like common sense to many staff and guests. Because such sentiments are currently so ubiquitous in the United

States, they make sense as the normal way to resolve homelessness. Thus, neither the majority of guests nor staff tended to question them. In fact, many shelter guests often sought more stringent staff surveillance and urged stronger disciplinary rules in the shelter. They understood surveillance of their selves as a mechanism for "helping."

Through the application of these shelter practices, the homeless person is turned into a case history, someone known via these diagnostic techniques as a set of individual disorders and symptoms. The staff and guest's determination of cause "types" the homeless person as a "kind" of client defined by "signs" of his or her "disorder." This "typing" thus drives subsequent treatment responses.

Once the staff and guests have detected and diagnosed the disorder(s) within a homeless person, they begin treatment. Gloria, a shelter staff member, explained this process: "I think many staff take the sort of disease model approach. Well, you know, if that's your problem, we'll hook you up with meetings, you'll do this, you'll go into this program, and that will cure your problem and fix you."

Within the shelter, biomedical language and practices focusing attention on diagnosing and treating pathologies understood to cause social problems are augmented by pseudo-scientific discourses arguing that the only "reasonable" way to help many people is through programs aimed at self-help. As a result, one of the first steps in developing a case history is to have the guest and staff look for the factors that caused that person to turn out the way he or she did. A defining feature of the diagnosis is that the homeless guest must be a willing collaborator in self-diagnosis. Guests are taught to ask, "How did I come to be this way?" It is this reflexive inquiry about the self that is at the heart of future reform efforts.

The vast majority of routine shelter treatment plans fall under the rubric of self-help and governing of the self. As Barbara Cruikshank concludes in her work on self-esteem programs for poor women, self-help and self-government promise "to deliver a technology of subjectivity that will solve social problems like homelessness and inequality by waging a social revolution, not against capitalism, racism, and gender inequality, but against the order of the self and the way we govern our selves" (1996:231). Let me illustrate this process with a few ethnographic examples.

Jerry, a 24-year-old white man, tried his hardest to work his way out of homelessness through paid employment. He came to the shelter shortly after being honorably discharged from the military and maintained a job at a local branch of a supermarket chain for over nine months. Jerry's strategy of attempting to resolve homelessness through paid employment is far from unique. In 1995, 74 (38 percent) of the 193 people who stayed at the shelter were employed. However, over 90 percent of those employed worked in either food service or in retail trade jobs with unsteady work schedules, low pay, and no health benefits. Those are the jobs available in this community.[10] Consequently, only four of the 193 shelter guests were able to secure an apartment or house in Northampton that year. When rents average approximately $650 per month for a one-bedroom apartment (Watson 1996:16) and there are thousands of people on the waiting list for subsidized housing, it is fairly difficult to afford rent with an income less than $200 per week.

Jerry was one homeless person who understood his low pay as the result of broader political-economic processes. After one particularly frustrating evening of work at the supermarket, Jerry and I had a long conversation about his working conditions. At one point, he argued, "It's just shit. If this was the 1950s, I wouldn't be homeless. My uncle graduated from high school and got a job right away in doing tool and die work. They gave him good pay and benefits and he was able to buy a house. There just aren't good jobs like that anymore. I work just as hard and I'm still stuck in this job and in the shelter."

Feeling powerless to alter the wages paid in the existing jobs in the community, he desperately wanted to go to college as a path toward a better job and more financial stability. However, he couldn't figure out a way to pay for school. He couldn't afford to rent a room in a rooming house, let alone pay for college. Jerry tried to hold down a second food service job, but the two sets of work hours conflicted too often and he was forced to quit the second job. He also persistently searched for better paying jobs in the community, but was unsuccessful in obtaining one.

After Jerry had been in the shelter several months, staff began to worry about how to help him move out. Weekly discussions at staff meetings ensued focusing on how to help Jerry. Some staff began to pressure him to work more closely with them on diagnosing the reasons for his homelessness and his inability to find a higher-paying job. Several staff members suggested that his inability to save enough money to move out of the shelter was a "sign" of deeper problems than simply a low-paying job. When Jerry and I countered that he was working long hours but was just not being paid enough to afford local rents, he was urged to think "realistically" about what he could do to afford a place to live.

When I again suggested that the problem might not be within Jerry but with the wages being paid locally, I was seen as diverting attention from "realistic" solutions. As Karen, a newer staff member, commented, "I agree that those are problems, but I wouldn't know where to start to solve those problems. I feel like all I can do is to do what I can to really help people on a practical level. And people here have real problems with personal issues." It was suggested that Jerry was unable to obtain a higher-paying job because of lingering depression and substance abuse. I then suggested that perhaps these conditions were the result of his current life circumstances. A few staff members thought that made sense, but, again, they had to be practical and work on what they could change. What they could change was Jerry.

Increased staff attention focused on helping Jerry resolve his "issues" of substance abuse and depression. At case management meetings, he was urged to look at past behaviors as possible indicators of disorders. In particular, drunken episodes in high school and the military were portrayed as symptoms of a substance abuse disorder. Even though he had only drunk alcohol two times during the previous two months, it was suggested that staff mandate that Jerry have bi-weekly meetings with a therapist and attend at least three Alcoholics Anonymous meetings each week as conditions for receiving further extended stays at the shelter.

He was encouraged to understand his homelessness as the result of traumatic stress related to his youth, insecurity about his sexuality, depression, and substance abuse. In fact, he was rewarded with extended staff "help" and extra time at the shelter for doing so and threatened with expulsion from the shelter if he did not work to reform his self. Several staff members urged him to quit his job so he could focus more energy on his self. He did not comply with that suggestion, but he did agree to seek therapy, to take antidepressant medication, and to attend self-help programs. Through these efforts, he soon came to articulate his problem as being within his self. What else could he do, but struggle to change his self? Clearly, nothing could be done about the fact that 45 percent of new jobs in the region are projected to pay wages below the federal poverty level for a family of two (Turner 1998). Likewise, nothing could be done about the fact that the supermarket chain Jerry worked for made $73 million in profits in 1995 and paid its CEO a base salary of $1.19 million while paying its workers wages inadequate to afford housing (Spain and Talbott 1996:1351). It was understood that nothing could be done about those circumstances. Therefore, the only reasonable path was to teach Jerry to reform his self.

A second example details a similar subject-making effect. On a June night in 1996, Maria came down the stairs of the shelter and asked if she could speak with me. Maria had entered the shelter approximately two months earlier. Like Raymond, she had a fairly extensive history of social activism around racial inequality in the region. She had also worked for many years in social service jobs. When she entered the shelter, both Maria and the staff believed she would quickly find a job and move out of the shelter. After two months of unsuccessful job searches, some staff began to understand Maria's problems as the result of a disorder within her self. At the same time, her relationship with the father of her children began to become difficult. Several staff counseled Maria and urged "self-empowerment" through focusing on the "issues within her own life." Maria was urged to stop seeking a job and to focus on her "issues."

Our conversation began with Maria stating that she was now willing to address a disorder of the self that a staff member had previously diagnosed. She explained that she was now willing to seek counseling and therapy for her depression. She said, "I'm starting to feel really low. It started at the end of the week, and by Friday and Saturday I didn't want to see anyone."

When I asked her why she now thought she needed therapy, she explained,

> I feel stuck here. I need a job. I've done everything I can think of to get a job. I even applied at Burger King for an assistant manager. I've sent out my resume to a thousand places, but I can't get a job. I'm starting to think that I must be doing something during the interviews to turn these people off. I know sometimes it's discrimination, because I'm someone who speaks my mind and people don't like Puerto Rican women who speak up, but I'm starting to blame myself also. Thinking that there's something wrong with me. . . . I think I'll call this woman I used to talk to on Monday. She was pretty good, except she tried to push the pills on me. A job don't come in no pill. If you got a pill that gets me a job, I'll take it.

Both Maria and Jerry are strong, bright, energetic people. After a few months of working with the shelter staff, however, both were contemplating medication for mental health problems. As Maria stated, "A job don't come in no pill," but neither she nor Jerry were provided with any way of understanding their inability to resolve homelessness that did not involve focusing on treating the individualized self. Within the dominant medicalized conceptual framework, it becomes common sense to understand the coping strategies of people surviving in homeless shelters as symptoms and evidence of mental illness. These people are thus understood as passive victims of biological disorders rather than situated social agents. Rather than providing a collective, social, or political understanding, shelter practices help to reproduce self-blame and self-governing.

People who come to believe that the solution to homelessness lies in treating or reforming the self are unlikely to engage in collective action. Within that discursive framework, collective action makes little sense because it does not involve working on individual issues. However, as Raymond Williams (1977) elucidates, hegemony is never totalizing. Peripheral discourses, although marginalized, do provide possibilities for resisting. Some shelter staff and some people who find themselves homeless, like Raymond, do voice a profound desire to change systemic conditions. Like Maria, they often articulate an analysis linking homelessness to class exploitation and social discrimination. However, these noncompliant staff and homeless people also remain enmeshed within the dominant medicalized discourse. In fact, any resistance to medicalizing discourses and practices is often itself medicalized and diagnosed as misplaced attention and further evidence of pathology. "The medical gaze is then a controlling gaze, through which active (although furtive) forms of protest are transformed into passive acts of 'breakdown'" (Lock and Scheper-Hughes 1990:68). Let me demonstrate this with an example.

After Raymond had several bouts with homelessness, a small majority of staff members voted to not allow him to return to the shelter. At the time, the shelter had a long waiting list, and the decision to bar Raymond was based on the argument that the shelter needed to prioritize those people they could really help. It was argued that it would be a waste of resources to allow him to return because he did not cooperate with prior case management procedures designed to "help" him. As Karen argued, "We can only help people if they are willing to work with us."

I suggested that maybe the staff was projecting a politically dangerous message by prioritizing who was worthy of shelter. Instead, I urged, we should argue that everyone was deserving of a safe place to live and engage in practices to accomplish that goal. Two other staff members, however, disagreed. They reminded us of what had happened a few years earlier when the shelter had let in everyone requesting a bed. They correctly reminded me that, at the time, I had agreed with them that it was an unhealthy and unhelpful effort.

I then stated that perhaps I was not being clear. I was not suggesting more shelters but, rather, that we work to decrease poverty and inequality and lessen the actual demand for shelters. They agreed with the sentiment but argued that they felt the shelter would alienate supporters with such practices and that we needed to be "realistic" and cognizant of the public sentiment that only those willing to help themselves were deserving of housing.

As one staff member, Leopoldina, reminded me, the shelter had just begun to obtain adequate funding from the state. A condition of the funding was that the shelter submit a monthly summary of how many guests staff had referred to treatment programs, job training programs, and similar reformative efforts. Leopoldina pointed out that it was quite telling that nowhere on the monthly form were there questions about efforts to politically organize homeless people, facilitate the development of collaborative efforts to decrease economic inequality in the community, alter the local wage scale, or address issues of housing cost or availability. In her mind, the state agency was sending a clear message about priorities and what practices the shelter staff must engage in if they wished to continue to receive funding. Not wanting to risk losing funding and, thus, the ability to shelter anyone, most staff complied with this message. No one was happy about turning away 20 to 40 people each night, but prioritizing those seeking shelter was understood by some as the most "practical" and "reasonable" response available.

As a result, Raymond's attention to the collective and racialized experience of homelessness was portrayed as an expression of his unwillingness to help himself. In fact, his focus on historical and political-economic conditions was sometimes represented as a symptom of a mental health disorder both by other shelter residents and by several staff. Other staff read Raymond's noncompliance (and perhaps his race) as a sign of drug use, and he was portrayed in staff meetings as a drug dealer and pimp despite the absence of any concrete evidence. In any case, he was punished for not complying with the idea that the proper way to respond to homelessness was through treating individualized deviancy. Other noncompliant guests have had similar experiences.

If a homeless person openly questions shelter helping efforts, he or she is understood as a problem. Staff use a variety of mechanisms to lessen the significance of such critiques. The homeless person is diagnosed as misplacing attention on "political" matters and not focusing on real individual issues. Often, these "political" concerns are understood as symptoms of mental illness and paranoia. Medication has been suggested as a means of "helping" more than a few people who spoke out against what they saw as misplaced shelter practices.

A slightly different set of practices surround a second noncompliant guest. Ariel, a white woman in her late fifties, first came to the shelter in May of 1993. Ariel had maintained a lower-middle-class life, doing light clerical work until the mid-1980s. When she was no longer able to find such work because of her age and computerization, she began to try to support herself through house cleaning. In 1993, she lost her room at a local rooming house when she was no longer able to secure enough work to pay rent. As soon as Ariel entered the shelter, staff members went to work trying to help her. The strategy used was that of uncovering the disorders within Ariel that resulted in her homelessness.

As with most of the hundreds of homeless people I have met, Ariel was full of self-blame and, consequently, was quite angry and upset over her situation when we first met. As she put it, "I didn't know what to do with this anger, so I blamed myself." Ariel's feelings of anguish would be manifested in her sometimes losing her patience with a fellow guest, becoming distraught, crying, and feeling unable to concentrate at times. She was clearly in a great deal of emotional pain. A few times, she was forgetful in the kitchen, and tea kettles were left on the stove unattended.

Ariel's emotions and behaviors were read by most staff as symptomatic of a mental illness. She was characterized as "clinically depressed" or suffering from post-traumatic stress disorder. Further evidence of a mental health disorder was gathered from her frequent suggestions for improving shelter policies and practices. Ariel's seemingly helpful suggestions, for example, that staff save dinners for shelter residents working the second shift, or her offer to wash the window curtains were read as directing attention away from the "cause" of her homelessness and as symptoms of her disorder. Staff members often did not respond to her suggestions because they did not want to "encourage her denial."

During July of 1993, this diagnosis resulted in a group of shelter staff developing a treatment plan for Ariel. The first step was to get her into counseling and on anti-depressant medications. When she resisted, staff devised a second plan to obtain money for Ariel by having her declared mentally disabled so that she would be eligible for social security disability payments. Ariel wanted nothing to do with that form of help. She explained that she was poor, not mentally ill.

Staff at the shelter continued to push the plan on Ariel. She was routinely called into a staff office for counseling sessions. At these sessions, well-meaning staff members would point out to Ariel how she was unable to care for herself. They would explain that they were concerned about her, but she could not stay at the shelter forever if she did not want to "help herself." Ariel told me how, during these meetings, staff members would tell her she was going to freeze to death or lose limbs from frostbite that winter if she did not comply with their helping efforts. When she still refused to comply, Ariel was denied further time at the shelter.

As a result of her resistance to medicalized shelter practices, Ariel was kicked out of the shelter for being difficult. *Being difficult* was defined as not claiming a mental health disability. The hope of the staff was that living on the streets would "break through her denial" once Ariel "hit bottom." Instead, her resistance to the medicalization of her body resulted in physical hardship. She survived outside from August through mid-December, when my constant advocacy, the empty shelter beds, the extreme cold, and the guilt of the Christmas season led staff to allow her to move back into the shelter. But then the efforts to push Ariel toward self-reform began anew.

Ariel described to me how some staff would ask her why she just wouldn't go along and comply. They could not understand how she could "keep living like this." Ariel told me, "The alternative is to commit suicide, and I'm not going to commit suicide. I'm willing to walk around with no place to live because I have no place to live. Because I'm willing to keep on living, that's why. I'm willing to walk around all night or sit up in Stop and Shop [a regional supermarket] because I'm not willing to jump off a bridge. Those are my options."

I asked, "And you think that getting social security payments so you can have a room in a rooming house wouldn't be living, it would be giving up?"

Ariel replied, "Right. I'm not going to lie. I'm going to tell them the truth. They better not declare me mentally disabled. I am not mentally disabled, but I do need money to get a place to live. It's like they're saying, 'We can't change the economy, so we have to change you.'"

Everyone in this situation did the best they could. Clearly, Ariel was resisting, but her resistance remained quite constrained. Let me be clear: I am not simply describing a case by mystification or false consciousness. Not everyone I worked with believes that homelessness is simply the result of deviancy within homeless people. As Stuart Hall notes, hegemony functions such that "ruling ideas may . . . set the limit to what will appear as rational, reasonable, credible, indeed sayable or thinkable" (1988:44). The hegemony of the medicalized discourse of deviancy operating within the homeless sheltering industry produces everyday practices of self-disclosure and self-government as routine habits that are accepted as "common sense."

The combination of a dominant medicalized discourse of deviancy, the belief in the naturalness and inevitability of capitalist exploitation, and widespread feelings of powerlessness to alter systemic conditions produce practices within the narrowly defined parameters of what is "reasonable" and "realistic" to think and do. The actual practices, even of noncompliant homeless people, remain enmeshed within the hegemony of the discourses of deviancy. To paraphrase Michel de Certeau, everyday practices enacted by noncompliant homeless people often allow them to "escape domination without leaving it" (1984:xiii). They are resisting the hegemony of the biomedical discourse by refusing to comply and collaborate in their oppression, but are not working collectively to escape or alter the systemic oppression that results in widespread inequality and homelessness.

Agents within the sheltering industry develop diagnostic tools, statistical representations, treatments, and reforms to make the homeless person into a new kind of self-blaming and self-governing person. Under these discursive conditions, the staff and guests function as institutional agents whose job it is to govern "the homeless" through a regime of surveillance, discipline, and personal enhancement. In short, a "normal" person is to be made by governing a "deviant" homeless person.

Those advocating governing the self as the solution to homelessness do not pay attention to the extent to which personal life is governed. The self (like poverty, homelessness, inequality, and racism) is not only personal but also the product of power relations, the outcome of strategies and technologies (Cruikshank 1996:248). Self-help, self-fulfillment, and self-reform are technologies that produce certain kinds of selves and marginalize the possibilities of producing alternative subjectivities. When statistical typologies and case histories diagnose disorders within homeless people and, thus, reinforce knowledge about homeless deviants, it becomes only "common sense" that helping efforts focus on treating these disorders of the self. Homeless subjectivities are made up through shelter helping practices such that it makes perfect sense for many people living in shelters to willingly comply with more surveillance and reform of their bodies and selves.

If we are to understand the durability of homelessness despite the well-meaning efforts of the sheltering industry, we must contemplate how *the homeless* and *homelessness,* as categories, are produced and resisted. These categories are products of discursive conditions that give rise to concrete ways of thinking and acting. This article focuses on one particular community and one shelter. Although not representative of all shelters, it does provide a case study by which to examine the ambiguous effects of adapting the "disease" model for responding to homelessness. We need to examine practices designed to validate the categories of *homelessness* and *the homeless* in a range of settings. Through that work, we can begin to uncover how dominant discursive conditions reinforce routine practices that normatively silence or devalue other possible ways of perceiving and being in regard to homelessness.

Notes

Correspondence may be addressed to the author at Department of Anthropology, Western Michigan University, Kalamazoo, MI 49008, e-mail: vincent.lyon-callo@wmich.edu.

1. The names of all homeless people and shelter staff referred to in this article have been changed. Everyone quoted formally agreed to take part in this study.

2. Many shelters were created as charitable institutions by religious organizations. In these shelters, a homeless person also often received a lecture or gospel reading as a condition for a night's stay.

3. As one example, New York City instituted a program in 1998 whereby the city paid shelter operators bonuses for moving homeless families and individuals into permanent housing. This was represented as an incentive to the shelters to develop more effective helping programs (Holloway 1998).

4. This is certainly not meant to suggest that some people do not display symptoms of what are commonly diagnosed as mental illnesses or substance abuse disorders prior to becoming homeless. However, I would argue that even in such cases, homelessness is a result of political and historical conditions. There is no inherent reason why mental illness or substance abuse must lead to homelessness. In fact, in other historical moments and geographic locations, it has not. Nor do all people displaying such behaviors in the United States today become homeless.

5. See Desjarlais 1997 for a related ethnographic study focused on practices within a shelter for people deemed mentally ill.

6. Activist ethnographic research, like advocacy or action research, strives to be accurate and non-biased without claiming to be value-free or neutral. For more detailed arguments on this research methodology, see Schensul and Schensul 1978 and Singer 1990.

7. I did not formally interview two staff members because of their time commitments outside the shelter. All shelter staff and regular volunteers agreed to participate in the study, sign consent forms, and allow me to tape weekly staff meetings.

8. In fact, several staff members and shelter residents frequently urged me to speak up and assert my views within the community, as if I had "the answer." I tried to explain that my goal was to push all of us to think more critically about our assumptions and practices so that we (including myself) could learn from each other.

9. Again, to be clear, I am not arguing that such engagement will lead people to see "the truth" or free them from the false consciousness hidden by ideological conditions. Instead, my hope was that new discursive practices might lead to different social outcomes, which, hopefully, would decrease the violence of structural inequalities and homelessness.

10. As in much of New England, deindustrialization has hit western Massachusetts quite hard. A 15 percent decrease in manufacturing jobs and a 12 percent increase in service sector jobs occurred countywide during the 1980s (Market Street Research 1994:14). This trend continued throughout the 1990s. According to the Northampton Chamber of Commerce, 42 percent of the jobs in Northampton in 1998 were in the service sector.

References

Burt, Martha
1992 Over the Edge: The Growth of Homelessness in the 1980s. Washington, DC: The Urban Institute Press.
Cruikshank, Barbara
1996 Revolutions Within: Self Government and Self Esteem. *In* Foucault and Political Reason: Liberalism, Neo-Liberalism, and Rationalities of Government. Andrew Barry, Thomas Osborne, and Nikolas Rose, eds. Pp. 231–252. Chicago: University of Chicago Press.
Dear, Michael, and Brendan Gleeson
1991 Community Attitudes Toward the Homeless. Urban Geography 12:155–176.
de Certeau, Michael
1984 The Practice of Everyday Life. Steven F. Rendall, trans. Berkeley: University of California Press.
Desjarlais, Robert
1997 Shelter Blues: Sanity and Selfhood among the Homeless. Philadelphia: University of Pennsylvania Press.
Dordick, Gwendolyn
1997 Something Left to Lose: Personal Relations and Survival among New York's Homeless. Philadelphia, PA: Temple University Press.

Farmer, Paul, Margaret Conners, and Janie Simmons, eds.
1996 Women, Poverty and AIDS: Sex, Drugs and Structural Violence. Monroe, ME: Common Courage Press.
Gounis, Kostas
1992 The Manufacture of Dependency: Shelterization Revisited. New England Journal of Public Policy 8(1):685–693.
Hacking, Ian
1986 Making Up People. *In* Reconstructing Individualism: Autonomy, Individualism, and the Self in Western Thought. Thomas Heller, Morton Sosna, and David Wellberry, eds. Pp. 222–236. Stanford, CA: Stanford University Press.
1995 Rewriting the Soul: Multiple Personality Disorder and the Science of Memory. Princeton, NJ: Princeton University Press.
Hall, Stuart
1988 The Toad in the Garden: Thatcherism among the Theorists. *In* Marxism and the Interpretation of Culture. Cary Nelson and Lawrence Grossberg, eds. Pp. 58–74. Urbana: University of Illinois Press.
Holloway, Lynette
1998 Shelter Operators to Get Bonuses for Finding Homes for the Homeless. The New York Times, September 6:B3.
Hopper, Kim
1988 More than Passing Strange: Homelessness and Mental Illness in New York City. American Ethnologist 15:155–167.
Hopper, Kim, Ezra Susser, and Sarah Conover
1985 Economics of Makeshift: Deindustrialization and Homelessness in New York City. Urban Anthropology 14:183–235.
Liebow, Elliot
1993 Tell Them Who I Am: The Lives of Homeless Women. New York: The Free Press.
Lock, Margaret, and Nancy Scheper-Hughes
1990 A Critical-Interpretive Approach in Medical Anthropology: Rituals and Routines of Discipline and Dissent. *In* Medical Anthropology: Contemporary Theory and Methods. Thomas M. Johnson and Carolyn F. Sargent, eds. Pp. 47–72. New York: Praeger Books.
Lyon-Callo, Vincent
1998 Constraining Responses to Homelessness: An Ethnographic Exploration of the Impact of Funding Concerns on Resistance. Human Organization 57:1–8.
Marcuse, Peter
1989 Gentrification, Homelessness, and the Work Process. Housing Studies 4: 211–220.
Market Street Research
1994 Health and Human Service Needs of Hampshire County Residents: Needs Assessment Report. Northampton, MA: Market Street Research, Inc.
Mathieu, Arlme
1993 The Medicalization of Homelessness and the Theater of Repression. Medical Anthropology Quarterly 7:170–184.
Morsy, Soheir
1990 Political Economy in Medical Anthropology. *In* Medical Anthropology: Contemporary Theory and Methods. Thomas M. Johnson and Carolyn F. Sargent, eds. Pp. 26–46. New York: Praeger Books.
Navarro, Vicente
1986 Crisis, Health, and Medicine: A Social Critique. New York: Tavistock.
Roofless Women's Action Research Mobilization
1996 A Hole in My Soul: Experiences of Homeless Women. *In* For Crying Out Loud: Women's Poverty in the United States. Diane Dujon and Ann Withorn, eds. Pp. 41–55. Boston: South End Press.

Rose, Nikolas
1990 Governing the Soul: The Shaping of the Private Self. London: Routledge
1996 The Death of the Social? Re-Figuring the Territories of Government. Economy and Society 25:327–356.
Ruddick, Susan
1995 Young and Homeless in Hollywood: Mapping Social Identities. London: Routledge.
Schensul, Stephen L., and Jean J. Schensul
1978 Advocacy and Applied Anthropology. *In* Social Scientists as Advocates: Views from the Applied Disciplines. George H. Weber and George J. McCall, eds. Pp. 121–165. Beverly Hills, CA: Sage.
Singer, Merrill
1990 Another Perspective on Advocacy. Current Anthropology 31:548–549.
1995 Beyond the Ivory Tower: Critical Praxis in Medical Anthropology. Medical Anthropology Quarterly 9:80–106.
Singer, Merrill, and Hans Baer
1996 Critical Medical Anthropology. Amityville, NY: Baywood.
Singer, Merrill, Freddie Valentin, Hans Baer, and Zhongke Jia
1992 Why Does Juan Garcia Have a Drinking Problem? Medical Anthropology 14(1):77–106.
Spain, James, and Robert Talbott
1996 Hoover's Handbook of American Businesses, 1996. Austin, TX: The Reference Press.
Turner, Maureen
1998 The Division of Labor: Employment Numbers Look Good on Paper, but They Hide Serious Weak Spots in the Market. The Valley Advocate, February 26:20–22.
Wagner, David
1993 Checkerboard Square: Culture and Resistance in a Homeless Community. Boulder, CO: Westview Press.
Watson, Bruce
1996 Tight Rental Market Aggravates Annual Housing Scramble. The Daily Hampshire Gazette, August 28:15–16.
Williams, Brett
1996 There Goes the Neighborhood: Gentrification, Displacement, and Homelessness in Washington, DC. *In* There's No Place Like Home: Anthropological Perspectives on Housing and Homelessness in the United States. Anna Lou Dehavenon, ed. Pp. 145–163. Westport, CT: Bergin and Garvey.
Williams, Raymond
1977 Marxism and Literature, Oxford: Oxford University Press.
Wright, Talmadge
1997 Out of Place: Homeless Mobilizations, Subcities, and Contested Landscapes. Albany: State University of New York Press.
Young, Alan
1995 The Harmony of Illusions: Inventing Post Traumatic Stress Disorder. Princeton, NJ: Princeton University Press.

Managing Institutional Careers and Identities

We have argued previously that the labeling ceremony or institutional processing can be viewed from two major perspectives—the institution's or the actor's. Thus far, the selections have dealt with processing primarily from the institution's perspective and little direct attention has been given to the actor's perceptions and responses. If we are to approach a more complete understanding of the range of effects that various types of bureaucratic processing can produce at selected stages, then we must try to assume the perspective of individuals who become caught up in the deviant-defining process. How, for example, does being identified, selected, and processed, and ultimately accorded the status of social deviant affect one's public and personal identity and one's self-image? Does the organizationally-created deviant accept his or her new status and associated labels, or does the newly-created deviant reject such organizational products and tags? Perhaps the patient will, in a therapeutic setting, accept the "sick role," but out on the ward the patient may reject the role and protest that he or she is not sick. Predicting which type of outcome is likely to occur is problematic.

Erving Goffman's work, "The Moral Career of the Mental Patient," examines contingencies such as these. Goffman is concerned with analyzing the *moral career* of the mental patient, particularly in terms of how patients perceive and respond to their treatment. Of major concern is the impact of the ward experience upon *self.* He points out initially that very few patients come willingly to the hospital. Rather, many arrive as a result of family or police action. (In this sense, the article further substantiates the discussion of the ways in which behavior in private domains may become regulated by some institution.) Goffman argues that the prepatient career can be analyzed in terms of an "extrusory model." In essence, this means that the patient initially has certain relationships and rights; however, he or she is left with very few after admission. Through Goffman's insightful analysis, one understands how the actor's public identity becomes transformed into a "deviant" identity—in this case, that of a mental patient. Important to this process are such phenomena as the "alienative coalition" and the "betrayal funnel." Goffman argues further that "the last step in the prepatient career can involve his realization—justified or not—that he has been deserted by society and turned out of relationships by those closest to him." At this stage the patient may begin to orient himself or herself to the "ward system." Some patients may, for example, accept the "sick role" and develop a set of rationalizations to "explain" their hospitalization. Such strategies enable the patient to regain and sustain a certain semblance of self—a self that has been subjected to a frontal assault from the institution, its personnel, family members and relatives, and, frequently, other patients. With his or her acceptance of this label, the individual begins to take on the identity of the secondary, or career, deviant.

Thomas J. Schmid and Richard S. Jones, in "Suspended Identity: Identity Transformation in a Maximum Security Prison," present an interesting variant of the identity change process. They examine inmates incarcerated in a maximum security prison. Of interest are not only the ways in which inmates may suspend their preprison identities but how inauthentic prison identities may be constructed. They note initially that most inmates have little in common prior to their imprisonment; they also have little knowledge about what prison is like. However, inmates are required to come to grips with the fact of their incarceration. An inmate often finds himself trying to manage a dualistic self, trying to balance his "true" identity (i.e., his preprison identity) with his "false" identity (i.e., his prison identity). The researchers note that this separation of identities "represents two conscious and interdependent identity-preservation tactics, formulated through self-dialogue and refined through tentative interaction with others." Schmid and Jones present an excellent diagram illustrating the major features involved in the identity change process. They conclude by discussing how an inmate's postprison identity may be influenced in various domains.

33 The Moral Career of the Mental Patient

Erving Goffman

Traditionally the term *career* has been reserved for those who expect to enjoy the rises laid out within a respectable profession. The term is coming to be used, however, in a broadened sense to refer to any social strand of any person's course through life. The perspective of natural history is taken: unique outcomes are neglected in favor of such changes over time as are basic and common to the members of a social category, although occurring independently to each of them. Such a career is not a thing that can be brilliant or disappointing; it can no more be a success than a failure. In this light, I want to consider the mental patient, drawing mainly upon data collected during a year's participant observation of patient social life in a public mental hospital,[1] wherein an attempt was made to take the patient's point of view.

One value of the concept of career is its two-sidedness. One side is linked to internal matters held dearly and closely, such as image of self and felt identity; the other side concerns official position, jural relations, and style of life, and is part of a publicly accessible institutional complex. The concept of career, then, allows one to move back and forth between the personal and the public, between the self and its significant society, without having overly to rely for data upon what the person says he thinks he imagines himself to be.

This paper, then, is an exercise in the institutional approach to the study of self. The main concern will be with the *moral* aspects of career—that is, the regular sequence of changes that career entails in the person's self and in his framework of imagery for judging himself and others.[2]

The category "mental patient" itself will be understood in one strictly sociological sense. In this perspective, the psychiatric view of a person becomes significant only in so far as this view itself alters his social fate—an alteration which seems to become fundamental in our society when, and only when, the person is put through the process of hospitalization.[3] I therefore exclude certain neighboring categories: the undiscovered candidates who would be judged "sick" by psychiatric standards but who never come to be viewed as such by themselves or others, although they may cause everyone a great deal of trouble;[4] the office patient whom a psychiatrist feels he can handle with drugs or shock on the outside; the mental client who engages in psychotherapeutic relationships. And I include anyone, however robust in temperament, who somehow gets caught up in the heavy machinery of mental hospital servicing. In this way the effects of being treated as a mental patient can be kept quite distinct from the effects upon a person's life of traits a clinician would view as psychopathological.[5] Persons who become mental hospital patients vary widely in the kind and degree of illness that a psychiatrist would impute to them, and in the attributes by which laymen would describe them. But once started on the way, they are confronted by some importantly similar circumstances and respond to these in some importantly similar ways. Since these similarities do not come from mental illness, they would seem to occur in spite of it. It is thus a tribute to the power of social forces that the uniform status of mental patient cannot only assure an aggregate of persons a common fate and eventually, because of this, a common character, but that this social reworking can be done upon what is perhaps the most obstinate diversity of human materials that can be brought together by society. Here there lacks only the frequent forming of a protective group-life by ex-patients to illustrate in full the classic cycle of response by which deviant subgroupings are psychodynamically formed in society.

This general sociological perspective is heavily reinforced by one key finding of sociologically oriented students in mental hospital research. As has been repeatedly shown in the study of nonliterate societies, the awesomeness, distastefulness, and barbarity of a foreign culture can decrease in the degree that the student becomes familiar with the point of view to life that is taken by his subjects. Similarly, the student of mental hospitals can discover that the craziness or "sick behavior" claimed for the mental patient is by and large a product of the claimant's social distance from the situation that the patient is in, and is not primarily a product of mental illness. Whatever the refinements of the various patients' psychiatric diagnoses, and whatever the special ways in which social life on the "inside" is unique, the researcher can find that he is participating in a community not significantly different from any other he has studied.[6] Of course, while restricting himself to the off-ward grounds community of paroled patients, he may feel, as some patients do, that life in the locked wards is bizarre; and while on a locked admissions or convalescent ward, he may feel that chronic "back" wards are socially crazy places. But he need only move his sphere of sympathetic participation to the "worst" ward in the hospital, and this too can come into social focus as a place with a livable and continuously meaningful social world. This in no way denies that he will find a minority in any ward or patient group that continues to seem quite beyond the capacity to follow rules of social organization, or that the orderly fulfillment of normative expectations in patient society is partly made possible by strategic measures that have somehow come to be institutionalized in mental hospitals.

The career of the mental patient falls popularly and naturalistically into three main phases: the period prior to entering the hospital, which I shall call the *prepatient phase;* the period in the hospital, the *inpatient phase;* the period after discharge from the hospital, should this occur, namely, the *expatient phase.*[7] This paper will deal only with the first two phases.

The Prepatient Phase

A relatively small group of prepatients come into the mental hospital willingly, because of their own idea of what will be good for them, or because of wholehearted agreement with the relevant members of their family. Presumably these recruits have found themselves acting in a way which is evidence to them that they are losing their minds or losing control of themselves. This view of oneself would seem to be one of the most pervasively threatening things that can happen to the self in our society, especially since it is likely to occur at a time when the person is in any case sufficiently troubled to exhibit the kind of symptom which he himself can see. As Sullivan described it,

> What we discover in the self-system of a person undergoing schizophrenic changes or schizophrenic processes, is then, in its simplest form, an extremely fear-marked puzzlement, consisting of the use of rather generalized and anything but exquisitely refined referential processes in an attempt to cope with what is essentially a failure at being human—a failure at being anything that one could respect as worth being.[8]

Coupled with the person's disintegrative re-evaluation of himself will be the new, almost equally pervasive circumstance of attempting to conceal from others what he takes to be the new fundamental facts about himself, and attempting to discover whether others too have discovered them.[9] Here I want to stress that perception of losing one's mind is based on culturally derived and socially engrained stereotypes as to the significance of symptoms such as hearing voices, losing temporal and spatial orientation, and sensing that one is being followed, and that many of the most spectacular and convincing of these symptoms in some instances psychiatrically signify merely a temporary emotional upset in a stressful situation, however terrifying to the person at the time. Similarly, the anxiety consequent upon this perception of oneself, and the strategies devised to reduce this anxiety, are not a product of abnormal psychology, but would be exhibited by any person socialized into our culture who came to conceive of himself as someone losing his mind. Interestingly, subcultures in American society apparently differ in the amount of ready imagery and encouragement they supply for such self-views, leading to differential rates of *self*-referral; the capacity to take this disintegrative view of oneself without psychiatric prompting seems to be one of the questionable cultural privileges of the upper classes.[10]

For the person who has come to see himself—with whatever justification—as mentally unbalanced, entrance to the mental hospital can sometimes bring relief, perhaps in part because of the sudden transformation in the structure of his basic social situations; instead of being to himself a questionable person trying to maintain a role as a full one, he can become an officially questioned person known to himself to be not so questionable as that. In other cases, hospitalization can make matters worse for the willing patient, confirming by the objective situation what has theretofore been a matter of the private experience of self.

Once the willing prepatient enters the hospital, he may go through the same routine of experiences as do those who enter unwillingly. In any case, it is the latter that I mainly want to consider, since in America at present these are by far the more numerous kind.[11] Their approach to the institution takes one of three classic forms: they come because they have been implored by their family or threatened with the abrogation of family ties unless they go "willingly"; they come by force under police escort; they come under misapprehension purposely induced by others, this last restricted mainly to youthful prepatients.

The prepatient's career may be seen in terms of an extrusory model; he starts out with relationships and rights, and ends up, at the beginning of his hospital stay, with hardly any of either. The moral aspects of this career, then, typically begin with the experience of abandonment, disloyalty, and embitterment. This is the case even though to others it may be obvious that he was in need of treatment, and even though in the hospital he may soon come to agree.

The case histories of most mental patients document offense against some arrangement for face-to-face living—a domestic establishment, a work place, a semipublic organization such as a church or store, a public region such as a street or park. Often there is also a record of some *complainant,* some figure who takes that action against the offender which eventually leads to his hospitalization. This may not be the person who makes the first move, but it is the person who makes what turns out to be the first effective move. Here is the *social* beginning of the patient's career, regardless of where one might locate the psychological beginning of his mental illness.

The kinds of offenses which lead to hospitalization are felt to differ in nature from those which lead to other extrusory consequences—to imprisonment, divorce, loss of job, disownment, regional exile, noninstitutional psychiatric treatment, and so forth. But little seems known about these differentiating factors; and when one studies actual commitments, alternate outcomes frequently appear to have been possible. It seems true, moreover, that for every offense that leads to an effective complaint, there are many psychiatrically similar ones that never do. No action is taken; or action is taken which leads to other extrusory outcomes; or ineffective action is taken, leading to the mere pacifying or putting off of the person who complains. Thus, as Clausen and Yarrow have nicely shown, even offenders who are eventually hospitalized are likely to have had a long series of ineffective actions taken against them.[12]

Separating those offenses which could have been used as grounds for hospitalizing the offender from those that are so used, one finds a vast number of what students of occupation call career contingencies.[13] Some of these contingencies in the mental patient's career have been suggested, if not explored, such as socio-economic status, visibility of the offense, proximity to a mental hospital, amount of treatment facilities available, community regard for the type of treatment given in available hospitals, and so on.[14] For information about other contingencies one must rely on atrocity tales: a psychotic man is tolerated by his wife until she finds herself a boyfriend, or by his adult children until they move from a house to an apartment; an alcoholic is sent to a mental hospital because the jail is full, and a drug addict because he declines to avail himself of psychiatric treatment on the outside; a rebellious adolescent daughter can no longer be managed at home because she now threatens to have an open affair with an unsuitable companion; and so on. Correspondingly there is an equally important set of contingencies causing the person to bypass this fate. And should the person enter the hospital, still another set of contingencies will help determine when he is to obtain a discharge—such as the desire of his family for his return, the availability of a "manageable" job, and so on. The society's official view is that inmates of mental hospitals are there primarily because they are suffering from mental illness. However, in the degree that the "mentally ill" outside hospitals numerically approach or surpass those inside hospitals, one could say that mental patients *distinctively* suffer not from mental illness, but from contingencies.

Career contingencies occur in conjunction with a second feature of the prepatient's career—the *circuit of agents*—and agencies—that participate fatefully in his passage from civilian to patient status.[15] Here is an instance of that increasingly important class of social system whose elements are agents and agencies, which are brought into systemic connection through having to take up and send on the same persons. Some of these agent-roles will be cited now, with the understanding that in any concrete circuit a role may be filled more than once, and a single person may fill more than one of them.

First is the *next-of-relation*—the person whom the prepatient sees as the most available of those upon whom he should be able to most depend in times of trouble; in this instance the last to doubt his sanity and the first to have done everything to save him from the fate which, it transpires, he has been approaching. The patient's next-of-relation is usually his next of kin; the special term is introduced because he need not be. Second is the *complainant,* the person who retrospectively appears to have started the person on his way to the hospital. Third are the *mediators*—the sequence of agents and agencies to which the prepatient is referred and through which he is relayed and processed on his way to the hospital. Here are included police, clergy, general medical practitioners, office psychiatrists, personnel in public clinics, lawyers, social service workers, school teachers, and so on. One of these agents will have the legal mandate to sanction commitment and will exercise it, and so those agents who precede him in the process will be involved in something whose outcome is not yet settled. When the mediators retire from the scene, the prepatient has become an inpatient, and the significant agent has become the hospital administrator.

While the complainant usually takes action in a lay capacity as a citizen, an employer, a neighbor, or a kinsman, mediators tend to be specialists and differ from those they serve in significant ways. They have experience in handling trouble, and some professional distance from what they handle. Except in the case of policemen, and perhaps some clergy, they tend to be more psychiatrically oriented than the lay public, and will see the need for treatment at times when the public does not.[16]

An interesting feature of these roles is the functional effects of their interdigitation. For example, the feelings of the patient will be influenced by whether or not the person who fills the role of complainant also has the role of next-of-relation—an embarrassing combination more prevalent, apparently, in the higher classes than in the lower.[17] Some of these emergent effects will be considered now.[18]

In the prepatient's progress from home to the hospital he may participate as a third person in what he may come to experience as a kind of *alienative coalition*. His next-of-relation presses him into coming to "talk things over" with a medical practitioner, an office psychiatrist, or some other counselor. Disinclination on his part may be met by threatening him with desertion, disownment, or other legal action, or by stressing the joint and explorative nature of the interview. But typically the next-of-relation will have set the interview up, in the sense of selecting the professional, arranging for time, telling the professional something about the case, and so on. This move effectively tends to establish the next-of-relation as the responsible person to whom pertinent findings can be divulged, while effectively establishing the other as the patient. The prepatient often goes to the interview with the understanding that he is going as an equal of someone who is so bound together with him that a third person could not come between them in fundamental matters; this, after all, is one way in which close relationships are defined in our society. Upon arrival at the office the prepatient suddenly finds that he and his next-of-relation have not been accorded the same roles, and apparently that a prior understanding between the professional and the next-of-relation has been put in operation against him. In the extreme but common case the professional first sees the prepatient alone, in the role of examiner and diagnostician, and then sees the next-of-relation alone, in the role of advisor, while carefully avoiding talking things over seriously with them both together.[19] And even in those nonconsultative cases where public officials must forcibly extract a person from a family that wants to tolerate him, the next-of-relation is likely to be induced to "go along" with the official action, so that even here the prepatient may feel that an alienative coalition has been formed against him.

The moral experience of being third man in such a coalition is likely to embitter the prepatient, especially since his troubles have already probably led to some estrangement from his next-of-relation. After he enters the hospital, continued visits by his next-of-relation can give the patient the "insight" that his own best interests were being served. But the initial visits may temporarily strengthen his feeling of abandonment; he is likely to beg his visitor to get him out or at least to get him more privileges and to sympathize with the monstrousness of his plight—to which the visitor ordinarily can respond only by trying to maintain a hopeful note, by not "hearing" the requests, or by assuring the patient that the medical authorities know about these things and are doing what is medically best. The visitor then nonchalantly goes back into a world that the patient has learned is incredibly thick with freedom and privileges, causing the patient to feel that his next-of-relation is merely adding a pious gloss to a clear case of traitorous desertion.

The depth to which the patient may feel betrayed by his next-of-relation seems to be increased by the fact that another witnesses his betrayal—a factor which is apparently significant in many three-party situations. An offended person may well act forbearantly and accommodatively toward an offender when the two are alone, choosing peace ahead of justice. The presence of a witness, however, seems to add something to the implications of the offense. For then it is beyond the power of the offended and offender to forget about, erase, or suppress what has happened; the offense has become a public social fact.[20] When the witness is a mental health commission, as is sometimes the case, the witnessed betrayal can verge on a "degradation ceremony."[21] In such circumstances, the offended patient may feel that some kind of extensive reparative action is required before witnesses, if his honor and social weight are to be restored.

Two other aspects of sensed betrayal should be mentioned. First, those who suggest the possibility of another's entering a mental hospital are not likely to provide a realistic picture of how in fact it may strike him when he arrives. Often he is told that he will get required medical treatment and a rest, and may well be out in a few months or so. In some cases they may thus be concealing what they know, but I think, in general, they will be telling what they see as the truth. For here there is a quite relevant difference between patients and mediating professionals; mediators, more so than the public at large, may conceive of mental hospitals as short-term medical establishments where required rest and attention can be voluntarily obtained, and not as places of coerced exile. When the prepatient finally arrives he is likely to learn quite quickly, quite differently. He then finds that the information given him about life in the hospital has had the effect of his having put up less resistance to entering than he now sees he would have put up had he known the facts. Whatever the intentions of those who participated in his transition from person to patient, he may sense they have in effect "conned" him into his present predicament.

I am suggesting that the prepatient starts out with at least a portion of the rights, liberties, and satisfactions of the civilian and ends up on a psychiatric ward stripped of almost everything. The question here is *how* this stripping is managed. This is the second aspect of betrayal I want to consider.

As the prepatient may see it, the circuit of significant figures can function as a kind of *betrayal funnel*. Passage from person to patient may be effected through a series of linked stages, each managed by a different agent. While each stage tends to bring a sharp decrease in adult free status, each agent may try to maintain the fiction that no further decrease will occur. He may even manage to turn the prepatient over to the next agent while sustaining this note. Further, through words, cues, and gestures, the prepatient is implicitly asked by the current agent to join with him in sustaining a running line of polite small talk that tactfully avoids the administrative facts of the situation, becoming, with each stage, progressively more at odds with these facts. The spouse would rather not have to cry to get the prepatient to visit a psychiatrist; psychiatrists would rather not have a scene when the prepatient learns that he and his spouse are being seen separately and in different ways; the police infrequently bring a prepatient to the hospital in a strait jacket, finding it much easier all around to give him a cigarette, some kindly words, and freedom to relax in the back seat of the patrol car; and finally, the admitting psychiatrist finds he can do his work better in the relative quiet and luxury of the "admission suite" where, as an incidental consequence, the notion can survive that a mental hospital is indeed a comforting place. If the prepatient heeds all of these implied requests and is reasonably decent about the whole thing, he can travel the whole circuit from home to hospital without forcing anyone to look directly at what is happening or to deal with the raw emotion that his situation might well cause him to express. His showing consideration for those who are moving him toward the hospital allows them to show consideration for him, with the joint result that these interactions can be sustained with some of the protective harmony characteristic of ordinary face-to-face dealings. But should the new patient cast his mind back over the sequence of steps leading to hospitalization, he may feel that everyone's *current* comfort was being busily sustained while his long-range welfare was being undermined. This realization may constitute a moral experience that further separates him for the time from the people on the outside.[22]

I would now like to look at the circuit of career agents from the point of view of the agents themselves. Mediators in the person's transition from civil to patient status—as well as his keepers, once he is in the hospital—have an interest in establishing a responsible next-of-relation as the patient's deputy or *guardian;* should there be no obvious candidate for the role, someone may be sought out and pressed into it. Thus while a person is gradually being transformed into a patient, a next-of-relation is gradually being transformed into a guardian. With a guardian on the scene, the whole transition process can be kept tidy. He is likely to be familiar with the prepatient's civil involvements and business, and can tie up loose ends that might otherwise be left to entangle the hospital. Some of the prepatient's abrogated civil rights can be transferred to him, thus helping to sustain the legal fiction that while the prepatient does not actually have his rights he somehow actually has not lost them.

Inpatients commonly sense, at least for a time, that hospitalization is a massive unjust deprivation, and sometimes succeed in convincing a few persons on the outside that this is the case. It often turns out to be useful, then, for those identified with inflicting these deprivations, however justifiably, to be able to point to the cooperation and agreement of someone whose relationship to the patient places him above suspicion, firmly defining him as the person most likely to have the patient's personal interest at heart. If the guardian is satisfied with what is happening to the new inpatient, the world ought to be.[23]

Now it would seem that the greater the legitimate personal stake one party has in another, the better he can take the role of guardian to the other. But the structural arrangements in society which lead to the acknowledged merging of two persons' interests lead to additional consequences. For the person to whom the patient turns for help—for protection against such threats as involuntary commitment—is just the person to whom the mediators and hospital administrators logically turn for authorization. It is understandable, then, that some patients will come to sense, at least for a time, that the closeness of a relationship tells nothing of its trustworthiness.

There are still other functional effects emerging from this complement of roles. If and when the next-of-relation appeals to mediators for help in the trouble he is having with the prepatient, hospitalization may not, in fact, be in his mind. He may not even perceive the prepatient as mentally sick, or, if he does, he may not consistently hold to this view.[24] It is the circuit of mediators, with their greater psychiatric sophistication and their belief in the medical character of mental hospitals, that will often define the situation for the next-of-relation, assuring him that hospitalization is a possible solution and a good one, that it involves no betrayal, but is rather a medical action taken in the best interests of the prepatient. Here the next-of-relation may learn that doing his duty to the prepatient may cause the prepatient to distrust and even hate him for the time. But the fact that this course of action may have had to be pointed out and prescribed by professionals, and be defined by them as a moral duty, relieves the next-of-relation of some of the guilt he may feel.[25] It is a poignant fact that an adult son or daughter may be pressed into the role of mediator, so that the hostility that might otherwise be directed against the spouse is passed on to the child.[26]

Once the prepatient is in the hospital, the same guilt-carrying function may become a significant part of the staff's job in regard to the next-of-relation.[27] These reasons for feeling that he himself has not betrayed the patient, even though the patient may then think so, can later provide the next-of-relation with a defensible line to take when visiting the patient in the hospital and a basis for hoping that the relationship can be re-established after its hospital moratorium. And of course this position, when sensed by the patient, can provide him with excuses for the next-of-relation, when and if he comes to look for them.[28]

Thus while the next-of-relation can perform important functions for the mediators and hospital administrators, they in turn can perform important functions for him. One finds, then, an emergent unintended exchange or reciprocation of functions, these functions themselves being often unintended.

The final point I want to consider about the prepatient's moral career is its peculiarly *retroactive* character. Until a person actually arrives at the hospital there usually seems no way of knowing for sure that he is destined to do so, given the determinative role of career contingencies. And until the point of hospitalization is reached, he or others may not conceive of him as a person who is becoming a mental patient. However, since he will be held against his will in the hospital, his next-of-relation and the hospital staff will be in great need of a rationale for the hardships they are sponsoring. The medical elements of the staff will also need evidence that they are still in the trade they were trained for. These problems are eased, no doubt unintentionally, by the case-history construction that is placed on the patient's past life, this having the effect of demonstrating that all along he had been becoming sick, that he finally became very sick, and that if he had not been hospitalized much worse things would have happened to him—all of which, of course, may be true. Incidentally, if the patient wants to make sense out of his stay in the hospital, and, as already suggested, keep alive the possibility of once again conceiving of his next-of-relation as a decent, well-meaning person, then he too will have reason to believe some of this psychiatric work-up of his past.

Here is a very ticklish point for the sociology of careers. An important aspect of every career is the view the person constructs when he looks backward over his progress; in a sense, however, the whole of the prepatient career derives from this reconstruction. The fact of having had a prepatient career, starting with an effective complaint, becomes an important part of the mental patient's orientation, but this part can begin to be played only after hospitalization proves that what he had been having, but no longer has, is a career as a prepatient.

The Inpatient Phase

The last step in the prepatient's career can involve his realization—justified or not—that he has been deserted by society and turned out of relationships by those closest to him. Interestingly enough, the patient, especially a first admission, may manage to keep himself from coming to the end of this trail, even though in fact he is now in a locked mental hospital ward. On entering the hospital, he may very strongly feel the desire not to be known to anyone as a person who could possibly be reduced to these present circumstances, or as a person who conducted himself in the way he did prior to commitment. Consequently, he may avoid talking to anyone, may stay by himself when possible, and may even be "out of contact" or "manic" so as to avoid ratifying any interaction that presses a politely reciprocal role upon him and opens him up to what he has become in the eyes of others. When the next-of-relation makes an effort to visit, he may be rejected by mutism, or by the patient's refusal to enter the visiting room, these strategies sometimes suggesting that the patient still clings to a remnant of relatedness to those who made up his past, and is protecting this remnant from the final destructiveness of dealing with the new people that they have become.[29]

Usually the patient comes to give up this taxing effort at anonymity, at not-hereness, and begins to present himself for conventional social interaction to the hospital community. Thereafter he withdraws only in special ways—by always using his nickname, by signing his contribution to the patient weekly with his initial only, or by using the innocuous "cover" address tactfully provided by some hospitals; or he withdraws only at special times, when, say, a flock of nursing students makes a passing tour of the ward, or when, paroled to the hospital grounds, he suddenly sees he is about to cross the path of a civilian he happens to know from home. Sometimes this making of oneself available is called "settling down" by the attendants. It marks a new stand openly taken and supported by the patient, and resembles the "coming out" process that occurs in other groupings.[30]

Once the prepatient begins to settle down, the main outlines of his fate tend to follow those of a whole class of segregated establishments—jails, concentration camps, monasteries, work camps, and so on—in which the inmate spends the whole round of life on the grounds, and marches through his regimented day in the immediate company of a group of persons of his own institutional status.[31]

Like the neophyte in many of these "total institutions," the new inpatient finds himself cleanly stripped of many of his accustomed affirmations, satisfactions, and defenses, and is subjected to a rather full set of mortifying experiences: restriction of free movement; communal living; diffuse authority of a whole echelon of people; and so on. Here one begins to learn about the limited extent to which a conception of oneself can be sustained when the usual setting of supports for it are suddenly removed.

While undergoing these humbling moral experiences, the inpatient learns to orient himself in terms of the "ward system."[32] In public mental hospitals this usually consists of a series of graded living arrangements built around wards, administrative units called services, and parole statuses. The "worst" level involves often nothing but wooden benches to sit on, some quite indifferent food, and a small piece of room to sleep in. The "best" level may involve a room of one's own, ground and town privileges, contacts with staff that are relatively undamaging, and what is seen as good food and ample recreational facilities. For disobeying the pervasive house rules, the inmate will receive stringent punishments expressed in terms of loss of privileges; for obedience he will eventually be allowed to reacquire some of the minor satisfactions he took for granted on the outside.

The institutionalization of these radically different levels of living throws light on the implications for self of social settings. And this in turn affirms that the self arises not merely out of its possessor's interactions with significant others, but also out of the arrangements that are evolved in an organization for its members.

There are some settings which the person easily discounts as an expression or extension of him. When a tourist goes slumming, he may take pleasure in the situation not because it is a reflection of him but because it so assuredly is not. There are other settings, such as living rooms, which the person manages on his own and employs to influence in a favorable direction other persons' views of him. And there are still other settings, such as a work place, which express the employee's occupational status, but over which he has no final control, this being exerted, however tactfully, by his employer. Mental hospitals provide an extreme instance of this latter possibility. And this is due not merely to their uniquely degraded living levels, but also to the unique way in which significance for self is made explicit to the patient, piercingly, persistently, and thoroughly. Once lodged on a given ward, the patient is firmly instructed that the restrictions and deprivations he encounters are not due to such things as tradition or economy—and hence dissociable from self—but are intentional parts of his treatment, part of his need at the time, and therefore an expression of the state that his self has fallen to. Having every reason to initiate requests for better conditions, he is told that when the staff feels he is "able to manage" or will be "comfortable with" a higher ward level, then appropriate action will be taken. In short, assignment to a given ward is presented not as a reward or punishment, but as an expression of his general level of social functioning, his status as a person. Given the fact that the worst ward levels provide a round of life that inpatients with organic brain damage can easily manage, and that these quite limited human beings are present to prove it, one can appreciate some of the mirroring effects of the hospital.[33]

The ward system, then, is an extreme instance of how the physical facts of an establishment can be explicitly employed to frame the conception a person takes of himself. In addition, the official psychiatric mandate of mental hospitals gives rise to even more direct, even more blatant, attacks upon the inmate's view of himself. The more "medical" and the more progressive a mental hospital is—the more it attempts to be therapeutic and not merely custodial—the more he may be confronted by high-ranking staff arguing that his past has been a failure, that the cause of this has been within himself, that his attitude to life is wrong, and that if he wants to be a person he will have to change his way of dealing with people and his conceptions of himself. Often the moral value of these verbal assaults will be brought home to him by requiring him to practice taking this psychiatric view of himself in arranged confessional periods, whether in private sessions or group psychotherapy.

Now a general point may be made about the moral career of inpatients which has bearing on many moral careers. Given the stage that any person has reached in a career, one typically finds that he constructs an image of his life course—past, present, and future—which selects, abstracts, and distorts in such a way as to provide him with a view of himself that he can usefully expound in current situations. Quite generally, the person's line concerning self defensively brings him into appropriate alignment with the basic values of his society, and so may be called an *apologia.* If the person can manage to present a view of his current situation which shows the operation of favorable personal qualities in the past and a favorable destiny awaiting him, it may be called a *success story.* If the facts of a person's past and present are extremely dismal, then about the best he can do is to show that he is not responsible for what has become of him, and the term *sad tale* is appropriate. Interestingly enough, the more the person's past forces him out of apparent alignment with central moral values, the more often he seems compelled to tell his sad tale in any company in which he finds himself. Perhaps he partly responds to the need he feels in others of not having their sense of proper life courses affronted. In any case, it is among convicts, "wino's," and prostitutes that one seems to obtain sad tales the most readily.[34] It is the vicissitudes of the mental patient's sad tale that I want to consider now.

In the mental hospital, the setting and the house rules press home to the patient that he is, after all, a mental case who has suffered some kind of social collapse on the outside, having failed in some overall way, and that here he is of little social weight, being hardly capable of acting like a full-fledged person at all. These humiliations are likely to be most keenly felt by middle-class patients, since their previous condition of life little immunizes them against such affronts; but all patients feel some downgrading. Just as any normal member of his outside subculture would do, the patient often responds to this situation by attempting to assert a sad tale proving that he is not "sick," that the "little trouble" he did get into was really somebody else's fault, that his past life course had some honor and rectitude, and that the hospital is therefore unjust in forcing the status of mental patient upon him. This self-respecting tendency is heavily institutionalized within the patient society where opening social contacts typically involve the participants' volunteering information about their current ward location and length of stay so far, but not the reasons for their stay—such interaction being conducted in the manner of small talk on the outside.[35] With greater familiarity, each patient usually volunteers relatively accept-able reasons for his hospitalization, at the same time accepting without open immediate question the lines offered by other patients. Such stories as the following are given and overtly accepted.

> I was going to night school to get a M.A. degree, and holding down a job in addition, and the load got too much for me.

> The others here are sick mentally but I'm suffering from a bad nervous system and that is what is giving me these phobias.

> I got here by mistake because of a diabetes diagnosis, and I'll leave in a couple of days. [The patient had been in seven weeks.]

> I failed as a child, and later with my wife I reached out for dependency.

> My trouble is that I can't work. That's what I'm in for. I had two jobs with a good home and all the money I wanted.[36]

The patient sometimes reinforces these stories by an optimistic definition of his occupational status: A man who managed to obtain an audition as a radio announcer styles himself a radio announcer; another who worked for some months as a copy boy and was then given a job as a reporter on a large trade journal, but fired after three weeks, defines himself as a reporter.

A whole social role in the patient community may be constructed on the basis of these reciprocally sustained fictions. For these face-to-face niceties tend to be qualified by behind-the-back gossip that comes only a degree closer to the "objective" facts. Here, of course, one can see a classic social function of informal networks of equals: they serve as one another's audi-ence for self-supporting tales—tales that are somewhat more solid than pure fantasy and somewhat thinner than the facts.

But the patient's *apologia* is called forth in a unique setting, for few set-tings could be so destructive of self-stories except, of course, those stories already constructed along psychiatric lines. And this destructiveness rests on more than the official sheet of paper which attests that the patient is of unsound mind, a danger to himself and others—an attestation, incidentally, which seems to cut deeply into the patient's pride, and into the possibility of his having any.

Certainly the degrading conditions of the hospital setting belie many of the self-stories that are presented by patients; and the very fact of being in the mental hospital is evidence against these tales. And of course, there is not always sufficient patient solidarity to prevent patient discrediting pa-tient, just as there is not always a sufficient number of "professionalized" attendants to prevent attendant discrediting patient. As one patient in-formant repeatedly suggested to a fellow patient:

> If you're so smart, how come you got your ass in here?

The mental hospital setting, however, is more treacherous still. Staff has much to gain through discreditings of the patient's story—whatever the felt reason for such discreditings. If the custodial faction in the hospital is to succeed in managing his daily round without complaint or trouble from him, then it will prove useful to be able to point out to him that the claims about himself upon which he rationalizes his demands are false, that he is not what he is claiming to be, and that in fact he is a failure as a person. If the psychiatric faction is to impress upon him its views about his personal make-up, then they must be able to show in detail how their version of his past and their version of his character hold up much better than his own.[37] If both the custodial and psychiatric factions are to get him to cooperate in the various psychiatric treatments, then it will prove useful to disabuse him of *his* view of their purposes, and cause him to appreciate that they know what they are doing, and are doing what is best for him. In brief, the difficulties caused by a patient are closely tied to his version of what has been happening to him, and if cooperation is to be secured, it helps if this version is discredited. The patient must "insightfully" come to take, or affect to take, the hospital's view of himself.

Notes

1. The study was conducted during 1955–56 under the auspices of the Laboratory of Social-environmental Studies of the National Institute of Mental Health. I am grateful to the Laboratory Chief, John A. Clausen, and to Dr. Winfred Overholser, Superintendent, and the late Dr. Jay Hoffman, then First Assistant Physician of Saint Elizabeth's Hospital, Washington, D.C., for the ideal cooperation they freely provided. A preliminary report is contained in Goffman, "Interpersonal Persuasion," pp. 117–193; in *Group Processes: Transactions of the Third Conference,* edited by Bertram Schaffner: New York, Josiah Macy, Jr. Foundation, 1957. A shorter version of this paper was presented at the Annual Meeting of the American Sociological Society, Washington, D.C., August 1957.

2. Material on moral career can be found in early social anthropological work on ceremonies of status transition, and in classic social psychological descriptions of those spectacular changes in one's view of self that can accompany participation in social movements and sects. Recently new kinds of relevant data have been suggested by psychiatric interest in the problem of "identity" and sociological studies of work careers and "adult socialization."

3. This point has recently been made by Elaine and John Cumming, *Closed Ranks;* Cambridge, Commonwealth Fund, Harvard Univ. Press, 1957; pp. 101–102. "Clinical experience supports the impression that many people define mental illness as 'That condition for which a person is treated in a mental hospital.' . . . Mental illness, it seems, is a condition which afflicts people who must go to a mental institution, but until they do almost anything they do is normal." Leila Deasy has pointed out to me the correspondence here with the situation in white collar crime. Of those who are detected in this activity, only the ones who do not manage to avoid going to prison find themselves accorded the social role of the criminal.

4. Case records in mental hospitals are just now coming to be exploited to show the incredible amount of trouble a person may cause for himself and others before anyone begins to think about him psychiatrically, let alone take psychiatric action against him. See John A. Clausen and Marian Radke Yarrow, "Paths to the Mental Hospital," *J. Social Issues* (1955) 11:25–32; August B. Hollingshead and Fredrick C. Redlich, *Social Class and Mental Illness;* New York, Wiley, 1958: pp. 173–174.

5. An illustration of how this perspective may be taken to all forms of deviancy may be found in Edwin Lemert, *Social Pathology;* New York, McGraw-Hill, 1951; see especially pp. 74–76. A specific application to mental defectives may be found in Stewart E. Perry, "Some Theoretic Problems of Mental Deficiency and Their Action Implications," *Psychiatry* (1954) 17: 45–73; see especially p. 68.

6. Conscientious objectors who voluntarily went to jail sometimes arrived at the same conclusion regarding criminal inmates. See, for example, Alfred Hassler, *Diary of a Self-made Convict;* Chicago, Regnery, 1954; p. 74.

7. This simple picture is complicated by the somewhat special experience of roughly a third of ex-patients—namely, readmission to the hospital, this being the recidivist or "repatient" phase.

8. Harry Stack Sullivan, *Clinical Studies in Psychiatry;* edited by Helen Swick Perry, Mary Ladd Gawel, and Martha Gibbon; New York, Norton, 1956; pp. 184–185.

9. This moral experience can be contrasted with that of a person learning to become a marihuana addict, whose discovery that he can be "high" and still "op" effectively without being detected apparently leads to a new level of use. See Howard S. Becker, "Marihuana Use and Social Control," *Social Problems* (1955) 3:35–44; see especially pp. 40–41.

10. See note 4: Hollingshead and Redlich, p. 187, Table 6, where relative frequency is given of self-referral by social class grouping.

11. The distinction employed here between willing and unwilling patients cuts across the legal one, of voluntary and committed, since some persons who are glad to come to the mental hospital may be legally committed, and of those who come only because of strong familial pressure, some may sign themselves in as voluntary patients.

12. Clausen and Yarrow; see note 4.

13. An explicit application of this notion to the field of mental health may be found in Edwin M. Lemert, "Legal Commitment and Social Control," *Sociology and Social Research* (1946) 30:370–378.

14. For example, Jerome K. Meyers and Leslie Schaffer, "Social Stratification and Psychiatric Practice: A Study of an Outpatient Clinic," *Amer. Sociological Rev.* (1954) 19:307–310, Lemert, see note 5; pp. 402–403. *Patients in Mental Institutions,* 1941; Washington, D.C., Department of Commerce, Bureau of Census, 1941; p. 2.

15. For one circuit of agents and its bearing on career contingencies, see Oswald Hall, "The Stages of a Medical Career," *Amer. J. Sociology* (1948) 53:227–336.

16. See Cumming, note 3; p. 92.

17. Hollingshead and Redlich, note 4; p. 187.

18. For an analysis of some of these circuit implications for the inpatient, see Leila C. Deasy and Olive W. Quinn, "The Wife of the Mental Patient and the Hospital Psychiatrist," *J. Social Issues* (1955) 11:49–60. An interesting illustration of this kind of analysis may also be found in Alan G. Gowman, "Blindness and the Role of Companion," *Social Problems* (1956) 4:68–75. A general statement may be found in Robert Merton, "The Role Set: Problems in Sociological Theory," *British J. Sociology* (1957) 8:106–120.

19. I have one case record of a man who claims he thought *he* was taking his wife to see the psychiatrist, not realizing until too late that his wife had made the arrangements.

20. A paraphrase from Kurt Riezler, "The Social Psychology of Shame," *Amer. J. Sociology* (1943) 48:458.

21. See Harold Garfinkel, "Conditions of Successful Degradation Ceremonies," *Amer. J. Sociology* (1956) 61:420–424.

22. Concentration camp practices provide a good example of the function of the betrayal funnel in inducing cooperation and reducing struggle and fuss, although here the mediators could not be said to be acting in the best interests of the inmates. Police picking up persons from their homes would sometimes joke good-naturedly and offer to wait while coffee was being served. Gas chambers were fitted out like delousing rooms, and victims taking off their clothes were told to note where they were leaving them. The sick, aged, weak, or insane who were selected for extermination were sometimes driven away in Red Cross ambulances to camps referred to by terms such as "observation hospital." See David Boder, *I Did Not Interview the Dead;* Urbana, Univ. of Illinois Press, 1949; p. 81; and Elie A. Cohen, *Human Behavior in the Concentration Camp;* London, Cape, 1954; pp. 32, 37, 107.

23. Interviews collected by the Clausen group at NIMH suggest that when a wife comes to be a guardian, the responsibility may disrupt previous distance from in-laws, leading either to a new supportive coalition with them or to a marked withdrawal from them.

24. For an analysis of these nonpsychiatric kinds of perception, see Marian Radke Yarrow, Charlotte Green Schwartz, Harriet S. Murphy, and Leila Calhoun Deasy, "The Psychological Meaning of Mental Illness in the Family," *J. Social Issues* (1955) 11:12–24; Charlotte Green Schwartz, "Perspectives on Deviance: Wives; Definitions of their Husbands' Mental Illness," *Psychiatry* (1957) 20:275–291.

25. This guilt-carrying function is found, of course, in other role-complexes. Thus, when a middle-class couple engages in the process of legal separation or divorce, each of their lawyers usually takes the position that his job is to acquaint his client with all of the potential claims and rights, pressing his client into demanding these, in spite of any nicety of feelings about the rights and honorableness of the ex-partner. The client, in all good faith, can then say to self and to the ex-partner that the demands are being made only because the lawyer insists it is best to do so.

26. Recorded in the Clausen data.

27. This point is made by Cumming, see note 3; p. 129.

28. There is an interesting contrast here with the moral career of the tuberculosis patient. I am told by Julius Roth that tuberculosis patients are likely to come to the hospital willingly, agreeing with their next-of-relation about treatment. Later in their hospital career, when they learn how long they yet have to stay and how depriving and irrational some of the hospital rulings are, they may seek to leave, be advised against this by the staff and by relatives, and only then begin to feel betrayed.

29. The inmate's initial strategy of holding himself aloof from ratifying contact may partly account for the relative lack of group-formation among inmates in public mental hospitals, a connection that has been suggested to me by William R. Smith. The desire to avoid personal bonds that would give license to the asking of biographical questions could also be a factor. In mental hospitals, of course, as in prisoner camps, the staff may consciously break up incipient group-formation in order to avoid collective rebellious action and other ward disturbances.

30. A comparable coming out occurs in the homosexual world, when a person finally comes frankly to present himself to a "gay" gathering not as a tourist but as someone who is "available." See Evelyn Hooker, "A Preliminary Examination of Group Behavior of Homosexuals," *J. Psychology* (1956) 42:217–225; especially p. 221. A good fictionalized treatment may be found in James Baldwin's *Giovanni's Room;* New York, Dial, 1956; pp. 41–63. A familiar instance of the coming out process is no doubt to be found among prepubertal children at the moment one of these actors sidles *back* into a room that had been left in an angered huff and injured *amour-propre*. The phrase itself presumably derives from a *rite-de-passage* ceremony once arranged by upper-class mothers for their daughters. Interestingly enough, in large mental hospitals the patient sometimes symbolizes a complete coming out by his first active participation in the hospital wide patient dance.

31. See Goffman, "Characteristics of Total Institutions," pp. 43–84; in *Proceedings of the Symposium of Preventive and Social Psychiatry;* Washington, D.C., Walter Reed Army Institute of Research, 1958.

32. A good description of the ward system may be found in Ivan Belknap, *Human Problems of a State Mental Hospital;* New York, McGraw-Hill, 1956; see especially p. 164.

33. Here is one way in which mental hospitals can be worse than concentration camps and prisons as places in which to "do" time; in the latter, self-insulation from the symbolic implications of the settings may be easier. In fact, self-insulation from hospital settings may be so difficult that patients have to employ devices for this which staff interpret as psychotic symptoms.

34. In regard to convicts, see Anthony Heckstall-Smith, *Eighteen Months;* London, Wingate, 1954; pp. 52–53. For "wino's" see the discussion in Howard G. Bain, "A Sociological Analysis of the Chicago Skid-Row Lifeway;" unpublished M.A. thesis, Dept. of Sociology, pp. 141–146. Bain's neglected thesis is a useful source of material on moral careers.

Apparently one of the occupational hazards of prostitution is that clients and other professional contacts sometimes persist in expressing sympathy by asking for a defensible dramatic explanation for the fall from grace. In having to bother to have a sad tale ready, perhaps the prostitute is more to be pitied than damned. Good examples of prostitute sad tales may be found in Sir Henry Mayhew, "Those that Will Not Work," pp. 210–272; in his *London Labour and the London Poor,* Vol. 4; London, Griffin, Bohn, and Cox, 1862. For a contemporary source, see *Women of the Streets,* edited by C. H. Rolph; London, Zecker, and Warburg, 1955; especially p. 6. "Almost always, however, after a few comments on the police, the girl would begin to explain how it was that she was in the life, usually in terms of self-justification." Lately, of course, the psychological expert has helped out the profession in the construction of wholly remarkable sad tales. See, for example, Harold Greenwald, *Call Girl;* New York, Ballantine, 1958.

35. A similar self-protecting rule has been observed in prisons. Thus, Hassler, see note 6, in describing a conversation with a fellow-prisoner: "He didn't say much about why he was sentenced, and I didn't ask him, that being the accepted behavior in prison" (p. 76). A novelistic

version for the mental hospital may be found in J. Kerkhoff, *How Thin the Veil: A Newspaper-man's Story of His Own Mental Crack-up and Recovery;* New York, Greenberg, 1952; p. 27.

36. From the writer's field notes of informal interaction with patients, transcribed as near verbatim as he was able.

37. The process of examining a person psychiatrically and then altering or reducing his status in consequence is known in hospital and prison parlance as *bugging,* the assumption being that once you come to the attention of the testers you either will automatically be labeled crazy or the process of testing itself will make you crazy. Thus psychiatric staff are sometimes seen not as *discovering* whether you are sick, but as *making* you sick; and "Don't bug me, man," can mean, "Don't pester me to the point where I'll get upset." Sheldon Messinger has suggested to me that this meaning of bugging is related to the other colloquial meaning, of wiring a room with a secret microphone to collect information usable for discrediting the speaker.

Suspended Identity: Identity Transformation in a Maximum Security Prison

Thomas J. Schmid
Richard S. Jones

The extent to which people hide behind the masks of impression management in everyday life is a point of theoretical controversy (Goffman 1959; Gross and Stone 1964; Irwin 1977; Douglas et al. 1980; Douglas and Johnson 1977; Messinger et al. 1962; Blumer 1969, 1972). A variety of problematic circumstances can be identified, however, in which individuals find it necessary to accommodate a sudden but encompassing shift in social situations by establishing temporary identities. These circumstances, which can range from meteoric fame (Adler and Adler 1989) to confinement in total institutions, place new identity demands on the individual, while seriously challenging his or her prior identity bases.

A prison sentence constitutes a "massive assault" on the identity of those imprisoned (Berger 1963:100–101). This assault is especially severe on first-time inmates, and we might expect radical identity changes to ensue from their imprisonment. At the same time, a prisoner's awareness of the challenge to his identity affords some measure of protection against it. As part of an ethnographic analysis of the prison experiences of first-time, short-term inmates, this article presents an identity transformation model that differs both from the gradual transformation processes that characterize most adult identity changes and from such radical transformation processes as brainwashing or conversion.

Data for the study are derived principally from ten months of participant observation at a maximum security prison for men in the upper midwest of the United States. One of the authors was an inmate serving a felony sentence for one year and one day, while the other participated in the study as an outside observer. Relying on traditional ethnographic data collection and analysis techniques, this approach offered us general observations of hundreds of prisoners, and extensive fieldnotes that were based on repeated, often daily, contacts with about fifty inmates, as well as on personal relationships established with a smaller number of inmates. We subsequently returned to the prison to conduct focused interviews with

Figure 1 ● Prison Images and Strategies of New Inmates

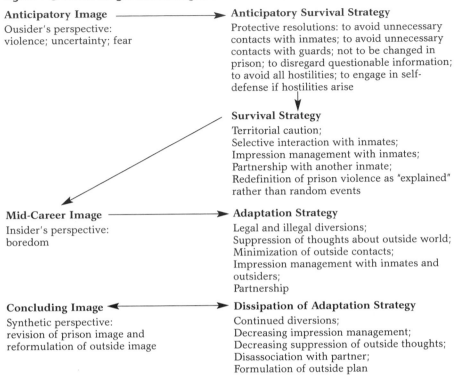

Anticipatory Image ⟶ **Anticipatory Survival Strategy**

Ousider's perspective: violence; uncertainty; fear

Protective resolutions: to avoid unnecessary contacts with inmates; to avoid unnecessary contacts with guards; not to be changed in prison; to disregard questionable information; to avoid all hostilities; to engage in self-defense if hostilities arise

Survival Strategy

Territorial caution; Selective interaction with inmates; Impression management with inmates; Partnership with another inmate; Redefinition of prison violence as "explained" rather than random events

Mid-Career Image ⟶ **Adaptation Strategy**

Insider's perspective: boredom

Legal and illegal diversions; Suppression of thoughts about outside world; Minimization of outside contacts; Impression management with inmates and outsiders; Partnership

Concluding Image ◀ ⟶ **Dissipation of Adaptation Strategy**

Synthetic perspective: revision of prison image and reformulation of outside image

Continued diversions; Decreasing impression management; Decreasing suppression of outside thoughts; Disassociation with partner; Formulation of outside plan

other prisoners; using information provided by prison officials, we were able to identify and interview twenty additional first-time inmates who were serving sentences of two years or less. See Schmid and Jones (1987) for further description of this study.

Three interrelated research questions guided our analysis: How do first-time, short-term inmates define the prison world, and how do their definitions change during their prison careers? How do these inmates adapt to the prison world, and how do their adaptation strategies change during their prison careers? How do their self-definitions change during their prison careers? Our analyses of the first two questions are presented in detail elsewhere (Schmid and Jones 1987, 1990); an abbreviated outline of these analyses, to which we will allude throughout this article, is presented in Figure 1. The identity transformation model presented here, based on our analysis of the third question, is outlined in Figure 2.

Preprison Identity

Our data suggest that the inmates we studied have little in common before their arrival at prison, except their conventionality. Although convicted of felonies, most do not possess "criminal" identities (cf. Irwin 1970:29–34).

Figure 2 ● Suspended Identity Dialectic

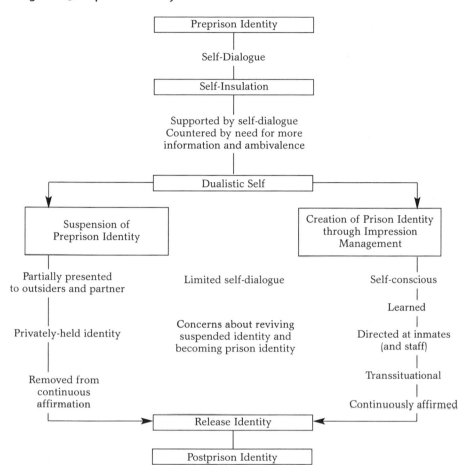

They begin their sentences with only a vague, incomplete image (Boulding 1961) of what prison is like, but an image that nonetheless stands in contrast to how they view their own social worlds. Their prison image is dominated by the theme of violence: they see prison inmates as violent, hostile, alien human beings, with whom they have nothing in common. They have several specific fears about what will happen to them in prison, including fears of assault, rape, and death. They are also concerned about their identities, fearing that—if they survive prison at all—they are in danger of changing in prison, either through the intentional efforts of rehabilitation personnel or through the unavoidable hardening effects of the prison environment. Acting on this imagery (Blumer 1969)—or, more precisely, on the inconsonance of their self-images with this prison image—they develop an anticipatory survival strategy (see Figure 1) that consists primarily of protective resolutions: a resolve to avoid all hostilities; a resolve to avoid all nonessential contacts with inmates and guards; a resolve to defend themselves in any way possible; and a resolve not to change, or to be changed, in prison.

A felon's image and strategy are formulated through a running self-dialogue, a heightened state of reflexive awareness (Lewis 1979) through which he ruminates about his past behavior and motives, and imaginatively projects himself into the prison world. This self-dialogue begins shortly after his arrest, continues intermittently during his trial or court hearings, and becomes especially intense at the time of his transfer to prison.

> You start taking a review—it's almost like your life is passing before your eyes. You wonder how in the heck you got to this point and, you know, what are—what's your family gonna think about it—your friends, all the talk, and how are you going to deal with that—and the kids, you know, how are they gonna react to it?. . . . All those things run through your head. . . . The total loss of control—the first time in all my life that some other people were controlling my life.

*   *   *

> My first night in the joint was spent mainly on kicking myself in the butt for putting myself in the joint. It was a very emotional evening. I thought a lot about all my friends and family, the good-byes, the things we did the last couple of months, how good they had been to me, sticking by me. I also thought about my fears: Am I going to go crazy? Will I end up fighting for my life? How am I going to survive in here for a year? Will I change? Will things be the same when I get out?

His self-dialogue is also typically the most extensive self-assessment he has ever conducted; thus, at the same time that he is resolving not to change, he is also initiating the kind of introspective analysis that is essential to any identity transformation process.

Self-Insulation

A felon's self-dialogue continues during the initial weeks and months of his sentence, and it remains a solitary activity, each inmate struggling to come to grips with the inconsonance of his established (preprison) identity and his present predicament. Despite the differences in their preprison identities, however, inmates now share a common situation that affects their identities. With few exceptions, their self-dialogues involve feelings of vulnerability, discontinuity, and differentiation from other inmates, emotions that reflect both the degradations and deprivations of institutional life (cf. Goffman 1961; Sykes 1958; and Garfinkel 1956) and their continuing outsiders' perspective on the prison world. These feelings are obviously the result of everything that has happened to the inmates, but they are something else as well: they are the conditions in which every first-time, short-term inmate finds himself. They might even be called the common attributes of the in-mates' selves-in-prison, for the irrelevance of their preprison identities within the prison world reduces their self-definitions, temporarily, to the level of pure emotion.[1] These feelings, and a consequent emphasis on the "physical self" (Zurcher 1977:176), also constitute the essential motivation for the inmates' self-insulation strategies.[2]

An inmate cannot remain wholly insulated within the prison world, for a number of reasons. He simply spends too much of his time in the presence of others to avoid all interaction with them. He also recognizes that his prison image is based on incomplete and inadequate information, and that he must interact with others in order to acquire first-hand information about the prison world. His behavior in prison, moreover, is guided not only by his prison image but by a fundamental ambivalence he feels about his situation, resulting from his marginality between the prison and outside social worlds (Schmid and Jones 1987). His ambivalence has several manifestations throughout his prison career, but the most important is his conflicting desires for self-insulation and for human communication.

Managing a Dualistic Self

An inmate is able to express both directions of his ambivalence (and to address his need for more information about the prison) by drawing a distinction between his "true" identity (i.e., his outside, preprison identity) and a "false" identity he creates for the prison world. For most of a new inmate's prison career, his preprison identity remains a "subjective" or "personal" identity while his prison identity serves as his "objective" or "social" basis for interaction in prison (see Weigert 1986; Goffman 1963). This bifurcation of his self (Figure 2) is not a conscious decision made at a single point in time, but it does represent two conscious and interdependent identity-preservation tactics, formulated through self-dialogue and refined through tentative interaction with others.

First, after coming to believe that he cannot "be himself" in prison because he would be too vulnerable, he decides to "suspend" his preprison identity for the duration of his sentence. He retains his resolve not to let prison change him, protecting himself by choosing not to reveal himself (his "true" self) to others. Expressions of a suspension of identity emerged repeatedly and consistently in both the fieldwork and interview phases of our research through such statements as

> I was reserved. . . . I wouldn't be very communicative, you know. I'd try to keep conversation to a minimum. . . . I wasn't interested in getting close to anybody . . . or asking a lot of questions. You know, try to cut the conversation short . . . go my own way back to my cell or go to the library or do something.

* * *

> I didn't want nobody to know too much about me. That was part of the act.

An inmate's decision to suspend his preprison identity emanates directly from his feelings of vulnerability, discontinuity and differentiation from other inmates. These emotions foster something like a "proto-sociological attitude" (Weigert 1986:173; see also Zurcher 1977), in which new inmates find it necessary to step outside their taken-for-granted preprison identities. Rather than viewing these identities and the everyday life experience in which they are grounded as social constructions, however, inmates see the *prison* world as an artificial construction, and judge their "naturally occurring" preprison identities to be out of place within this construction. By attempting to suspend his preprison identity for the time that he spends in prison an inmate believes that he will again "be his old self" after his release.

While he is in confinement, an inmate's decision to suspend his identity leaves him with little or no basis for interaction. His second identity tactic, then, is the creation of an identity that allows him to interact, however cautiously, with others. This tactic consists of his increasingly sophisticated impression management skills (Goffman 1959; Schlenker 1980), which are initially designed simply to hide his vulnerability, but which gradually evolve into an alternative identity felt to be more suitable to the prison world. The character of the presented identity is remarkably similar from inmate to inmate:

> Well, I learned that you can't act like—you can't get the attitude where you are better than they are. Even where you might be better than them, you can't strut around like you are. Basically, you can't stick out. You don't stare at people and things like that. I knew a lot of these things from talking to people and I figured them out by myself. I sat down and figured out just what kind of attitude I'm going to have to take.

*   *   *

> Most people out here learn to be tough, whether they can back it up or not. If you don't learn to be tough, you will definitely pay for it. This toughness can be demonstrated through a mean look, tough language, or an extremely big build. . . . One important thing is never to let your guard down.

An inmate's prison identity, as an inauthentic presentation of self, is not in itself a form of identity transformation but is rather a form of identity construction. His prison identity is simply who he must pretend to be while he is in prison. It is a false identity created for survival in an artificial world. But this identity nonetheless emerges in the same manner as any other identity: it is learned from others, and it must be presented to, negotiated with, and validated by others. A new inmate arrives at prison with a general image of what prisoners are like, and he begins to flesh out this image from the day of his arrival, warily observing others just as they are observing him. Through watching others, through eavesdropping, through cautious conversation and selective interaction, a new inmate refines his understanding of what maximum security prisoners look like, how they talk, how they move, how they act. Despite his belief that he is different from these other prisoners, he knows that he cannot appear to be too different from them, if he is to hide his vulnerability. His initial image of other prisoners, his early observations, and his concern over how he appears to others thus provide a foundation for the identity he gradually creates through impression management.

Impression management skills, of course, are not exclusive to the prison world; a new inmate, like anyone else, has had experience in the creation of his prison identity. He has undoubtedly even had experience in presenting a "front" to others, and he draws upon his experience in projecting the very attributes—strength, stoicism, aplomb—required by his prison identity. Impression management in prison differs, however, in the totality with which it governs interactions and in the perceived costs of failure: humiliation, assault, or death. For these reasons the entire impression management process becomes a more highly conscious endeavor. When presenting himself before others, a new inmate pays close attention to such minute details of his front as eye contact, posture, and manner of walking:

> I finally got out of orientation. I was going out with the main population, going down to get my meals and things. The main thing is not to stare at a bunch of people, you know. I tried to just look ahead, you know, not stare at people. 'Cause I didn't really know; I just had to learn a little at a time.

*   *   *

> The way you look seems to be very important. The feeling is you shouldn't smile, that a frown is much more appropriate. The eyes are very important. You should never look away; it is considered a sign of weakness. Either stare straight ahead, look around, or look the person dead in the eyes. The way you walk is important. You shouldn't walk too fast; they might think you were scared and in a hurry to get away.

To create an appropriate embodiment (Weigert 1986; Stone 1962) of their prison identities, some new inmates devote long hours to weightlifting or other body-building exercises, and virtually all of them relinquish their civilian clothes—which might express their preprison identities—in favor of the standard issue clothing that most inmates wear. Whenever a new inmate is open to the view of other inmates, in fact, he is likely to relinquish most overt symbols of his individuality, in favor of a standard issue "prison inmate" appearance.

By acting self-consciously, of course, a new inmate runs the risk of exposing the fact that he *is* acting. But he sees no alternative to playing his part better; he cannot "not act" because that too would expose the vulnerability of his "true" identity. He thus sees every new prison experience, every new territory that he is allowed to explore, as a test of his impression management skills. Every nonconfrontive encounter with another inmate symbolizes his success at these skills, but it is also a social validation of his prison identity. Eventually he comes to see that many, perhaps most, inmates are engaging in the same kind of inauthentic presentations of self (cf. Glaser and Strauss 1964). Their identities are as "false" as his, and their validations of his identity may be equally false. But he realizes that he is powerless to change this state of affairs, and that he must continue to present his prison identity for as long as he remains in prison.

A first-time inmate enters prison as an outsider, and it is from an outsider's perspective that he initially creates his prison identity. In contrast to his suspended preprison identity, his prison identity is a *shared* identity, because it is modeled on his observations of other inmates. Like those of more experienced prisoners, his prison identity is tied directly to the social role of "prison inmate" (cf. Scheff 1970; Solomon 1970); because he is an outsider, however, his prison identity is also severely limited by his narrow understanding of that role. It is based on an outsider's stereotype of who a maximum security inmate is and what he acts like. It is, nonetheless, a *structural* identity (Weigert 1986), created to address his outsider's institutional problems of social isolation and inadequate information about the prison world.

By the middle of his sentence, a new inmate comes to adopt what is essentially an insider's perspective on the prison world. His prison image has evolved to the point where it is dominated by the theme of boredom rather than violence. (The possibility of violence is still acknowledged and feared, but those violent incidents that do occur have been redefined as the consequences of prison norm violations rather than as random predatory acts; see Schmid and Jones 1990.) His survival strategy, although still extant, has been supplemented by such general adaptation techniques as legal and illegal diversionary activities and conscious efforts to suppress his thoughts about the outside world (Figure 1). His impression management tactics have become second nature rather than self-conscious, as he routinely interacts with others in terms of his prison identity.

An inmate's suspension of his preprison identity, of course, is never absolute, and the separation between his suspended identity and his prison identity is never complete. He continues to interact with his visitors at least partially in terms of his preprison identity, and he is likely to have acquired at least one inmate "partner" with whom he interacts in terms of his preprison as well as his prison identity. During times of introspection, however—which take place less frequently but do not disappear—he generally continues to think of himself as being the same person he was before he came to prison. But it is also during these periods of self-dialogue that he begins to have doubts about his ability to revive his suspended identity.

That's what I worry about a lot. Because I didn't want to change. . . . I'm still fighting it, 'cause from what I understood, before, I wasn't that bad—I wasn't even violent. But I have people say stuff to me now, before I used to say "O.k., o.k."—but now it seems like I got to eye them back, you know.

*   *   *

I don't know, but I may be losing touch with the outside. I am feeling real strange during visits, very uncomfortable. I just can't seem to be myself, although I am not really sure what myself is all about. My mind really seems to be glued to the inside of these walls. I can't even really comprehend the outside. I haven't even been here three months, and I feel like I'm starting to lose it. Maybe I'm just paranoid. But during these visits I really feel like I'm acting. I'm groping for the right words, always trying to keep the conversation going. Maybe I'm just trying to present a picture that will relieve the minds of my visitors, I just don't know.

*   *   *

I realized that strength is going to be an important factor whether I'm going to turn into a cold person or whether I'm going to keep my humanitarian point of view. I knew it is going to be an internal war. It's going to take a lot of energy to do that. . . . I just keep telling myself that you gotta do it and sometimes you get to the point where you don't care anymore. You just kinda lose it and you get so full of hate, so full of frustration, it gets wound up in your head a lot.

At this point, both the inmate's suspended preprison identity and his created prison identity are part of his "performance consciousness" (Schechner 1985), although they are not given equal value. His preprison identity is grounded primarily in the memory of his biography (Weigert 1986) rather than in self-performance. His concern, during the middle of his sentence, is that he has become so accustomed to dealing with others in terms of his prison identity—that he has been presenting and receiving affirmation of this identity for so long—that it is becoming his "true" identity.[3]

An inmate's fear that he is becoming the character he has been presenting is not unfounded. All of his interactions within the prison world indicate the strong likelihood of a "role-person merger" (Turner 1978). An inmate views his presentation of his prison identity as a necessary expression of his inmate status. Unlike situational identities presented through impression management in the outside world, performance of the inmate role is transsituational and continuous. For a new inmate, prison consists almost exclusively of front regions, in which he must remain in character. As long as he is in the maximum security institution, he remains in at least partial view of the audience for which his prison identity is intended: other prison inmates.[4] Moreover, because the stakes of his performance are so high, there is little room for self-mockery or other forms of role distance (Ungar 1984; Coser 1966) from his prison identity, and there is little possibility that an inmate's performance will be "punctured" (Adler and Adler 1989) by his partner or other prison acquaintances. And because his presentation of his prison identity is continuous, he also receives continuous affirmation of this identity from others—affirmation that becomes more significant in light of the fact that he also remains removed from day-to-day reaffirmation of his preprison identity by his associates in the outside world. The inauthenticity of the process is beside the point: Stone's (1962:93) observation that "one's identity is established when others *place* him as a social object by assigning him the same words of identity that he appropriates for himself or *announces*" remains sound even when both the announcements and the placements are recognized as false.

Standing against these various forms of support for an inmate's prison identity are the inmate's resolve not to be changed in prison, the fact that his sentence is relatively brief (though many new inmates lose sight of this brevity during the middle of their careers) and the limited reaffirmation of his preprison identity that he receives from outsiders and from his partner. These are not insubstantial resources, but nor do they guarantee an inmate's future ability to discard his prison identity and revive the one he has suspended.

Identity Dialectic

When an inmate's concerns about his identity first emerge, there is little that he can do about them. He recognizes that he has no choice but to present his prison identity so, following the insider's perspective he has now adopted, he consciously attempts to suppress his concerns. Eventually, however, he must begin to consider seriously his capacity to revive his suspended identity; his identity concerns, and his belief that he must deal with them, become particularly acute if he is transferred to the minimum security unit of the prison for the final months of his sentence.[5] At the conclusion of his prison career, an inmate shifts back toward an outsider's perspective on the prison world (see Figure 1); this shift involves the dissipation of his maximum security adaptation strategy, further revision of his prison image, reconstruction of an image of the outside world, and the initial development of an outside plan.[6] The inmate's efforts to revive his suspended identity are part of this shift in perspectives.

It is primarily through a renewed self-dialogue that the inmate struggles to revive his suspended identity—a struggle that amounts to a dialectic between his suspended identity and his prison identity. Through self-dialogue he recognizes, and tries to confront, the extent to which these two identities really do differ. He again tries to differentiate himself from maximum security inmates.

> There seems to be a concern with the inmates here to be able to dis-
> tinguish . . . themselves from the other inmates. That is—they feel they
> are above the others. . . . Although they may associate with each other,
> it still seems important to degrade the majority here.

And he does have some success in freeing himself from his prison identity.

> Well, I think I am starting to soften up a little bit. I believe the identity
> I picked up in the prison is starting to leave me now that I have left the
> world of the [maximum security] joint. I find myself becoming more
> and more involved with the happenings of the outside world. I am even
> getting anxious to go out and see the sights, just to get away from this
> place.

But he recognizes that he *has* changed in prison, and that these changes run
deeper than the mask he has been presenting to others. He has not returned
to his "old self" simply because his impression management skills are used
less frequently in minimum security. He raises the question—though he
cannot answer it—of how permanent these changes are. He wonders how
much his family and friends will see him as having changed. As stated by
one of our interview respondents:

> I know I've changed a little bit. I just want to realize how the people I
> know are going to see it, because they [will] be able to see it more than
> I can see it. . . . Sometimes I just want to go somewhere and hide.

He speculates about how much the outside world—especially his own network of outside relationships—has changed in his absence. (It is his life,
not those of his family and friends, that has been suspended during his
prison sentence; he knows that changes have occurred in the outside
world, and he suspects that some of these changes may have been with-
held from him, intentionally or otherwise.) He has questions, if not serious
doubts, about his ability to "make it" on the outside, especially concerning
his relationships with others; he knows, in any case, that he cannot simply
return to the outside world as if nothing has happened. Above all, he repeatedly confronts the question of who he is, and who he will be in the
outside world.

An inmate's struggle with these questions, like his self-dialogue at the
beginning of his prison career, is necessarily a solitary activity. The identity he claims at the time of his release, in contrast to his prison identity,
cannot be learned from other inmates. Also like his earlier periods of self-
dialogue, the questions he considers are not approached in a rational, systematic manner. The process is more one of rumination—of pondering one
question until another replaces it, and then contemplating the new question until it is replaced by still another, or suppressed from his thoughts.
There is, then, no final resolution to any of the inmate's identity questions.
Each inmate confronts these questions in his own way, and each arrives at
his own understanding of who he is, based on this unfinished, unresolved

self-dialogue. In every case, however, an inmate's release identity is a synthesis of his suspended preprison identity and his prison identity.[7]

Postprison Identity

Because each inmate's release identity is the outcome of his own identity dialectic, we cannot provide a profile of the "typical" release identity. But our data do allow us to specify some of the conditions that affect this outcome. Reaffirmations of his preprison identity by outsiders—visits and furloughs during which others interact with him as if he has not changed— provide powerful support for his efforts to revive his suspended identity. These efforts are also promoted by an inmate's recollection of his preprison identity (i.e., his attempts, through self-dialogue, to assess who he was before he came to prison), by his desire to abandon his prison identity, and by his general shift back toward an outsider's perspective. But there are also several factors that favor his prison identity, including his continued use of diversionary activities; his continued periodic efforts to suppress thoughts about the outside world; his continued ability to use prison impression management skills; and his continuing sense of injustice about the treatment he has received. Strained or cautious interactions with outsiders, or unfulfilled furlough expectations, inhibit the revival of his preprison identity. And he faces direct, experiential evidence that he has changed: when a minimum security resident recognizes that he is now completely unaffected by reports of violent incidents in maximum security, he acknowledges that he is no longer the same person that he was when he entered prison. Turner (1978:1) has suggested three criteria for role-person merger: "failure of role compartmentalization, resistance to abandoning a role in the face of advantageous roles, and the acquisition of role-appropriate attitudes"; at the time of their release from prison, the inmates we studied had already accrued some experience with each of these criteria.

Just as we cannot define a typical release identity, we cannot predict these inmates' future, postprison identities, not only because we have restricted our analysis to their prison experiences but because each inmate's future identity is inherently unpredictable. What effect an ex-inmate's prison experience has on his identity depends on how he, in interaction with others, defines this experience. Some of the men we have studied will be returned to prison in the future; others will not. But all will have been changed by their prison experiences. They entered the prison world fearing for their lives; they depart with the knowledge that they have survived. On the one hand, these men are undoubtedly stronger persons by virtue of this accomplishment. On the other hand, the same tactics that enabled them to survive the prison world can be called upon, appropriately or not, in difficult situations in the outside world. To the extent that these men draw upon their prison survival tactics to cope with the hardships of the outside world—to the extent that their prison behavior becomes a meaningful part of their "role repertoire" (Turner 1978) in their everyday lives—their prison identities will have become inseparable from their "true" identities.

The Suspended Identity Model

As identity preservation tactics, an inmate's suspension of his preprison identity and development of a false prison identity are not, and cannot be, entirely successful. At the conclusion of his sentence, no inmate can ever fully revive his suspended identity; he cannot remain the same person he was before he came to prison. But his tactics do not fail entirely either. An inmate's resolve not to change, his decision to suspend his preprison identity, his belief that he will be able to revive this identity, and his subsequent struggle to revive this identity undoubtedly minimize the identity change that would otherwise have taken place. The inmate's tactics, leading up to his suspended identity dialectic, constitute an identity transformation process, summarized in Figure 2, that differs from both the gradual, sequential model of identity transformation and models of radical identity transformation (Strauss 1959). It also shares some characteristics with each of these models.

As in cases of brainwashing and conversion, there is an external change agency involved, the inmate does learn a new perspective (an insider's perspective) for evaluating himself and the world around him, and he does develop new group loyalties while his old loyalties are reduced. But unlike a radical identity transformation, the inmate does not interpret the changes that take place as changes in a *central* identity; the insider's perspective he learns and the new person he become in prison are viewed as a false front that he must present to others, but a front that does not affect who he really is. And while suspending his preprison identity necessarily entails a weakening of his outside loyalties, it does not, in most cases, destroy them. Because he never achieves more than a marginal status in the prison world, the inmate's ambivalence prevents him from accepting an insider's perspective too fully, and thus prevents him from fully severing his loyalties to the outside world (Schmid and Jones 1987). He retains a fundamental, if ambivalent, commitment to his outside world throughout his sentence, and he expects to reestablish his outside relationships (just as he expects to revive his suspended identity) when his sentence is over.

Like a religious convert who later loses his faith, an inmate cannot simply return to his old self. The liminal conditions (Turner 1977) of the prison world have removed him, for too long, from his accustomed identity bearings in everyday life. He does change in prison, but his attempts to suspend and subsequently revive his preprison identity maintain a general sense of identity continuity for most of his prison career. As in the gradual identity transformation process delineated by Strauss (1959), he recognizes changes in his identity only at periodic "turning points," especially his mid-career doubts about his ability to revive his suspended identity and his self-dialogue at the end of his sentence. Also like a gradual identity transformation, the extent of his identity change depends on a balance between the situational adjustments he has made in prison and his continuing commitments to the outside world (Becker 1960, 1964). His identity depends, in other words, on the outcome of the dialectic between his prison identity and his suspended preprison identity.

The suspended identity model is one component and a holistic analysis of the experiences of first-time, short-term inmates at a specific maximum security prison. Like any holistic analysis, its usefulness lies primarily in its capacity to explain the particular case under study (Deising 1971). We nonetheless expect similar identity transformation processes to occur under similar circumstances: among individuals who desire to preserve their identities despite finding themselves involved in temporary but encompassing social situations that subject them to new and disparate identity demands and render their prior identities inappropriate. The suspended identity model presented here provides a basis for further exploration of these circumstances.

Acknowledgments

We wish to thank Jim Thomas, Patricia A. Adler and the reviewers of *Symbolic Interaction* for their useful comments and suggestions.

Notes

1. This is a matter of some theoretical interest. Proponents of existential sociology (cf. Douglas and Johnson 1977) view feelings as the very foundation of social action, social structures, and the self. From this theoretical framework, a new inmate would be viewed as someone who has been stripped to that core of primal feelings that constitutes his existential self; the symbolic construction of his former world, including his cognitive definition of himself (learned from the definitions that others hold of him) are exposed as artificial, leaving the individual at least partially free to choose for himself what he wants to be and how he wants to present himself to others. Whether or not we view the feelings of vulnerability, discontinuity, and differentiation as the core of an inmate's self, or even as attributes of his self, we must note that the inmate does not reject his earlier self-image (or other symbolic constructions) as artificial. He continues to hold on to his preprison identity as his "true" self and he continues to view the outside world as the "real" world. It is the prison world that is viewed as artificial. His definitions of the outside world and the prison world do change during his prison career, but he never fully rejects his outsider's perspective.

2. There are four principal components to the survival strategies of the inmates we studied, in the early months of their prison sentences. "Selective interaction" and "territorial caution" are essentially precautionary guidelines that allow inmates to increase their understanding of the prison world while minimizing danger to themselves. "Partnership" is a special friendship bond between two inmates, typically based on common backgrounds and interests (including a shared uncertainty about prison life) and strengthened by the inmates' mutual exploration of a hostile prison world. The fourth component of their strategies, impression management, is discussed in subsequent sections of this article.

3. Clemmer (1958:299) has defined "prisonization" as the "taking on in greater or less degree of the folkways, mores, customs, and general culture of the penitentiary." Yet new inmates begin to "take on" these things almost immediately, as part of the impression they are attempting to present to other inmates. Thus, we would argue instead that prisonization (meaning assimilation to the prison world) begins to occur for these inmates when their prison identities become second nature—when their expressions of prison norms and customs are no

longer based on self-conscious acting. A new inmate's identity concerns, during the middle of his sentence, are essentially a recognition of this assimilation. For other examples of problems associated with double identity, see Warren and Ponse (1977) and Lemert (1967); Adler and Adler (1989) describe self-diminishment problems, as well as self-aggrandizement effects, that accompany even highly valued identity constructions.

4. This finding stands in contrast to other works on total institutions, which suggest that inmates direct their impression management tactics toward the staff. See, for example, Goffman (1961:318) and Heffernan (1972; chapter VI). First-time, short-term inmates certainly interact with guards and other staff in terms of their prison identities, but these personnel are neither the primary source of their fear nor the primary objects of their impression management. Interactions with staff are limited by a concern with how other inmates will define such interactions; in this sense, presentation of a new inmate's prison identity to staff can be viewed as part of the impression he is creating for other inmates.

5. Not all prisoners participate in this unit; inmates must apply for transfer to the unit, and their acceptance depends both on the crimes for which they were sentenced and staff evaluation of their potential for success in the unit. Our analysis focuses on those inmates who are transferred.

6. There are three features of the minimum security unit that facilitate this shift in perspectives: a more open physical and social environment; the fact that the unit lies just outside the prison wall (so that an inmate who is transferred is also physically removed from the maximum security prison); and greater opportunity for direct contact with the outside world, through greater access to telephones, an unrestricted visitor list, unrestricted visiting hours and, eventually, weekend furloughs.

7. This is an important parallel with our analysis of the inmate's changing prison definitions: his concluding prison image is a synthesis of the image he formulates before coming to prison and the image he holds at the middle of his prison career; see Schmid and Jones (1990).

References

Adler, Patricia A. and Peter Adler. 1989. "The Gloried Self: The Aggrandizement and the Constriction of Self." *Social Psychology Quarterly* 52:299–310.

Becker, Howard S. 1960. "Notes on the Concept of Commitment." *American Journal of Sociology* 66:32–40.

———. "Personal Change in Adult Life." 1964. *Sociometry* 27:40–53.

Berger, Peter L. 1963. *Invitation to Sociology: A Humanistic Perspective.* Garden City, NY: Doubleday Anchor Books.

Blumer, Herbert. 1969. *Symbolic Interactionism: Perspective and Method,* Englewood Cliffs, NJ: Prentice Hall.

———. 1972. "Action vs. Interaction: Review of *Relations in Public* by Erving Goffman." *Transaction* 9:50–53.

Boulding, Kenneth. 1961. *The Image.* Ann Arbor: University of Michigan Press.

Clemmer, Donald. 1958. *The Prison Community.* New York: Holt, Rinehart & Winston.

Coser, R. 1966. "Role Distance, Sociological Ambivalence and Traditional Status Systems." *American Journal of Sociology* 72:173–187.

Deising, Paul. 1971. *Patterns of Discovery in the Social Sciences.* Chicago: Aldine-Atherton.

Douglas, Jack D., Patricia A. Adler, Peter Adler, Andrea Fontana, Robert C. Freeman, and Joseph A. Kotarba. 1980. *Introduction to the Sociologies of Everyday Life.* Boston: Allyn and Bacon.

Douglas, Jack D. and John M. Johnson. 1977. *Existential Sociology.* Cambridge: Cambridge University Press.

Garfinkel, Harold. 1956. "Conditions of Successful Degradation Ceremonies." *American Journal of Sociology* 61:420–424.

Glaser, Barney G. and Anselm L. Strauss. 1964. "Awareness Contexts and Social Interaction." *American Sociological Review* 29:269–279.

Goffman, Erving. 1959. *The Presentation of Self in Everyday Life.* Garden City, NY: Doubleday Anchor Books.

———. 1961. *Asylums.* Garden City, NY: Doubleday Anchor Books.

———. 1963. *Stigma: Notes on the Management of Spoiled Identity.* Englewood Cliffs, NJ: Prentice Hall.

Gross, Edward and Gregory P. Stone. 1964. "Embarrassment and the Analysis of Role Requirements." *American Journal of Sociology* 70:1-15.

Heffernan, Esther. 1972. *Making It in Prison: The Square, the Cool and the Life.* New York: Wiley-Interscience.

Irwin, John. 1970. *The Felon.* Englewood Cliffs, NJ: Prentice Hall.

———. 1977. *Scenes.* Beverly Hills: Sage.

Lemert, Edwin. 1967. "Role Enactment, Self, and Identity in the Systematic Check Forger." Pp. 119-134 in *Human Deviance, Social Problems and Social Control.* Englewood Cliffs, NJ: Prentice Hall.

Lewis, David J. 1979. "A Social Behaviorist Interpretation of the Median I." *American Journal of Sociology* 84:261-287.

Messinger, Sheldon E., Harold Sampson, and Robert D. Towne. 1962. "Life as Theater: Some Notes on the Dramaturgic Approach to Social Reality." *Sociometry* 25:98-111.

Schechner, Richard. 1985. *Between Theater and Anthropology.* Philadelphia: University of Pennsylvania Press.

Scheff, Thomas. 1970. "On the Concepts of Identity and Social Relationships" Pp. 193-207 in *Human Nature and Collective Behavior,* edited by T. Shibutani. Englewood Cliffs, NJ: Prentice Hall.

Schlenker, B. 1980. *Impression Management: The Self Concept, Social Identity and Interpersonal Relations.* Belmont, CA: Wadsworth.

Schmid, Thomas and Richard Jones. 1987. "Ambivalent Actions: Prison Adaptation Strategies of New Inmates." American Society of Criminology, annual meetings, Montreal, Quebec.

———. 1990. "Experiential Orientations to the Prison Experience: The Case of First-Time, Short-Term Inmates." Pp. 189-210 in *Perspectives on Social Problems,* edited by Gale Miller and James A. Holstein. Greenwich, CT: JAI Press.

Solomon, David N. 1970. "Role and Self-Conception: Adaptation and Change in Occupations." Pp. 286-300 in *Human Nature and Collective Behavior,* edited by T. Shibutani. Englewood Cliffs, NJ: Prentice Hall.

Stone, Gregory P. 1962. "Appearance and the Self." Pp. 86-118 in *Human Behavior and Social Processes,* edited by Arnold Rose. Boston: Houghton Mifflin.

Strauss, Anselm L. 1959. *Mirrors and Masks: The Search for Identity.* Glencoe: The Free Press.

Sykes, Gresham. 1958. *The Society of Captives: A Study of a Maximum Security Prison.* Princeton: Princeton University Press.

Turner, Ralph H. 1978. "The Role and the Person." *American Journal of Sociology* 84:1-23.

Turner, Victor. 1977. *The Ritual Process: Structure and Anti-Structure.* Ithaca, NY: Cornell University Press.

Ungar, Sheldon. 1984. "Self-Mockery: An Alternative Form of Self-Presentation." *Symbolic Interaction* 7:121-133.

Warren, Carol A. and Barbara Ponse. 1977. "The Existential Self in the Gay World." Pp. 273-289 in *Existential Sociology,* edited by Jack D. Douglas and John M. Johnson. Cambridge: Cambridge University Press.

Weigert, Andrew J. 1986. "The Social Production of Identity: Metatheoretical Foundations." *Sociological Quarterly* 27:165-183.

Zurcher, Louis A. 1977. *The Mutable Self.* Beverly Hills: Sage.

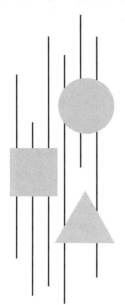

PART ——— V

Building Deviant
Careers and Identities

In Part IV, we described how institutional careers and identities may be produced. The material in that section examined how various types of institutional typing and processing may affect an actor's personal and public identity, as well as self-image. An equally important concern is the way in which noninstitutional careers evolve. As we noted earlier, such careers or activities generally arise as a result of an actor's own desires and needs; this means that frequently the actor plays an assertive role in moving into a particular type of activity, consciously structuring and presenting a specific image of self to others. Often, as the general introduction indicates, there may be a degree of overlap between institutional and noninstitutional careers. For instance, prostitutes, skid-row alcoholics, homosexuals, and thieves may be arrested and thus pulled into, rather than intentionally entering, an institutional career. Although the distinction between institutional and noninstitutional careers is useful analytically, we must recognize that if an actor is to assume the status of a secondary or career deviant, he or she must become familiar with and act in accord with existing ideology, culture, practices, and traditions. Obtaining a more complete understanding of how a deviant career or identity is actually built, however, requires that we initially examine an occupation's or profession's underlying organizational structures and associated ideologies. Once such elements have been located, characterized, described, and set, we are in a much better position to understand such processes as recruitment and socialization.

Organizational Structures, Ideologies, and Recruitment: The Noninstitutional Backdrop

"The Social Organization of Deviants," by Joel Best and David F. Luckenbill, provides an excellent framework for understanding the social organizations in which deviants become involved. The authors make an initial distinction between the social organization of *deviants* and the social organization of *deviance*. The former refers to the "patterns of relationships between deviant actors," whereas the latter refers to the "patterns of relationships between the various roles performed in deviant transactions." Best and Luckenbill elect to focus on the social organization of deviants. Deviant organizations, they reason, can vary along certain dimensions, most notably in terms of their sophistication (i.e., complexity, degree of coordination, and purposiveness). For example, with regard to complexity, organizations can have varying divisions of labor, degrees of stratification, and degrees of role specialization. Best and Luckenbill note that, in terms of sophistication, deviants organize in identifiable ways. They discuss five organizational forms: loners, colleagues, peers, mobs, and formal organizations. Each of these forms can be analyzed relative to four variables: whether the deviants associate with each other, whether they engage in deviance together, whether there is an elaborate division of labor, and whether activities extend over time and space. The authors describe various types of each organizational form. They then examine the consequences of organizing as loners, colleagues, peers, mobs, or formal organizations. Best and Luckenbill argue that the degree of sophistication of a deviant organization has consequences for deviants and social-control agents. Five propositions are advanced in support of this argument. The authors' second hypothesis is especially relevant for the next section on entering and learning about deviant cultures. Specifically, they hypothesize that "the more sophisticated the form of deviant organization, the more elaborate the socialization of its members." The underlying assumption here is that "neophyte deviants" not only must learn how to perform deviant acts and attain the appropriate skills and techniques, but they must also develop a *cognitive perspective* (e.g., learn the relevant rationalizations and language). For example, loners do not depend on others for instruction, but pool hustlers do.

Phyllis Coontz, in "Managing the Action: Sports Bookmakers as Entrepreneurs," examines the social organizational and occupational features of bookmaking. Bookmaking shares many common features with other forms of deviance. For example, getting into the business requires contact with others—current or former participants—and learning the skills and attitudes favorable to bookmaking occurs through interaction. To be successful in any deviant career requires a level of individual and organizational sophistication; this is true of bookies, who cannot openly advertise their services but who are dependent on "paying customers." Minimizing risk is essential both with regard to avoiding apprehension by social-control agents and with regard to avoiding economic loss. Possessing and applying specialized skills and knowledge help the bookie continue to operate. Coontz also shows that certain organizational features contribute directly to the length of a bookie's career. She demonstrates that bookmaking is significantly different in a number of ways (e.g., career duration) from many other deviant careers.

Coontz's analysis suggests that in many ways, the social organization of bookmaking shelters bookies from arrest, prosecution, jail or prison time, and the like. There are also several features that serve an insulating function. Initially, there is no material exchange, and taking the bet requires only a verbal agreement between the one placing the bet and the bookmaker. Further, face-to-face interaction is not required, and there are no middlemen—no producers, no suppliers, no vendors. These features minimize the risk of detection and help to solidify and extend the deviant career.

One of the many interesting observations revolves around the relationships that exist between the bookmaker and the client in deviant transactions. Bookies have no legal recourse for clients who do not pay their debts. It is essential, therefore, that the bookie operate honestly and with integrity with each customer. Commitment to conventional values such as these contributes to long-term career paths by reducing competition and insuring faithful clientele and suggests an entrepreneurial approach to deviant careers such as bookmaking.

35 The Social Organization of Deviants

Joel Best
David F. Luckenbill

Ethnographic research on particular social scenes provides data for general, grounded theories (Glaser and Strauss, 1967). For the study of deviance, field studies have supplied the basis for the development of general theories of the social psychology of deviance (Goffman, 1963; Lofland, 1969; Matza, 1969). However, while several reports about specific forms of deviance focus on social organization (Einstader, 1969; McIntosh, 1971; Mileski and Black, 1972; Shover, 1977; Zimmerman and Wieder, 1977), there is no satisfactory general theory of the social organization of deviance.

Sociologists of varying perspectives have debated the nature of social organization among juvenile delinquents, professional criminals, organized criminals and white-collar criminals. Others have developed typologies of deviants that include social organizational features (Clinard and Quinney, 1973; Gibbons, 1965, 1977; Miller, 1978). However, these statements of social organization suffer from several flaws. First, they are often too narrow, focusing on a single type of deviance, such as burglary or more broadly, crime. Second, they usually are content with describing the organizational forms of different types of deviance. They fail to locate such forms along a dimension of organization or examine the consequences of organizational differences for deviants and social control agents. Third, they typically confuse two different bases for analyzing social organization: a general theory must distinguish between the social organization of *deviants* (the patterns of relationships between deviant actors) and the social organization of *deviance* (the patterns of relationships between the various roles performed in deviant transactions).

In this paper, we present a framework for understanding the social organization of deviants.[1] By examining reports of field research, several forms of social organization are identified and located along a dimension of organizational sophistication. Then some propositions are developed regarding the consequences of organizational variation for deviants and social control agents. Finally, some implications for the study of social organization are considered.

Forms of Deviant Organization

The social organization of deviants refers to the structure or patterns of relationships among deviant actors in the context of deviant pursuits. The social organization of deviants varies along a dimension of sophistication. Organizational sophistication involves the elements of complexity, coordination and purposiveness (cf. Cressey, 1972). Organizations vary in the complexity of their division of labor including the size of membership, degree of stratification, and degree of specialization of organizational roles. Organizations also vary in their coordination among roles including the degree to which rules, agreements, and codes regulating relationships are formalized and enforced. Finally, organizations vary in the purposiveness with which they specify, strive toward, and achieve their objectives. Forms of organization which display high levels of complexity, coordination, and purposiveness are more sophisticated than those forms with lower levels.

Research reports suggest that deviants organize in several identifiable ways along the dimension of sophistication. Beginning with the least sophisticated, we will discuss five forms: loners, colleagues, peers, mobs and formal organizations. These organizational forms can be defined in terms of four variables: (1) whether the deviants associate with one another; (2) whether they participate in deviance together; (3) whether their deviance requires an elaborate division of labor; and (4) whether their organization's activities extend over time and space (see Table 1). *Loners* do not associate with other deviants, participate in shared deviance, have a division of labor, or maintain their deviance over extended time and space. *Colleagues* differ from loners because they associate with fellow deviants. *Peers* not only associate with one another, but also participate in deviance

Table 1 Characteristics of Different Forms of the Social Organization of Deviants

	Type of Organization				
Variable	Loners	Colleagues	Peers	Mobs	Formal Organizations
Mutual association	−	+	+	+	+
Mutual participation	−	−	+	+	+
Division of labor	−	−	−	+	+
Extended organization	−	−	−	−	+

together. In *mobs,* the shared participation requires an elaborate division of labor. Finally, *formal organizations* involve mutual association and participation, an elaborate division of labor, and deviant undertakings extended over time and space.

The descriptions of these forms of organization must be qualified in two ways. First, the forms are presented as ideal types. There is variation among the types of deviants within each form, as well as between one form and another. The intent is to sketch out the typical features of each form, recognizing that particular types of deviants may not share all of the features of their form to the same degree. Organizational sophistication can be viewed as a continuum, with deviants located between, as well as on, the five points. Describing a number of forms along this continuum inevitably understates the complexities of social life. Second, the descriptions of these forms draw largely from field studies of deviance in the contemporary United States, and attempt to locate the deviants studied along the dimension of organizational sophistication. A particular type of deviant can be organized in various ways in different societies and at different times. The references to specific field studies are intended to place familiar pieces of research within this framework; they are not claims that particular types of deviants invariably organize in a given way.

Loners

Some deviants operate as individuals. These loners do not associate with other deviants for purposes of sociability, the performance of deviant activities, or the exchange of supplies and information. Rather, they must supply themselves with whatever knowledge, skill, equipment and ideology their deviance requires. Loners lack deviant associations, so they cannot receive such crucial forms of feedback as moral support or information about their performance, new opportunities, or changes in social control strategies. They often enter deviance as a defensive response to private troubles (Lofland, 1969). Because their entry does not require contact with other deviants, as long as they can socialize themselves, loners frequently come from segments of the population which are less likely to be involved in the more sophisticated forms of deviance; it is not uncommon for loners to be middle-aged, middle-class or female. Because their deviance often is defensive, and because they lack the support of other deviants, loners' careers typically are short-lived. Examples of loners include murderers (Luckenbill, 1977), rapists (Amir, 1971), embezzlers (Cressey, 1953), check forgers (Lemert, 1967:99–134; Klein and Montague, 1977), physician narcotic addicts (Winick, 1961), compulsive criminals (Cressey, 1962), heterosexual transvestites (Buckner, 1970), amateur shoplifters (Cameron, 1964), some gamblers (Lesieur, 1977), and many computer criminals (Parker, 1976).[2]

Colleagues

Like loners, colleagues perform as individuals. Unlike loners, however, colleagues associate with others involved in the same kind of deviance. Colleagues thus form a simple group which provides important services for members. First, colleagues often socialize newcomers, providing training in deviant skills as well as an ideology which accounts for and justifies their deviance. Association also offers sociability among members with whom one's deviant identity need not be concealed: an actor can take down his or her guard without fear of discovery by agents of social control (Goffman, 1959, 1963). Also, association provides a source of information about ways to obtain deviant equipment, new techniques, new opportunities for engaging in deviance, and strategies for avoiding sanctioning. Colleagues learn and are held to a loose set of norms which direct conduct in both deviant and respectable activities. "Don't inform on a colleague" and "Never cut in on a colleague's score" exemplify such norms. The moral climate established by these expectations increases the stability of colleagues' social scene. At the same time, only some deviant activities and some people are suited for such a loose form of organization. A successful career as a colleague depends ultimately on the individual's performance when operating alone. As a result, newcomers often sample the scene and, when they encounter difficulties, drift away. Only the more successful colleagues maintain extended deviant careers. Some examples of colleagues include most prostitutes (Hirschi, 1962; Bryan, 1965, 1966), pimps (Milner and Milner, 1972), and pool hustlers (Polsky, 1967).

Peers

Like colleagues, peers associate with one another and benefit from services provided by their fellows. Peers are involved in the socialization of novices, considerable sociable interaction, and the maintenance of a loose, unwritten code of conduct to be followed by individuals who wish to remain in the peer group. Unlike colleagues, peers participate in deviant acts together; they are involved in deviant transactions at the same time and in the same place. In some cases, such mutual participation is required by the nature of the deviant activity. This is exemplified in the performance of homosexual acts, or in the "task force raids" where a collection of young men engages in simple acts of violence such as gang fighting or rolling drunks (Cressey, 1972). In other cases, mutual participation is required because peers form a network for supplying one another with essential goods and services, as found in the distribution of illicit drugs. In either event, peers interact basically as equals; there is a minimal division of labor and specialized roles are uncommon. Although individuals pass through these social scenes, peer groups often are quite stable, perhaps because peer groups solve structural problems within society for their members. Two common varieties of deviant peers are young people who have not yet entered integrated adult work roles, and those who frequent a deviant marketplace and depend on their contacts with one another for the satisfaction of illicit needs. Examples of peers include hobos (Anderson, 1923), homosexuals (Humphreys, 1970; Mileski and Black, 1972; Warren, 1974), group-oriented gamblers (Lesieur, 1977), swingers (Bartell, 1971), gang delinquents (Shaw, 1930; Matza, 1964; Rosenberg and Silverstein, 1969), motorcycle outlaws (Thompson, 1966), skid row tramps (Wiseman, 1970; Rubington, 1978), and illicit drug users (Blumer, 1967; Carey, 1968; Feldman, 1968; Stoddart, 1974).

Mobs

Mobs are small groups of professional or career deviants organized to pursue specific, profitable goals.[3] Their deviance requires the coordinated actions of members performing specialized roles—a more sophisticated division of labor than that found among peers. Thus, work is divided among confidence artists (the inside man and the outside man), pickpockets (the tool and the stall), or card and dice hustlers (the mechanic and the shootup man; Maurer, 1962, 1964; Prus and Sharper, 1977). Ordinarily, at least one of the roles in the mob is highly skilled, requiring considerable practice and training to perfect. This training (normally via apprenticeship), the need for on-the-job coordination, and the common practice of traveling from city to city as a mob lead to intensive interaction between mobsters. Elaborate technical argots develop, as well as elaborate codes specifying mobsters' obligations to each other.

Mobs have complex links to outsiders. They are organized to accomplish profitable yet safe crimes. McIntosh (1971) describes the historical shift from craft thieving, where mobs develop routine procedures for stealing relatively small sums from individuals, to project thieving, where larger amounts are taken from corporate targets using procedures specifically tailored to the particular crime. In either case, mob operations are planned and staged with an eye toward avoiding arrest. Also, mobs may attempt to neutralize the criminal justice system by bribing social control agents not to make arrests, "fixing" those cases where arrests take place, or making restitution to victims in return for dropped charges. Mobs also have ties to others who purchase stolen goods, provide legal services, and supply information and deviant equipment. Finally, a network of sociable and business contacts ties mobs to one another, enabling strategic information to spread quickly. These arrangements ensure that mobs can operate at a consistently profitable level with minimal interference. Consequently, the careers of individual mobsters, as well as those of specific mobs, seem to be more stable than those of deviants organized in less sophisticated ways.[4] Examples of mobs are the groups of professional criminals specializing in confidence games (Sutherland, 1937; Maurer, 1962), picking pockets (Maurer, 1964), shoplifting (Cameron, 1964), armed robbery (Einstader, 1969; Letkemann, 1973), burglary (Shover, 1977), and card and dice hustling (Prus and Sharper, 1977).

Formal Organizations

Formal organizations of deviants differ from mobs in the scope of their actions.[5] Normally they involve more people, but, more importantly, their actions are coordinated to efficiently handle deviant tasks on a routine basis over considerable time and space. While mobsters work as a group in a series of episodic attacks, formal organizations are characterized by delegated responsibility and by routine and steady levels of productivity. In many ways, formal organizations of deviants share the features which characterize such respectable bureaucracies as military organizations, churches, and business firms. They have a hierarchal division of labor, including both vertical and horizontal differentiation of positions and roles and established channels for vertical and horizontal communication. A deviant formal organization may contain departments for planning, processing goods, public relations and rule enforcement, with positions for strategists, coordinators, accountants, lawyers, enforcers, and dealers in illicit goods. There may be recruitment policies for filling these diversified positions, and entry into the organization may be marked by a ritual ceremony of passage. Formal organizations usually have binding, but normally unwritten, rules and codes for guiding members in organizational action, and these rules are actively enforced.

Formal organizations of deviants can make large profits by operating efficiently. At the same time, they must protect themselves from harm or destruction. As in less sophisticated forms of organization, loyal members are expected to maintain the group's secrets. In addition, deviant formal organizations attempt to locate power in the office, rather than in an individual charismatic leader. Although charismatic leadership obviously plays a part in some deviant formal organizations, the successful organization is able to continue operations when a leader dies or is arrested. Finally, deviant formal organizations typically invest considerable energy in neutralizing the criminal justice system by corrupting both high- and low-level officials. The scope and efficiency of their operations, their organizational flexibility, and their ties to agencies of social control make formal organizations of deviants extremely stable. Examples of such deviant formal organizations include very large urban street gangs (Keiser, 1969; Dawley, 1973), smuggling rings (Green, 1969), and organized crime "families" (Cressey, 1969; Ianni, 1972).

The Significance of the Social Organization of Deviants

The identification and description of these different organizational forms permit a comparative analysis. What are the consequences of organizing as loners, colleagues, peers, mobs, or formal organizations? A comparison suggests that the sophistication of a form of deviant social organization has several consequences for both deviants and social control agents. Five propositions can be advanced.

I. *The more sophisticated the form of deviant organization, the greater its members' capability for complex deviant operations.* Deviant activities, like conventional activities, vary in their complexity. The complexity of a deviant operation refers to the number of elements required to carry it through; the more component parts to an activity, the more complex it is.[6] Compared to simple activities, complex lines of action demand more careful preparation and execution and take longer to complete. The complexity of a deviant activity depends upon two identifiable types of elements. First, there are the *resources* which the actors must be able to draw upon. Some activities require that the deviant utilize special knowledge, skill, equipment, or social status in order to complete the operation successfully, while simple acts can be carried out without such resources. Second, the *organization of the deviant transaction* affects an activity's complexity.[7] Some deviant acts can be accomplished with a single actor, while others require two or more people. The actors in a transaction can share a common role, as in a skid row bottle gang, or the transaction may demand different roles, such as offender and victim or buyer and seller. Furthermore, the degree to which these roles must be coordinated, ranging from the minimal coordination of juvenile vandals to the precision routines performed by mobs of pickpockets, varies among situations. The more people involved, the more roles they perform; and the more coordination between those roles, the more complex the deviant transaction's organization. The more resources and organization involved in a deviant operation, the more complex the operation is.

In general, deviants in more sophisticated forms of organization commit more complex acts.[8] The deviant acts of loners tend to be simple, requiring little in the way of resources or organization. Although colleagues work apart from one another, they generally share certain resources, such as shared areas. The hustlers' pool hall and the prostitutes' red light district contain the elements needed to carry out deviant operations, including victims and clients. Peers may interact in situations where they are the only ones present, performing complementary or comparable roles, as when two people engage in homosexual intercourse or a group of motorcycle outlaws makes a "run." Peers also may undertake activities which involve nonmembers, as when members of a delinquent gang rob a passerby. The activities carried out by mobs involve substantially more coordination among the members' roles. In an armed robbery, for instance, one member may be assigned to take the money, while a second provides "cover" and a third waits for the others in the car, ready to drive away on their return. Finally, the activities of formal organizations tend to be particularly complex, requiring substantial resources and elaborate organization. Major off-track betting operations, with staff members at local, district and regional offices who carry out a variety of clerical and supervisory tasks on a daily basis,, represent an exceedingly complex form of deviance.

The relationship between the sophistication of organization and the complexity of deviant activities is not perfect. Loners can engage in acts of considerable complexity, for example. The computer criminal who single-handedly devises a complicated method of breaking into and stealing from computerized records, the embezzler who carries through an elaborate series of illicit financial manipulations, and the physician who juggles drug records in order to maintain his or her addiction to narcotics are engaged in complex offenses requiring substantial resources. However, these offenses cannot be committed by everyone. These loners draw upon resources which they command through their conventional positions, turning them to deviant uses. The computer criminal typically is an experienced programmer, the embezzler must occupy a position of financial trust, and the physician has been trained in the use of drugs. Possessing these resources makes the loner's deviance possible. Thus, the more concentrated the resources necessary for a deviant operation, the less sophisticated the form of organization required. However, when resources are not concentrated, then more sophisticated forms of organization are necessary to undertake more complex deviant operations.

Sophisticated forms of deviant organization have advantages beyond being able to undertake complex operations by pooling resources distributed among their members. Some deviant activities require a minimal level of organization; for example, homosexual intercourse demands the participation of two parties. In many other cases, it may be possible to carry out a deviant line of action using a relatively unsophisticated form of organization, but the task is considerably easier if a sophisticated form of organization can be employed. This is so because more sophisticated forms of deviant organization enjoy several advantages: they are capable of conducting a larger number of deviant operations; the operations can occur with greater frequency and over a broader range of territory; and, as discussed below, the members are better protected from the actions of social control agents. Of course, sophisticated organizations may engage in relatively simple forms of deviance, but the deviant act is often only one component in a larger organizational context. Taking a particular bet in the policy racket is a simple act, but the racket itself, handling thousands of bets, is complex indeed. Similarly, a murder which terminates a barroom dispute between two casual acquaintances is very different from an execution which is ordered and carried out by members of a formal organization, even though the two acts may appear equally simple. In the latter case, the killing may be intended as a means of maintaining discipline by demonstrating the organization's ability to levy sanctions against wayward members.

II. *The more sophisticated the form of deviant organization, the more elaborate the socialization of its members.* Neophyte deviants need to acquire two types of knowledge: (1) they must learn how to perform deviant acts, and how to gain appropriate *skills and techniques;* (2) they must develop a *cognitive perspective,* a distinctive way of making sense of their new, deviant world (cf. Shibutani, 1961:118–127). Such a perspective includes an ideology which accounts for the deviance, the individual's participation in deviance, and the organizational form, as well as a distinctive language for speaking about these and other matters.

As forms of deviant organization increase in sophistication, socialization becomes more elaborate. Loners do not depend upon other deviants for instruction in deviant skills or for a special cognitive perspective; they learn through their participation in conventional social scenes. Murderers, for instance, learn from their involvement in conventional life how to respond in situations of interpersonal conflict, and they employ culturally widespread justifications for killing people (Bohannon, 1960; Wolfgang and Ferracuti, 1967). Embezzlers learn the technique for converting a financial trust in the course of respectable vocational training, adapting justifications such as "borrowing" from conventional business ideology (Cressey, 1953). In contrast, colleagues teach one another a great deal. Although pool hustlers usually know how to shoot pool before they enter hustling, their colleagues provide a rich cognitive perspective, including a sense of "we-ness," some norms of behavior, a system for stratifying the hustling world, and an extensive argot (Polsky, 1967).[9] Peers receive similar training or, in some cases, teach one another through a process of emerging norms (Turner, 1964). Juvenile vandals, for example, can devise new offenses through their mutually constructed interpretation of what is appropriate to a particular situation (Wade, 1967). Sometimes, the knowledge peers acquire has largely symbolic functions that affirm the group's solidarity, as when a club of motorcycle outlaws devises a written constitution governing its members (Reynolds, 1967:134–136). In mobs and formal organizations, the cognitive perspective focuses on more practical matters; their codes of conduct specify the responsibilities members have in their dealings with one another, social control agents and others. Greater emphasis is also placed on the acquisition of specialized skills, with an experienced deviant coaching an apprentice, frequently over an extended period of time.

Two circumstances affect the socialization process in different forms of deviant organization. First, the sophistication of the organization affects the scope and style of the training process. The amount of training tends to increase with the sophistication of the organization. The skills required to perform deviant roles vary, but there is a tendency for more sophisticated forms of organization to incorporate highly skilled roles. Further, the more sophisticated forms of organization often embody cognitive perspectives of such breadth that the deviant must acquire a large body of specialized knowledge. In addition, the socialization process tends to be organized differently in different forms of deviant organization. While loners serve as their own agents of socialization, and colleagues and peers may socialize one another, mobs and formal organizations almost always teach newcomers through apprenticeship to an experienced deviant. Second, the socialization process is affected by the newcomer's motivation for entering deviance. Loners, of course, choose deviance on their own. In the more sophisticated forms, newcomers may ask for admission, but they often are recruited by experienced deviants. While peers may recruit widely, as when a delinquent gang tries to enlist all of the neighborhood boys of a given age, mobs and formal organizations recruit selectively, judging the character and commitment of prospective members and sometimes demanding evidence of skill or prior experience. For loners, entry into deviance frequently is a defensive act, intended to ward off some immediate threat. Peers, on the other hand, often are using deviance to experience stimulation; their deviance has an adventurous quality (Lofland, 1969). In contrast, mobs and formal organizations adopt a more professional approach: deviance is instrumental, a calculated means of acquiring economic profits.[10] These differences in the scope of socialization, the way the process is organized, and the neophyte's motivation account for the relationship between sophistication of organization and the elaborateness of the socialization.

III. *The more sophisticated the form of deviant organization, the more elaborate the services provided its members.* Every social role poses practical problems for its performers. In some cases these problems can be solved by providing the actors with supplies of various sorts. Actors may require certain *equipment* to perform a role. They may also need *information* about their situation in order to coordinate their behavior with the ongoing action and successfully accomplish their part in an operation. One function of deviant social organization is to solve such practical problems by supplying members with needed equipment and information. More sophisticated forms of social organization are capable of providing more of these services.

Deviants differ in their requirements for equipment. Some need little in the way of equipment; a mugger may be able to get by with a piece of pipe. In other cases, deviants make use of specialized items which have few, if any, respectable uses (e.g., heroin or the booster boxes used in shoplifting).[11] Most loners require little equipment. When specialized needs exist, they are met through conventional channels accessible to the deviants, as when a physician narcotic addict obtains illicit drugs from hospital or clinic supplies. Colleagues also supply their own equipment, for the most part, although they may receive some assistance; pool hustlers, for example, provide their own cues, but they may rely on financial backers for funding.

Peers adopt various patterns toward equipment. In some cases, peer groups develop to facilitate the distribution and consumption of deviant goods, such as illicit drugs. In other instances, peers use equipment as a symbol of their deviant status, as when gang members wear special costumes. The equipment used by mobsters is more utilitarian; many of their trades demand specialized tools, for safecracking, shoplifting and so forth. In addition to a craftsman's personal equipment, the mob may require special materials for a specific project. Norms often exist that specify the manner in which these equipment purchases will be financed. In still other instances, some mobsters with expensive pieces of equipment may cooperate with several different mobs who wish to make use of them (such as the "big store" which is centrally located for the use of several confidence mobs). Formal organizations also have extensive equipment requirements. Because their operations extend over considerable time, formal organizations may find it expedient to invest in an elaborate array of fixed equipment. Off-track bookmaking, for example, may involve the purchase or rental of offices, desks, calculators, computer lines, special telephone lines, office supplies and automobiles. Special staff members may have the responsibility for maintaining this equipment (Bell, 1962:134). In addition, some formal organizations are involved in producing or distributing deviant equipment for the consumption of other deviants; drug smuggling offers the best example.

Deviants need information in order to determine their courses of action. To operate efficiently, they need to know about new opportunities for deviant action; to operate safely, they need to know about the movements of social control agents. The more sophisticated forms of organization have definite advantages in acquiring and processing information. Loners, of course, depend upon themselves for information; opportunities or threats outside their notice cannot be taken into account. Colleagues and peers can learn more by virtue of their contacts with the deviant "grapevine," and they may have norms regarding a member's responsibility to share relevant information. In mobs, information is sought in more systematic ways. In the course of their careers, mobsters develop perceptual skills, enabling them to "case" possible targets (Letkemann, 1973). In addition, some mobs rely on outsiders for information; spotters may be paid a commission for pointing out opportunities for theft. A formal organization can rely upon its widely distributed membership for information and its contacts with corrupted social control agents.

The degree to which deviants need special supplies varies with the requirements of their operations, the frequency with which they interact with victims or other nondeviants, and their visibility to social control agents. Supplies other than equipment and information may be required in some instances. However, for most supply problems, sophisticated forms of social organization enjoy a comparative advantage.

IV. *The more sophisticated the form of deviant organization, the greater its members' involvement in deviance.* Complex deviant operations require planning and coordinated action during the deviant act. Socialization and supply also involve interaction among an organization's members. More sophisticated forms of deviant organization, featuring complex operations and elaborate socialization and supply, are therefore more likely to involve intensive social contact with one's fellow deviants. Furthermore, because deviants face sanctions from social control agents and respectable people, their contacts with other deviants are an important source of social support. The differences in the ability of forms and social organization to provide support for their members have important social psychological consequences for deviants' careers and identities.

The dimensions of deviant careers vary from the form of deviant organization. Longer deviant careers tend to occur in more sophisticated forms of organization. For naive loners, deviance can comprise a single episode, a defensive act to ward off an immediate threat. For systematic loners, and many colleagues and peers, involvement in deviance is limited to one period in their life. Prostitutes grow too old to compete in the sexual marketplace, delinquents move into respectable adult work roles, and so forth. Members of mobs and formal organizations are more likely to have extended careers. Where the roles are not too physically demanding, deviance can continue until the individual is ready to retire from the work force (Inciardi, 1977). Deviant careers also vary in the amount of time they demand while the individual is active; some kinds of deviance take up only a small portion of the person's hours, but other deviant roles are equivalent to full-time, conventional jobs. Although the relationship is not perfect, part-time deviance is associated with less sophisticated forms of deviant organization.[12]

Social organization is also related to the relative prominence of the deviant identity in the individual's self-concept. Individuals may view their deviance as tangential to the major themes in their lives, or as a central focus, an identity around which much of one's life is arranged. The latter pattern is more likely to develop in sophisticated forms of deviant organization, for, as Lofland (1969) points out, several factors associated with deviant social organization facilitate the assumption of deviant identity, including frequenting places populated by deviants, obtaining deviant equipment, and receiving instruction in deviant skills and ideology. These factors also would appear to be associated with the maintenance of deviance as a central identity. Loners seem especially adept at isolating their deviance, viewing it as an exception to the generally conventional pattern their lives take. This is particularly true when the deviance was initially undertaken to defend that conventional life style from some threat. Even when an individual is relatively committed to deviance, normal identities can serve as an important resource. In his discussion of the World War II underground, Aubert (1965) notes that normal identities served to protect its members. In the same way, an established normal status shields the deviant from the suspicion of social control agents and, if the members refrain from revealing their conventional identities to one another, against discovery brought about by deviant associates who invade their respectable lives. Such considerations seem to be most important in middle-class peer groups organized around occasional leisure-time participation in a deviant marketplace, such as homosexuality and swinging.[13] Other deviants, particularly members of mobs and formal organizations, may associate with their fellows away from deviant operations, so that both their work and their sociable interaction take place among deviants. This is also true for peer groups that expand into "communities" and offer a wide range of services to members. Active members of urban gay communities can largely restrict their contacts to other homosexuals (Harry and Devall, 1978; Wolf, 1979). In these cases there is little need to perform conventional roles, aside from their obvious uses as concealment, and the deviant identity is likely to be central for the individual.

The degree to which an individual finds a deviant career and a deviant identity satisfying depends, in part, on the form of deviant organization of which he or she is a part. As in any activity, persons continue to engage in deviance only as long as the rewards it offers are greater than the rewards which could be obtained through alternative activities. The relevant rewards vary from one person to the next and from one type of deviance to another; a partial list includes money, physical and emotional satisfaction, valued social contacts, and prestige. Because the relative importance of these rewards varies with the individual, it is impossible to measure the differences in rewards between forms of deviant organization. There is some evidence that monetary profits are generally higher in more sophisticated forms of deviant organization. While an occasional loner can steal a very large sum through an embezzlement or a computer crime, most mobs can earn a reasonably steady income, and rackets run by formal organizations consistently bring in high profits. A more revealing measure of satisfaction is career stability; members of more sophisticated forms of deviant organization are more likely to remain in deviance. Loners' careers are short-lived, even when they are involved in systematic deviance. Lemert's (1967) account of the failure of professional forgers to remain at large suggests that the lack of social support is critical. As noted above, persons frequently drift out of their roles as colleagues and peers when other options become more attractive. The long-term careers of members of mobs and formal organizations suggest that these forms are more likely to satisfy the deviant.[14]

V. *The more sophisticated the form of deviant organization, the more secure its members' deviant operations.* The social organization of deviants affects the interaction between deviants and social control agents. This relationship is complicated because increased sophistication has consequences which would seem to make social control effects both easier and more difficult. On the one hand, the more sophisticated the deviant organization, the greater its public visibility and its chances of being subject to social control actions. Because more sophisticated forms of organization have more complex deviant operations, there are more people involved with the organization as members, victims, customers and bystanders. Therefore, there are more people capable of supplying the authorities with information about the identities, operations, and locations of organizational members. On the other hand, more sophisticated forms of organization are more likely to have codes of conduct requiring their members to be loyal to the organization and to maintain its secrets. Further, more sophisticated forms of organization command resources which can be used to protect the organization and its members from social control agents. While highly sophisticated organizations find it more difficult to conceal the fact that deviance is taking place, they often are more successful at shielding their members from severe sanctions.

Notes

1. A second paper, in preparation, will discuss the social organization of deviance.

2. Following Lemert (1967), loners can be subdivided into naive loners, for whom deviance is an exceptional, one-time experience, and systematic loners, whose deviance forms a repeated pattern. Lemert's analysis of the problems confronting systematic check forgers, who have trouble maintaining a deviant identity with little social support, suggests that systematic loners may have particularly instable careers.

3. The term "mob," as it is used here, is drawn from the glossary in Sutherland: "A group of thieves who work together; same as 'troupe' and 'outfit'" (1937:239; cf. Maurer, 1962, 1964). A more recent study uses the term "crew" (Prus and Sharper, 1977).

4. Although the mob is able to accomplish its ends more efficiently, the same tasks are sometimes handled by loners. For example, see Maurer (1964:166–168) and Prus and Sharper (1977:22).

5. Our use of the term "formal organization" is not meant to imply that these organizations have all of the characteristics of an established bureaucracy. Rather, "formal" points to the deliberately designed structure of the organization—a usage consistent with Blau and Scott (1962:5).

6. The complexity of a deviant activity must be distinguished from two other types of complexity. First, the definition of organizational sophistication, given above, included the complexity of the division of labor among the deviants in a given organizational form as one criterion of sophistication. Second, the complexity of an activity should not be confused with the complexity of its explanation. A suicide, for example, can be easily accomplished, even though a complex social-psychological analysis may be required to explain the act.

7. This point illustrates the distinction, made earlier, between the social organization of deviance (the pattern of relationships between the roles performed in a deviant transaction) and the social organization of deviants (the pattern of relationships between deviant actors). The former, not the latter, affects an activity's complexity.

8. In most cases, loners do not possess the resources required for more than one type of complex deviance; physicians, for instance, are unable to commit computer thefts. In contrast, members of more sophisticated forms of organization may be able to manage several types of operations, as when a mob's members shift from picking pockets to shoplifting in order to avoid the police, or when an organized crime family is involved in several different rackets simultaneously (Maurer, 1964; Ianni, 1972:87–106).

9. Within a given form of organization, some cognitive perspectives may be more elaborate than others. While pool hustlers have a strong oral tradition, founded on the many hours they share together in pool halls, prostitutes have a relatively limited argot. Maurer (1939) argues that this is due to the restricted contact they have with one another during their work.

10. Here and elsewhere, colleagues represent a partial exception to the pattern. Colleagues resemble members of mobs and formal organizations in that they adopt an instrumental

perspective, view deviance as a career, are socialized through apprenticeship to an experienced deviant, and accept deviance as a central identity. While peers have a more sophisticated form of organization, their mutual participation in deviance is based on their shared involvement in an illicit marketplace or leisure-time activity. In contrast, colleagues usually are committed to deviance as means of earning a living.

Yet, because colleagues share a relatively unsophisticated form of organization, they labor under restrictions greater than those faced by mobs and formal organizations. Socialization is of limited scope; call girls learn about handling money and difficult clients, but little about sexual skills (Bryan, 1965). The code of conduct governing colleagues is less encompassing and less binding than those for more sophisticated forms, and the deviance of colleagues is usually less profitable. The absence of the advantages associated with organizational sophistication leads colleagues, despite their similarities to mobs and formal organizations, into an unstable situation where many individuals drift away from deviance.

11. Sometimes such equipment is defined as illicit, and its possession constitutes a crime.

12. Two reasons can be offered to explain this relationship. If a type of deviance is not profitable enough to support the individual, it may be necessary to take other work, as when a pool hustler moonlights (Polsky, 1967). Also, many loners have only a marginal commitment to deviance and choose to allocate most of their time to their respectable roles. This is particularly easy if the form of deviance requires little time for preparation and commission.

13. Swingers meeting new couples avoid giving names or information which could be used to identify them (Bartell, 1971:92–95); and Humphreys (1970) emphasizes that many tearoom participants are attracted by the setting's assurance of anonymity.

14. During their careers, deviants may shift from one organizational form or one type of offense to another. The habitual felons interviewed by Petersilia et al. (1978) reported that, while many of their offenses as juveniles involved more than one partner (presumably members of a peer group), they preferred to work alone or with a single partner on the crimes they committed as adults. The most common pattern was for juveniles who specialized in burglaries to turn to robbery when they became adults.

References

Amir, Menachem
    1971 Patterns in Forcible Rape. Chicago: University of Chicago Press.
Anderson, Nels
    1923 The Hobo. Chicago: University of Chicago Press.
Aubert, Vilhelm
    1965 The Hidden Society. Totowa, N.J.: Bedminster.
Bartell, Gilbert
    1971 Group Sex. New York: New American.
Bell, Daniel
    1962 The End of Ideology. Revised edition. New York: Collier.
Blau, Peter M. and W. Richard Scott
    1962 Formal Organizations. San Francisco: Chandler.
Blumer, Herbert
    1967 The World of Youthful Drug Use. Berkeley: University of California Press.
Bohannon, Paul
    1960 African Homicide and Suicide. Princeton: Princeton University Press.
Bryan, James H.
    1965 "Apprenticeships in prostitution." Social Problems 12:287–297.
    1966 "Occupational ideologies and individual attitudes of call girls." Social Problems 13:441–450.
Buckner, H. Taylor
    1970 "The transvestic career path." Psychiatry 33:381–389.
Cameron, Mary Owen
    1964 The Booster and the Snitch. New York: Free Press.
Carey, James T.
    1968 The College Drug Scene. Englewood Cliffs, N.J.: Prentice Hall.

Clinard, Marshall B. and Richard Quinney
1973 Criminal Behavior Systems: A Typology. Second edition. New York: Holt, Rinehart and Winston.
Cressey, Donald R.
1953 Other People's Money. New York: Free Press.
1962 "Role theory, differential association, and compulsive crimes." Pp. 443–467 in Arnold M. Rose (ed.), Human Behavior and Social Processes. Boston: Houghton Mifflin.
1969 Theft of the Nation. New York: Harper & Row.
1972 Criminal Organization. New York: Harper & Row.
Dawley, David
1973 A Nation of Lords. Garden City, N.Y.: Anchor.
Einstader, Werner J.
1969 "The social organization of armed robbery." Social Problems 17:64–83.
Feldman, Harvey W.
1968 "Ideological supports to becoming and remaining a heroin addict." Journal of Health and Social Behavior 9:131–139.
Gibbons, Don C.
1965 Changing the Lawbreaker. Englewood Cliffs, N.J.: Prentice-Hall.
1977 Society, Crime, and Criminal Careers. Third edition. Englewood Cliffs, N.J.: Prentice-Hall.
Glaser, Barney G. and Anselm L. Strauss
1967 The Discovery of Grounded Theory. Chicago: Aldine.
Goffman, Erving
1959 The Presentation of Self in Everyday Life. Garden City, N.Y.: Anchor.
1963 Stigma. Englewood Cliffs, N.J.: Prentice-Hall.
Green, Timothy
1969 The Smugglers. New York: Walker.
Harry, Joseph and William B. Devall
1978 The Social Organization of Gay Males. New York: Praeger.
Hirschi, Travis
1962 "The professional prostitute." Berkeley Journal of Sociology 7:33–49.
Humphreys, Laud
1970 Tearoom Trade. Chicago: Aldine.
Ianni, Francis A. J.
1972 A Family Business. New York: Sage.
Inciardi, James A.
1977 "In search of the class cannon." Pp. 55–77 in Robert S. Weppner (ed.), Street Ethnography. Beverly Hills, Calif.: Sage.
Keiser, R. Lincoln
1969 The Vice Lords. New York: Holt, Rinehart and Winston
Klein, John F. and Arthur Montague
1977 Check Forgers. Lexington, Mass.: Lexington.
Lemert, Edwin M.
1967 Human Deviance, Social Problems, and Social Control. Englewood Cliffs, N.J.: Prentice-Hall.
Lesieur, Henry R.
1977 The Chase. Garden City, N.Y.: Anchor.
Letkemann, Peter
1973 Crime as Work. Englewood Cliffs, N.J.: Prentice-Hall.
Lofland, John
1969 Deviance and Identity. Englewood Cliffs, N.J.: Prentice-Hall.
Luckenbill, David F.
1977 "Criminal homicide as a situated transaction." Social Problems 25:176–186.

Matza, David
    1964 Delinquency and Drift. New York: Wiley.
    1969 Becoming Deviant. Englewood Cliffs, N.J.: Prentice-Hall.
Maurer, David W.
    1939 "Prostitutes and criminal argots." American Journal of Sociology 44:346–350.
    1962 The Big Con. New York: New American.
    1964 Whiz Mob. New Haven, Conn.: College and University Press.
McIntosh, Mary
    1971 "Changes in the organization of thieving." Pp. 98-133 in Stanley Cohen (ed.), Images of Deviance. Baltimore, Maryland: Penguin.
Mileski, Maureen and Donald J. Black
    1972 "The social organization of homosexuality." Urban Life and Culture 1:131-166.
Miller, Gale
    1978 Odd Jobs: The World of Deviant Work. Englewood Cliffs, N.J.: Prentice-Hall.
Milner, Christina and Richard Milner
    1972 Black Players. Boston: Little, Brown.
Parker, Donn B.
    1976 Crime by Computer. New York: Scribner's.
Petersilia, Joan, Peter W. Greenwood and Marvin Lavin
    1978 Criminal Careers of Habitual Felons. Santa Monica, Calif.: Rand.
Polsky, Ned
    1967 Hustlers, Beats, and Others. Chicago: Aldine.
Prus, Robert C. and C. R. D. Sharper
    1977 Road Hustler. Lexington, Mass.: Lexington.
Reynolds, Frank
    1967 Freewheelin' Frank. New York: Grove.
Rosenberg, Bernard and Harry Silverstein
    1969 Varieties of Delinquent Experience. Waltham, Mass.: Blaisdell.
Rubington, Earl
    1978 "Variations in bottle-gang controls." Pp. 383-391 in Earl Rubington and Martin S. Weinberg (eds.), Deviance: The Interactionist Perspective. Third edition. New York: Macmillan.
Shaw, Clifford R.
    1930 The Jack-Roller. Chicago: University of Chicago Press.
Shibutani, Tamotsu
    1961 Society and Personality. Englewood Cliffs, N.J.: Prentice-Hall.
Shover, Neal
    1977 "The social organization of burglary." Social Problems 20:499-514.
Stoddart, Kenneth
    1974 "The facts of life about dope." Urban Life and Culture 3:179-204.
Sutherland, Edwin H.
    1937 The Professional Thief. Chicago: University of Chicago Press.
Thompson, Hunter S.
    1966 Hell's Angels. New York: Ballantine.
Turner, Ralph H.
    1964 "Collective behavior." Pp. 382-425 in Robert E. L. Faris (ed.), Handbook of Modern Sociology. Chicago: Rand McNally.
Wade, Andrew L.
    1967 "Social processes in the act of juvenile vandalism." Pp. 94-109 in Marshall B. Clinard and Richard Quinney (eds.), Criminal Behavior Systems: A Typology. New York: Holt, Rinehart and Winston.

Warren, Carol A. B.
  1974 Identity and Community in the Gay World. New York: Wiley.
Winick, Charles
  1961 "Physician narcotic addicts." Social Problems 9:174–186.
Wiseman, Jacqueline P.
  1970 Stations of the Lost. Englewood Cliffs, N.J.: Prentice-Hall.
Wolf, Deborah G.
  1979 The Lesbian Community. Berkeley: University of California Press.
Wolfgang, Marvin E. and Franco Ferracuti
  1967 The Subculture of Violence. London: Tavistock.
Zimmerman, Don H. and D. Lawrence Wieder
  1977 "You can't help but get stoned." Social Problems 25:198–207.

36 Managing the Action: Sports Bookmakers as Entrepreneurs

Phyllis Coontz

More and more states have moved to legalize various forms of gambling as a viable way to raise substantial revenues. And while some have considered adding sports betting to their menu of games, Nevada continues to be the only state where placing a bet on sports events is legal. This is both puzzling and ironic considering the popularity of gambling and the prominence of sports. Despite the lack of concrete knowledge about illegal sports betting, two justifications for keeping it illegal have dominated the public debate. The first has to do with whether legal sports betting could successfully compete with illegal operations were it to be legalized and the second has to do with a purported link between gambling on sports and organized crime.

This paper focuses on the second line of argument and examines the social, organizational, and occupational features of bookmaking. If bookmakers are conduits for organized crime, as is claimed, there should be evidence of this in the day-to-day activities of bookmaking and in the career trajectories of bookmakers. The analysis is based upon interviews with 47 sports bookmakers working in the Rust Belt region. Drawing upon what sports bookies themselves have to say about their experiences in the business and their career trajectories, there appears to be little merit to the organized crime link argument. The analysis suggests that unlike other types of deviance, the social organization of bookmaking insulates bookies from the more typical consequences associated with frequent and prolonged deviant activity, for example, getting arrested, being prosecuted, serving time in prison, and forced association with other criminals. In fact, the findings suggest that bookies are more like entrepreneurs than criminals. While a single study cannot resolve the normative question about whether sports bookmaking should be criminalized, the findings do show that the social construction of bookmaking and bookmakers found in the public debate and popular culture does not reflect the reality of sports bookmaking.

504

Introduction

As a cultural phenomenon, gambling in the United States has been an enduring contradiction—while it is widespread it is also heavily regulated. Despite the growth of commercialized gambling since the 1960s, some forms of gambling remain off limits. One of these is sports betting.[1] Betting on sports events is illegal in every state except Nevada. This is somewhat puzzling given the popularity of both gambling and sports.

One of the ironies of this is that while Nevada is the only state that allows sports betting, one of the accoutrements for gambling on sports, i.e., the "line"[2] or "point spread," can be found everywhere. It appears daily in the sports section of most major newspapers; it is a link on numerous sports news websites; it is central to sports commentary about winners, losers, and outcomes on network and cable television; it is packaged as advice that can be purchased through various sports services through 900 telephone numbers; and it is woven into conversations that take place at work, in restaurants, classrooms, dorms, country clubs, bars, and parties every day around the country. It is even available through one of the more than 700 gambling casinos operating on the Internet.

Some have suggested that sports betting might be the number one form of gambling (legal or illegal) in the United States (Scarne 1974; Reuter 1983; Congressional Hearings 1995). Industry analysts (e.g., Moody's and Standard and Poor) report that sports betting is one of the biggest growth areas in commercialized gambling (Moody's Industry Review 1995:L46). For example, by the end of fiscal year 1996, bookmakers in Las Vegas handled $2.5 billion in wagers (O'Brien 1998). And according to the Gaming Control Board of Nevada, the amount wagered on sports events has been increasing every year and more sports events are being added to the menu. For example, sports books in Las Vegas added last year's Women's World Cup soccer final to their array of events. Focusing on only a single event, the Super Bowl, the amount wagered almost doubled from $40 million in 1991 to $70 million in 1997 (personal communication, Research Division, June 1998). While illicit wagers are far more difficult to track, it is estimated that in 1997

---

[1] Congress passed legislation in 1992 that prevents any state from legalizing sports betting well into the future.

[2] The daily line refers to betting odds. It consists of the number of points a favored team is penalized in order to win. Since the majority of sports events do not involve equally matched teams in terms of talent, performance, or record, the superior team would almost always win the contest. Such predictability is not very interesting. Although there is a lack of consensus about the origin of the line, it was not widely used until after World War II. The line makes a game more interesting because it equalizes unevenly matched teams with a handicap. For example in the 1999 Super Bowl, the Denver Broncos were the defending Super Bowl champions and favored to beat Atlanta by 7½ points. Denver was assessed a 7½ point deficit while Atlanta was given a 7½ point advantage to the final score. This meant that Denver had to win by more than 7½ points and Atlanta could lose by less than 7½ points for bettors to win. The final score was 34 to 19 in Denver's favor. Denver won the game and bettors that took Denver won their bets.

alone, over $100 billion was wagered illegally on sports (U.S. News & World Report 1997).

Given the magnitude of legal or illegal sports betting and the popularity of sports, it is difficult to understand why it continues to be outlawed. Of course, sociologists have long recognized that a behavior's legal status has little to do with its popularity, intrinsic harm, or even desirability. Far more important in determining legal status is the way the behavior is socially constructed. In the case of sports betting, we see that one of the dominant social constructions involves bookmakers as unsavory characters with ties to the underworld. For example, supporters of the Professional and Amateur Sports Protection Act of 1992 argued that "[I]nstead of standing for healthy competition through team work and honest preparation, professional sport contests would come to represent the fast buck, the quick fix, and the desire to get something for nothing. Betting would undermine the integrity of team sports and public confidence in them. . . . Fans could not help but wonder if a missed free throw, a dropped fly ball, or a missed extra point was part of a player's scheme to fix the game" (S-474, pg S-7302 Temp. Record). Other advocates of criminalization allege a link between bookmaking and organized crime and argue that it is a major source of its total gambling revenue (Cressey 1969; The President's Commission on Law Enforcement and Administration of Justice 1967; Clark 1971). The criminal construction is also common in our popular culture, particularly in films such as *Wiseguy 1986, Goodfellas 1990,* and *Casino 1995* and novels such as Gay Talese's *Honor Thy Father,* Mario Puzo's *The Godfather,* and most recently Bill Bonanno's *Bound by Honor.*

How closely do the social constructions presented in the public debate and the popular culture mirror reality? The research on bookmaking shows that what is known about sports bookies, their methods of operation, career trajectories, life styles, and relationships with each other is limited, fragmented, and largely inferred. Some research on bookmaking generally suggests that instead of being members of a larger criminal syndicate, bookmakers are more likely to operate as a loose confederation of independents that may at times cooperate with one another (Chambliss 1978; Anderson 1979; Reuter and Rubinstein 1982; Reuter 1983; Rosencrance 1987; Sasuly 1982). Despite the lack of empirical evidence about the nature of sports bookmaking, the image of the sports bookie as criminal is pervasive.

This study set out to learn about sports bookmaking from those who do it. The assumption was that if sports bookies are a part of an organized crime syndicate, then there should be some evidence of it in the day-to-day operations of bookmaking. The study examines the social organization of bookmaking and the occupational features of being a sports bookie. This approach is useful because it allows us to move beyond the criminal aspects of sports bookmaking and consider what is actually involved in operating a sports book. That is, what sorts of skills, knowledge, processes, and contexts are needed to get into and manage a sports book.

The analysis draws upon face-to-face interviews with 47 different book-makers operating in Western Pennsylvania. This researcher examines how one becomes a sports bookmaker; how sports bookmakers manage and grow their business; their relationships with bettors, other sports book-makers, law enforcement officials, and family; and finally, how they exit the business. If sports bookmaking is indeed a part of a larger criminal or-ganization then it is reasonable to expect that entry into and departure from the business would be determined by the larger organization; that the day-to-day operations would follow norms and practices dictated and moni-tored by an outside organization; and that the conditions under which bookmakers transact business with bettors would involve criminal ele-ments such as coercion, dishonesty, and bribery.

Background for the Study

Although I have been interested in deviant behavior for more than 20 years, I became interested in sports betting only recently through a friend. It happened during dinner with this friend about six years ago when she excused herself so that she could call her bookie to place a bet on a foot-ball game. I didn't know she gambled on sports, and she certainly did not fit my image of someone who would know a bookie. She was a professional and civic minded and did not resemble my image of someone who associ-ated with bookies. This contradiction between my friend and my beliefs piqued my curiosity and is what led to this research.

When I thought about the source of my beliefs, I realized they came mostly from the literature on organized crime and popular culture. I did a thorough literature review and discovered that there was little empirical knowledge about sports bookmaking. In order to learn what sports book-making was all about I would need to do some field work and find bookies who were willing to talk about bookmaking. Like most field work on illicit activities, one needs a contact to gain access. I explained my growing inter-est to my friend and asked whether she would vouch for me with her bookie. My plan was to place bets with her bookie, develop a relationship with him, and then explore whether he would talk to me about the business. For the next several months I placed bets on different football games for an entire season. Eventually, I shared my research interest with my bookie and he agreed to be interviewed. The first interview took place in my home. Si-multaneously, I began talking more openly and frequently with friends, ac-quaintances, and colleagues about betting on sports events and discovered that many of the people I came into contact with—both socially and profes-sionally—bet on sporting events. These interactions led to contacts with other bookies, many of whom agreed to be interviewed. Over the course of a two-year period I interviewed a total of 47 bookies at least once and had follow-up interviews with 11 of them. All of the interviews were tape recorded, transcribed, and analyzed using NUD*IST (a computer based text analysis program). The findings presented here reflect major aspects of the organizational and occupations dimensions of the bookmaking business.

With the exception of the interviews with my bookie, all other interviews took place in locations selected by the bookmakers. Typically we met in restaurants, private clubs, and bars. The interview format focused on the process by which sports bookmakers got involved in the business; their strategies for building and maintaining their business; the duration of their involvement in the business; their relationships with other bookmakers; experiences with outside pressure (from law enforcement, other bookmakers, or professional criminals); the size of their business; the volume of the action; their families and friends; and their perceptions of the business, themselves, and its legal status. I begin the analysis with a general profile of the bookies that participated in this study.

Demographic and General Information about Sports Bookies

All bookmakers were male and ranged in age from 22–72 years old. The mean age for this group was 46. When asked about female bookmakers, I was told that none operated in this region, although some had heard about female sports bookies working elsewhere. All of my informants were originally from the region. All but two of my informants were currently married or living with someone, and all but five had children. Five had gotten divorced as a result of their bookmaking activities, and four remarried. Ninety-one percent ($n = 43$) were currently employed or self-employed in a legitimate job and five reported relying solely on earnings from bookmaking at different times. Four of my informants did not finish high school, 34 completed high school, and 7 completed college. Of those who completed college, one had a graduate degree and another was studying for an MBA.

On average these men had been involved in bookmaking for 17 years, ranging from a low of 2 years to a high of 45 years. None would reveal the amount of income earned from their bookmaking activities explaining their actual income was contingent on a number of factors such as the amount of a bet, the kind of bet made, the number of winners and losers, and whether losers paid their losses. However, all of the bookies in this study reported making money from bookmaking.[3] Most experienced occasional "off" periods meaning they paid out more than they brought in. And one informant revealed he lost $96,000 the first year he went into business.

---

[3] The informant with the legal island sports book (available through the Internet and 900 access) confided that he made "so much money it would make you crazy." Another informant was under a federal indictment for income tax evasion on an estimated $12 million allegedly made over a nine-month period.

Like other illegal markets, sports betting is a cash business—all transactions are conducted with cash. Payouts were usually made midweek (typically Wednesdays) while collections were made the first part of the week (typically Mondays) and took place at designated locations, which were typically public. If a customer was unable to pay their losses in full, terms were established without an interest penalty. Although there are numerous kinds of wagers that can be made, the four most common were: straight bets,[4] over and under bets,[5] teasers,[6] and parlays.[7] The amount wagered varied by customer, but the average wager was $50.00 per game. All of these bookies established a minimum and maximum amount they would accept with the majority not willing to accept wagers over $5,000. Five, however, accepted bets for $10,000 and occasionally more. The majority accepted wagers only on the day of the game (and usually approximately 30 minutes before the start of a game), but some would accept bets when the line first came out.

The Mechanics of Sports Bookmaking

The "line" which is the basis for taking bets serves two general purposes: (1) to encourage the gambling public to gamble on both opponents playing a game and (2) to balance the amount of money wagered equally between both teams so that amount is equally divided between both teams. According to the "Roxy" Roxborough, the guru of the Las Vegas Line, "the fundamental concept of bookmaking is to force people to gamble . . . at odds favorable to the house. The line is used to encourage gambling by equalizing the contest" (Cook 1992). Sports bookies could care less about who wins or loses a game; they are interested in the final score and whether they have more losers than winners for any given game. The point spread then is the bookie's management tool for balancing the betting action on individual games.

The following illustrates how the point spread works. The Super Bowl is the final championship game between the two Conferences in the National Football League (NFL). Although each Conference has a champion,

---

[4] A straight bet is based on the point spread. If the game is between the Denver Broncos and New York Jets and 12 points favor Denver, and the bettor took Denver to win, then Denver would need to win by a score of at least 12 points. The New York Jets on the other hand would receive 12 points and they could lose by a total of 7 points, but a bettor would still win the bet if they took the Jets because there was still 5 points leeway.

[5] For over and under bets, the bettor is gambling on whether the teams will score above the total for the game or below the total. In the Denver Bronco/New York Jet example, suppose the total was 55 points—the bettor would either gamble that the total score would be above 55 or below 55 depending on the direction the bet was made.

[6] In teasers, the bettor is given 5 points to add to the team the gamble is on and 7 points on the over and under point spread. In the Denver Bronco/New York Jet example, if the bettor were taking a teaser on Denver, in the over and under bets and Denver is favored by 12, then they would be given 5 points to subtract from the 12 points in the point spread and 7 points to add or subtract from the total score of 55—either a total of 62 or 48 depending on the direction.

[7] Parlays involve making wagers on multiple (2 or 3) teams at a time. The odds are better, but to win, all teams included in the parlay must win.

one is usually perceived to be stronger than the other (this is based on a combination of record, performance, and hype). In Super Bowl XXX (for the 1995–96 season) the Dallas Cowboys (the National Football Conference [NFC] champions) and the Pittsburgh Steelers (the American Football Conference [AFC] champions) played for the championship. At the time, the NFC and Dallas Cowboys were perceived to be superior to the AFC and Pittsburgh Steelers. Based on this alone, the outcome of the game was seen as a foregone conclusion—Dallas would win.

If you know the outcome of a game before it starts, it will not be very interesting. Because so many matchups are between unequal teams, the line equalizes the contest by giving the underdog an advantage. When the line came out for Super Bowl XXX it was set at 14 points, favoring Dallas. Translated, a 14-point spread meant that the Cowboys would need to win by more than two touchdowns. The question raised by such a high point spread for the bettor, and the question the bookie hopes the bettor will ask, is whether the Cowboys can beat the Steelers by more than 14 points.[8] The line alters what is otherwise a foregone conclusion and entices bettors to put money on the underdog.

Getting into the Business

As argued earlier, if sports bookmaking is controlled by outside interests, then getting into the business should be determined by those associated with these interests. At a minimum, if the external control allegation has merit, there should be accounts of being recruited, coerced, pressured, or getting permission to get started from bookies. None of the bookies reported external pressure—all entered the business voluntarily and most viewed their entry as an opportunity to make money. The oldest bookie in the study, Artie, started out as a numbers runner for another bookmaker when he was only 8 years old. In fact, he told me that during his early years (which he characterized as "hard times") he was the sole support for his family (including his parents and siblings). Artie was the only bookie I interviewed who progressed from numbers to sports bookmaking. He worked in the numbers business for over 30 years and then moved into sports bookmaking when he was in his early 40s.

> I ran numbers and made a pretty nice income for a kid. If you hustled $400–$500 worth, you could make a nice piece of change. I took care of my family—I literally paid the bills. I learned from one of the smartest guys in the area. He's dead now, but he was smart, very wise— he was a cousin of my mother's. He liked me, and he took me under his wing. I used to hang around him and one day he asked me if I

---

[8] If the difference in the score is exactly 14 points, the game is a "push" which means there are no winners and no losers.

wanted to do something for him. He sent me out to pick up the day's business—in a paper bag. I brought it back and he put me to work. He trusted me even though I was just a kid, he had confidence in me. You can't imagine how good I felt 'cause I looked up to him, he had something and everybody, they admired him too. He trusted me—this skinny kid. My mother didn't like it, but at the time, I was the only one working and bringing any money in. I made enough to pay the rent, food, and utilities. Times were hard back then.

Before setting up their own bookmaking operations, betting on sports had been an integral part of every bookie's everyday experiences. Joe, who is in his 50s and operated a legitimate sports book in the Caribbean, grew up around bookies and bettors. He entered the business as a young man while working in the steel mills and began his involvement as a favor to a coworker.

I was helping a guy I worked with out. A lotta guys bet with him and he couldn't handle it one weekend cause he was sick. We were buddies, he trusted me and asked me to help him out. I took all the action that weekend even though I didn't know what I was doin'. After spending that weekend on the phone I told my buddy I wanted to work with him and I did. The rest is history as they say. After a while I went on my own, I worked every day which is tough when you're workin too, especially during basketball and baseball season. You're takin action all day and all night long. You gotta time everything. You're on the phone all day and sometimes all night. How many games are played in a day during March Madness? You could have a couple dozen games in one day. My first wife really hated it cause I couldn't leave, we didn't go out—I worked all week and I was on the phone all weekend till the games were over. And if I had a bad day, if I got upset—I was an animal. One time I got so upset, I threw a chair through the TV. That was a long time ago, I'm still embarrassed by it. My kids hated it, too. Like now, they'd never get involved with it cause they saw what it did to me—my wife left me 'cause of it—it's your whole life. Things are different now though. The business in the islands, it's legitimate, it's totally different. I have time to enjoy all my hard work—I'm making so much money down there it'd make you crazy. I'm paying taxes, everything's legitimate. My second wife and I can travel, we can go wherever we want and do whatever we want. I could never make this kind of money at anything else. And the way I look at it, I've earned it 'cause I worked hard for over 30 years.

Steve, a student studying for his MBA at an area university at the time I interviewed him, said he was motivated by what he saw was a way to make money. Steve explains:

There was a guy in the dorm and everyone bet with him. I started watching him and saw the potential for making money and thought to myself, 'hey I can do that.' So, one Saturday I started, just like that, with just a few guys I knew. At first I used the local line in the newspaper and I'd talk to other guys to see what they were gettin. I only deal with students around here, so it's not too complicated. I mean, at first I kept track of everything in my head, but as I took on more customers I had to write things down—I couldn't keep them straight. I was doin pretty well and after a couple of months I had over 70 regulars. Then I got a couple of friends of mine involved, 'cause I needed the help—I give 'em a few bucks to help me out. You know, I'm not doin this forever, but for right now it pays the bills—I'm paying for school. I really don't want to have any debt when I graduate.

There was no evidence of coercion, pressure, or an apprenticeship to get into the business. The two main routes through which bookies got into the business were through their personal relationships and perceived economic opportunities. In all cases, entry was voluntary and situational.

Managing and Building the Business

Since bookies can never be certain of the number of bets that will be made on a given game or the amount wagered, being successful involves more than simply taking the action. While several factors affect success, five appear to be common among all bookies: knowledge of sports, building a credible customer base, volatility in the market, productivity of the bookmaker, and avoiding arrest. Roger, a young former bookie who now operates a legitimate sports betting advice service, explains how knowledge of sports plays an integral role in bookmaking and succeeding in the business.

I read everything that's printed about the games and players. I did that when I was in the business and I'm doing it right now. Every morning I'm on the Internet reading what the sports writers have to say, looking at statistics, checkin' the weather conditions, going over last year's statistics, everything. I study; study so I can handicap each game. Half my day is spent digesting information. We offer 1 or 2 picks each week—and my track record is pretty good on this, mostly winners. I miss it now and then, but when you put all the facts and figures together with what the sports experts are saying, then you're more likely to come up with winners. Even though I'm on the other side of the business now, the same rules apply. Rule number one is that you've got to pay attention to the details. When I was takin bets, the only way you could make money was if your people picked losers. They're always looking at the Internet, the paper, and checkin with friends. So if you're gonna make money, you gotta have a solid line—one that's based on the facts and figures of the game. I handicapped all my games, see some guys get their lines from the books in Vegas, but not me, I did it myself. I always prided myself on offering a precise line especially on close games—you know, ½ point difference or maybe a 1 point difference on a close game can make a huge difference. And ½ point is appealing to a lot of bettors. You gotta be firm about your line too. Once you set it, it's the same for everybody. I like to think of myself as an expert on these games—you know, Jimmy the Greek. I've studied them all my life—ask me anything and I can tell you. Bettors are emotional, so they don't think about that ½ point difference—they're gonna go with their hearts. If the bookie's gonna make money, you gotta get 'em to go with their favorites and you do that by a solid line. You don't have to be perfect all the time, 50% of the time will do.

The illegal status of bookmaking limits what bookmakers can do to attract customers. They cannot advertise or make cold calls from the phonebook or random digit dialing, yet a successful bookmaking business requires a customer base. How do bookies build a customer base? Jimmy, a 22-year veteran, claims that the customers are just there waiting for bookies because of the popularity of sports.

Who doesn't like sports? Everybody loves sports—and betting on them is part of the entertainment. Ever been to a Steelers game? Look around right before a game. You see all these guys on the horn talking to guys like me. Betting makes a game interesting. Every guy I ever knew from my neighborhood and school bet on games. My Dad even bet—on boxing matches. My brother bet. Since I got into the business, I never had any trouble findin' customers. Listen, they're just there waiting to give you their business. Some of my customers I've known since school, some of 'em I work with, some I've met here or there. I've even had guys give me customers. You know my brother brought customers to me. My sister's husband bets with me. My biggest problem is keeping it manageable and making sure I got good people. I don't want too many customers, you know I work and that complicates things a little. Fifty, sixty's about all I can handle at a time. It seems like if I lose one, then I pick up another one or two.

In addition to building a customer base, bookmakers assume the financial risks in their business. Like any for profit business, the focus is on the bottom line which means bookies must be attuned to the market, especially patterns and changes in betting action. Volatility of the market affects success and while the line enables the bookie to balance the action between opposing teams, it is insufficient by itself for ensuring a profit. Knowing this, bookies take other steps to minimize potential risks from dramatic swings in the action. According to Carl, who has been in the business for 18 years, limiting your customer base and setting a maximum limit on wagers are two such steps.

If you're gonna hold everything yourself, you've got to have a minimum of 40 players. Right now I got about 100 people. You've gotta have a strong limit, say $500 and not take any more on a game from any one person because if you get 20 of those people giving you a $500 bet, you've got $10,000 you could lose.

An instrumental factor that affects success is knowing how closely specific customers fit the average customer profile. For example, bookies know that bettors tend to wager on multiple games. Multiple game bettors always work to the bookie's advantage and Tony, who has been in the business for 25 years, explains why:

> As you research this, you'll find out that the more games people play, the more chance the bookie has to make money. They gotta pick about 66% to break even. They don't realize it 'cause everybody thinks if they pick 50% they're even, but they're not, they're losing money cause you gotta pay the juice.[9] For the customer to come out ahead, they gotta pick about 66% of the time. There's only one way to make money betting and that's to bet one game. Of course, most people bet a lot of games and they bet their hearts—which is good for the bookie.

Like many small businesses, bookmaking requires a high degree of commitment from the bookie. I frequently heard this level of commitment described in terms of bookmaking being a bookie's life. Bookmaking has a higher priority than other activities. To sustain a business for any length of time, bookies must set aside their other interests and be on call for their customers. Depending on the sports season this could range from every day to every weekend of that season. The bookie must learn to manage his time and balance his bookmaking responsibilities against other responsibilities. Sam describes the various ways that bookmaking consumes the bookie's life.

> You can work year round or you can work a couple seasons. See there's a sport for every season. I work year round. Football's not so bad, but basketball, baseball, and hockey'll kill you—every single day, six and seven days a week. If you're gonna work year round, you basically have no life outside of this. It's not over just 'cause the phones stop ringin' either. You gotta keep track of everything and I don't know many guys who can just turn out the light after the phones stop. I have my set times see, so half hour before a game starts I'm taking action. I get all my 7 and 8:00 games startin at 6:30. Now Sunday football, I've got my 1:00 games and I start around 12:40, my 4:00 games I start around 3:40, and my 9:00 game I start at 8:45. You've gotta little free time in between, but then you're watchin the game to see whether you're makin money. Some games don't end till after midnight. Then I gotta get up and go to work. My wife complains, less now than she used to. I guess she's used to it now. I think the extra money helps. She likes to go out, so I get someone to take over for a day or night. I got a couple of guys who'll do that, you know, answer the phone for me. We always go away in the summer, but I don't relax, 'cause I'm worrying about things. I'm checking every day when I'm away. It's just part of you, it's there all the time.

With the exception of online sports books (who accept credit cards), bookmaking is strictly a cash business. Thus, having customers who are

[9] The "juice" refers to the fee the customer pays the bookie when he loses a bet.

willing to pay their losses is essential for profitability. In lieu of a credit report, the bookie depends on informal means of scrutinizing customers. Typically customers are acquired in two ways: either by referral from other customers (which happened in my case) or directly by knowing the customer. What happens when a customer refuses to pay the bookie? Although proponents of criminalization argue that bookies resort to the corruption and extortion to collect gambling debts, none of the bookies I talked to engaged in these practices. Instead, they avoid potential losses by screening their customer. Ray, who has been in the business for 35 years, describes how this process works:

> You see, it's not illegal to place a bet, but you can't take bets—that's why you always gotta watch yourself; most guys know that. You gotta know who you're dealing with. I don't take on anybody I don't know. I check, check, check. Say some guy calls me and wants me to take his action. If I don't know him, I won't do it 'cause I don't need the aggravation. I had to learn this though. There was a guy—oh this was about 15 years ago—who bet with a bunch of different guys. Back then what I thought was important was the numbers. I didn't know the guy so well, but I took his bets anyway. He ran up quite a number with me—he owed me about $10,000. I'd call him and he'd tell me he'd have something for me next week. Well, he never gave me a thing—this happened over and over again. Then one night I see the guy out, and he's buying drinks for everybody, playing the big shot. The guy owes me $10,000 and he's buying people drinks. I was mad. I went up to him and said, 'hey where's my money?' The guy was a jerk; he stammered around and told me that if I didn't leave him alone he'd call the feds. He owes me and he's gonna call the feds. I don't want the feds bothering me, I'm not interested in goin' to prison and I don't want anybody checking up on what I'm doing. I knew right then I'd never see any of it and that the guy was a jerk. So what I did was put the word out that he wasn't paying up, that he wasn't good for his bets. You gotta understand, this is a disease for someone like this guy—he just has to bet and there's nothin worse you can do to somebody who likes to bet than to cut him off. When the word is out, nobody will take their action. The only way someone would take his action is if he put money up first.

As discussed earlier, the line is used to balance the action between two teams. There are times however when the betting public is not enticed by fluctuations in the line. When there is more money wagered on one team than another, the bookie could end up having to pay out more than he takes in—a situation he wants to avoid. A degree of bettor psychology is relevant in such cases. Bookies know that sentimentality motivates many bettors. Sentimentality is the tendency to bet on the hometown team—or as one bookie described it, to "bet with your heart." For example, in the recent NBA championship game between the Indiana Pacers and the Los Angeles Lakers, the majority of bettors in the L.A. area bet on the Lakers while the majority of bettors from the Midwest bet on the Pacers. Sentimentality also can explain regional variations in betting patterns, and bookies must always be aware of potential regional differences in betting patterns, and adjust accordingly. When it is impossible to balance the action, bookies can hedge their losses by selling their action to other bookmakers. This practice is called "laying off." Every bookmaker in this study had connections with a layoff bookmaker. Sam, a 17-year veteran, discusses the way sentimentality works:

> What you wanna do is get equal amounts of money on both sides. This is a Steeler town so when the line first came out at 14 then 13½ for the Super Bowl (1995), all the money was on Pittsburgh. I lowered it to 12, but still everyone was takin' Pittsburgh. Even at 12—nobody was taking Dallas. Even though I thought Dallas would win, I was worried. You know, Super Bowl is big, big, big. I was holding a lotta money. I checked around to see what was happening and after thinkin about it, I figured I'd better get rid of it, that's called a layoff, and if I hadn't gotten rid of it, I'd a been ruined.

Layoff bookmakers charge a fee for taking unwanted action. This can be thought of in terms of 'juice.' The existence of layoff operations is essential precisely because of the sentimentality factor. If movement in the line does not affect the direction of incoming wagers on a Pittsburgh/Dallas game, then the Pittsburgh layoff bookie could layoff with a Dallas bookie. Six of the bookies in this study took layoff action from other bookies and would sometimes layoff their layoff action with larger operators. It is important to distinguish the relationships bookies have with layoff bookies from organized crime associations. Bookies choose whether to layoff their action and they have choices of who to lay it off with. Instead of reflecting organized crime connections, these relationships more closely resemble what Reuter (1983:42) calls networks. Occasionally, bookies in these networks combined their bookmaking business with social activities, but this appears to be infrequent.

Although the typical bettor is the bookie's bread and butter, there are always exceptions to typicality and in bookmaking the exception is the wiseguy. The wiseguy almost always beats the bookie. Since bookies lose money to wiseguys they must know who the wiseguy bettors are and limit the action they will accept from them. Eddy, a 52-year-old who has been in the business since high school, differentiates the wiseguy from the typical bettor.

> The wiseguy is someone who follows the games—they really do. They know who they wanta bet before the line comes out of Las Vegas—oh, that's the outlaw line that comes out on Sunday night. They'll bet the game with you Sunday night. They know who they want to bet. They take a chance on the line going up or down. They're sharp, but remember this is their livelihood, that's what they do, they don't do anything else. The way it works is that when the game plays, the line might

be at 16 and they're locked in at 10. Being locked in they have an option, they can keep the bet at 10 or take the 16 backup with somebody else and hope it falls in between, take the game, and make twice the money. They always bet with a couple of people and they study the games. I did that myself one Saturday a couple of weeks ago, it was the playoff games. I took 17 basketball games. I bet a couple of hundred per game. I was trying to catch it in the middle. I made $17,000 that afternoon. A lot of bookies have quit basketball because you can get destroyed with basketball. If you get a wiseguy who's hot, he'll beat you to death. Those guys just don't bet $100, they want to bet your limit—whatever it is, $500, $1,000, $5,000 whatever, and if they're hot, they'll win 9 out of 10 games.

In addition to developing a reliable client base and learning how to avoid losses, sports bookies can affect their profits by the number of hours they work and the sports they will accept. If they choose to, bookies can work year round or limit their business to particular seasons. Harry, who operated one of the larger businesses, took action on all sports events and explains the relation of this to being successful.

I got into this for the money; I figured that the more I worked, the more money I'd make. And I'm good at this. But I've had to put in hundreds of thousands of hours at this thing and that's year round. I mean I take every kind of game there is. I take horses, baseball, boxing, football, the baskets, hockey, jai lai, you name it. If there's some esoteric thing going on, I'll take it too. You should see my house, I got TVs everywhere. I got one of those dishes so I can watch what's going on all over the world and I got a computer to keep up with the scores and see what other people are doin'. If you wanta make money you've got to put the hours in and you have to know what's going on. See it's not the bookie that puts the fix in, but gamblers. You see they're lookin for the big win. But like anything else, if you wanna make money you gotta have a work ethic and you gotta know what's going on. I'll buy whatever I need that gives me an edge.

One of the biggest risks from any form of illicit activity is arrest, but unlike other forms of deviant behavior bookies are not afraid of getting arrested. In fact, none of the bookies in this study had been arrested for their bookmaking activities. Tony explains why:

The cops don't care about guys like me. I don't cause any trouble. I don't drink or do drugs and I don't know of any guys who do, 'cause for one thing you gotta be alert in this business and drinking and drugs will mess up your thought processes. So what kind of a danger am I? What I'm doing is providing a service, that's all, like any other service type of business. That doesn't mean I'm out there advertising what I'm doin', no way. I just don't do anything that's gonna draw attention to me. My customers are happy. So I'm clean, my people are happy, and everything's okay. The idea that we go out and break people's legs is something you see on TV. What sense does that make? I mean, if I broke some guy's legs, I'd get arrested. Just doin this, nobody's gonna arrest me.

Retiring from Bookmaking

Like getting into the business, retirement is a personal and voluntary decision. While not all of the bookies talked about retirement, those who did identified three factors that influenced their decision to leave the business: the desire to spend more time with family, having achieved their economic goals, and retirement from their legitimate job. Pete, who has been in the business approximately 15 years plans to retire within the next year because he wants to spend more time with his family. Pete discusses how the business interferes with spending time with his family and the preparation involved in leaving the business.

> I don't need to do this any more. Financially, things are different now, my wife is working a little and I'm working a lot of hours, I've got seniority. I'm thinking in about a year this thing will come to an end. I mean I don't have the time anymore. I'm coaching my kids, spending a lotta time with them. With the money I've made, I've put it into my house. We couldn't afford the house we're in without this. When I look back on the years, they've been good to me. I made some money where I could buy some things—my house, I got Debbie a new car, and for my kids I've been putting money away for their tuition for school. You know I don't want them going to public school. With my kids, when I'm doing this, they're with me. And to be honest with you, I don't want them growing up with this thing all the time. Everyone in my family, even my wife's family, knows what I do. The way things are now, when there's a family thing, I'm tied up with this—I can't go 'cause I'm answering the phone all the time. I've talked about leaving with George, he doesn't have the responsibilities I have with my family and all, so he can just step right in 'cause the business is running smoothly. He wants to take it over, it's a good deal for him—I've got good customers, I know them, there's no trouble, and things are real good now.

Unlike Pete, Joe's retirement plan does not involve a successor; instead he shifted his business to the Caribbean where he owns a legitimate sports book. Joe views the earnings from his legitimate enterprise as his retirement cushion. In the following excerpt, Joe discusses how his legitimate operation will provide a comfortable lifestyle without the worry that accompanies an illegal operation.

> The island operation is easy. You can advertise. We do, we have a full page advertisement in Las Vegas, in fact, even in some of the local papers we've got ads with a sports book number. You can call, set up an account. You can use a credit card, wire money, or send us a certified

check. Somebody puts money into their account, we give them 10% interest on their money, sometimes 15% depending on the amount they have and the type of bets they make. If somebody puts a considerable amount of money in there, we give 'em 15% right off the bat. If the person is a bettor, you have the money in an account, you know you're getting paid, and that's a big part of the business, getting paid. So we give 'em those extra bucks back to use. It works, it works great. Your regular bettors, guys that have the money and want to bet have no problem puttin' the money up front. It's a beautiful way to do business. So, I'm looking at this as my retirement plan. 'Cause, I'm out of everything here and I don't work any work. I've got eight people employed around the clock there and the action comes in 24 hours a day and a woman who manages the operation for me. She's real good. The business grows each week. Even though I worked all my life, I'm not depending on Social Security to live on—I never trusted the government, I gotta look out for myself. So by the time I'm 65, I'll have enough money saved up from this business to continue to enjoy my life. Like I told you before, me and my wife like to travel, so this way, we can do whatever we want. You know, I'm not a flamboyant guy, I drive a modest car and we live in a nice house, but nothing outrageous. People know me, I belong to the club here, me and my wife come up here a couple times a week, have dinner, watch a game here and there. I'm just beginning to enjoy all that time I've put into this thing 'cause I'll tell you I've worked hard in this business, all those hours. For years, I couldn't leave the house 'cause I was on the phone all day and all night. But now, I can relax now.

Frank, who is 60, is planning to retire from his legitimate job and quit bookmaking at the same time within a year.

I plan to retire in a year and I've been savin' the money I've made so I can enjoy myself. I got this house in Florida, so as soon as I retire I'm gone. I don't have anybody to worry about, my wife left me 30 years ago, no kids, so it's just me. I saved up a little nest egg so I can go here or there. If I wanta go to Atlantic City or out to Vegas every now and then for a week or so, I'll go. You know, I like to play blackjack. Right now, I'm only working with about 45 people anyway, so when I leave they can find somebody else. Some of my people already work with a couple of bookies, so I'm not worrying, they're set up.

Although Pete, Joe, and Frank give different reasons for leaving the business, their accounts show that retirement is their choice. Pete wants to spend more time with his family and has designated a successor; Joe has worked hard and wants to enjoy his life more fully and is depending on the income from his Caribbean operation; and Frank is planning to retire from bookmaking when he retires from his legitimate job and expects his customers to find another bookie. In all three cases, the decision to retire was voluntary. The different paths to retirement further indicate that not only is the decision to retire voluntary, but also the way that one retires is a choice.

Ties to Organized Crime

I asked about the alleged link to organized crime and found no support in bookies' accounts. Joe offers an interesting counterperspective suggesting that the allegation is a government ploy to control competition from bookies.

> The idea that the Mafia is pullin the strings on guys like me is a myth. We keep sports honest, believe me. If you're looking for the crooked angle, then government's the real criminal 'cause they really don't want competition from independents like me. So they keep betting illegal. The truth is that the independents do a better job than the government. Look, our payout is higher, we don't use gimmicks—think about all the gimmicks for the lottery—we don't have the overhead, and we don't cheat. Remember that Nick Perry incident?[10] Bookies have integrity. You gotta have integrity, 'cause if I cheated I'd be outta business. And remember this, we're not on every corner or in every retail store either, pushing people to gamble. But the government can't do it right 'cause they're greedy and most people know that. Just look at the OTB (Off Track Betting). How could you lose money with horses? Think about it. When the government's involved there are too many hands in the till. Guys like me make the government look bad 'cause we know what we're doin' and they don't want us out there. So they gotta make it seem like we're a bunch of thugs fixin' games and workin' players. The only games I ever heard about being fixed are the ones you read about in the paper. I'm not saying that it never happens, but when it does, bookies aren't doing the fixin. It's usually gamblers.

According to Sasuly (1982), all of the major sporting associations (i.e., the NCAA, NBA, NFL, and Thoroughbred Tracks of America) maintain contact with illegal bookmakers as a way of monitoring irregularities. Bookies can be thought of as barometers of irregularities for the world of sports.

Since there have been numerous reports of athletes shaving points, I asked whether bookies had first hand knowledge of professional athletes betting on games. None of the bookies I talked to knew of any instances where athletes placed bets on or against teams they played for. However, bookies did acknowledge having customers who were professional athletes and who wagered on sports events. Roger describes his experiences with a professional athlete who bets with him.

> I knew players who gambled. I took bets from _____. He didn't call me every week, but once in a while he'd bet on this game or that game. Sometimes he'd win and sometimes he'd lose. If you're askin' whether he'd bet his own game, the answer is no. In fact, he wouldn't bet on any games while he was playing. You know, he had to keep it low key because he could be kicked out of the pros if anyone ever found out. So we kept it quiet. We'd meet at _____, you know a lot of

---

[10] Nick Perry was the television announcer for the Pennsylvania Daily Lottery drawing who was convicted of fixing the live drawing on April 24, 1980.

guys worked out there, you could be sorta invisible there, and you know no one noticed, so we'd square up in the locker room. Players gamble. Believe me, all the players know what the line is on their own game and every other game. But me, personally, I've never known a player who bet his own game. I have known guys who are no longer in the pros who bet on their team. The way I look at it is, it's just part of sports.

When unusual or irregular betting patterns emerge, bookies stop taking bets on the game. This practice is referred to as "taking it off the board." It would not be in the bookie's best interests to try to rig or fix games since it is the bookie that stands to lose. Moreover, rigged games would disrupt the logic of bookmaking and the inherent parity in sports betting.

Discussion and Conclusions

Contrary to the image found in the public debate and popular culture, namely that bookies are slick operators looking for the "fast buck, the quick fix, or the desire to get something for nothing"[11] and have ties to organized crime, this analysis shows that bookmakers work hard, are dedicated, possess skill and specialized knowledge, and operate with integrity. Bookies put in long hours and make many sacrifices in other parts of their life in order to build a successful business.

Despite the maxim that "you can't beat the bookie," bookies need paying customers and since they cannot recruit or solicit their customers openly, they must devise ways that weed out the poor risks. Bookies must also be attuned to betting patterns and know when to raise or lower the line in order to balance the action. When it is not possible to balance the action, bookies need to know when to layoff with another bookmaker to avoid heavy losses. Finally, successful bookies operate with honesty and integrity. The relationship between the bookie and his customer is based on trust, and bookies know that if they cheat their customers they will lose them.

While the findings show that bookies are fully aware that what they are doing is illegal (Ray captures this by saying "You see, it's not illegal to place a bet, but you can't take bets—that's why you always gotta watch yourself"), they do not define themselves or other bookies as deviant or criminal. Instead they perceive themselves as providing a service to a niche market. What accounts for this nondeviant identity? One possible explanation has to do with the way bookmaking is socially organized. To the lay observer deviance appears to lack order, but sociologists know that like the social world of which it is a part, deviance is highly organized. The social organization of all forms of deviance is a microcosm of

[11] From the Professional Amateur Sports Protection Act of 1992.

society—there are distinct roles, norms of interaction, relationships, and distinct settings and contexts for its occurrence. Best and Luckenbill (1994) argue that the social organization of deviance is an endless source of knowledge because it is where the relationship between the individual and the larger society is mediated (5).

Like many service transactions, the product in the transaction (i.e., the bet) is nonmaterial—it consists of a verbal agreement about the outcome of a sports event. But unlike most illegal service transactions, the bet does not require face-to-face interaction. This fact sets bookmaking apart from other types of deviant transactions. Bookies and customers communicate by phone which means that the transaction can take place anywhere—at work, at home, in a car, in a restaurant, or even while walking down the street. This distances the bookie and the bettor from typical deviant or subcultural settings such as back alleys, street corners, or designated areas like redlight districts. The deviant transaction is integrated into the rhythms of everyday actions within the context of normal everyday settings.

In addition to occurring outside a criminal milieu, the structure of the transaction is unlike other illegal transactions because it is nonhierarchical. No middlemen are involved. While it is true that most bookies get their line from oddsmakers (usually working out of Las Vegas), the line nevertheless is in the public domain; you can find it anywhere. Consequently, nothing in the transaction requires the involvement of suppliers, venders, or front men. Because the transaction is between the bookie and the bettor, bookies have autonomy, discretion, control, and independence over their business.

There are three major phases of the bookmaking process: establishing the terms for betting, taking bets, and settling accounts. Within each of these processes, the bookies maintain independence, autonomy, discretion, and control. The conditions and terms for the transaction are determined by the bookie. This involves making decisions about what the line will be, the maximum and minimum amount to be accepted, the types of bets that will be accepted (a straight bet, over/under bet, parlay, etc.), and whether to extend credit to customers. Bookies know that if their terms are not competitive with other bookies, they could lose customers. Taking the bet consummates the transaction. Bettors tell the bookie who they want to wager on, the amount of the bet, and the type of bet they want to make. Bookies repeat this information back to the customer so that there is no misunderstanding about the wager and both wait for the outcome. Settling accounts involves the transfer of money either from losing bettors to bookies or from bookies to winning bettors and is the only phase that involves face-to-face interaction. Since bookmaking is illegal, bookies have no legal right to collect monies owed them nor can bettors demand monies owed to them. Instead of being coercive, settling accounts is based on trust between the bookie and bettor. In every aspect of the bookmaking process we see that bookies are the innovators, decision makers, and risk-takers. They initiate their involvement in bookmaking and see it as an opportunity to provide a service to a growing market; they hone their skills, gather the resources, and manage the process of building their own business.

There is further evidence that bookies differ from other types of deviants when we examine their career trajectories. On average, the bookies in this study were involved in bookmaking for 17 years, which can only be thought of in terms of a lengthy career. Throughout this period, the majority held full-time legitimate jobs, were committed to their families, planned for the future of their families, set economic goals, were involved in community activities, and generally were committed to conventional values. It also is worth noting that only one of the bookies in this study had ever been arrested. Yet in the literature on deviant careers, it is argued that prolonged deviant involvement requires rejecting conventional values (Stebbins 1971:63).

Best and Luckenbill (1994:235–237) argue that the social organization of deviance affects the duration of deviant careers in at least four ways. First, most deviant careers are dependent on the support of other deviants; the more contacts they have with other deviants, the longer the career. Second, career deviants have connections to other deviant organizations because of the resources such organizations offer. Third, since illegal activities are characterized by unregulated competition, career deviants must minimize competition, and this is usually done through negotiating with other deviants and by sharing or dividing the territory or resources. The final way career length is affected is through contacts with social control agents—the more contacts the higher the risk and the shorter the career. The analysis shows that bookmakers' careers are distinct from other deviant careers in the following ways. First, while bookies may associate with other bookies, this occurs only occasionally. Most importantly, their bookmaking business does not depend on these associations or on other deviants. In short, bookies are independent of other deviants. Second, since bookies assume all of the risks (financial and otherwise) involved in the bookmaking enterprise, they do not need to divide or share their customers nor do they have ties to other deviant organizations. Third, the most effective device against competition is the bookie's honesty and integrity. Finally, bookies are buffered from contact with social control agents because the enterprise has such low criminal visibility. Gambling on sports is integrated into the rhythms of everyday life, particularly male culture, and the bookie is a feature of that culture.

This leads to the question of whether it is time that the organized crime, corruption, and sports betting link be put to rest. The findings presented here provide a compelling argument for doing so. Although there is evidence showing organized crime's involvement in bookmaking, the findings presented here show bookies to be small entrepreneurs who operate independently. They see themselves as providing a service that is in great demand. It could be argued that major media that promote sports events increase the demand for this service. The line is readily available to the public and is very much a part of the hype that accompanies sports events. The line increases public interest in sporting events and betting on events ensures that millions of fans will watch them. Given the ubiquity of these accoutrements of gambling on sports, it is not surprising that sports betting is widespread and that our anti-gambling policies against it have little impact.

Although the sample for this study is small, confined to a single geographical area, and was selected by word of mouth, the accounts show remarkable consistency. It is possible that the bookies I interviewed represent an unusual group of bookies. Since there is no way of knowing just how large the population of bookies is, it is difficult to assess the representativeness of this study's sample. More research is needed, particularly research done in other geographical areas. Nevertheless, the findings presented here show that while bookmaking is illegal, sports betting is widespread, and that bookmakers are more like small business entrepreneurs than petty criminals.

References

Anderson, Annelies. 1979. *The Business of Organized Crime.* Stanford, CA: Hoover Institute.

Best, Joel, and David Luckenbill. 1994. *Organizing Deviance.* Englewood Cliffs, NJ: Prentice Hall.

Bonanno, Bill. 1999. *Bound by Honour.* NY: St. Martin's Press.

Chambliss, William. 1978. *On the Take.* Bloomington, IN: University of Indiana Press.

Clark, Ramsey. 1971. *Crime in America.* New York: Simon and Schuster.

Congressional Hearings for H.R. 497, National Gambling Impact and Policy Commission Act, September, 1995.

Cook, James. "If Roxborough Says the Spread is 7 it's 7." *Forbes*, September 14, 1992, pp. 350–363.

Cressey, Donald. 1969. *Theft of the Nation.* New York: Harper & Row.

DeFina, B., J. P. Reidy (Producers), and M. Scorsese (Director). (1995). *Casino* [Film]. (Available from Universal Pictures).

DeFina, B., B. Pustin, and I. Winkler (Producers), and M. Scorsese (Director). (1990). *Goodfellas* [Film]. (Available from Warner Bros).

Holcomb, R., and P. D. Marshall (Directors). (1987). *Wiseguy* [Film]. (Available from Cannell Films).

McGraw, Dan. "The National Bet." *U.S. News & World Report*, April 7, 1997, pp. 50–55.

Moody's Industry Review. Gaming. April 6, 1995.

National Amateur and Professional Sports Protection Act, S. 474, 1992.

Nevada Gaming Commission and State Gaming Control Board, personal communication with Research Division, June 1998.

O'Brien, Timothy. 1998. *Bad Bet.* New York: Times Business.

President's Commission on Law Enforcement and the Administration of Justice. 1967. *Task Force Report: Organized Crime.* Washington, DC: U.S. Government Printing Office.

Puzo, Mario. 1969. *The Godfather.* New York: Putnum.

Reuter, Peter. 1983. *Disorganized Crime: Illegal Markets and the Mafia.* Cambridge, MA: MIT Press.

Reuter, Peter, and Jonathan Rubinstein. 1982. *Illegal Gambling in New York.* Washington, DC: National Institute of Justice.

Rosencrance, John. 1987. "Bookmaking: A Case Where Honesty is the Best Policy." *Sociology and Social Research* 72(1):7–11.

Sasuly, Richard. 1982. *Bookies and Bettors: Two Hundred Years of Gambling.* New York: Holt Rinehart and Winston.

Scarne, John. 1974. *Scarne's New Complete Guide to Gambling.* New York: Simon and Schuster.

Shapiro, Joseph, Penny Loeb, Kenan Pollack, Timothy Ito, and Gary Cohen. "America's Gambling Fever." *U.S. News & World Report,* January 15, 1996, pp. 52–60.

Stebbins, Robert. 1971. *Commitment to Deviance.* Westport, CT: Greenwood.

Talese, Gay. 1971. *Honor Thy Father.* New York: World Publishing.

Entering and Learning Deviant Cultures and Practices: The Building of Deviant Careers and Identities

The statements by Best and Luckenbill indicate that deviant organizations can be characterized in terms of their relative degree of sophistication. Best and Luckenbill also emphasize that a person can gain initial entry to organizations through various channels. Once individuals gain entry, however, they must, if they elect to stay, learn the existing culture and traditions. A similar requirement exists with respect to the institutional deviant. Failure to meet expectations may result in such penalties as ostracism or exclusion from the group. (The general social-psychological processes involved in learning deviant cultures were highlighted in our discussion of the cultural transmission model in Part II.) The selections in this section deal primarily with entry routes and offer specific illustrations of how actors become socialized into deviant or semideviant careers.

In "Drifting into Dealing: Becoming a Cocaine Seller," Sheigla Murphy, Dan Waldorf, and Craig Reinarman outline the various modes and levels of entry into the world of cocaine sales. Their observations are based on interviews with eighty ex-cocaine sellers. All had sold cocaine for at least a year; however, none had done so for a period of six months prior to the interviews. Actual entry into the world of cocaine sales is, according to the researchers, a fluid process, with most sellers drifting into their dealing career. The authors go on to describe five basic ways that people begin to sell cocaine. The first mode of entry is the *go-between*, in which a person who initially buys for his or her friends begins to envision the profits that may result from selling. The second avenue is the *stash dealer*, in which a user sells small amounts to support his or her own cocaine needs. The *connoisseur*, the third mode of entry, includes those who seek to buy high-quality drugs through wholesale purchases, and the fourth entry route entails the *apprenticeship*, a trainee-style of connection. In this situation, the novice takes over all aspects of an established dealer's business after learning the ropes. The fifth and final entry route described involves what is termed the *product line expansion*. Here dealers start selling other drugs (e.g., marijuana) and then move into cocaine sales when a supply becomes available. Of importance, too, is the authors' analysis of how a seller may exhibit a subtle transformation of his or her identity. Once situated in the role of the dealer, selling often becomes viewed as a job or career. Significant, too, is the observation that the "dealer identity" did not seem to replace former "legitimate" identities but was, instead, added to a subject's other conventional identities. Thus, sellers would, depending upon the situation, emphasize different aspects of their identities. The researchers end by describing some of the values and expectations that characterize the business relationships existing between sellers and customers.

In "Confronting Deadly Disease: The Drama of Identity Construction among Gay Men with AIDS," Kent L. Sandstrom uses interview data to describe how gay men attempt to construct an AIDS-related identity and integrate it with other positive aspects of self; this is a particularly important requirement for those who are afflicted with AIDS. Persons with AIDS (PWAs), the author notes, are acutely aware of the stigma associated with their illness, and they often encounter some very difficult emotional and social reactions. How do PWAs deal with such responses? The researcher sheds some light on this question by describing a range of identity management strategies (e.g., passing, covering, isolation, and insulation) that can be used to avoid potentially threatening social occasions and interactions. Whether a specific technique is useful or not depends on several factors. If, for example, facial lesions are apparent or one has a pale complexion, then passing or covering is not especially effective. Pursuing isolation also produces differential effects on PWAs. Exclusive reliance on such attempts to shield one's self from the stigma of AIDS not only is defensive in nature but is not associated with any significant efforts to reformulate or reconstruct one's personal and public identity, or view of self. Sandstrom then outlines the various types of *identity work* that PWAs engage in, with the most prominent one being *identity embracement*. Through use of new memberships and support groups, PWAs build and come to embrace a positive AIDS-related identity. They reject public imputations that they are "AIDS victims" and promote a different image. The view promoted might be that PWAs are individuals who are "living and thriving with the illness." Sandstrom concludes by describing how subcultures and such processes as ideological embracement are used by PWAs to revitalize their identities and views of self. His concluding comments are especially relevant to those sections of this book in which we describe how deviant categories are created (Part I) and how they may be transformed (Part VI). In this case, the category of "AIDS victim" and its associated range of negative labels appear to have undergone some significant redefinition. Hence, anyone occupying this status may, both in terms of self and other perceptions, be cast in a more positive light.

Drifting into Dealing: Becoming a Cocaine Seller

Sheigla Murphy
Dan Waldorf
Craig Reinarman

Introduction

No American who watched television news in the 1980s could have avoided images of violent drug dealers who brandished bullets while driving BMW's before being hauled off in handcuffs. This new stereotype of a drug dealer has become a staple of popular culture, the very embodiment of evil. He works for the still more vile villains of the "Colombian cartel," who make billions on the suffering of millions. Such men are portrayed as driven by greed and utterly indifferent to the pain from which they profit.

We have no doubt that some such characters exist. Nor do we doubt that there may be a new viciousness among some of the crack cocaine dealers who have emerged in ghettos and barrios already savaged by rising social problems and failing social programs. We have grave doubts, however, that such characterizations tell us anything about cocaine sellers more generally. If our interviews are any guide, beneath every big-time dealer who may approximate the stereotype there are hundreds of smaller sellers who do not.

This paper describes such sellers, not so much as a way of debunking a new devil but rather as a way of illuminating how deviant careers develop and how the identities of the individuals who move into this work are transformed. Along with the many routine normative strictures against drug use in our culture, there has been a mobilization in recent years for a "war on drugs" which targets cocaine dealers in particular. Many armaments in the arsenal of social control from propaganda to prisons have been employed in efforts to dissuade people from using/selling such substances. In such a context it is curious that ostensibly ordinary people not only continue to use illicit drugs but also take the significant additional step of becoming drug sellers. To explore how this happens, we offer an analysis of eighty depth interviews with former cocaine sellers. We sought to learn

528

something about how it is that otherwise conventional people—some legally employed, many well educated—end up engaging in a sustained pattern of behavior that their neighbors might think of as very deviant indeed.

Deviant Careers and Drift

Our reading of this data was informed by two classic theoretical works in the deviance literature. First, in *Outsiders,* Howard Becker observed that, "The career lines characteristic of an occupation take their shape from the problems peculiar to that occupation. These, in turn, are a function of the occupation's position vis-a-vis other groups in society" (1963:102). He illustrated the point with the dance musician, caught between the jazz artist's desire to maintain creative control and a structure of opportunities for earning a living that demanded the subordination of this desire to mainstream musical tastes. Musicians' careers were largely a function of how they managed this problem. When the need to make a living predominated, the basis of their self conceptions shifted from art to craft.

Of course, Becker applied the same proposition to more deviant occupations. In the next section, we describe five discrete modes of becoming a cocaine seller which center on "the problems peculiar to" the world of illicit drug use and which entail a similar shift in self conception. For example, when a drug such as cocaine is criminalized, its cost is often greatly increased while its availability and quality are somewhat limited. Users are thus faced with the problems of avoiding detection, reducing costs, and improving availability and quality. By becoming involved in sales, users solve many of these problems and may also find that they can make some money in the bargain. As we will show, the type of entree and the level at which it occurs are functions of the individual's relationship to networks of other users and suppliers. At the point where one has moved from being a person who *has* a good connection for cocaine to a person who *is* a good connection for cocaine, a subtle shift in self conception and identity occurs.

Becker's model of deviant careers entails four basic steps, three of which our cocaine sellers took. First, the deviant must somehow avoid the impact of conventional commitments that keep most people away from intentional non-conformity. Our cocaine sellers passed this stage by ingesting illegal substances with enough regularity that the practice became normalized in their social world. Second, deviant motives and interests must develop. These are usually learned in the process of the deviant activity and from interaction with other deviants. Here too our cocaine sellers had learned the pleasures of cocaine by using it, and typically were moved toward involvement in distribution to solve one or more problems entailed in such use. Once involved, they discovered additional motivations which we will describe in detail below.

Becker's third step in the development of deviant careers entails public labeling. The person is caught, the rule is enforced, and his or her public identity is transformed. The new master status of "deviant," Becker argues, can be self fulfilling when it shapes others' perceptions of the person and limits his or her possibilities for resuming conventional roles and activities. Few of our respondents had been publicly labeled deviant, but they did describe a gradual change in identity that may be likened to self-labeling. This typically occurred when they deepened their deviance by dealing on top of using cocaine. This shift in self conception for our subjects was more closely linked to Becker's fourth step—movement into an organized deviant group in which people with a common fate and similar problems form subcultures. There they learn more about solving problems and ideologies which provide rationales for continuing the behavior, thus further weakening the hold of conventional norms and institutions and solidifying deviant identities. In the case of our subjects, becoming sellers further immersed them into deviant groups and practices to the point where many came to face the problems of, and to see themselves as, "dealers."

The fact that these processes of deeper immersion into deviant worlds and shifts in self conception were typically gradual and subtle brought us to a second set of theoretical reference points in the work of David Matza (1964; 1969).[1] In his research on delinquency, Matza discovered that most so-called delinquents were not self-consciously committed to deviant values or lifestyles, but on the contrary continued to hold conventional beliefs. Most of the time they were law abiding, but because the situation of "youth" left them free from various restraints, they often *drifted* in and out of deviance. Matza found that even when caught being delinquent, young people tended to justify or rationalize their acts through "techniques of neutralization" (Sykes and Matza, 1957) rooted in conventional codes of morality. Although we focus on *entering* selling careers, we found that Matza's concept of drift (1964) provided us with a useful sensibility for making sense of our respondents' accounts. The modes of entree they described were as fluid and non-committal as the drift into and out of delinquency that he described.

None of the career paths recounted by our subjects bear much resemblance to stereotypes of "drug dealers."[2] For decades the predominant image of the illicit drug dealer was an older male reprobate sporting a long, shabby overcoat within which he had secreted a cornucopia of dangerous consciousness-altering substances. This proverbial "pusher" worked school yards, targeting innocent children who would soon be chemically enslaved repeat customers. The newer villains have been depicted as equally vile but more violent. Old or new, the ideal-typical "drug dealer" is motivated by perverse greed and/or his own addiction, and has crossed a clearly marked moral boundary, severing most ties to the conventional world.

The cocaine sellers we interviewed, on the other hand, had more varied and complex motives for selling cocaine. Moreover at least within their subcultures, the moral boundaries were both rather blurry and as often wandered along as actually crossed. Their life histories reminded us of Matza's later but related discussion of the *overlap* between deviance and conventionality:

> Overlap refers to . . . the marginal rather than gross differentiation between deviant and conventional folk and the considerable though variable interpenetration of deviant and conventional culture. Both themes sensitize us to the regular exchange, traffic, and flow—of persons as well as styles and precepts—that occur among deviant and conventional worlds. (1969:68)

Our subjects were already seasoned users of illicit drugs. For years their drug use coexisted comfortably with their conventional roles and activities; having a deviant dimension to their identities appeared to cause them little strain. In fact, because their use of illicit drugs had gone on for so long, was so common in their social worlds, and had not significantly affected their otherwise normal lives, they hardly considered it deviant at all.

Thus, when they began to sell cocaine as well as use it, they did not consider it a major leap down an unknown road but rather a series of short steps down a familiar path. It was not as if ministers had become mobsters; no sharp break in values, motives, world views, or identities was required. Indeed, few woke up one morning and made a conscious decision to become sellers. They did not break sharply with the conventional world and actively choose a deviant career path; most simply drifted into dealing by virtue of their strategies for solving the problems entailed in using a criminalized substance, and only then developed additional deviant motives centering on money.

To judge from our respondents, then, dealers are not from a different gene pool. Since the substances they enjoy are illegal, most regular users of such drugs become involved in some aspect of distribution. There is also a growing body of research on cocaine selling and distribution that has replaced the simplistic stereotype of the pusher with complex empirical evidence about underground economies and deviant careers (e.g., Langer, 1977; Waldorf et al., 1977, 1991; Adler, 1985; Plasket and Quillen, 1985; Morales, 1986a, 1986b; Sanchez and Johnson, 1987; Sanabria, 1988; and Williams, 1989). Several features of underground economies or black markets in drugs contribute to widespread user participation in distribution. For example, some users who could obtain cocaine had other user-friends who wanted it. Moreover, the idea of keeping such traffic among friends offered both sociability and safety. For others, cocaine's high cost inspired many users to become involved in purchasing larger amounts to take advantage of volume discounts. They then sold part of their supply to friends in order to reduce the cost of personal use. The limited supply of cocaine in the late seventies and early eighties made for a sellers' market, providing possibilities for profits along with steady supplies. For most of our subjects, it was not so much that they learned they could make money and thus decided to become dealers but rather, being involved in distribution anyway, they learned they could make money from it. As Becker's model suggests, deviant motives are learned in the course of deviant activities; motivation follows behavior, not the other way around.

After summarizing our sampling and interviewing procedures, we describe in more detail (1) the various modes and levels of entree into cocaine sales; (2) some of the practices, rights and responsibilities entailed in dealing; and (3) the subtle transformation of identity that occurred when people who consider themselves rather conventional moved into careers considered rather deviant.

Sample and Methods

The sample consists of 80 ex-sellers who sold cocaine in the San Francisco Bay Area. We interviewed them in 1987 and 1988. Most had stopped selling before crack sales peaked in this area. Only five of the eighty had sold crack or rock. Of these five, two had sold on the street and two had sold in "rock party houses"[3] as early as 1978. It is important to note, therefore, that the sellers we describe are very likely to be different from street crack dealers in terms of the product type, selling styles, visibility, and thus the risks of arrest and attendant violence.

The modes and levels of entree we describe should not be considered exhaustive. They are likely to vary by region, subculture, and level of dealing. For example, our sample and locus differed from those of Adler (1985), who studied one community of *professional* cocaine dealers at the *highest levels* of the distribution system. Her ethnographic account is rich in insights about the lifestyles and career contingencies of such high-level dealers and smugglers. These subjects decided to enter into importing and/or dealing and to move up the ranks in this deviant occupation in order to obtain wealth and to live the sorts of lives that such wealth made possible. Adler's dealers were torn, however, between the lures of fast money and the good life and the stress and paranoia inherent in the scene. Thus, she reported "oscillations" wherein her dealers moved in and out of the business, usually to be lured back in by the possibility of high profits. Our dealers tended to have different motivations, career trajectories, and occupational exigencies. Most were lower in the hierarchy and non-professional (some maintained "straight" jobs); few set out to achieve success in an explicitly deviant career, to amass wealth, or to live as "high rollers." Moreover, our study was cross-sectional rather than longitudinal, so our focus was on how a wide variety of cocaine sellers entered careers rather than on the full career trajectories of a network of smugglers and sellers.

To be eligible for the study our respondents had to have sold cocaine steadily for at least a year and to have stopped selling for at least 6

Levels of Sales	Number of Interviews
Smugglers	2
Kilograms/pounds	13
Parts of kilos and pounds	6
Ounce dealers	18
Part-ounce dealers	13
Gram dealers	12
Part-gram dealers	11
Crack dealers	5
Total	80

months. We designed the study to include only *former* sellers so that respondents would feel free to describe all their activities in detail without fear that their accounts could somehow be utilized by law enforcement authorities.

They spoke of six different levels or types of sellers: smugglers, big dealers, dealers, sellers (unspecified), bar dealers, and street dealers. The social organization of cocaine sales probably varies in other areas. We located and interviewed ex-sellers from the full range of these dealer-identified sales levels, but we have added two categories in order to provide a more detailed typology. Our eight levels of sales were defined according to the units sold rather than the units bought. So, for example, if a seller bought quarters or eighths of ounces and regularly sold grams, we categorized him or her as a gram dealer rather than a part-ounce dealer.

Unlike most other studies of dealing and the now infamous street crack dealers, the majority of our respondents sold cocaine hydrochloride (powder) in private places. There are a number of styles of selling drugs—selling out of homes, selling out of rock houses and shooting galleries, selling out of party houses, selling out of rented "safe houses" and apartments, delivery services (using telephone answering, answering machines, voice mail and telephone beepers), car meets,[4] selling in bars, selling in parks, and selling in the street. Within each type there are various styles. For example, in some African-American communities in San Francisco a number of sellers set up business on a street and respond to customers who come by on foot and in automobiles. Very often a number of sellers will approach a car that slows down or stops to solicit customers; drugs and money are exchanged then and there. Such sales activities are obvious to the most casual observers; even television camera crews often capture such transactions for the nightly news. On certain streets in the Mission District, a Latino community in San Francisco, street drug sales are less blatant. Buyers usually walk up to sellers who stand on the street among numerous other people who are neither buyer nor sellers. There, specific transactions rarely take place on the street itself; the participants generally retreat to a variety of shops and restaurants. Buyers seldom use cars for transactions and sellers tend not to approach a car to solicit customers.

Despite the ubiquity of street sales in media accounts and the preponderance of street sellers in arrest records, we set out to sample the more hidden and more numerous sellers who operate in private. Most users of cocaine hydrochloride are working- or middle-class. They generally avoid street sellers both because they want to avoid being observed and because they believe that most street sellers sell inferior quality drugs (Waldorf et al., 1991). Further, we found that people engaged in such illegal and furtive transactions tend to prefer dealing with people like themselves, people they know.

We located our respondents by means of chain referral sampling techniques (Biernacki and Waldorf, 1981; Watters and Biernacki, 1989). This is a method commonly used by sociologists and ethnographers to locate hard-to-find groups and has been used extensively in qualitative research on drug use (Lindesmith, 1947; Becker, 1953; Feldman, 1968; Preble and Casey, 1969; Rosenbaum, 1981; Biernacki, 1986). We initiated the first of our location chains in 1974–1975 in the course of a short-term ethnography of cocaine use and sales among a small friendship network (Waldorf et al., 1977). Other chains were developed during a second study of cocaine cessation conducted during 1986–1987 (Reinarman et al., 1988; Macdonald et al., 1988; Murphy et al., 1989; Waldorf et al., 1991). Another three chains were developed during the present study. We located the majority of our respondents via referral chains developed by former sellers among their previous customers and suppliers. Initial interviewees referred us to other potential respondents whom we had not previously known. In this way we were able to direct our chains into groups of ex-sellers from a variety of backgrounds.

We employed two interview instruments: an open-ended, exploratory interview guide designed to maximize discovery of new and unique types of data, and a more structured survey designed to gather basic quantifiable data on all respondents. The open-ended interviews were tape-recorded, transcribed, and content-analyzed. These interviews usually took from 2 to 4 hours to complete, but when necessary we conducted longer and/or follow-up interviews (e.g., one woman was interviewed for 10 hours over three sessions). The data analyzed for this paper was drawn primarily from the tape-recorded depth interviews.

There is no way to ascertain if this (or any similar) sample is representative of all cocaine sellers. Because the parameters of the population are unknowable, random samples on which systematic generalizations might be based cannot be drawn. We do know that, unlike other studies of drug sellers, we placed less emphasis on street sellers and included dealers at all levels. We also attempted to get a better gender and ethnic mix than studies based on captive samples from jails or treatment programs. Roughly one in three (32.5%) of our dealers are female and two of five (41.2%) are persons of color.

Table 1   Demographics (*N* = 80)

		Number	Percent[a]
Age: Range = 18–60 years			
Mean = 37.1			
Median = 35.4			
Sex:			
Male		54	67.5
Female		26	32.5
Ethnicity:			
African-American		28	35.0
White		44	58.8
Latino(a)		4	5.0
Asian		1	1.2
Education:			
Less than high school grad		11	13.8
High school graduate		18	22.5
Some college		31	38.8
B.A. or B.S. degree		12	15.0
Some graduate		3	3.8
Graduate degree		5	6.3

[a]Percentages may not equal 100% due to rounding.

Our respondents ranged in age from 18 to 60, with a mean age of 37.1 years. Their education level was generally high, presumably an indication of the relatively large numbers of middle-class people in the sample.

Dealers

Dealers are people who are "fronted" (given drugs on consignment to be paid for upon sale) and/or who buy quantities of drugs for sale. Further, in order to be considered a dealer by users or other sellers a person must: (1) have one or more reliable connections (suppliers); (2) make regular cocaine purchases in amounts greater than a single gram (usually an eighth of an ounce or greater) to be sold in smaller units; (3) maintain some consistent supplies for sale; and (4) have a network of customers who make purchases on a regular basis. Although the stereotype of a dealer holds that illicit drug sales are a full-time occupation, many dealers, including members of our sample, operate part-time and supplement income from a legal job.

As we noted in the introduction, the rather average, ordinary character of the respondents who fit this definition was striking. In general, without prior knowledge or direct observation of drug sales, one would be unable to distinguish our respondents from other, non-dealer citizens. When telling their career histories, many of our respondents invoked very conventional, middle-class American values to explain their involvement in dealing (e.g., having children to support, mortgages or rent to pay in a high-cost urban area, difficulty finding jobs which paid enough to support a family). Similarly, their profits from drug sales were used in "normal" ways—to buy children's clothes, to make house or car payments, to remodel a room. Moreover, like Matza's delinquents, most of our respondents were quite law-abiding, with the obvious exception of their use and sales of an illicit substance.

When they were not dealing, our respondents engaged in activities that can only be described as mainstream American. For example, one of our dealers, a single mother of two, found herself with a number of friends who used cocaine and a good connection. She needed extra income to pay her mortgage and to support her children, so she sold small amounts of cocaine within her friendship network. Yet while she sold cocaine, she worked at a full-time job, led a Girl Scout troop, volunteered as a teacher of cardio-pulmonary resuscitation (CPR) classes for young people, and went to Jazzercize classes. Although she may have been a bit more civic-minded than many others, her case served to remind us that cocaine sellers do not come from another planet.

Modes of Entree into Dealing

Once they began selling cocaine, many of our respondents moved back and forth between levels in the distribution hierarchy. Some people dealt for short periods of time and then quit, only to return several months later at another level of sales.[5] The same person may act as a broker on one deal, sell a quarter gram at a profit to a friend on another, and then pick up an ounce from an associate and pass it on to another dealer in return for some marijuana in a third transaction. In a few instances each of these roles were played by the same person within the same twenty-four hour period.

But whether or not a dealer/respondent moved back and forth in this way, s/he usually began selling in one of five distinct ways. All five of these modes of entree pre-suppose an existing demand for cocaine from people known to the potential dealers. A person selling any line of products needs two things, a group of customers and a product these customers are interested in purchasing. Cocaine sellers are no different. In addition to being able and willing to pay, however, cocaine customers must also be trustworthy because these transactions are illegal.

The first mode of entree, *the go-between*, is fairly straightforward. The potential seller has a good cocaine connection and a group of friends who place orders for cocaine with him/her. If the go-between's friends use cocaine regularly enough and do not develop their own connections, then a period of months or even years might go by when the go-between begins to spend more and more time and energy purchasing for them. Such sellers generally do not make formal decisions to begin dealing; rather, opportunities regularly present themselves and go-betweens gradually take advantage of them. For example, one 30-year-old African-American who became a gram dealer offered this simple account of his passage from go-between to seller:

> Basically, I first started because friends pressured me to get the good coke I could get. I wasn't even making any money off of it. They'd come to me and I'd call up my friend who had gotten pretty big selling a lot of coke. (Case # E-5)

This went on for six months before he began to charge his friends money for it. Then his connection started fronting him eighths of ounces at a time, and he gradually became an official dealer, regularly selling drugs for a profit. Others who began in this way often took only commissions-in-kind (a free snort) for some months before beginning to charge customers a cash mark-up.

Another African-American male began selling powdered cocaine to snorters in 1978 and by the mid-eighties had begun selling rock cocaine (crack) to smokers. He described his move from go-between to dealer as follows:

> Around the time I started indulging [in cocaine] myself, people would come up and say, "God, do you know where I can get some myself?" I would just say, "Sure, just give me your money," I would come back and either indulge with them or just give it to them depending on my mood. I think that's how I originally set up my clientele. I just had a certain group of people who would come to me because they felt that I knew the type of people who could get them a real quality product.
>
> And pretty soon I just got tired of, you know, being taken out of situations or being imposed upon. . . . I said that it would be a lot easier to just do it myself. And one time in particular, and I didn't consider myself a dealer or anything, but I had a situation one night where 5 different people called me to try to get cocaine . . . not from me but it was like, "Do you know where I can get some good cocaine from?" (Case # E-11)

Not all go-betweens-cum-dealers start out so altruistically. Some astute businessmen and women spot the profit potential early on and immediately realize a profit, either in-kind (a share of the drugs purchased) or by tacking on a surcharge to the purchase price. The following respondent, a 39-year-old African-American male, described this more profit-motivated move from go-between to formal seller:

> Well, the first time that I started it was like I knew where to get good stuff . . . and I had friends that didn't know where to get good stuff. And I knew where to get them really good stuff and so I would always

put a couple of dollars on it, you know, if I got it for $20 I would sell it to them for $25 or $30 or whatever.

It got to be where more and more people were coming to me and I was going to my man more and I would be there 5 or 6 times a day, you know. So he would tell me, "Here, why don't you take this, you know, and bring me x-amount of dollars for it." So that's how it really started. I got fronted and I was doing all the business instead of going to his house all the time, because he had other people that were coming to his house and he didn't want the traffic. (Case # E-13)

The second mode of entree is the *stash dealer,* or a person who becomes involved in distribution and/or sales simply to support or subsidize personal use. The name is taken from the term "stash," meaning a personal supply of marijuana (see Fields, 1985, on stash dealers in the marijuana trade). This 41-year-old white woman who sold along with her husband described her start as a stash dealer this way:

Q: So what was your motivation for the sales?
A: To help pay for my use, because the stuff wasn't cheap and I had the means and the money at the time in order to purchase it, where our friends didn't have that amount of money without having to sell something. . . . Yeah, friendship, it wasn't anything to make money off of, I mean we made a few dollars. . . . (Case # E-7)

The respondents who entered the dealing world as stash dealers typically started out small (selling quarter and half grams) and taking their profits in product. However, this motivation contributed to the undoing of some stash dealers in that it led to greater use, which led to the need for greater selling, and so on. Unless they then developed a high-volume business that allowed them to escalate their cocaine use and still make profits, the reinforcing nature of cocaine tempted many of them to use more product than was good for business.

Many stash dealers were forced out of business fairly early on in their careers because they spent so much money on their own use they were financially unable to "re-cop" (buy new supplies). Stash dealers often want to keep only a small number of customers in order to minimize both the "hassle" of late-night phone calls and the risk of police detection, and they do not need many customers since they only want to sell enough to earn free cocaine. Problems arise, however, when their small group of customers do not buy the product promptly. The longer stash dealers had cocaine in their possession, the more opportunities they had for their own use (i.e., for profits to "go up your nose"). One stash dealer had an axiom about avoiding this: "It ain't good to get high on your own supply" (Case # E-57). The predicament of using rather than selling their product often afflicts high-level "weight dealers" as well, but they are better able to manage for longer periods of time due to larger volumes and profit margins.

The third mode of entry into cocaine selling had to do with users' desire for high-quality, unadulterated cocaine. We call this type the *connoisseur*. Ironically, the motivation for moving toward dealing in this way is often health-related. People who described this mode of entree described their concerns, as users, about the possible dangers of ingesting the various adulterants or "cuts" commonly used by dealers to increase profits. User folklore holds that the larger the quantity purchased, the purer the product. This has been substantiated by laboratory analysis of the quality of small amounts of street drugs (typically lower) as opposed to larger police seizures (typically higher).

The connoisseur type of entry, then, begins with the purchase of larger quantities of cocaine than they intend to use in order to maximize purity. Then they give portions of the cocaine to close friends at a good price. If the members of the network start to use more cocaine, the connoisseurs begin to make bigger purchases with greater regularity. At some point they begin to feel that all this takes effort and that it makes sense to buy large quantities not only to get purer cocaine but to make some money for their efforts. The following 51-year-old, white business executive illustrated the connoisseur route as follows:

> I think the first reason I started to sell was not to make money or even to pay for my coke, because I could afford it. It was to get good coke and not to be snorting a lot of impurities and junk that people were putting into it by cutting it so much. So I really think that I started to sell it or to get it wholesale so that I would get the good stuff. And I guess my first. . . . what I did with it in the beginning, because I couldn't use all that I had to buy to get good stuff, I sold it to some of my friends for them to sell it, retail it. (Case # E-16)

Connoisseurs, who begin by selling unneeded quantities, often found they unlearned certain attitudes when they moved from being volume buyers looking for quality toward becoming dealers looking for profit. It was often a subtle shift, but once their primary motivation gradually changed from buying-for-purity to buying-to-sell they found themselves beginning to think and act like dealers. The shift usually occurred when connoisseurs realized that the friends with whom they had shared were in fact customers who were eager for their high quality cocaine and who often made demands on their time (e.g., friends seeking supplies not merely for themselves, but for other friends a step or two removed from the original connoisseur). Some connoisseurs also became aware of the amount of money that could be made by becoming business-like about what had been formerly friendly favors. At such points in the process they began to buy-to-sell, for a profit, as well as for the purpose of obtaining high-quality cocaine for personal use. This often meant that, rather than buying sporadically, they had to make more regular buys; for a successful businessperson must have supplies when customers want to buy or they will seek another supplier.

The fourth mode of entree into cocaine selling is an *apprenticeship.* Like the other types, apprentices typically were users who already had loosened conventional normative strictures and learned deviant motives by interacting with other users and with dealers; and they, too, drifted into dealing. However, in contrast to the first three types, apprentices moved toward dealing less to solve problems inherent in using a criminalized substance than to solve the problems of the master dealer. Apprenticeships begin in a personal relationship where, for example, the potential seller is the lover or intimate of a dealer. This mode was most often the route of entry for women, although one young man we interviewed learned to deal from his father. Couples often start out with the man doing the dealing—picking up the product, handling the money, weighing and packaging, etc. The woman gradually finds herself acting as an unofficial assistant—taking telephone messages, sometimes giving people prepackaged cocaine and collecting money. Apprentices frequently benefit from being involved with the experienced dealer in that they enjoy both supplies of high-quality cocaine and indirect financial rewards of dealing.

Some of our apprentices moved into official roles or deepened their involvement when the experienced dealer began to use too much cocaine to function effectively as a seller. In some such cases the abuse of the product led to an end of the relationship. Some apprentices then left dealing altogether while others began dealing on their own. One 32-year-old African-American woman lived with a pound dealer in Los Angeles in 1982. Both were freebasers (cocaine smokers) who sold to other basers. She described her evolution from apprentice to dealer this way:

> I was helping him with like weighing stuff and packaging it and I sort of got to know some of the people that were buying because his own use kept going up. He was getting more out of it, so I just fell into taking care of it partly because I like having the money and it also gave me more control over the situation, too, for awhile, you know, until we both got too out of it. (Case # E-54)

The fifth mode of entree into cocaine selling entailed the *expansion of an existing product line.* A number of the sellers we interviewed started out as marijuana salespersons and learned many aspects of the dealers' craft before they ever moved to cocaine. Unlike in the other modes, in this one an existing marijuana seller already had developed selling skills and established a network of active customers for illicit drugs. Expansion of product line (in business jargon, horizontal integration) was the route of entry for many of the multiple-ounce and kilo cocaine dealers we interviewed. The combination of the availability of cocaine through their marijuana connection and their marijuana customers' interest in purchasing cocaine, led many marijuana sellers to add cocaine to their product line.

Others who entered dealing this way also found that expanding from marijuana to cocaine solved some problems inherent in marijuana dealing. For example, cocaine is far less bulky and odoriferous than marijuana and thus did not present the risky and costly shipping and storage problems of multiple pounds of marijuana. Those who entered cocaine selling via this product line expansion route also recognized, of course, that there was the potential for higher profits with cocaine. They seemed to suggest that as long as they were already taking the risk, why shouldn't they maximize the reward? Some such dealers discontinued marijuana sales altogether and others merely added cocaine to their line. One white, 47-year-old mother of three grown children described how she came to expand her product line:

Q: How did you folks [she and her husband] get started dealing?
A: The opportunity just fell into our lap. We were already dealing weed and one of our customers got this great coke connection and started us onto dealing his product. We were selling him marijuana and he was selling us cocaine.
Q: So you had a network of weed buyers, right? So you could sell to those . . . ?
A: There was a shift in the market. Yeah, because weed was becoming harder [to find] and more expensive and a bulkier product. The economics of doing a smaller, less bulkier product and more financially rewarding product like cocaine had a certain financial appeal to the merchant mentality. (Case # E-1)

Conscious Decision to Sell

As noted earlier, the majority of our sample were middle class wholesalers who, in the various ways just described, drifted into dealing careers. The few street sellers we interviewed did not drift into sales in the same way. We are obliged to note again that the five modes of entry into cocaine selling we have identified should not be taken as exhaustive. We have every reason to believe that for groups and settings other than those we have studied there are other types of entree and career trajectories. The five cases of street sellers we did examine suggest that entree into street-level sales was more of a conscious decision of a poor person who decided to enter an underground economy, not an effort to solve a user's problems. Our interviews with street sellers suggest that they choose to participate in an illicit profit-generating activity largely because licit economic opportunities were scarce or nonexistent. Unlike our other types, such sellers sold to strangers as well as friends, and their place of business was more likely to be the street corner rather than homes, bars, or nightclubs. For example, one 30-year-old Native American ex-prostitute described how she became a street crack dealer this way:

I had seen in the past friends that were selling and stuff and I needed extra money so I just one day told one of my friends, you know, if he could help me, you know, show me more or less how it goes. So I just went by what I seen. So I just started selling it. (Case # E-AC 1)

A few higher-level dealers also made conscious decisions to sell (see Adler, 1985), particularly when faced with limited opportunity structures. Cocaine selling, as an occupation, offers the promise of lavish lifestyles otherwise unattainable to most ghetto youth and other impoverished groups. Dealing also provides an alternative to the low-paying, dead-end jobs typically available to those with little education and few skills. A 55-year-old African-American man who made his way up from grams to ounce sales described his motivation succinctly: "The chance presented itself to avoid the 9 to 5" (Case # E-22).

Street sellers and even some higher-level dealers are often already participating in quasi-criminal lifestyles; drug sales are simply added to their repertoire of illicit activities. The perceived opportunity to earn enormous profits, live "the good life," and set your own work schedule are powerful enticements to sell. From the perspective of people with few life chances, dealing cocaine may be seen as their only real chance to achieve the "American Dream" (i.e., financial security and disposable income). Most of our sample were not ghetto dwellers and/or economically disadvantaged. But for those who were, there were different motivations and conscious decisions regarding beginning sales. Popular press descriptions of cocaine sellers predominantly portray just such street sellers. Although street sellers are the most visible, our data suggest that they represent what might be called the tip of the cocaine dealing iceberg.

Levels of Entry

The levels at which a potential dealer's friends/connections were selling helped determine the level at which the new dealer entered the business. If the novitiate was moving in social scenes where "big dealers" are found, then s/he is likely to begin by selling grams and parts of grams. When supplies were not fronted, new dealers' personal finances, i.e., available capital, also influenced how much they could buy at one time.

Sellers move up and down the cocaine sales ladder as well as in and out of the occupation (see Adler, 1985). Some of our sellers were content to remain part-ounce dealers selling between a quarter and a half an ounce a week. Other sellers were more ambitious and eventually sought to become bigger dealers in order to increase profits. One interviewee reported that her unusually well organized suppliers had sales quotas, price fixing, and minimum purchase expectations which pushed her toward expansion. The levels of sales and selling styles of the new dealer's suppliers, then, interacted with personal ambitions to influence eventual sales careers.

Another important aspect of beginning to sell cocaine is whether the connection is willing to "front" the cocaine (risk a consignment arrangement) rather than requiring the beginner to pay in full. Having to pay "up front" for one's inventory sometimes slowed sales by tying up capital, or even deterred some potential dealers from entering the business. Fronted cocaine allowed people with limited resources to enter the occupation. Decisions to front or not to front were based primarily on the connection's evaluation of the new seller's ability to "move" the product. This was seen as a function of the potential volume of business the beginning seller could generate among his/her networks of friends and/or customers. The connection/fronter also evaluates the trustworthiness of the potential dealer, as well as their own capability of absorbing the loss should the deal "go bad" and the frontee be unable to pay. The judgment of the fronter is crucial, for a mistake can be very costly and there is no legal recourse.

Learning to Deal

In the go-between, stash and connoisseur modes of entree, novices gradually learn the tricks of the trade by observing the selling styles of active dealers, and ultimately by doing. Weighing, packaging, and pricing the product are basic techniques. A scale, preferably a triple-beam type . . . accurate to the tenth of a gram, is a necessary tool. In the last ten years answering machines, beepers, and even cellular phones have become important tools as well. Learning how to manage customers and to establish selling routines and rules of procedure are all essential skills that successful dealers must master.

The dealers who enter sales through the apprenticeship and product line expansion modes have the advantage of their own or their partner/seller's experience. Active marijuana sellers already have a network of customers, scales, familiarity with metric measures, and, most important, a connection to help them move into a new product line. Apprentices have lived with and/or observed the selling styles of their dealer/mentors and have access to their equipment, connections and customers. Both apprentices and marijuana dealers who have expanded into cocaine also know how to "maintain a low profile" and avoid any kind of attention that might culminate in arrest. In this way they were able to reduce or manage the paranoia that often inheres in drug dealing circles.

Many sellers learn by making mistakes, often expensive mistakes. These include: using too much cocaine themselves, fronting drugs to people who do not pay for them, and adding too much "cut" (usually an inactive adulterant such as vitamin B) to their product so they develop a reputation for selling inferior cocaine and sometimes have difficulty selling the diluted product. One 32-year-old African-American male made one such error in judgment by fronting to too many people who did not "come through." It ended up costing him $15,000:

> It was because of my own recklessness that I allowed myself to get into that position. There was a period where I had a lot of weight that I just took it and just shipped it out to people I shouldn't have shipped it out

> to. . . . I did this with 10 people and a lot of them were women to be exact. I had a lot of women coming over to my house and I just gave them an ounce apiece one time. . . . So when maybe 6 of those people didn't come through . . . there was a severe cramp in my cash flow. This made me go to one of the family members to get the money to re-cop. (Case # E-11)

Business Sense/People Sense

Many people have a connection, the money to make the initial buy, a reputation for being reliable, and a group of friends interested in buying drugs, but still lack the business sense to be a successful dealer. Just because a person drifts into dealing does not mean that he or she will prosper and stay in dealing. We found a variety of ways in which people initially became dealers, few of which hinged on profits. But what determined whether they continued dealing was their business sense. Thus even though a profit orientation had little to do with becoming a dealer, the ability to consistently realize profits had a major influence over who remained a dealer. In this sense, cocaine selling was like any other capitalist endeavor.

According to our respondents, one's ability to be a competent dealer depended on being able to separate business from pleasure. Success or failure at making this separation over time determined whether a profit was realized. Certain business practices were adopted by prosperous dealers to assist them in making this important distinction. For example, prepackaging both improves quality control and helps keep inventory straight; establishing rules for customers concerning when they can purchase and at what prices reduces the level of hassle; limiting the amount of fronting can reduce gross sales volume, but it also reduces financial risk and minimizes the amount of debt collection work; and limiting their own personal use keeps profits from disappearing up one's nose or in one's pipe.

Being a keen judge of character was seen as another important component of being a skilled dealer. Having the "people skills" to judge whether a person could be trusted to return with the money for fronted supplies, to convince people to pay debts that the dealer had no legal mechanisms for collecting, and to engender the trust of a connection when considerable amounts of money were at stake, are just a few of the sophisticated interpersonal skills required of a competent dealer.

Adler also discusses the importance of a "good personal reputation" among upper level dealers and smugglers:

> One of the first requirements for success, whether in drug trafficking, business enterprise broadly, or any life undertaking, is the establishment of a good personal reputation. To make it in the drug world, dealers and smugglers had to generate trust and likability. (1985:100)

Adler's general point applies to our respondents as well, although the experiences of some of our middle and lower level dealers suggested a slight amendment: A likable person with a good reputation could sell a less than high quality product, but an unlikable person, even one with a bad reputation, could still do a considerable amount of business if s/he had an excellent product. One 47-year-old white woman described her "difficult" husband/partner, "powder keg Paul":

> He would be so difficult, you couldn't believe it. Somebody [this difficult] better have a super primo product to make all this worthwhile. . . . He's the kind of guy you don't mind buying from because you know you'll get a good product, but he's the kind of guy you never want to sell to . . . he was that difficult. (Case # E-1)

High quality cocaine, in other words, is always at a premium in this subculture, so even without good people skills a dealer or connection with "good product" was tolerated.

From User to Dealer: The Transformation of Identity

In each of our respondents' deviant careers there occurred what Becker referred to as a change in self conception. Among our respondents, this took the form of a subtle shift in identity from a person who *has* a good connection for cocaine to a person who *is* a good connection for cocaine. There is a corresponding change in the meaning of, and the motives for, selling. The relationship between the seller and the customer undergoes a related transformation, from "picking up something for a friend" to conducting a commercial transaction. In essence, dealing becomes a business quite like most others, and the dealer gradually takes on the professional identity of a business person. Everett Hughes, writing on the sociology of work, urged social scientists to remember that when we look at work,

> We need to rid ourselves of any concepts which keep us from seeing that the essential problems of men at work are the same whether they do their work in the laboratories of some famous institution or in the messiest vat of a pickle factory. (1951:313)

When they had fully entered the dealer role, our respondents came to see selling cocaine as a job—work, just like other kinds of work save for its illegality. For most, selling cocaine did not mean throwing out conventional values and norms. In fact, many of our respondents actively maintained their conventional identities (see Broadhead, 1983). Such identities included those of parents, legally employed workers, neighbors, church-goers and softball players, to list just a few. Dealer identities tended not to replace former, "legitimate" identities but were added to a person's repertoire of more conventional identities.

Like everyone else in modern life, sellers emphasized one or another dimension of their identities as appropriate to the situation. In his study of heroin addicts Biernacki notes that, "The arrangement of identities must continuously be managed in such a way as to stress some identities at certain points in particular social worlds and situations, and at the same time to de-emphasize others" (1986:23). Our sellers, too, had to become adept at articulating the proper identity at the proper time. By day, one woman dealer was a concerned mother at her daughter's kindergarten field trip, and that same evening she was an astute judge of cocaine quality when picking up an ounce from her connection. At least for our interviewees, selling cocaine rarely entailed entirely terminating other social roles and obligations.

Yet, at some point in all of our sellers' careers, they found themselves transformed from someone who has a good connection to someone who is a good connection, and they gradually came to accept the identity of dealer as a part of their selves. Customers began to treat them like a salesperson, expecting them to be available to take calls and do business and even for services such as special off-hour pick-ups and deliveries or reduced rates for volume purchases. When dealers found themselves faced with such demands, they typically began to feel *entitled* to receive profits from selling. They came to be seen as dealers by others, and in part for this reason, came to see themselves as dealers. As Becker's (1963) model suggests, selling *behavior* usually preceded not only motivation but also changes in attitude and identity. As one 38-year-old white woman put it,

> I took over the business and paid all my husband's debts and started to make some money. One day I realized I was a coke dealer. . . . It was scary, but the money was good. (Case # E-75)

Acceptance of the dealer identity brings with it some expectations and values shared by dealers and customers alike. Customers have the expectation that the dealer will have a consistent supply of cocaine for sale. Customers also expect that the dealer will report in a fairly accurate manner the quality of his/her present batch of drugs within the confines of the *caveat emptor* philosophy that informs virtually all commercial activities in market societies. Buyers do not expect sellers to denigrate their product, but they do not expect the dealer to claim that their product is "excellent" if it is merely "good." Customers assume the dealer will make a profit, but dealers should not be "too greedy." A greedy dealer is one who makes what is estimated by the buyer to be excessive profits. Such estimations of excessiveness vary widely among customers and between sellers and buyers. But the fact that virtually all respondents spoke of some unwritten code of fairness suggests that there is, in E. P. Thompson's (1971) phrase, a "moral economy" of drug dealing that constrains the drive for profit maximization even within an illicit market.[6]

For their part, dealers expect that customers will act in a fashion that will minimize their chances of being arrested by being circumspect about revealing their dealer status. One simply did not, for example, bring to a dealer's house friends whom the dealer had not met. Dealers want customers to appreciate the risks undertaken to provide them with cocaine. And dealers come to feel that such risks deserve profits. After all, the seller is the one who takes the greatest risks; s/he could conceivably receive a stiff jail sentence for a sales conviction. While drifting into dealing and selling mostly to friends and acquaintances mitigated the risks of arrest and reduced their paranoia, such risks remained omnipresent.

In fact, the growing realization of such risks—and the rationalization it provided for dealing on a for-profit basis—was an integral part of becoming a cocaine seller. As our 38-year-old white woman dealer put it, "When it's all said and done, I'm the one behind bars, and I had better have made some money while I was selling or why in the hell take the risk?" (Case # E-75)

Acknowledgment

The research reported herein was funded by a grant from the National Institute of Justice (#7-0363-9-CA-IJ), Bernard A. Gropper, Ph.D., Program Manager, Drugs, Alcohol and Crime Programs, Center for Crime Control Research. The views expressed herein are those of the authors alone. The authors are grateful to the anonymous reviewers of *Qualitative Sociology* for helpful comments.

Address correspondence to Sheigla Murphy, Institute for Scientific Analysis, 2235 Lombard Street, San Francisco, CA, 94123.

Notes

1. Adler also refers briefly to Matza's formulations within her discussion of becoming a dealer (pp. 127–128, 1985).

2. It must be noted at the outset that the predominately white, working and middle-class cocaine sellers we interviewed are very likely to differ from inner-city crack dealers depicted in the media. While there is now good reason to believe that both the profits and the violence reported to be endemic in the crack trade have been exaggerated (e.g., Reuter, 1990, and Goldstein et al., 1989, respectively), our data are drawn from a different population, selling a different form of the drug, who were typically drawn to selling for different reasons. Thus the exigencies they faced and their responses to them are also likely to differ from those of inner-city crack sellers.

3. Rock party houses are distinct from "rock houses" or "crack houses." In the former, sellers invite only selected customers to their homes to smoke rock and "party." Unlike crack houses, where crack is sold to all comers, outsiders are never invited to rock party houses, and the arrangement is social and informal. Proprietors of both types, however, charge participants for the cocaine.

4. Car meets are transactions that take place in cars. Arrangements are made over the telephone in advance and both buyer and seller arrange to meet at parking lots, usually at busy shopping centers, and exchange drugs and money. Each arrives in his or her own car and leaves separately.

5. These movements back and forth among different levels of involvement in dealing were different from the "shifts and oscillations" found among the cocaine dealers studied by Adler (1985:133–141). She studied a circle of high-level dealers over an extended period of field work and found that the stresses and strains of dealing at the top of the pyramid often led her participants to attempt to get out of the business. While many of our interviewees felt similar

pressures later in their careers and subsequently quit, our focus here is on becoming a cocaine seller.

6. In addition to lore about "righteous" and "rip off" dealers, there were present other norms that suggested the existence of such an unwritten code or moral economy, e.g., refusing to sell to children or to adults who "couldn't handle it" (i.e., had physical, familial, or work-related problems because of cocaine use).

References

Adler, P. (1985). *Wheeling and Dealing: An Ethnography of an Upper-Level Drug Dealing Community.* New York: Columbia University Press.

Becker, H. S. (1953). "Becoming a marijuana user." *American Journal of Sociology* 59:235-242.

Becker, H. S. (1963). *Outsiders.* New York: Free Press.

Becker, H. S. (1986). *Pathways from Heroin Addiction.* Philadelphia: Temple University Press.

Biernacki, P., and Waldorf, D. (1981). "Snowball sampling: problems and techniques of chain referral sampling." *Sociological Methods and Research* 10:141-163.

Broadhead, R. (1983). *The Private Lives and Professional Identity of Medical Students.* New Brunswick, NJ: Transaction Books.

Feldman, H. W. (1968). "Ideological supports to becoming and remaining a heroin addict." *Journal of Health and Social Behavior* 9:131-139.

Fields, A. (1985). "Weedslingers: a study of young black marijuana dealers." *Urban Life* 13:247-270.

Goldstein, P., Brownstein, H., Ryan, P., and Belucci, P. (1989). "Crack and homicide in New York City, 1988." *Contemporary Drug Problems* 16:651-687.

Grinspoon, L., and Bakalar, J. (1976). *Cocaine: A Drug and Its Social Evolution.* New York: Basic Books.

Hughes, E. (1951). "Work and the self." In John Rohrer and Muzafer Sherif (eds.), *Social Work at the Crossroads.* New York: Harper and Brothers, 313-323.

Langer, J. (1977). "Drug entrepreneurs and dealing culture." *Social Problems* 24:377-386.

Lindesmith, A. (1947). *Addiction and Opiates.* Chicago: Aldine Press.

Macdonald, P., Waldorf, D., Reinarman, C., and Murphy, S. (1988). "Heavy cocaine use and sexual behavior." *Journal of Drug Issues* 18:437-455.

Matza, D. (1964). *Delinquency and Drift.* New York: Wiley.

Matza, D. (1969). *Becoming Deviant.* Englewood Cliffs, NJ: Prentice Hall.

Morales, E. (1986a). "Coca culture: the white gold of Peru." *Graduate School Magazine of City University of New York* 1:4-11.

Morales, E. (1986b). "Coca and cocaine economy and social change in the Andes in Peru." *Economic Development and Social Change* 35:143-161.

Morales, E. (1988). *Cocaine: The White Gold Rush in Peru.* Tucson, AZ: University of Arizona Press.

Murphy, S., Reinarman, C., and Waldorf, D. (1989). "An eleven year follow-up of a network of cocaine users." *British Journal of the Addictions* 84:427-436.

Plasket, B., and Quillen, E. (1985). *The White Stuff.* New York: Dell Publishing Company.

Preble, E., and Casey, J. H., Jr. (1969). "Taking care of business: the heroin user's life on the streets." *The International Journal of the Addictions* 4:1-24.

Reinarman, C., Waldorf, D., and Murphy, S. (1988). "Scapegoating and social control in the construction of a public problem: empirical and critical findings on cocaine and work." *Research in Law, Deviance and Social Control* 9:37-62.

Reuter, P. (1990). *Money from Crime: The Economics of Drug Dealing.* Santa Monica, CA: Rand Corporation.

Rosenbaum, M. (1981). *Women on Heroin.* New Brunswick, NJ: Rutgers University Press.

Sanabria, H. (1988). *Coca, Migration and Socio-Economic Change in a Bolivian Highland Peasant Community.* Ph.D. thesis, University of Wisconsin.

Sanchez, J., and Johnson, B. (1987). "Women and the drug crime connection: crime rates among drug abusing women at Riker's Island." *Journal of Psychoactive Drugs* 19:205–215.

Sykes, G., and Matza, D. (1957). "Techniques of neutralization." *American Sociological Review* 22:664–670.

Thompson, E. P. (1971). "The moral economy of the English crowd in the eighteenth century." *Past and Present* 50:76–136.

Waldorf, D., Reinarman, C., Murphy, S., and Joyce, B. (1977). *Doing Coke: An Ethnography of Cocaine Snorters and Sellers.* Washington, DC: Drug Abuse Council.

Waldorf, D., Reinarman, C., and Murphy, S. (1991). *Cocaine Changes.* Philadelphia: Temple University Press.

Watters, J. K., and Biernacki, P. (1989). "Targeted sampling: options for the study of hidden populations." *Social Problems* 36:416–430.

Williams, T. (1989). *The Cocaine Kids.* New York: Addison-Wesley.

Confronting Deadly Disease: The Drama of Identity Construction among Gay Men with AIDS

Kent L. Sandstrom

The phenomenon of AIDS (acquired immunodeficiency syndrome) has been attracting increased attention from sociologists. A number of observers have examined the social meanings of the illness (Conrad 1986; Sontag 1989; Palmer 1989), the social influences and behavior involved in its onset and progression (Kaplan et al. 1987) and the larger social consequences of the AIDS epidemic (Ergas 1987). Others have studied the "psychosocial" issues faced by individuals who are either diagnosed with the illness (Nichols 1985; Baumgartner 1986; Weitz 1989) or closely involved with someone who has been diagnosed (Salisbury 1986; Geiss, Fuller and Rush 1986; Macklin 1988).

Despite this growing interest in the social and psychosocial dimensions of AIDS, little attention has been directed toward the processes of social and self-interaction (Denzin 1983) by which individuals acquire and personalize an AIDS-related identity. Further, given the stigmatizing implications of AIDS, there has been a surprising lack of research regarding the strategies of stigma management and identity construction utilized by persons with this illness.

This article presents an effort to address these issues. It examines the dynamics of identity construction and management which characterize the everyday lives of persons with AIDS (PWAs). In doing so, it highlights the socially ambiguous status of PWAs and considers (a) the processes through which they personalize the illness, (b) the dilemmas they encounter in their interpersonal relations, (c) the strategies they employ to avoid or minimize potentially discrediting social attributions, and (d) the subcultural networks and ideologies which they draw upon as they construct, avow and embrace AIDS-related identities. Finally, these themes are situated within the unfolding career and lived experience of people with AIDS.

Method and Data

The following analysis is based on data gathered in 56 in-depth interviews with 19 men who had been diagnosed with HIV (human immunodeficiency virus) infections. On the average, each individual was interviewed on three separate occasions and each of these sessions lasted from 1 to 3 hours. The interviews, conducted between July 1987 and February 1988, were guided by 60 open-ended questions and were audiotaped. Most interviews took place in the participants' homes. However, a few participants were interviewed in a private university office because their living quarters were not conducive to a confidential conversation.

Participants were initially recruited through two local physicians who treat AIDS patients and through a local self-help organization that provides support groups and services for people with HIV infections. Those individuals who agreed to be interviewed early in the study spoke with friends or acquaintances and encouraged them to become involved. The majority of interviews were thus obtained through "snowball" or chain-referral sampling.

By employing a snowball sampling procedure, we were able to gain fairly rapid access to persons with AIDS-related diagnoses and to discuss sensitive issues with them. However, due to its reliance on self-selection processes and relatively small social networks, this method is not likely to reflect the range of variation which exists in the population of persons with advanced AIDS-related infections. This study is thus best regarded as exploratory.

All respondents were gay males who lived in a metropolitan area in the Midwest. They varied in age, income, and the stage of their illness. In age, they ranged from 19 to 46 years, with the majority in the 28 to 40 age bracket. Six persons were currently employed in professional or white-collar occupations. The remaining 13 were living marginally on Social Security or disability benefits. Several members of this latter group had previously been employed in either blue-collar or service occupations. Seven individuals were diagnosed with AIDS, 10 were diagnosed with ARC (AIDS-related complex), and 2 were diagnosed as HIV positive but both had more serious HIV-related health complications (e.g., tuberculosis).

On Becoming a PWA: The Realization of an AIDS Identity

For many of these men, the transformation of physical symptoms into the personal and social reality of AIDS took place most dramatically when they received a validating diagnosis from a physician. The following account reveals the impact of being officially diagnosed:

> She [the doctor] said, "Your biopsy did come out for Kaposi's sarcoma. I want you to go to the hospital tomorrow and to plan to spend most of

the day there." While she is telling me this, the whole world is buzzing in my head because this is the first confirmation coming from outside as opposed to my own internal suspicions. I started to cry—it (AIDS) became very real . . . *very real* . . . .

Anyway, everything started to roller coaster inside me and I was crying in the office there. The doctor said "You knew this was the way it was going to come out, didn't you?" She seemed kind of shocked about why I was crying so much, not realizing that no matter how much you are internally aware of something, to hear it from someone else is what makes it real. For instance, the first time I really accepted being gay was when other people said "You are gay!" . . . It's a social thing—you're not real until you're real to someone else.

This quote illustrates the salience of social processes for the validation and realization of an identity—in this case, an AIDS-related identity. Becoming a PWA is not simply a matter of viral infection, it is contingent on interpersonal interaction and definitions. As depicted in the quote, a rather momentous medical announcement facilitates a process of identity construction which, in turn, entails both interpersonal and subjective transformation. Within the interpersonal realm, the newly diagnosed "AIDS patient" is resituated as a social object and placed in a marginal or liminal status. He is thereby separated from many of his prior social moorings. On the subjective level, this separation produces a crisis, or a disruption of the PWA's routine activities and self-understanding. The diagnosed individual is prompted to "make sense" of the meaning of his newly acquired status and to feel its implications for future conceptions and enactments of self . . . .

Interpersonal Dilemmas Encountered by PWAs

Stigmatization

Stigmatization is one of the most significant difficulties faced by people with AIDS as they attempt to fashion a personal and social meaning for their illness. The vast majority of our informants had already experienced some kind of stigma because of their gay identities. When they were diagnosed with AIDS, they usually encountered even stronger homophobic reactions and discreditation efforts. An especially painful form of stigmatization occurred when PWAs were rejected by friends and family members after revealing their diagnosis. Many respondents shared very emotional accounts of how they were ostracized by parents, siblings, or colleagues. Several noted that their parents and family members had even asked them to no longer return home for visits. However, rejections were not always so explicit. In many cases, intimate relationships were gradually and ambiguously phased out rather than abruptly or clearly ended.

A few PWAs shared stories of being stigmatized by gay friends or acquaintances. They described how some acquaintances subtly reprimanded them when seeing them at gay bars or repeatedly reminded them to "be careful" regarding any sexual involvements. Further, they mentioned that certain gay friends avoided associating with them after learning of their AIDS-related diagnoses. These PWAs thus experienced the problem of being "doubly stigmatized" (Kowalewski 1988), that is, they were devalued within an already stigmatized group, the gay community.

PWAs also felt the effects of stigmatization in other, more subtle ways. For example, curious and even sympathetic responses on the parts of others, especially strangers, could lead PWAs to feel discredited. One PWA, reflecting on his interactions with hospital staff, observed:

> When they become aware [of my diagnosis], it seemed like people kept looking at me . . . like they were looking for something. What it felt like was being analyzed, both physically and emotionally. It also felt like being a subject or guinea pig . . . like "here's another one." They gave me that certain kind of look. Kind of that look like pity or that said "what a poor wretch," not a judgmental look but rather a pitying one.

An experience of this nature can precipitate a crisis of identity for a person with AIDS. He finds himself being publicly stigmatized and identified as a victim. Such an identifying moment can seriously challenge prior conceptions of self and serve as a turning point from which new self-images or identities are constructed (Charmaz 1980). That is, it can lead a PWA to internalize stigmatizing social attributions or it can incite him to search for involvements and ideologies which might enable him to construct a more desirable AIDS identity.

Counterfeit Nurturance

Given the physical and social implications of their illness, PWAs typically desire some kind of special nurturing from friends, partners, family members, or health practitioners. Yet displays of unusual concern or sympathy on the part of others can be threatening to self. People with AIDS may view such expressions of nurturance as counterfeit or harmful because they highlight their condition and hence confirm their sense of difference and vulnerability.

The following observation illustrates the sensitivity of PWAs to this problem:

> One thing that makes you feel kind of odd is when people come across supportive and want to be supportive but it doesn't really feel like they are supportive. There is another side to them that's like, well, they are being nice to you because they feel sorry for you, or because it makes them feel good about themselves to help someone with AIDS, not because they really care about you.

PWAs often find themselves caught in a paradox regarding gestures of exceptional help or support. They want special consideration at times, but if they accept support or concern which is primarily focused on their condition, they are likely to feel that a "victim identity" is being imposed on them. This exacerbates some of the negative self-feelings that have already been triggered by the illness. It also leads PWAs to be more wary of the motivations underlying others' expressions of nurturance.

Given these dynamics, PWAs may reach out to each other in an effort to find relationships that are more mutually or genuinely nurturing. This strategy is problematic, though, because even PWAs offer one another support which emphasizes their condition. They are also likely to remind each other of the anomalous status they share and the "spoiled" features (Goffman 1963) of their identities qua PWAs.

Ultimately, suspicions of counterfeit nurturance can lead those diagnosed with AIDS to feel mistreated by almost everyone, particularly by caregivers who are most directly involved in helping them. Correctly or incorrectly, PWAs tend to share some feelings of ambivalence and resentment towards friends, lovers, family members, and medical personnel.

Fears of Contagion and Death Anxiety

Fears of contagion present another serious dilemma for PWAs in their efforts to negotiate a functional social identity. These fears are generated not only by the fact that people with AIDS are the carriers of an epidemic illness but also because, like others with a death taint, they are symbolically associated with mass death and the contagion of the dead (Lifton 1967). The situation may even be further complicated by the contagion anxiety which homosexuality triggers for some people.

In general, others are tempted to withdraw from an individual with AIDS because of their fears of contracting the virus. Even close friends of a PWA are apt to feel more fearful or distant toward him, especially when first becoming aware of the diagnosis. They may feel anxious about the possibility of becoming infected with the virus through interactions routinely shared with him in the past (e.g., hugging and kissing). They may also wish to avoid the perils of being stigmatized themselves by friends or associates who fear that those close to a PWA are a potential source of contagion.

Another dimension of contagion anxiety is reflected in the tendency of significant others to avoid discussing issues with a PWA that might lead them to a deeper apprehension of the death-related implications of his diagnosis. As Lifton (1967) suggested, the essence of contagion anxiety is embodied in the fear that "if I come too close to a death tainted person, I will experience his death and his annihilation" (p. 518).

This death-related contagion anxiety often results in increased strain and distance in a PWA's interactions with friends or family members. It can also inhibit the level of openness and intimacy shared among fellow PWAs when they gather together to address issues provoked by their diagnoses. Responses of grief, denial, and anxiety in the face of death make in-depth discussions of the illness experience keenly problematic. According to one respondent:

> Usually no one's ever able to talk about it [their illness and dying] without going to pieces. They might start but it only takes about two minutes to break into tears. They might say something like "I don't know what to do! I might not even be here next week!" Then you can just see the ripple effect it has on the others sitting back and listening. You have every possible expression from anger to denial to sadness and all these different emotions on people's faces. And mostly this feeling of "what can we do? Well . . . Nothing!"

Problems of Normalization

Like others who possess a stigmatizing attribute, people with AIDS come to regard many social situations with alarm (Goffman 1971) and uncertainty (Davis 1974). They soon discover that their medical condition is a salient aspect of all but their most fleeting social encounters. They also quickly learn that their diagnosis, once known to others, can acquire the character of a *master status* (Hughes 1945; Becker 1963) and thus become the focal point of interaction. It carries with it, "the potential for inundating the expressive boundaries of a situation" (Davis 1974, 166) and hence for creating significant strains or rupture in the ongoing flow of social intercourse.

In light of this, one might expect PWAs to prefer interaction contexts characterized by "closed" awareness (Glaser and Strauss 1968). Their health status would be unknown to others and they would presumably encounter fewer problems when interacting. However, when in these situations, they must remain keenly attuned to controlling information and concealing attributes relevant to their diagnosis. Ironically, this requirement to be dramaturgically "on" may give rise to even more feelings of anxiety and resentment.

The efforts of persons with AIDS to establish and maintain relationships within more "open" contexts are also fraught with complications. One of the major dilemmas they encounter is how to move interactions beyond an atmosphere of fictional acceptance (Davis 1974). A context of fictional acceptance is typified by responses on the part of others which deny, avoid, or minimize the reality of an individual's diagnosis. In attempting to grapple with the management of a spoiled identity, PWAs may seek to "break through" (Davis 1974) relations of this nature. In doing so, they often try to broaden the scope of interactional involvement and to normalize problematic elements of their social identity. That is, they attempt to project "images, attitudes and concepts of self which encourage the normal to identify with [them] (i.e., 'take [their] role') in terms other than those associated with imputations of deviance" (Davis 1974, 168).

Yet even if a PWA attains success in "breaking through," it does not necessarily diminish his interactional difficulties. Instead, he can become caught in an ambiguous dilemma with respect to the requisites of awareness and normalization. Simply put, if others begin to disregard his diagnosis and treat him in a normal way, then he faces the problem of having to remind them of the limitations to normalcy imposed by this condition. The person with AIDS is thus required to perform an intricate balancing act between encouraging the normalization of his relationships and ensuring that others remain sensitized to the constraining effects of such a serious illness. These dynamics promote the construction of relationships which, at best, have a qualified sense of normalcy. They also heighten the PWA's sense that he is located in an ambiguous or liminal position.

Avoiding or Minimizing Dilemmas

In an attempt to avoid or defuse the problematic feelings, attributions, and ambiguities which arise in their ongoing interactions, PWAs engage in various forms of identity management. In doing so, they often use strategies which allow them to minimize the social visibility of their diagnoses and to carefully control interactions with others. These strategies include *passing, covering, isolation, and insulation.*

The particular strategies employed vary according to the progression of their illness, the personal meanings they attach to it, the audiences serving as primary referents for self-presentations, and the dynamics of their immediate social situation.

Passing and Covering

As Goffman (1963) noted in his classic work on stigma, those with a spoiled identity may seek to pass as normal by carefully suppressing information and thereby precluding others' awareness of devalued personal attributes. The PWAs we interviewed mentioned that "passing" was a maneuver they had used regularly. It was easily employed in the early stages of the illness when more telltale physical signs had not yet become apparent and awareness of an individual's diagnosis was [confined] to a small social circle.

However, as the illness progresses, concealing the visibility of an AIDS-related diagnosis becomes more difficult. When a person with AIDS begins to miss work frequently, to lose weight noticeably, and to reduce his general level of activity, others become more curious or suspicious about what ailment is provoking such major changes. In the face of related questions, some PWAs elected to devise a "cover" for their diagnosis which disguised troubling symptoms as products of a less discrediting illness.

One informant decided to cover his AIDS diagnosis by telling co-workers that he was suffering from leukemia:

> There was coming a point, I wasn't feeling so hot. I was tired and the quality of my life was decreasing tremendously because all of my free time was spent resting or sleeping. I was still keeping up with work but I thought I'd better tell them something before I had to take more days off here and there to even out the quality of my life. I had already had this little plan to tell them I had leukemia . . . but I thought how am I going to tell them, what am I going to tell them, how am I going to convince them? What am I going to do if someone says, "You don't have leukemia, you have AIDS!"? This was all stuff clicking around in my mind. I thought, how could they possibly know? They only know as much as I tell them.

This quote reveals the heightened concern with information control that accompanies decisions to conceal one's condition. Regardless of the psychic costs, though, a number of our informants opted for this remedial strategy. A commonly used technique consisted of informing friends, parents, or co-workers that one had cancer or tuberculosis without mentioning that these were the presenting symptoms of one's AIDS diagnosis. Covering attempts of this kind were most often employed by PWAs when relating to others who were not aware of their gay identity. These relationships were less apt to be characterized by the suspicions or challenges offered by those who knew that an individual was both gay and seriously ill.

Isolation and Insulation

For those whose diagnosis was not readily visible, dramaturgical skills, such as passing and covering, could be quite useful. These techniques were not so feasible when physical cues, such as a pale complexion, emaciated appearance, or facial lesion made the nature of a PWA's condition more apparent. Under these circumstances, negotiations with others were more alarming and they were more likely to include conflicts engendered by fear, ambiguity, and expressions of social devaluation.

In turn, some PWAs came to view physical and social isolation as the best means available to them for escaping from both these interpersonal difficulties and their own feelings of ambivalence. By withdrawing from virtually all interaction, they sought to be spared the social struggles and psychic strains that could be triggered by others' recognition of their condition. Nonetheless, this strategy was typically an unsuccessful one. Isolation and withdrawal often exacerbated the feelings of alienation that PWAs were striving to minimize in their social relationships. Moreover, their desire to be removed from the interactional matrix was frequently overcome by their need for extensive medical care and interpersonal support as they coped with the progressive effects of the illness.

Given the drawbacks of extreme isolation, a number of PWAs used a more selective withdrawal strategy. It consisted of efforts to disengage from many but not all social involvements and to interact regularly with only a handful of trusted associates (e.g., partners, friends, or family members). Emphasis was placed on minimizing contacts with those outside of this circle because they were likely to be less tolerant or predictable. PWAs engaging in this type of selective interaction tried to develop a small network of intimate others who could insulate them from potentially threatening interactions. Ideally, they were able to form a reliable social circle within which they felt little need to conceal their diagnosis. They could thereby experience some relief from the burden of stigma management and information control.

Building and Embracing an AIDS Identity

Strategies such as passing, covering, isolation, and insulation are used by PWAs, especially in the earlier stages of their illness, to shield themselves from the stigma and uncertainty associated with AIDS. However, these strategies typically require a high level of personal vigilance, they evoke concerns about information control, and they are essentially defensive in nature. They do not provide PWAs with a way to reformulate the personal meaning of their diagnosis and to integrate it with valued definitions of self.

In light of this, most PWAs engage in more active types of *identity work* which allow them to "create, present and sustain personal identities which are congruent with and supportive of the(ir) self-concept[s]" (Snow and Anderson 1987, 1348). Certain types of identity work are especially appealing because they help PWAs to gain a greater sense of mastery over their condition and to make better use of the behavioral possibilities arising from their liminal condition.

The most prominent type of identity work engaged in by the PWAs we interviewed was embracement. As Snow and Anderson (1987) argued, embracement refers to "verbal and expressive confirmation of one's acceptance of and attachment to the social identity associated with a general or specific role, a set of social relationships, or a particular ideology" (p. 1354). Among the PWAs involved in this study, embracement was promoted and reinforced through participation in local AIDS-related support groups.

Support Groups and Associational Embracement

People facing an existential crisis often make use of new memberships and social forms in their efforts to construct a more viable sense of self (Kotarba 1984). The vast majority of respondents in this study became involved in PWA support groups in order to better address the crisis elicited by their illness and to find new forms of self-expression. They typically joined these groups within a few months of receiving their diagnosis and continued to attend meetings on a fairly regular basis.

By and large, support groups became the central focus of identity work and repair for PWAs. These groups were regarded as a valuable source of education and emotional support that helped individuals to cope better with the daily exigencies of their illness. At support group meetings, PWAs could exchange useful information, share feelings and troubles, and relate to others who could see beyond the negative connotations of AIDS.

Support groups also facilitated the formation of social ties and feelings of collective identification among PWAs. Within these circles, individuals learned to better nurture and support one another and to emphasize the shared nature of their problems. Feelings of guilt and isolation were transformed into a sense of group identification. This kind of *associational embracement* (Snow and Anderson 1987) was conveyed in the comments of one person who proclaimed:

> I spend almost all of my time with other PWAs. They're my best friends now and they're the people I feel most comfortable with. We support one another and we know that we can talk to each other any time, day or night.

For some PWAs, especially those with a troubled or marginal past, support group relationships provided an instant "buddy system" that was used to bolster feelings of security and self-worth. Recently formed support group friendships even took on primary importance in their daily lives. Perhaps because of the instability and isolation which characterized their life outside of support groups, a few of these PWAs tended to exaggerate the level of intimacy which existed in their newly found friendships. By stressing a romanticized version of these relationships, they were able to preserve a sense of being cared for even in the absence of more enduring social connections.

Identity Embracement and Affirmation

Most of the PWAs we interviewed had come to gradually affirm and embrace an AIDS-related identity. Participation in a support group exposed them to alternative definitions of the reality of AIDS and an ongoing system of identity construction. Hence, rather than accepting public imputations which cast them as "AIDS victims," PWAs learned to distance themselves from such designations and to avow more favorable AIDS-associated identities. In turn, the process of *identity embracement* was realized when individuals proudly announced that they were PWAs who were "living and thriving with the illness."

Continued associations with other PWAs could also promote deepening involvement in activities organized around the identity of being a person with AIDS. A case in point is provided by a man who recounted his progression as a PWA:

> After awhile, I aligned myself with other people with AIDS who shared my beliefs about taking the active role. I began writing and speaking

> about AIDS and I became involved in various projects. I helped to create and promote a workshop for people with AIDS. . . . I also got involved in organizing a support group for family members of PWAs.

As involvement in AIDS-related activities increases, embracement of an AIDS-centered identity is likely to become more encompassing. In some cases, diagnosed individuals found themselves organizing workshops on AIDS, coordinating a newsletter for PWAs, and delivering speeches regularly at schools and churches. Virtually all aspects of their lives became associated with their diagnosis. Being a PWA thus became both a master status and a valued career. This process was described by a person who had been diagnosed with ARC for two years:

> One interesting thing is that when you have AIDS or ARC and you're not working anymore, you tend to become a veteran professional on AIDS issues. You get calls regularly from people who want information or who want you to get involved in a project, etc. You find yourself getting drawn to that kind of involvement. It becomes almost a second career!

This kind of identity embracement was particularly appealing for a few individuals involved in this study. Prior to contracting an AIDS-related infection, they had felt rejected or unrecognized in many of their social relationships (e.g., family, work, and friendships). Ironically, their stigmatized AIDS diagnosis provided them with an opportunity for social affirmation. It offered them a sense of uniqueness and expertise that was positively evaluated in certain social and community circles (e.g., public education and church forums). It could even serve as a springboard for a new and more meaningful biography.

Ideological Embracement: AIDS as a Transforming Experience

Support groups and related self-help networks are frequently bases for the production and transmission of subcultural perspectives which controvert mainstream social definitions of a stigma. As Becker (1963) argued, when people who share a deviant attribute have the opportunity to interact with one another, they are likely to develop a system of shared meanings emphasizing the differences between their definitions of who they are and the definitions held by other members of the society. "They develop perspectives on themselves and their deviant [attributes] and on their relations with other members of the society" (p. 81). These perspectives guide the stigmatized as they engage in processes of identity construction and embracement.

Subcultural perspectives contain ideologies which assure individuals that what they do on a continuing basis has moral validity (Lofland 1969). Among PWAs, these ideologies were grounded in metaphors of transformation which included an emphasis on *special mission* and *empowerment*.

One of the most prominent subcultural interpretations of AIDS high-lighted the spiritual meaning of the illness. For PWAs embracing this view-point, AIDS was symbolically and experientially inverted from a "curse" to a "blessing" which promoted a liberating rather than a constricting form of identity transformation. The following remarks illustrate this perspective:

> I now view AIDS as both a gift and a blessing. That sounds strange, I suppose, in a limited context. It sounds strange because we [most peo-ple] think it's so awful, but yet there are such radical changes that take place in your life from having this illness that's defined as terminal. You go through this amazing kind of *transformation.* You look at things for the first time, in a powerful new way that you've never looked at them before in your whole life.

A number of PWAs similarly stressed the beneficial personal and spiritual transitions experienced as a result of their diagnosis. They even regarded their illness as a motivating force that led them to grapple with important existential questions and to experience personal growth and change that otherwise would not have occurred.

For many PWAs, *ideological embracement* (Snow and Anderson 1987) en-tailed identity constructions based on a quasi-religious sense of "special mission." These individuals placed a premium on disseminating informa-tion about AIDS and promoting a level of public awareness which might inhibit the further transmission of this illness. Some felt that their diagno-sis had provided them with a unique opportunity to help and educate oth-ers. They subsequently displayed a high level of personal sacrifice and commitment while seeking to spread the news about AIDS and to nurture those directly affected by this illness. Most crucially, their diagnosis pro-vided them with a heightened sense of power and purpose:

> Basically I feel that as a person with ARC I can do more for humanity in general than I could ever do before. I never before in my life felt like I belonged here. For the most part, I felt like I was stranded on a hos-tile planet—I didn't know why. But now with the disease and what I've learned in my life, I feel like I really have something by which I can help other people. It gives me a special sense of purpose.
>
> I feel like I've got a mission now and that's what this whole thing is about. AIDS is challenging me with a question and the question it asks is: If I'm not doing something to help others regarding this illness, then why continue to use up energy here on this earth?

The idea of a "special mission" is often a revitalizing formulation for those who carry a death taint (Lifton 1967). It helps to provide PWAs with a sense of mastery and self-worth by giving their condition a more positive or redemptive meaning. This notion also gives form and resolu-tion to painful feelings of loss, grief, guilt, and death anxiety. It enables individuals to make use of these emotions, while at the same time tran-scending them. Moreover, the idea of special mission provides PWAs with a framework through which they can moralize their activities and continuing lives.

Beliefs stressing the empowering aspects of AIDS also served as an important focus of identity affirmation. These beliefs were frequently rooted in the sense of transformation provoked by the illness. Many of those interviewed viewed their diagnosis as empowering because it led them to have a concentrated experience of life, a stronger sense of purpose, a better understanding of their personal resources and a clearer notion of how to prioritize their daily concerns. They correspondingly felt less constrained by mundane aspects of the AIDS experience and related symptoms.

A sense of empowerment could additionally be derived from others' objectification of PWAs as sources of danger, pollution, or death. This was illustrated in the remarks of an informant who had Kaposi's sarcoma:

> People hand power to me on a silver platter because they are afraid. It's not fear of catching the virus or anything, I think it is just fear of identification with someone who is dying.

The interactional implications of such attributions of power were also recognized by this same informant:

> Because I have AIDS, people leave me alone in my life in some respects if I want them to. I never used to be able to get people to back off and now I can. I'm not the one who is doing this, so to speak. They are giving me the power to do so.

Most PWAs realized their condition offered them an opportunity to experience both psychological and social power. They subsequently accentuated the empowering dimensions of their lived experience of AIDS and linked these to an encompassing metaphor of transformation.

Summary and Conclusions

People with AIDS face many obstacles in their efforts to construct and sustain a desirable social identity. In the early stages of their career, after receiving a validating diagnosis, they are confronted by painful self-feelings such as grief, guilt, and death anxiety. These feelings often diminish their desire and ability to participate in interactions which would allow them to sustain favorable images of self.

PWAs encounter additional difficulties as a result of being situated (at least initially) as liminal persons. That is, their liminal situation can heighten negative self-feelings and evoke a sense of confusion and uncertainty about the social implications of their illness. At the same time, however, it releases them from conventional roles, meanings, or expectations and provides them with a measure of power and maneuverability in the processes of identity construction.

In turn, as they construct and negotiate the meaning of an AIDS-related identity, PWAs must grapple with the effects of social reactions such as stigmatization, counterfeit nurturance, fears of contagion, and death anxiety. These reactions both elicit and reinforce a number of interactional ambiguities, dilemmas, and threats to self.

In responding to these challenges, PWAs engage in various types of identity management and construction. On one hand, they may seek to disguise their diagnoses or to restrict their social and interactional involvements. PWAs are most likely to use such strategies in the earlier phases of the illness. The disadvantage of these strategies is that they are primarily defensive. They provide PWAs with a way to avoid or adjust to the effects of problematic social reactions, but they do not offer a means for affirming more desirable AIDS-related identities.

On the other hand, as their illness progresses and they become more enmeshed in subcultural networks, most PWAs are prompted to engage in forms of identity embracement which enable them to actively reconstruct the meaning of their illness and to integrate it with valued conceptions of self. In essence, through their interactions with other PWAs, they learn to embrace affiliations and ideologies which accentuate the transformative and empowering possibilities arising from their condition. They also acquire the social and symbolic resources necessary to fashion revitalizing identities and to sustain a sense of dignity and self-worth.

Ultimately, through their ongoing participation in support networks, PWAs are able to build identities which are linked to their lived experience of AIDS. They are also encouraged to actively confront and transform the stigmatizing conceptions associated with this medical condition. Hence, rather than resigning themselves to the darker implications of AIDS, they learn to affirm themselves as "people with AIDS" who are "living and thriving with the illness."

References

Baumgartner, G. 1986. *AIDS: Psychosocial factors in the acquired immune deficiency syndrome.* Springfield, IL: Charles C. Thomas.

Becker, H. S. 1963. *Outsiders.* New York: Free Press.

Charmaz, K. 1980. The social construction of pity in the chronically ill. *Studies in Symbolic Interaction* 3:123–45.

Conrad, P. 1986. The social meaning of AIDS. *Social Policy* 17:51–56.

Davis, F. 1974. Deviance disavowal and the visibly handicapped. In *Deviance and liberty,* edited by L. Rainwater, 163–72. Chicago: Aldine.

Denzin, N. 1983. A note on emotionality, self and interaction. *American Journal of Sociology* 89:402–9.

Ergas, Y. 1987. The social consequences of the AIDS epidemic. *Social Science Research Council/Items* 41:33–39.

Geiss, S., R. Fuller, and J. Rush. 1986. Lovers of AIDS victims: Psychosocial stresses and counseling needs. *Death Studies* 10:43–53.

Goffman, E. 1963. *Stigma.* Englewood Cliffs, NJ: Prentice Hall.

———. 1971. *Relations in public.* New York: Harper & Row.

Glaser, B. S., and A. L Strauss. 1968. *Awareness of dying*. Chicago: Aldine.

Hughes, E. C. 1945. Dilemmas and contradictions of status. *American Journal of Sociology* 50:353–59.

Kaplan, H., R. Johnson, C. Bailey, and W. Simon. 1987. The sociological study of AIDS: A critical review of the literature and suggested research agenda. *Journal of Health and Social Behavior* 28:140–57.

Kotarba, J. 1984. A synthesis: The existential self in society. In *The existential self in society,* edited by J. Kotarba and A. Fontana, 222–33. Chicago: Aldine.

Kowalewski, M. 1988. Double stigma and boundary maintenance: How gay men deal with AIDS. *Journal of Contemporary Ethnography* 7:211–28.

Lifton, R. J. 1967. *Death in life*. New York: Random House.

Lofland, J. 1969. *Deviance and identity*. Englewood Cliffs, NJ: Prentice Hall.

Macklin, E. 1988. AIDS: Implications for families. *Family Relations* 37:141–49.

Nichols, S. 1985. Psychosocial reactions of persons with AIDS. *Annals of Internal Medicine* 103:13–16.

Palmer, S. 1989. AIDS as metaphor. *Society* 26:45–51.

Salisbury, D. 1986. AIDS: Psychosocial implications. *Journal of Psychosocial Nursing* 24 (12): 13–16.

Snow, D., and L. Anderson. 1987. Identity work among the homeless: The verbal construction and avowal of personal identities. *American Journal of Sociology* 1336–71.

Sontag, S. 1989. *AIDS and its metaphors*. New York: Farrar, Straus & Giroux.

Weitz, R. 1989. Uncertainty and the lives of persons with AIDS. *Journal of Health and Social Behavior* 30:270–81.

Deviant Careers and Identities: Some Additional Forms and Shapes— Peers, Gangs, and Organizations

As the preceding descriptions reveal, deviant or semideviant occupations vary in terms of their sophistication and corresponding organizational structure; the house prostitute, given the particular nature of the profession, is subjected to a more elaborate and intense degree of socialization than is the call girl. This means that deviance and the deviant career can exhibit a variety of patterns, each with its own recruiting offices, entry routes, career lines, socialization mechanisms, and career shifts. Deviant pursuits can also exhibit (in accord with Best and Luckenbill's concern over the social organization of deviance) a range of mutually beneficial relationships; this is especially evident in the next two selections.

Patricia Yancey Martin and Robert A. Hummer, in "Fraternities and Rape on Campus," note that fraternities are rarely examined in terms of their underlying structure, values, and group processes. The authors focus specifically on those organizational contexts and associated practices that create an abusive social context for women. The researchers, in their examination of rapes in college fraternities, draw on data obtained from a range of newspaper accounts, judges, attorneys, and fraternity members. They initially find that fraternities are vitally concerned with promoting the image of *masculinity*. The researchers observe that fraternities work hard to create a macho image and context, and, accordingly, they avoid any suggestions or indicators of "wimpishness," homosexuality, and femininity. Not only are such values as winning, athleticism, willingness to drink, and sexual prowess stressed, but prospective members who do not measure up to such standards are rejected. Alcohol and activities associated with its use form the cornerstones of the fraternity's social life. Martin and Hummer then move to an analysis of the status and norms associated with pledgeship. Of significance is their description of how the new recruit, who is given a trial membership, is actually socialized by other brothers, most notably by his "Big Brother." It is during this process that the prevailing norms and values are inculcated in the pledge. The pledging experience itself can involve physical abuse, harsh discipline, demands to obey and follow orders, and demeaning activities and rituals. Such emphasis on toughness and obedience to superiors creates a brother who is non-caring and insensitive. Once the status of brother is actually occupied, it is expected that the occupant abide by the practices of brotherhood. At this point, the researchers describe the practices that are especially conducive to the sexual exploitation and coercion of women. For example, the use of alcohol to obtain sex is pervasive. It is often used as a weapon to counter sexual resistance or reluctance. The researchers present materials illustrating how this works, both individually and collectively. Martin and Hummer conclude by describing how women are treated as commodities (i.e., how "fraternities knowingly, and intentionally, *use* women for their benefit"). In this respect, they are used as bait to attract new members, as servers of the members' needs, and as sexual prey. Here, Martin and Hummer describe how the group known as "Little Sisters," because of its virtual lack of affiliation with any other groups (e.g., sororities) and its lack of peer group support, is particularly susceptible to forced sexual encounters with the brothers. Access to such women for sexual gratification is not only a presumed benefit of membership but, and at the individual and collective levels, the brothers develop and execute strategies aimed at achieving sexual gratification. Getting a woman drunk, or inviting women to fraternity parties, getting them drunk, and then forcing sex on them, are but two of the strategies frequently employed. If such organizational contexts and associated practices remain intact, we can expect to obtain outcomes similar to those noted in this research. Clearly, such observations emphasize the need for the complete elimination or radical restructuring of those institutions which, by way of a particularly demeaning ideology, place selected categories of actors in especially vulnerable or susceptible positions. Part VI of this book examines how those perceived as powerless by organizations can be empowered to effect change in an agency's underlying organizational structure, theory of the office, diagnostic stereotypes, working ideology, and staff-socializing practices. Part VI also calls for increased monitoring of the activities and routines of bureaucrats and others.

Andrew Szasz, in "Corporations, Organized Crime, and the Disposal of Hazardous Waste: An Examination of the Making of a Criminogenic Regulatory Structure," offers another interesting account of the types of relationships that can exist among legitimate and illegitimate enterprises or entrepreneurs. He focuses on the disposal of toxic waste, particularly the way in which organized crime became involved in its disposal. Szasz argues that corporate generators of hazardous waste products helped to create a regulatory structure that was accessible and attractive to organized crime. Szasz begins by describing how attempts were made to regulate the disposal of hazardous waste—efforts that resulted in the creation of the federal Resource Conservation and Recovery Act (RCRA). RCRA established procedures for the safe disposal of hazardous substances and authorized states to register the corporate generators of the waste. RCRA also mandated the licensing of hauling and disposal firms. Given organized crime's traditionally heavy involvement in garbage hauling and landfilling, extension of their influence to the illegal disposal of hazardous wastes was relatively straightforward. For example, when RCRA mandated the licensing of firms, mob-connected haulers acquired state permits and called themselves hazardous waste haulers. Organized crime also controlled some final disposal sites; hence, it was easy to have the manifest signed and then state that the waste had been disposed of properly. Other organized crime figures seized control of phony disposal sites and treatment facilities. Szasz continues by describing those political and social-structural factors that enabled organized crime to "'colonize' the hazardous waste disposal industry." Specifically, lax implementation and incompetent enforcement of the provisions of RCRA allowed organized crime to gain a strong foothold in the hazardous waste business. Interim licenses were granted and the manifest system was monitored loosely. Szasz also points to the role of generators of waste. For example, corporate generators lobbied for narrow definitions of hazardous waste as well as less stringent rules for disposal.

39 Fraternities and Rape on Campus

Patricia Yancey Martin
Robert A. Hummer

Rapes are perpetrated on dates, at parties, in chance encounters, and in specially planned circumstances. That group structure and processes, rather than individual values or characteristics, are the impetus for many rape episodes was documented by Blanchard (1959) 30 years ago (also see Geis 1971), yet sociologists have failed to pursue this theme (for an exception, see Chancer 1987). A recent review of research (Muehlenhard and Linton 1987) on sexual violence, or rape, devotes only a few pages to the situational contexts of rape events, and these are conceptualized as potential risk factors for individuals rather than qualities of rape-prone social contexts.

Many rapes, far more than come to the public's attention, occur in fraternity houses on college and university campuses, yet little research has analyzed fraternities at American colleges and universities as rape-prone contexts (cf. Ehrhart and Sandler 1985). Most of the research on fraternities reports on samples of individual fraternity men. One group of studies compares the values, attitudes, perceptions, family socioeconomic status, psychological traits (aggressiveness, dependence), and so on, of fraternity and nonfraternity men (Bohrnstedt 1969; Fox, Hodge, and Ward 1987; Kanin 1967; Lemire 1979; Miller 1973). A second group attempts to identify the effects of fraternity membership over time on the values, attitudes, beliefs, or moral precepts of members (Hughes and Winston 1987; Marlowe and Auvenshine 1982; Miller 1973; Wilder, Hoyt, Doren, Hauck, and Zettle 1978; Wilder, Hoyt, Surbeck, Wilder, and Carney 1986). With minor exceptions, little research addresses the group and organizational context of fraternities or the social construction of fraternity life (for exceptions, see Letchworth 1969; Longino and Kart 1973; Smith 1964).

Gary Tash, writing as an alumnus and trial attorney in his fraternity's magazine, claims that over 90 percent of all gang rapes on college campuses involve fraternity men (1988, p. 2). Tash provides no evidence to substantiate this claim, but students of violence against women have been concerned with fraternity men's frequently reported involvement in rape episodes (Adams and Abarbanel 1988). Ehrhart and Sandler (1985) identify over 50 cases of gang rapes on campus perpetrated by fraternity men, and their analysis points to many of the conditions that we discuss here. Their analysis is unique in focusing on conditions in fraternities that make gang rapes of women by fraternity men both feasible and probable. They identify excessive alcohol use, isolation from external monitoring, treatment of women as prey, use of pornography, approval of violence, and excessive concern with competition as precipitating conditions to gang rape (also see Merton 1985; Roark 1987).

The study reported here confirmed and complemented these findings by focusing on both conditions and processes. We examined dynamics associated with the social construction of fraternity life, with a focus on processes that foster the use of coercion, including rape, in fraternity men's relations with women. Our examination of men's social fraternities on college and university campuses as groups and organizations led us to conclude that fraternities are a physical and sociocultural context that encourages the sexual coercion of women. We make no claims that all fraternities are "bad" or that all fraternity men are rapists. Our observations indicated, however, that rape is especially probable in fraternities because of the kinds of organizations they are, the kinds of members they have, the practices their members engage in, and a virtual absence of university or community oversight. Analyses that lay blame for rapes by fraternity men on "peer pressure" are, we feel, overly simplistic (cf. Burkhart 1989; Walsh 1989). We suggest, rather, that fraternities create a sociocultural context in which the use of coercion in sexual relations with women is normative and in which the mechanisms to keep this pattern of behavior in check are minimal at best and absent at worst. We conclude that unless fraternities change in fundamental ways, little improvement can be expected.

Methodology

Our goal was to analyze the group and organizational practices and conditions that create in fraternities an abusive social context for women. We developed a conceptual framework from an initial case study of an alleged gang rape at Florida State University that involved four fraternity men and an 18-year-old coed. The group rape took place on the third floor of a fraternity house and ended with the "dumping" of the woman in the hallway of a neighboring fraternity house. According to newspaper accounts, the victim's blood-alcohol concentration, when she was discovered, was .349 percent, more than three times the legal limit for automobile driving and an almost lethal amount. One law enforcement officer reported that sexual intercourse occurred during the time the victim was unconscious: "She was in a life-threatening situation" (*Tallahassee Democrat*, 1988b). When the victim was found, she was comatose and had suffered multiple scratches and abrasions. Crude words and a fraternity symbol had been written on her thighs (*Tampa Tribune,* 1988). When law enforcement officials tried to investigate the case, fraternity members refused to cooperate. This led, eventually, to a five-year ban of the fraternity from campus by the university and by the fraternity's national organization.

In trying to understand how such an event could have occurred, and how a group of over 150 members (exact figures are unknown because the fraternity refused to provide a membership roster) could hold rank, deny knowledge of the event, and allegedly lie to a grand jury, we analyzed newspaper articles about the case and conducted open-ended interviews with a variety of respondents about the case and about fraternities, rapes, alcohol use, gender relations, and sexual activities on campus. Our data included over 100 newspaper articles on the initial gang rape case; open-ended interviews with Greek (social fraternity and sorority) and non-Greek (independent) students (*N* = 20); university administrators (*N* = 8, five men, three women); and alumni advisers to Greek organizations (*N* = 6). Open-ended interviews were held also with judges, public and private defense attorneys, victim advocates, and state prosecutors regarding the processing of sexual assault cases. Data were analyzed using the grounded theory method (Glaser 1978; Martin and Turner 1986). In the following analysis, concepts generated from the data analysis are integrated with the literature on men's social fraternities, sexual coercion, and related issues.

Fraternities and the Social Construction of Men and Masculinity

Our research indicated that fraternities are vitally concerned—more than with anything else—with masculinity (cf. Kanin 1967). They work hard to create a macho image and context and try to avoid any suggestion of "wimpishness," effeminacy, and homosexuality. Valued members display, or are willing to go along with, a narrow conception of masculinity that stresses competition, athleticism, dominance, winning, conflict, wealth, material possessions, willingness to drink alcohol, and sexual prowess vis-à-vis women.

Valued Qualities of Members

When fraternity members talked about the kind of pledges they prefer, a litany of stereotypical and narrowly masculine attributes and behaviors was recited and feminine or woman-associated qualities and behaviors were expressly denounced (cf. Merton 1985). Fraternities seek men who are "athletic," "big guys," good in intramural competition, "who can talk college sports." Males "who are willing to drink alcohol," "who drink socially," or "who can hold their liquor" are sought. Alcohol and activities associated with the recreational use of alcohol are cornerstones of fraternity social life. Non-drinkers are viewed with skepticism and rarely selected for membership.[1]

Fraternities try to avoid "geeks," nerds, and men said to give the fraternity a "wimpy" or "gay" reputation. Art, music, and humanities majors, majors in traditional women's fields (nursing, home economics, social work, education), men with long hair, and those whose appearance or dress violate current norms are rejected. Clean-cut, handsome men who dress well (are clean, neat, conforming, fashionable) are preferred. One sorority woman commented that "the top ranking fraternities have the best looking guys."

One fraternity man, a senior, said his fraternity recruited "some big guys, very athletic" over a two-year period to help overcome its image of wimpiness. His fraternity had won the interfraternity competition for highest grade-point average several years running but was looked down on as "wimpy, dancy, even gay." With their bigger, more athletic recruits, "our reputation improved; we're a much more recognized fraternity now." Thus a fraternity's reputation and status depends on members' possession of stereotypically masculine qualities. Good grades, campus leadership, and community service are "nice" but masculinity dominance—for example, in athletic events, physical size of members, athleticism of members—counts most.

Certain social skills are valued. Men are sought who "have good personalities," are friendly, and "have the ability to relate to girls" (cf. Longino and Kart 1973). One fraternity man, a junior, said: "We watch a guy [a potential pledge] talk to women . . . we want guys who can relate to girls." Assessing a pledge's ability to talk to women is, in part, a preoccupation with homosexuality and a conscious avoidance of men who seem to have effeminate manners or qualities. If a member is suspected of being gay, he is ostracized and informally drummed out of the fraternity. A fraternity with a reputation as wimpy or tolerant of gays is ridiculed and shunned by other fraternities. Militant heterosexuality is frequently used by men as a strategy to keep each other in line (Kimmel 1987).

Financial affluence or wealth, a male-associated value in American culture, is highly valued by fraternities. In accounting for why the fraternity involved in the gang rape that precipitated our research project had been recognized recently as "the best fraternity chapter in the United States," a university official said: "They were good-looking, a big fraternity, had lots of BMWs [expensive, German-made automobiles]." After the rape, newspaper stories described the fraternity members' affluence, noting the high number of members who owned expensive cars (*St. Petersburg Times,* 1988).

The Status and Norms of Pledgeship

A pledge (sometimes called an associate member) is a new recruit who occupies a trial membership status for a specific period of time. The pledge period (typically ranging from 10 to 15 weeks) gives fraternity brothers an opportunity to assess and socialize new recruits. Pledges evaluate the fraternity also and decide if they want to become brothers. The socialization experience is structured partly through assignment of a Big Brother to each pledge. Big Brothers are expected to teach pledges how to become a brother and to support them as they progress through the trial membership period. Some pledges are repelled by the pledging experience, which can entail physical abuse; harsh discipline; and demands to be subordinate, follow orders, and engage in demeaning routines and activities, similar to those used by the military to "make men out of boys" during boot camp.

Characteristics of the pledge experience are rationalized by fraternity members as necessary to help pledges unite into a group, rely on each other, and join together against outsiders. The process is highly masculinist in execution as well as conception. A willingness to submit to authority, follow orders, and do as one is told is viewed as a sign of loyalty, togetherness, and unity. Fraternity pledges who find the pledge process offensive often drop out. Some do this by openly quitting, which can subject them to ridicule by brothers and other pledges, or they may deliberately fail to make the grades necessary for initiation or transfer schools and decline to reaffiliate with the fraternity on the new campus. One fraternity pledge who quit the fraternity he had pledged described an experience during pledgeship as follows:

> This one guy was always picking on me. No matter what I did, I was wrong. One night after dinner, he and two other guys called me and two other pledges into the chapter room. He said, "Here, X, hold this 25 pound bag of ice at arms' length 'til I tell you to stop." I did it even though my arms and hands were killing me. When I asked if I could stop, he grabbed me around the throat and lifted me off the floor. I thought he would choke me to death. He cussed me and called me all kinds of names. He took one of my fingers and twisted it until it nearly broke. . . . I stayed in the fraternity for a few more days, but then I decided to quit. I hated it. Those guys are sick. They like seeing you suffer.

Fraternities' emphasis on toughness, withstanding pain and humiliation, obedience to superiors, and using physical force to obtain compliance contributes to an interpersonal style that de-emphasizes caring and sensitivity but fosters intragroup trust and loyalty. If the least macho or most critical pledges drop out, those who remain may be more receptive to, and influenced by, masculinist values and practices that encourage the use of force in sexual relations with women and the covering up of such behavior (cf. Kanin 1967).

Norms and Dynamics of Brotherhood

Brother is the status occupied by fraternity men to indicate their relations to each other and their membership in a particular fraternity organization or group. Brother is a male-specific status; only males can become brothers, although women can become "Little Sisters," a form of pseudomembership. "Becoming a brother" is a rite of passage that follows the consistent and often lengthy display by pledges of appropriately masculine qualities and behaviors. Brothers have a quasi-familial relationship with each other, are normatively said to share bonds of closeness and support, and are sharply set off from nonmembers. Brotherhood is a loosely defined term used to represent the bonds that develop among fraternity members and the obligations and expectations incumbent upon them (cf. Marlowe and Auvenshine [1982] on fraternities' failure to encourage "moral development" in freshman pledges).

Some of our respondents talked about brotherhood in almost reverential terms, viewing it as the most valuable benefit of fraternity membership. One senior, a business-school major who had been affiliated with a fairly high-status fraternity throughout four years on campus, said:

> Brotherhood spurs friendship for life, which I consider its best aspect, although I didn't see it that way when I joined. Brotherhood bonds and unites. It instills values of caring about one another, caring about community, caring about ourselves. The values and bonds [of brotherhood] continually develop over the four years [in college] while normal friendships come and go.

Despite this idealization, most aspects of fraternity practice and conception are more mundane. Brotherhood often plays itself out as an overriding concern with masculinity and, by extension, femininity. As a consequence, fraternities comprise collectivities of highly masculinized men with attitudinal qualities and behavioral norms that predispose them to sexual coercion of women (cf. Kanin 1967; Merton 1985; Rapaport and Burkhart 1984). The norms of masculinity are complemented by conceptions of women and femininity that are equally distorted and stereotyped and that may enhance the probability of women's exploitation (cf. Ehrhart and Sandler 1985; Sanday 1981, 1986).

Practices of Brotherhood

Practices associated with fraternity brotherhood that contribute to the sexual coercion of women include a preoccupation with loyalty, group protection and secrecy, use of alcohol as a weapon, involvement in violence and physical force, and an emphasis on competition and superiority.

Loyalty, group protection, and secrecy   Loyalty is a fraternity preoccupation. Members are reminded constantly to be loyal to the fraternity and to their brothers. Among other ways, loyalty is played out in the practices of group protection and secrecy. The fraternity must be shielded from criticism. Members are admonished to avoid getting the fraternity in trouble and to bring all problems "to the chapter" (local branch of a national social fraternity) rather than to outsiders. Fraternities try to protect themselves from close scrutiny and criticism by the Interfraternity Council (a quasi-governing body composed of representatives from all social fraternities on campus), their fraternity's national office, university officials, law enforcement, the media, and the public. Protection of the fraternity often takes precedence over what is procedurally, ethically, or legally correct. Numerous examples were related to us of fraternity brothers' lying to outsiders to "protect the fraternity."

Group protection was observed in the alleged gang rape case with which we began our study. Except for one brother, a rapist who turned state's evidence, the entire remaining fraternity membership was accused by university and criminal justice officials of lying to protect the fraternity. Members consistently failed to cooperate even though the alleged crimes were felonies, involved only four men (two of whom were not even members of the local chapter), and the victim of the crime nearly died. According to a grand jury's findings, fraternity officers repeatedly broke appointments with law enforcement officials, refused to provide police with a list of members, and refused to cooperate with police and prosecutors investigating the case (*Florida Flambeau*, 1988).

Secrecy is a priority value and practice in fraternities, partly because full-fledged membership is premised on it (for confirmation, see Ehrhart and Sandler 1985; Longino and Kart 1973; Roark 1987). Secrecy is also a boundary-maintaining mechanism, demarcating in-group from out-group, us from them. Secret rituals, handshakes, and mottoes are revealed to pledge brothers as they are initiated into full brotherhood. Since only brothers are supposed to know a fraternity's secrets, such knowledge affirms membership in the fraternity and separates a brother from others. Extending secrecy tactics from protection of private knowledge to protection of the fraternity from criticism is a predictable development. Our interviews indicated that individual members knew the difference between right and wrong, but fraternity norms that emphasize loyalty, group protection, and secrecy often overrode standards of ethical correctness.

Alcohol as weapon   Alcohol use by fraternity men is normative. They use it on weekdays to relax after class and on weekends to "get drunk," "get crazy," and "get laid." The use of alcohol to obtain sex from women is pervasive—in other words, it is used as a weapon against sexual reluctance. According to several fraternity men whom we interviewed, alcohol is the major tool used to gain sexual mastery over women (cf. Adams and Abarbanel 1988; Ehrhart and Sandler 1985). One fraternity man, a 21-year-old senior, described alcohol use to gain sex as follows: "There are girls that you know will fuck, then some you have to put some effort into it. . . . You have to buy them drinks or find out if she's drunk enough. . . . "

A similar strategy is used collectively. A fraternity man said that at parties with Little Sisters: "We provide them with 'hunch punch' and things get wild. We get them drunk and most of the guys end up with one." "'Hunch punch,'" he said, "is a girls' drink made up of overproof alcohol and powdered Kool-Aid, no water or anything, just ice. It's very strong. Two cups will do a number on a female." He had plans in the next academic term to surreptitiously give hunch punch to women in a "prim and proper" sorority because "having sex with prim and proper sorority girls is definitely a goal." These women are a challenge because they "won't openly consume alcohol and won't get openly drunk as hell." Their sororities have "standards committees" that forbid heavy drinking and easy sex.

In the gang rape case, our sources said that many fraternity men on campus believed the victim had a drinking problem and was thus an "easy make." According to newspaper accounts, she had been drinking alcohol on the evening she was raped; the lead assailant is alleged to have given her a bottle of wine after she arrived at his fraternity house. Portions of the rape occurred in a shower, and the victim was reportedly so drunk that her assailants had difficulty holding her in a standing position (*Tallahassee Democrat*, 1988a). While raping her, her assailants repeatedly told her they were members of another fraternity under the apparent belief that she was too drunk to know the difference. Of course, if she was too drunk to know who they were, she was too drunk to consent to sex (cf. Allgeier 1986; Tash 1988).

One respondent told us that gang rapes are wrong and can get one expelled, but he seemed to see nothing wrong in sexual coercion one-on-one. He seemed unaware that the use of alcohol to obtain sex from a woman is grounds for a claim that a rape occurred (cf. Tash 1988). Few women on campus (who also may not know these grounds) report date rapes, however; so the odds of detection and punishment are slim for fraternity men who use alcohol for "seduction" purposes (cf. Byington and Keeter 1988; Merton 1985).

Violence and physical force   Fraternity men have a history of violence (Ehrhart and Sandler 1985; Roark 1987). Their record of hazing, fighting, property destruction, and rape has caused them problems with insurance companies (Bradford 1986; Pressley 1987). Two university officials told us that fraternities "are the third riskiest property to insure behind toxic waste dumps and amusement parks." Fraternities are increasingly defendants in legal actions brought by pledges subjected to hazing (Meyer 1986; Pressley 1987) and by women who were raped by one or more members. In a recent alleged gang rape incident at another Florida university, prosecutors failed to file charges but the victim filed a civil suit against the fraternity nevertheless (*Tallahassee Democrat*, 1989).

Competition and superiority   Interfraternity rivalry fosters in-group identification and out-group hostility. Fraternities stress pride of membership and superiority over other fraternities as major goals. Interfraternity rivalries take many forms, including competition for desirable pledges, size of pledge class, size of membership, size and appearance of fraternity house, superiority in intramural sports, highest grade-point averages, giving the best parties, gaining the best or most campus leadership roles, and, of great importance, attracting and displaying "good looking women." Rivalry is particularly intense over members, intramural sports, and women (cf. Messner 1989).

Fraternities' Commodification of Women

In claiming that women are treated by fraternities as commodities, we mean that fraternities knowingly, and intentionally, *use* women for their benefit. Fraternities use women as bait for new members, as servers of brothers' needs, and as sexual prey.

Women as bait Fashionably attractive women help a fraternity attract new members. As one fraternity man, a junior, said, "They are good bait." Beautiful, sociable women are believed to impress the right kind of pledges and give the impression that the fraternity can deliver this type of woman to its members. Photographs of shapely, attractive coeds are printed in fraternity brochures and videotapes that are distributed and shown to potential pledges. The women pictured are often dressed in bikinis, at the beach, and are pictured hugging the brothers of the fraternity. One university official says such recruitment materials give the message: "Hey, they're here for you, you can have whatever you want," and, "we have the best looking women. Join us and you can have them too." Another commented: "Something's wrong when males join an all-male organization as the best place to meet women. It's so illogical."

Fraternities compete in promising access to beautiful women. One fraternity man, a senior, commented that "the attraction of girls [i.e., a fraternity's success in attracting women] is a big status symbol for fraternities." One university official commented that the use of women as a recruiting tool is so well entrenched that fraternities that might be willing to forgo it say they cannot afford to unless other fraternities do so as well. One fraternity man said, "Look, if we don't have Little Sisters, the fraternities that do will get all the good pledges." Another said, "We won't have as good a rush [the period during which new members are assessed and selected] if we don't have these women around."

In displaying good-looking, attractive, skimpily dressed, nubile women to potential members, fraternities implicitly, and sometimes explicitly, promise sexual access to women. One fraternity man commented that "part of what being in a fraternity is all about is the sex" and explained how his fraternity uses Little Sisters to recruit new members:

> We'll tell the sweetheart [the fraternity's term for Little Sister], "You're gorgeous; you can get him." We'll tell her to fake a scam and she'll go hang all over him during a rush party, kiss him, and he thinks he's done wonderful and wants to join. The girls think it's great too. It's flattering for them.

Women as servers　The use of women as servers is exemplified in the Little Sister program. Little Sisters are undergraduate women who are rushed and selected in a manner parallel to the recruitment of fraternity men. They are affiliated with the fraternity in a formal but unofficial way and are able, indeed required, to wear the fraternity's Greek letters. Little Sisters are not full-fledged fraternity members, however; and fraternity national offices and most universities do not register or regulate them. Each fraternity has an officer called Little Sister Chairman who oversees their organization and activities. The Little Sisters elect officers among themselves, pay monthly dues to the fraternity, and have well-defined roles. Their dues are used to pay for the fraternity's social events, and Little Sisters are expected to attend and hostess fraternity parties and hang around the house to make it a "nice place to be." One fraternity man, a senior, described Little Sisters this way: "They are very social girls, willing to join in, be affiliated with the group, devoted to the fraternity." Another member, a sophomore, said: "Their sole purpose is social—attend parties, attract new members, and 'take care' of the guys."

Our observations and interviews suggested that women selected by fraternities as Little Sisters are physically attractive, possess good social skills, and are willing to devote time and energy to the fraternity and its members. One undergraduate woman gave the following job description for Little Sisters to a campus newspaper:

> It's not just making appearances at all the parties but entails many more responsibilities. You're going to be expected to go to all the intramural games to cheer the brothers on, support and encourage the pledges, and just be around to bring some extra life to the house. [As a Little Sister] you have to agree to take on a new responsibility other than studying to maintain your grades and managing to keep your checkbook from bouncing. You have to make time to be a part of the fraternity and support the brothers in all they do. (*The Tomahawk*, 1988)

The title of Little Sister reflects women's subordinate status; fraternity men in a parallel role are called Big Brothers. Big Brothers assist a sorority primarily with the physical work of sorority rushes, which, compared to fraternity rushes, are more formal, structured, and intensive. Sorority rushes take place in the daytime and fraternity rushes at night so fraternity men are free to help. According to one fraternity member, Little Sister status is a benefit to women because it gives them a social outlet and "the protection of the brothers." The gender-stereotypic conceptions and obligations of these Little Sister and Big Brother statuses indicate that fraternities and sororities promote a gender hierarchy on campus that fosters subordination and dependence in women, thus encouraging sexual exploitation and the belief that it is acceptable.

Women as sexual prey　Little Sisters are a sexual utility. Many Little Sisters do not belong to sororities and lack peer support for refraining from unwanted sexual relations. One fraternity man (whose fraternity has 65 members and 85 Little Sisters) told us they had recruited "wholesale" in the prior year to "get lots of new women." The structural access to women that the Little Sister program provides and the absence of normative supports for refusing fraternity members' sexual advances may make women in this program particularly susceptible to coerced sexual encounters with fraternity men.

Access to women for sexual gratification is a presumed benefit of fraternity membership, promised in recruitment materials and strategies and through brothers' conversations with new recruits. One fraternity man said: "We always tell the guys that you get sex all the time, there's always new girls. . . . After I became a Greek, I found out I could be with females at will." A university official told us that, based on his observations, "no one [i.e., fraternity men] on this campus wants to have 'relationships.' They just want to have fun [i.e., sex]." Fraternity men plan and execute strategies aimed at obtaining sexual gratification, and this occurs at both individual and collective levels.

Individual strategies include getting a woman drunk and spending a great deal of money on her. As for collective strategies, most of our undergraduate interviewees agreed that fraternity parties often culminate in sex and that this outcome is planned. One fraternity man said fraternity parties often involve sex and nudity and can "turn into orgies." Orgies may be planned in advance, such as the Bowery Ball party held by one fraternity. A former fraternity member said of this party:

> The entire idea behind this is sex. Both men and women come to the party wearing little or nothing. There are pornographic pinups on the walls and usually porno movies playing on the TV. The music carries sexual overtones. . . . They just get schnockered [drunk] and, in most cases, they also get laid.

When asked about the women who come to such a party, he said: "Some Little Sisters just won't go. . . . The girls who do are looking for a good time, girls who don't know what it is, things like that."

Other respondents denied that fraternity parties are orgies but said that sex is always talked about among the brothers and they all know "who each other is doing it with." One member said that most of the time, guys have sex with their girlfriends "but with socials, girlfriends aren't allowed to come and it's their [members'] big chance [to have sex with other women]." The use of alcohol to help them get women into bed is a routine strategy at fraternity parties.

Conclusions

In general, our research indicated that the organization and membership of fraternities contribute heavily to coercive and often violent sex. Fraternity houses are occupied by same-sex (all men) and same-age (late teens, early twenties) peers whose maturity and judgment is often less than ideal. Yet fraternity houses are private dwellings that are mostly off-limits to, and away from scrutiny of, university and community representatives, with the result that fraternity house events seldom come to the attention of outsiders. Practices associated with the social construction of fraternity brotherhood emphasize a macho conception of men and masculinity, a narrow, stereotyped conception of women and femininity, and the treatment of women as commodities. Other practices contributing to coercive sexual relations and the cover-up of rapes include excessive alcohol use, competitiveness, and normative support for deviance and secrecy (cf. Bogal-Allbritten and Allbritten 1985; Kanin 1967).

Some fraternity practices exacerbate others. Brotherhood norms require "sticking together" regardless of right or wrong; thus rape episodes are unlikely to be stopped or reported to outsiders, even when witnesses disapprove. The ability to use alcohol without scrutiny by authorities and alcohol's frequent association with violence, including sexual coercion, facilitates rape in fraternity houses. Fraternity norms that emphasize the value of maleness and masculinity over femaleness and femininity and that elevate the status of men and lower the status of women in members' eyes undermine perceptions and treatment of women as persons who deserve consideration and care (cf. Ehrhart and Sandler 1985; Merton 1985).

Androgynous men and men with a broad range of interests and attributes are lost to fraternities through their recruitment practices. Masculinity of a narrow and stereotypical type helps create attitudes, norms, and practices that predispose fraternity men to coerce women sexually, both individually and collectively (Allgeier 1986; Hood 1989; Sanday 1981, 1986). Male athletes on campus may be similarly disposed for the same reasons (Kirshenbaum 1989; Telander and Sullivan 1989).

Research into the social contexts in which rape crimes occur and the social constructions associated with these contexts illumine rape dynamics on campus. Blanchard (1959) found that group rapes almost always have a leader who pushes others into the crime. He also found that the leader's latent homosexuality, desire to show off to his peers, or fear of failing to prove himself a man are frequently an impetus. Fraternity norms and practices contribute to the approval and use of sexual coercion as an accepted tactic in relations with women. Alcohol-induced compliance is normative, whereas, presumably, use of a knife, gun, or threat of bodily harm would not be because the woman who "drinks too much" is viewed as "causing her own rape" (cf. Ehrhart and Sandler 1985).

Our research led us to conclude that fraternity norms and practices influence members to view the sexual coercion of women, which is a felony crime, as sport, a contest, or a game (cf. Sato 1988). This sport is played not between men and women but between men and men. Women are the pawns or prey in the interfraternity rivalry game; they prove that a fraternity is successful or prestigious. The use of women in this way encourages fraternity men to see women as objects and sexual coercion as sport. Today's societal norms support young women's right to engage in sex at their discretion, and coercion is unnecessary in a mutually desired encounter. However, nubile young women say they prefer to be "in a relationship" to have sex while young men say they prefer to "get laid" without a commitment (Muehlenhard and Linton 1987). These differences may reflect, in part, American puritanism and men's fears of sexual intimacy or perhaps intimacy of any kind. In a fraternity context, getting sex without giving emotionally demonstrates "cool" masculinity. More important, it poses no threat to the bonding and loyalty of the fraternity brotherhood (cf. Farr 1988). Drinking large quantities of alcohol before having sex suggests that "scoring" rather than intrinsic sexual pleasure is a primary concern of fraternity men.

Unless fraternities' composition, goals, structures, and practices change in fundamental ways, women on campus will continue to be sexual prey for fraternity men. As all-male enclaves dedicated to opposing faculty and administration and to cementing in-group ties, fraternity members eschew any hint of homosexuality. Their version of masculinity transforms women, and men with womanly characteristics, into the out-group. "Womanly men" are ostracized; feminine women are used to demonstrate members' masculinity. Encouraging renewed emphasis on their founding values (Longino and Kart 1973), service orientation and activities (Lemire 1979), or members' moral development (Marlowe and Auvenshine 1982) will have little effect on fraternities' treatment of women. A case for or against fraternities cannot be made by studying individual members. The fraternity qua group and organization is at issue. Located on campus along with many vulnerable women, embedded in a sexist society, and caught up in masculinist goals, practices, and values, fraternities' violation of women—including forcible rape—should come as no surprise.

Note

1. Recent bans by some universities on open-keg parties at fraternity houses have resulted in heavy drinking before coming to a party and an increase in drunkenness among those who attend. This may aggravate, rather than improve, the treatment of women by fraternity men at parties.

References

Allgeier, Elizabeth. 1986. "Coercive Versus Consensual Sexual Interactions." G. Stanley Hall Lecture to American Psychological Association Annual Meeting, Washington, DC, August.

Adams, Aileen and Gail Abarbanel. 1988. *Sexual Assault on Campus: What Colleges Can Do.* Santa Monica, CA: Rape Treatment Center.

Blanchard, W. H. 1959. "The Group Process in Gang Rape." *Journal of Social Psychology* 49:259–66.

Bogal-Allbritten, Rosemarie B. and William L. Allbritten. 1985. "The Hidden Victims: Courtship Violence Among College Students." *Journal of College Student Personnel* 43:201–4.

Bohrnstedt, George W. 1969. "Conservatism, Authoritarianism and Religiosity of Fraternity Pledges." *Journal of College Student Personnel* 27:36–43.

Bradford, Michael. 1986. "Tight Market Dries Up Nightlife at University." *Business Insurance* (March 2):2, 6.

Burkhart, Barry. 1989. Comments in Seminar on Acquaintance/Date Rape Prevention: A National Video Teleconference, February 2.

Burkhart, Barry R. and Annette L. Stanton. 1985. "Sexual Aggression in Acquaintance Relationships." Pp. 43–65 in *Violence in Intimate Relationships,* edited by G. Russell. Englewood Cliffs, NJ: Spectrum.

Byington, Diane B. and Karen W. Keeter. 1988. "Assessing Needs of Sexual Assault Victims on a University Campus." Pp. 23–31 in *Student Services: Responding to Issues and Challenges.* Chapel Hill: University of North Carolina Press.

Chancer, Lynn S. 1987. New Bedford, Massachusetts, March 6, 1983–March 22, 1984: The 'Before and After' of a Group Rape. *Gender & Society* 1:239–60.

Ehrhart, Julie K. and Bernice R. Sandler. 1985. *Campus Gang Rape: Party Games?* Washington, DC: Association of American Colleges.

Farr, K. A. 1988. "Dominance Bonding Through the Good Old Boys Sociability Network." *Sex Roles* 18:259–77.

Florida Flambeau. 1988. "Pike Members Indicted in Rape." (May 19):1, 5.

Fox, Elaine, Charles Hodge, and Walter Ward. 1987. "A Comparison of Attitudes Held by Black and White Fraternity Members." *Journal of Negro Education* 56:521–34.

Geis, Gilbert. 1971. "Group Sexual Assaults." *Medical Aspects of Human Sexuality* 5:101–13.

Glaser, Barney G. 1978. *Theoretical Sensitivity: Advances in the Methodology of Grounded Theory.* Mill Valley, CA: Sociology Press.

Hood, Jane. 1989. "Why Our Society Is Rape-Prone." *New York Times,* May 16.

Hughes, Michael J. and Roger B. Winston, Jr. 1987. "Effects of Fraternity Membership on Interpersonal Values." *Journal of College Student Personnel* 45:405–11.

Kanin, Eugene J. 1967. "Reference Groups and Sex Conduct Norm Violations." *The Sociological Quarterly* 8:495–504.

Kimmel, Michael, ed. 1987. *Changing Men: New Directions in Research on Men and Masculinity.* Newbury Park, CA: Sage.

Kirshenbaum, Jerry. 1989. "Special Report, An American Disgrace: A Violent and Unprecedented Lawlessness Has Arisen Among College Athletes in all Parts of the Country." *Sports Illustrated* (February 27):16–19.

Lemire, David. 1979. "One Investigation of the Stereotypes Associated with Fraternities and Sororities." *Journal of College Student Personnel* 37:54–57.

Letchworth, G. E. 1969. "Fraternities Now and in the Future." *Journal of College Student Personnel* 10:118–22.

Longino, Charles F., Jr., and Cary S. Kart. 1973. "The College Fraternity: An Assessment of Theory and Research." *Journal of College Student Personnel* 31:118–25.

Marlowe, Anne F. and Dwight C. Auvenshine. 1982. "Greek Membership: Its Impact on the Moral Development of College Freshmen." *Journal of College Student Personnel* 40:53–57.

Martin, Patricia Yancey and Barry A. Turner. 1986. "Grounded Theory and Organizational Research." *Journal of Applied Behavioral Science* 22:141–57.

Merton, Andrew. 1985. "On Competition and Class: Return to Brotherhood." *Ms.* (September):60–65, 121–22.

Messner, Michael. 1989. "Masculinities and Athletic Careers." *Gender & Society* 3:71–88.

Meyer, T. J. 1986. "Fight Against Hazing Rituals Rages on Campuses." *Chronicle of Higher Education* (March 12):34–36.

Miller, Leonard D. 1973. "Distinctive Characteristics of Fraternity Members." *Journal of College Student Personnel* 31:126–28.

Muehlenhard, Charlene L. and Melaney A. Linton. 1987. "Date Rape and Sexual Aggression in Dating Situations: Incidence and Risk Factors." *Journal of Counseling Psychology* 34:186–96.

Pressley, Sue Anne. 1987. "Fraternity Hell Night Still Endures." *Washington Post* (August 11):B1.

Rapaport, Karen and Barry R. Burkhart. 1984. "Personality and Attitudinal Characteristics of Sexually Coercive College Males." *Journal of Abnormal Psychology* 93:216–21.

Roark, Mary L. 1987. "Preventing Violence on College Campuses." *Journal of Counseling and Development* 65:367–70.

Sanday, Peggy Reeves. 1981. "The Socio-Cultural Context of Rape: A Cross-Cultural Study." *Journal of Social Issues* 37:5–27.

——. 1986. "Rape and the Silencing of the Feminine." Pp. 84–101 in *Rape,* edited by S. Tomaselli and R. Porter. Oxford: Basil Blackwell.

St. Petersburg Times. 1988. "A Greek Tragedy." (May 29):1F, 6F.

Sato, Ikuya. 1988. "Play Theory of Delinquency: Toward a General Theory of 'Action.'" *Symbolic Interaction* 11:191–212.

Smith, T. 1964. "Emergence and Maintenance of Fraternal Solidarity." *Pacific Sociological Review* 7:29–37.

Tallahassee Democrat. 1988a. "FSU Fraternity Brothers Charged" (April 27):1A, 12A.

——. 1988b. "FSU Interviewing Students About Alleged Rape" (April 24):1D.

——. 1989. "Woman Sues Stetson in Alleged Rape" (March 19):3B.

Tampa Tribune. 1988. "Fraternity Brothers Charged in Sexual Assault of FSU Coed." (April 27):6B.

Tash, Gary B. 1988. "Date Rape." *The Emerald of Sigma Pi Fraternity* 75(4):1–2.

Telander, Rick and Robert Sullivan. 1989. "Special Report, You Reap What You Sow." *Sports Illustrated* (February 27):20–34.

The Tomahawk. 1988. "A Look Back at Rush, A Mixture of Hard Work and Fun" (April/May):3D.

Walsh, Claire. 1989. Comments in Seminar on Acquaintance/Date Rape Prevention: A National Video Teleconference, February 2.

Wilder, David H., Arlyne E. Hoyt, Dennis M. Doren, William E. Hauck, and Robert D. Zettle. 1978. "The Impact of Fraternity and Sorority Membership on Values and Attitudes." *Journal of College Student Personnel* 36:445–49.

Wilder, David H., Arlyne E. Hoyt, Beth Shuster Surbeck, Janet C. Wilder, and Patricia Imperatrice Carney. 1986. "Greek Affiliation and Attitude Change in College Students." *Journal of College Student Personnel* 44:510–19.

Corporations, Organized Crime, and the Disposal of Hazardous Waste: An Examination of the Making of a Criminogenic Regulatory Structure

40

Andrew Szasz

The generation of hazardous waste is a necessary side effect of modern industrial production. Factories must cope daily with large accumulations of unrecyclable chemical byproducts generated by normal production techniques. The processing or disposal of these byproducts is a significant cost of production, a cost that, like all other costs of production, the prudent owner or manager minimizes.

Until recently, industrial hazardous waste was not legally distinguished from municipal garbage and other solid wastes. It was disposed of with ordinary garbage, at very low cost to the generator, mostly in coastal waters or in landfills unfit to adequately contain it. However, concern grew during the 1970s that improper disposal of hazardous waste was creating an environmental and public health burden of unknown but potentially massive scale. This concern finally moved some states and eventually the federal government to begin to legislate new regulations. The centerpiece of this regulatory effort was the federal Resource Conservation and Recovery Act (RCRA) of 1976. On paper, RCRA mandated comprehensive mechanisms to guarantee the safe disposal of hazardous waste. It established standards and procedures for classifying substances as hazardous. It authorized the states to register corporate generators of hazardous waste and license hauling and disposal firms. It mandated the creation of a manifest system that would document the movement of hazardous waste "from cradle to grave," from the generator, through the hands of the transporter, to the shipment's final destination at a licensed disposal site.

By legally distinguishing hazardous waste from other wastes and by directing that such wastes be treated differently than municipal solid waste, the new regulations dramatically increased, almost overnight, the demand for hazardous waste hauling and disposal services. Unhappily, recent state and federal investigations have documented both that illegal waste disposal is widespread (U.S. General Accounting Office, 1985; U.S. House of Representatives, 1980) and that organized crime elements traditionally active

in garbage hauling and landfilling have entered this burgeoning and potentially profitable new market (Block and Scarpitti, 1985; U.S. House of
Representatives, 1980, 1981a). Although the exact extent of organized
crime involvement in hazardous waste hauling and disposal is uncertain,[1]
the fact of that involvement is beyond question. A situation exists, then, in
which corporations, some at the heart of the American economy, discharge
their regulatory obligations under RCRA by entering into direct contractual
relationships with firms dominated by organized crime. The goal in this
paper is to analyze in detail the complex nature of this relationship between
corporate generators of hazardous waste and elements of organized crime
that are active in industrial waste disposal. This goal will be approached
by analyzing the formation and implementation of RCRA legislation.

The subject of this paper speaks to two distinct criminological litera-
tures: works that examine the relationship between legitimate and illicit
enterprise and works that examine crimogenic market structures. Recent
scholarship has challenged the commonsense distinction between legitimate business and organized crime. Schelling (1967), Smith and Alba
(1979), Smith (1980), and Albanese (1982) all argue that the most fundamental aspect of organized crime is that it is a form of entrepreneurial
activity and that its ethnic or conspiratorial nature is of secondary importance. Recent scholarship also challenges the equally widely held belief
that the relationship between the underworld and legitimate business consists solely of the former exploiting the latter through extortion, racketeering, and so on (Drucker, 1981). At minimum, it is argued that the
relationship is one of mutually beneficial interdependence (Martens and
Miller-Longfellow, 1982). This is clearly supported by excellent case studies of labor racketeering (Block and Chambliss, 1981), organized crime on
the waterfront (Block, 1982), and arson (Brady, 1983). Chambliss (1978:
181–182) argues the even stronger view that organized crime can exist only
because the structure of the legitimate economy and its accompanying political organization make its emergence possible and even inevitable. In a
similar vein, Smith (1980) and Smith and Alba (1979) challenge the very
distinction between business and organized crime and begin to dissolve
that distinction in the common dynamic of a market economy. The study
of organized crime participation in hazardous waste disposal presents an
opportunity to once again examine this relationship between legitimate and
illegitimate entrepreneurship.

The story of RCRA may also have links to the concept of crimogenic
market processes. Farberman's (1975) and Leonard and Weber's (1977)
studies of auto retailing and Denzin's (1977) study of the liquor industry
showed that the normal operating logic of an industry may force some
sectors of that industry into illegal activity in order to survive, much less
thrive, in doing their part of the business. Needleman and Needleman
(1979) subsequently expanded the concept by describing a second type
of criminogenesis in which the criminal activity is not forced. It is, in-

stead, an unwelcome drain on business, but it is unavoidable because the conditions that make it possible are necessary to the overall functioning of that industry and could not be altered without fundamentally affecting how business is conducted in that industry. Needleman and Needleman discussed securities fraud as an example of what they call a "crime-facilitative," as opposed to a "crime-coercive" market sector. The fact that RCRA not only cannot prevent illegal hazardous waste dumping but has also attracted organized crime participation in illegal hazardous waste activity suggests that the concept of criminogenesis may be fruitfully extended to regulatory processes as well.

In the first sections of this paper, some background is presented on hazardous waste as a social issue and the nature and extent of organized crime involvement in hazardous waste hauling and disposal is summarized. At the core of the paper, the conditions that made this involvement possible are analyzed. It is shown that the most common explanations—lax implementation and enforcement by state and local officials—are incomplete. Analysis of the formation of RCRA legislation shows that corporate generators of hazardous waste were instrumental in securing a regulatory structure that would prove highly attractive to and well suited for organized crime participation. In other words, generators are deeply implicated in the creation of conditions that have made their relationship to organized crime possible. This finding is used to critique two explanations of this relationship suggested during Congressional hearings, generator "ignorance" and generator "powerlessness." It is then argued that the relationship has two other important aspects: generators did not consciously desire or intend this outcome, but they nonetheless benefited from it once it occurred. The paper concludes with a discussion of the relevance of the findings to the two areas of criminological research mentioned above.

The Issue Background: Hazardous Waste Facts

The Environmental Protection Agency (EPA) defines waste products as "hazardous" if they are flammable, explosive, corrosive, or toxic. Major industries central to the modern national economy, such as the petroleum, chemical, electronic, and pharmaceutical industries, generate copious amounts of hazardous waste. Although there is still great uncertainty about the exact effect of industrial hazardous waste on public health (Greenberg and Anderson, 1984:84–105), improper management may result in explosions, fires, pollution of water resources, and other uncontrolled releases that put surrounding communities at risk and may result in physical harm ranging from skin irritation to increased incidence of cancer, lung disease, birth defects, and other serious illnesses.

How much hazardous waste has accumulated? How much is currently generated? Neither question can be answered confidently at this time. The generation and disposal of hazardous waste was completely unregulated until the late 1970s. In the absence of regulation, there was no systematic data-gathering effort. Consequently, there is great uncertainty about the magnitude and composition of hazardous waste accumulated up to the passage of the RCRA. Estimates have risen regularly as more sites are located and assessed. The EPA's most recent estimate is that there are 25,000 sites nationally that contain some hazardous waste. Of these, about 2,500 are priority sites judged by the EPA to be imminently hazardous to public health. More recent research by the General Accounting Office (GAO) and the Office of Technology Assessment (OTA) suggests that there may be 378,000 total sites nationally, perhaps 10,000 of them requiring priority attention (Shabecoff, 1985).

In theory, at least, the availability of data should have improved greatly following passage of the RCRA. Generators of hazardous waste were now required to create written documentation—the manifest—of the amount and content of every shipment of hazardous waste signed over to outside haulers and disposers. This documentation would be forwarded to state agencies following final disposition of each waste shipment. However, the actual quality of the data produced was compromised by several factors. First, there was little agreement over what substances should be defined as hazardous. Congressional and EPA testimony (U.S. Environmental Protection Agency, 1976, 1979; U.S. House of Representatives, 1975, 1976; U.S. Senate, 1974, 1979) shows that industrial spokesmen argued that too many substances had been unjustifiably included, while environmentalists argued that some materials had been improperly excluded. Second, firms generating less than one metric ton (2,200 lbs.) of hazardous waste per month are exempt from RCRA regulation (U.S. House of Representatives, 1983:56, 60). There are over four million privately owned industrial sites in the nation. The "small generator" exemption leaves all but a few tens of thousands of these sites out of RCRA's registration and manifest system. Third, some firms that generate significant amounts of hazardous waste have either failed to cooperate with EPA requests for data (Williams and Matheny, 1984:436–437) or have failed to identify themselves to the EPA as regulable generators (U.S. General Accounting Office, 1985:14–20). Fourth, even those firms that appear to comply with reporting requirements may not be reporting accurately the types and quantities of hazardous waste they generate (U.S. GAO, 1985:20–23). Consequently, knowledge of the amount and content of current hazardous waste generation is still imprecise. Estimates, like estimates of historical accumulation, have been rising. In 1974, the EPA was estimating hazardous waste generation at 10 million metric tons per year (U.S. Senate, 1974:70). In 1980, the EPA estimate had risen to 40 million metric tons. In 1983, new research led the EPA to nearly quadruple its estimate to 150 million metric tons (Block and Scarpitti, 1985:46), while the OTA was estimating 250 million metric tons per year (U.S. House of Representatives, 1983:1).[2]

Where does hazardous waste end up? In response to EPA inquiries in 1981, 16% of generating firms reported treating their wastes completely on site and another 22% reported treating part of their wastes on site. The remaining 62% contracted with other parties to handle all of their wastes (Block and Scarpitti, 1985:48–49). Where do transported wastes actually end up? The exemptions and noncooperation cited above leave an unknown fraction of total hazardous waste movement out of the paperwork of the manifest system (U.S. GAO, 1985:3–4, 14–24). The manifests that are filed are poorly monitored and vulnerable to undetected falsification (Greenberg and Anderson, 1984:242; U.S. GAO, 1985:25–31; U.S. House of Representatives, 1980:140, 1981b:124). Consequently, this question also cannot be answered with great certainty. On the basis of admittedly poor and incomplete data, the OTA estimates that no more than 10% to 20% of all hazardous waste is rendered harmless by incineration or by chemical or biological treatment. There are few facilities that can treat wastes in these ways and the price of treatment is much higher than the price of other means of disposal (U.S. House of Representatives, 1983:2, 5–6). The remaining 80% to 90% is either landfilled or disposed of illegally. Only a small proportion of hazardous waste goes into landfills that have the siting studies, proper containment practices, and continuous monitoring to be fully licensed by the EPA, since there are only about 200 such landfills in the nation (Block and Scarpitti, 1985:49; U.S. House of Representatives, 1981b:187). Even these top landfills are only required by the EPA to keep wastes contained for 30 years (U.S. House of Representatives, 1983:2).[3] Most hazardous waste goes to landfills that have only interim license to operate, landfills that are of much poorer quality and are likely to pollute the surrounding land and water within a few years.

Illegal hazardous waste dumping is even more likely to have adverse short-term environmental and public health consequences. The full extent of illegal hazardous waste disposal is not known. State officials interviewed by the GAO agreed that illegal disposal was occurring, but had no firm information on the scope of this activity (U.S. GAO, 1985:10). One study done for the EPA surveyed hazardous waste generators in 41 cities and estimated that one in seven generators had illegally disposed of some of their wastes during the two years preceding the study (U.S. GAO, 1985:10). A wide array of illegal disposal practices have been documented. Waste shipments may end up commingled with ordinary garbage. A 20 cubic yard "dumpster" full of dry garbage can be made to absorb up to sixty 55 gallon drums of liquid hazardous waste (U.S. House of Representatives, 1980:63) and then be deposited in unlicensed municipal landfills never designed to contain hazardous waste. Liquid hazardous waste may be released along a roadway. An 8,000 gallon truck can be emptied in 8 minutes (U.S. House of Representatives, 1980:101). Shipments may simply be stockpiled at sites awaiting alleged transfer that never happens or at disposal facilities that have no real disposal capability (U.S. House of Representatives, 1980:10).

Wastes may be drained into local city sewer systems, rivers, and oceans, or dumped in out-of-the-way rural spots (U.S. House of Representatives, 1980:93). Flammable hazardous waste may be commingled with fuel oil and sold as pure heating oil (U.S. House of Representatives, 1980:63–64) or sprayed on unsuspecting communities' roads for dust control (U.S. House of Representatives, 1980:151).

Organized Crime Participation in the Hazardous Waste Disposal Industry

Congressman Albert Gore: "At what point did companies picking up garbage begin to get into the toxic waste disposal business?"

Harold Kaufman: "To my knowledge, it's when the manifest system came out is when they found out the profit motive" (U.S. House of Representatives, 1980:8).

New Jersey Attorney General John J. Degnan pointed out to a Congressional audience that organized crime activity accounts for only a fraction of the illegal dumping taking place in the United States (U.S. House of Representatives, 1980:87). Nonetheless, organized crime was ideally suited to develop the methodology of illegal hazardous waste practices to the fullest. In those parts of the nation where garbage hauling and landfilling was historically controlled by organized crime, their movement into the newly created hazardous waste market was an obvious extension of current activity. In New Jersey, for example, organized crime had controlled the garbage industry through ownership of garbage hauling firms, through ownership of or control of landfills, and through labor racketeering (U.S. House of Representatives, 1981:1–45). The new regulations governing hazardous waste would have had to have been carefully written and tenaciously enforced were organized crime to be kept from applying this highly developed infrastructure to the new market. In fact, as will be shown below, the opposite happened and organized crime easily entered both the hauling and the disposal phases of the hazardous waste handling industry.

Hauling. Organized crime had dominated traditional garbage hauling in states like New York and New Jersey for decades. Once associates of organized crime owned a number of hauling firms in any geographical area, they established an organizational infrastructure that governed their relationships and ensured high profits. Threats and violence persuaded other firms to join that infrastructure and abide by its rules or to sell and get out. The keystone of this infrastructure was the concept of "property rights" or "respect." Municipal solid waste hauling contracts were illegally apportioned among haulers. Having a property right meant that a hauler held rights to continue picking up the contract at sites he currently serviced without competition from others. Other firms would submit artificially high bids or would not bid at all when a contract came up for renewal, thereby assuring that the contractor kept his traditional site. This system of *de facto* territorial monopolies permitted noncompetitive pricing and made the lowly business of garbage hauling a very lucrative activity. Property rights were recognized and enforced by organized crime authorities. Conflicts were adjudicated in meetings of the Municipal Contractors Association. Decisions of the MCA were enforced by threats and, if necessary, violence (U.S. House of Representatives, 1981a:1–42).[4] As is shown below, when the RCRA mandated the licensing of firms deemed fit to transport hazardous waste, mob-connected garbage haulers found it easy to acquire state permits and declare themselves to be hazardous waste haulers. Quite naturally, they brought their traditional forms of social organization with them. Individual haulers holding established property rights assumed that they would transfer those property rights to a new type of waste (U.S. House of Representatives, 1980:22). They also met as a group to set up a Trade Waste Association modeled after the Municipal Contractors Association to apportion and enforce property rights in the new market (U.S. House of Representatives, 1980:9–10, 1981a:1–12, 212).

Disposal. The manifest system requires that someone will be willing to sign off on the manifest and declare that a waste shipment has been properly disposed of. This means, as Congressman Florio (Democrat, New Jersey) pointed out (U.S. House of Representatives, 1980:30), that mob control over hauling is not enough: organized crime figures had to have ownership of, or at least influence over, final disposal sites. This requirement did not prove to be a serious stumbling block, however. Many landfills were already owned wholly or in part by organized crime figures, a legacy of past mob involvement in the garbage business. These sites readily accepted dubious shipments of hazardous waste thinly disguised as ordinary municipal waste (U.S. House of Representatives 1981a:228, 1981b). Landfill owners not directly associated with organized crime could be bribed to sign manifests for shipments never received or to accept hazardous waste that was manifested elsewhere (U.S. House of Representatives, 1980:70, 90). In addition, known organized crime figures started or seized control of a network of phony disposal and "treatment" facilities such as Chemical Control Corporation, Elizabeth, New Jersey; Modern Transportation, Kearny, New Jersey; and Duane Marine, Perth Amboy, New Jersey.[5] Licensed by the state, these outfits could legally receive hazardous waste and sign off on the manifest. They would then either stockpile it on site (where it would stay until it exploded, burned, or otherwise came to the attention of authorities) or dump it along roadways, down municipal sewers, into the ocean, or elsewhere (Block and Scarpitti, 1985:145, 158, 298; U.S. House of Representatives, 1980:25). In the extreme, actual ownership of or access to disposal sites was unnecessary for those willing to file totally fanciful manifests. Congressman Gore cited one case in which several major corporations signed over their wastes to an out-of-state facility that subsequently was shown to simply not exist (U.S. House of Representatives, 1980:70, 135).[6]

Enabling Causes: The Making of a Vulnerable Regulatory Structure

In retrospect, it is hardly surprising that, given the opportunity, organized crime would enter the newly created market for hazardous waste handling. It was an extension of their current business activity. They had the equipment and organization. They had both the know-how and the will to corrupt the manifest system. It was an attractive prospect. Both the potential size of the market and the potential profits were enormous. Even if they charged only a fraction of the true price of legitimate disposal, that price would be much higher than the price they charged to move the same stuff when it was legally just garbage, but their operating expenses would stay the same (if they commingled hazardous waste with ordinary garbage) or decrease (if they simply dumped). Why organized crime would want to enter into a relationship with corporate generators when the opportunity presented itself needs no subtle unraveling. The more complex task is to determine what political and social-structural conditions made it possible for them to "colonize" the hazardous waste disposal industry.

Lax Implementation, Incompetent and/or Corrupt Enforcement

Explanations of organized crime presence in hazardous waste handling focused on lax implementation and improper enforcement. Congressional hearings produced dramatic evidence that, at least in New Jersey, the state where organized crime intrusion into hazardous waste is most thoroughly documented, the major provisions of the RCRA were poorly implemented and enforced. Interim hauling and disposal licenses were freely granted. The manifest system was not sufficiently monitored.

Interim Licensing.   Congress had mandated an extended transition period during which both transporters and disposal firms would operate under temporary permits until an adequate national hazardous waste industry developed. Generators lobbied quite heavily on this point (U.S. EPA, 1976:238, 1979:153, 307; Gansberg, 1979) and Congress had to agree to this provision because the shortage of adequate hazardous waste facilities was so severe. American industry would have choked in its own accumulating wastes had it not been permitted to continue to use less-than-adequate means of disposal. A reasonable concession to economic realities, implementation of interim licensing was poorly managed. House of Representatives testimony shows that New Jersey issued hauling permits to any applicant who paid a nominal $50 fee (U.S. House of Representatives, 1980:14–15). Existing landfills and even totally bogus firms with no real disposal facilities found it equally easy to get interim disposal permits (U.S. House of Representatives, 1980:10).

> Harold Kaufman (key FBI informant on mob involvement in hazardous waste disposal, testifying about his old firm, Duane Marine): The State licensed us. We were the first ones licensed . . . .
> Gore: And this was a chemical waste disposal facility, is that right?
> Kaufman: Well, that is what it was called. It never disposed of anything, but you can call it that.

Manifest Oversight.   Once a license was obtained, lax supervision of the manifest system made illegal and unsafe disposal of hazardous waste a relatively straightforward, low-risk activity (U.S. House of Representatives, 1980:140).

> Gore: What enforcement efforts are you making to prevent the abuse of the manifest system?
> Edwin Stier (New Jersey Division of Criminal Justice): The only way the manifest system is going to be properly, effectively enforced is through the proper analysis of the information that comes from the manifest. . . . Anyone who assumes that a manifest system which looks good on paper can control the flow and disposition of toxic waste without the kind of support both technical and manpower support that is necessary to make it effective, I think, is deluding himself. [However] . . . we aren't looking specifically for manifest case violations. We aren't pulling every manifest in that is filed with the department of environmental protection and looking for falsification of manifests specifically because we don't have the time, the resources, or the specific lead information to do that.

Congressional testimony revealed that until 1980 New Jersey did not have a single person assigned to monitor the manifests being filed in Trenton (U.S. House of Representatives, 1981b:124). A recent study by the General Accounting Office (U.S. GAO, 1985:25–31) found that the manifest system does not detect illegal disposal, in part because of inadequate monitoring.

Congressional hearings also produced evidence suggesting that the relevant New Jersey agencies—the Interagency Hazardous Waste Strike Force, the Division of Criminal Justice, and the Division of Environmental Protection—were incapable of producing effective enforcement even when tipped off to specific instances of hazardous waste dumping (U.S. House of Representatives, 1980:144–146, 1981b:110–124). Block and Scarpitti (1985) present many other examples that appear to show corruption or, at best, ineptitude on the part of state officials responsible for investigation and prosecution of illegal hazardous waste practices.

Lax implementation and enforcement undoubtedly played a big role in facilitating organized crime entry into the hazardous waste disposal industry. There are, however, more fundamental conditioning factors that logically and temporally preceded these causes. RCRA is a regulatory structure ripe with potential for subversion. Why did Congress create a regulatory structure so vulnerable to lax enforcement? A review of RCRA's legislative history shows quite clearly that corporate generators moved decisively to shape the emerging federal intervention to their liking. They determinedly fought for and achieved a regulatory form that would demand of them the least real change and a form that would minimize their liability for potential violations of the new regulations.

Generators' Strategic Intervention in the Legislative Debate over the Form of Policy

Compared to the regulatory mechanism written into the final language of the RCRA, some potential alternative forms that were proposed and then rejected would have proved much less hospitable to noncompliance in general and to the entry of organized crime in particular. The federal government could have mandated specific treatment and disposal practices, or directed generators to treat all of their wastes themselves, or legislated that generators retain full responsibility for their wastes even if they assign them to other parties for shipping and disposal. Generators, led by representatives of major oil and chemical corporations, explicitly and vigorously opposed any such language. They hammered away with striking unanimity at two fundamental points: that the government should in no way interfere in firms' production decisions, and that generators should not be held responsible for the ultimate fate of their hazardous wastes.

Generators repeatedly warned Congress neither to appropriate to itself the power to intervene in production processes nor to require generators to follow specific waste treatment practices. They stressed, instead, that regulatory controls are more properly imposed at the stage of final disposition. Here are some representative statements:

> We believe that the disposal of wastes ought to be regulated instead of regulating the nature and use of the product or the type of manufacturing process used (E.I. DuPont de Nemours and Co., U.S. Senate, 1974:454).

> Authority to control production, composition, and distribution of products . . . would be devastating to free enterprise commerce (Dow Chemical, U.S. Senate, 1974:1,478).

> [Stauffer Chemical opposes generator permits which] would place controls on raw materials, manufacturing processes, products and distribution (Stauffer, U.S. Senate, 1974:1,745).

> . . . legislation should not impede the natural interaction of raw materials, market and other forces that ultimately control the nature, quality,

price, and success of products developed in our free enterprise system (Union Carbide, U.S. Senate, 1974:1,748).

No specific requirements or prohibitions should be set governing the recovery, reuse or disposal of industrial wastes. . . . Generators should be free to increase or decrease waste production rates, terminate waste production, treat their own wastes, and negotiate treatment or disposal service contracts in a free and competitive market (American Petroleum Institute, U.S. EPA, 1976:1,406, 1,410).

. . . the generator should be free to decide whether to treat or dispose of wastes (Manufacturing Chemists Association, U.S. EPA, 1976:565).

. . . economic incentive alone should determine the degree of waste re-cycle and recovery. . . . We are opposed to regulations specifying the kind and amount of processing and recycle of wastes [by the genera-tor]. [The] greatest emphasis should be placed on establishing standards which assure that the ultimate disposal method is satisfactory (DuPont, U.S. EPA, 1976:72–73).[7]

Generator unanimity was equally impressive on the second issue of re-sponsibility. They were willing to have limited responsibility, to label their wastes, and make sure they contracted only with firms approved by state authorities, but they vehemently opposed the idea that generators should bear legal responsibility for their wastes from cradle to grave. They argued that responsibility should pass to the party in physical possession of the hazardous waste. Under such a system, they further pointed out, only the hauler and disposer need to be licensed and the government should not li-cense generators. Here are some representative statements:

We agree that the generator has some responsibility in the area, . . . [i.e.] make some determination that the disposer is competent and has the proper permits for disposal. . . . However, the waste hauler and disposer have responsibility to assure, respectively, that the wastes are delivered for disposal at the proper location and are properly disposed. Irrespon-sible action is invited if the person holding the waste has no responsi-bility for it (DuPont, U.S. EPA, 1976:73–74).

[The generator should] confirm the competence and reliability of trans-porters, treaters and processors to whom the waste may be trans-ferred. . . . Each transporter, treater and disposer should be responsible for his individual activities while the waste is in his possession (Mon-santo, U.S. EPA, 1976:410–411).

MCA recommends that the responsibility for the waste should be asso-ciated with physical possession of the waste, so that the generator should not be held liable for negligence of the transporter and the dis-poser of the waste. (Manufacturing Chemists Association, U.S. EPA, 1976:565).

> We feel that permits should only be required of the disposal site operator (B.F. Goodrich, U.S. Senate, 1974:1,441).

> . . . permits for both generation and disposal of hazardous waste is doubly redundant. . . . A permit system for generators of wastes is unneeded and would tend to stagnate technology at the level prevailing at the time the permit was issued (Dow Chemical, U.S. Senate, 1974:1,478–1,479).

> . . . we consider permits for the generation of hazardous wastes to be unneeded, and could result in unnecessary restriction of manufacturing operations (Union Carbide, U.S. Senate, 1974:464).[8]

The generators also lobbied for the other provisions to their liking—a narrow definition of what substances should be regulated as hazardous, flexible time frames for implementation, and less stringent rules for on-site disposal[9]—but the two points above were the heart of their legislative intervention. In the end, they didn't get everything they wanted. The government would make generators register with the EPA. On-site, generator self-disposal would be subject to the same rules that governed off-site disposal firms. However, the overall forms of RCRA passed by Congress embodied both of their major demands.

The Legacy of Generator Inattention and Inaction

The generators also contributed indirectly to the shaping of RCRA legislation through their historical lack of attention to proper hazardous waste disposal. The EPA estimated in 1974 that ocean dumping and improper landfilling cost about 5% of the price of environmentally adequate disposal and it reported that

> Given this permissive legislative climate, generators of waste are under little or no pressure to expend resources for adequate management of their hazardous wastes. (U.S. Senate, 1974:71)

Lack of generator demand for adequate disposal facilities discouraged the inflow of investment capital, and an adequate waste disposal industry had failed to develop by the time RCRA legislation was being debated. Had legislators ignored this situation and required an immediate shift to proper disposal, a production crisis could have been triggered as wastes accumulated and firms found few legal outlets for them. Industrial spokesmen predicted dire consequences. In a representative statement, a Union Carbide spokesman warned legislators:

> Those wastes which are non-incinerable and have no commercial value must be disposed of. To deny opportunity for disposal would effectively eliminate much of the chemical process industry. Disposal in or on the

land or disposal in the oceans are the only viable alternatives available. (U.S. Senate, 1974:461)

Neither individual officeholders nor whole governments stay in office long if they pass legislation which, even for the best and most popular of reasons, brings to a halt industrial sectors central to the national economy. Congressmen had to be realistic and mandate years of transition during which hazardous waste would be hauled and disposed by operators having only interim licenses. This reasonable concession to the reality of the situation, a legacy of generator inattention, created a loophole through which many less-than-qualified parties could legally participate as providers in the hazardous waste market.[10]

Notes

I wish to gratefully acknowledge that this paper has benefited from comments by Frank Henry, Judith Gerson, Wendy Strimling, Vern Baxter, John Campbell, Carroll Estes, members of the Pew Writing Seminar, and several anonymous reviewers.

1. The extent of involvement is unclear for two reasons:

First, investigation has focused on the New York, Connecticut, and New Jersey region. This is a strategic site for investigation because so much hazardous waste is produced in the Tri-State area (for example, New Jersey ranks number one in the nation in annual hazardous waste generation) and because mob involvement in garbage in this region has been thoroughly documented. But, for the same reasons, this region may not be typical of the rest of the nation. Recent investigatory reporting concerning environmental pollution and political corruption in Louisiana (Getschow and Petzinger, 1984; Petzinger and Getschow, 1984a, 1984b; Snyder, 1985a, 1985b, 1985c, 1985d, 1985e, 1985f) shows that waste disposal is a corrupt business there as well, but that corruption grows out of the specific history of oil industry domination of that state's economy and its politics and appears to be quite different from patterns of corruption in the Northeast. This suggests that the post-RCRA relationship between corporate generators and waste disposers may be heavily influenced by variations in regional history predating RCRA.

Second, on a more theoretical level, the boundary between organized crime and legitimate business is, at points, somewhat ambiguous. Take, for example, SCA, the nation's third largest hazardous waste company. SCA undertook a vigorous acquisition program in New Jersey and quickly bought up about 20 garbage hauling and landfill companies. Some of these were formerly owned by organized crime figures. SCA is a corporation whose stock is traded on the New York Stock Exchange and its corporate board boasts outside directors associated with IBM, Houghton-Mifflin Co., MIT, and the Boston Co. (U.S. House of Representatives, 1980, 1981a), but Congressional testimony indicates that when SCA bought mob-owned firms, it hired the former owners as managers and appears to have allowed them free hand to run their business as they had before acquisition.

2. Methods of estimation are discussed in depth by Greenberg and Anderson (1984).

3. It is generally admitted that even the best landfill is only temporary and inadequate: "No landfill can be made safe from all substances"—Albert Gore (U.S. House of Representatives, 1983:2). George J. Tyler, Assistant Commissioner of the New Jersey Department of Environmental Protection, speaking about the Lone Pine landfill in Freehold, New Jersey (U.S. House of Representatives, 1981b:188): "The landfill is leaking into the water, but so does every landfill in the country." The landfill at Wilsonville, Illinois, owned and operated by SCA (see Note 1), is, according to Dr. Raymond D. Harbison, a toxicologist, EPA consultant, and professor of pharmacology at Vanderbilt University, "the most scientific landfill in this country" (U.S. House of Representatives, 1981a:267). Geological and soil permeability feasibility tests were conducted before construction was begun. Trenches were carefully dug. Arriving waste is sampled and tested, then buried in either nonleaking 55 gallon drums or double-walled paper bags. Monitoring wells surround the site. Yet subsequent studies show that the soil is more

porous than originally thought and water is seeping in at rates greater than predicted. Furthermore, the landfill is built over an abandoned coal mine and feasibility tests underestimated the likelihood of "subsidence," land sinkage that may compromise the site's ability to keep substances safely contained. If this is the best site in the nation, the Office of Technology Assessment is right to worry that current efforts to clean up the worst abandoned sites under the Superfund program only transfer the problem to other places and future times (Shabecoff, 1985:31).

4. Of parenthetical interest here is the methodological similarity between organized crime's property rights system in garbage and price-fixing by Westinghouse, General Electric, and other firms in the famous heavy electrical equipment price fixing scandal of 1961 (Geis, 1977).

5. Modern Transportation, a firm that would ultimately receive half the manifested hazardous waste originating in northern New Jersey, was incorporated in 1972 by Richard Miele, co-owner with known organized crime figures of numerous garbage-related firms and landfills (Block and Scarpitti, 1985:297). Chemical Control Corporation was taken over by Johnny Albert, one of the organizers of the New Jersey Trade Waste Association (Block and Scarpitti, 1985:256–260; U.S. House of Representatives, 1980:10). Duane Marine was so enmeshed in organized crime networks and activities that its former employee, Harold Kaufman, became the central federal informant on these activities.

6. Albert Gore in the case of Capital Recovery: "The subcommittee's investigation has uncovered evidence that since August, 1976, major industrial companies, such as Koppers, Inc., in one case Exxon, Union Chemical Company in the state of New Jersey certified that over 270,000 gallons of chemical waste were delivered to an out-of-state facility in Wilmington, Delaware, named Capital Recovery. From all the available evidence, Capital Recovery is nothing more than a paper corporation. It has no offices or any site in Wilmington. There is no phone listing, no city or State real estate tax or business tax information; no annual report has been filed . . . " (U.S. House of Representatives, 1980:135–136).

7. Other companies and associations making the same argument during these hearings included Monsanto, Exxon, B.F. Goodrich, Alcoa, the Texas Chemical Council, and the Western Oil and Gas Association.

8. The same point was also raised by Stauffer Chemicals, Marathon Oil, American Cyanamid, Berylco, Shell, Alcoa, the Texas Chemical Council, the Western Oil and Gas Association, the American Petroleum Institute, and the New Jersey Manufacturers Association.

9. The issue of flexible time frames was raised by the National Association of Manufacturers (U.S. House of Representatives, 1976:190) and Exxon (U.S. EPA, 1976:940). Arguing for a restricted definition of what is regulable hazardous waste were DuPont (U.S. EPA, 1976:69), the American Iron and Steel Institute (U.S. EPA, 1976:100), American Cyanamid (U.S. EPA, 1976:1,550), B.F. Goodrich (U.S. Senate, 1974:1,440), Stauffer (U.S. Senate, 1974:1,746). Monsanto (U.S. EPA, 1976:406–407), and Dow (U.S. EPA, 1976:956), argued for fewer restrictions for on-site disposal.

10. It should be noted that generators intervened not only in policy formation but also engaged in ongoing efforts to weaken regulatory impact during implementation. They appeared at EPA implementation hearings to emphasize that the criteria for declaring substances hazardous were still too broad, that proposed disposal requirements were too stringent, that interim standards were burdensome and inflexible, and that recordkeeping and reporting requirements were onerous. Especially active in this period were trade associations such as the Manufacturing Chemists Association, the Synthetic Organic Chemists Manufacturing Association, the American Petroleum Institute, and the National Paint and Coatings Association, as well as large individual corporations such as Dow and DuPont (U.S. EPA, 1979; U.S. Senate, 1979). EPA officials complained privately that "the millions of pages of testimony filed by representatives of industry on virtually each clause of every implementation proposal" created "a major obstacle" to timely implementation of RCRA (Shabecoff, 1979:1).

References

Albanese, Jay S.
    1982 What Lockheed and La Cosa Nostra have in common: The effect of ideology on criminal justice policy. Crime and Delinquency 28:211–232.
Barnett, Harold C.
    1981 Corporate capitalism, corporate crime. Crime and Delinquency 27:4–23.

Block, Alan A.
1982 "On the Waterfront" revisited: The criminology of waterfront organized crime. Contemporary Crisis 6:373–396.
Block, Alan A. and William J. Chambliss
1981 Organizing Crime. New York: Elsevier.
Block, Alan A. and Frank R. Scarpitti
1985 Poisoning for Profit: The Mafia and Toxic Waste in America. New York: William Morrow.
Brady, James
1983 Arson, urban economy and organized crime: The case of Boston. Social Problems 31:1–27.
Chambliss, William J.
1978 On the Take: From Petty Crooks to Presidents. Bloomington: Indiana University Press.
Clinard, Marshall B., Peter C. Yeager, Jeanne M. Brissette, David Petrashek, and Elizabeth Harries
1979 Illegal Corporate Behavior. Washington, DC: U.S. Government Printing Office.
Clinard, Marshall B. and Peter C. Yeager
1980 Corporate Crime. New York: The Free Press.
Crenson, Matthew A.
1971 The Un-Politics of Air Pollution: A Study of Non-Decisionmaking in the Cities. Baltimore: Johns Hopkins University Press.
Denzin, Norman K.
1977 Notes on the crimogenic hypothesis: A case study of the American liquor industry. American Sociological Review 42:905–920.
Drucker, Peter P.
1981 What is business ethics? The Public Interest 63:18–36.
Etzioni, Amitai
1985 Shady corporate practices. New York Times. November 15.
Farberman, Harvey A.
1975 A crimogenic market structure: The automobile industry. Sociological Quarterly 16:438–457.
Gansberg, Martin
1979 New Jersey Journal. New York Times. January 21.
Geis, Gilbert
1977 The heavy electrical equipment antitrust cases of 1961. In Gilbert Geis and Robert F. Meier (eds.), White-Collar Crime: Offenses in Business, Politics, and the Professions (rev. ed.). New York: Free Press.
Getschow, George and Thomas Petzinger, Jr.
1984 Oil's legacy: Louisiana marshlands, laced with oil canals, are rapidly vanishing. The Wall Street Journal. October 24.
Governor's Commission on Science and Technology for the State of New Jersey.
1983 Report of the Governor's Commission on Science and Technology.
Greenberg, Michael R. and Richard F. Anderson
1984 Hazardous Waste Sites: The Credibility Gap. Piscataway, NJ: Center for Urban Policy Research.
Leonard, William N. and Marvin G. Weber
1977 Automakers and dealers: A study of crimogenic market forces. In Gilbert Geis and Robert F. Meier (eds.), White-Collar Crime: Offenses in Business, Politics, and the Professions (rev. ed.). New York: Free Press.
Martens, Frederick T. and Colleen Miller-Longfellow
1982 Shadows of substance: Organized crime reconsidered. Federal Probation 46:3–9.

Marx, Karl
1967 Capital: A Critique of Political Economy, Vol. 1. New York: International Publishers.
Needleman, Martin L. and Carolyn Needleman
1979 Organizational crime: Two models of crimogenesis. Sociological Quarterly 20:517–528.
Petzinger, Thomas, Jr. and George Getschow
1984a Oil's legacy: In Louisiana, big oil is cozy with officials and benefit is mutual. The Wall Street Journal. October 22.
1984b Oil's legacy: In Louisiana, pollution and cancer are rife in the petroleum area. The Wall Street Journal. October 23.
Shabecoff, Philip
1979 House unit attacks lags on toxic waste. New York Times. October 14.
1985 Toxic waste threat termed far greater than U.S. estimates. New York Times. March 10.
Schelling, Thomas C.
1967 Economics and criminal enterprise. The Public Interest 7:61–78.
Smith, Dwight C., Jr.
1980 Paragons, pariahs, and pirates: A spectrum-based theory of enterprise. Crime and Delinquency 26:358–386.
Smith Dwight C., Jr., and Richard D. Alba
1979 Organized crime and American life. Society 3:32–38.
Snyder, David
1985a Toxic scars crisscross Louisiana. The New Orleans Times-Picayune. September 8.
1985b Early action was met with disbelief. The New Orleans Times-Picayune. September 8.
1985c Wastes choke scenic bayous of St. Charles. The New Orleans Times-Picayune. September 10.
1985d Chemical specter fills Cajun paradise with sense of fear. The New Orleans Times-Picayune. September 11.
1985e He won't be stopped, landfill operator warns. The New Orleans Times-Picayune. September 11.
1985f 10-year struggle to shut down waste site stymied by state. The New Orleans Times-Picayune. September 12.
Szasz, Andrew
1982 The dynamics of social regulation: A study of the formation and evolution of the Occupational Safety and Health Administration. Unpublished doctoral dissertation. Madison: University of Wisconsin.
1984 Industrial resistance to occupational safety and health legislation: 1971–1981. Social Problems 32:103–116.
U.S. Environmental Protection Agency
1976 Hazardous Waste Management: Public Meetings. December 2–11.
1979 Public Hearings on the Proposed Regulations Implementing Sections 3001 to 3004 of the Resource Conservation and Recovery Act. February 22–23.
U.S. General Accounting Office
1985 Illegal Disposal of Hazardous Waste: Difficult to Detect or Deter. Comptroller General's Report to the Subcommittee on Investigations and Oversight, Committee on Public Works and Transportation, House of Representatives.
U.S. House of Representatives
1975 Waste Control Act of 1975. Hearings held by the Subcommittee on Transportation and Commerce, Committee on Interstate and Foreign Commerce. April 8–11, 14–17.

1976 Resource Conservation and Recovery Act of 1976. Hearings held by the Subcommittee on Transportation and Commerce, Committee on Interstate and Foreign Commerce. June 29–30.

1980 Organized Crime and Hazardous Waste Disposal. Hearings held by Subcommittee on Oversight and Investigations, Committee on Interstate and Foreign Commerce. December 16.

1981a Organized Crime Links to the Waste Disposal Industry. Hearings held by Subcommittee on Oversight and Investigations, Committee on Energy and Commerce. May 28.

1981b Hazardous Waste Matters: A Case Study of Landfill Sites. Hearings held by Subcommittee on Oversight and Investigations, Committee on Energy and Commerce, June 9.

1982 Hazardous Waste Enforcement. Hearings held by Subcommittee on Oversight and Investigations, Committee on Energy and Commerce. December.

1983 Hazardous Waste Disposal. Hearings held by Subcommittee on Oversight and Investigations. Committee on Science and Technology. March 30 and May 4.

U.S. Senate

1974 The Need for a National Materials Policy. Hearings held by the Subcommittee on Environmental Pollution, Committee on Public Works. June 11–13, July 9–11, 15–18.

1979 Oversight of RCRA Implementation. Hearings held by the Subcommittee on Environmental Pollution and Resource Protection, Committee on Environmental and Public Works. March 28–29.

Williams, Bruce A. and Albert R. Matheny

1984 Testing theories of social regulation: Hazardous waste regulation in the American states. Journal of Politics 46:428–458.

Managing Deviant Careers and Identities

As explained by Johann le Roux and Cheryl Sylvia Smith, in "Is the Street Child Phenomenon Synonymous with Deviant Behavior," street children evoke strong feelings from those who wish to help and those who wish to get rid of them. While the individual biographies among street children vary, once homeless, each of these youth is confronted with his or her marginal social position. This is a group with few safety nets, precisely because they are alienated from society and seen as "social junk." The authors show that because of the negative attitudes toward street children, as well as the frequent contact with social-control agents, by virtue of their behavior being defined as deviant, it is very difficult to maintain a healthy self-concept.

Because of a lack of resources, the experience of living on the street may also require involvement in other forms of deviance. Engaging in additional forms of deviance serves not only to further antagonize an already impatient community but also to provide rationale for punitive attitudes and actions against them. A significant concern is whether the harsh reality of the streets and the process of labeling pushes these children more deeply into a path of primary and secondary deviance. One of the few buffers against developing a negative self-perception may be the support they receive from other street children. However, one significant barrier to energized programs designed to intervene and help these children is "probably due to street children's marginality to society." Street children carry stigma and are discredited.

Adina Nack examines how stigma is managed in her article, "Damaged Goods: Women Managing the Stigma of STDs." The social construction of chronic STD infections in American culture is related to social values. Managing stigma, therefore, is a significant concern for those infected, since sexual health is assumed to be connected to morality. She notes that women become "engaged in a three-stage process [passing for healthy and/or covering; stigma transference; and disclosure] of reconciling their spoiled sexual selves." Virtually all of the women in Nack's study "altered the way that they saw themselves as sexual beings." To deal with the stigma, these women utilized various strategies, ranging from concealment and deception to selective disclosure. Strategies for preserving an acceptable self-concept may take other forms as well. Nack's observations reveal a stigma management strategy not previously addressed by other deviance theorists: stigma transference. This strategy was used by most of the women in her study. Stigma transference is the process of deflecting the blame for negative traits assigned to the disceditable individual onto such others as previous or current sexual partners, or imaginary others. In essence, stigma transference is an attempt to manage the burdens of stigma by externalizing the origins of the illness and redirecting the finger of blame to selected others.

41 Is the Street Child Phenomenon Synonymous with Deviant Behavior?

Johann le Roux
Cheryl Sylvia Smith

Introduction

Street children are subjected to physical assault, sexual abuse, harassment from the public, intimidation by gang members and criminals, and arrest by the police (Richter, 1988b). This victimization frequently repeats what has occurred in the home. Though often victims themselves, street children, according to Swart (1988c), are regarded as irresponsible and lawless and a serious financial burden to society.

Richter (cited in the *Natal Mercury,* June 15, 1988) has stated that the phenomenon of street children has become an emotional issue, evoking strong feelings among those committed to helping them, as well as those determined to get rid of them (see also Swart-Kruger and Donald, 1994; Donald and Swart-Kruger, 1994; Jayes, 1985). Further, Richter (1991a, 1991b) has noted that these children live on the periphery of society, and as a result they are often misunderstood.

Characterizing Street Children

The term street children can be applied to a large number of youths, all of whom spend a great deal of time away from home, but do not necessarily share other characteristics (Agnelli, 1986). Definitions vary, but they generally have three main elements in common: (1) these children live or spend a significant amount of time on the street; (2) the street is the children's source of livelihood; and (3) they are inadequately cared for, protected, or supervised by responsible adults. Richter (1988c, 1991b) has pointed out that the characteristics of runaways, or homeless youths, in First World countries differ from those of working Third World street children. These differences will be considered in the context of South Africa.

A survey of the literature on street children reveals that three groups are frequently identified: children with continuous family contacts, who work on the street, usually go to school, and go home to their families at the end of the day; children with occasional family contacts, who work on the street, do not go to school, and seldom go home to their families; and children without family contacts, who consider the street their home, and it is there that they seek shelter, food, and a sense of belonging among peers. Lusk (1992) has emphasized the psychological characteristics of four groups of street children: poor, working children who return to their families at night and usually attend school—they are not likely to exhibit delinquent behavior; independent street workers, whose family ties are in the process of breaking down—their school attendance is erratic and they exhibit increasing delinquency; children who live and work with their families on the street—poverty is the overwhelming reason for their presence; and children who have broken off all contact with their families—they live full time on the streets and are the "real" street children. Aptekar (1994) divides the process into stages, beginning with the child spending a small amount of time away from home, and progressing to the total adoption of the street lifestyle and culture (compare Baizerman, 1988; Visano, 1990).

Richter (1988a), Konanc (1989), Cosgrove (1990), and Aptekar (1995a) have stated that street children can be defined according to their relationships with family. Children *of* the street have left home permanently and usually have little or no contact with their families. Children *on* the street, who constitute the largest group, return home from time to time, usually contributing to the financial support of their families (Ennew, cited in Richter, 1988c; compare Aptekar, 1994).

Thus, street children encompass various categories. In addition, this term is commonly used in Africa, while in Europe, the Americas, and Australia, the terms homeless children, runaways, throwaways, and pushouts are more common.

The United Nations has developed its own definition of street children: "any girl or boy . . . for whom the street in the widest sense of the word, including unoccupied dwellings, wasteland, and so on, has become his or her habitual abode and/or source of livelihood, and who is inadequately protected, supervised, or directed by responsible adults" (Inter-NGO, cited in Swart-Kruger and Donald, 1994, p. 108). Cockburn (1991), noting that most differences in definitions are largely semantic, has defined street children as "those who have abandoned their homes, schools and immediate communities, before they are sixteen years of age, and have drifted into a nomadic street life" (p. 12). Richter (1988a) would add, "or those who have been abandoned by their families." Keen (1989) has proposed the following definition: "A street child is regarded as one who has run away from home and is living on the streets apart from any adult supervision or care" (p. 11). Cosgrove (1990) has emphasized the degree of family involvement and the amount of deviant behavior: a street child is "any individual under the age of eighteen whose behavior is predominantly at variance with community norms, and whose primary support for his/her developmental needs is not a family or family substitute" (p. 192). A recent report by the Human Sciences Research Council (HSRC) of South Africa (cited in Schurink and Mathye, 1993) has put forward the following definition: "A street child is any girl or boy who is under the age of eighteen and who has left his/her home environment part time or permanently (because of problems at home and/or in school, or to try to alleviate those problems) and who spends most of his/her time unsupervised on the street as part of a subculture of children who live an unprotected communal life and who depend on themselves and each other, and not on an adult, for the provision of physical and emotional needs, such as food, clothing, nurturance, direction and socialization" (p. 5).

According to Aptekar (1995a), it has been a common practice to refer to street children as a more or less unified group. However, the uniqueness of each street child should be acknowledged: "The term street children and youth embraces a diverse group of young people dislocated, to various degrees, from family, school and community, who tend to congregate in inner-city areas. Their reasons for being on the street vary, as do their probable educational and adjustment outcomes" (Richter and Swart-Kruger, 1995, p. 31).

It has also been suggested that children who have adjusted to street life are not easily convinced that there is a better alternative (Agnelli, 1986). Samper, cited in Aptekar (1995a), has gone so far as to refer to these children as a "plague."

Aptekar (1995a) has argued that, in most cases, street children are lumped together with working children who return to their families at the end of the day to live a normal but impoverished family life. This serves to make the problem of homelessness seem much greater than it actually is. In fact, the great majority—well over three-quarters and as many as ninety percent in various developing countries—live at home but work on the streets to earn money for their families (Aptekar, 1994).

Geddes (1993), however, has stated that although few street children are actually homeless or orphans, they are functionally homeless. Their parents are incapable of caring for them due to such problems as substance abuse and poverty (similar findings have been reported by Ennew, 1986, 1994; Lusk, 1992; Myers, 1989; Ojanuga, 1990; Patel, 1990; UNICEF, 1986).

A useful typology developed by UNICEF (cited in Aptekar, 1994) has classified street children in relation to their development. It reflects the belief that the experience of children who work on the street is considerably different from children who must look to a peer group or gang for the fulfillment of primary needs, such as protection, sustenance, and nurture. Aptekar (1994) has noted that some researchers classify street children by the different types of experiences they have, including the quality of their play and work and their relations with peers and authority figures. In addition, age and gender are important factors.

There is also the popular misconception that equates street children with gangs (compare Scharf et al., 1986; Swart, 1988a). Unfortunately both the police and the public are predisposed to characterize street children in this way.

Visano (1990) has claimed that street children are defined mainly by two dimensions: the amount of time spent on the streets and the absence of contact with responsible adults. However, this ignores the individual differences among them, such as coping style.

Deviance

Highly charged reactions to street children make it difficult to remain objective. Thus, the children's ability to survive under the most trying circumstances may be understated, or their problems minimized, making them appear as modern-day Huckleberry Finns. According to Aptekar et al. (1995), "it is so difficult to know to what degree the children are honest, to what degree one's perception of them is accurate, and how what is written about them will be perceived by readers" (pp. 2–3).

Adults' negative interpretations of the lifestyle and hostile, condemnatory responses to street children would seem to make it almost impossible for them to retain healthy self-esteem (Richer, 1989a; compare Scharf et al., 1986; Swart, 1988b). Wilson and Arnold (1986) have stated that "their silent scream and inner rage surface as they cut loose and take to the streets. There are few safety nets for them, because they are alienated from our society and because we regard them as 'deviants' and 'social junk'" (p. 7). Further, "they feel exploited by almost everyone: the media, the pushers, the sex purchasers, the sociologists, and the do-gooders" (p. 6).

South African street children are generally thought of as sly, manipulative, deceitful troublemakers. According to Richter (1991b), "like all stereotypes, these cameos contain a little bit of truth, often enough to reinforce and maintain the stereotype" (p. 6). In addition, these negative appraisals are predominantly all-embracing, and no concessions are made that bad behavior may be temporary or situational (Richter, 1989b).

According to Goliath (1989), "street children are a burden on society. These children often become the adult layabouts and criminals of the future" (p. 5). The literature, on the whole, reveals that by society's standards, street children deviate from social, moral, and legal norms. Swart (1988c) has stated that although some people condone the behavior of street children as that which is to be expected under the circumstances, it is generally "considered deviant in terms of childhood and community norms" (p. 8). Further, Swart-Kruger and Donald (1994) have stated that "it is not surprising . . . that lying and deceit are fundamental tools of survival in an adult world which has aligned itself against them" (p. 120).

Hansson (1991), citing Posel (1990), has claimed that since 1976, when many black children left their homes to take up the political struggle against apartheid, the media have depicted them as being symbols of "anarchy, barbarism, criminality and spiraling violence" (p. 8). According to Hansson, this explains why most programs have been aimed at reinstating adult control and resocializing such children by getting them off the streets and back into some form of schooling. Similarly, Richter (1988c) has pointed out that "one of the chief difficulties in trying to help street children is to find ways of bringing them back into so-called normal society. . . . Their socialization into this lifestyle has been prematurely and, often, traumatically ended" (p. 3).

Richter (1988a) has noted that the longer the children spend on the streets, the more likely it is that they will enter into criminal activities. It would appear that street children engage in criminal activities mainly to ensure their own survival. According to Agnelli (1986), "street children as such are not delinquent, but only immediate candidates for delinquency if their needs are not met" (p. 112).

Society's negative opinion of these children, the low expectations of them, and the closing of legitimate avenues of opportunity may push them into delinquency, resulting in a self-fulfilling prophecy. According to Swart (1988a), a few street children, feeling humiliated and frustrated, have even threatened adults with violence for making their lives unbearable. Paton (1990) has noted that "a child is more often delinquent because he has been deprived of . . . the fundamental needs of security, affection and outlets for his creative and emotional impulses. The change in him is remarkable when these deep needs are satisfied" (p. 99).

In general, street children are perceived by the public as being "deviant" (Swart, 1988b; Mangwana, 1992; Konanc, 1989). Haralambos and Holborn (1992) define deviance as "those activities which bring disapproval from members of society" (pp. 580–581). Richter's (1988a) findings indicate that about one fifth of street children may be involved in antisocial activities, with some having acquired a set of attitudes and beliefs congruent with criminality. Further, "the high visibility of criminal or delinquent activities, even among a small group of street children, tends to antagonize the communities in which they occur, and they provide the authorities with a rationale for adopting a punitive attitude towards all street children" (Richter, 1988a, p. 13).

Agnelli (1986) has stated that the outcome of having to adjust, often alone, in a hostile environment is involvement in delinquent activities. Cemane (1990) has taken a more categorical stance: "street children have no incentive to conform to social sanctions that inhibit antisocial behavior, and will seize any opportunity to engage in deviant behavior" (p. 2).

The brutality of street life and negative interactions with authorities may set into motion a process of primary and secondary deviance, with terrible consequences. Involvement in petty crime, or even proximity to such crime, has frequently made street children victims of violence. Dewees and Klees (1995), citing research from Childhope, have stated that, between 1988 and 1990, an estimated 4,611 Brazilian children and adolescents were murdered by renegade police and vigilante groups.

It is possible that the labeling of street children as deviant pushes them more deeply into antisocial behavior. They may even come to accept society's perceptions of them. This labeling serves to further isolate them from society, intensifying their victimization (Alexander, 1987; O'Connor, 1989; Olson et al., 1980; Aptekar, 1988). Kennedy (1987) has stated that being labeled homeless carries many connotations: dirty, lazy, alcoholic, delinquent, and drug addicted. Perceptions beget attitudes, which, regarding street children, are negative—they are troublesome, they are undeserving. "So we provide *separate* services for them in *separate* hostels or houses, and what services there are, are provided not by the statutory bodies but by underfunded voluntary agencies. This in turn reinforces society's attitudes towards these children, that they don't deserve any better" (Kennedy, 1987, p. 19).

Commenting on street children in the Americas, Connolly (1990) has stated that, on the whole, these children are regarded as either delinquent or deviant. The fact that children who have spent a considerable amount of time on the streets frequently run away from both government and private programs is used as evidence to support the common belief that they are uneducable and incorrigible (see also Balanon, 1989; Konanc, 1989; Hickson and Gaydon, 1989). According to Richter (1989b), UNICEF has identified the inhibition of self-confidence and self-esteem, brought about by society's negative perception of street children and their work, as a significant element in their exploitation (compare Keen, 1990; Richter, 1988a).

Labeling theory views the determination of deviance as a dynamic process. Who is to be considered deviant comes about in the interplay between the powerless and the powerful (Thio, 1988). That the majority expect street children to be criminals as adults (Swart, 1988d) therefore has important repercussions.

Haskell and Yablonsky (1987) have stated that "a youth is defined as a juvenile delinquent when that status is conferred upon him by a court" (p. 7). Thus, when arrested, street children are often incarcerated with adult offenders, who instruct them in the tricks of the trade. This may lead to the entrenchment of a criminal career (Swart, 1988a; compare Olson et al., 1980; Nye, 1980; Gullotta, 1979; Young et al., 1983).

Conclusions

Increasing numbers of children live on the streets (Cemane, 1990; Richter, 1991a; Peacock, 1994). Once there, the attitudes and perceptions of society become that catalyst for the mainly negative self-perceptions that street children have of themselves (Konanc, 1989). The support of other street children, however, may act as a significant emotional buffer (Donald and Swart-Kruger, 1994).

According to Richter (1991a), "children are most especially harmed on the streets by the harsh physical conditions, by violence and harassment, by labor exploitation, by absorption into criminal networks, and by denial of their right to receive an education that will equip them to achieve a better life" (p. 8). Interventions have ranged from government programs to projects by volunteers. These efforts, until recently, have been minimal, probably due to street children's marginality to society (Cockburn, 1991).

Richter, citing Agnelli (1986), has claimed that the presence of street children is an indictment of the way society construes its priorities. These children, who endure significant hardship but hope one day to rejoin the community as productive members, are ignored by a society that systematically excludes them (Richter, 1989a).

References

Agnelli, S. (1986). *Street children: A growing urban tragedy.* London: Weidenfeld & Nicolson.

Alexander, M. (1987). *Street children: Towards global awareness and action. A study of resources available to homeless children in Guatemala, C.A.* Unpublished honors dissertation, Newcomb College, Tulane University.

Aptekar, L. (1988). *The street children of Cali.* Durham, NC: Duke University Press.

———. (1994). Street children in the developing world: A review of their condition. *Cross-Cultural Research, 28*(3), 195–224.

———. (1995a). *Educating the public about the coping strategies of street children.* Paper presented at the Tenth National Congress of the South African Association for Child and Adolescent Psychiatry (Children of Africa: Risk, Resilience, Challenge and Change), Durban.

———. (1995b). *Street children: A cross-cultural perspective.* Paper presented at the HSRC Conference (Street Children: From Resolutions to Action), Pretoria.

Aptekar, L., Cathey, P. J., Ciano, L., & Giardino, G. (1995). Street children in Nairobi, Kenya. *African Urban Quarterly, 10,* 1–26.

Baizerman, M. (1988). Street kids: Notes for designing a program for the youth of and on the streets. *The Child Care Worker, 6*(11), 13–15.

Balanon, L. G. (1989). Street children: Strategies for action. *Child Welfare, 68*(2), 159–166.

Cemane, K. B. (1990). The street-child phenomenon. *Social Work Practice, 1*(90), 2–5.

Cockburn, A. (1991). Street children: An overview of the extent, causes, characteristics and dynamics of the problem. *The Child Care Worker, 9*(1), 12–13.

———. (1995). *Looking after street children: A model indigenous to South Africa.* Paper presented at the Tenth Biennial Conference of the National Association of Child Care Workers, Cape Town.

Connolly, M. (1990). Adrift in the city: A comparative study of street children in Bogota, Colombia, and Guatemala City. In B. Boxhill (Ed.), *Homeless children: The watchers and the waiters* (pp. 129–149). New York: Haworth Press.

Cosgrove, J. (1990). Towards a working definition of street children, *International Social Work, 33,* 185–192.

Dewees, A., & Klees, S. J. (1995). Social movements and the transformation of national policy: Street and working children in Brazil. *Comparative Education Review, 39*(1), 76–100.

Donald, D., & Swart-Kruger, J. (1994). The South African street child: Developmental implications. *South African Journal of Psychology, 24*(24), 169–174.

Ennew, J. (1986). Children of the streets. *New Internationalist, 164,* 10–11.

———. (1994). Parentless friends: A cross-cultural examination of networks among street children and street youth. In F. Nesman & K. Hurrelman (Eds.), *Social networks and social support in childhood and adolescence.* London: De Gruyter.

Geddes, F. (1993). *The drugging patterns and attitudes towards substance abuse in a group of Johannesburg street children.* Unpublished master's thesis, University of the Witwatersrand, Johannesburg.

Goliath, D. (1989). The problem that grows and grows. *Prisma, 4,* 4–5.

Gullotta, T. (1979). Leaving home: Family relationships of the runaway child. *Social Casework, 60*(2), 111–114.

Hansson, D. (1991). *We the invisible: A feminist analysis of the conception of "street children" in South Africa.* Cape Town: Institute of Criminology, University of Cape Town.

Haralambos, M., & Holborn, M. (1992). *Sociology: Themes and perspectives* (3rd ed.). London: Harper Collins.

Haskell, M. R., & Yablonsky, L. (1987). *Juvenile delinquency.* Chicago: Rand McNally College Publishing.

Hickson, J., & Gaydon, V. (1989). Counselling in South Africa: The challenge of apartheid. *Journal of Multicultural Counselling and Development, 17*(2), 85–94.

Jayes, C. S. (1985). *Some characteristics of a group of coloured runaway boys aged 8–16 years and factors that these boys and their mothers perceived as contributing to their runaway behavior.* Unpublished master's thesis, University of Cape Town.

Keen, J. (1989). *A window on the world: A study into the values, interests, perceptions and aspirations of female street children.* Research project, University of Cape Town.

Keen, J. (1990). Dealing with street children. *The Child Care Worker, 8*(11), 8–9.

Kennedy, S. (Ed.). (1987). *Streetwise: Homelessness among the young in Ireland and abroad.* Glendale Press.

Konanc, E. (1989). Street children and children working in the street: Preliminary results of a field study in Turkey. *The Child Care Worker, 7*(11), 13–15.

Lusk, M. (1992). Street children of Rio de Janeiro. *International Social Work, 35,* 293–305.

Mangwana, T. (1992). Working with street children: Hints for child care workers. *The Child Care Worker, 10*(5), 14–15.

Maphatane, M., & Schurink, W. (1993). Legislation and welfare policy regarding street children. In W. Schurink (Ed.), *Street children.* Pretoria: HSRC.

Myers, W. (1989). Urban working children: A comparison of four surveys from South Africa. *International Labor, 128,* 321–335.

Natal Mercury. (1988, June 15). Durban. Page 3.

Nye, F. I. (1980). A theoretical perspective on running away. *Journal of Family Issues, 1*(2), 14–19.

O'Connor, I. (1989). *Our homeless children: Their experiences.* Report to the National Inquiry into Homeless Children by the Human Rights and Equal Opportunity Commission. Sydney: The Printing Place.

Ojanuga, D. (1990). Kaduma beggar children: A study of child abuse and neglect in northern Nigeria. *Child Welfare, 69,* 371–380.

Olson, L., Liebow, E., Mannino, F. V., & Shore, M. F. (1980). Runaway children twelve years later: A follow-up. *Journal of Family Issues, 1*(2), 176–185.

Patel, S. (1990). Street children, hotel boys and children of pavement dwellers and construction workers in Bombay: How they meet their daily needs. *Environment and Urbanization, 2,* 9–26.

Paton, A. (1990). *Diepkloof: Reflections on Diepkloof Reformatory.* Cape Town: David Philip.

Peacock, R. (1994). Street children. *Africa Insight, 24*(2), 138–143.

Richter, L. (1988a). Street children: The nature and scope of the problem in Southern Africa. *The Child Care Worker, 6*(7), 11–14.

——. (1988b). *A psychological study of street children in Johannesburg: An investigation requested by "Street-Wise," Johannesburg* (Report 89–01). Pretoria: Unisa.

——. (1988c). *Thinking on your feet in the street: Discussion to determine the educational potential of a group of "street children" in Johannesburg.* Address delivered at the Open Day of the Unit for Cognitive Development. Pretoria: Vista University.

——. (1989a). *South African street children: Comparisons with Anglo-American runaways.* Pretoria: Unisa.

——. (1989b). *Descriptions of self, family and society given by street children in Johannesburg.* Paper presented at the Seventh National Congress of the South African Association for Child and Adolescent Psychiatry and Allied Disciplines, Cape Town.

——. (1991a). Street children in South Africa: General theoretical introduction—Society, family and childhood. *The Child Care Worker, 9*(8), 7–9.

——. (1991b). Street children in South Africa: Street children in rich and poor countries. *The Child Care Worker, 9*(9), 5–7.

Richter, L., & Swart-Kruger, J. (1995). AIDS risk among street children and youth: Implications for intervention. *South African Journal of Psychology, 25*(1), 31–38.

Scharf, W., Powell, M., & Thomas, E. (1986). Strollers: Street children of Cape Town. In S. Burman & P. Reynolds (Eds.), *Growing up in a divided society: The context of childhood in South Africa.* Johannesburg: Ravan Press.

Schurink, W., & Mathye, M. (1993). Orientation. In W. Schurink (Ed.), *Street children.* Pretoria: HSRC.

Swart, J. (1986). My professional life on the streets. In N. J. Pines (Ed.), *Street children: Four perspectives.* The Institute for the Study of Man in Africa (ISMA Paper No. 40). Johannesburg: University of the Witwatersrand.

——. (1987). Street children: Refugees, drop-outs or survivors? *The Child Care Worker, 5*(10), 6–8.

——. (1988a). "Street-wise": Opening the way to self-actualization for the street child. *Africa Insight, 18*(1), 33–41.

——. (1988b). Community perceptions of street children in Hillbrow. *The Child Care Worker, 6*(6), 11–13.

——. (1988c). *Community and self-perceptions of the black South African street child.* Paper presented at the International Workshop on the Ethnography of Childhood, Cambridge University, Cambridge.

——. (1988d). *An anthropological study of street children in Hillbrow, Johannesburg, with special reference to their moral values.* Master's thesis, University of South Africa, Pretoria.

Swart-Kruger, J., & Donald, D. (1994). Children of the South African streets. In A. Dawes & D. Donald (Eds.), *Childhood and adversity: Psychological perspectives from South African research.* Cape Town: David Philip.

Thio, A. (1988). *Deviant behavior* (3rd ed.). New York: Harper & Row.

UNICEF. (1986). *Children in especially difficult circumstances: Exploitation of working and street children.* New York: United Nations Children Fund.

Visano, L. (1990). The socialization of street children: The development and transformation of identities. *Sociological Studies of Child Development, 3,* 139–161.

Wilson, P., & Arnold, J. (1986). *Street kids: Australia's alienated young.* Victoria: Collins Dove.

Young, R. L., Godfrey, W., & Adams, G. R. (1983). Runaways: A review of negative consequences. *Family Relations, 32,* 16–24.

Damaged Goods: Women Managing the Stigma of STDs

Adina Nack

The HIV/AIDS epidemic has garnered the attention of researchers from a variety of academic disciplines. In contrast, the study of other sexually transmitted diseases (STDs) has attracted limited interest outside of epidemiology and public health. In the United States, an estimated three out of four sexually active adults have human papillomavirus infections (HPV—the virus that can cause genital warts); one out of five have genital herpes infections (Ackerman 1998; Centers for Disease Control and Prevention [CDC] 1998a). In contrast, the nationwide rate of HIV infection is approximately 1 out of 300 (CDC 1998b). Current sociological research on the interrelationships between sexual health, stigma, and the self has focused overwhelmingly on HIV/AIDS (Sandstrom 1990; Siegel and Krauss 1991; Weitz 1989).

The social psychological perspective has addressed the role of social learning and psychological factors on shaping the meaning and practice of sexuality in different cultures and on developing sexual orientations and identities with regard to choice of sexual partners (Strong, DeVault, and Sayad 1996). A research focus has been psychosexual development: "factors that form a person's sexual feelings, orientations, and patterns of behavior" (Kelly 1998:157). Symbolic interactionist accounts of sexuality have addressed "the process of becoming sexual—something that is learnt and negotiated in a complex sequence of events" (Walby 1990:114). However, there has been a lack of theory building around the question of how individuals' conceptions of themselves as sexual beings exist in relation to their core or overall self-concepts.

This article focuses on how the sexual self-concept is transformed when the experience of living with a chronic STD casts a shadow of disease on the health and desirability of a woman's body, as well as on her perceived possibilities for future sexual experiences. The term *sexual self* means something fundamentally different from *gender identity* or *sexual identity*. Invoking the term *sexual self* is meant to conjure up the innately intimate parts of individuals' self-concepts that encompass how they think of themselves with regard to their experienced and imagined sensuality. Components of a sexual self may include the following: level of sexual experience, emotional memories of sexual pleasure (or lack thereof), perception of one's body as desirable, and perception of one's sexual body parts as healthy.

Prior studies have found that adolescents and adults use emotion-focused coping strategies for health problems (Folkman and Lazarus 1980; Spirito, Stark, and Williams 1988). These studies have drawn on social psychological theories of the self that offer insights on components of coping with various illnesses. Pioneers in researching the connection between self-conception and sexual health, Swanson and Chenitz (1993) used qualitative methods to examine the relationship between herpes infections and a "valued" self. Although these researchers theorized a three-stage model of regaining a valued sense of self after a herpes diagnosis, the findings of this study indicate a more complex process. In a related psychological study, researchers used quantitative methods to analyze the coping strategies of adolescent girls with STDs (Rosenthal et al. 1995). Although their findings highlight a typology of coping strategies, the authors concluded by emphasizing the need for further research into how young women cope with STDs as both a medical and an interpersonal problem.

To understand the individual-level experience of living with a chronic STD, it is important to take into account how these infections are symbolically constructed in American culture. The meanings that Americans give to being infected with an STD are intersubjectively formed during interactions. Individuals' experiences of health, illness, and medical care "are connected to the particular historically located social arrangements and the cultural values of any society" (Conrad and Kern 1994:5). Present American social values reflect the longstanding connections between sexual health and morality: Interactions with medical practitioners and lay people are the conduit through which the stigma of STDs is reinforced (Brandt 1987). Pryce (1998) pointed to a critical gap—the "missing" sociology of sexual disease—and asserted that this application of sociology should focus on the social construction of the body as central in the medical and social iconography of STDs.

In answer to Pryce's (1998) challenge, this research expands on the work of Swanson and Chenitz by sociologically analyzing the impact of genital herpes and HPV on women's sexual selves. This study adds to this research area by examining sexual self-transformation, starting from the point of how individuals' sexual selves are transformed by the lived experiences of being diagnosed and treated for chronic STDs. Beginning from a premise that the majority of people grow up feeling sexually invincible, a variety of traumas have the capacity to disrupt a positive sexual self-concept (e.g., molestation, rape, and illness). Social–interactional traumas also transmit messages that can damage sexual selves: Some physical bodies are undesirable; some sexual preferences are unacceptable; some levels of sexual experience are immoral.

This article addresses the process of how women manage the stigma of having an STD. First, I describe the research setting and methods. Second, I develop a conceptual framework for understanding the relationship between stigma management strategies and sexual self-transformation. Then, I analyze the women's self-narratives to evaluate both internal and interactional processes: (a) nonacceptance of stigma, (b) deflection of the stigma onto scapegoats, and (c) reflexive dynamics of stigma acceptance through disclosure. Finally, I conclude by exploring how their stories highlight the adaptation of individual stigma management strategies to a form of deviance that neither takes over core identities nor opens the door to social networks of collective stigma management. The connection between stigma management and identity transformation is explored by applying a narrative metaphor for the self to the women's struggles to keep their core self-concepts insulated from the stigma of STD infections.

Setting and Method

The motivation for this study stems from my personal experience with STDs. My "complete membership role" (Adler and Adler 1987) stems from legitimacy and acceptance by other women with STDs as a member of this unorganized and stigmatized group. At 20, sexual health became the center of my world when I was diagnosed with mild cervical dysplasia, the result of an HPV infection. I began an informal self-education process that helped me manage the stress of my treatments. My commitment to managing my sexual health status would become the foundation for this research project and provide me with the personal insights needed to connect with others facing STDs and the clinical knowledge necessary to be a sexual health researcher.

As a campus sexual health educator, I began to question what sexual health services were not provided. Seeing that women and men were being diagnosed and treated for STDs without receiving follow-up education and counseling, I developed a women-only support group for individuals dealing with STDs. Because of the topic's sensitive nature, I chose a gender-segregated approach to the support group and, ultimately, to the research. Contemporary gender scholars have demonstrated that sexuality "is socially organized and critically structured by gender inequality" (Walby 1990:121).

Unfortunately, only one woman used the support group. Initially disheartened, I began to question why people flocked to other support groups that were based on shared stigma (e.g., eating disorders and alcoholism) but failed to use this sexual health support group. Even persons living with HIV and AIDS used support groups to collectively manage their stigma. Clearly, I was a member without a group.

To investigate the failure of this support group, I conducted a survey among patients using a local women's health care clinic. During a month chosen at random, clinic staff gave each patient who came in for an appointment an anonymous survey about a new service being offered: a women's sexual health support group. In all, 279 completed surveys were collected ($N = 279$). Owing to the population from which the sample was drawn, generalizability is restricted to the population of women who receive women's health care services from this clinic. Further, the survey instrument was self-administered, thereby eliminating the possibility of participants getting clarification of confusing wording and so forth. Thirty-nine surveys contained missing data on one or more of the variables and were excluded from analysis.

I performed a multiple regression analysis on the data, the results of which supported the hypothesis that a person who has been diagnosed with a STD is less likely to be interested in a sexual health support group. The standardized coefficient ($-.149971$) reflects a moderately strong, negative relationship, significant at the .05 level. One of the most revealing findings was that only 23.3 percent of the women were definitely interested ("yes") in a sexual health support group. Of those who answered no (31.5 percent) or maybe (30.5 percent), most commented on their desire to keep sexual health matters private—even to the exclusion of others living with similar STDs. These findings lessen the effectiveness of a focus-group method for data collection.

I interpreted this finding to reflect that the stigma of having an STD is so severe that the perceived cost of disclosing this sexual health status to strangers outweighs the possible benefits. Because there has yet to be a moral entrepreneurial campaign to destigmatize STDs in our society, the norm remains secrecy (Brandt 1987). Therefore, to attend an STD support group is to make semipublic what the affected individuals strive to keep secret.

On the basis of these findings, I determined that in-depth interviews were my best chance for obtaining valid data. I constructed my research methods to reflect a reciprocal intention: As the women gave their stories to me, I would offer my support and resources as a sexual health educator. The challenge was to locate myself as a researcher on the "same critical plane as the overt subject matter" (Harding 1987:8). In this way, my values and actions as the researcher were viewed as empirical knowledge that might either support or weaken my findings.

My first hurdle was to achieve approval from the campus Human Research Committee. Their main concern was the participants' confidentiality. Because of the confidential nature of individuals' STD diagnoses, I was not allowed to directly recruit participants. Rather, they had to approach me, usually after hearing about my research project from other participants or women's health care practitioners with whom I had consulted. Once interview participants contacted me, I gained entrée and acceptance through my status as a sexual health peer educator and a complete member. In this way, I used snowball sampling to generate interviews (Biernacki and Waldorf 1981).

Many researchers have gone against traditional methods of interviewing that emphasize distance, instead answering participants' questions, providing important educational information during interviews, and maintaining friendships with participants long after studies reached completion (Nielson 1990). Semistructured or unstructured interviewing has been favored by many feminist researchers because it "produces nonstandardized information that allows researchers to make full use of differences among people" (Reinharz 1990:19). During the interviews, I used researcher self-disclosure to create and maintain rapport, and I included self-reflexive reporting of the interview process as part of the transcribed data that I analyzed (Reinharz 1990).

I conducted 28 conversational, unstructured interviews with consensual participants, who ranged in age from 19 to 56. The interview gave each woman the opportunity to discuss with me, one on one, her unfolding experiences with specific sexual health issues. I conducted the interviews in participants' preferred locations: their homes, my home, or other private settings. The interviews lasted from 1 to 2 hours and were tape recorded with the participants' permission. When appropriate, I concluded the interview with offers to provide sexual health information and resources, either in the form of health education materials or referrals to resources.

I then analyzed the data according to the principles of grounded theory (Glaser and Strauss 1967). Using constant comparative methods developed by Glaser and Strauss (1967; Glaser 1978), I analyzed the interview data by adjusting analytical categories to fit the emerging theoretical concepts. Over time, I verified these categories as similar patterns from previous interviews reappeared. On the basis of introspection (Ellis 1991), I began by hypothesizing stages of the transformation process of the sexual self as affected by the diagnosis and treatment of an STD. With each interview, I started to cluster participants' experiences around particular stages to check the validity of my initial model. The six stages of sexual self-transformation, in chronological order, are as follows: sexual invincibility, STD suspicion, diagnostic crisis, damaged goods, healing/treatment, and integration. Each of these stages had subcomponents that detailed the impact on the women's sense of sexual self from one part of the process to the next. I then looked through my field notes and transcriptions of interviews for illustrations of these stages and their properties, examining each example to further check the validity of my conceptualizations.

Once certain stages emerged, I began to ask about them more specifically in interviews, checking for the boundaries and variations as applied concepts. I also searched for connections between different stages and subcomponents, searching to understand how these conceptualizations interacted with each other. When particular stages emerged as more dominant themes in interviews, I began to delve into them further and to center my thinking around them as key analytical concepts. By this time, I had discarded some of the preliminary conceptualizations that appeared less relevant or theoretically inconsequential. The result of this evolving analysis was what Wiseman (1970) called a "total pattern," a sequence of events that held true for the group studied. I followed this plan of data collection and analysis to maximize the validity of my findings.

Stigma and the Sexual Self

For all but 1 of the 28 women, their STD diagnoses radically altered the way that they saw themselves as sexual beings. Facing both a daunting medical and social reality, the women used different strategies to manage their new stigma. Each stigma management strategy had ramifications for the transformation of their sexual selves.

Stigma Nonacceptance

Goffman (1963) proposed that individuals at risk for a deviant stigma are either "the discredited" or "the discreditable." The discrediteds' stigma was known to others either because the individuals revealed the deviance or because the deviance was not concealable. In contrast, the discreditable were able to hide their deviant stigma. Goffman found that the majority of discreditables were "passing" as nondeviants by avoiding "stigma symbols," anything that would link them to their deviance, and by using "disidentifiers," props or actions that would lead others to believe they had a nondeviant status. Goffman (1963) also noted that individuals bearing deviant stigma might eventually resort to "covering," one form of which he defined as telling deceptive stories. To remain discreditable in their everyday lives, 19 of the women used the individual stigma management strategies of passing and/or covering. In contrast, 9 women revealed their health status to select friends and family members soon after receiving their diagnoses.

Passing   The deviant stigma of women with STDs was essentially concealable, though revealed to the necessary inner circle of health care and health insurance providers. For the majority, passing was an effective means of hiding stigma from others, sometimes even from themselves.

Hillary, a 22-year-old White college senior, recalled the justifications she had used to distance herself from the reality of her HPV infection and to facilitate passing strategies.

> At the time, I was in denial about it. I told myself that that wasn't what it was because my sister had had a similar thing happen, the dysplasia. So, I just kind of told myself that it was hereditary. That was kinda funny because I asked the nurse that called if it could be hereditary, and she said

> "No, this is completely sexually transmitted"—I really didn't accept it until a few months after my cryosurgery.

Similarly, Gloria, a Chicana graduate student and mother of four, was not concerned about a previous case of gonorrhea she had cured with antibiotics or her chronic HPV "because the warts went away." Out of sight, out of her sex life: "I never told anybody about them because I figured they had gone away, and they weren't coming back. Even after I had another outbreak, I was still very promiscuous. It still hadn't registered that I needed to always have the guy use a condom."

When the women had temporarily convinced themselves that they did not have a contagious infection, it was common to conceal the health risk with partners because the women themselves did not perceive the risk as real. Kayla, a lower middle-class White college senior, felt justified in passing as healthy with partners who used condoms, even though she knew that condoms could break. Cleo, a White 31-year-old mother of a toddler, had sex with a partner after being diagnosed with HPV.

> So at the time I had sex with him, yes, I knew but, no, I hadn't been treated yet. That gets into the whole "I never told him," and I didn't. Part of me thought I should, and part of me thought that having an STD didn't fit with my self-concept so much that I just couldn't [disclose].

Francine, a White 43-year-old professional and mother of a fourth grader, had never intended to pass as healthy, but she did not get diagnosed with herpes until after beginning a sexual relationship with her second husband.

> I think there was all the guilt: What if I bring this on you? So, I felt guilt in bringing this into the relationship. Because he had not been anywhere near as sexually active as I had. So, I started feeling remorse for having been so sexually active during the period of time between marriages. So, I think I always felt a little more guilty because I might have exposed him to something through my actions.

Similarly, Tasha, a White graduate student, found out that she might have inadvertently passed as healthy when her partner was diagnosed with chlamydia. "I freaked out—I was like, 'Oh my God! I gave you chlamydia. I am so sorry! I am so sorry!' I felt really horrible, and I felt really awful." Sara, a Jewish upper middle-class 24-year-old, expressed a similar fear of having passed as healthy and exposed a partner to HPV. "Evan called me after we'd been broken up and told me he had genital warts. And, I was with another guy at the time, doing the kinda-sorta-condom-use thing. It was like, 'Oh, my gosh, am I giving this person something?'" Even if the passing is done unintentionally, it still brings guilt to the passer.

The women also tried to disidentify themselves from sexual disease in their attempts to pass as being sexually healthy. Rather than actively using a verbal or symbolic prop or action that would distance them from the stigma, the women took a passive approach. Some gave nonverbal agreement to putdowns of other women who were known to have STDs. For example, Hillary recalled such an interaction.

> It's funny being around people that don't know that I have an STD and how they make a comment like "That girl, she's such a slut. She's a walking STD." And how that makes me feel when I'm confronted with that, and having them have no idea that they could be talking about me.

Others kept silent about their status and tried to maintain the social status of being sexually healthy and morally pure. Kayla admitted to her charade: "I guess I wanted to come across as like really innocent and everything just so people wouldn't think that I was promiscuous, just because inside I felt like they could see it even though they didn't know about the STD." Putting up the facade of sexual purity, these women distanced themselves from any suspicion of sexual disease.

Covering When passing became too difficult, some women resorted to covering to deflect family and friends from the truth. Cleo summed up the rationale by comparing her behavior to what she had learned growing up with an alcoholic father. "They would lie, and it was obvious that it was a lie. But I learned that's what you do. Like you don't tell people those things that you consider shameful, and then, if confronted, you know, you lie."

Hillary talked to her parents about her HPV surgery, but never as treatment for an STD. She portrayed her moderate cervical dysplasia as a precancerous scare, unrelated to sex. "We never actually talked about it being a STD, and she kind of thought that it was the same thing that my sister had which wasn't sexually transmitted." When Tasha's sister helped her get a prescription for pubic lice, she actually provided the cover story for her embarrassed younger sister. "She totally took control, and made a personal inquiry: 'So, how did you get this? From a toilet seat?' And, I was like, 'a toilet seat,' and she believed me." When I asked Tasha why she confirmed her sister's misconception, she replied, "Because I didn't want her to know that I had had sex." For Anne, a 28-year-old lower middle-class graduate student, a painful herpes outbreak almost outed her on a walk with a friend. She was so physically uncomfortable that she was actually waddling. Noticing her strange behavior, her friend asked what was wrong. Anne told her that it was a hemorrhoid; that was only a partial truth because herpes was the primary cause of her pain. As Anne put it, telling her about the hemorrhoid "was embarrassing enough!"

Deception and guilt The women who chose to deny, pass as normal, and use disidentifiers or cover stories shared more than the shame of having an STD—they had also told lies. With lying came guilt. Anne, who had used the hemorrhoid cover story, eventually felt extremely guilty. Her desire to conceal the truth was in conflict with her commitment to being an honest person. "I generally don't lie to my friends. And I'm generally very truthful with people and I felt like a sham lying to her." Deborah, a 32-year-old White professional from the Midwest, only disclosed to her first sexual partner after she had been diagnosed with HPV; she passed as healthy with all other partners. Deborah reflected, "I think my choices not to disclose have hurt my sense of integrity." However, her guilt was resolved during her last gynecological exam when the nurse practitioner confirmed that after years of "clean" pap smear results Deborah was not being "medically unethical" by not disclosing to her partners. In other words, her immune system had probably dealt with the HPV in such a way that she might never have another outbreak or transmit the infection to sexual partners.

When Cleo passed as healthy with a sexual partner, she started "feeling a little guilty about not having told." However, the consequences of passing as healthy were very severe for Cleo:

> No. I never disclosed it to any future partner. Then, one day, I was having sex with Josh, my current husband, before we were married, and we had been together for a few months, maybe, and I'm like looking at his penis, and I said, "Oh, my goodness! You have a wart on your penis! Ahhh!" All of a sudden, it comes back to me.

Cleo's decision to pass left her with both the guilt of deceiving and infecting her husband.

Surprisingly, those women who had unintentionally passed as being sexually healthy (i.e., they had no knowledge of their STD status at the time) expressed a similar level of guilt as those who had been purposefully deceitful. Violet, a middle-class, White 36-year-old, had inadvertently passed as healthy with her current partner. Even after she had preventively disclosed to him, she still had to deal with the guilt over possibly infecting him.

> It hurt so bad that morning when he was basically furious at me thinking I was the one he had gotten those red bumps from. It was the hour from hell! I felt really majorly dirty and stigmatized. I felt like "God, I've done the best I can: If this is really caused by the HPV I have, then I feel terrible."

When using passing and covering techniques, the women strove to keep their stigma from tainting social interactions. They feared reactions that Lemert (1951) has labeled the *dynamics of exclusion:* rejection from their social circles of friends, family, and, most important, sexual partners. For most of the women, guilt surpassed fear and became the trigger to disclose. Those who had been deceitful in passing or covering had to assuage their guilt: Their options were either to remain in nonacceptance, disclose, or transfer their guilt to somebody else.

Stigma Deflection

As the women struggled to manage their individual stigma of being sexually diseased, real and imaginary social interactions became the conduit for the contagious label of damaged goods. Now that the unthinkable had happened to them, the women began to think of their past and present partners as infected, contagious, and potentially dangerous to themselves or other women. The combination of transferring stigma and assigning blame to others allowed the women to deflect the STD stigma away from themselves.

Stigma transference   I propose the concept of stigma transference to capture this element of stigma management that has not been addressed by other deviance theorists. Stigma transference is not a specialized case of projection that "in a psychoanalytic context describes the unconscious process in which the individual attributes to others his or her own emotions and impulses—a common defense mechanism, used by the ego to control unacceptable feelings, thereby helping to reduce anxiety" (Marshall 1994:421). Stigma is neither an emotion nor an impulse; rather, it is a formal concept that captures a relationship of devaluation (Goffman 1960). Although the participants attributed their devalued relationship with sexual health ideals to real and imaginary others, they were not controlling unacceptable feelings. Rather, stigma transference manifests as a clear expression of anger and fear, and the women did not connect this strategy to a reduction in their levels of anxiety; in fact, several discussed it in relation to increased anxiety.

Cleo remembered checking her partner's penis for warts after her doctor told her that she could detect them by visual inspection. It became a habit for Kayla to check her partner for any visible symptoms of an STD. Gloria was more careful about checking future partners and asking if they had anything. Tasha explained, "I just felt like I was with someone who was dirty." In all four cases, the women were only sure of their own STD infections, yet in their minds these partners had become diseased.

Transference of stigma to a partner became more powerful when the woman felt betrayed by her partner. When Hillary spoke of the "whole trust issue" with her ex-partner, she firmly believed he had lied to her about his sexual health status and that he would lie to others. Even though she had neither told him about her diagnosis nor had proof of him being infected, she fully transferred her stigma to him.

> He's the type of person who has no remorse for anything. Even if I did tell him, he wouldn't tell the people that he was dating. So it really seemed pretty pointless to me to let him know because he's not responsible enough to deal with it, and it's too bad knowing that he's out there spreading this to God knows how many other people.

Kayla also transferred the stigma of sexual disease to an ex-partner, never confronting him about whether he had tested positive for STDs. The auxiliary trait of promiscuity colored her view of him: "I don't know how sexually promiscuous he was, but I'm sure he had had a lot of partners." Robin, a 21-year-old White undergraduate, went so far as to tell her ex-partner that he needed to see a doctor and "do something about it." He doubted her ability to pinpoint contracting genital warts from him and called her a slut. Robin believed that he was the one with the reputation for promiscuity and decided to trash him by telling her two friends who hung out with him. Robin hoped to spoil his sexual reputation and scare off his future partners. In the transference of stigma, the women ascribed the same auxiliary traits onto others that others had previously ascribed to them.

In a different twist, Anne did not transfer her stigma to her partner, as they both felt that he had been betrayed by his ex-girlfriend.

> He felt terrible about his own infection—he was angry at the woman who infected him because she didn't tell him. They had a verbal agreement that they were having a monogamous relationship, and then she was not monogamous with him. She infected him with a sexually transmitted infection. And he was just really upset and felt like he didn't want to pass that on. He didn't want to continue that cycle. So then when he infected me, he felt horrible.

Anne's partner had revealed his herpes status to her before they had become sexually intimate. His disclosure, "being so up front—before he even kissed me," ended up preventing him from being the target of stigma transference.

In all cases, it was logical to assume that past and current sexual partners may also have been infected. However, the stigma of being sexually diseased had far-reaching consequences in the women's imaginations. The traumatic impact on their sexual selves led most to infer that future, as yet unknown partners were also sexually diseased. Kayla summed up this feeling: "After I was diagnosed, I was a lot more cautious and worried about giving it to other people or getting something else because somebody hadn't told me." They had already been damaged by at least one partner. Therefore, they expected that future partners, ones who had not yet come into their lives, held the threat of also being damaged goods.

For Hillary, romantic relationships held no appeal anymore. She had heard of others who also had STDs but stayed in non-acceptance and never changed their lifestyle of having casual, unprotected sex:

> I just didn't want to have anything to do with it. A lot of it was not trusting people. When we broke up, I decided that I was not having sex. Initially, it was because I wanted to get an HIV test. Then, I came to kind of a turning point in my life and realized that I didn't want to do the one-night-stand thing anymore. It just wasn't worth it. It wasn't fun.

At this stage in her sexual self-transformation, Hillary imagined the world of possible partners having been polluted with contagion.

Anne's lesbian friends introduced her to a theory about which future partners should be suspected of being dangerous. One friend claimed that her secret to sexual health was to only have sex with female partners. In a therapeutic disclosure to another lesbian friend, Anne recalled her friend's reaction. "Those rotten men! You should just leave them alone. It's clear that you should be with women, and it's safer and better that way. Women don't do this kind of thing to each other." Her friends' guidance was an overt attempt to encourage Anne to believe that only potential male partners bore the stigma.

Instead of going by gender, Gloria, a self-identified Chicana, made a distinction based on ethnicity as a predictor of sexual health status:

> Now, if it was a White man, I made 'em wear a condom because I got it from a White man, and so I assumed that there had to be something with their culture—they were more promiscuous. But, one thing I do know culturally and with the times is that Chicano men were more likely to have a single partner.

These women felt justified in their newfound attitudes about sexual partners. What was only supposed to happen to "bad" women had happened to them. Overall, these women transitioned from blaming their own naiveté to blaming someone else for not being more cautious or more honest.

Blame   The women's uses of stigma transference techniques were attempts to alleviate their emotional burdens. First, the finger of shame and guilt pointed inward, toward the women's core sexual selves. Their sexual selves became tainted, dirty, damaged. In turn, they directed the stigma outward to both real and fictional others. Blaming others was a way for all of the women to alleviate some of the internal pressure and turn the anger outward. This emotional component of the damaged goods stage externalized the pain of their stigma.

Francine recalled how she and her first husband dealt with the issue of genital warts. "We kind of both ended up blaming it on the whole fraternity situation. I just remember thinking that it was not so much that we weren't clean, but that he hadn't been at some point, but now he was." Francine's husband had likely contracted genital warts from his wild fraternity parties: "We really thought of it as, that woman who did the trains [serial sexual intercourse]. It was still a girl's fault kind of thing." By externalizing the blame to the promiscuous women at fraternity parties, Francine exonerated not only herself but also her husband.

Similarly, Sara found a way to blame the other woman. In the process of internalizing her new stigmatized sexual reality, she wanted to set the blame away from herself, and even away from her ex-partner because she was contemplating getting back together with him:

> So, then I thought, oh, he was with that floozy, dirty woman before we got back together: the last time. And, then I thought, [the genital warts] could be latent—for up to 18 months. I'm like, that falls within the 18-month guideline; it was definitely her. So, I decided it was her who gave it to him, who gave it to me.

For Violet, it was impossible to neatly deflect the blame away from both herself and her partner.

> I remember at the time just thinking, "Oh man! He gave it to me!" While he was thinking, "God, [Violet]! You gave this to me!" So, we kind of just did a truce in our minds. Like, OK, we don't know who gave it— just as likely both ways. So, let's just get treated. We just kind of dropped it.

Clearly, the impulse to place blame was strong even when there was no easy target.

Often, the easiest targets were men who exhibited the auxiliary traits of promiscuity and deception. Tasha wasn't sure which ex-partner had transmitted the STD. However, she rationalized blaming a particular guy. "He turned out to be kind of huge liar, lied to me a lot about different stuff. And, so I blamed him. All the other guys were, like, really nice people, really trustworthy." Likewise, when I asked Violet from whom she believed she had contracted chlamydia, she replied, "Dunno, it could've been from one guy, because that guy had slept with some unsavory women, so therefore he was unsavory." Later, Violet contracted HPV, and the issue of blame contained more anger:

> I don't remember that discussion much other than, being mad over who I got it from: "Oh it must have been Jess because he had been with all those women." I was mad that he probably never got tested. I was o.k. before him.

The actual guilt or innocence of these blame targets was secondary. What mattered to the women was that they could hold someone else responsible.

Stigma Acceptance

Eventually, every woman in the study stopped denying and deflecting the truth of her sexual health status by disclosing to loved ones. The women disclosed for either preventive or therapeutic reasons. That is, they were either motivated to reveal their STD status to prevent harm to themselves or others or to gain the emotional support of confidants.

Preventive and therapeutic disclosures　The decision to make a preventive disclosure was linked to whether the STD could be cured. Kayla explained,

> Chlamydia went away, and I mean it was really bad to have that, but I mean it's not something that you have to tell people later 'cause you know, in case it comes back. Genital warts, you never know.

Kayla knew that her parents would find out about the HPV infection because of insurance connections. Before her cryosurgery, Kayla decided to tell her mom about her condition.

> I just told her what [the doctor] had diagnosed me with, and she knew
> my boyfriend and everything, so—it was kind of hard at first. But, she
> wasn't upset with me. Main thing, she was disappointed, but I think
> she blamed my boyfriend more than she blamed me.

Sara's parents also reacted to her preventive disclosure by blaming her boyfriend: They were disappointed in their daughter, but angry with her
boyfriend.

Preventive disclosures to sexual partners, past and present, were a more
problematic situation. The women were choosing to put themselves in a position where they could face blame, disgust, and rejection. For those reasons,
the women put off preventive disclosures to partners as long as possible. For
example, Anne made it clear that she would not have disclosed her herpes to
a female sexual partner had they not been about to have sex. After "agonizing
weeks and weeks and weeks before trying to figure out how to tell," Diana,
a 45-year-old African American professional, finally shared her HPV and
herpes status before her current relationship became sexual. Unfortunately,
her boyfriend had a negative reaction: "He certainly didn't want to touch me
anywhere near my genitals." In Cleo's case, she told her partner about her
HPV diagnosis because she wasn't going to be able to have sexual intercourse
for a while after her cryosurgery. Violet described the thought process that
lead up to her decision to disclose her HPV status to her current partner:

> That was really scary because once you have [HPV], you can't get rid
> of the virus. And then having to tell my new partner all this stuff. I just
> wanted to be totally up front with him: We could use condoms. Chances
> are he's probably totally clean. I'm like, "Oh my god, here I am tainted
> because I've been with, at this point, 50 guys, without condoms. Who
> knows what else I could have gotten?" [long pause, nervous laugh] So,
> that was tough.

For Summer, a 20-year-old Native American administrative assistant, and
Gloria, their preventive disclosures were actually a relief to their sexual
partners. Summer decided to disclose her genital warts to a new boyfriend
after they had been "getting hot n' heavy." Lying in bed together, she said, "I
need to tell you something." After she disclosed, he lay there, staring at the
ceiling for a couple of minutes before deeply exhaling, "I thought you were
going to tell me you had AIDS." Similarly, one of Gloria's partners sighed in
relief when she revealed that she had herpes; he thought she was going to
say she was HIV positive.

Many of the therapeutic disclosures were done to family members. The
women wanted the support of those who had known them the longest. Finally willing to risk criticism and shame, they hoped for positive outcomes:
acceptance, empathy, sympathy—any form of nonjudgmental support.
Tasha disclosed to her mother right after she was diagnosed with chlamydia.

> My family died—"Guess what, mom, I got chlamydia." She's like,
> "Chlamydia? How did you find out you got chlamydia?" I'm like, "Well,

my boyfriend got an eye infection." [laughter] "How'd he get it in his eye?" [laughter] So, it was the biggest joke in the family for the longest time!

In contrast, Rebecca, a White professional in her mid-50s, shared her thought process behind not disclosing to her adult children.

> I wanted to tell my younger one—I wanted very much for him to know that people could be asymptomatic carriers because I didn't want him to unjustly suspect somebody of cheating on him—and I don't believe I ever managed to do it—it's hard to bring something like that up.

The women often unburdened their feelings of shame and guilt onto their close friends. Cleo shared her feelings with her roommate: "I told her that I was feeling weird about having had sex with this second guy, knowing that I had an STD." Kayla's therapeutic disclosure was reciprocal with her best friend. "At that time, she was also going through a similar situation with her boyfriend, so I felt okay finally to talk about it." Lily, a 41-year-old White mother of a teenage son, disclosed to a male friend and found relief, as she could share her fear about what was happening to her. He was able to be emotional and supportive. Deborah only disclosed to a handful of female friends, never to any male friends. In Anne's case, her therapeutic disclosure to a friend was twofold: both to seek support and to apologize for initially having used the hemorrhoid cover story. Anne explained to her friend that she had felt too uncomfortable to tell the truth. "I remember later when I did tell her the truth, I was embarrassed and said, 'I need to tell you that I wasn't completely honest with you before.'"

Consequences of disclosure With both therapeutic and preventive disclosure, the women experienced some feelings of relief in being honest with loved ones. However, they still carried the intense shame of being sexually diseased women. The resulting emotion was anxiety over how their confidants would react: rejection, disgust, or betrayal. Francine was extremely anxious about disclosing to her husband. "That was really tough on us because I had to go home and tell Damon that I had this outbreak of herpes." When asked what sorts of feelings that brought up, she immediately answered. "Fear. You know I was really fearful—I didn't think that he would think I had recently had sex with somebody else—but, I was still really afraid of what it would do to our relationship." Hillary's anxiety over her deviant status getting leaked almost prevented her from taking advantage of a sexual health support group.

> I think one of the biggest fears for me was walking into a support group and seeing someone that I knew there. But then I turned it around and decided that they were just as vulnerable as I was—But, I think the biggest part was just having people find out about what I had somehow.

Even though the other women in the support group would have been strangers, each participant represented a potential gossip.

Overall, disclosing intensified the anxiety of having their secret leaked to others in whom they would never have chosen to confide. In addition, each disclosure brought with it the possibility of rejection and ridicule from the people whose opinions they valued most. For Gloria, disclosing was the right thing to do but had painful consequences when her partner's condom slipped off in the middle of sexual intercourse.

> I told him it doesn't feel right. "You'd better check." And, so he checked, and he just jumped off me and screamed, "Oh fuck!" And, I just thought, oh no, here we go. He just freaked and went to the bathroom and washed his penis with soap. I just felt so dirty.

The risk paid off for Summer, whose boyfriend asserted, "I don't ever want to be *that guy*—the one who shuns people and treats them differently." He borrowed sexual health education materials and spent over an hour asking her questions about various STDs. Even in this best-case scenario, the sexual intimacy in this relationship became problematized (e.g., having to re-search modes of STD transmission and safe-sex techniques). Disclosures were the interactional component of self-acceptance. The women became fully grounded in their new reality when they realized that the significant people in their lives were now viewing them through the discolored lenses of sexual disease.

Conclusion

The women with STDs went through an emotionally difficult process, testing out stigma management strategies, trying to control the impact of STDs on both their self-concepts and on their relationships with others. In keeping with Cooley's ([1902] 1964) "looking glass self," the women derived their sexual selves from the imagined and real reactions of others. Unable to immunize themselves from the physical wrath of disease, they focused on mediating the potentially harmful impacts of STDs on their sexual self-concepts and on their intimate relationships.

Ironically, most of the women first tried to deny this deviant health status —one that was virtually secret through the protection of doctor–patient confidentiality laws. Although many used passing and covering techniques that relied on deceiving others, self-deception was impossible to maintain. The medical truth began to penetrate their sexual self-conceptions as soon as they fabricated their first lie. To strategize a successful ruse, it was necessary to know the scope of what they were trying to hide.

When guilt caught up with them, making it hard to pass as healthy, their goal shifted to stigma deflection. Those who engaged in stigma transference imagined forcing blamed others to look into the same mirror of judgment in which they had been forced to look into. However, this only delayed the inevitable—a deviant sexual self that penetrated the women's prior conceptions of their sexual selves.

After mentally transferring their stigma to real and imaginary others, all of the women finally accepted their tainted sexual health status through the reflexive dynamics of disclosure. Voluntary disclosure to intimate others took their sexual health status out of the doctor's office and into their lives. Each time they told their story to a friend, family member, lover, or ex-lover, they revised the story of who they were as sexual beings. The new stories gained veracity in the verbal and nonverbal responses of the trusted few. The women's sexual selves moved along a deviant career path by means of the interactive dynamics of their stigma management strategies.

One model of deviant identity formation treats the process as involving three distinct linear stages: primary, secondary (Lemert 1967), and tertiary deviance (Kitsuse 1980). The women began the move into primary deviance when they engaged in the initial act of deviance: contraction of a sexually transmitted disease. However, the actual moment of STD transmission was imperceptible and did not result in a deviant label. Rather, in private interactions, medical practitioners named the deviance through STD diagnoses, thus completing the women's transitions into primary deviance.

Movement into secondary deviance began as the women contemplated how they would manage the stigma of sexual disease in their "real" lives, beyond the sterile doors of the examination rooms. As the women made choices on which stigma management strategies to use, they grappled with the ramifications of internalizing this new label. Choosing passing and covering techniques meant they could remain in non-acceptance and put off stigma internalization. When they deflected the stigma onto others by means of stigma transference, the women glimpsed the severity of an STD stigma as reflected in the presumed sexual selves of real and imaginary others. Finally, the women's disclosures confirmed the new story of their tainted sexual selves.

For the women with STDs, the stigma penetrated only the portions of their self-concepts that addressed sexuality. They were forced to reconcile new, "dirty" sexual self-concepts with their prior conceptions of unspoiled sexual health. However, all of them succeeded in compartmentalizing the deviant identity of being sexually diseased into the sexual part of their self-concepts, never making the complete transition to secondary deviance. Their experience of partial secondary deviance significantly differs from Lemert's (1967) conception, in which the deviant identity becomes fully integrated into one's core self-concept. Unlike the people in ethnographic studies of other medically deviant groups (Herman 1993; Karp 1992; Sandstrom 1990), the women in this study learned to accept a tainted sexual self but did not end up with an internalized deviant identity that spoiled their entire self-concepts.

These data highlight the limitations of this three-stage model for explaining the process of deviant identity development for women with STDs. The fragmented nature of the women's movement into secondary deviance stems from the situational nature of the STD stigma. Unlike the stigma of HIV/AIDS—which carries the threat of life-changing illness, death, and contagion beyond the scope of sexual behaviors—the STD stigma lends itself to compartmentalization. The women were able to hide their shame, guilt, and fear (of further health complications, of contaminating others, of rejection, etc.) in the sexual part of their self-concept. They recognized that this part of their self-concept did not have to affect their entire identity. Medically speaking, an STD need only affect the decisions and interactions connected with sexual and reproductive behavior. If the impact of the STDs on their sex lives ever became too emotionally painful, the women could always decide to distance themselves from this role: choosing temporary or permanent celibacy.

The "narrative metaphor" for self (Hermans 1996) views the self as multivoiced. Historically, James ([1890]1902) and Mead (1934) discussed the distinctions between the objective and subjective self. Whereas the subjective self engages in self-reflexivity to negotiate an identity, information provided through interactions with external others continues to shape the objective self. In this way, the externally constructed self mediates internal conversations about identity. During these dialogues between the "I" and the "me," one's negotiated identities become incorporated into the self-concept.

James ([1890]1902) posited the distinction between "I" and "me." However, Mancuso and Sarbin (1983) and Sarbin (1986) posited an interpretation of James ([1890]1902) and Mead (1934) that frames the I–Me distinction as a narrative of the self. From a narrative perspective, I is the author of the story about Me, the protagonist of the story being constructed about the self. The ability to construct such a narrative comes from the I's ability to reinvent the past, hypothesize the future, and describe her- or himself as the actor (Crites 1986). In this way, the construction of self-narratives becomes the means by which people organize experiences, behaviors, and their accounts of these events (Sarbin 1986).

A narrative model of the self proposes that personal myths create the self and become "the stories we live by" (McAdams 1996:266). I propose that we seek to understand the significance of the stories we choose not to live by. Personal STD "stories" are rarely told in American mass culture. McAdams (1996:22) proposed that "carrying on affairs in secret"—maintaining a discreditable stigma—is a way to keep stigmatizing stories from occupying center stage in people's personal myth. However, these data suggest that individuals manage identity transformations, especially transformations into deviant identities, by constructing and sharing self-narratives through disclosure interactions. Although the women do not maintain secrecy, they do keep their STD stories from center stage.

When the distasteful or spoiled self can be contained to the private sphere (such as the sex life), the I uses stigma management strategies that protect the core self from the spoiled part of the self. To accomplish this, the I authors a peripheral narrative about the deviant aspect of the Me. Disclosures are the telling of this peripheral narrative. This type of narrative is connected, yet fails to contaminate, the core narrative, in which the Me, as protagonist, is insulated from the stigma contained in the peripheral narrative.

The incompleteness of the women's transitions into secondary deviance is explained by their choice to incorporate the stigma into a peripheral rather than core self-narrative. Although this strategy enables them to protect their core self-narrative from stigma, the women face challenges in maintaining this compartmentalization. Whereas celibacy is an obvious aid in using this stigma management strategy (three participants were celibate), the norm of sexual activity repeatedly makes the sexual self a salient part of women's self-concepts. In modern American culture, "heterosexual activity is seen not only as desirable but also as necessary for a 'normal' healthy life, [and] the pressures on women to marry or cohabit with a man, with all the consequent forms of servicing, are increased" (Walby 1990:127).[1]

In many ways, the creation of a deviant peripheral self-narrative may be the ultimate stigma management strategy. The apparent effectiveness of this particular stigma management strategy would seem to appeal to all individuals who struggle with deviant stigma. The rarity of its use can be explained by the organizational complexity of those who share a particular deviant stigma. The existence of a deviant subculture promotes secondary deviance by implying membership requirements: acceptance of deviant norms, values, social support, and so forth (Best and Luckenbill 1980). Deviant subcultures also allow for the existence of collective stigma management groups that may encourage individuals to move into tertiary deviance and embrace their deviant identities (Kitsuse 1980). The inclusion of stigmatized individuals into deviant subcultures exposes them to others who have rewritten their core self-narratives to reflect their deviant identities. Such groups function to remove the negative connotation of the deviance by offering inclusion to their deviant circles (Lemert 1951). However, micro-level interactions between deviant individuals and collective stigma management groups encourage the incorporation of the stigmatized label into core self-narratives.

These data on how women manage the stigma of chronic STDs have significant implications for the study of isolated deviants and the study of self-transformation of deviants in general: They highlight the role of isolation in protecting a core self-narrative from stigma. Individuals, such as women with STDs, remain loners because their deviant labels do not provide them

---

[1]The next phase of this study will focus on men living with chronic STDs and compare the gendered dimensions of this experience.

with membership to deviant subcultures (Lowery and Wetli 1982) and, possibly, to collective stigma management groups. When society constructs a type of deviance as "loner," affected individuals need not enter complete secondary deviance and internalize the deviant label into their core self-narrative. Isolated in their experience of this stigma, these individuals have great flexibility in their decision to rewrite their deviant transformations into either core or peripheral self-narratives. Further research on loner deviants would be helpful in testing the efficacy of peripheral self-narratives for managing stigma.

References

Ackerman, Sandra J. 1998. "HPV: Who's Got It and Why They Don't Know." *HPV News* 8(2):1, 5-6.

Adler, Patricia A. and Peter Adler. 1987. *Membership Roles in Field Research.* Newbury Park, CA: Sage.

Best, Joel and David F. Luckenbill. 1980. "The Social Organization of Deviants." *Social Problems* 28(1): 14-31.

Biernacki, Patrick and Dan Waldorf. 1981. "Snowball Sampling." *Sociological Research Methods* 10:141-63.

Blumer, Herbert, 1969. *Symbolic interactionism: Perspective and method.* Berkeley: University of California Press.

———. 1973. "A Note on Symbolic Interactionism." *American Sociological Review* 38(6):797-98.

Brandt, Allan M. 1987. *No magic bullet: A social history of venereal disease in the United States since 1880.* New York: Oxford University Press.

Centers for Disease Control and Prevention. 1998a. "Genital Herpes." *National Center for HIV, STD & TB Prevention.* Retrieved from the World Wide Web February 4, 1998: URL.

———. 1998b. "HIV/AIDS Surveillance Report." *National Center for HIV, STD & TB Prevention.* Retrieved from the World Wide Web February 4, 1998: URL.

Conrad, Peter, and Rochelle Kern, eds. 1994. *The Sociology of Health & Illness: Critical Perspectives.* 4th ed. New York: St. Martin's Press.

Cooley, Charles H. [1902] 1964. *Human nature and the social order.* New York: Schocken Books.

Crites, Stephen. 1986. "Storytime: Recollecting the Past and Projecting the Future." Pp. 152-73 in *Narrative Psychology: The Storied Nature of Human Conduct,* edited by T. R. Sarbin. New York: Praeger.

Ellis, Carolyn. 1991. "Sociological Introspection and Emotional Experience." *Symbolic Interaction* 14(1):23-50.

Folkman, Susan and Richard S. Lazarus. 1980. "An Analysis of Coping in a Middle-Aged Community Sample." *Journal of Health and Social Behavior* 21:219-39.

Glaser, Barney G. 1978. *Theoretical sensitivity.* Mill Valley, CA: Sociological Press.

Glaser, Barney G. and Anselm L. Strauss. 1967. *The Discovery of Grounded Theory: Strategies for Qualitative Research.* Chicago: Aldine.

Goffman, Erving. 1963. *Stigma.* Englewood Cliffs, NJ: Prentice Hall.

Harding, Sandra, ed. 1987. *Feminism and Methodology.* Bloomington: Indiana University Press.

Herman, Nancy J. 1993. "Return to Sender: Reintegrative Stigma-Management Strategies of Ex-Psychiatric Patients." *Journal of Contemporary Ethnography* 22(3):295-330.

Hermans, Hubert J. M. 1996. "Voicing the Self: From Information Processing to Dialogical Interchange." *Psychological Bulletin* 119:31–50.

James, William. [1890] 1902. *The Principles of Psychology.* Vol. 1. London: Macmillan.

Karp, David A. 1992. "Illness Ambiguity and the Search for Meaning: A Case Study of a Self-Help Group for Affective Disorders." *Journal of Contemporary Ethnography* 21(2):139–70.

Kelly, Gary F. 1998. *Sexuality Today: The Human Perspective.* Boston: McGraw-Hill.

Kitsuse, John. 1980. "Coming Out All Over: Deviants and the Politics of Social Problems." *Social Problems* 28:1–13.

Lemert, Edwin. 1951. *Social Pathology.* New York: McGraw-Hill.

———. 1967. *Human Deviance, Social Problems and Social Control.* Englewood Cliffs, NJ: Prentice-Hall.

Lowery, Shearon A. and Charles V. Wetli. 1982. "Sexual Asphyxia: A Neglected Area of Study." *Deviant Behavior,* 3:19–39.

Mancuso, James C. and Theodore R. Sarbin. 1983. "The Self-Narrative in the Enactment of Roles." Pp. 254–73 in *Studies in Social Identity,* edited by T. R. Sarbin and K. Scheibe. New York: Praeger.

Marshall, Gordon. 1994. *The Concise Oxford Dictionary of Sociology.* Oxford: Oxford University Press.

McAdams, Dan P. 1996. *The stories we live by: Personal myths and the making of the self.* New York: Guilford Press.

Mead, George Herbert. 1934. *Mind, Self, and Society.* Chicago: University of Chicago Press.

Nielson, Joyce M., ed. 1990. *Feminist Research Methods.* Boulder, CO: Westview.

Pryce, Anthony, 1998. "Theorizing the Pox: A Missing Sociology of VD." Presented to the International Sociological Association.

Reinharz, Shulamit. 1990. *Feminist Methods in Social Research.* Oxford, England: Oxford University Press.

Rosenthal, Susan L., Frank M. Biro, Shelia S. Cohen, Paul A. Succop, and Lawrence R. Stanberry, 1995. "Strategies for Coping with Sexually Transmitted Diseases by Adolescent Females." *Adolescence* 30(119):655–66.

Sandstrom, Kent L. 1990. "Confronting Deadly Disease: The Drama of Identity Construction among Gay Men with AIDS." *Journal of Contemporary Ethnography,* 19(3):271–94.

Sarbin, Theodore R. 1986. "The Narrative as a Root Metaphor for Psychology." Pp. 3–21 in *Narrative Psychology: The Storied Nature of Human Conduct,* edited by T. R. Sarbin. New York: Praeger.

Siegel, Karolynn and Beatrice J. Krauss. 1991. "Living with HIV Infection: Adaptive Tasks of Seropositive Gay Men." *Journal of Health and Social Behavior* 32(1):17–32.

Spirito, Anthony, Lori J. Stark, and Connie Williams, 1988. "Development of a Brief Coping Checklist for Use with Pediatric Populations." *Journal of Pediatric Psychology* 13:555–74.

Strong, Bryan, Christine DeVault, and Barbara Werner Sayad. 1996. *Core Concepts in Human Sexuality.* Mountain View, CA: Mayfield.

Swanson, Janice M. and W. Carole Chenitz. 1993. "Regaining a Valued Self: The Process of Adaptation to Living with Genital Herpes." *Qualitative Health Research* 3(3):270–97.

Walby, Sylvia. 1990. *Theorizing Patriarchy.* Oxford, England: Basil Blackwell.

Weitz, Rose. 1989. "Uncertainty and the Lives of Persons with AIDS." *Journal of Health and Social Behavior* 30(3):270–81.

Wiseman, Jacqueline P. 1970. *Stations of the Lost.* Chicago: University of Chicago Press.

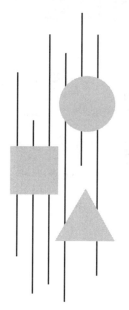

PART

Changing Deviance

Parts IV and V offered materials that demonstrate how, both voluntarily and involuntarily, a person's public identity becomes transformed into a "deviant" identity. Central to this process, at least in terms of bureaucratic processing, is the "status denunciation ceremony," in which a collective effort is made to place an institutional tag upon a person. This status-conferring process was especially evident in those articles dealing with the involuntary processing of clients. The articles also helped to underscore the fact that the institutional deviant has relatively little to say about his or her processing. It has been emphasized, too, that the identity-transformation process is generally rather routine.

How the organizationally labeled deviant actually perceives and responds to institutional processing is often difficult to judge. As we have seen, some will accept the label, while others will either reject or ignore it. The individual's response is critical in the alteration of a deviant career and identity—that is, in moving from a deviant to a nondeviant status, with the deviant label being removed during the process of change. For example, if an individual rejects an institutional label, he or she can expect to encounter various types of difficulties. The plight of McMurphy (discussed in the general introduction) offers an illustration of this. Not only did he reject the "sick role," but his resistance, when viewed from the institution's perspective, was taken as a sign that he needed help. In this instance, the prognosis for change—again from the institution's viewpoint (i.e., its theory of the office and associated diagnostic stereotypes)—was extremely poor. A patient may, however, accept the label and act according to institutional expectations. Such patients thus become willing parties in the transformation process.

Even if individuals decide to conform to social norms, they will most certainly encounter numerous structural and individual barriers—

barriers that often reduce the probability that they will elect to change their behavior. The ex-deviant, as we have noted in the general introduction, frequently experiences difficulty finding housing and employment, primarily because others, in general, continue to react to the person as a deviant. Institutional processing is very systematic and efficient in tagging individuals as deviants. The reverse process, however, is anything but systematic and efficient. Specifically, there are few, if any, institutional mechanisms that can be used to systematically remove deviant labels (and the associated stigma) from individuals. Thus, deviants are often left to fend for themselves. Obviously, giving ex-cons a bit of money and a suit of clothes, without helping them to deal with potential structural barriers (e.g., having to indicate they are ex-cons on job applications) and individual problems (e.g., feelings of low self-esteem), is not going to do much by way of "rehabilitating" them. A viable model of change or "rehabilitation" must incorporate a concern for both individual and structural factors. Even this, however, is not enough.

Clearly, if the underlying images, conceptions, and categories of deviance are altered (as discussed in Part I), then the picture of deviance and the deviant must undergo some corresponding changes. Analytically, it is useful to think in terms of the transformation of deviant categories, as well as the transformation of actors and structures. As an example, certain crimes may become decriminalized, and acts that were formerly perceived as deviant may become acceptable. The selections in this part explore possibilities such as these.

 ## Transforming Deviance: Conceptions, Actors, and Organizations

A central theme in Part I was the idea that the reactions of social observers provide acts with meanings—that is, indicate whether the acts are deviant or nondeviant. In "Reform the Law: Decriminalization," Samuel Walker provides a provocative analysis of how removing selected types of behavior from the statutes may affect the picture of crime and deviance. He begins by drawing most heavily upon the classic work by Morris and Hawkins, *The Honest Politician's Guide to Crime Control*, and notes that these authors propose to decriminalize acts in seven areas: (1) drunkenness, (2) narcotics and drug abuse, (3) gambling, (4) disorderly conduct and vagrancy, (5) abortion, (6) sexual behavior, and (7) juvenile delinquency. The rationale for decriminalizing these domains is predicated primarily upon three arguments: Many of the existing laws, in their applications, are "criminogenic" (i.e., produce more crime); they overburden the justice system; and they violate individual rights. Walker's working proposition, which centers on a major concern of his, is that "with the possible exception of heroin policy, decriminalization is simply irrelevant to the control of robbery and burglary." Hence, he is concerned mainly with what he views as being serious crime. In an effort to establish, as well as substantiate, the irrelevance of a link between most victimless crimes and the serious crimes of robbery and burglary, the author offers a balanced and insightful examination of the arguments and evidence associated with each of the areas listed by Morris and Hawkins. For example, in terms of the proposal to decriminalize most sexual activities (e.g., adultery, fornication, cohabitation, prostitution, and the like), he contends that many good arguments—some of which he reviews briefly—have been advanced for doing so. Walker does caution us, however, that decriminalization in a selected area may not reduce the ancillary crime connected with it. Customers may still be mugged or robbed before, during, or after their sexual encounter with a prostitute.

As we have suggested, noninstitutional deviants (e.g., drug addicts and prostitutes) and institutional deviants (e.g., mental patients and delinquents) who elect to change their deviant behavior can expect to encounter a range of structural and individual roadblocks—roadblocks that may ultimately produce a relapse or further deviance.

J. David Brown, in "The Professional Ex-: An Alternative for Exiting the Deviant Career," offers an interesting twist on the processes involved in exiting from deviant careers. He notes that most material on exiting focuses on an actor's abandonment of deviant behavior, identity, and ideologies. Brown, however, contends that the exiting process does not have to entail the total abandonment of a deviant career and identity. Rather, the professionalization of a deviant identity might be more in order for selected types of occupations. In a sense, the contours of a deviant status can be expanded, redefined, and professionalized. And in a sense, a niche can be carved out for the institutionally perceived ex-deviant. Brown illustrates how this process works by using data obtained from interviews with some 35 professional "ex-s" who work in a variety of institutions that provide care for people with drug, drinking, and eating problems. He observes four main stages in the exiting and resocialization process: (1) the emulation of one's therapist, (2) the call to a counseling career, (3) status-set realignment, and (4) credentialization. For example, not only do many of the ex-s come to embrace the counseling profession but, through a process of resocialization and identity transformation, they create a counseling-related identity for themselves. Brown concludes by noting that many organizations are using ex-s in their social control efforts. He cites as examples the prison counselors who counsel delinquents, and the gang counselors who counsel present gang members.

As is evident throughout this book, it is the social actor—usually a person who is relatively powerless—who becomes selected out and processed as a deviant by some type of people-processing or people-changing institution. As we have already argued, it is the actor who must alter behavior. Placing the burden for change exclusively upon the individual, however, means that the decision makers and their organizations escape scrutiny. Yet there is solid evidence of the need for such examinations, and Shichor's examination of the privatization of prisons within a corporate context and Meehan's analysis of gang statistics (Part IV) help to substantiate such a requirement. Such research also offers an important caveat about trying to effect any significant policy changes: If an institution's underlying organizational structure (i.e., its theory of the office, diagnostic stereotypes, career lines, and staff socializing procedures) remains unaltered, then selected categories of clients can expect to be typed and treated in a routinized, stereotypical, and uncaring fashion; this is often a fact of bureaucratic life. And, predictably, when the homeless in Lyon-Callo's study (Part IV) became caught up in a working ideology presuming individual pathology, not only were they forced to accept their perfunctory care and the associated and enduring stigmatization, but failure to do so (i.e., go along with the "program") could produce serious consequences: They could be dropped from the program. Their problems, according to the prevailing ideology, were individual in nature and not systemic, structural, or societal. This ingrained, bureaucratic tendency to operate on the basis of, or to promote, an individual-clinical-medical model of change, whereby the burden for change is placed directly upon the client, is not unique to only a selected few institutions but, rather, generally characterizes most people-processing and people-changing organizations. And probably one of the best, graphic, and most alarming illustrations of this can be found in the educational classifying, sorting, and processing of low-income, minority, and other generally disadvantaged students (Kelly, Part IV). Not only are such students, when compared with their counterparts, often viewed as lacking any significant educational ability, but such a presumption (i.e., the presumption of differential ability) virtually guarantees that a preponderance of the failures, dropouts, and deviants manufactured by our educational systems will be, necessarily, concentrated among these categories of students. Again, it is not that the educational system has failed the individual but, rather, it is the individual who has failed the system. Again, too, the educational system and its decision makers escape scrutiny. This often-overlooked need for dissecting and examining underlying organizational structures and embedded ideologies applies not only to such formal bureaucratic entities as educational systems but to other less formal groupings and organizations as well. Hence, if the values, normative configurations, and associated ideologies of deviant enterprises, activities, and organizations remain intact, recruits, once effectively socialized, will exhibit attitudes and behaviors commensurate with these elements (Part V). Logically, then, if any significant or desired change in outcomes is to occur, it must come initially from an overhaul or redefinition of those values, norms, and ideologies that are inculcated within a social actor. The same type of scenario applies aptly to those formal social control agents who are given the task of policing deviant categories and processing those who are perceived as violating the categories. As an example, if the prevailing content of the diagnostic stereotypes was such that *all* police officers were inculcated with the presumption that the likelihood of committing a crime is equally distributed across racial and ethnic lines and if, further, *all* officers acted in accordance with such a working ideology, then the phenomena of racial and/or ethnic profiling should either be eliminated or else substantially reduced. And in more general terms, such an operating or official institutional perspective should reduce the probability that a range of extra legal factors (e.g., one's race, ethnicity, gender, looks, and the like) will be used as the primary or sole basis upon which to select out actors to play the role of the social deviant.

Jim Leitzel, in the final selection, "Race and Policing," offers additional commentary on points such as these, especially those problems associated with trying to effect changes in organizational ideologies and practices. He notes that preventing crime from occurring is a significant concern for those who police deviant categories and for citizens. Actually preventing crime, however, requires being able to identify those individual characteristics that would enable one to reliably predict future criminal activity. And while criminal profiling has been useful, on an individual basis, in identifying perpetrators of particular crimes, the use of such profiles in *proactive* policing is fraught with significant problems, since race is frequently included as a major component of any profile that may be applied. Leitzel not only points out that using race as the basis for traffic stops is associated with a range of rather predictable negative consequences and criticisms, but he also poses a solution: Do not allow the use of race in policing. For Leitzel, "the operational rule of thumb for police officers who are considering stopping or searching a black person (or potentially a Latino or another minority) should be: would I stop or search this person if he or she was white?"

Quite clearly, then, whether race is invoked as a basis for a stop or search falls squarely on the shoulders of the officer, and even though official policy may advise against such use, the officer may still do it. To counteract this, we would contend that an effective officer monitoring or tracking system must be established and maintained, not only for all police agencies but for social control agencies in general; this will allow for an empirical and ongoing analysis of just how a social control agency's official perspective or working ideology is actually translated into action by its agents. The need for gathering the relevant data is long overdue.

43 Reform the Law: Decriminalization

Samuel Walker

The "first principle" advanced by Norval Morris and Gordon Hawkins in the 1970 book, *The Honest Politician's Guide to Crime Control,* involved removing a broad range of crimes from the statutes. Decriminalization of certain types of behavior has long been a major item on the liberal crime control agenda. In his book *Crime and Punishment: A Radical Solution,* Aryeh Neier, then Executive Director of the ACLU, offered decriminalization as his most substantive crime reduction proposal.[1]

For liberals the problem is what Morris and Hawkins call the "overreach" of the criminal law. It covers too wide a range of human behavior. Too much of it expresses the moralistic concerns of particular groups who are offended by the behavior of others. Morris and Hawkins urge us to "strip off the moralistic excrescences on our criminal justice system so that it may concentrate on the essential." They propose decriminalization in seven general areas:

1. **Drunkenness.** Public drunkenness shall cease to be a criminal offense.
2. **Narcotics and drug abuse.** Neither the acquisition, purchase, possession, nor the use of any drug will be a criminal offense. The sale of some drugs other than by a licensed chemist (druggist) and on prescription will be criminally proscribed; proof of possession of excessive quantities may be evidence of a sale or of intent to sell.
3. **Gambling.** No form of gambling will be prohibited in the criminal law; certain fraudulent and cheating gambling practices will remain criminal.
4. **Disorderly conduct and vagrancy.** Disorderly conduct and vagrancy laws will be replaced by laws precisely stipulating the conduct proscribed and defining the circumstances in which the police should intervene.

5. **Abortion.** Abortion performed by a qualified medical practitioner in a registered hospital shall cease to be a criminal offense.

6. **Sexual behavior.** Sexual activities between consenting adults in private will not be subject to the criminal law. [In the following areas,] adultery, fornication, illicit cohabitation, statutory rape and carnal knowledge, bigamy, incest, sodomy, bestiality, homosexuality, prostitution, pornography, and obscenity . . . the role of the criminal law is excessive.

7. **Juvenile delinquency.** The juvenile court should retain jurisdiction only over conduct by children which would be criminal were they adult.

The Rationale

The rationale for decriminalization consists of three arguments. First, and of primary concern to us here, many of these laws are criminogenic. They produce crime through at least three different means: labeling, secondary deviance, and the creation of a crime tariff. According to labeling theory, the criminal process itself encourages criminal careers. Any contact with the system—arrest, prosecution, conviction, or incarceration— imposes a "criminal label" on the individual. The person internalizes the label and proceeds to act out the role, committing additional and more serious crimes. Decriminalization advocates argue that the laws covering essentially harmless behavior launch people onto criminal careers. Abolish those laws and these people will never become entangled in the criminal justice system to begin with. As a result, crime will be reduced.[2] The laws also create what is known as "secondary deviance." A person becomes addicted to heroin and then, because the drug is illegal and expensive, must turn to crime to support the habit. If addiction were handled as a medical problem, with appropriate treatment or maintenance programs, addicts would not have to rob and steal. Thus we would reduce much of the drug-related crime. Criminologists also refer to the "crime tariff" problem in this regard. Making a product illegal only drives up the price. Not only does this effect raise the amount of money the person needs to obtain illegally, but it encourages the development of criminal syndicates seeking to control the market. Thus, many decriminalization advocates charge that our gambling statutes are responsible for sustaining organized crime.

Overly broad criminal statutes undermine respect for the law. Prohibition is the classic example. The law made criminals out of millions of people who simply wanted a recreational drink. Today, it is argued that many young people lost respect for the law and the legal system by the illegal status of marijuana, a relatively harmless recreational drug.

In addition to actively generating more crime, the laws in question overburden the criminal justice system. Morris and Hawkins, along with many others, maintain that the police waste far too much time dealing with vagrancy, disorderly conduct, and public intoxication when they should be concentrating on serious crimes against people and property. Moreover, insofar as the gambling statutes sustain organized crime, they are also responsible for the most serious patterns of corruption in the criminal justice system.

The final decriminalization argument is that the laws violate individual rights. Much of the behavior covered by criminal statutes is a private matter: one's sexual preference or the decision to have an abortion, for example. As long as the behavior harms no one, it should not be criminalized. Most of the items on the Morris and Hawkins list are referred to as "victimless crimes."

There is room for debate on many of these issues. To what extent gambling should be legalized is an important social policy question, involving many considerations. Abortion is perhaps the most politically controversial moral issue in the United States today. Whether or not the drug addict is a "victim" is arguable. The debate between the libertarians, who wish to restrict the scope of the criminal law in order to enhance individual liberty, and the legal moralists, who argue that the law can and should reflect fundamental moral principles, has been going on for over a hundred years and will likely continue.

Here we are concerned with the control of serious crime. On the question of decriminalization, our position is:

> PROPOSITION 26: With the possible exception of heroin policy, decriminalization is simply irrelevant to the control of robbery and burglary.

Placing decriminalization at the center of a crime control policy, as Morris and Hawkins and Neier do, evades the issue. There are no easy answers to the problem of serious crime. Conservatives and liberals respond to this dilemma in different ways. Conservatives focus on serious crime but tend to propose unworkable solutions. Liberals tend to shift the subject and talk about social reforms that are not directly related to serious crime at all.

The one possible exception to the general irrelevance of decriminalization involves heroin policy. The connection between heroin addiction and crime is clear, although experts disagree about the nature and extent of that connection. Nonetheless, as we shall see, there is no consensus on the effective solution to the heroin problem. Decriminalization is only one possible alternative, and its efficacy is not clearly established.

Victimless Crimes and Serious Crime

To establish the irrelevance of the connection between most of the victimless crimes and the serious crimes of robbery and burglary we should examine each of the items on Morris and Hawkin's list.

Public drunkenness, disorderly conduct, and vagrancy are public nuisances rather than predatory crimes. They harm no one, even though they may offend the sensibilities of many people. Traditionally, these three crimes have consumed the bulk of police time and energy.[3] In the nineteenth century as many as 80 percent of all arrests were in these three categories, and they still make up the largest single group of arrests. In 1981, they accounted for 18.5 percent of all arrests, or as many as all eight of the Index crimes and three times as many as robbery and burglary.

The public nuisance arrests are indeed a burden on the police, the lower courts, and city jails. There are many good reasons for decriminalizing all three offense categories. From our standpoint, the question is whether or not this step would help reduce serious crime, as it potentially could in two different ways.

The most direct effect would take the form of more efficient police work. In theory, police would be freed from about 20 percent of their arrest work load and would be able to concentrate on the more serious crimes against people and property. There are two reasons why this shift in police priorities would not significantly reduce serious crime. In our discussion of the conservative proposal to add more cops and/or improve detective work, we found that there are some basic limits to the crime control capacity of the police. Decriminalization is simply the liberal means to the same end of making more cops available for serious crime. For all the same reasons, it will not achieve the intended results. In poorly managed departments the savings in officer time will not be effectively used. In well-managed departments, as we have already learned, more patrol and more detectives will not lower the crime rate.

To a great extent, the decriminalization of public nuisances has been occurring gradually over the past fifteen years as a result of two factors. First, courts and legislatures have decriminalized some of the offenses in question. In *Easter v. District of Columbia*, a U.S. District Court ruled that chronic alcoholism was a condition and not a crime. Meanwhile, a number of states have repealed their public intoxication statutes and some cities have replaced arrest with referral to detoxification programs. These steps reflect a growing consensus that criminalization is not the appropriate response to social and medical problems. The arguments of the decriminalization advocates, in other words, have found some acceptance.[4]

On a de facto basis, the police have shifted their priorities away from public nuisance offenses. The percentage of all arrests in the categories of public intoxication, disorderly conduct, and vagrancy fell from 39.7 percent in 1969 to 18.5 percent in 1981. It is unlikely that the number of drunks and unemployed vagrants has declined in those years. If anything, their numbers have probably increased. Instead, the police have simply shifted their priorities to devote more time to serious crime. The redirection effort was probably not the result of a formal policy directive from the chief. Rather, individual patrol officers, perhaps in consultation with their sergeants, made a common-sense judgment about what was important.[5]

Not everyone, however, supports this reordering of police priorities. George L. Kelling and James Q. Wilson argue that the police should devote more attention to the little nuisance problems that define the quality of life on the neighborhood level. Police should be more aggressive in keeping drunks off the street (or at least out of the neighborhood), for example, as a way of maintaining a sense of public safety among law-abiding residents. The police neglect of the small, "quality of life" issues, according to Kelling and Wilson, contributes to neighborhood deterioration.[6]

The second way in which decriminalization of nuisance offenses might reduce serious crime is by negating the labeling effect. The theory is generally applied to juvenile delinquents—and even then its validity remains a matter of debate. The people who are arrested for public intoxication and vagrancy are not the kind who graduate to predatory crime. For the most part they are the chronic alcoholics and the chronically unemployed. Often in helpless condition, they are commonly the victims of crime. Police frequently arrest them, in fact, in order to provide them some protection from either the elements or potential muggers. Being arrested does not encourage them to become predatory criminals. They are not the young, healthy, and aggressive males who become career criminals. Decriminalization of public intoxication, disorderly conduct, and vagrancy may well be sound social policy; but it is not a solution to the problem of serious crime.[7]

Much has happened since Morris and Hawkins recommended the decriminalization of abortion in 1970. Three years later the Supreme Court did just that in *Roe v. Wade*. One can debate the morality of abortion and the wisdom of the *Roe* decision as social policy. But it is hard to establish the connection between the old policy of criminal abortion and serious crime. There is nothing to suggest that a person is transformed into a robber or burglar because abortions are illegal. By the same token, the argument of many Right to Life advocates that abortion undermines the moral fabric of the nation, and thereby contributes to crime, is without foundation. Abortion is a supremely important social policy question, but it has no bearing on serious crime.

Much the same can be said for the proposal to decriminalize various sexual activities between consenting adults. The statutes are still filled with laws criminalizing adultery, fornication, cohabitation, statutory rape, homosexuality, and prostitution. Whether or not these activities are acceptable is a significant moral question. Good arguments can be advanced for removing them from their criminal status and, for the most part, police have accommodated themselves to changing moral standards by simply not enforcing them. Decriminalization, however, will not in any way reduce the level of predatory crime. The one possible exception is prostitution. A certain amount of ancillary crime accompanies this activity. Customers are occasionally mugged and robbed before or after their transactions with prostitutes. But those instances represent only a minor part of the total robbery picture.

A good case can be made that gambling sustains organized crime in America. Most experts on the subject agree that criminal syndicates generate not only a majority of revenues but their steadiest and most secure revenues from gambling. Our social policy of making many forms of gambling illegal creates a potentially lucrative area of enterprise for anyone willing to assume the risks of providing the necessary goods and services. The pernicious effects of criminal syndicates on our society are well known. Organized crime money is the major corruptive force in the criminal justice system and a significant corrupter in politics. Criminal syndicates also invest their money in legitimate businesses and, using their accustomed methods, pervert the free enterprise system. Organized crime does generate some violent crime, but these murders and assaults are directed against other members of the criminal syndicates. To be sure, some threats and actual violence are directed against nonmembers—for example, owners of legitimate businesses that the syndicates are attempting to take over. But this category represents at most a tiny fraction of the violent crimes in this country. Decriminalization of gambling may or may not be a wise social policy. It may or may not strike at the roots of organized crime, as many people believe. But it will not reduce the incidence of robbery and burglary.

The Heroin Problem

The one area in which decriminalization might help reduce crime involves heroin. There is no question that heroin is a terrible problem in our society and that a lot of predatory crime is committed by heroin addicts. Decriminalization is one possible remedy for these related problems, but it is not a self-evident solution. There is considerable disagreement over three central points: the number of heroin addicts, the amount of crime committed by addicts, and whether methadone maintenance or some other form of treatment effectively reduces addiction and crime.

The drug problem, unfortunately, has attracted more than its share of crusaders and quacks. Much of the information put out by drug crusaders is grossly wrong. Sorting our way through the misinformation is a difficult task by itself.

The first question concerns the number of heroin addicts in the United States. Official estimates range from 200,000 to 900,000, with about half of them in New York City alone. Use of the term "addict" is part of the problem. Not everyone who uses heroin is physically addicted. Antidrug propagandists created the myth that even the smallest use results in addiction. But there are large numbers of "weekend chippers" who use heroin occasionally as just another recreational drug. There are also many regular users who are not truly addicted. Even among addicts, there are great differences in the intensity of the addiction and the amount of heroin needed. As we shall see, these differences are important in estimating the amount of crime committed by heroin addicts. For the sake of the argument, let us accept the lower estimates and assume that there are between 200,000 and 300,000 regular users of heroin, including addicts, in the country and that 40 percent to 50 percent of them are in New York City.[8]

The second question is the amount of crime that is the direct result of heroin addiction. Or, to put it another way, how much crime could be eliminated by an effective heroin control policy (leaving the exact policy open for the moment)? On this issue we must sort our way through some truly fantastic estimates. The Rand Corporation estimated in 1969 that heroin addicts were responsible for $2 billion to $5 billion worth of crime in New York City. Frightening estimates of this sort are routine in the drug control business. They bear little relationship to reality, however.

In the pages of *The Public Interest,* Max Singer performed a devastating critique of the Rand heroin/crime estimates. If there were 100,000 addicts in New York City who needed $30 a day to maintain their habit, they would have to raise $1.1 billion over the course of a year (100,000 × $30 × 365). But criminals must sell their stolen goods to fences, who give them at most 25 percent of actual value (Singer may have been overly generous; some goods yield only 10 percent of their value from fences). Thus, the total value of stolen property would be in the neighborhood of $4 to $5 billion in New York City alone. By looking at the figures for particular crimes, Singer found that amount to be utterly absurd. Retail sales in New York City totaled $15 billion annually, and if addicts were responsible for half of the estimated 2 percent inventory loss they would realize only $150 million during the year. Likewise, 500,000 burglaries at an average loss of $200 would yield the addicts another $100 million. In 1969, however, there were only 196,397 reported burglaries in New York City (or about 400,000 total burglaries, if we assume that only half were reported). The same absurdity applies to robbery. At an average take of $100 (high by most recent estimates), 800,000 robberies would yield the addicts $80 million. Unfortunately there were only 61,209 reported robberies, or an estimated 120,000 actual robberies in New York City in 1969. Singer concludes that addicts are responsible for, at most, only one-tenth the amount of crime attributed to them by the Rand report.[9]

How could the Rand report and most of the other drug experts be so wrong? Easy. You begin with a high estimate of heroin users and assume that all users are addicts. Then you multiply the result by a relatively high estimate of the price of satisfying an intense level of addiction each day. This calculation ignores some well-known facts about heroin usage. Not all users are addicts. Neither regular users nor addicts have the same daily need. Some addicts can meet their needs through lawfully gained income. The cases of the addicted physicians and musicians are well known. Some blue-collar and now even white-collar workers can continue to work while addicted. Many addicts meet their financial needs through prostitution, pimping, and drug dealing. Only some heroin addicts, then, must turn to predatory crime to feed their habits. They are indeed responsible for a lot of crime, but it is much less than most of the sensational estimates would have us believe.

A realistic estimate of the amount of crime committed by heroin addicts must take into account the fluctuating intensity of addiction. During a "run" or a period of heavy addiction, an addict/criminal may rob or steal six times as much as during a period of less intense addiction.[10] Estimates based on interviews with addicts who report their needs during peak periods will inevitably result in gross exaggerations of the total heroin/crime picture. In short, there is no such thing as the "average" heroin addict (even forgetting, for the moment, about the nonaddicted users) and, as we discussed in relation to the problem of estimating average offense rates for career criminals, no meaningful "average" amount of crime committed by addicts.

The question of whether heroin causes predatory street crime has been hotly debated. The drug crusaders traditionally paint a picture of the addict driven to crime by the need to supply his or her habit. In this scenario, heroin causes crime. Criminologists tend to take a different view. Research has indicated that among addicts/criminals, the first arrest preceded the first use of heroin by about a year and a half. Crime and heroin use are seen as two parts of a deviant lifestyle, without a strong causal relationship working in either direction. Many factors lead people into this deviant lifestyle, but criminologists have yet to isolate any one of them as taking priority over the others. From our perspective this lack of established causality signifies that the effective control of heroin (by whatever means) would not in and of itself keep substantially more people from entering lives of crime.[11]

We now turn to the question of decriminalization as a method of controlling heroin-related crime. It is only one of several alternatives available. Law enforcement strategies may be divided into two classes: "supply reduction" and "demand reduction."[12] The former attempts to reduce the amount of heroin available on the streets, either by interdicting importation or by cracking down on major dealers. Decades of law enforcement effort have proven this approach to be a will-of-the-wisp. The potential sources of supply are simply too numerous and there are too many people willing to take the risks of becoming importers and major dealers. A number of supply reduction campaigns may actually have backfired. Supply reduction, of course, raises the price of the commodity in question and thus may only force current addicts to increase their criminal activity to meet the higher price. Or it may cause drug users to turn to other drugs to meet their recreational or physical needs.

Nor does demand reduction appear to be any more promising. The most notable effort in this regard is the 1973 New York drug law. . . . Despite its Draconian penalties, the law did not reduce the level of drug usage in New York City. Deterring people from wanting heroin is not a realistic goal.[13]

These lines of reasoning bring us to decriminalization. Many thoughtful observers have argued, quite persuasively, that the criminalization of heroin use has done incalculable damage to our society and our criminal justice system. Criminal penalties have brought suffering to addicts, sustained criminal syndicates, corrupted the criminal justice system, and brought the law and law enforcement into disrepute by exposing their helplessness. As a policy, decriminalization does not mean a total legalization of and disregard for heroin. Advocates of decriminalization acknowledge that the drug is a terribly destructive commodity that requires control. Decriminalization usually means removing criminal penalties for its *use* but not for its sale and distribution. Thus, the individual addict would not face criminal penalties. Heroin trafficking, however, would remain a crime. At the same time, most decriminalization proposals call for some form of treatment or maintenance for the addict. Methadone is the most popular form of maintenance, although some experts propose maintaining addicts through medically prescribed heroin.

The story of methadone maintenance is another example of a familiar syndrome in the treatment literature: a new treatment is announced, its proponents claim amazing success rates amid great publicity, independent evaluations reveal that the successes are greatly exaggerated, and a powerful backlash sets in. In the case of methadone maintenance, Vincent Dole, Marie Nyswander, and Alan Warner claimed, in the pages of the December 1968 issue of the *Journal of the American Medical Association,* a 90 percent success rate in treating heroin addicts. After four years of treatment through methadone maintenance, 88 percent of their 750 addicts with criminal records remained arrest-free. By comparison, 91 percent of the group had had some jail experience before entering treatment. Only 5.6 percent of the group were arrested and convicted while in methadone treatment. Dole, Nyswander, and Warner professed to have saved New York City over $1 million per day in prevented crime. A year later, Dr. Francis Gearing, of Columbia University School of Public Health, asserted that after three years of methadone maintenance his group of heroin addicts had an arrest rate lower than that of the general population.[14]

The backlash was not long in coming. A reevaluation of the Dole, Nyswander, and Warner data showed that while 94 percent of the addicts had not been arrested in the year following treatment, only 80 percent had not been arrested the year before treatment—a drop of but 14 percent. Further studies indicated that many methadone programs were not careful to ensure enrollment of true addicts rather than occasional heroin users. Some provided methadone but no other treatment services. Levels of dosage varied widely. Not all programs monitored the behavior of their clients carefully to ensure that they were not selling their methadone. As is the case with so many evaluations in other forms of correctional treatment, evaluators failed to use adequate controls, and the resulting findings are not reliable. Arnold Trebach concludes that there are "no definitive answers in the 'scientific' studies." The backlash reached its apogee with Edward Jay Epstein's 1974 article, "Methadone: the Forlorn Hope." Appearing in *The Public Interest* in the same year that the magazine published Martinson's "What Works?" article, Epstein's article denounced methadone as a complete failure. Not only was there no evidence of its success but, in many respects, it was as damaging as heroin itself.[15]

The truth is that methadone maintenance is partially but not completely successful. John Kaplan estimates that it achieves permanent success with about 40 percent of the addicts who receive treatment. That may not seem like a terribly high success rate, but, Kaplan argues, it is "about as well as we can do." Methadone maintenance is "the most cost-effective treatment we have today" for this destructive drug that has resisted every form of control and treatment. With respect to crime, it appears that methadone maintenance reduces but does not eliminate criminal activity. In one California experiment, income from criminal activity dropped from $3,900 to $400 a year for one group of former addicts, and from $7,200 to $1,700 for another group. Another study by Dr. Paul Cushman found that arrest rates for addicts fluctuated from 3.1 per 100 person/years before addiction to 35.1 per 100 during addiction (confirming other data indicating that addicts do indeed commit large numbers of crimes). During methadone maintenance, arrest rates dropped from 5.9 per 100 and then rose to 9.0 per 100 after the clients were discharged from the program. We can view this "success" from different perspectives. Discharged clients were committing about three times as much crime after treatment as before addiction, but less than during their addiction period.[16]

As John Kaplan suggests, heroin is indeed "the hardest drug." It is the hardest not just in terms of its addictive powers but also because it has resisted all our attempts to control it. He suggests that decriminalization is the wisest approach to this terrible problem. But he has no illusions about its being a total cure. Decriminalization, with methadone maintenance and accompanying treatment, might make some difference. But it will neither completely reduce addiction nor eliminate heroin-related crime.

Notes

1. Norval Morris and Gordon Hawkins, *The Honest Politician's Guide to Crime Control* (Chicago: University of Chicago Press, 1970), chap. 1; Aryeh Neier, *Crime and Punishment: A Radical Solution* (New York: Stein and Day, 1976).

2. Edwin M. Schur, *Crimes without Victims* (Englewood Cliffs, NJ: Prentice Hall, 1965).

3. Raymond T. Nimmer, *Two Million Unnecessary Arrests* (Chicago: American Bar Foundation, 1971).

4. Nimmer, *Two Million Unnecessary Arrests*.

5. David E. Aaronson, C. Thomas Dienes, and Michael C. Mushneno, *Public Policy and Police Discretion* (New York: Clark Boardman, 1984).

6. George L. Kelling and James Q. Wilson, "Broken Windows: The Police and Neighborhood Safety," *Atlantic Monthly* 249 (March 1982), reprinted in James Q. Wilson, *Thinking about Crime,* rev. ed. (New York: Basic Books, 1983), chap. 5.

7. Nimmer, *Two Million Unnecessary Arrests,* chap. 2.

8. John Kaplan, *The Hardest Drug: Heroin and Public Policy* (Chicago: University of Chicago Press, 1983).

9. Max Singer, "The Vitality of Mythical Numbers," *The Public Interest* 23 (Spring 1971):3–9.

10. Kaplan, *The Hardest Drug,* pp. 55–57.

11. Kaplan, *The Hardest Drug,* p. 55.

12. Mark H. Moore, "Controlling Criminogenic Commodities: Drugs, Guns, and Alcohol," in James Q. Wilson, ed., *Crime and Public Policy* (San Francisco: ICS Press, 1983), pp. 125–144.

13. U.S. Department of Justice, *The Nation's Toughest Drug Law: Evaluating the New York Experience* (Washington, DC: U.S. Government Printing Office, 1978).

14. Arnold Trebach, *The Heroin Solution* (New Haven, CT: Yale University Press, 1982), pp. 259–260.

15. Edward Jay Epstein, "Methadone: The Forlorn Hope," *The Public Interest* 36 (Summer 1974).

16. Kaplan, *The Hardest Drug,* p. 222; Trebach, *The Heroin Solution,* p. 261.

The Professional Ex-: An Alternative for Exiting the Deviant Career

J. David Brown

This study explores the careers of professional ex-s, persons who have exited their deviant careers by replacing them with occupations in professional counseling. During their transformation professional ex-s utilize vestiges of their deviant identity to legitimate their past deviance and generate new careers as counselors.

Recent surveys document that approximately 72% of the professional counselors working in the over 10,000 U.S. substance abuse treatment centers are former substance abusers (NAADAC 1986; Sobell and Sobell 1987). This attests to the significance of the professional ex- phenomenon. Though not all ex-deviants become professional ex-s, such data clearly suggest that the majority of substance abuse counselors are professional ex-s.[1]

Since the inception of the notion of deviant career by Goffman (1961) and Becker (1963), research has identified, differentiated, and explicated the characteristics of specific deviant career stages (e.g., Adler and Adler 1983; Luckenbill and Best 1981; Meisenhelder 1977; Miller 1986; Shover 1983). The literature devoted to exiting deviance primarily addresses the process whereby individuals abandon their deviant behaviors, ideologies, and identities and replace them with more conventional lifestyles and identities (Irwin 1970; Lofland 1969; Meisenhelder 1977; Shover 1983). While some studies emphasize the role of authorities or associations of ex-deviants in this change (e.g., Livingston 1974; Lofland 1969; Volkman and Cressey 1963), others suggest that exiting deviance is a natural process contingent upon age-related, structural, and social psychological variables (Frazier 1976; Inciardi 1975; Irwin 1970; Meisenhelder 1977; Petersilia 1980; Shover 1983).

Although exiting deviance has been variously conceptualized, to date no one has considered that it might include adoption of a legitimate career premised upon an identity that embraces one's deviant history. Professional ex-s exemplify this mode of exiting deviance.

647

Ebaugh's (1988) model of role exit provides an initial framework for examining this alternative mode of exiting the deviant career. Her model suggests that former roles are never abandoned but, instead, carry over into new roles. I elaborate her position and contend that one's deviant identity is not an obstacle that must be abandoned prior to exiting or adopting a more conventional lifestyle. To the contrary, one's lingering deviant identity facilitates rather than inhibits the exiting process.

How I gathered data pertinent to exiting, my relationship to these data, and how my personal experiences with exiting deviance organize this article, follow. I then present a four stage model that outlines the basic contours of the professional ex- phenomenon. Finally I suggest how the professional ex- phenomenon represents an alternative interpretation of exiting deviance that generalizes to other forms of deviance.

Methods

Data for this research consists of introspective and qualitative material.

Introspective Data

My introspections distill 20 years of experience with substance abuse/ alcoholism, social control agents/agencies, and professional counselor training. I spent 13 years becoming a deviant drinker and entered substance abuse treatment in 1979. For 5 years (1981–1986), I was a primary therapist and family interventionist for a local private residential treatment facility.

"Systematic sociological introspection" (Ellis 1987, 1990), "auto-ethnography" (Hayano 1979), and "opportunistic research" (Reimer 1977) accessed the introspective data. Each group status—abuser, patient, therapist—indicates the "complete membership role" (Adler and Adler 1987) that combines unique circumstances with personal expertise to enhance research. The four stage model of exiting described later is, in part, informed by reexamination of the written artifacts of my therapeutic/recovery experiences (e.g., alco-biography, moral inventory, daily inventory journal) and professional counselor training (e.g., term paper, internship journal).

Qualitative Data

Qualitative data were collected over a six month period of intensive interviews with 35 counselor ex-s employed in a variety of community, state, and private institutions that treat individuals with drug, alcohol, and/or eating disorder problems.[2]

These professional ex-s worked in diverse occupations prior to becoming substance abuse counselors. A partial list includes employment as accountants, managers, salespersons, nurses, educators, and business owners. Although they claimed to enter the counseling profession within two years of discharge from therapy, their decision to become counselors usually came within one year. On the average they had been counselors for four and one half years. Except one professional ex- who previously counseled learning disabled children, all claimed they had not seriously considered a counseling career before entering therapy.

The Exit Process

Ebaugh (1988) contends that the experience of being an "ex" of one kind or another is common to most people in modern society. Emphasizing the sociological and psychological continuity of the ex- phenomenon she states, "[I]t implies that interaction is based not only on current role definitions but, more important, past identities that somehow linger on and define how people see and present themselves in their present identities" (p. xiii). Ebaugh defines the role exit as the "process of disengagement from a role that is central to one's self-identity and the reestablishment of an identity in a new role that takes into account one's ex-role" (p. 1).

Becoming a professional ex- is the outcome of a four stage process through which ex-s capitalize on the experience and vestiges of their deviant career in order to establish a new identity and role in a respectable organization. This process comprises emulation of one's therapist, the call to a counseling career, status-set realignment, and credentialization.

Stage One: Emulation of One's Therapist

The emotional and symbolic identification of these ex-s with their therapists during treatment, combined with the deep personal meanings they imputed to these relationships, was a compelling factor in their decisions to become counselors. Denzin (1987, pp. 61–62) identifies the therapeutic relationship's significance thus: "Through a process of identification and surrender (which may be altruistic), the alcoholic may merge her ego and her self in the experiences and the identity of the counselor. The group leader . . . is the group ego ideal, for he or she is a successful recovering alcoholic. . . . An emotional bond is thus formed with the group counselor. . . . "

Professional ex-s not only developed this emotional bond but additionally aspired to have the emotions and meanings once projected toward their therapists ascribed to them. An eating disorders counselor discussed her relationship with her therapist and her desire to be viewed in a similar way with these words:

> My counselor taught me the ability to care about myself and other people. Before I met her I was literally insane. She was the one who showed me that I wasn't crazy. Now, I want to be the person who says, "No, you're not crazy!" I am the one, now, who is helping them to get free from the ignorance that has shrouded eating disorders.

Counselors enacted a powerfully charismatic role in professional ex-s' therapeutic transformation. Their "laying on of verbal hands" provided initial comfort and relief from the ravaging symptoms of disease. They came to represent what ex-s must do both spiritually and professionally for themselves. Substance abuse therapy symbolized the "sacred" quest for divine grace rather than the mere pursuit of mundane, worldly, or "profane" outcomes like abstinence or modification of substance use/abuse behaviors; counselors embodied the sacred outcome.

Professional ex-s claimed that their therapists were the most significant change agent in their transformation. "I am here today because there was one very influential counselor in my life who helped me to get sober. I owe it all to God and to him," one alcoholism counselor expressed. A heroin addiction counselor stated, "The best thing that ever happened in my life was meeting Sally [her counselor]. She literally saved my life. If it wasn't for her I'd still probably be out there shootin' up or else be in prison or dead."

Subjects' recognition and identification of a leader's charismatic authority, as Weber (1968) notes, is decisive in validating that charisma and developing absolute trust and devotion. The special virtues and powers professional ex-s perceived in their counselors subsequently shaped their loyalty and devotion to the career.

Within the therapeutic relationship, professional ex-s perform a priestly function through which a cultural tradition passes from one generation to the next. While knowledge and wisdom pass downward (from professional ex- to patient), careers build upward (from patient to professional ex-). As the bearers of the cultural legacy of therapy, professional ex-s teach patients definitions of the situation they learned as patients. Indeed, part of the professional ex- mystique resides in once having been a patient (Bissell 1982). In this regard,

> My counselor established her legitimacy with me the moment she disclosed the fact that she, too, was an alcoholic. She wasn't just telling me what to do, she was living her own advice. By the example she set, I felt hopeful that I could recover. As I reflect upon those experiences I cannot think of one patient ever asking me about where I received my professional training. At the same time, I cannot begin to count the numerous times that my patients have asked me if I was "recovering."

Similar to religious converts' salvation through a profoundly redemptive religious experience, professional ex-s' deep career commitment derives from a transforming therapeutic resocialization. As the previous examples suggest, salvation not only relates to a changed universe of discourse; it is also identified "with one's personal therapist."[3]

At this stage, professional ex-s trust in and devote themselves to their counselors' proselytizations as a promissory note for the future. The promise is redemption and salvation from the ever-present potential for self-destruction or relapse that looms in their mental horizon. An eating disorders counselor shared her insights in this way:

> I wouldn't have gotten so involved in eating disorders counseling if I had felt certain that my eating disorder was taken care of. I see myself in constant recovery. If I was so self assured that I would never have the problem again there would probably be less of an emphasis on being involved in the field but I have found that helping others, as I was once helped, really helps me.

The substance abuse treatment center transforms from a mere "clinic" occupied by secularly credentialed professionals into a moral community of single believers. As Durkheim (1915) suggests, however, beliefs require rites and practices in order to sustain adherents' mental and emotional states.

Stage Two: The Call to a Counseling Career

At this juncture, professional ex-s begin to turn the moral corner on their deviance. Behaviors previously declared morally reprehensible are increasingly understood within a new universe of discourse as symptoms of a much larger disease complex. This recognition represents one preliminary step toward grace. In order to emulate their therapist, however, professional ex-s realize they must dedicate themselves to an identity and lifestyle that ensure their own symptoms' permanent remission. One alcoholism counselor illustrated this point by stating:

> I can't have my life, my health, my family, my job, my friends, or anything, unless I take daily necessary steps to ensure my continued recovery. My program of recovery has to come first. Before I can go out there and help my patients I need to always make sure that my own house is in order.

As this suggests, a new world-view premised upon accepting the contingencies of one's illness while maintaining a constant vigilance over potentially recurring symptoms replaces deviant moral and social meanings. Professional ex-s' recognition of the need for constant vigilance is internalized as their moral mission from which their spiritual duty (a counseling career) follows as a natural next step.

Although professional ex-s no longer engage in substance abuse behaviors, they do not totally abandon deviant beliefs or identity. "Lest we become complacent and forget from whence we came," as one alcoholism counselor indicated the significance of remembering and embracing the past.

Professional ex-s' identification with their deviant past undergirds their professional, experiential, and moral differentiation from other professional colleagues. A heroin addiction counselor recounted how he still identified himself as an addict and deviant:

> My perspective and my affinity to my clients, particularly the harder core criminals, is far better than the professor and other doctors that I

> deal with here in my job. We're different and we really don't see things
> the same way at all. Our acceptance and understanding of these peo-
> ple's diseases, if you will, is much different. They haven't experienced
> it. They don't know these people at all. It takes more than knowing
> about something to be effective. I've been there and, in many respects,
> I will always be there.

In this way, other counselors' medical, psychiatric, or therapeutic skills
are construed as part of the ordinary mundane world. As the quotation indicates, professional ex-s intentionally use their experiential past and therapeutic transformations to legitimate their entrance into and authority in
counseling careers.

Professional ex-s embrace their deviant history and identity as an in-
valuable, therapeutic resource and feel compelled to continually reaffirm
its validity in an institutional environment. Certainly, participating in "12
Step Programs"[4] without becoming counselors could help others but professional ex-s' call requires greater immersion than they provide. An alcoholism counselor reflected upon this need thus:

> For me, it was no longer sufficient to only participate "anonymously" in
> A.A. I wanted to surround myself with other spiritual and professional
> pilgrims devoted to receiving and imparting wisdom.

Towards patients, professional ex-s project a saintly aura and exemplify
an "ideal recovery." Internalization of self-images previously ascribed to
their therapist and now reaffirmed through an emotional and moral commitment to the counseling profession facilitate this ideation. Invariably,
professional ex-s' counseling careers are in institutions professing treatment ideologies identical to what they were taught as patients. Becoming
a professional ex- symbolizes a value elevated to a directing goal, whose
pursuit predisposes them to interpret all ensuing experience in terms of
relevance to it.

Stage Three: Status-Set Realignment

Professional ex-s' deep personal identification with their therapist provides
an ego ideal to be emulated with regard to both recovery and career. They
immerse themselves in what literally constitutes a "professional recovery
career" that provides an institutional location to reciprocate their counselors' gift, immerse themselves in a new universe of discourse, and effectively lead novitiates to salvation. "I wouldn't be here today if it wasn't for
all of the help I received in therapy. This is my way of paying some of those
people back by helping those still in need," one alcoholism counselor related this.

Professional ex-s' identities assume a "master status" (Hughes 1945) that
differs in one fundamental respect from others' experiencing therapeutic
resocialization. Specifically, their transformed identities not only become

the "most salient" in their "role identity hierarchy" (Stryker and Serpe 1982), but affect all other roles in their "status-sets" (Merton 1938). One alcoholism counselor reflected upon it this way:

> Maintaining a continued program of recovery is the most important thing in my life. Everything else is secondary. I've stopped socializing with my old friends who drink and have developed new recovering friends. I interact differently with my family. I used to work a lot of overtime but I told my old boss that overtime jeopardized my program. I finally began to realize that the job just didn't have anything to do with what I was really about. I felt alienated. Although I had been thinking about becoming a counselor ever since I went through treatment, I finally decided to pursue it.

Role alignment is facilitated by an alternative identity that redefines obligations associated with other, less significant, role identities. In the previous example, the strains of expectations associated with a former occupation fostered a role alignment consistent with a new self-image. This phenomenon closely resembles what Snow and Machalek (1983, p. 276) refer to as "embracement of a master role" that "is not merely a mask that is taken off or put on according to the situation. . . . Rather, it is central to nearly all situations. . . . " An eating disorders counselor stated the need to align her career with her self-image, "I hid in my former profession, interacting little with people. As a counselor, I am personally maturing and taking responsibility rather than letting a company take care of me. I have a sense of purpose in this job that I never had before."

Financial remuneration is not a major consideration in the decision to become a professional ex-. The pure type of call, Weber (1968, p. 52) notes, "disdains and repudiates economic exploitation of the gifts of grace as a source of income. . . . " Most professional ex-s earned more money in their previous jobs. For instance, one heroin addiction counselor stated:

> When I first got out of treatment, my wife and I started an accounting business. In our first year we cleared nearly sixty thousand dollars. The money was great and the business showed promise but something was missing. I missed being around other addicts and I knew I wanted to do more with my life along the lines of helping out people like me.

An additional factor contributing to professional ex-s' abandonment of their previous occupation is their recognition that a counseling career could resolve lingering self-doubts about their ability to remain abstinent. In this respect becoming a professional ex- allows "staying current" with their own recovery needs while continually reaffirming the severity of their illness. An eating disorders counselor explained:

> I'm constantly in the process of repeating insights that I've had to my patients. I hear myself saying, to them, what I need to believe for myself. Being a therapist helps me to keep current with my own recovery. I feel that I am much less vulnerable to my disease in this environment. It's a

> way that I can keep myself honest. Always being around others with similar issues prevents me from ignoring my own addiction clues.

This example illustrates professional ex-s' use of their profession to secure self-compliance during times of self-doubt. While parroting the virtues of the program facilitates recognition that they, too, suffer from a disease, the professional ex- role, unlike their previous occupations, enables them to continue therapy indirectly.

Finally, the status the broader community ascribes to the professional ex- role encourages professional ex-s' abandonment of previous roles. Association with an institutional environment and an occupational role gives the professional ex- a new sense of place in the surrounding community, within which form new self-concepts and self-esteem, both in the immediate situation and in a broader temporal framework.

The internal validation of professional ex-s' new identity resides in their ability to successfully anticipate the behaviors and actions of relevant others. Additionally, they secure validation by other members of the professional ex- community in a manner atypical for other recovering individuals. Affirmation by this reference community symbolizes validation by one's personal therapist and the therapeutic institution, as a heroin addiction counselor succinctly stated:

> Becoming a counselor was a way to demonstrate my loyalty and devotion to helping others and myself. My successes in recovery, including being a counselor, would be seen by patients and those who helped me get sober. It was a return to treatment, for sure, but the major difference was that this time I returned victorious rather than defeated.

External validation, on the other hand, comes when others outside the therapeutic community accord legitimacy to the professional ex- role. In this regard, a heroin addiction counselor said:

> I remember talking to this guy while I was standing in line for a movie. He asked me what I did for a living and I told him that I was a drug abuse counselor. He started asking me all these questions about the drug problem and what I thought the answers were. When we finally got up to the door of the theater he patted me on the back and said, "You're doing a wonderful job. Keep up the good work. I really admire you for what you're trying to do." It really felt good to have a stranger praise me.

Professional ex-s' counseling role informs the performance of all other roles, compelling them to abandon previous work they increasingly view as mundane and polluting. The next section demonstrates how this master role organizes the meanings associated with their professional counselor training.

Stage Four: Credentialization

One characteristic typically distinguishing the professions from other occupations is specialized knowledge acquired at institutions of higher learning (Larson 1977; Parsons 1959; Ritzer and Walczak 1986, 1988). Although mastering esoteric knowledge and professional responsibilities in a therapeutic relationship serve as gatekeepers for entering the counseling profession, the moral and emotional essence of being a professional ex- involves much more.

Professional ex-s see themselves as their patients' champions. "Knowing what it's like" and the subsequent education and skills acquired in training legitimate claims to the "entitlements of their stigma" (Gusfield 1982), including professional status. Their monopoly of an abstruse body of knowledge and skill is realized through their emotionally lived history of shame and guilt as well as the hope and redemption secured through therapeutic transformation. Professional ex-s associate higher learning with their experiential history of deviance and the emotional context of therapy. Higher learning symbolizes rediscovery of a moral sense of worth and sacredness rather than credential acquisition. This distinction was clarified by an alcoholism counselor:

> Anymore, you need to have a degree before anybody will hire you. I entered counseling with a bachelors but I eventually received my MSW about two years ago. I think the greatest benefit in having the formal training is that I have been able to more effectively utilize my personal alcoholism experiences with my patients. I feel that I have a gift to offer my patients which doesn't come from the classroom. It comes from being an alcoholic myself.

These entitlements allow professional ex-s to capitalize on their deviant identity in two ways: the existential and phenomenological dimensions of their lived experience of "having made their way from the darkness into the light" provide their experiential and professional *legitimacy* among patients, the community, and other professionals, as well as occupational *income.* "Where else could I go and put bulimic and alcoholic on my resume and get hired?" one counselor put it.

Professional ex-s generally eschew meta-perspective interpretations of the system in which they work. They desire a counseling method congruent with their fundamental universe of discourse and seek, primarily, to perpetuate this system (Peele 1989; Room 1972, 1976). The words of one educator at a local counselor training institute are germane:

> These people [professional ex-s] . . . are very fragile when they get here. Usually, they have only been in recovery for about a year. Anyone who challenges what they learned in therapy, or in their program of recovery [i.e., A.A., Narcotics Anonymous, Overeaters Anonymous] . . . is viewed as a threat. Although we try to change some of that while

they're here with us, I still see my role here as one of an extended therapist rather than an educator.

Information challenging their beliefs about how they, and their patients, should enact the rites associated with recovery is condemned (Davies 1963; Pattison 1987; Roizen 1977). They view intellectual challenges to the disease concept as attacks on their personal program of recovery. In a Durkheimian sense, such challenges "profane" that which they hold "sacred."

Within the walls of these monasteries professional ex-s emulate their predecessors as one generation of healers passes on to the next an age old message of salvation. Although each new generation presents the path to enlightenment in somewhat different, contemporary terms, it is already well lit for those "becoming a professional ex-."

Discussion

Focusing on their lived experiences and accounts, this study sketches the central contours of professional ex-s' distinctive exit process. More generally, it also endeavors to contribute to the existing literature on deviant careers.

An identity that embraces their deviant history and identity undergirds the professional ex-s' careers. This existing mode is the outcome of a four stage process enabling professional ex-s to capitalize on their deviant history. They do not "put it all behind them" in exchange for conventional lifestyles, values, beliefs, and identities. Rather, they use vestiges of their deviant biography as an explicit occupational strategy.

My research augments Ebaugh's (1988) outline of principles underlying role exit in three ways. First, her discussion suggests that people are unaware of these guiding principles. While this holds for many, professional ex-s' intentional rather than unintentional embracement of their deviant identity is the step by which they adopt a new role in the counseling profession. Second, Ebaugh states that significant others' negative reactions inhibit or interrupt exit. Among professional ex-s, however, such reactions are a crucial precursor to their exit mode. Finally, Ebaugh sees role exit as a voluntary, individually initiated process, enhanced by "seeking alternatives" through which to explore other roles. Professional ex-s, by contrast, are compelled into therapy. They do not look for this particular role. Rather, their alternatives are prescribed through their resocialization into a new identity.

Organizations in American society increasingly utilize professional ex-s in their social control efforts. For example, the state of Colorado uses prisoners to counsel delinquent youth. A preliminary, two year, follow-up study suggests that these prisoner-counselors show only 13% recidivism (Shiller 1988) and a substantial number want to return to college or enter careers as guidance counselors, probation officers, youth educators, or law enforcement consultants. Similarly, a local effort directed toward curbing gang violence, the Open Door Youth Gang Program, was developed by a professional ex- and uses former gang members as counselors, educators, and community relations personnel.

Further examination of the modes through which charismatic, albeit licensed and certified, groups generate professional ex- statuses is warranted. Although the examples just described differ from the professional ex-s examined earlier in this research in terms of therapeutic or "medicalized" resocialization, their similarities are even more striking. Central to them all is that a redemptive community provides a reference group whose moral and social standards are internalized. Professional ex- statuses are generated as individuals intentionally integrate and embrace rather than abandon their deviant biographies as a specific occupational strategy.

Notes

1. Most individuals in substance abuse therapy do not become professional ex-s. Rather, they traverse a variety of paths not articulated here including (1) dropping out of treatment, (2) completing treatment but returning to substance use and/or abuse, and (3) remaining abstinent after treatment but feeling no compulsion to enter the counseling profession. Future research will explore the differences among persons by mode of exit. Here, however, analysis and description focus exclusively on individuals committed to the professional ex- role.

2. I conducted most interviews at the subject's work environment, face-to-face. One interview was with a focus group of 10 professional ex-s (Morgan 1988). Two interviews were in my office, one at my home, and one at a subject's home. I interviewed each individual one time for approximately one hour. Interviews were semi-structured, with open-end questions designed to elicit responses related to feelings, thoughts, perceptions, reflections, and meaning concerning subjects' past deviance, factors facilitating their exit from deviance, and their counseling career.

3. I contend that significantly more professional ex-s pursue their careers due to therapeutic resocialization than to achieving sobriety/recovery exclusively through the 12 Step Program (e.g., A.A.). It is too early, however, to preclude that some may enter substance abuse counseling careers lacking any personal therapy. My experiences and my interviews with other professional ex-s suggest that very few professional ex-s enter the profession directly through their contacts with the 12 Step Program. The program's moral precepts—that "sobriety is a gift from God" that must be "given freely to others in order to assure that one may keep the gift"—would appear to discourage rather than encourage substance abuse counseling careers. Financial remuneration for assisting fellow substance abusers directly violates these precepts. Further, professional ex-s are commonly disparaged in A.A. circles as "two hatters" (cf. Denzin 1987). They are, therefore, not a positive reference group for individuals recovering exclusively through the 12 Step Program. Sober 12 Step members are more inclined to emulate their "sponsors" than pursue careers with no experiential referents or direct relevance to their recovery. Further data collection and analysis will examine these differences. Extant data, however, strongly indicate that therapeutic resocialization and a professional role model provide the crucial link between deviant and substance abuse counseling careers.

4. "12 Step Program" refers to a variety of self-help groups (e.g., A.A., Narcotics Anonymous, Overeaters Anonymous) patterning their recovery model upon the original 12 Steps and 12 Traditions of A.A.

References

Adler, Patricia, and Peter Adler. 1983. "Shifts and Oscillations in Deviant Careers: The Case of Upper-Level Drug Dealers and Smugglers." *Social Problems* 31: 195–207.

——. 1987. *Membership Roles in Field Research.* Newbury Park, CA: Sage.

Becker, Howard. 1963. *Outsiders: Studies in the Sociology of Deviance.* New York: Free Press.

Best, Joel, and David F. Luckenbill. 1982. *Organizing Deviance.* Englewood Cliffs, NJ: Prentice Hall.

Bissell, LeClair. 1982. "Recovered Alcoholism Counselors." Pp. 810–817 in *Encyclopedic Handbook of Alcoholism,* edited by E. Mansell Pattison and Edward Kaufman. New York: Gardner.

Davies, D. L. 1963. "Normal Drinking in Recovered Alcoholic Addicts" (comments by various correspondents). *Quarterly Journal of Studies on Alcohol* 24:109–121, 321–332.

Denzin, Norman. 1987. *The Recovering Alcoholic.* Beverly Hills: Sage.

Durkheim, Emile. 1915. *The Elementary Forms of the Religious Life.* New York: Free Press.

Ebaugh, Helen Rose Fuchs. 1988. *Becoming an Ex: The Process of Role Exit.* Chicago: University of Chicago Press.

Ellis, Carolyn. 1987. "Systematic Sociological Introspection and the Study of Emotions." Paper presented to the annual meeting of the American Sociological Association, Chicago.

———. 1990. "Sociological Introspection and Emotional Experience." *Symbolic Interaction* 13(2).

Frazier, Charles. 1976. *Theoretical Approaches to Deviance.* Columbus: Charles Merrill.

Glassner, Barry, Margret Ksander, Bruce Berg, and Bruce D. Johnson. 1983. "A Note on the Deterrent Effect of Juvenile vs. Adult Jurisdiction." *Social Problems* 31:219–221.

Goffman, Erving. 1961. *Asylums.* Garden City, NY: Anchor.

Gusfield, Joseph. 1982. "Deviance in the Welfare State: The Alcoholism Profession and the Entitlements of Stigma." *Research in Social Problems and Public Policy* 2:1–20.

Hayano, David. 1979. "Auto-Ethnography: Paradigms, Problems and Prospects." *Human Organization* 38:99–104.

Hughes, Everett. 1945. "Dilemmas and Contradictions of Status." *American Journal of Sociology* L:353–359.

Inciardi, James. 1975. *Careers in Crime.* Chicago: Rand McNally.

Irwin, John. 1970. *The Felon.* Englewood Cliffs: Prentice Hall.

Larson, Magali. 1977. *The Rise of Professionalism.* Berkeley: University of California Press.

Livingston, Jay. 1974. *Compulsive Gamblers.* New York: Harper and Row.

Lofland, John. 1969. *Deviance and Identity.* Englewood Cliffs: Prentice Hall.

Luckenbill, David F., and Joel Best. 1981. "Careers in Deviance and Respectability: The Analogy's Limitations." *Social Problems* 29:197–206.

Meisenhelder, Thomas. 1977. "An Exploratory Study of Exiting from Criminal Careers." *Criminology* 15:319–334.

Merton, Robert. 1938. *Social Theory and Social Structure.* Glencoe: Free Press.

Miller, Gale. 1986. "Conflict in Deviant Occupations." Pp. 373–401 in *Working: Conflict and Change,* 3rd ed., edited by George Ritzer and David Walczak. Englewood Cliffs: Prentice Hall.

Morgan, David L. 1988. *Focus Groups as Qualitative Research.* Beverly Hills: Sage.

NAADAC. 1986. *Development of Model Professional Standards for Counselor Credentialing.* National Association of Alcoholism and Drug Abuse Counselors. Dubuque: Kendall/Hunt.

Parsons, Talcott. 1959. "Some Problems Confronting Sociology as a Profession." *American Sociological Review* 24:547–559.

Pattison, E. Mansell. 1987. "Whither Goals in the Treatment of Alcoholism." *Drugs and Society* 2/3:153–171.

Peele, Stanton. 1989. *The Diseasing of America: Addiction Treatment Out of Control.* Toronto: Lexington.

Petersilia, Joan. 1980. "Criminal Career Research: A Review of Recent Evidence." Pp. 321–379 in *Crime and Justice: An Annual Review of Research,* vol. 2, edited by Norval Morris and Michael Tonry. Chicago: University of Chicago Press.

Reimer, Jeffrey. 1977. "Varieties of Opportunistic Research." *Urban Life* 5:467–477.

Ritzer, George, and David Walczak. 1986. *Working: Conflict and Change.* 3rd ed. Englewood Cliffs: Prentice Hall.

––––––. 1988. "Rationalization and the Deprofessionalization of Physicians." *Social Forces* 67:1–22.

Roizen, Ron. 1977. "Comment on the Rand Report." *Quarterly Journal of Studies on Alcohol* 38:170–178.

Room, Robin. 1972. "Drinking and Disease: Comment on the Alcoholist's Addiction." *Quarterly Journal of Studies on Alcohol* 33:1049–1059.

––––––. 1976. "Drunkenness and the Law: Comment on the Uniform Alcoholism Intoxication Treatment Act." *Quarterly Journal of Studies on Alcohol* 37:113–144.

Shiller, Gene. 1988. "A Preliminary Report on SHAPE-UP." Paper presented to the Colorado District Attorneys Council, Denver.

Shover, Neil. 1983. "The Later Stages of Ordinary Property Offenders' Careers." *Social Problems* 31:208–218.

Snow, David, and Richard Machalek. 1983. "The Convert as a Social Type." Pp. 259–289 in *Sociological Theory 1983,* edited by Randall Collins. San Francisco: Jossey-Bass.

Sobell, Mark B., and Linda C. Sobell. 1987. "Conceptual Issues Regarding Goals in the Treatment of Alcohol Problems." *Drugs and Alcohol* 2/3:1–37.

Stryker, Sheldon, and Richard Serpe. 1982. "Commitment, Identity Salience, and Role Behavior: Theory and Research Example." Pp. 199–218 in *Personality, Roles, and Social Behavior,* edited by William Ickes and Eric S. Knowles. New York: Springer-Verlag.

Volkman, Rita, and Donald Cressey. 1963. "Differential Association and the Rehabilitation of Drug Addicts." *American Journal of Sociology* 69:129–142.

Weber, Max. 1968. *On Charisma and Institution Building.* Edited by S. N. Eisenstadt. Chicago: University of Chicago Press.

45 Race and Policing

Jim Leitzel

Police in the United States seem to be doing something right: serious crime has been plummeting, declining by more than 20 percent since 1991. The reduction in the number of murders has been even more spectacular, dropping by more than 36 percent between 1993 and 1999: the murder rate in 1999 was lower than in every year since 1966. Simultaneously, many public areas have become decidedly more hospitable. Aggressive "quality-of-life" policing, such as that employed in New York City to clean up the subway or rid the city of "squeegeemen," may be partly responsible for both the drop in the crime rate and improvements in public spaces.

These successes, however, are tarnished by ongoing controversy concerning the role of race in policing. Race has been an element in some high-profile incidents, such as the February 1999 killing of unarmed African immigrant Amadou Diallo by four white New York City police officers, or the 1997 police torture of Haitian immigrant Abner Louima. But the racial disparities in policing appear to go well beyond isolated cases of abuse. Generally speaking, black people, particularly young black males, tend to have much worse experiences with the police than do white Americans. These experiences range from the annoying—frequent traffic stops for minor or imagined violations—to the fatal, as in the Diallo case. To some extent, racial disparities in citizen-police interactions are deliberate, as criminal "profiles" compiled by the police formally or informally employ race as one factor in identifying potential miscreants. In practice, race appears often to be a decisive element in whether a stop is initiated, or in how an encounter is handled.

Given the success evidenced by falling crime rates, it might be thought that the way forward in crime control is to continue with present policing strategies, while redoubling efforts to eliminate the abuses of racist and brutal police. Surely there is wide consensus that such bad cops should be rooted out and prosecuted for their misdeeds. But it is the use of racial profiling, not its abuse, that is the more fundamental problem: even if all abuses associated with race-based policing could somehow be eliminated, racial profiling would remain a bad idea. Race-based policing is counter-productive: it leads to more crime, not less.

Is There Race-Based Policing in the U.S.?

Perhaps the characterization of racial disparities in policing as a problem is itself misguided. Perhaps there are no actual racial disproportions in police-citizen encounters; or, if disparities do exist, they are a necessary evil, the price that has to be paid for a well-policed society.

Do disparities exist? With respect to traffic regulations, for instance, are blacks and other minorities stopped more frequently, for a given level of violations of the law? Statistics on race, age, sex, and other information from traffic stops are not routinely collected. But information that is available suggests wide racial disparities. The Maryland State Police, in settling a lawsuit, agreed to collect racial information on traffic stops. On Interstate 95, 70 percent of the drivers who were stopped by the state police between January 1995 and December 1997 were African Americans, though African Americans comprised only some 17.5 percent of the drivers (and of the speeding drivers). Videotapes of stops for drug interdiction in Volusia County, Florida, also on I-95, indicated that blacks comprised 5 percent of the drivers, but 70 percent of those who were stopped. Other statistics suggest that the war on drugs is waged primarily against the non-white segment of the population. According to a report written by David Harris for the American Civil Liberties Union (ACLU), "Today, blacks constitute 13 percent of the country's drug users; 37 percent of those arrested on drug charges; 55 percent of those convicted; and 74 percent of all drug offenders sentenced to prison."

Racial disparities in policing exist; indeed, it would be surprising if they did not exist, since race is used as one of the indicators in criminal profiling. Are such disparities understandable, the result of scrupulous policing? While young black males are treated with more suspicion by the police it might be argued that this is natural, because young black males cause a disproportionate amount of trouble. When attempting to prevent or solve street crime, police shouldn't devote much time to tailing elderly women (except perhaps as potential victims of crime)—young males are the likely perpetrators. Conscientious, unbiased policing would seem to require that police focus their suspicions on the most probable threats. By this reckoning, young black males should have more frequent and maybe even less pleasant police encounters than does the rest of the population.

As a seeming bolster to the notion that race-based policing is essential, an appeal might be made to the behavior of private citizens, as opposed to the police. When walking alone down the street at night, suddenly you notice some individuals walking toward you. If you perceive them as a threat, you may want to quickly take evasive action, such as crossing the street or returning to some more populated area. But you only have a few seconds in which to make this decision. The only basis that you have for choosing your route is the small amount of information that you can visually gather, and your prior beliefs about likely and unlikely perpetrators. In a quick glance, you can only learn a few basic facts: the number of individuals, perhaps their size, their sex, and roughly, their age, their manner of dress, and their general comportment. If the strangers are two elderly women, you continue on your way, rightly confident that you are not about to become a crime victim. If they are two young adult males, you might implement your evasion plan. You might be even more likely to take evasive action if it is two black males. You would not be alone in such a reaction: Rev. Jesse Jackson notably mentioned back in 1993 his own pain at subconsciously associating blackness with potential criminality in street encounters.

Private behavior, in making judgments about potential criminality, discriminates on the basis of sex, age, race, and other factors. It seems unavoidable that when better information is not available—and in a chance meeting in the street, only a few characteristics will be observable—group reputations, even if mistaken, play a dominant role in determining private actions. And group reputations can quite easily be mistaken. Few of us actually know how much more likely it is that we will be victimized by a black man than a white man, if indeed it is more likely—most crime involves victims and perpetrators of the same race. Nor would knowledge of crime statistics necessarily resolve the issue. If the police focus their crime-fighting resources on young black men, they will end up arresting such suspects more often than others, even if there is no sex- or race-based differential in the actual amount of crime. Group reputations for criminality might then yield the appearance of validity, even when they are actually mistaken.

Nevertheless, young men on average are widely believed to be more inclined to predatory violence than elderly women, and without better information, many people will respond to this perception. Such private actions based on group reputation by people who are not racist cannot simply be condemned as inappropriate. In the words of Harvard Law professor Randall Kennedy (whose overall approach to race-based policing is closely paralleled here), those who legally employ race as a signal of potential criminality, "like everyone, are caught up in a large tragedy that will require more than individual good will and bravery to resolve."

Should good cops, then, behave as good private citizens often do? Perhaps surprisingly, the answer is: no. Police should, in general, not use race as a basis for deciding whom to watch, or, after a crime has been committed, whom to question or arrest on grounds of suspicion. This conclusion is not driven by some philosophical perspective that places a higher weight on racial equality than on crime control. Just the opposite: it -

derives solely from a concern with crime. As in many other policy arenas, the best long-term approach to crime control appears counterproductive in the short-run.

Costs of Race-Based Policing

Effective crime control in a democracy requires voluntary cooperation between the police and the citizenry. Voluntary cooperation requires trust. Race-based policing undermines trust. Reduced trust means lessened deterrence of crime, as minorities become unwilling to report crime—a not insignificant concern, given that approximately one-half of serious crime in the United States is not reported to the police. Further, hostility between minorities and the police creates an unwillingness to testify at trials, and, when serving on juries, an unwillingness to convict defendants. This lack of cooperation, brought on by racial disparities in policing, reduces criminal deterrence.

Beyond lowering deterrence, race-based policing also provides positive inducements to disobey the law. When all young black males are thought to be and treated as criminals, a law-abiding black male cannot easily overcome this perception through his own virtuous behavior. Being thought a scoundrel in any event, the reward to virtue falls. The perception of criminality that is inherent in race-based policing prevents well-behaving minority youths from distinguishing themselves from those who are criminals, reducing the incentive to be law-abiding.

The problem is not bad or racist cops in an otherwise workable system. Rather, the problem is the hostility and distrust created among police and minority citizens. This pool of hostility between a group of citizens and the police is not the work of a single cop—especially a single good cop—or based on the activities of a single day. Rather, the pool of hostility is created by long-term, numerous interactions between the police and the citizenry. The activities of any single cop over a short period are essentially irrelevant in determining the size of the hostility "pool": they are literally a drop in the ocean. So when a conscientious police officer is doing his (or her) job, he ignores the effect that his actions have on the sea of hostility, because his actions make no noticeable difference. But the sea of hostility is in fact made up of unpleasant police-citizen encounters in the aggregate, despite the fact that any individual encounter, short of an obviously abusive encounter, is of little or no consequence.

Conscientious policing as described above may not only lead to a general mistrust of the police within a minority community, it also can hold rather severe adverse consequences for specific individuals. Police officers who use race and other noisy indicators unrelated to behavior in profiling potential criminals might "rationally" ignore the fact that the same indicators that lead them to make a stop will also lead other officers to do so, too.

Thus their stop is often far from an isolated event for the individual in question, but just one in a continuing series of stops, as the famous "San Diego walker" case [*Kolender v. Lawson* 461 U.S. 352 (1983)] demonstrated. Further, police actions to some extent serve as guides for the behavior of citizens. When private citizens see or learn about racial profiling by police, their own attitudes toward and treatment of minorities are likely to be influenced.

Race-based practices also harm police, even beyond the mistrust that such practices engender. While race-based policing makes it hard for law-abiding young minority males to distinguish themselves from lawbreakers, it simultaneously leads to a parallel stereotyping of police. Race-based policing generates an unfair perception that many or most police officers are best insensitive to the concerns of minorities or, at worst, racists. So good and honest cops also pay a price from the countenancing of race-based policing, as they become perceived as rough equivalents to those few police whose motivations and acts actually are racist.

Race-based policing presents a familiar scenario, where rational individual behavior does not serve the social good. National defense, the paradigmatic "public good," provides an analogy. Whether or not a particular individual pays his or her taxes has essentially no influence upon the amount of government military spending. Nevertheless, the amount spent on national defense depends on the aggregate amount of taxes paid. If tax payments were voluntary, we would expect too little defense to be supplied: people would recognize that their individual contribution would essentially not matter for the amount of defense provided to them, so they might as well not contribute. Unconstrained individual incentives do not serve society's interests with respect to public goods. Taxes, therefore, are not voluntary. Similarly, citizen hostility towards the police is a "public bad," and individual police officers, acting rationally, will create or "supply" too much of it in the aggregate. Unconstrained individual incentives do not serve society's interests with respect to public bads, either.

An Imperfect Solution

The remedy to the distorted individual incentives that characterize race-based policing is the same as with taxes: we must not allow the use of race in policing to be voluntary. A stringent ban on race-based policing must be adopted. The operational rule of thumb for police officers who are considering stopping or searching a black person (or potentially a Latino or another minority) should be: would I stop or search this person if he or she was white? If the answer is no, then the black person should not be stopped or searched, either, even if, for instance, the neighborhood is predominately white and blacks stopped in the area have been associated with crime in the past. Police "profiles" of drug couriers or other classes of criminals should not include race, even (as is currently done) as one of a panoply of characteristics.

If a description of a suspect is available, race should then be taken into account in attempting to apprehend the suspect. Even here, however, police must be careful to prevent using a description that includes race to cast too wide a net, or as a pretext for a stop unrelated to the crime for which the description was secured.

Important questions remain about how to enforce a ban on race-based policing, and enforcement surely will be imperfect. But the current federal standard, which allows the police to use race not in isolation, but as one of several factors that determine their profiling of potential criminals, is likewise hard to enforce. In fact, evasion of the current standard cannot be prevented, as it is a simple matter to fabricate other, non-race-based factors to accompany race as rationales for police stops or searches. Perhaps the ban on race-based policing will also be easily evaded. But over time, if good police sincerely adopt it, the rule can alter the behavior of all officers, and reduce the pool of hostility towards the police that now exists among many black Americans.

Because using racial indicators of potential criminality appears to be a rational approach for individual police officers (as for private citizens), a conscientious police officer who currently engages in race-based policing is likely to believe that he or she is doing the right thing, something socially desirable. Adoption of formal rules prohibiting race-based policing will at least make it clear that society does not share that judgment. Race-based activity by police, then, can no longer serve as an open source of pride in a job well done, and this too can reduce the extent of race-based policing over time, even if the prohibition is hard to enforce.

Not all disparities in police-citizen encounters will be eliminated when race-based policing is no longer countenanced: policing high crime areas might require more stops than in other neighborhoods, for instance, and minorities are more likely to live in such neighborhoods. But minorities will also be the beneficiaries of this increased scrutiny, which will be more acceptable when it is not part of an explicit or implicit race-based policing strategy.

Outlawing race-based policing may require other changes. Possibly it might mean an increase in the number of police officers that are required to guard some neighborhoods. It may also mean stopping more citizens in the aggregate, encompassing a broader range than those who are habitually stopped today. (Professor Randall Kennedy discussed these alternatives more fully in his presentation to the National Institute of Justice.) This latter measure would spread more widely the costs imposed by policing, and should not be viewed as necessarily a bad thing. It is easy to support certain laws and police practices if you are unlikely to be burdened by them. But will support for the many searches that take place in the name of the war on drugs, for instance, survive a broadening of the citizenry that is subject to such searches? A rule prohibiting race-based policing will not only serve the long-run goal of controlling crime, but will also help to protect, for all citizens, constitutionally guaranteed rights against illegal search and seizure. One area in which a prohibition on race-based policing might require supplementary measures is in traffic patrolling. The complexity of traffic laws guarantees available pretexts for race-based stops, and as a result, differential traffic stops occasioned by race-based policing currently appear to be widespread. But as traffic stops are more formal than street-to-street encounters (and typically constrained to take place within a short distance of the patrol car), they can be more closely monitored. Videotaping stops (which already occurs in some jurisdictions), and the collection of statistics on the race of stopped drivers (which is now done by law in some states by executive order for federal law enforcers, and voluntarily by other police departments), offer means to ensure that strictures against race-based policing are not ignored.

The formal repudiation of race-based policing can be complemented with a strategy to enforce strict limits on the actions that the state can take in the absence of more compelling evidence of wrongdoing than noisy signals like gender, race, and age. In the drug search example, for instance, the searches can be limited to be of only a few minutes duration, and restrictions can be placed on the extent of their intrusiveness. Whether race-based policing is countenanced or not, there must be strict ceilings to what actions the state can take in the absence of information more incriminating than "suspicion" or group reputation. Otherwise, outrages such as the U.S. internment of Japanese-Americans during World War II, or the mundane, daily outrages that some members of targeted groups are subjected to by police, will continue to be repeated.

In the long run, there is no tradeoff between crime control and race-neutral policing: more of one does not mean less of the other. Indeed, just the opposite. But the immediate rejection of race-based policing will not immediately reduce distrust between police and minority communities. The distrust has been fostered over many years, and it will take sustained changes in police policy and behavior to reduce the sea of hostility. The time to make the change to race-neutral policing, then, is when crime is relatively low. What the police have been doing right has helped to bring about the low crime rates that we currently enjoy. We should take advantage of these low crime rates to change, now, what the police, generally in good faith, have been doing wrong.

Suggested Further Readings

Cole, David. *No Equal Justice: Race and Class in the American Criminal Justice System.* New York: The New Press, 1999

Davis, Marcia. "Traffic Violation: Racial Profiling Is a Reality for Black Drivers." *Emerge,* pp. 42–48, June 1999.

Harris, David. "Driving While Black: Racial Profiling on our Nation's Highways." American Civil Liberties Union Special Report, June 1999, available at www.aclu.org/profiling/report/index.html.

Kennedy, Randall. *Race, Crime, and the Law.* New York: Random House, 1997.

——. "Race, the Police, and 'Reasonable Suspicion.'" Presentation to the National Institute of Justice, February 3, 1998. Perspectives on Crime and Justice: 1997–1998 Lecture Series, available at *www.ojp.usdoj.gov/nij/pubs-sum/172851.htm.*

Merida, Kevin. "Capital Scene: Decriminalizing 'Driving While Black.'" *Emerge,* p. 26, December/January 1999.

Acknowledgments

1. Jack P. Gibbs, "Conceptions of Deviant Behavior: The Old and the New," *Pacific Sociological Review*, Spring 1996, pp. 9–11. Reprinted by permission of JAI Press.

2. Druann Maria Heckert, "Positive Deviance: A Classificatory Model." Reprinted by permission of Free Inquiry.

3. Howard S. Becker, "Moral Entrepreneurs: The Creation and Enforcement of Deviant Categories," reprinted by permission of The Free Press, a Division of Simon & Schuster, Inc. From *Outsiders*, by Howard S. Becker. Copyright © 1963 by The Free Press.

4. Justin L. Tuggle and Malcolm D. Holmes, "Blowing Smoke: Status Politics and the Shasta County Smoking Ban," reprinted from *Deviant Behavior*, vol. 18, 1997, pp. 77–93. Copyright 1997 from *Deviant Behavior* by Tuggle and Holmes. Reproduced by permission of Taylor & Francis, Inc., http://www. routledge-ny.com.

5. Stephen Spitzer, "The Production of Deviance in Capitalist Society," reprinted from *Social Problems*, vol. 22, no. 5, June 1975, pp. 641–646. Copyright © 1975 by The Society for the Study of Social Problems. Reprinted by permission of the University of California Press Journals.

6. Peter Conrad, "The Discovery of Hyperkinesis: Notes on the Medicalisation of Deviant Behavior," Copyright © 1975 by The Society for the Study of Social Problems. Reprinted from *Social Problems* vol. 23, no. 1, October 1975, pp.12–21, by permission of the University of California Press Journals.

7. Emile Durkheim, "The Normal and the Pathological," reprinted by permission of The Free Press, a Division of Simon & Schuster, Inc. from THE RULES OF SOCIOLOGICAL METHOD by Emile Durkheim, translated by Sarah A. Solovay and John H. Mueller. Edited by George E.G. Catlin. Copyright © 1938 by George E.G. Catlin; copyright renewed 1966 by Sarah A. Solovay, John H. Mueller, George E.G. Catlin.

8. Kai T. Erikson, "On the Sociology of Deviance," reprinted with the permission of Simon & Schuster from the Macmillan College Division title of *Wayward Puritans*, by Kai T. Erikson. Copyright © 1966 by Macmillan Publishing Company.

9. Thorsten Sellin, "The Conflict of Conduct Norms," reprinted from *Culture Conflict and Crime*, a report of the Subcommittee on Delinquency of the Committee on Personality and Culture, *Social Science Research Council Bulletin 41* (New York, 1938).

10. Jeffrey H. Reiman, "A Radical Perspective on Crime." Reprinted by permission of Pearson Education.

11. Rudolph Alexander, Jr., and Jacquelyn Gyamerah, Journal of Black Studies (28:1) pp. 97–111, Copyright © 1997 Reprinted by Permission of Sage Publications, Inc.

12. Gresham M. Sykes and David Matza, "Techniques of Neutralization: A Theory of Delinquency," reprinted from *American Sociological Review*, vol. 22, 1957, pp. 666–670.

13. Donald McCabe, "Influence of Situational Ethics on Cheating Among College Students," from *Sociological Inquiry*, vol. 82, no. 3, 1992, pp. 365–374. Copyright © 1992 by *Sociological Inquiry*. Reprinted by permission of Blackwell Publishers.

14. Robert K. Merton, "Social Structure and Anomie," reprinted from *American Sociological Review*, vol, 3, 1938, pp. 672–682.

15. John M. Hagedorn, "Homeboys, Dope Fiends, Legits, and New Jacks," reprinted by permission of The American Society of Criminology from *Criminology*, vol. 32, no. 2, May 1994, pp. 197–219. Copyright © 1963 by The Free Press; copyright renewed 1991 by Howard S. Becker.

16. Travis Hirschi, "A Control Theory of Delinquency," reprinted from *Causes of Delinquency*, 2001, pp. 16–26. Reprinted by permission of Transaction Publishers. Copyright 2001 © by Transaction Publishers.

17. Neal Shover and David Honaker, "The Socially Bounded Decision Making of Persistent Property Owners," reprinted from *Howard Journal*, vol. 31, 1992, pp. 276–293.

18. Howard S. Becker, "Career Deviance," reprinted by permission of The Free Press, a Division of Simon & Schuster. From *Outsiders*, by Howard S. Becker. Copyright © 1963 by The Free Press.

19. Frank Tannenbaum, "Definition and Dramatization of Evil," reprinted from *Crime and Community*, pp. 17–22. Copyright © 1938 by Columbia University Press. Reprinted by permission of Columbia University Press.

20. Jeffrey T. Ulmer, "Commitment, Deviance, and Social Control," reprinted from *The Sociological Quarterly*, vol. 41, no. 3, Summer 2000, pp. 315–336. Copyright © 2000 by The Midwest Sociological Society. Reprinted by permission of the University of California Press Journals.

21. Erving Goffman, "The Moral Career of the Mental Patient," reprinted from *Psychiatry*, vol. 22, 1959, pp. 123–142. Copyright © 1963 by Prentice Hall. Reprinted by permission of The Guilford Press.

22. Peter and Patricia Adler, "Tiny Dopers: A Case Study of Deviant Socialization." Copyright © 1978. Reprinted by permission of the authors.

23. Karolynn Siegal, Howard Lune, and Han H. Meyer, "Stigma Management Among Gay/Bisexual Men with HIV/AIDS," reprinted from *Qualitative Sociology*, vol. 21, no. 1, 1998. Reprinted with kind permission from Kluwer Academic Publishers.

24. Rhonda D. Evans, "Examining the Informal Sanctioning of Deviance in a Chat Room Culture," reprinted from *Deviant Behavior*, vol. 22, 2001, pp. 195–210. Copyright © 2001 from *Deviant Behavior* by Rhonda D. Evans. Reproduced by permission of Taylor & Francis, Inc., http://www.routledge-ny.com.

25. Delos H. Kelly, "Bureaucratic Slots and Client Processing," from *Creating School Failure, Youth Crime, and Deviance*, by Delos H. Kelly, Los Angeles: Trident Shop, 1982. Copyright © by Delos Kelly.

26. David Shicor, "The Corporate Context of Private Prisons," reprinted from *Crime, Law and Social Change*, vol. 20, 1993, pp. 113–138. Reprinted with kind permission from Kluwer Academic Publishers.

27. Jennifer Hunt and Peter K. Manning, "The Social Context of Police Lying," reprinted from *Symbolic Interaction*, vol. 14, no. 1, pp. 51–70 (Spring, 1991). Reprinted by permission of JAI Press.

28. Troy Duster, "The Epistemological Challenge of the Early Attack on 'Rate Construction,'" reprinted from *Social Problems*, vol. 48, no. 1, pp. 134–136. Copyright © 2001 by The Society for the Study of Social Problems. Reprinted by permission of the University of California Press Journals.

29. Albert J. Mehan, "The Organizational Career of Gang Statistics: The Politics of Policing Gangs," reprinted from *The Sociological Quarterly*, vol. 41, no. 3, Summer 2000, pp. 337–370. Copyright © 2000 by The Midwest Sociological Society. Reprinted by permission of the University of California Press Journals.

30. Richard Gosden, "The Medicalisation of Deviance," reprinted from *Social Alternatives*, vol. 16, no. 2, April 1997, pp. 58–60.

31. Nora S. Gustavson and Ann E. MacEachron, "Criminalizing Women's Behavior," reprinted from *Journal of Drug Issues*, vol. 27, no. 3, 1997, pp. 673–687. Copyright © 1997 by the *Journal of Drug Issues*s. Reprinted by permission of the *Journal of Drug Issues*.

32. Vincent Lyon-Callo, "Medicalizing Homelessness: The Production of Self-Blame and Self-Governing within Homeless Shelters," reprinted from *Medical Anthropology Quarterly*, vol. 14, no. 3, 2000, pp. 328–345. Copyright © 2000 by American Anthropological Association. Not for sale or further reproduction.

33. Erving Goffman, "Information Control and Personal Identity: The Discredited and the Discreditable," reprinted by permission of Prentice Hall, a division of Simon & Schuster. From *Stigma*, 1962, pp. 41–48. Copyright © 1995 assigned to Prentice Hall, a Trade Division of Simon & Schuster, Inc.

34. Thomas J. Schmid and Richard S. Jones, "Suspended Identity: Identity Transformation in a Maximum Security Prison," reprinted from *Symbolic Interaction*, vol. 14, no. 4, Winter 1991, pp. 415–432. Copyright © 1991 by JAI Press. Reprinted by permission of University of California Press.

35. Joel Best and David F. Luckenbill, Social Problems (28:1) Copyright © 1980 by the Society for the Study of Social Problems. Reprinted by Permission of the University of California Press.

36. Phyllis Coontz, "Managing the Action: Sports Bookmakers as Entrepreneurs," reprinted from *Deviant Behavior*, vol. 22., 2001, pp. 239–266. Copyright © 2001 from *Deviant Behavior* by Phyllis Coontz. Reproduced by permission of Taylor & Francis, Inc., http://www.routledge-ny.com.

37. Sheigla Murphy, Dan Waldorf, and Craig Reinarman, "Drifting into Dealing: Becoming a Cocaine Seller," reprinted from *Qualitative Sociology*, vol. 13, no. 4, Winter 1990, pp. 321–343. Copyright © 1990. Reprinted by kind permission of Kluwer Academic Publishers.

38. Kent L. Sandstrom, "Confronting Deadly Disease: The Drama of Identity Construction among Gay Men with AIDS," reprinted from the *Journal of*

Contemporary Ethnography, vol. 19, no. 3, October 1990, pp. 271–294. Copyright © 1990 by Sage Publications. Reprinted by permission of Sage Publications, Inc.

39. Patricia Yancey Martin, Robert A. Hummer, "Fraternities and Rape on Campus," reprinted from *Gender and Society*, vol. 3, no. 4 (December 1989), pp. 457–473. Copyright © 1989 by Sage Publications. Reprinted by permission of Sage Publications, Inc.

40. Andrew Szasz, "Corporations, Organized Crime, and the Disposal of Hazardous Waste: An Examination of the Making of a Criminogenic Regulatory Structure," reprinted by permission of The American Society of Criminology from *Criminology*, vol. 24, no. 1, February 1986, pp. 1–15.

41. Johann Le Roux and Cheryl Sylvia Smith, "Is the Street Child Phenomenon Synonymous with Deviant Behavior?" reprinted from *Adolescence*, vol. 33, no. 132, Winter 1998. Copyright © 1998 by Libra Publishers. Reprinted by permission of Libra Publishers, Inc.

42. Adina Nack, "Damaged Goods: Women Managing the Stigma of STDs," reprinted from *Deviant Behavior*, vol. 21, 2001, pp. 95–121. Copyright © 2001 from *Deviant Behavior* by Adina Nack. Reprinted by permission of Taylor & Francis, Inc., http://www.routledge-ny.com.

43. Samuel Walker, "Reform the Law: Decriminalization," from *Sense and Nonsense About Crime: A Policy Guide, 1st edition,* by Walker © 1985. Reprinted with permission of Wadsworth, an imprint of the Wadsworth Group, a division of Thomson Learning. Fax 800-730-2215.

44. J. David Brown, "The Professional Ex-: An Alternative for Exiting the Deviant Career," *The Sociological Quarterly*, vol. 32, no. 2, 1991, pp. 219–230. Reprinted by permission of University of California Press.

45. Jim Leitzel, "Race and Policing," reprinted from *Society*, vol. 28, no. 3, 2002, pp. 38–42. Reprinted by permission of Transaction Publishers. Copyright © 2001 by Transaction Publishers.

Index